THE BATTLE OF THE BULGE IN LUXEMBOURG
THE SOUTHERN FLANK: DECEMBER 1944 - JANUARY 1945
Vol.II THE AMERICANS

Roland Gaul

THE SOUTHERN FLANK
December 1944 - January 1945
Vol.II THE AMERICANS

THE BATTLE
OF THE BULGE
IN LUXEMBOURG

Roland Gaul

Schiffer Military/Aviation History
Atglen, PA

Translated from the German by Edward Force.

Book Design by Robert Biondi.

Printed in the United States of America.
ISBN: 0-88740-746-3

We are interested in hearing from authors with book ideas on related topics.

Published by Schiffer Publishing Ltd.
77 Lower Valley Road
Atglen, PA 19310
Please write for a free catalog.
This book may be purchased from the publisher.
Please include $2.95 postage.
Try your bookstore first.

AUTHOR'S PREFACE

During my five years of research to put the two parts of this book together, I was asked very often by former soldiers on both sides, as well as by numerous civilians, why I was so interested in this gloomy period of time at all.

I should be happy that I was not yet born in those troubled times, and I should not bring those terrible events back into their awareness or tear old wounds open.

I generally told them that even as a child, during the "Uuchten" (uuchten=evening meeting of neighboring families to exchange news and to socialize – children normally participated to listen to stories) that were still customary at that time, I was confronted time and time again with the subject of war, which was always brought up by choice in the course of pleasant get-togethers with my elders.

Out of this there developed, over the course of years, the general interest in the events of the war in the immediate vicinity of my home town of Diekirch, Luxembourg which was intensified by many discoveries of abandoned American and German military equipment, that we youngsters found, while playing "Cowboys and Indians" in the nearby woods.

Fascinated by the many individual experiences, I gradually understood that I, as a history enthusiast, had the great advantage of being able to locate considerable numbers of witnesses who were still alive.

So I told those whom I interviewed how important oral history is, and that their experiences should be preserved for coming generations, where they fit into the historical framework like pieces of a jigsaw puzzle.

"How can my few meager recollections be of help?" was often the reply.

It usually turned out, though, that the interviewees, in the course of a conversation in which I helped them with dates or events known to them, very quickly "warmed up", so that one 90-minute audio cassette was often not enough for an interview.

In this way I attempted to recapture the thoughts, feelings and actions of people in certain situations with which people who have had similar experiences can identify easily.

The combination of Germans, Americans and Luxembourg civilians contributes a great deal to objectivity and to the completion of this historical study.

This second part is meant to allow the reader a better understanding of the events that were portrayed (from German viewpoints) in the first part, and thus afford a synoptic situation. As in the first part, I have tried to recapture in written language what was told to me by former American soldiers and inhabitants of the area around Diekirch, without taking a position myself. I have made conscious changes to what they have said only to correct factual errors on the basis of official documents. This applies particularly to dates and places.

Once again, I would like to thank those people without whose help this second volume could scarcely have been completed. They are:

First of all, my wife Nicole and daughter Carine, as well as my parents.

The officers of the "Dikircher Geschichtsfrenn" (Diekirch Historical Society), the city government of Diekirch, as well as the personnel of the U.S. and German embassies in Luxembourg.

Tessy Goedert, Aloyse Liefgen, Josy Lorentz and Roland Schleich for their photographic work. I am also very indebted to my historian colleagues who always stood beside me in word and deed:

From Luxembourg,	Germany,	and the USA
Prof. Paul Jost†	Mr. Paul Krischer†	Prof. Frank Edwards
Mr. Fred Karen	Mr. Klaus Ritter	Col. Rob. Waggoner
Mr. Henri Koch-Kent	Mr. Günter von der Weiden	
Prof. Roland Lacaf		
Prof. Claude Lanners		
Mr. Han Makkinga		
Prof. Ben Molitor†		
Mr. Frank Rockenbrod		
Mr. Jules Roulling		
Dr. Marc Rosch		
Mr. Jean-Paul Sassel		
Mr. Marion Schaaf		

As well as the Archives de l'Etat, Luxembourg; Archives de la Croix Rouge, Luxembourg; Ministère de la Force publique, Luxembourg; Armée luxembourgeoise; Militärgeschichtliches Archiv, Freiburg i. Breisgau; Bundesarchiv, Koblenz; Center of Military History, Washington D.C.; Suitland Federal Archives, Maryland; DAVA Audiovisual Dept. of the Pentagon, Washington D.C.; Imperial War Museum, London; National Archives, Washington D.C.

Above all, my thanks go to those people listed at the end of this book, whose reports on their experiences furnished me the raw material for this second volume on the Battle of the Bulge.

Diekirch, March 30, 1987
Roland Gaul

CONTENTS

FOREWORD

From the latter part of December, 1944 until the end of February, 1945, I was stationed in the Grand Duchy of Luxembourg as Executive Officer of the 10th U.S. Regimental Combat Team of the Fifth Infantry Division. Our mission was to liberate the Grand Duchy as rapidly as possible. Needless to say this presented us with a few problems.

Luxembourg, with its hills, rivers and heavily forested areas, offered ideal positions for the defense and formidable problems for the offense. Another problem for us was a lack of knowledge of the area. I am sure that a large part of our success was due to the 100% cooperation and assistance of the people of the country. Any assistance needed was given voluntarily and enthusiastically.

The same spirit is obvious in the author of this book and his compatriots of the "Dikircher Geschichtsfrenn." They have established a museum which memorializes the "Bulge" with particular emphasis on what took place in the area of the Sauer River. The author, in addition to his efforts for the museum, has spent many hours in travel and research for his book.

All of this has been done by a group of people who were not even born, for the most part, at the time of the "Bulge." They deserve a tremendous amount of credit for a job very well done. They also deserve our thanks for memorializing our efforts during the winter of 1944-45.

W. M. Breckinridge
Major General, U.S. Army
(Retired).

FOREWORD

On December 15, 1944, the Allied Forces in Western Europe were hard against – or barely across – the western border of Nazi Germany. Those on the front line, as well as troops and leaders in supporting and headquarters units in the rear, bedded down that night, be it in foxhole or cha^teau, confident that victory was close due to overwhelming superiority in forces and material. A rude awakening was only hours away.

Before dawn on December 16, that rude awakening was accomplished by enemy concentrations of accurate artillery and mortar fire on front line strongpoints, headquarters and communication centers, supporting fire units, and supply crossroads. The "Battle of the Bulge" had begun.

Trapped in the crossfire – as inhabited areas have been since the beginning of warfare – was the town of Diekirch, Luxembourg, close to the border with Germany. After invasion and occupation by German forces during the offensive to the Atlantic Ocean, Diekirch was liberated by the U.S. Army in September 1944 as the Allied Forces pushed toward Germany. Now the U.S. Army – specifically the 109th Infantry Regiment of the 28th Infantry Division with attached and supporting units – was deployed in its defense on the German border, the relatively narrow and shallow Our River. The confident Americans were preparing to thrust into German territory on order of their high commanders.

As the battle developed, many an American soldier must have wondered why he was trapped in such a situation, thousands of miles from home, his very life threatened by violent extinction daily if not hourly. The civilians of Diekirch and vicinity must also have wondered why they were caught between the conflicting military forces. This narrative will help to explain what happened to the military forces in this small area of the "Bulge" and to the civilians trapped in the area. Perhaps it will also answer the question of "why."

Mr. Roland Gaul's detailed and persistent research led him to me as a source of information for his book. I was pleased to provide facts on the actions of the 109th Infantry Regiment around Diekirch. The citizens of Luxembourg are fortunate to have such a dedicated historian among them. The recorded history of the nation has benefitted from his work."

Harry M. Kemp
Colonel U.S. Army
(Retired)

CHAPTER I

HISTORICAL OVERVIEW

U.S. UNITS IN ACTION IN THE SAUER AND OUR RIVER AREA
DURING THE OFFENSIVE

D iekirch and the surrounding villages were liberated on September 11, 1944
by units of the 5th U.S. Armored Division. Because of a too-fast advance,
made easier by hasty German withdrawal without major combat, as well
as by the onset of supply difficulties, a possible attack of the U.S. forces on German
soil at that time was halted.

Here the front line ran parallel to the natural border featured by the flow of the
Our and Sauer rivers and the West Wall located behind them. The 5th Armored
Division was replaced in October by units of the 8th U.S. Infantry Division. They
remained in defensive and observation positions built along the Our until the middle
of November and carried out numerous missions to gain knowledge of the country.

These units of the 8th U.S. Infantry Division were followed in turn by the
109th U.S. Infantry Regiment of the 28th U.S. Infantry Division, known as the
"Keystone Division" or the "Bloody Bucket."

This dependable infantry regiment, though severely tested during the offensive, can be proud, and rightfully so, to look back on a history of the unit covering
more than a hundred years.

The regiment was first founded under this denomination on August 14, 1877,
but bore the additional name of "Scranton City Guards" and thus belonged to the
Pennsylvania National Guard. Numerous organizational changes were undertaken
during the course of the twentieth century before the regiment itself was released
from its National Guard status as a kind of territorially limited guard unit for the
state of Pennsylvania, and called into federal service.

On February 17, 1941 the regiment was "activated" as a main combat unit of its
mother division, the 28th Infantry Division, which was also the largest defensive
organization on the American state of Pennsylvania. At that time all the soldiers
serving in this division were natives of northwestern or central Pennsylvania.

In the following months, the regiment took part in large-scale maneuvers, which
took place partly in the eastern, partly in the southern states of the USA. The following camps then served the 109th Infantry Regiment as headquarters during its
stringent training: Indiantown Gap, Pennsylvania; Camp Livingstone, Louisiana;
Camp Gordon Jonston, Florida; Camp Pickett, Virginia; and Camp Miles Standish,
Massachusetts.

Since the "U.S. Army" was still being built up at the beginning of the war, fully
trained soldiers were frequently transferred from the regiment to become the cadres
of newly formed units, and the 109th Infantry Regiment was gradually filled, dur-

ing maneuvers and training, with young soldiers from all over the USA who were to do their military service there.

At the end of September 1943, the regiment was shipped from Boston, Massachusetts to a support point in Wales, Great Britain, in order to prepare in all ways for the war with Germany on the continent. In expectation of the invasion, rough field training was frequently held in Wales. On July 20, 1944 the regiment, as a following wave, landed in the "Omaha Beach" sector of Normandy and began slowly but surely to move along its long trail to Germany.

As a combat unit of the 28th Infantry Division, the regiment pushed forward in the direction of Paris and took part in the hard and costly fighting around Gathemo and Elboeuf, focal points in the U.S. attack from Normandy. On August 28, 1944 the regiment, at full strength, proudly took part in the 28th Infantry Division's triumphal parade in liberated Paris.

The line of march continued ceaselessly in the direction of Germany, where the resistance gradually became stronger. Finally, as one of the very first units of the U.S. forces on German soil, two patrols of the B Company of the regiment broke through to cross the boundary between Luxembourg and Germany along the Our near Stolzembourg. A major battle ensued at Sevenig (on German soil) between September 13 and 20, 1944 as strong enemy defensive forces made further progress impossible.

On October 25 the regiment, with its mother division, was transferred to the Hürtgenwald north of Aachen, Germany to prepare for an attack from the village of Hürtgen toward the Rhine. For the three infantry regiments of the division, this attack began simultaneously at 9:00 AM on November 2, 1944, and the 109th Regiment was supposed to push forward in a northerly direction. In the thick underbrush of the forest and the German minefields, this attack took a high toll of blood under intense mortar fire. Ceaseless artillery fire allowed scarcely any gain in territory and inspired the name "Hell at Hürtgen Forest." The combat continued until November 18, when the regiment was replaced by the 8th Infantry Division because of overly high losses in men and materials, and was then moved southward into a line of defensive positions on the border between Germany and Luxembourg. For recovery and reorganization, the 109th Regiment was sent into the Diekirch area. On December 8, Lt. Col. Daniel Strickler departed as Regimental Executive Officer, and Lt. Col. James Rudder, formerly commander of the 2nd Ranger Battalion, who had made a name for himself in Normandy on June 6 by climbing the "Pointe du Hoc", became the regiment's commander.

Originating in its earlier status, the regimental motto on its coat of arms was "Cives Arma Ferant", meaning "Let the citizens bear arms."

Structure of a U.S. Division and a Regiment
(Example: 28th U.S. Infantry Division/109th Regiment)

All U.S. combat units established in or after 1941 were formed according to the "triangular division" pattern. Thus a division included three regiments, each regiment had three battalions, and each battalion was divided into three infantry or rifle companies plus one heavy or weapons company.

The 28th U.S. Infantry Division was thus structured as follows:

Division Headquarters   109th Regiment
and Infantry   110th Regiment (a regiment then had
                             112th regiment more than 3000 men)

Also belonging to the division were:

Its own artillery   107th Field Artillery Battalion
(with 105 mm howitzers)   108th Field Artillery Battalion (with
                             155 m howitzers)
                             109th Field Artillery Battalion
                             229th Field Artillery Battalion

Plus
Its support units   28th Reconnaissance Troop
                             28th Quartermaster Company
                             28th Military Police Platoon
                             28th Signal Company
                             103rd Engineer Battalion
                             103rd Medical Battalion
                             728th Ordnance Company
                             447th Anti Aircraft Artillery Battalion
                             630th Tank Destroyer Battalion
                             707th Tank Battalion (sometimes, for tank support)

The infantry weapons used were:
                             M1 Rifle (30.06 caliber)
                             M1 Carbine (.30M1 caliber)
                             (Self-loading weapons for NCOs and men)
                             Browning or Colt .45 caliber pistols
                             for officers
                             Thompson M1 A1 or M3 submachine guns
                             (.45 caliber)
                             Browning machine gun (air- and water-
                             cooled), .30.06 caliber (M 1917 A1,
                             M 1919 A4, M 1919 A6)
                             Browning M2 heavy machine gun, .50 caliber
                             60 mm (mortar)
                             81 mm (mortar)
                             2-36 inch Bazooka (antitank weapon
                             similar to the German Panzerschreck)
                             57 mm antitank gun

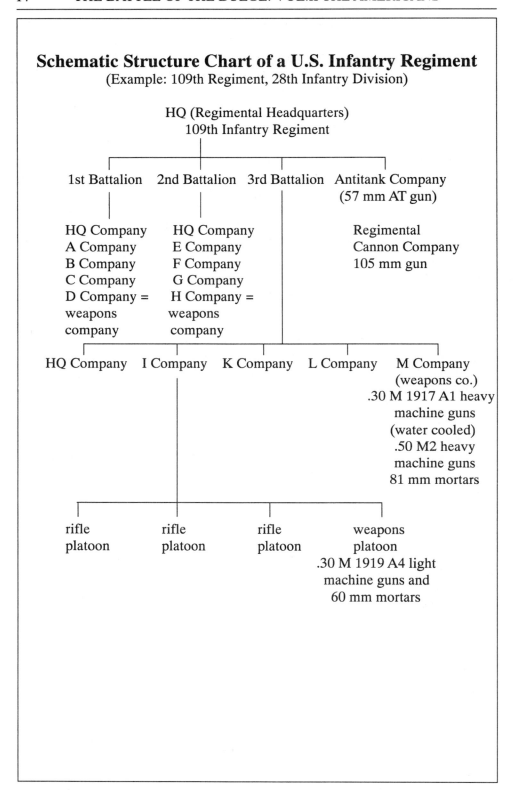

Here are a few clarifications: A normal regiment of a U.S. infantry division, formed by the "triangular system", consisted of three infantry battalions, which were subdivided into four companies plus one "headquarters company."

The first three companies of a battalion (for example, A, B and C in the first battalion) were known as "rifle companies" and armed with the customary light infantry weapons. A "rifle company" itself was composed of four platoons, including three "rifle platoons" and a fourth platoon equipped with heavy or collective weapons, such as the 60 mm mortar or the Browning .30 M 1917A1 (water-cooled) machine gun on heavy tripods.

The fourth company (in this case the D company) was known as the "weapons company") and provided support with heavy infantry weapons, which were normally mounted on vehicles. Such weapons were chiefly the 81 mm mortar, which fired explosive, white phosphorus and illuminating ammunition, and the .50 Browning machine gun, which could be used both in infantry combat and to fight off aircraft and lightly armored vehicles. when needed or requested, the "weapons company" was detailed to the various "rifle companies" for their support in combat, or applied in groups at lightly occupied or easily damaged points.

The infantry regiment also included an "antitank company", whose special task was to take on tanks in combat. This company was equipped with 57 mm antitank guns, which turned out to be outdated and were replaced by more effective weapons in early 1945. In order to give the infantry companies direct artillery support in times of need, since normally the effective range of the 81 mm mortar was limited to 2000 meters, the regiment also included its own "cannon company" with several 105 mm M3 howitzers.

The division very often detached a company of an engineer, signal-or medical battalion and put it under the command of the regimental commander to afford greater tactical mobility. In addition, this solution turned out to be the most suitable in practice, so that only in the rarest cases were these support units in action at full battalion strength.

When a unit was further strengthened by a section of division artillery, a tank- or tank destroyer unit, it formed a so-called "task force", which was called by the name of the officer who commanded it. Often, though, and particularly during the course of the offensive, a "task force" consisted only of several strengthened companies with tank support.

The 5th U.S. Infantry Division "Red Diamond"

The "Red Diamond" Division, so called because of its emblem (a red diamond), was constituted at Camp Hogan, Texas in December of 1917 and sent overseas in May of 1918. It took part in the battles at St-Dié and Villers-en-Haye in Lorraine as well as the military operations at St-Mihiel and in the "Meuse-Argonne" area.

Despite tough German resistance, it succeeded in crossing the Meuse, and at the end of World War I the 5th Infantry Division was located at Thionville and Metz. After the Armistice, the division remained in Luxembourg as an occupation unit, returned to the USA in July of 1919, and was deactivated there in October of 1921.

Only on October 16, 1939 was the division mobilized again at Fort McClelland, Alabama and ordered to Fort Benjamin Harrison, Indiana, later to Fort Custer, Michigan, and in May and June of 1941 it took part in the Tennessee maneuvers, as well as in field training in Louisiana from August to October. In September of 1941, during its training, the 10th Infantry Regiment was sent to Iceland as one of the first contingents of the U.S. armed forces; at the end of 1941 and in the spring of 1942 the other units of the division followed.

In August of 1943 the 5th Infantry Division was transferred to England. Its commanding general during this period and through April 1945 was Major General Stafford Leroy Irwin. The powerful "Red Diamond" landed in the "Utah Beach" sector of Normandy on June 9, 1944 and formed a defensive line near Caumont four days later. Thanks to a successful attack at Vidouville on July 26, the division moved southeast toward St-Lô, took Angers on August 10, crossed the Seine at Fontainebleau on August 23, liberated Reims across the Marne on August 30 and thus reached the area to the east of Verdun. Here the division prepared to attack Metz. In mid-September it succeeded in reaching a bridgehead over the Mosel south of Metz despite strong resistance. A first attempt to capture the fortress of Metz failed with heavy losses, and the "Red Diamond" drew back in mid-October 1944 to attack again on November 9. After a hard and bloody ten-day battle, Metz fell.

On December 4 the division, as part of Patton's Third Army, crossed the German border, took Lauterbach on December 5, and reached the banks of the Saar with its advance guard on the next day. When the last German major offensive began on December 16, the 5th Infantry Division was applied on the south flank of the "Bulge" as of December 18, and late in January of 1945 it was able to push back the German front on the Sauer. In February and March of 1945 the division crossed the lower Sauer, broke through the Siegfried Line, reached and crossed the Rhine on March 22, and pushed on toward Frankfurt am Main, taking the city and its surroundings at the end of March.

In April of 1945 it took part in breaking through the Ruhr pocket, and then moved on to the Czechoslovakian border around May 1; it was at Volary and Vimpek when Germany surrendered.

IT was particularly the infantry regiments of the division that saw service in the Diekirch area, the 2nd, 10th and 11th Regiments, which liberated the Sauer valley on January 18-22. Thus the history of these units during the Ardennes offensive deserve our closer observation.

Structure of the "Red Diamond"

The 5th Infantry Division was constituted as follows:

Infantry	2nd Infantry Regiment
	10th Infantry Regiment
	11th Infantry Regiment

Artillery	19th Field Artillery Battalion (105 mm 21st Field Artillery Battalion (155 mm howitzers) 46th Field Artillery Battalion (105 mm how.) 50th Field Artillery Battalion (105 mm how.)
A-A Artillery	449th Anti Aircraft Artillery Battalion (attached) (fully mobile)
Division Support Units	Division Headquarters Company with special units (Military Police Platoon, etc.) 7th Engineer Battalion 5th Medical Battalion 5th Quartermaster Company 5th Signal Company 5th Reconnaissance Troop 705th Ordnance Company
Attached Tank and Tank Destroyer Units	735th Tank Battalion (at times) 303rd Tank Destroyer Battalion * 818th Tank Destroyer Battalion * 737thth Tank Battalion

* Both tank destroyer units were equipped with M-10 and M-18, later M-36 gun motor vehicles (tank destroyers)

The 4th U.S. Infantry Division "Ivy Leaves"

As one of the very first U.S. units to take part in the invasion on June 6, 1944, the 8th Infantry Regiment of the 4th U.S. Infantry Division landed in Normandy and relieved the 82nd Airborne Division which was surrounded at Ste-Mère-Eglise; the 4th Infantry Division then mopped up the Contentin peninsula and helped to take Cherbourg.

After hard fighting near Périers from July 6 to 12, 1944, the division broke through the left wing of the 7th German Army and helped to hinder enemy pressure on Avranches.

At the end of August, the division had advanced to shortly before Paris, where it took part in the city's liberation by French troops.

The division then swung toward Belgium, reached the Schnee-Eifel via Houffalize on September 14 and thus reached the Siegfried Line, where it achieved several breakthroughs.

Further penetration into Germany went very slowly; only on November 6 did the division reach the Hürtgenwald, where heavy and bloody fighting until early December cost it numerous casualties. (Here the 4th Infantry Division partially relieved the hard-pressed 28th Infantry Division.) Ordered to Luxembourg to recover, the division was involved in the combat of the Ardennes offensive. Although its line was thin, the "Ivy Leaves" were able to hold out against the German attack especially successfully at Osweiler and Dickweiler. In mid-January the division attacked in the Sauer sector along with the 5th U.S. Infantry Division and rolled over German positions from Fouhren to before Vianden. Only at Prüm, where it met heavy enemy resistance in February, was the division's advance halted, and thus it turned toward Olzheim on February 28 and crossed the Kyll on March 7, 1945.

After a short rest, the division crossed the Rhine near Worms on March 29, took Würzburg and established a stable bridgehead on the Main at Ochsenfurt on April 3. Advancing in a southerly direction through Bavaria, it reached the Isar near Miesbach on May 2, 1945; here the division was relieved and ordered to serve as an occupation unit. On July 10, 1945 the division returned to the United States. Its commanding general until December of 1945 was Major General Raymond O. Barton.

Structure (like that of the 5th Inf.Div.)

8th Infantry Regiment	4th Signal Company	377th AAA Battalion
12th Infantry Regiment	704th Ordnance Co.	(anti-aircraft)
22nd Infantry Regiment	4th Quartermaster Co.	70th Tank Battalion
20th FA Battalion	4th Reconnaissance Tr	801st TD Battalion
(155 mm howitzer)		
29th FA Battalion*	4th Engineer Batt.	802nd TD Battalion
42nd FA Battalion*	4th Medical Batt.	803rd TD Battalion
44th FA Battalion*	4th CIC Detachment	(only at times)
* 105 mm howitzers		

The 9th U.S. Armored Division "Phantom Division"

In the late autumn of 1944, the 9th U.S. Armored Division landed in Normandy, where it was given its specific mission on October 23: to take a position in Luxembourg along the German border. When the Ardennes offensive began, the situation changed suddenly for the young, still combat-inexperienced division.

It was hard pressed and had to fight spread out as a non-unified unit (its three main battle groups or combat commands, CCA, CCB and CCR (Combat Command, corresponding roughly to a present-day brigade) fought isolated from each other. Its focal points were St. Vith (Belgium), Echternach (Luxembourg), Beaufort (Luxembourg) and Bastogne (Belgium).

Its positions around Bastogne delayed the German advance, which allowed the 101st Airborne Division, which had been detached for defensive purposes, to settle and hold its position in and around Bastogne. (Units of CCA considerably slowed down the German advance on the south flank of the "Bulge" in the Wallendorf-Beaufort, Grundhof sector).

At the end of January the division was prepared to advance over the Roer line. On February 28, 1945 this offensive began, and the 9th Armored Division moved through Roes toward Reimbach, and from there its spearhead and motorized patrols advanced toward Remagen.

They found the Ludendorff Bridge undamaged; it was taken by troops of the 9th Armored Division on March 7 before the main explosive charge could be detonated to destroy the bridge late in the afternoon. The resulting bridgehead was quickly enlarged and the division moved on to the south and east across the Lahn to Limburg, where it liberated thousands of Allied prisoners of war from the prison camps there. From Frankfurt it was sent out to take part in a pincer movement that enclosed the Ruhr pocket. Leipzig was taken by it in April, and the division was moving southward toward Czechoslovakia when the war ended in Europe.

During the offensive, the main units in the greater Diekirch area were the 60th Armored Infantry Battalion and the 3rd Field Artillery Battalion (105 mm howitzers on M7 tracked vehicles called "Priest", a kind of self-propelled armored howitzer on Sherman tank chassis).

The commanding general as of October 1942 was Major General John W. Leonard.

Structure

27th Armored Infantry Battalion	89th Cavalry Reconn. Squadron
52nd Armored Infantry Battalion	9th Armored Engineer Battalion
60th Armored Infantry Battalion	2nd Armored Medical Battalion
2nd Tank Battalion	131st Armored Ordnance Battn.
14th Tank Battalion	149th Armored Signal Battalion
19th Tank Battalion	509th CIC Detachment
3rd Armored Field Artillery Battalion	482nd Anti Aircraft Battalion
16th Armored Field Artillery Battalion	811th Tank Destroyer Battalion
73rd Armored Field Artillery Battalion	656th Tank Destroyer Battalion

The 10th U.S. Armored Division "Tiger Division"

On September 23, 1944 the 10th U.S. Armored Division entered France at the harbor of Cherbourg and took part in a month-long maneuver near Theurteville, France, before it was sent into action. On October 25 it made its first contact with the enemy at Mars-la-Tour. In mid-November the division went on the offensive, crossed the Mosel near Malling and attacked across the Saar north of Metz.

The division staff was just about to make plans for Patton's Third Army to advance across the Rhine when the news came that the Germans had broken through on December 16.

The 10th Armored Division was transferred to the north immediately to take part in the ensuing battles. Several operations were carried out along the Sauer by units of the division before the division itself did a fine job of fighting against the hard-fighting enemy at Noville, Bras and Bastogne.

At the beginning of January the division was transferred again to occupy a line of defensive positions east of the Saar and south of the Maginot Line. On February 20, 1945 the division attacked again and did its part in mopping up the Saar-Mosel triangle. Attacking in a northerly direction, the 10th Armored Division took the city of Trier on March 15. Further focal points on its advance were Kaiserslautern, Mannheim, Oehringen, Heilbronn and Kirchheim.

On April 23-25, 1945 it crossed the Danube and took Oberammergau. When Germany capitulated, the division was near Innsbruck.

The commanding general (from July to November 1944) was Major General F. B. Prickett, and as of November 1944 Major General Morris.

Structure

20th Armored Infantry Battalion	796th Anti Aircraft Battalion
54th Armored Infantry Battalion	638th Tank Destroyer Battalion
61st Armored Infantry Battalion	609th Tank Destroyer Battalion
3rd Tank Battalion	90th Cavalry Reconn. Squadron
11th Tank Battalion	55th Armored Engineer Battalion
21st Tank Battalion	80th Armored Medical Battalion
419th Armored FA Battalion	132nd Armored Ordnance Battalion
420th Armored FA Battalion	150th Armored Signal Battalion
423rd Armored FA Battalion	510th CIC Detachment

Notes: FA = Field Artillery. Field Artillery and Tank Destroyer battalions were self-propelled. Like the 9th Armored Division, this was divided into Combat Command A, B and R (= Reserve). Variations in division structures are possible, as various support units were detailed to them temporarily.

CHAPTER II

U.S. MILITARY OPERATIONS BETWEEN THE SAUER AND OUR RIVERS

The second part of this book is devoted principally to those U.S. units that fought in the area between the Sauer and Our shortly before December 16, 1944 or during the course of the Ardennes offensive, but it would not be proper not to mention that division that liberated our country for the first time, including Diekirch and its surroundings, on September 10 and 11, 1944, namely the 5th U.S. Armored Division under major General Lunsford E. Oliver.

With the long-awaited appearance of the 5th U.S. Armored Division on the border between Luxembourg and Germany, the people's fear of a continuation of the war on Luxembourg's soil gradually disappeared.

A patrol of the 85th Reconnaissance Squadron (the division's reconnaissance unit) made history as one of the very first U.S. units to set foot on German soil near Stolzembourg. (A similar patrol was carried out on the same day by reconnaissance units of the 28th Infantry Division.) The most important events will be presented here briefly in chronological order, thus remembering the 5th Armored Division, which allowed our country to breathe free again after four years of Nazi oppression. (Source: U.S. Federal Archives, Suitland, Md., 319.1.GNNJG).

September 1944

On September 9, 1944 the German resistance gradually stiffened along the border of Luxembourg and Belgium to oppose the units of the 5th U.S. Armored Division rolling in from France. Around 4:45 PM, tank duels took place east of Bascharage, and Combat Command A of the 5th Armored Division reported advancing German tanks (Panther PzKpw V) from the direction of Luxembourg. About 10:00 PM, Combat Command A was located some seven kilometers west of our capital and occupied some of the most important approaches to Luxembourg. According to official sources, the approach roads to Arlon were heavily mined; Arlon was thus circumvented by Combat Command R, which arrived in the areas south of Useldingen only late in the evening. On September 9, twelve German tanks and some seventy other vehicles were destroyed by U.S. air forces.

The advance continued steadily, and Combat Command A took Luxembourg city about 9:45 AM on September 10, 1944. At 10:00 AM an escort accompanied the division commander and Prince Felix and Crown-Prince Jean, our present Grand-Duke, then a 1st Lieutenant in the Irish Guards, through the liberated capital city. After a short exchange of fire with several German antitank guns, which were able to delay the U.S. spearheads for about an hour and a half, the first U.S. tanks reached

Mersch, where the bridge was blown up by the retreating Germans at the moment when Combat Command R arrived. The railroad bridge there was mined and prepared for demolition, but its destruction could be prevented at the last minute.

Engineers of Combat Command R removed the explosive charges, and thus the bridge could be crossed quickly. Combat Command B was ordered to divide itself between CCA and CCR and fan out into the area of Ermsdorf. About 10:30 PM on September 10, 1944, a column was two kilometers west of Rammeldange. CCB was in Blaschette and parts of CCR had advanced to Schrondweiler. In order to protect the capital, a task force was assembled and separated from CCA to take over the protection of Luxembourg city. On this day the Germans had 225 losses to report, as well as some 180 prisoners, while the low-flying U.S. fighter-bombers were able to destroy many more German vehicles. Without further enemy opposition, CCB advanced on the following day (Sept. 11, 1944) as far as Brucherhof (Ermsdorf-Stegen), and from there they undertook several reconnaissance missions as far as the German border.

Warner W. Holzinger

The author had the good fortune to correspond with the former U.S. sergeant, probably the very first American soldier on German soil. Sgt. Holzinger (85th Cavalry Reconnaissance Squadron) wrote to the author in 1984:

"When the staff sergeant informed me that Lt. McGuinness had suggested men from the 2nd Platoon, me among others, for a patrol along the descending road to Stolzembourg, I heard only the grumbling of my men; nobody volunteered willingly. So I had no choice but to choose them quickly. Among others, Lt. Lionel A. de Lille, T/5 Coy Locke, the driver of my reconnaissance Jeep, equipped with a machine gun, and I set out. Lt. de Lille was a Frenchman. In 1940 he was a captain of the French artillery and was taken prisoner. Later he broke out and joined us in Dreux, France, and stayed with us until Germany surrendered. Our leadership granted him the rank of a first lieutenant. As we set out, we heard that CCB had set up its headquarters near Schlinder, north of Diekirch.

It was a sunny day as we set out in the Jeep. In Stolzembourg we heard from the people who lived there that there were no longer any German soldiers in the vicinity. Here I learned how important it is to know foreign languages. I spoke quite good German and could also write it fairly well, and also knew a few words of French. Lt. de Lille spoke English fluently and also knew some German. After was had searched the village, we saw that the Germans had only partly damaged the small bridge over the Our. So it was possible for us to cross the bridge on foot, although we could just as easily have driven through the river with the Jeep. On the opposite side there was a bunker, disguised as a barn . . . abandoned. Lt. de Lille spoke with a German farmer somewhat farther from the river. The man told us that he had seen the last German soldiers the day before. He also told us that we should follow the road up to the hill, from which we would have a view directly at the first line of bunkers. So we went carefully about a mile and a half farther, along with the farmer, until we had a sufficient field of vision. Besides Lt. de Lisle, Pfc McColligan was with us. We scanned the line of bunkers with our binoculars. It turned out that none of the bunkers was occupied. We turned back to Stolzembourg and reported on our observations to Lt. Loren Vipond, who led the other patrol. Lt. Vipond immediately passed the information on by radio to CCB, which immediately let the whole world know that the first Allies had set foot in Germany.

But since the division was under strict standards of secrecy, at first it was not mentioned that it had been a patrol of the 5th Armored Division.

On the next day we were to undertake another scouting patrol under the command of Lt. Vipond, and so Lt. de Lille, T/5 Coy Locke and I prepared to set out. At the last minute, though, Lt. Vipond decided to go alone, and we were supposed to wait for a platoon of the 81st Tank Battalion, a small unit of light tanks under the command of Captain Harold D. Schiering. But since the terrain on the German side was extremely impassable, the unit with its commander, Lt. Henry Plass, stayed back. Meanwhile Coy Locke, Lt. de Lille and I had climbed to the hilltop again to have another look at the bunker. After we had ventured about a mile farther than on the previous day, we made sketches of the situation of the bunker and of its nature. During this time Captain Schiering, Commander of D Company of the 81st Tank Battalion, along with NCO's Robert C. Moore and Warren S. Nitschke, had been questioning the inhabitants of an isolated house beyond Stolzembourg. We went to Captain Nitschke at once and told him of our observations. But now as we looked from the highlands on the Luxembourg side toward Germany, we suddenly saw a column of German soldiers far away. The enemy troops were coming from the north and moving along another ridge of hills in the direction of Bauler. There were about sixty men. They carried heavy packs and machine guns, and six to ten men remained in every bunker that the column passed. The last bunker was occupied only minutes after our patrol had left German soil. The Germans moved around quite freely, and it seemed that they had not noticed our presence. So a hasty report was made to headquarters that the occupation of the West Wall bunkers in this sector had just begun. On the next day the Vth Corps ordered fire concentrated on the enemy bunker locations along the border. At 3:00 PM the division's heavy guns, plus numerous tanks and tank destroyers, concentrated heavy fire on the bunkers. No reaction came from the German side. Here Sgt. Holzinger's account ends."

About 7:00 PM (Sept. 11, 1944), CCA received the command to occupy the transmitting station of Radio Luxembourg in Junglinster with a fast-moving battle group and protect it from possible sabotage by the enemy. A similar occupation force remained in the Villa Louvigny (broadcasting headquarters of Radio Luxembourg) in Luxembourg city.

About 10:35 PM a report from the headquarters of the Vth U.S. Corps arrived, saying that effective immediately, the 112th Infantry Regiment of the 28th Infantry Division was transferred to the 5th Armored Division, and that from now on the main task of the division consisted of cleaning any remaining German pockets of resistance out of the northern part of Luxembourg and keeping them out. Finally the 85th Reconnaissance Cavalry Squadron (without Troops A, B and C, which were still engaged in reconnaissance missions on the Our along the border) took over the protection of the capital city in place of the CCA task force.

On September 11, close to midnight, the division had reached a line that ran southward along the Our from Rodershausen, following the course of the Sauer to the vicinity of Grevenmacher on the Moselle river.

Combat Command A (CCA) reported at 8:50 AM on the following day (September 12, 1944) that Radio Luxembourg at Junglinster had been taken intact; thereupon a part of the 112th Infantry Regiment (28th Infantry Division) relieved the CCA unit and protected the radio transmitter; the rest of the unit was transferred to the vicinity of Oberanven.

On September 13, on order from the Corps, a demonstration of concerted fire on the Siegfried Line bunkers was carried out. Directed by the "Divisional Artillery HQ", as of 3:00 PM guns, tanks and tank destroyers took the Western Wall under fire. At the same time, small CCA patrols encountered road barricades and enemy resistance around Grevenmacher. CCR fired on and destroyed several heavy bunkers between Ammeldingen and Gentingen, but received no enemy artillery fire in return, to the surprise of all. Obviously these bunkers were no longer occupied since the Germans had made a hasty retreat.

Wallendorf

The 1st Battalion of the 112th Regiment was brought back to CCR at about 12:00 noon on September 14; this strengthened unit then attacked forcefully and crossed the confluence of the Sauer and Our near Wallendorf. About 1:30 PM CCR reported heavy enemy resistance, chiefly from automatic weapons. Then the U.S. artillery took the opposite slope under fire with a deadly rain of white phosphorus and forced the bunker crews to leave their positions. B Company of the 47th Armored Infantry Battalion, strengthened by a platoon of Sherman tanks, attacked Wallendorf at once in order to take the heights beyond it. Early in the afternoon the 112th Regiment, 28th Inf. Division, (1st Battalion!) was still working to clean out numerous pockets of resistance in Wallendorf, while the eastern edge of the village was already taken.

At the same time, CCA encountered a German cycle unit that was trying to reach the border near Moestroff. CCR moved up quickly, and about 6:25 PM the greater part of the unit was across the Sauer and thus reached the heights to the east of Wallendorf. At both ends of the village there were now several tank destroyers that were there to safeguard the advance of the 1st Battalion of the 112th Regiment in a northerly direction. Artificial fog and bitter resistance made CCR's attack more difficult. CCA reported that no straggling German units had succeeded in reaching the German side of the Our.

At 6:20 PM the attack of CCR came to a stop near Biesdorf; the valley was too strongly defended, as the enemy had the advantage of excellent observation of the territory.

Several superbly camouflaged German antitank guns were recognized and reported at the right time by the 112th Regiment. CCR now took over firing on the concrete bunkers, most of which were connected with each other by underground tunnels. Only on September 15 could the attack be continued. Sight conditions in the valley were very poor, and around 10:00 numerous German tanks and tank destroyers unexpectedly appeared. With their 8.8 cm guns they were able to knock out the Sherman tanks that had advanced. The commander of CCR then moved his unit immediately into the country between Hommerdingen and Kruchten. Biesdorf was retaken by the 1st Battalion of the 112th Regiment about 12:40 PM.

On the night before September 16, CCA reported the loss of three Shermans to enemy antitank-gun fire, as well as stubborn infantry resistance by machine guns and light antitank guns along the Sauer shore.

At 9:30 AM, units of CCB received the order to move as far as Reisdorf and then cross the Sauer there. South of Niedersgegen German tanks were sighted again, firing shell after shell accurately into the U.S. columns. In the neighborhood of Wettlingen the enemy attacked the flank of CCR.

On the afternoon of September 17 the road blockades of CCB between Wallendorf and Reisdorf received heavy mortar and machine-gun fire. At 7:45 AM the U.S. artillery succeeded in destroying several German tanks near Wettlingen; the 1st Battalion of the 112th Regiment, which meanwhile had fought its way to just short of Wettlingen, was held down there under heavy German artillery fire. At 7:15 PM CCA reported that the Germans were still defending the bridgeheads at Echternach, Wasserbillig and Grevenmacher tenaciously with heavy machine guns, heavy mortars and light artillery. CCB had to halt the attack under heavy defensive fire and received a command to fight only on the defensive.

Only on the night of September 17 had the U.S. bridgehead attained its greatest size, resembling a horseshoe in its shape. It reached from Gentingen on the east bank of the Our through Hüttingen and Mettendorf southeastward to Stockem, to the point where CCR had been pushed back from Bettingen. The southernmost extreme lay between Wallendorf and Bollendorf.

On this day the Germans lost 325 men, 15 tanks and 12 halftracks, and 89 German soldiers were taken prisoner.

On September 18 the division's headquarters were moved to Moestroff. A reconnaissance unit of CCB sent the news that an enemy column was moving in the direction of Gentingen; a second would advance toward Körperich and Hüttingen. The two columns were on foot and marched very slowly; the enemy had obviously been able to advance to the American lines during the night and lay mines, which now had to be located, a laborious job. Shortly thereafter, the Germans fired rockets at this sector, and three Sherman tanks went up in flames. The 1st Battalion of the 112th Regiment suffered serious losses and was pulled back, along with the A Company of the 628th Tank Destroyer Battalion, for its protection. Mettendorf was burning but was still reported as being heavily occupied!

In the morning of September 19 the enemy attacked CCR with infantry and a tank unit. But CCR was able to beat off this attack, in which, according to the unit's report, eighteen Panzer IV tanks were lost or had to be towed back because of shot damage.

At 11:30 AM German infantry attacked the occupied bridge in Wallendorf and was able to take it for a short time; but about 2:55 PM the bridge was in American hands again, though CCR and CCB were again under heavy artillery fire.

At 6:30 PM CCR was assigned the 2nd Battalion of the 112th Infantry Regiment to protect its flank; a part of CCR was then moved back to Diekirch. CCB was given the order to continue to hold its defensive positions, until the order came on September 20 to follow CCR.

In the early morning of September 20, CCR set up its command post south of Gilsdorf, while the greatest part of the division's artillery was placed in positions on the west bank of the Sauer. CCR, as ordered, moved back unit by unit and reached its assigned zone near Diekirch at 5:00 AM. In the morning the two battalions of the 112th Infantry Regiment were attacked but, despite heavy rocket fire and close combat that flared up at times, were able to hold the bridge at Wallendorf. During the night, though, a German command was able to blow up the bridge in Wallendorf and mine its approaches on the German side.

On September 21 the P-47 "Thunderbolt" fighter-bombers of the 9th U.S. Air Force were able to destroy a heavy cannon battery disguised as a private house. When CCB reported twenty German tanks near Niedersgegen around 5:00 PM, the U.S. Air Force attacked successfully there, too, and stopped their advance, though only one tank was said to have been destroyed!

At 7:30 PM, CCB received a radio message that the entire unit was to draw back to the west bank of the Sauer immediately. Under the protection of CCR, the column was to move from Wallendorf through Reisdorf, Bettendorf, Gilsdorf and Diekirch to Ingeldorf. The division's artillery would guarantee the necessary harassing fire.

On September 23 the remaining parts of CCR, which were still in position along the Sauer, were also to be moved back to Diekirch. But when CCR came under artillery and mortar fire around noon, this plan was given up. Units of CCR then maintained their positions along the border.

According to the subsequent order from the division, only as many forces were to remain along the border as were absolutely necessary for the defense of the American bridgehead. In the late afternoon of September 23, a combat team of the 83rd Infantry Division was also to be brought up to strengthen the southernmost wing of the division. The same division was to arrive there at full strength on September 25. The V. Corps arranged that during this troop movement all the artillery units in the sector, plus available fighter-bombers, were to concentrate a withering fire on all known targets. As soon as the 2nd Combat Team of the 83rd Infantry Division had arrived, the hard-pressed 112th Regiment was to be transferred back to its mother division (28th Infantry Division). CCA was to move northward, and on orders from the Corps, the 5th Armored Division was to take over immediately and assume the responsibility and provide protection for the northern half of Luxembourg. CCR, though, remained in a mobile reserve position in Diekirch.

On September 26 too, that unit of the 85th Reconnaissance Cavalry Squadron returned to the squadron, which was still stationed in Luxembourg city.

Around 6:00 PM on the next day, CCA had reached its assigned zone near Consthum; at the same time, the U.S. Air Force bombed Godendorf, Wallendorf and Ammeldingen. At 9:00 PM an American truck fell into the hands of a German scouting party not far from Roder; the village of Roder was immediately recognized as a transition point for German patrols, and appropriate countermeasures were undertaken at once.

Around 11:30 on September 28, the V. Corps received a report that the enemy had moved into Hosingen and the unit of the 28th Infantry Division that had been there had left the town. CCA was ordered to clean out and hold Hosingen in co-operation with units of the 28th Infantry Division. At the same time, Combat Command A reported a vigorous contact with a German company east of Weiler.

The division's artillery reported around noon that enemy troops were at the pontoon bridge and on the west shore of the Our near Vianden.

In the further course of the day, CCA cleaned out the strip of land from Dorscheid to Rodershausen and reported it cleared of enemies around 6:00 PM. German troop movements and Luftwaffe activity were sighted south of Wallendorf. September 29 passed without any contact with the enemy other than one 15-man enemy patrol near Hosingen.

On that day the division's artillery fired on a large German column of vehicles in the area of Dahnen and Bollendorf.

The entire 5th Armored Division, as ordered by the Corps, was to move back, after being relieved by the troops of the VIII. US Corps (Middleton), through the line of the 28th Infantry Division and the 4th Infantry Division and gather in the vicinity of Faymonville, Belgium. The 5th Armored Division was then to take over the major role in the V. Corps' planned attack on the Siegfried Line in the north.

The Vth Corps gave the division permission to move its sector gradually toward the Born-Recht line as of September 30, 1944, if necessary. Although the 5th Armored Division had suffered many losses of men and materials in the heavy fighting around the Wallendorf bridgehead, it was still able to inflict heavy losses on the enemy within two weeks; the extent of these losses, as seen in the following list of destroyed German material, provides a picture of the heavy fighting at that time:

Destroyed tanks: 61
Destroyed or captured vehicles: 398
Destroyed guns (incl. Flak, Pak, heavy mortars and rocket launchers): 138
Destroyed heavy infantry weapons: 192
German soldiers lost: 3387
German soldiers captured: 3078

In addition, the units of the 5th Armored Division captured eight intact German aircraft, several hundred cycles and a storehouse with Luftwaffe material to the value of (at that time) two million U.S. dollars.

The American losses during the whole month of September 1944, most of which were suffered in the fighting around Wallendorf, amounted to 792 dead, including 55 officers, and 13 missing, 19 tanks, 73 trucks and 32 lighter vehicles. (Author's note: The designations CCA, CCB and CCR naturally refer only to parts of units (which together made up a combat command), that is, a battle group consisting of infantry with tank and artillery support).

The following text, sung to the well-known melody of the Boy Scout song "Héich de Bokkel voll Gepäck", became very popular in Diekirch in the first few weeks after the liberation. It is still sung happily by the ladies of Diekirch at social occasions and recalls an unforgettable time.

D'si vill Jongen op der Welt
Mä d'as keen dee mir gefällt
Wi mein USA aus Amerika
Su e schéine flotte Jong
Su een hun ech gär am Fong
Well hien huet nach Schokkela

All mein Denken bleiwt drun henken
un dem Zockerjong aus Amerika . . .

[Translator's note: the Luxembourg text says that of all the young men in the world, the singer likes none as well as the handsome young American (soldier) who gives her chocolate.]

CHAPTER *III*

TWO LUXEMBOURGERS IN SERVICE WITH THE 5TH ARMORED DIVISION

THE BROTHERS ALOYSE AND RENÉ SCHILTZ

Chance surely played a major role in the fact that in September of 1944 Aloyse and René Schiltz, both (brothers) of whom were born in Ettelbrück, suddenly arrived a few days apart and under different conditions and met after three years' separation while serving with the 5th Armored Division, the first American unit to liberate Luxembourg.

Aloyse Schiltz

Aloyse Schiltz was already taking part in underground action against the German occupying forces at Ettelbrück in June of 1941, including the burning of the "Eierepaart" (gate of honor) that had been set up by the Nazis in the center of Ettelbrück. On August 28, 1941 he fled with his friend, the "Passeur" ("passeurs" assisted persons prosecuted by the Nazis to escape to unoccupied zones of France at the risk of their own lives) Albert Ungeheuer, over the border from Luxembourg to France at Differdange. In 1942, after spending time in Montpelier, Besançon, Digne and finally Lyon, he was able to obtain papers and a passport from the American consulate and thus be able to leave France. In August of 1942 he arrived in Portugal, departed by sea and arrived at Southampton, England, on September 2, 1942. With the support of the Luxembourg government in exile in London, he volunteered for service in the FFL (Forces Françaises Libres [Free French Forces]) and entered the "Ecole des Cadets de la France Libre" (FFL officer cadet school) at Ribbesford. After concluding all of his training at the school, he was appointed an officer of the FFL, but he remained at the "Bureau Central de Renseignements et d'Actions" (Central Bureau of Intelligence and Operations) and took part in several special training courses in Scotland.

Only in August of 1944 was he parachuted into France in the vicinity of Mézières-Charleville, with the assignment to join the FFI (Forces Françaises de l'Interieur [French Interior Forces]) within the framework of a large-scale action against the Wehrmacht, which was then in the process of withdrawing. Above all, their task was to scatter the Germans away from their retreat routes by numerous ambushes, acts of sabotage and explosions.

Aloyse Schiltz reports: "On September 5, 1944 we were on both sides of a main road in the vicinity of Nouzonville with our weapons ready to fire and waiting to attack at any moment where a German convoy was expected, when suddenly several American scout cars and Jeeps with heavy machine guns came along. Since I recognized them immediately, I jumped onto the road and prevented any unwanted shooting. The men with whom I had prepared the ambush were trembling with excitement, and a premature shot could have been fired all too easily.

The Americans, including a captain, immediately stopped and talked with us and found out about the organization and actions of the FFI, but urged us forcefully to stay away from the main lines of communication because of the American advance, since confusion could result all too easily. The captain, who was amazed at my language ability, advised me to make my services available to the G-2 (intelligence) section of the 5th Armored Division, and took me to headquarters. I agreed but made one request of my superiors, who got in touch with the "Etat-Major" (Headquarters) of General König in England about the corps. He released me for the time being and "detached" me from the FFI to the 5th Armored Division. Thus I came under the command of Lt. Col. McFarland, Chief of the G-2 section of the division. My immediate superior was Captain Ryan, liaison officer of G-2 to the corps. From now on I wore an American uniform with the French insignia of a lieutenant, plus the "kepi", which I usually traded with an American steel helmet.

On September 9, taking part in a large-scale reconnaissance mission with the advance guard of the division, I crossed the border from Belgium into Luxembourg near Athus-Pétange. That same night the G-2 section was quartered in the woods near Bascharage. After almost three years I was back in my homeland again! Just before that. though, I had driven with the Vth corps commander, General Gerow, to Bouillon, where the division had just been given the order to liberate Luxembourg, when it had become clear that Prince Félix and Crown Prince Jean would be present for the liberation. So I took part in the liberation of the capital city on September 10 – a feeling that is indescribable. I was immediately given the task of making contact with the former members of the city government as far as that was possible. So I went by Jeep to "Verlorenkost" (suburb of Luxembourg city) to see Gust Jacquemart, whom I knew well. From Sandweiler we were fired on by the Germans with mortar fire which, thank God, did not do us any great harm. Via Gust Jacquemart I quickly made contact with the mayor, Gaston Diderich, and reported to him of the division's intentions in liberating the capital city. Through another acquaintance, Mr. Edy Gerson, I learned that my brother René had deserted from the Wehrmacht and was hiding in the church at Pfaffenthal. I could scarcely believe it, there he stood . . . and around "Dräi Eechelen" there were still Germans! Late in the afternoon of September 11 I took part in the occupation of the transmitters of Radio Luxembourg in Junglinster by troops of the CCA (Combat Command A) of the division. At this point in time the division's headquarters were located in a forest along the road between Angelsberg and Fels. Here on September 12 I got together with my brother again, who had meanwhile made himself available to the division as an interpreter. Unfortunately we did not stay together, as we were given different assignments.

My most urgent order was to obtain maps and sketches of the Siegfried Line bunkers along the Our and Sauer for the G-2 section, as far as possible through contact with the civilian population of Luxembourg. A friend of former days, the geometry specialist François Scheifer, turned out to be a real magician. Within the framework of his professional activities, he had secretly been making minute maps, accurate to the millimeter, of the German occupying forces' facilities, and now the Americans could make good use of them.

Another mission consisted of bringing in information about the vicinity of Vianden. Thus I drove with Lieutenant d'Avy, an American officer of French ancestry, via Diekirch to Fouhren, where the division had an observation post. Vianden itself was not occupied by our troops. As we drove around, we suddenly came under German machine-gun and mortar fire.

The division's CCR had meanwhile pushed forward through Mersch to Ermsdorf, On the evening of September 13, the order came from the corps to take Wallendorf and thus break through the German Western Wall on the border. On the basis of maps, it had been seen that Wallendorf was most suitable to this purpose because of its bridges. As far as I can remember, no reconnaissance missions took place here. After four to five hours of artillery preparation, using all available guns, the tanks and other vehicles with infantrymen crossed the Sauer at the appointed place on the morning of September 14. The bridge was blown up, but the attack moved along smoothly, and by evening the spearhead had reached the plateau beyond Wallendorf, which gave easy access to the country farther on. In Wallendorf itself, white flags hung out of the windows, and while we marched across the Sauer, which I myself crossed in a Jeep, not a shot was fired. Only in the evening, after one of our engineer columns had come to repair the damaged bridge, did they suddenly come under unexpected heavy fire from Wallendorf. We ourselves dug in for the night on the high ridge beyond Wallendorf, in order to continue the attack on the next morning. Gradually the German opposition flared up, unorganized at first, then suddenly intensifying in the next few days and growing into genuine counterattacks. supported by tanks and heavy guns. Bitter fighting followed, in which about 25% of our materials were lost. Our flanks in particular were unprotected and constantly exposed to German artillery and 8.8 cm anti-aircraft fire. When our attack failed, the 112th Infantry Regiment of the 28th Infantry Division was finally moved up to safeguard the tactical withdrawal called for by the division. In the process, the infantry suffered numerous losses. On September 22 and 23, all the troops were withdrawn, step by step, from the Wallendorf sector and the division was regrouped. Later I went to the division's headquarters in Waismes, Belgium. Here I met Jos Michels, an acquaintance from Ettelbrück, whom the Americans had picked up. He looked terrible, very emaciated, with prison clothes under his coat. It turned out that he had escaped from Hinzert concentration camp and made his way through Germany to where we were. Since he had told the Americans he came from Luxembourg but they had not believed him, they questioned him about Luxembourg. When he finally mentioned Ettelbrück, they asked him if he knew an Aloyse Schiltz. He said yes and assured the captain that he had gone to school along with Schiltz. Finally they called me in . . . and at first I did not recognize him!

After the fall of Aachen, I was called back to Luxembourg by the Luxembourg government, which had returned from exile.

René Schiltz

Schiltz escaped from the Wehrmacht, where he had been forced to join an infantry-engineer battalion, in Berlin in August of 1943, while troops were being transported, and made his way to Luxembourg with false papers, which had been provided to him by Mr. Gerson. He remained hidden there in the church of Pfaffenthal and was cared for by the pastor, J. P. Ries. As if by a miracle, he and a comrade, also an escapee, avoided a large-scale Gestapo raid in Pfaffenthal.

During this time the other brother, Joseph Schiltz, who had been arrested in November of 1941 and imprisoned at Hinzert, Wittlich and Natzweiler concentration camps, was brought to Schönberg in the Palatinate, and was in custody there. The father, Pierre Schiltz, captured in October of 1943, was likewise at Schönberg after being held at Hinzert, Trier and Natzweiler. His mother and sister were forcefully resettled in Koblenz by the Nazis.

As already related, René Schiltz met his brother Aloyse again on September 12, and Aloyse helped him to become an interpreter with the 5th Armored Division.

"At first I went to the 112th Infantry Regiment of the 28th Infantry Division," says René Schiltz, "which was then attached to the 5th Armored Division. Like my brother Aloyse, I was assigned there to make contact with the civilian population in order to obtain information that was important to the reconnaissance service. Among other things, I took part in forest search actions in the area of Brouch (Wecker), Grevenmacher and Wasserbillig from September 13 to 20, in an attempt to round up and capture strayed Germans. Here, to my amazement, I came upon my old professor Jos. Goedert, who had been resettled and had finally escaped in the general confusion of the German withdrawal and returned to Luxembourg. He was pleasantly surprised when the Americans immediately freed him and he recognized me as a GI after I had taken off my steel helmet. He, who had had to sneak through all the border towns secretly, was able to give the Americans valuable information.

After the 5th Armored Division's attack had been halted at Wallendorf, I was called back and sent to General Regnier at the CCA headquarters in Luxembourg, that unit having taken over the protection of the capital city. In the Arbed Building we had a small communications office, the purpose of which was to maintain contact with the authorities and the population until the actual "Civil Affairs "Authority" was established.

With the reorganization of the 5th Armored Division, I was sent to the CCA headquarters at Consthum with the same function. From there I took part in numerous patrols along the Our and tried as much as possible to gain information from the population of the villages along the border of Luxembourg. Around October 5, 1944 the whole division was transferred northward to the area of Malmédy, as well as to the Monschau-Rötgen front line in the Eifel. Heavy and costly fighting took place here until the beginning of December; I was not directly involved, to be sure, but was often near the front with my GI comrades Vic Barton and John Brookens, carrying out reconnaissance missions. Probably the most spectacular operation in which I participated was the so-called 'Lontzen Raid'.

Shortly before the Ardennes offensive began on December 16, the 5th Armored Division was in a defensive position in the area of Eupen. Here I took part in the arrests and house searches of collaborators and informants who worked for the Germans; this was done by a detachment of the 505th Counter Intelligence Corps. I myself was directly involved in the capture of fifteen known spies in Lontzen, Belgium. In their trials I also served as an interpreter. Even on December 17, 1944, after the German major offensive had begun, we were still able to capture several saboteurs who were wearing American uniforms. Later it turned out that the U.S. vehicles, which were used by the troop set up by SS Obersturmbannführer Skorzeny to cause confusion behind the American lines, were for the most part vehicles of the 5th Armored Division that had been abandoned in the attack on Wallendorf-Cruchten.

On January 31, 1945 the government of Luxembourg called me back to Luxembourg, where I was assigned as a sergeant to the SHAEF (Supreme Headquarters, Allied Expeditionary Forces) mission of Colonel Frazer, and more particularly to the newly-formed Ministry of Economy (Minister Guill, Konsbrück). My work for the ministry consisted above all of working with civil and military organizations to carry out missions in destroyed Eislek (Eislek is the Luxembourg name for the Ardennes) and caring, as far as was possible, for cattle which the German side had moved there during the Ardennes offensive, and returning them to the farmers in Luxembourg. I was very astounded when a farmer from Ingeldorf was recognized by one of his horses that the Germans had taken along across the Our when they retreated in January of 1945, and that was now in a German border town. Finally, as of May 1945, I helped to reconstitute and organize the new Luxembourg Army, in which I eventually remained."

Chapter IV
Return to Order

Immediately after the liberation of Luxembourg by the aforementioned 5th Armored Division, the Vth U.S. Corps set up a provisional military government whose task it was to restore order and justice to war-torn Luxembourg until the civil authorities of Luxembourg could take over this task again.

It is probable that numerous "collaborators" were saved from "lynch justice" at the hands of the perturbed populace by the measures taken by the U.S. "Civil Affairs" authorities to keep order for the time being, and were turned over to the authorities for their own protection. Just a few days after the arrival of the first U.S. tanks in Diekirch, the U.S. Civil Affairs detachment office was established in the "Maison rouge" (today the Hotel du Parc).

Major Matthews

Matthews commanded the responsible "Detachment B1F1" until the beginning of the Ardennes offensive. In bright autumn weather, his unit, which was also under the control of the Vth Corps, reached Luxembourg via Sedan along with the combat units of the 5th U.S. Armored Division. After spending two days in the celebrating capital, Major Matthews and his detachment were ordered to Diekirch to take up their specific and surely not exactly simple task there within the framework of the 5th Armored Division. When reading the following report, which Major, later Lt.Col. Matthews based on his diary, it must be remembered that thanks to the work of "Detachment B1F1" of "Civil Affairs", numerous problems that appeared suddenly after the liberation were disposed of quickly for the welfare of the population, and a more regulated life gradually came into being again.

Major Charles Matthews reports:

"On our arrival on September 13, 1944, everything seemed to me to be quiet, unnaturally quiet. We found out very soon that most of the leaders of the former Nazi regime had already been arrested by the militia or had gone into hiding somewhere; in some cases they had been able to move to Germany with the retreating Wehrmacht contingents. On that same afternoon, the former Mayor Theis had been given his earlier office again, after which a discussion took place among him, the previous District Commissioner François, and my officers. On the next day a similar meeting took place, involving my personnel who were to take over a specific office and several former local officials and other persons. At this point, positive and constructive planning was already in action, but one could clearly sense by the almost hesitant behavior of the officials that the population of Diekirch had just been released from Nazi domination a few days ago. Mayor Theis offered me his chair but was surprised when I declined out of respect for his age.

The greatest problem was that the bridges in the vicinity of Diekirch had been blown up during the German withdrawal. For this reason I called in another discussion, in which all the mayors in the district participated." Painfully precise considerations and planning were necessary to organize the necessary transport which was to supply the whole district regularly with food and other goods.

In this situation, Major Matthews found himself compelled to seek out several headquarters, including Army, Corps and Division HQ. In these conferences he was usually accompanied by Lieutenant Lent, the officer for public safety, as well as Major Leonard (executive officer) and his adjutant Captain Houghton. The last two officers were British.

In these conferences it was determined that it would be useful to appoint a liaison officer in the capital city of Luxembourg, who was to maintain the necessary communications between the Detachment and SHAEF (Supreme Headquarters, Allied Expeditionary Forces) in Luxembourg, and who could intervene directly in case of difficulties. The choice fell upon the British Major Seignior, who remained in Luxembourg City and took care of "Civil Affairs" in Diekirch twice a day by means of a mobile information service. Scarcely had Major Matthews and his staff undertaken an orientation trip over the border to the German shore on September 17 when a noticeable uneasiness became obvious among the population of Diekirch, who feared that the Germans might return. This fear of the inhabitants of the town on the Sauer was all the more justified as the German resistance at the border had gradually become stronger against the advancing units of the 5th U.S. Armored Division, and on account of the overly fast advance of the U.S. combat forces, they were widely separated from each other and thus were not in an ideal situation to hold off a beaten but bitterly fighting German army successfully. But as the U.S. artillery fired ceaselessly toward Germany, and as armored patrols frequently brought back German prisoners or wiped out pockets of resistance along the border, the fear slowly disappeared and the people felt confident again.

Increasing problems, though, made it necessary to open a second "Civil Affairs" office in Ettelbrück, administered by Captain Kappanadze. In his function, he was mainly in charge of the still-applicable measures that limited civilian travel. The Detachment was often warned to be extremely careful in carrying out missions, since danger from enemy patrols still did not seem to be ruled out; on Saturday, September 30, 1944 the first fatalities occurred. During a mission to oversee work, Pfc. Conrad drove into a trap and was wounded, while the two other persons in his Jeep were killed by a hand grenade that was thrown into it.

The result of this incident was a general ban on driving civilian vehicles, but this was lifted just two days later. The newly installed Luxembourg government was gradually able to assume power. One of the first measures taken by it, with the help of "Civil Affairs", was that of disarming all so-called Luxembourg militiamen or those who claimed to be such and regularly carried a weapon. Only the men who had reported as auxiliary policemen were allowed to keep their weapons. Numerous checks of this matter were carried out by the Detachment, since violent acts of revenge against former collaborators were still feared.

At the beginning of October 1944, the 5th Armored Division was relieved by the 8th Infantry Division after hard fights near Wallendorf. For several days, almost no American soldiers other than Major Matthews' detachment could be seen in Diekirch, until the troop transfer had been carried out. A result of this was that Major Matthews set out to take care of quartering the newly arrived troops. Thus he was able to make use of his familiarity with the locality for the good of the troops.

For some days a large number of military policemen were on duty in Diekirch, until the troops had settled in.

New connections with the responsible "Civil Affairs" officers of the VIIIth Corps and the divisions (8th and 28th Infantry) that belonged to it were established at once. During this time the nearby front line that was set up across the boundary was turned over by the 9th Army to the 1st Army. During the entire month of September, Major Matthews was very indebted to Captain Crawford, who was very capable of raising the morale of the population and reinforcing it again and again. In addition, Captain English, who spoke fluent French, saw to it that the American and Luxembourg flags were always flying at the eastern end of the city, to the joy and comfort of the inhabitants.

Gradually, though, refugees from the border towns of Vianden and Bettel came to Diekirch on account of the more and more frequent patrol activities of the Germans, as well as by smaller fights that flared up along the Our line. Thanks to the action of Major Matthews, these people were housed quickly, their cattle was divided among nearby farms for stabling, and their vehicles and possessions were housed as well as possible.

After a long period of work and planning, a still embryonic civil court was gradually established, since an uneasy feeling about the "political" prisoners, who were under U.S. jurisdiction and could not be tried, had already existed for several weeks. Thus this uneasy situation gradually relaxed. Another problem was the financial situation. Three weeks after the liberation, the German Reichsmark was still in circulation as currency, and the value of this hated money was kept stable, since no new currency had yet appeared.

Around October 7, the general situation had begun to calm down; the schools were opened again and the typical everyday life gradually returned. Nobody thought any longer that the Germans could ever return. Now and then, though, inhabitants of the border towns were wounded by German artillery fire on the U.S. units stationed there. The regular food supply service functioned superbly; food and rations were apportioned to all the towns.

In addition, the livestock of the refugees in the overfilled stables of the Diekirch farms was carefully registered and then assigned to farms located farther to the south. The public service agencies expanded, and a start was made at clearing and repairing damaged roads and paths. This was especially true of blown-up bridges and approach roads. "Among the population we found several Russians and Poles," Major Matthews reports, "who, thanks to Captain Kappanadze, who spoke both languages fluently, were able to describe to us their long story since their deportation from their home towns by the Germans in 1942."

Friday the 13th of October was a bad-luck day for the superstitious and the day when the Detachment ceased to function as a British-American institution. Higher authorities had decided that the regions near the front should be under the supervision of just one nation, and so the British officers were ordered back. The seven remaining U.S. officers had to take on the other jobs, and Captain Kappanadze became adjutant to Major Matthews.

Although daily life in daylight hours passed without problems, at night there were often individual shots heard in and near Diekirch. Unknown persons fired several times at night on the Glyco building, where a number of political prisoners were still interned. Thus Major Matthews strengthened the watch to protect them.

On the way back from Luxembourg, Corporal Wietsma and Mathes were compelled to abandon their Jeep when they were suddenly fired on in the darkness just outside Diekirch. The vehicle was brought back undamaged the next morning. This incident was proof that it was still not safe in the region at night. The danger consisted not only of the fact that German patrols in captured Jeeps often ventured into Luxembourg and sometimes exchanged fire, but also that our own troops, believing a German scouting party was before them, would open fire. In any case, this incident was never explained clearly.

Because of this and similar incidents in Diekirch, the military command posts located there were transferred to Ettelbrück for reasons of security, as many high-ranking officers regarded Diekirch as "too hot." Only the 121st Regiment of the newly arrived 8th Infantry Division rotated its battalions from Diekirch along the Our front line, alternating in readiness and resting positions.

Traffic limitations still prevailed, and the civilian population was not allowed to be on the streets after 7:00 PM; most of the people accepted this without objection.

Meanwhile, the provisional government of Luxembourg had named new authorities to take over various administrative functions. In addition, the German place and street names were torn down, and the "French" signs that were customary before the war were put up in place of them.

Even leisure-time activities seemed to be reappearing slowly when the only movie house in town was given permission to show films on Saturday and Sunday. The first film to be shown, "Desert Victory", with French subtitles, was a great success.

Currency reform was instituted gradually, after the Detachment had been plagued often enough with an abundance of currencies: Reichsmark, French and Belgian Francs, as well as the Allied military currencies, the last of which, though, had no legal value. Finally only Luxembourg and Belgian Francs were in circulation.

As of October 25 there came the request that on every Monday, Wednesday and Friday one officer and two men of "Civil Affairs" were to be sent to Luxembourg to take part in Detachment A1C1 planning, which had a very positive effect. In addition, Major Matthews' men found this to be a pleasant change from the still-prevailing limitations of social life.

On October 18, Prince Felix of Luxembourg visited the Detachment and signed his name in the unit's guest book. After a talk with Major Matthews, he drove back in his own car amid the cheers and flowers of the local population, who filled the streets with jubilation.

The Detachment set up a radio news service in Diekirch and Ettelbrück; BBC news, taken down in shorthand by Corporal Williams, was turned over to various authorities in both towns in English, and they translated it into Luxembourgeois and broadcast it every afternoon via loudspeakers that had been set up.

On October 30 the British flag was lowered during a brief ceremony, at the division's command; as of then, only the American flag flew, another sign of the change from Allied to exclusively American personnel.

On November 1 the French Lieutenant Duprat was detailed to Major Matthews to help the homeless French refugees who had come to Diekirch. He himself proved to be of great value in many other situations as well. Then on November 2 the Diekirch soccer team invited the Detachment to a game. Since not enough men were available to Major Matthews to make up a team, he turned to the 1st Battalion of the 121st Infantry Regiment (8th Infantry Division), which was resting in Diekirch.

As representatives from the Detachment, Corporal Wietsma and Private d'Aloja were members of the assembled American team, the latter only on the reserves' bench. The game took place at the Diekirch soccer stadium on Sunday afternoon, November 5, 1944. The score was Diekirch 9, U.S. Army 3!

Major Matthews received instructions from Luxembourg that the border towns, such as Wallendorf, Hoesdorf, etc., were to be regarded as "German territory" in the event that medals were awarded for combat days. Thus the Detachment received its third Battle Star as a unit decoration, in addition to its first, gained in Normandy, and its second, in the French campaign. On the evening of November 6, five U.S. trucks arrived in Diekirch. Their drivers, five black soldiers, had obviously overshot because of blackout driving regulations. They were given a hot meal and a night's lodging in the former Gestapo headquarters, the Villa Konter, before setting out the next morning with accurate directions.

From November 8 to 11, Major Matthews took part in a lengthy conference in the capital, where he learned that he had been chosen to take command of Detachment A1C1 in Luxembourg. Major Lewis now took his place in Diekirch.

Before his departure, Major Matthews said that he regretted having to leave Diekirch, and the town's representatives as well as his subordinates thanked him for his excellent work and exemplary leadership. At the same time, the 8th Infantry Division was replaced by the 28th Infantry Division, which had suffered heavy losses at Vossenack and Hürtgen.

On November 13, Major Matthews took command of Detachment A1C1 of "Civil Affairs" in Luxembourg, replacing Lt.Col. Jett.

On the following Saturday, though, he returned to Diekirch, where Major Lewis had already taken command a week ago. It was known that A1C1 was to be subordinated to the XIIth Army Group in Luxembourg and the B1F1 Detachment was to be transferred to Luxembourg; in addition, Major Matthews was to take over his old unit again.

On November 21, all the officers except Major Lewis reported in Luxembourg. Sergeant Rothstein and Corporal William were sent along as the unit's advance guard. The rest of the Detachment meanwhile stood ready in Diekirch with their trucks and all their administrative materials fully packed, awaiting new orders. On November 22, clarity finally came: A1C1 was sent to Verdun and B1F1 was to take over the available space and civilian vehicles on the following day.

Major Lewis remained in Diekirch until November 26, in order to instruct the newly arrived units of the 28th Infantry Division and acquaint them with the population and the region.

It became clear to Major Matthews in Luxembourg very soon that the situation there was totally different from that in Diekirch. Luxembourg, with its many headquarters of divisions, the 9th U.S. Air Force, the SHAEF mission as well as the new government of Luxembourg, represented a gigantic administrative center, and new problems arose and had to be solved every day.

Unlike those of Diekirch, the inhabitants of the capital city had a wealth of leisure-time activities and a normal social life.

Soldiers and civilians could move freely until 11:00 PM, civilian traffic functioned normally, almost all restaurants and cafes were open and nobody in Luxembourg city even thought about a front that was more than forty kilometers away, although the capital was still located in a division's sector.

Only the hundreds of military vehicles, trucks, tanks, Jeeps, and the numerous squares that had been turned into repair shops, reminded the people that there was still a war on. Sirens often howled during the night, and fire from U.S. anti-aircraft guns soon followed. V-1 rockets could also be seen often moving across the sky with their characteristic sound and fiery tail.

The 83rd Infantry Division, whose headquarters had been in Luxembourg since the end of September 1944, and whose units were along the southwestern front, was finally moved out of that sector; in its place came the 4th Infantry Division, sent to recuperate in the "quiet" Luxembourg sector after heavy and costly fighting in the Hürtgenwald.

On December 9, Major Matthews' Detachment was assigned to the 4th Infantry Division on orders from the VIIIth (Gen. Troy Middleton) Corps. Since the liberation of Luxembourg in September, the front seemed to have gone to sleep; other than a few patrol clashes, the line had not changed. The front sector that was now taken over by the VIIIth Corps was spread far out and occupied very sparsely in places.

On the evening of December 15, a staff dinner took place in Luxembourg, at the quarters of Colonel Frazer, the commanding officer of Civil Affairs of the Army Group; among others, Prince Felix and numerous officers participated. On December 16, the Detachment was visited in Luxembourg by several high officers, including Lt.Gen. Grasset (British officer with SHAEF), Colonel Ryan (G-5 Officer, XIIth Army Group), Colonel Gunn (G-5 Officer, 1st U.S. Army), and Lt.Col. Hatch, the G-5 Officer of the VIIIth Corps.

During the subsequent luncheon at the Hotel Cravat, the officers' mess of Major Matthews' Detachment, there came the alarming news that Diekirch had been fired on heavily by the German artillery in the early morning hours, and the Germans had crossed the Our with forces whose numbers were as yet unknown.

Alarm!

Shortly thereafter, the BBC reported that the enemy had broken through the entire line of the 1st U.S. Army from Malmedy to Echternach, and that the situation was to be regarded as serious. Two focal points, as Malmedy and in the Vianden-Hosingen sector, were particularly alarming; in addition, there was considerable pressure on the lines of the 4th Infantry Division near Consdorf.

Radio messages from Diekirch reached the capital and urgently requested additional fire-extinguishing materials.

During the night of December 17-18, Major Matthews ordered two fully equipped fire engines of the Luxembourg professional fire brigade to Diekirch to help prevent a growing catastrophe. Another fire truck was sent to Diekirch the next day for further protection.

In addition, Diekirch and Ettelbrück urgently needed additional beds and covers for the many wounded civilians there. Miss Morgan, the representative of the American Red Cross who had been attached to the Detachment since September, did the work of several people for many days.

During the first two days of the German breakthrough, approximately sixty wounded civilians from the vicinity of Diekirch were evacuated quickly via Ettelbrück to Luxembourg. The local hospitals were immediately emptied of patients who were no longer in need of urgent medical care, so as to make room for urgent emergency cases. Numerous homeless people who had also been housed in hospital rooms were housed with families who had large houses, through measures taken by the Red Cross.

Although the army did everything to calm the population, the people of Diekirch and Ettelbrück, along with many inhabitants of the surrounding villages, preferred to move to safe places as quickly as possible.

Numerous schools were immediately set up as emergency hospitals by the personnel of the Luxembourg Red Cross, since a further influx of severely wounded patients had to be expected. For that reason the casino in the capital, which served as a home for other homeless persons, was emptied and the people there were quartered in the southern part of the country. On Monday, December 18, it became known in Luxembourg that the enemy had already advanced to Diekirch and Ettelbrück, but numerous reconnaissance patrols, which brought additional firefighting materials with them, reported that only German shells had struck the two cities, and that no German had been seen in Diekirch as yet. Blocks and individual sections of Diekirch had been completely destroyed. The Hotel du Midi by the railway station, the Hotel de l'Europe, the city jail and several other buildings had been damaged by German artillery and partially burned out. No deaths had been reported as yet. At the same time when the flood of refugees from the north had jammed the roads, army transports with fresh troops and tremendous amounts of supplies were coming from the south. The 10th U.S. Armored Division and the 80th U.S. Infantry Division arrived at almost the same time; the latter set up its headquarters in Dommeldingen. The 5th Infantry Division, which had taken Metz, and the 26th U.S. Infantry Division arrived gradually. Luxembourg became the headquarters of the IIIrd and the XIIth Corps. In addition, the 6th U.S. Armored Division arrived somewhat later.

In the capital itself, a tangled mass of troops prevailed. When General Patton set up his tactical headquarters in Luxembourg on December 20, the capital was already the headquarters of the 12th Army Group, the XIIth Corps, the 9th Air Force, the 3rd Army and the 4th U.S. Infantry Division.

Kilometer-long military convoys streamed through the city day and night. The main road from Thionville to Luxembourg resounded with the rattle of tank tracks. New types of tanks appeared in Luxembourg for the first time: the M 36 tank destroyer with its 90 mm gun, very effective against German tanks, as well as the self-propelled 155 mm heavy artillery gun.

Here and there, German fighters flew over the area, and the sound of their motors was broken abruptly at night by the howling of sirens and bursts of anti-aircraft fire.

Unfortunately (as if Hitler himself had a hand in the game), it began to snow the night before December 21, 1944, and by early morning everything was covered by a thick layer of snow. Even before that, a bad-weather zone and lack of visibility had made it impossible for the U.S. Air Force to fly missions against the German attack; now the snowy weather made any attempt impossible.

At the end of December, the Germans unexpectedly fired on the capital city with new types of long-range explosive shells. At times members of the civilian population were wounded, and these shells also damaged the cathedral and the city hall.

When the American troops finally went on the offensive in mid-January and numerous focal points on the "Bulge" (the American term for the Ardennes offensive) were captured, it became more important than ever for Civil Affairs to make contact with the civilian population. In ice-cold weather, Major Matthews made many trips to the Sauer in an open Jeep to gain information, and on January 21, along with Major Turner and several local authorities, he entered Diekirch, which was still a front city and had been liberated by units of the 5th Infantry Division only two days before. In the following week, the Detachment's personnel made numerous visits to Diekirch and Ettelbrück in order to learn the extent of the damage in the two ghost cities.

Even before the first groups of inhabitants who had been evacuated returned to Diekirch, U.S. engineer units, on instructions from Major Matthews, had disarmed and removed many dud shells or mines that could have been fatal, particularly to incautious children.

Chapter V

EVENTS FROM OCTOBER TO MID-DECEMBER 1944

The 687th Field Artillery Battalion

This light artillery battalion, armed with twelve 105 mm caliber howitzers, entered French territory in the Utah Beach area, fought in Normandy, and was used as a support unit of several divisions in Brittany until the capture of Brest on September 28, 1944.

The unit, commanded by Lt.Col. Max Billingsley, was then withdrawn from France and transferred to Luxembourg, where it served as a fire-support unit to the companies on the 8th U.S. Infantry Division located along the Our front line in the greater Diekirch area.

The structure of the 687th Field Artillery Battalion was composed of Batteries A, B and C, which constituted the actual artillery unit (firing unit) with four guns apiece, plus a command unit or HQ Company and a Service Battery whose task it was to supply the necessary ammunition to the guns and also to be responsible for food, spare parts and means of transportation.

As listed in the commander's notes, the officers of the battalion were:
Battalion Commander: Lt. Col. Max Billingsley
Executive Officer: Major Edgar P. German
Headquarters Company (Battery) Commander: Captain William Roadstrum
A Battery Commander: 1st Lt. Norris D. McGinnis
B Battery Commander: Captain Eldon Bowers
C Battery Commander: Captain John Mitchell
Service Battery Commander: Captain Edmund Brown

Immediately on its arrival, the artillery unit, as constituted above, occupied raised firing positions in various locations, some of them far apart from each other. The headquarters for communications and fire direction center, plus the command post, were quartered in a hotel in Bourscheid. A Battery took up a position on the "Koeppchen" in Erpeldingen, thus overlooking Diekirch, B Battery went to Michelau, C Battery to Lipperscheid, but the Service Battery remained in Diekirch.

Nels Block, then First Sergeant in B Battery, recalls: "When it gradually began to get colder, only the crews remained at the guns in our position at Michelau, since we had no warm winter clothing other than our woolen overcoats.

The rest of the battery's men were quartered in the village and took turns doing sentry and readiness duty at the gun positions, which were covered with camouflage nets to avoid being spotted by the enemy from the air.

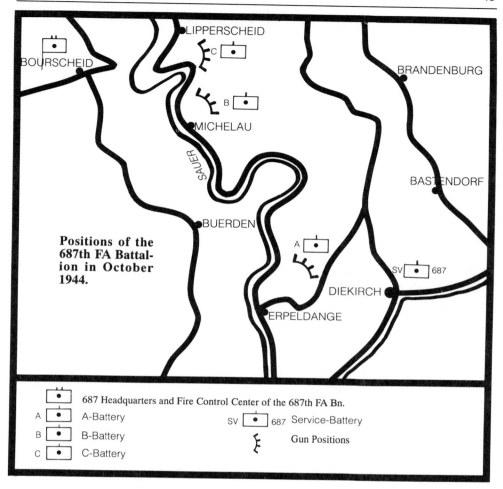

Positions of the 687th FA Battalion in October 1944.

687	Headquarters and Fire Control Center of the 687th FA Bn.
A	A-Battery
B	B-Battery
C	C-Battery
SV 687	Service-Battery
	Gun Positions

Our position was located on a high plateau east of Michelau, with an excellent view on several highland roads as well as the boundary on the horizon. The battery itself numbered over 100 men and had its own field kitchen mounted on a GMC truck, but often the food, especially for the cannoneers lying in readiness at the guns, consisted of rations, which everyone had to prepare himself. I myself often had the good fortune to drive to Diekirch on service trips, and on this occasion, in mid-October, I had myself photographed by a photographer who was active there; I sent the picture to my family members in Iowa.

At the end of November the battery was removed and transferred to just this side of Bastogne, in order to test a new kind of ammunition there, using the "Pozit Fuze" approach ignition. Through this transfer we escaped the German attack on the rest of the batteries on December 18, in which the battalion had many losses to report after two days of fighting."

Until December 16, 1944 the battalion, with the exception of B Battery, re-mained in these positions and fired numerous harassing-fire missions, as well as surface fire on known targets identified by scouting troops; our fire was guided by infantry units on the front lines through fire-control officers and observers.

As of November 19, 1944 the battalion was left on its own as the 8th Infantry Division was slowly withdrawn. This unit was later replaced by parts of the 28th Infantry Division, to which the 687th FA Battalion was subordinated. This resulted in a position change, though it was carried out only by the "firing" units.

A Battery was moved to Bastendorf, B Battery to Landscheid until its transfer to the Bastogne area, and C Battery to Consthum.

After numerous losses, in part to the effects of German artillery, the positions were given up on December 17, 1944, and the rest of the battalion was quickly ordered into the area around Wiltz; the Service Battery was sent to Eschdorf.

The combat on December 16 and 17 is described in the following short report from correspondence with Lt.Col. Billingsley:

"On December 16 the 687th FA Battalion was subordinated to the VIIIth Corps Middleton to strengthen the defense line held by the 110th and 109th Infantry Regiments of the 28th U.S. Infantry Division. The battalion was no longer at its full fighting strength, as B Battery had been transferred out; our gun positions stretched for several kilometers in very hilly terrain.

On December 16, 1944 several units of the enemy were able to break through the defense line formed by our infantry in front of the battalion and surround some of the gun positions. In addition, the command post and gun positions were under heavy German artillery fire. The gun crews were able, with ceaseless and well-aimed barrage fire at short ranges, to beat back several storming attacks; often the cannoneers themselves had to grab their rifles and fight off shock troops who had gotten through. C Battery near Consthum reported over thirty dead Germans in their sector. Shortly after that, the observation and fire-control and spotter aircraft of C Battery came under enemy fire; despite slight damage, the plane took off immediately, while several heavy machine guns took over the necessary fire protection during the takeoff. B Battery was immediately ordered by radio to return to the battalion, since its position was very endangered. Late in the evening of December 16 it arrived there and was immediately directed to a new position on the heights at Michelau. About 3:00 AM the plane's landing strip was hit by several shells. The pilot, who had previously fought along with the ground crew and had personally shot down a German vehicle with a bazooka, flew the Piper to Wiltz at daybreak.

Finally, on command from higher up, the whole battalion, including B Battery, was ordered to give up the position and transferred to the Wiltz area. At this time, though, the advanced observation posts of A and C Batteries had been rolled over by the enemy, and all the personnel were missing. Again detailed to the 28th Infantry Division, the 687th FA Battalion helped in the successful defense of Wiltz on December 18 and 19. Under constantly increasing pressure, though, the rest of the battalion had to draw back through Büderscheid, where the column came under enemy fire again. Finally the unit made it to Sibret, Belgium, where it partially took over the defense of the 28th Infantry Division headquarters.

At the end of the offensive, the 687th FA Battalion had suffered eight casualties. Another 134 men were wounded, some severely, or were missing. Nine guns in all were damaged and lost.

During the first half of December, the hard-hit regiment finally enjoyed some rest and slowly recovered from the strains of a very costly battle near Schmidt and Vossenack in the Hürtgenwald; every opportunity was utilized to entertain the worn-out troops, reorganize them and help them learn from the experience they had gained by providing appropriate training.

"A Paradise for Weary Troops"

Truly a paradise for war-weary troops – that was the general description of Luxembourg in the period from October to mid-December of 1944 among the GIs. who were moved out of a "hot" sector of the front and transferred here to rest.

Thousands of U.S. soldiers from the most varied combat, support and staff units were guests in our country at that time, and it was soon said by all the troops that the Americans would be welcomed with open arms everywhere by the thankful population. Meanwhile, life had more or less returned to normal, as the "Civil Affairs" of the U.S. military government disposed of many problems, that had appeared immediately after the liberation in September, for the good of the people.

There was scarcely a single town in Luxembourg where U.S. soldiers were not quartered, some for only a few days, others for longer periods. Along the border formed by the Sauer and Our in particular there were large masses of troops in observation and defensive positions, but often after a week of service they were sent back to the rear areas to rest and replaced by fresh troop units and reinforcements. As the weather grew colder, the Americans preferred to find quarters in barns, sheds or private houses, and the inhabitants regarded them practically as members of their families out of their great gratitude for regaining their freedom. Despite the language barrier, everyone had "his own American" with whom he was on particularly friendly terms. Often it was the children who learned the first bits of English and thus contributed very much to understanding as genuine little interpreters. The Americans took an active part in the everyday life of the population, some of them learned Luxembourg customs and partook of local specialties, served to them by beaming families, as a pleasant change.

Among the troops, their service during times of rest was used to make numerous scouting trips along the border and the West Wall. In addition, combat training was undertaken in the country, vehicles, weapons and equipment were repaired in great numbers, and new procedures were introduced. Often the U.S. artillery also fired "greetings" at the bunkers of the West Wall – to the particular joy of the inhabitants. Many a brass cartridge case, left behind by the Americans and polished to a high gloss, still decorates many a mantelpiece today as a souvenir.

In general it should be noted that this period of time was characterized by hopes for a quick end to the war, since the other side "over there" was very quiet. But there were sporadic clashes between enemy scouting parties in which shots were fired. Whenever the German artillery fired, the fire was often returned with multitudes of grenade "blessings" from the American side.

Especially after the fall of Aachen, there were more and more frequent rumors that Germany would probably surrender before Christmas.

CHAPTER VI

DEFENSIVE COMBAT
OF THE 109TH REGIMENT
(28TH INFANTRY DIVISION)

During the first half of December, the hard hit regiment finally enjoyed some rest and slowly recovered from the strains of a very costly battle near Schmidt and Vossenack in the Hürtgenwald; every opportunity was utilized to entertain the worn-out troops, reorganize them and help them learn from the experience they had gained by providing appropriate training.

A Brief Chronological Overview
December 1944
Officers who had lost their lives were replaced at once, the decimated ranks were refilled with new arrivals; in addition, every man finally received new clothing, and missing pieces of equipment were replaced.

During this period, the leadership gave a high priority to preparation of materials and weapons. On December 7, the former regimental commander, Colonel Gibney, was transferred to the division's headquarters as Chief of Staff, and on December 8 Lt.Col. James Rudder, who had won renown as the commander of the 2nd Ranger Battalion in the ascent of the "Pointe du Hoc" in Normandy on June 6, 1944, took his place. On December 11, Lt.Col. Daniel Strickler, the later "defender" of Wiltz, became Executive Officer of the 110th Regiment. When the German offensive began on December 16, the 28th Infantry Division was attacked along its entire defensive line by nine enemy divisions. During the ensuing battles, the division's own 109th Regiment, although pushed back at first, was able to slow the enemy advance considerably and likewise weaken it significantly.

If the 109th Regiment had drawn back at once, as it was advised to by the 9th U.S. Armored Division, then the units of the 352nd VGD surely would have been able to take the strategically important heights and intersections near Mertzig, Heinerscheid and Grosbous in a short time and without opposition.

By their tough and bitter defensive fighting, the units of the 109th Regiment were able to cripple the German advance almost completely during the first days of the offensive, so that the enemy could achieve practically no noteworthy gain in territory.

The correct behavior at the critical moment was thus decisive for the defeat of the Germans on the south wing of the line of attack; the 109th Regiment was later awarded a "Presidential Citation" for this. 1944 was a tough year for the regiment; scarcely a month passed in which it was not fighting against a fanatical foe. Many of its men were killed in action, many hundreds were hospitalized in France or Britain. There were only a few who remained from the original cadre of the regiment, whose traditional spirit and fighting morale were not changed by the many new arrivals and reinforcements.

Detailed Chronology
December 1-9, 1944

During this time the regiment again occupied the west bank of the Our in a defensive position and carried out much field training as well as an inclusive reorganization program.

On December 3, Company A (1st Battalion), on orders form the regiment, made a surprise attack on the enemy shore of the Our for the purpose of bringing in prisoners. On the next day the patrols returned successfully to the headquarters of the 1st Battalion. As it turned out, one of the captured Germans was from the 915th Grenadier Regiment. This provided evidence of a suspected troop movement; the 916th Grenadier Regiment of the 352nd VGD had been replaced only a short time before.

On December 8 Lt.Col. Rudder took command of the regiment, in place of Col. Gibney.

December 10

On this day the 2nd Battalion of the 109th Regiment was replaced in the vicinity of Beaufort by the 60th Armored Infantry Battalion of the 9th U.S. Armored Division (CCA = Combat Command A: subordinated unit); the 2nd Battalion was immediately transferred to Bastendorf in place of the 1st Battalion of the 110th Regiment. This transfer had as a result the modification of the regimental boundaries: Bettendorf became the center of the right battalion on the line of the 109th Regiment, Bastendorf the left, while the reserve battalion remained in Diekirch.

December 11-15, 1944

Effective December 12, Lt.Col. Daniel Strickler, Executive Officer of the 109th Regiment, was transferred to the 110th Regiment; in all, the regimental leadership underwent several modifications and staff changes on that day. In place of Lt.Col. Noto, Major Maroney, formerly the regiment's S-3 officer, became Commander of the 2nd Battalion, Lt.Col. Merriam became the new Executive Officer, while Major Martin took over the position of S-3 (Operations Officer).

In addition, the regimental headquarters were moved to Ettelbrück, so that on December 13 the situation was as follows: The 1st Battalion remained in Diekirch as a reserve, while the 2nd and 3rd Battalions had taken up positions on the defensive line along the Our in the regiment's sector (approximately from Vianden to Wallendorf).

December 16, 1944

At 5:45 AM the 2nd and 3rd Battalions, as well as the Antitank Company, reported to the regiment that there was heavy enemy fire by artillery and launcher shells in

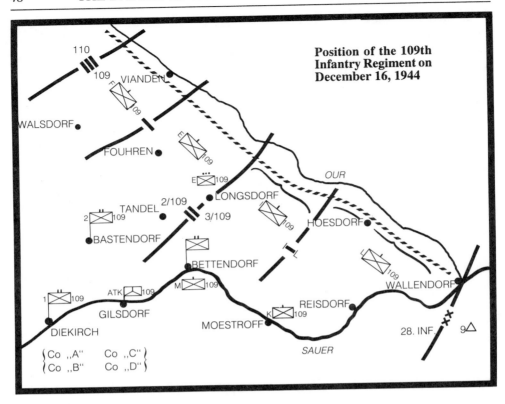

Position of the 109th Infantry Regiment on December 16, 1944

their respective sectors. The regiment in Ettelbrück ordered the highest level of alarm for all its units and ordered that the enemy should be opposed under all conditions in the event that crossing the Our was attempted. The reserve (1st) battalion in Diekirch was immediately put in readiness when, at 8:20 AM, the front units reported the presence of large enemy forces on the west (Luxembourg) bank of the Our.

Two of the enemy's main thrusts had been recognized near Bettendorf and Reisdorf as well as at Vianden (Roth on the Our). The two battalions on the defensive line immediately reacted with heavy infantry-weapons fire and requested artillery support. All positions held and cost the enemy numerous losses in the first attack, this being on account of the favorable defensive situation (steeply falling terrain from the American positions down to the Our).

Company E (2nd Battalion) reported a little later that the enemy had already broken through its flank near Longsdorf. On orders from the regiment, Reserve company G of the 2nd Battalion was transferred immediately from Brandenbourg to the neighboring Company F in order to close a dangerous gap. All companies now reported heavier artillery and launcher fire as well as isolated contact with the enemy. The 2nd Divisions, artillery battalions (107th and 108th FA Battalions) immediately directed a withering and well-aimed defensive fire at the German lines at the Our crossing points, and thus scattered the massive infantry attack that had begun.

At 2:25 PM the Commander of the 2nd Battalion, Major Maroney, reported that vocal contact with E Company (Author's note: this was a platoon of E Company) had been lost; from the last radio message that had been received, it appeared that the unit had come under German mortar fire and, shortly thereafter, had been attacked by the enemy in battalion strength. Company A and several Sherman tanks of the 707th Medium Tank Battalion were sent out from Diekirch to Longsdorf immediately in relief, to restore contact with the enclosed unit. South of Longsdorf, though, A Company came to a stop late in the afternoon when three German Jagdpanzer turned up. Thereupon B Company was immediately ordered to head toward Brandenbourg to build up a barrier there.

Only around 7:00 PM was C Company also moved out of Diekirch and sent to Brandenbourg, with orders to hold the village at all costs. All of these troop movements were completed by 10:00 PM. At midnight the 3rd Battalion still held its positions on the right wing of the regiment's line and had successfully driven back the enemy on the Bettendorf-Hoesdorf highland line several times; the 2nd Battalion was in Fouhren along with the remaining men of E Company, while F and G Companies were west of Walsdorf.

December 17, 1944

The second day of the offensive began around 5:00 AM with brief but extremely heavy German artillery fire. The 3rd Battalion reported an attack in company strength near Hoesdorf and on the plateau at Reisdorf but was able to beat it back successfully, as an extensive minefield prevented the Germans from advancing to a great degree.

On the Vianden-Fouhren road a firefight developed in the 2nd Battalion's sector, against a German infantry company supported by three assault guns.

G Company was able to capture approximately twenty Germans and, in concerted defense with Company F, to cost the enemy numerous losses.

Despite the tank support, Company A was not able to push forward to Longsdorf, since the village was already firmly in enemy hands and parts of E Company had probably been wiped out and taken prisoner already. There followed a firefight of the Antitank Company, which had taken positions halfway up the slopes at the Diekirch-Bettendorf road intersection and south of Tandel, against the approaching assault guns. The gun crews of the Antitank Company scored many hits, but the 57 mm shells were obviously ineffective against the heavily armored German assault guns. During the battle, the German tanks were able to knock two guns out of action, and the crews were lost.

East of Brandenbourg an advancing German assault gun was shot down by a bold bazooka man in close combat. Early in the afternoon another massive German infantry attack on the heights of Reisdorf took place, but it could be repelled successfully with mortar support. In this attack the 352nd VGD lost approximately 150 men (dead and wounded), and had to leave 22 prisoners behind. Meanwhile, though, the enemy had succeeded in rolling over the field kitchen of Company F and destroying that of D Company by artillery fire. Thereupon Lt. Col. Rudder ordered every field kitchen of the regiment still present in the sector of the 109th Regiment to evacuate to Ettelbrück immediately. This operation was carried out successfully by the S-4 officer without further losses. After a position of the Cannon Company had been overrun, the rest of the gun crews were able to set up a new defensive position farther back within a short time.

From the division there came the alarming news that the enemy had overrun most of the positions on the left flank and thus pushed the regiment's border in. The division ordered some of the remaining antitank guns transferred immediately into the sector of the 110th Regiment. Particularly endangered points were now the gun positions of Battery A of the 107th FA Battalion, as well as Battery C of the 108th FA Battalion.

At extremely short ranges, and practically defenseless for having almost no infantry weapons, the cannoneers had to provide their own defensive fire on the steep slopes with explosive shells.

Lt.Col. Rosborough, Commander of the 107th Field Artillery Battalion, was able at this critical moment to organize a task force out of available units, with two tanks and a platoon of infantry, and thus saved the situation. After a hard fight he was able to push forward to the endangered battery and rescue the guns.

Company B received permission to resupply the units, which were dangerously short of ammunition and supplies, but this was not possible until 11:00 PM on account of constantly arising small-scale combat. The commander of the 1st Battalion thereupon ordered Company B to carry out this thankless task only at daybreak.

December 18, 1944

During the night the enemy directed undirected harassing fire on all the defensive positions, and achieved several minor breakthroughs by means of night infiltration. Early in the morning Company A was able to make connections with the 2nd Battalion south of Longsdorf.

Around noon, Company K could not hold out any longer; a large part of it was overrun and taken prisoner near Reisdorf after its ammunition had run out. About 3:00 PM three German Jagdpanzer broke through the barrier on the Longsdorf-Tandel fork and reached the intersection at the "Bleesbreck." Since the whole defensive line could not be held any longer, the regiment called for a withdrawal an ordered a unit of the 103rd Engineer Battalion to prepare all bridges needed in the withdrawal to be blown up.

The 60th Armored Infantry Battalion of the 9th U.S. Armored Division moved back to Ermsdorf, while the major part of the 110th Regiment was already on the way to Wiltz as ordered. General Cota (Commander of the 28th Infantry Division) arranged for a combat team, which was later to be called the "Task Force Rudder", to move back with the 9th Armored Division so as not to endanger its open left flank. Under such artillery support as was still available, the exhausted 109th Regiment withdrew slowly, its withdrawal routes and bridges were blown up, and several roads that could have been of use in the enemy advance were mined. The withdrawal to a new defensive line was concluded about 2:00 AM on December 19.

According to statistics from the Ordnance Depot, on these three days 280,000 rounds of infantry-weapon ammunition, 5000 mortar shells, 3000 hand grenades and 300 bazooka rockets were fired.

December 19, 1944

Surprisingly, the enemy did not take advantage of the regiment's withdrawal, which made it easier to build up a new, favorably located line of defense. But during the withdrawal of the right wing, Bettendorf was heavily fired on with Nebelwerfer ("screaming Mimie") rockets, which resulted in losses in the ranks of the withdrawing 3rd Battalion.

Helped by the situation, the 81 mm mortars of the heavy companies of the 109th Regiment in particular were able to inflict serious losses on the German units that began to move late in the afternoon. About 6:00 PM the unmistakable sounds of German tracked vehicles were heard, and the G-2 Intelligence Section (reconnaissance unit) at the division headquarters reported that during the night, or early in the morning of December 20 at the latest, a German tank attack could be expected. When night fell and the German artillery became active again, the command to withdraw came from the division again; accordingly the 109th Regiment had to take up the following new defensive positions: along with the 9th Armored Division, the 2nd Battalion moved back in the direction of Colmar-Berg, the 1st Battalion westward beyond Ettelbrück. After all the units had passed through Ettelbrück, where it had been located for their protection, the 3rd Battalion was split up. Company I was sent to Feulen, K to Mertzig and L to Grosbous. The approach roads and bridges to Ettelbrück were mined and blown up during the withdrawal. Only early in the morning of December 20 were the Germans able, under cover of darkness, to push forward to Ingeldorf, where it could be – and was – seen easily and fired on by surrounding U.S. artillery units.

December 20, 1944

On this day a stronger enemy patrol, equipped with snow suits, attacked Company F, which was able to fight off this attack that was meant to bring in some American prisoners for questioning. In the firefight, though, a German officer who was carrying several maps with important information and notations on them was captured. For example, it was learned that the 352nd VGD was to advance via Feulen and Heiderscheid in the general direction of Arlon (Belgium).

December 21-30, 1944

On December 21, communications officers of the 80th U.S. Infantry Division pushed through to the lines of the 3rd Battalion in Mertzig and inquired as to the possibility of moving their 318th and 319th Regiments through the line of defense. Thereupon the parts of the 109th Regiment that were on hand (mainly Company L of Captain Embert Fossum, which was renamed Task Force L) moved back to Grosbous, from where they were likewise supposed to retard the German advance.

In the further course of their ordered withdrawal, the units of the 109th Regiment finally encountered the 26th U.S. Infantry Division near Schandel. From here, parts of the regiment were separated and ordered to Stegen, from where they were to join tanks of the 90th Reconnaissance Squadron of the 10th U.S. Armored Division in an attack on Gilsdorf and Moestroff on December 24.

As ordered, Combat Team 109 (consisting of an antitank company of the 2nd Battalion, units of the 707th Tank Battalion, 630th Tank Destroyer Battalion, 107th and 108th FA Battalions plus Company B), along with the 90th Reconnaissance Squadron, attacked Moestroff at 3:00 PM; part of the town was taken, but the enemy was able to destroy the Sauer bridge so that the other bank of the river could not be returned to.

Gilsdorf was cleaned out and given up by the penetrating German troops around 6:30 PM, and the engineers blew up the footbridge built by the Germans over the blown-up Sauer bridge. Then the U.S. task force withdrew to a defensive line overlooking much of the Sauer valley; numerous tanks detailed to the 90th Reconnaissance Squadron continued to fire on the Diekirch-Bettendorf road, almost completely wiping out a returning German cycle column.

On December 26 the regiment was to be replaced by units of the 6th U.S. Armored Division, after which it would rejoin the 28th Infantry Division, meanwhile located at Neufchâteau.

On December 28 the 1st Battalion was transferred to Recogne, the 2nd to the vicinity of St. Pierre, and the 3rd to Libramont, with orders to close off these sectors from possible infantry attacks. But the enemy was able to apply only single aircraft. Finally the regiment was sent westward of Recogne to protect the arriving anti-aircraft units of the 87th Infantry Division.

Total Losses, December 1-31, 1944
Strength on Dec. 1, 1944: 145 officers, 5 warrant officers, 2817 NCO and men
Dead: 5 officers, 93 men
Wounded: 19 officers, 294 men
Missing: 5 officers, 154 men
Other losses, including captured, sick, frostbitten: 14 officers, 590 men
Source: Regimental journal + diary of John McDonald

The following reports, which fit into the framework of the 109th Regiment, are the results of years of correspondence with former U.S. soldiers of this unit. No one else but the all-too-often nameless "GI", like his German adversary, is capable of presenting such a precise picture of the extremely tough and hard-bitten withdrawal fighting on the 109th Infantry Regiment.

This withdrawal combat, which was directed tactically so that it slowed the German advance between the Sauer and Our, is the reason why a great many of the inhabitants of this area could reach safety at the right time despite the rush of events.

The interviewed ex-soldiers often related the events of that time with tears in their eyes, and it seems impossible to capture their feelings and emotions in words.

The following reports of the surviving soldiers should be seen as a respectful memorial to the sacrifices of their comrades who fell in the fight for our freedom from December 16, 1944 to the end of January 1945.

Numerous patrols that extended in part to the German side of the Our were carried out by the 109th Regiment at the beginning of December. (see also Vol.I: The Germans). Alternatively, the individual companies tried to gain insight into the strength of the enemy troops in the sector of land across the river, the presence of bunkers and their types, minefields and the like, through nightly scouting forays in the defensive sectors assigned to them, all this in regard to a planned breakthrough into the German positions on the part of the regiment. The leader of such a patrol squad was Sgt. Charles Frawley, member of A Company (1st Battalion), wrote to the author in 1984:

"Our entire patrol, at about double platoon strength, left Bettendorf on trucks which were also loaded with several rubber rafts on which we were to cross the Our. Before daybreak we reached Hoesdorf, unloaded the boats in haste and dragged them down to the Our. According to our instructions, we were supposed to try to bring back several prisoners, whom we were to turn over to the regiment for questioning.

At this time (December 3) the water in the Our was high, the meadows along the shores were partly flooded, and the current in midstream was unusually strong. With some difficulty we reached the German shore and immediately disappeared into the darkness in groups. One man stayed behind and was supposed to remain on the Luxembourg side and be ready at an appointed time to pull the boats back by a line stretched just above the surface of the water.

Working our way cautiously along a dirty little village street, we reached a small group of deserted houses (Ammeldingen?) and hid ourselves in the village church while the other groups took up observation posts in the nearby barns. We all waited until it was dark to work our way forward to the known line of bunkers.

Several German dugouts were stormed quickly, there was wild shooting with wounded men on both sides, and the Germans also lost a few men. My group had succeeded in subduing a German sentry and take him prisoner. We tied his hands and gagged him, then ran back in the direction of the Our with the other groups and took cover immediately to await the time when the man on the other shore was supposed to bring the first boatload back. (Note: see also Vol.I: The Germans report by Friedrich Schmaschke, G.R.916").

We waited half an hour, but nothing happened. It grew dark gradually, and we had wounded men who needed to be treated quickly. The man who was supposed to take the first group across simply did not show up. Had he been captured by a German patrol during the same night? We never found out.

So there was nothing for us to do but cross the Our ourselves on the rope that was stretched across. I was the first to volunteer to do this, in order to test its condition. So I reached the other shore, located a boat, tied it to the line and, pulling on the line with great difficulty, pulled it to the other shore.

First the wounded men got onto the boat with a few companions and were brought across. Then soldiers from the other groups followed in turn, with the German prisoners.

On the third trip the boat tipped over, pulled loose, and the men fell into the icy water. Among them was a soldier from my group, Private Harry Dahm, who was pulled under and drowned, as he could not get rid of his equipment fast enough. The boat was lost, as it was torn away quickly by the current.

So there was nothing left for the rest of the men to do but cross the Our hanging onto the rope. I helped several slightly injured soldiers cross, as well as the Germans whom we had taken prisoner.

The men hung onto me tightly, so as not to slip away from the rope, which was barely twenty centimeters above the foaming surface of the water.

Harry Dahm was found farther downstream several days later.

Thus I lost one of my best men in this patrol. The German prisoners whom the rest of my group brought in were able to tell nothing that was not already known to the regimental staff. A high price for a blank!"

Chapter VII

Eyewitness Reports on the Units of the 109th Regiment

At the age of twenty, Bob Meyer, whose ancestors originated from Hamburg, was one of the oldest soldiers in A Company. The former machine-gunner, who brought his memories of past combat service back to life on the spot in the autumn of 1980, was taken prisoner by the Germans in a fir forest not far from Longsdorf on December 18, 1944, after his company had been almost completely wiped out.

A Company, 109th Infantry

After a careful study of his interview as to the localities he named, and checking on the basis of maps of the terrain, it turned out that on that December 18, 1944 Bob Meyer and Friedrich Schmäschke (GR 916) had been on opposite sides in a forest battle (see Vol.I: The Germans). (His story also matches the report given by Günter Bach, Vol.I: The Germans).

(When Friedrich Schmäschke was also on hand and pointed out the German situation before Longsdorf, this hypothesis was proved.) Fate intended that Bob Meyer would be taken prisoner on that day, while Friedrich Schmäschke was injured by artillery fire on the same afternoon.

Since the two reports complement each other in terms of time and place, when juxtaposed they provide a realistic picture of the fighting for a small wooded height just before Longsdorf that cost so many young soldiers on both sides their lives. Because of their common interest in their own past and sacrificed youth, the enemies of those days have become friends today, and have retained one lesson from their bitter experiences of December 1944: hopefully, NEVER AGAIN WAR.

But let us allow Private First Class Bob Meyer tell his story:

"For me, the war in Europe began at the beginning of October 1944, when I was transferred, as a brand-new GI, from a training unit at Camp Rucker, Alabama to the 112th Regiment (28th Infantry Division) for my baptism of fire. The fight for the village of Vossenack south of Aachen soon ended in a catastrophic defeat with astonishingly high losses in men and material. I was very happy to come out of this terrible, unforgettable battle unharmed and be ordered to the 109th Regiment of the same division as a replacement, since it had been hit even harder. Nobody knew or could suspect in the least that we were falling out of the hot frying pan straight into the glowing fire, for it was to get even worse.

Arrival in Luxembourg

As mentioned, after the hastily carried-out reorganization, we were loaded onto trucks with all our remaining equipment one day in November and transported by a direct route to Bettendorf in Luxembourg. At that time we had as good as no idea of what Luxembourg was; most of us believed we were already in Germany or even in France. Lousy and dirty, we arrived in Bettendorf and heard only that we were to replace units of the 8th U.S. Infantry Division located here. The castle in Bettendorf had been set up as our housing and we moved into our quarters.

Several companies of the 109th Regiment must have been present in Bettendorf at this time, since a rather large motor pool, with troop carriers bearing other companies' emblems, was still located here several days after we arrived.

After several days' rest and refreshing sleep after all the hardships we had been through, the world gradually looked different again, and it seemed to us that paradise would open to us after all that we had been through. A Company had to sacrifice almost 70% of its total effective strength; new replacements arrived gradually, all of them very young soldiers fresh from training in America and without any combat experience. In addition, lost weapons and damaged parts were replaced and repaired, so that within a short time the company had attained almost its full fighting strength again. We learned that the units in Bettendorf were intended as a reserve, and at the same time we heard something from the front lines at Reisdorf and Wallendorf, which ran along the natural border of the small Our River, to which we would soon be transferred as defensive readiness troops.

The days passed under the last autumn sun, and it became increasingly damp and cold. From the bitter experiences in the Hürtgenwald we tried to derive new tactical knowledge for forest fighting; in any case, field training took place every day now, which instructed us greenhorns again and again as to how we were supposed to behave in various situations under fire. At night we frequently undertook short patrols, so as to acquaint ourselves with the terrain, as the pitch-dark nights allowed only a very limited view. At this point we envied our comrades in other companies who were staying as a mobile reserve in Diekirch, the "parodies of relaxation", as it was called, and which we now knew only from stories we heard.

After weeks of "surviving" on K rations, there were finally three hot meals a day and plenty of army rations again since our arrival in Bettendorf, prepared to our applause at the ever-smoking field kitchen located in the cobblestone yard of the castle. Several times there were even extra supplies of fresh roast pork, vegetables and desserts, all of this intended to put us on our feet again and improve our morale.

We really felt that we were slowly blooming, and our will to live was reawakening. Even our breakfast regularly consisted of scrambled eggs with bacon, cornmeal pancakes with syrup and butter, where previously we had only had powdered eggs on rare occasions, and they were hated by everybody because of their medicinal aftertaste. Only the inhabitants of Bettendorf seemed to take pleasure in them, and we distributed quantities of them, along with corned beef, peanut butter, jam and such. The field kitchen was regularly surrounded by a crowd of children, and we had fun with them. For the begging young hands there was chocolate, of which we had plenty, chewing gum, which they obviously were not familiar with, jellybeans and powdered soft drinks, of which they could never get enough.

I received a brand new .30 Browning machine gun as my weapon and was definitively named machine-gunner in the "weapons squad" of the 2nd Platoon of A Company.

Front-line Activities

On orders from the regiment, we were soon transferred to the front line at Reisdorf, and only here did it become clear to us that we were just a shot away from the Germans in the so-called West Wall. At times we could clearly see bunkers whose natural camouflage of forest soil and branches had been ripped away by previous artillery fire so that the meter-thick concrete structures, all of which showed the scars of shots, came into view. Only the Our divided the valley, over which we had an excellent view, and thus formed a natural barrier. As machine-gunner I was assigned to a gun position that had already been constructed by the previous unit; so I was happy that I did not have to dig my own foxhole along with my loader. Three times a day, almost exactly on schedule, a field phone called us down to a nearby observation post to get our food, while another team briefly replaced us at the machine gun during chow call.

Nothing moved anyway, although often, especially at night, we heard sounds from the other side. It was clear to us, though, that the enemy was present permanently, for several young German soldiers who were captured on German soil and brought in by a night patrol confirmed this suspicion.

Because of the poor view in the darkness, numerous mine traps, so-called "booby traps" and flare mines had been placed on the slope down to the Our and in the sector that I was supposed to watch over, so as to betray and halt any possible nocturnal invasion of our positions at the very beginning.

During our surveillance activity, my loader and I were supplied with four boxes of machine-gun ammunition one afternoon in late November, with the order to fire the four belts of 250 rounds each at the German side within ten minutes on receiving a certain signal. They told us the regiment had ordered a "firepower demonstration" on the entire line along the Our in order to make the enemy think there were larger numbers of troops there and make him nervous. Shortly thereafter, every soldier opened a blindly aimed but well-nourished fire, accompanied by the fire of the available 60 mm mortars, in the direction of the bunkers. I personally thought this was nothing but a waste of ammunition, of which we were constantly in short supply a short time before.

As ordered, I emptied the fabric belts; the barrel of the machine gun glowed bright red from the heat of friction, and our foxhole filled up with empty cartridge cases.

After a week of service there, we went back to Bettendorf as a reserve; there we could rest and, in part, finally obtain new clothes from the quartermaster depot set up in the Catholic convent. At the end of November I was ordered to the front lines again, but this time I was sent to Wallendorf and also had to exchange my machine gun, since it was apparently needed more urgently in Reisdorf, for a BAR (Browning Automatic Rifle). I was not unhappy about that, for despite its weight, the BAR was still handier than the .30 machine gun.

The days passed quickly without any particular incidents. Only once, during a nightly trip, did I hear sounds along a wall by the road and was scared to death when I saw something black moving on the upper edge of the wall. When I got no answer after calling, "Stop, who's there?", I fired a burst. Splinters of stone flew, but thank God it turned out to have been a cat that had scared me.

At Rest in Diekirch

Finally the entire 1st Battalion was taken out of this sector and transferred to Diekirch for rest and reserve duty. The boys rejoiced, since they already knew Diekirch from hearsay; it was already rumored that Marlene Dietrich would come to Diekirch in the middle of December to put on a show there.

How happy we were finally to be able to sleep in a new building instead of a two-man tent or a barn. Our company was billeted in a three-story building, almost brand new, not far from the cemetery in Diekirch (probably the present Dr. Mambourg street). Right after our arrival in Diekirch, showers were set up in the present-day brewery not far from the railroad station, and finally we could thoroughly wash off the dirt and dust that still stuck to us.

At the exit from the shower room, which was located in the back courtyard of the brewery, the Quartermaster Company had put up its clothing depot, where everybody had to exchange his ragged uniform and underwear for brand new, neatly pressed clothes. In addition, each of us received two pairs of woolen socks and an extra supply of clean underwear, including warm winter clothes, for the weather was turning distinctly colder.

So the days passed with theoretical training, weapon cleaning, troop movies, recreational evenings and the like, and in fact, Marlene Dietrich entertained us for a couple hours in the festivity hall of the city hall on December 10, 1944, which excited all of us; the hall threatened to burst from the crowd of jubilant GIs.

Our company commander informed us that on December 16 we were to take part in a parade, at which several men of the 109th Regiment would be decorated. For this purpose, to the accompaniment of a band, the division had a marching drill on a square near the church (Place Guillaume), in which we all took part in new uniforms and coats. Carefree, we went to sleep on the evening of that foggy, cold, damp December 15, some of us annoyed about the parade to be held the next morning, where everything had to be "spit-polished."

One explosion after another woke us up in the lower part of town about 5:30 AM. We were immediately ordered, since we were sleeping on the top floor of our assigned house, to get to the ground floor and the cellar as fast as possible. Everything was confused on account of this sudden shelling. The firing continued until about daybreak, but we had already been placed in alarm readiness before that. Although the situation was not known, we had to stay ready with our equipment and marching rations. At 10:00 AM we were told: "Get out and hand over your personal belongings and other baggage"; so we were to move out. Shortly before noon the time came: our company marched out.

As we passed the church, German shells struck again. In a quick march we went through the inner city under a hail of shells and down to the Sauer, where we hurried along the left riverbank in the direction of Gilsdorf and Bettendorf. In the background of one of the houses near the Sauer river, a man called for help; his arm had been struck by a shell fragment and was just hanging by the skin above his elbow. A mother was holding a baby in her arms. Another splinter had cut the child and pierced the woman's chest. I quickly bandaged the man's arm as best as I could and then ran to catch up with the company. Several times we had to hit the dirt as whistling artillery shells landed in the garden along the Sauer and their iron fragments flew around us. Without losses our company reached the intersection near Bleesbrück. Small arms fire could already be heard farther ahead, so the Germans, as already suspected, had broken through! That was also the reason for this concentration of artillery fire. Close to the gable of the last house in Bleesbrück there was a weapons carrier (Dodge truck), and we were given additional ammunition. It was mainly hand grenades that were given out. In addition, D rations were handed out, small bars of vitamin-rich hard chocolate in waxed boxes, on which one could live for several days, if need be, when surrounded by the enemy.

I hurried along the roadside ditch with the rest of the machine-gun squad in the direction of the "Seltz", for according to orders we were to go to Longsdorf to block the road that led to Diekirch.

A shell that hit close to the railroad track (Benny line) killed a first sergeant and injured several man of the hastening platoon. Suddenly three assigned Sherman tanks of the 707th Tank Battalion rumbled up, and we gave a sigh of relief. From the wooded hills to the right of the "Seltz" there came the noise of machine weapons. With our nerves tensed to the breaking point, we approached the bend of the road to Longsdorf, protected by the tanks, when suddenly someone ahead of us called out that something had moved in the house on the left side of the road. The front tank immediately turned its turret to the 10 o'clock position and fired an explosive shell from its 75 mm tank gun into the house. The exploding shot tore a hole in the gable. To our amazement, which suddenly turned into tremendous horror, the cries of feminine voices rang out, and two totally disoriented women, in shock, were brought out of the house. Thank God they had not been injured. They were immediately taken care of and sent to safety.

All at once the German artillery fire that had fallen on the area sporadically came to a stop. In place of it, to our surprise, we were fired on from a house on the right side of the street where the road bent toward Longsdorf. Again the Sherman fired a shell into the building, and this time we were successful. When the smoke had cleared somewhat, and after several bursts of fire had been shot into the house from our automatic weapons, we suddenly heard "Nicht schiessen, no shoot, no shoot!" from inside.

After they had thrown their weapons out, several German soldiers, shaken by the force of the explosions, came outside. Some of them were still half-grown children. Several of the men following us immediately took them back and called a medic to take care of the wounded among them. When we searched the building, we found several stacked-up cases of 8 cm mortar ammunition as well as several primed Panzerfaust weapons. Thank God the tank had fired first. We left the house and took up a position in the wooded range of hills on the left side of the road to Longsdorf.

Thick underbrush prevented any fairly good view of the road. In order to keep the prescribed sector under sufficient view all the same, the company spread far out. My loader and I crouched in a small hollow not far from an old beech tree about in the middle of the downhill slope.

Suddenly shots rang out ahead of us. We exchanged fire blindly, without knowing exactly where the shots came from. But one thing was clear now: the enemy was within rifle range, no more than 500 meters away from us.

I checked our ammunition supply again; the hand grenades hanging on the D rings of my suspenders calmed me a little, but still they did not decrease my anxiety about the possibility of close combat. Above me was our platoon leader, a young second lieutenant who had likewise been transferred to our company just a short time ago. He carried a walkie-talkie with him, by which he was in contact with the commander of a Sherman tank. Since our tanks could not push forward toward the suspected German line on account of the thick underbrush and the sloping terrain, they had advanced along a bumpy field path at the upper edge of the woods to about the height of our position.

Here they were keeping themselves in readiness in a meadow, their engines thundering; through an opening in the trees at the edge of the woods I could make out the turret with its gun ready to fire, when it was finally reported to us that the tanks would now advance farther and attack the woods in which the Germans were presumably located.

Individual shots were fired. We had not left our position until then; it was getting dark slowly. On command from our lieutenant, I had worked my way forward to the edge of the woods, from where I could see the whole meadow between the two patches of woods and fire on it with my machine gun. The Shermans had in fact advanced somewhat, far apart from each other, but as yet had not fired a shot. In the midst of a sudden exchange of fire, in which I could finally recognize the source of the German muzzle flashes, there was a loud explosion, followed by a cluster of bright sparks (see Vol.I: The Germans). The leading Sherman had been hit by a Panzerfaust, shot by a man who had worked his way up to it. Obviously, though, the Panzerfaust shot had ricocheted off to the side, and thus the explosive power of the hollow charge had been weakened somewhat; in any case, the tank, despite giving off oily smoke, turned away shortly thereafter while another Sherman covered the area with fire from its heavy machine gun. Fortunately we were given no more orders to work our way farther forward during the night. While I ate a piece of chocolate, the 3rd Platoon and another machine-gun group were moved into the woodlands below the road.

The night was comparatively quiet. Here and there a flare lit up the pitch-black sky and bathed the damp, foggy meadow in an eerily beautiful light for a short time. I looked up in fright at every sound and bent my finger around the trigger, but did not fire. Now and then there were shots from various directions.

At the first light of day, there came the order to push farther forward through the thick underbrush in the direction of Longsdorf, for we were supposed to relieve an apparently prepared platoon of the 2nd Battalion. During the night our tanks had drawn back and were now behind us on the road, which offered the enemy fewer opportunities to fire a Panzerfaust from under cover.

We had covered barely fifty meters when concentrated infantry-weapon fire came at us. Tracer bullets hissed by me and bored into the trees. I threw myself down immediately on the forest floor, which had been softened by the fog, and as soon as my loader had set the machine gun on its tripod, I fired in the direction from which the fire came. I was now located about at the upper field path, close to the edge of the woods, from which I could get a very good view of the German position in the patch of fir trees ahead of us.

Most of the German fire, though, came out of the underbrush to our left. The exchange of fire lasted the whole day without our being able to win any ground. Now and then, during pauses in firing, calls for a medic could be heard on both sides.

When it finally got dark, we could see figures moving in front of us between the flashes of muzzle fire. Suddenly a hissing German stick grenade landed not far in front of my ditch. Instinctively I pressed myself into the wet bushes, pulled my head in and opened my mouth. A second later there was an ear-splitting crash. Splinters flew around, clumps of earth sprayed out and fell on the ground with a thud. I was unharmed and immediately fired in the direction in which I presumed the grenade thrower was. I was fired on at once by a German machine gun. But it fired too high, for the bullets whistled by and bored into the trees behind me. Shots were heard from all over again. Cries rang out! Damned forest combat! Why didn't our three tanks down on the road fire to take the pressure off us? The penetrating German shock troops would have been easy to neutralize, though!

The thought of being lost now inspired the strangest feelings in me.

Things Got Worse

In the afternoon, after the infantry fire fight, to my surprise, things had calmed down a little. Suddenly I heard a rushing sound over us, and a fraction of a second later a salvo of 8 cm mortar shells struck not far behind me. Then I also heard the characteristic sound of the next launch, and shortly after that the ear-splitting explosions of the projectiles. If only we were out of this damned forest! Between the explosions I heard again and again the rattling fire of a German machine gun.

The German mortar position must have been very close by and firing very steeply, since we could hear the sound of the mortar's muzzle flash very clearly. It was even possible to count the firings. Until evening came, we scarcely dared to move, but fired now and then to return the infantry fire, or more likely to calm ourselves inside.

Many of our men had been killed or wounded by the rushing iron splinters of the German shells.

When it got dark, a sergeant slipped up to our foxhole and let us know that our tanks would move back to be refueled. They would not return until the next morning. Otherwise they could be knocked out all too easily in the darkness.

Shortly after that I heard them depart. "Hang on," we were told, "in the morning troops will come to relieve you." About 5:00 AM on December 18, after the distant rumbling of artillery had kept us awake the whole night, suddenly the noise of tanks was heard again. We heard the sounds of motors coming closer but could not tell from which direction they came.

"Thank God," I thought, "that is the promised reinforcements." Then a horrified cry rang out from below: "Take cover, the tanks are German." There was a loud crash already. The German tanks, of which there were three, as I could see later when daylight dawned, took the wooded slope under fire.

One of the tanks had a rotating turret with a German cross painted on it and was in my estimation a Panzer IV type, while the other two were very flat in shape and, as I recall, without turrets but with sharply sloping sides (Hetzer?) (see Vol.I: The Germans)

The tanks fired several explosive shells into our lines, again resulting in numerous dead and wounded. Shortly thereafter, when the first dim light of morning allowed a poor view of the road, I saw from above that the big tank was moving farther forward in the direction of the "Seltz" intersection; obviously its intention was to cut off our retreat path to Diekirch. Suddenly German infantry attacked, appearing out of nowhere in the morning mist, out of the wooded slope and onto the road. Our concerted fire drove the first attack off; then came the order to withdraw along the field path above the edge of the woods.

But then heavy machine-gun fire came at us again from the patch of woods opposite us. We fired back bitterly and pushed ahead to the upper field path, for it would have been senseless to hold the woods. Down on the road there was a seething mass of Germans. A foot race to the "Seltz" began. I had no more ammunition but did not want the machine gun to be used against us by the Germans, so I hid it under a knobby mass of roots in a drainage ditch. I hastily covered the projecting butt of the Browning machine gun with branches. Tank shells were exploding very close to me again.

I raced out of this damned forest, ran straight across the field path and was just about to climb over a fence when I was fired on from the side. I threw myself back down into the hedge along the path and ducked down. Too late! I already saw Germans coming toward the hedge from below. I tried desperately to break through sideways and made panicky sounds in the process . . . twigs snapped . . . the hedge was fired on. Submachine gun bullets whistled past my helmet. Branches broke off with a splintering sound. "Hands up!" someone shouted to me. Fearfully I answered "Ja, ja!" I spoke and understood some German, and called: "Hier Kamerad, nicht schiessen!" – "Come out fast!" an older and obviously more experienced German soldier stepped up to me as I crept out of the bushes on all fours, and I looked into the threatening muzzle of his assault rifle. With a kick in the side he knocked me to the ground and ordered me to lie on my belly and fold my hands behind my head. The same thing happened to several of my comrades who were near me; they too were taken prisoner.

We were searched hastily; I had no individual weapon with me, which was what they were obviously looking for. Among us captured Americans there was also the unidentified young Luxembourger who had accompanied us since we left Diekirch. He might have been about sixteen years old and served the company commander as a pathfinder, since he knew the region thoroughly and seemed to know every tree, every bush.

When we had brought the German soldiers out of the house in the "Seltz" on December 16, he had taken a submachine gun and the magazine pouch that went with it from one of them, and during the last two days he had used it to fight alongside us in the woods of Longsdorf. Thank God he had thrown the weapon away before he was captured.

The Path to POW Camp

I was fully determined to risk everything and escape at the first opportunity. So now we lay there, our faces in the muddy earth of the field, and were searched. Suddenly I heard a single pistol shot behind me. "No, my God, that can't be" . . . a terrible thought flashed through my mind . . . "they're simply shooting us." If there had been another shot, I made up my mind to jump up quickly and run, although my chances were exactly zero. But I did not want to be passive and let myself be executed, and I was ready to jump up. But there was no second shot. Instead of that, the German poked me in the ribs with the barrel of his MP 44 and ordered me tersely: "Turn over and get up."

In a row, one close behind another, we were led down the slope to the road by three young German soldiers with their guns ready to fire. Since we had to keep our hands over our heads, I stumbled and fell down several times. When I got up I saw that there was a large number of captured Americans. Down on the road there was a crowd of Germans. Here too, most of them were only half-grown, and at the age of twenty I began to feel like an old man (see Vol.I: The Germans). One of the young soldiers shoved me and said sarcastically: "Pennsylvania, Pittsburgh, strawberry shortcake." The emblem of our division was the keystone, a symbol that originally came from Pennsylvania. His sarcastic laughter seemed so out of place to me at that moment that I could have screamed, but I only nodded nervously and tried to give a barely visible smile. The young Luxembourger was led off by an officer in the direction of the "Seltz." In my thoughts I said farewell to him, whose name I did not even know – a brave young man. Surely they would shoot him as a partisan.

But we heard no shots as we were made to march off in the direction of Longsdorf under a heavy guard. There at the side of the road stood the German tanks that had caused us so many losses, being refueled from gas cans by soldiers from Longsdorf. Suddenly, out of the mass of soldiers, we were approached by several SS men, whom we recognized at once by their black uniforms with characteristic collar patches. While we had to wait to the side of the street with our hands raised, a lively discussion arose between the SS men and several non-commissioned officers of the Wehrmacht; it became louder all the time. It obviously concerned us, and we already feared the worst. (Author's note: probably SD men of the Klöcker Group, who were seen later in Diekirch.)

Our suspicion seemed to be coming true in the worst way when one of the SS men suddenly climbed onto the turret of the Panzer IV and aimed the machine gun in our direction. Fear shot through our bodies: "They're going to shoot us down – the rumors that the SS often made short work of burdensome prisoners must be true after all."

But the vigorous discussion developed in our favor, since the SS men suddenly departed and we had to step back out onto the road. A soldier knocked the helmet off my head since I had not understood that we were supposed to take our helmets off. Then we were searched thoroughly again and had to empty all the pockets of our fatigues and turn them inside out. All our personal possessions were thrown on the ground in front of us.

In my jacket pocket there were still a bible, a GI spoon and a picture of my girl friend, which the Germans took from me. I did not dare to say that I would at least like to keep the picture.

Silently the German who had just searched me went on to the next man and left these three items lying in the dirt in front of me. I didn't dare to bend down.

A young soldier stepped up to me, picked up my three belongings, looked at the picture of my girl friend and, to my amazement, put the three things back in my pocket. He smiled at me, and I nodded thankfully – obviously we had the same feeling; despite the situation, there were sometimes still decent human feelings.

Finally we went farther. We were already out of the forest that was divided by the narrow road, and Longsdorf came into view. Then suddenly our own artillery fired on us with heavy-caliber guns (probably 155 mm guns of the 108th FA Battalion, from a position south of "Friedhaff" near Diekirch; author's note). There were explosions in the trees, pieces of wood flew through the air, the forest floor was torn up, hissing iron fragments and clods of earth flew around.

There was panic among both us and our German captors. The road had taken several direct hits all at once. We squeezed ourselves into the damp roadside ditches, almost growing into the ground, so as not to become victims of our own shells. Even so, several of our men were killed by U.S. shell fragments!

Early in the afternoon, when the artillery fire had quieted down somewhat and a shot howled along only at irregular intervals, we passed through Longsdorf at a quick march under close guard. While we were leaving the village, several German trucks approached and we walked past them. We crossed the Our on a makeshift bridge, made partly of heavy farm wagons standing in the water.

We went on at a quick march on the other banks until, in the twilight of December 18, we reached a farm on a hill, where were immediately herded into the barn together. One after another, we were questioned in a gloomy cellar room, isolated and guarded until we were all finished, in order to make sure that we could not talk to each other.

The German NCO who questioned me was in a splendid, victorious mood. "This offensive can no longer be stopped," he asserted. "By Christmas we'll be back in Paris. In three weeks Germany will have won the war." After he had questioned me as to our unit, position, etc., and I had told him only my name, rank and a few unimportant details, he commented: "You are surely of German ancestry, since you have a German name."

I agreed and told him that my ancestors came from Hamburg. "So why are you shooting at your German brothers?" – "For the same reason that you are shooting at the Americans," was my prompt reply.

I expected him to be furious, but the Feldwebel's drunk-with-glory mood did not let anything perturb him; he called to the guard and I was taken away. Finally they brought in several buckets of drinking water, a thin vegetable soup with added fat, and several loaves of black bread. Each of us received a quarter of a loaf of bread. We were very hungry and eagerly ate everything, even though we Americans, who were accustomed to good-tasting rations, normally would have scorned bread and water.

Never before had we lived on bread and water, even during the battle in the Hürtgenwald. But in times of need, everything tastes good. In the last few days I had lived on nothing but D bars, strengthening chocolate rations, anyway.

Only in Bitburg did we get slimy oat soup again, which we ate straight out of the steaming pot or out of the outer helmet of one man whom the Germans had allowed to keep it. There was also one roasted potato per man. Despite everything that had happened, I considered myself fairly lucky and was happy that the Germans had let me keep my aluminum spoon in Longsdorf. In the ensuing days, Bitburg filled with American prisoners; even crewmen of shot-down U.S. bombers were among them. In all, there must have been several hundred from various units. After Bitburg was bombed by the U.S. Air Force at Christmas, leaving numerous dead and wounded among us Americans again through our own action, not to mention the many dead among the civilian population and the German occupying forces, we had to gather in groups along with refugees, crying children and all their possessions that could still be rescued out of the flames, and go to Wittlich. I will never forget this long march through the Eifel at night. The impossible terrain robbed us of all our strength. In Wittlich we were locked in a chapel and given scarcely anything to eat. Hunger even impelled us to chew on the wax candles that were there, in order to suppress our feelings of hunger.

After several days we went on without stopping. Shortly before our departure, each of us was given a can of meat and half a loaf of army bread, which we ate immediately. Because of the threat of air attacks, the whole bunch of prisoners had to spend the days resting at farms. Here I stole two sugar beets, which I hid in my coat pocket after cutting them up with the handle of my spoon so they would not be noticeable.

While we marched on at night, I chewed on a piece of beet now and then, sucking all the sugary juice out before I swallowed the rest. Often, though, a German farmer took pity on us wretched figures and handed us a few cooked potatoes, which we took gratefully. We even ate the potato skins that we found in pig troughs.

We went on and on, farther into Germany. Finally, worn out and starving, we reached Stalag XII near Limburg. After two weeks behind barbed wire in this prisoner-of-war camp, we were loaded into cattle cars and transported by rail to Stalag IIA in Neubrandenburg.

Thank God it was not much longer until we were liberated by Russian units and sent back to our own forces.

Action of B Company, 109th Infantry Regiment

James Christy, now living in Florida as a retired mathematics teacher, then held the rank of First Lieutenant and served as Executive Officer of B Company within the structure of the 109th Regiment.

On his visit in the autumn of 1982, he recalled:

Our entry into Diekirch took place in November of 1944, when the 28th Infantry Division was pulled out of the Aachen area after bloody battles and transferred to Luxembourg for regrouping and recovery. Around November 22 we reached

Diekirch, and my company was quartered in the Hôtel de l'Europe in the center of town.

I still remember very precisely that on the day following our arrival, our own company field kitchen prepared a wonderful Thanksgiving dinner for us exhausted and emaciated soldiers. For us tradition-conscious Americans, this meal was very important, and nobody would have wanted to miss it, even under war conditions. Alluring good smells were already issuing forth from the steaming kitchen in the morning, and the whole company waited impatiently with their eating utensils in their hands, for this was an extremely welcome change after everything that we had gone through up to then. After all, our main nourishment during the combat in the Hürtgenwald consisted almost exclusively of K rations.

To the vast appreciation of the hungry soldiers, the desired meal was apportioned shortly before noon. There was turkey, mashed potatoes with gravy, cooked berries, applesauce and sweet corn.

"Uncle Sam" really took good care of his sons overseas. We could scarcely believe it. The turkeys had been sent from the USA in a deep-frozen condition just three days before!

Every one of us enjoyed the holiday meal heartily and ate several portions, as everything was available in abundance and the mess sergeant dished it out again and again.

The result of this was that our stomachs, which had lived on canned food and concentrated chocolate for weeks, could no longer handle the fatty food; almost every one of us had to suffer from cramps, flatulence and other digestive disorders that lasted for days. We did not hang around Diekirch very long, and after staying there for two days we were taken by truck to Ettelbrück for delousing. Here we could finally take a bath, wash ourselves thoroughly with warm water and real soap, and were finally issued new clothes and replacements for missing pieces of equipment from brand new army stocks.

My men also underwent a medical examination in an "Evacuation Hospital" stationed in Ettelbrück at the time. All in all, the morale of the hard-hit troops increased steadily, and life gradually developed back into a garrison routine with additional possibilities for spare-time activities: movies, dances organized by the civilian population, plus lengthened free-time limits for the resting troops reawakened the spirits of the soldiers, some of whom were still very young.

"The front is only three or four miles away," I told several doctors that same evening as we ate together in the officers' casino, whereupon their faces fell a bit, and lively conversations developed. I was probably the first to tell them of the enemy's position, which I myself had learned only from the S-2 Officer of the 1st Battalion.

After a good night's sleep we went back to Diekirch the next day, and on orders from the regiment, we were immediately transferred to a guard position on the Our front.

The 109th Regiment was located on the right wing of the division's defense line, and my company was given an area to guard that stretched several hundred meters from the Our up to a ridge about two kilometers long.

Our neighbor on the right, at the extreme right of the division, was A Company, whose positions stretched to the place where the Our flowed into the Sauer near Wallendorf. Since at that time (early December 1944) the 1st Battalion's headquarters were located on a big farm at the edge of Bettendorf, C Company, as far as I know, stayed in the town as a reserve and to protect the headquarters, and only detailed a platoon to our left wing. We had approximately two weeks' front service, and during this period an active patrol activity in the enemy's country developed, on orders from the battalion. Blankets of fog that remained in the morning, often accompanied by drizzling rain or damp showers of snow, helped this small undertaking. In addition, we dug additional fox holes on the ridge of the hill, later to be used by the 3rd Battalion, which was supposed to relieve us, and built and camouflaged numerous mine traps in the thick underbrush on the slope down to the Our.

On December 9 or 10 we were relieved according to plan and transferred to Diekirch again, where our 1st Battalion was supposed to stay, for Colonel Rudder had arranged for two battalions to form the regiment's defense line, while a third was to keep itself in readiness nearby as a mobile reserve.

In Diekirch itself my company had numerous courses of training and theoretical instruction, and we received new arrivals to fill the holes that still existed in our ranks. Despite that, our company never attained its specified strength.

I myself, as company executive, then took part in a staff discussion, which resulted in the following:

In the night between Friday and Saturday, December 15-16, a patrol mission carried out by parts of my company was to cross the Our front line, get into enemy territory, attack a bunker position known to us, destroy it with explosives and, if possible, bring back German prisoners.

I was supposed to lead this undertaking myself, and for it I chose twenty men with sufficient combat experience. Two engineers of the platoon of the 103rd Engineer Battalion attached to our battalion were supposed to support us with the necessary equipment for blowing up a bunker. According to the plan, we were supposed to cross the Our in the vicinity of the blown-up bridge at Vianden on the evening of December 15 and then work our way forward to the right under cover of darkness. Three rubber boats were supposed to be ready for the crossing.

The main purpose of the undertaking was actually to bring in German prisoners, who were to be turned over to the regiment for questioning about the enemy's position. Every one of the soldiers chosen by me for this mission believed that practically nothing had moved during our period of watching along the Our. I myself remained skeptical, though, for the quiet on the German side was downright uncanny.

In addition I presumed that, in the event that we blew up the bunker shaft with a "beehive" charge, consisting of forty pounds of TNT — a new type of hollow charge — scarcely any of the crew had a chance of survival, and that therefore the chance of taking out living prisoners was extremely unlikely.

I made my thoughts on this undertaking known, but the regiment insisted on its being carried out, since similar missions that had been carried out previously had been partially successful.

Thus on the afternoon of Friday, December 15, I held a last, detailed briefing of my men in order to give them the necessary tactical information. About 5:00 PM they were all standing ready in front of the Hotel de l'Europe with blackened faces and camouflaged weapons, waiting for the arrival of the truck that was supposed to take us to Vianden, from which we were to acquaint ourselves with the terrain in the last light of evening.

Astonishingly, a few minutes later an officer drove up in a Jeep and reported that Lt.Col. Harmon, Commander of the 1st Battalion, had aborted the undertaking and postponed it for one day. I was never given a reason for this, but in any case we were informed that we should go back to our quarters and amuse ourselves and rest, and the men were not unhappy about that.

I myself was invited to an officers' party that took place at the headquarters of the 1st Battalion in the Hotel du Midi, not far from the railroad station. Before I left my men, I told the platoon leader that at 10:00 the next morning we were supposed to take part in a parade of the 1st Battalion (on the Kluster; author's note), in which two men of my company were also to be decorated. So I instructed that everyone was to have his uniform and his footwear in order!

Intensive artillery fire awakened us abruptly on the early morning hours of the dawning day. At first it did not bother us much, although several shells had fallen in the area of the railroad station, and the loud noise of the explosions penetrated almost unabated as far as the Hotel de l'Europe. Since we had experienced much worse in the Hürtgenwald, each one of us tried to get back to sleep after we had moved down to the lower floor for safety's sake.

In spite of that, we were no longer able to close our eyes, for the heaviness of the fire increased. Shells were already landing in the heart of the city, and a messenger rushed in and told us excitedly that our battalion's motor pool had taken several direct hits and several vehicles were burning. In addition, several of the regiment's service locations in Diekirch had been hit very accurately, and it was generally obvious that the German artillery fire was concentrated almost exclusively on areas occupied by the military. Even the Hôtel du Midi, where I myself had taken part in a party just a few hours previously, was burning. That could not have happened just by chance!

Obviously, the rumors about German spies among the civilian population of Diekirch (see Vol.I: The Germans), which had been going around for a long time, apparently must have been true. The battalion immediately ordered alarm conditions and sent several patrols that were supposed to search for an artillery-fire leader. The military police of the headquarters company, along with several volunteer helpers from the inhabitants, were instructed to see to it that the population remained in the cellars and kept quiet.

In fact, a security patrol found a German radio set a short time afterward, after the fire had let up somewhat, in a shoemaker's shop not far from the Hotel de l'Europe. This shoemaker's shop had specialized in making pistol holsters out of grained leather, which were much desired by numerous GIs who had captured German handguns during the previous combat. I myself had been one of their customers, since I had always carried with me since the combat around Vossenack, as a second weapon, a Luger 08 pistol that I had taken from a captured German Unteroffizier. So I had likewise had a shoulder holster made for me, and I received it promptly in two days. In this shop there was also a good-looking blonde, who was known to the men for other things than pistol holsters; in any case, she was always surrounded by men on account of her alluring beauty, so that the shoemaker's business flourished and his shop was always full.

I myself had taken a good look at her, but there were always too many others ahead of me. In fact, it turned out that the blonde worked for the Germans. So it was not surprising that she knew how to learn more and more from her "American admirers and suitors"; as we found out later, she asked particularly about those buildings that were occupied by American soldiers.

This information was passed on through intermediaries in the German intelligence service to the staffs, so that the German artillery command posts could work out precisely exact firing data. Apparently there were several other agents arrested in addition to her. According to rumors, the blonde was said to have been shot. In spite of that, fire began again around noon.

The company leader, Captain Lawrence, immediately called off the planned parade and ordered the highest level of alarm readiness. Shortly after that, his adjutant, 1st Lieutenant Witney, appeared and called half the company to come out with their equipment and weapons. It was said that we would be taken at once to the sector of the 2nd Battalion, which was on the Our line.

About 10:30 AM we finally found out what the situation was, when it was reported to us that the Germans had crossed the Our in the early morning hours and begun to attack the regiment's sector. In addition, similar bad news had been received from the VIII. Corps and the division, so that everything pointed to a blitz offensive by the Wehrmacht.

Meanwhile, three Sherman tanks of the detailed 707th Tank Battalion had moved forward, and the 1st Platoon of B Company was immediately ordered to get aboard them. It was said that the situation in the Vianden area was especially alarming and the 2nd Battalion had made an urgent request for help. The 2nd Platoon was put under my command and was to make ready to march out. The Weapons Platoon was likewise on hand and awaiting orders. The 2nd Platoon likewise set out and followed the first tank in the direction of Vianden.

Shortly before that, about 9:30 AM, a Jeep with an excited medical officer had pulled up in front of the Hotel de l'Europe and the officer had asked me about the situation. Very perturbed, he asked if the situation indicated that the hospital had to be evacuated, whereupon I answered satirically: "We've finished with the 'Jerries' by now; it won't be so bad." – "You are the first one who has given me a little hope," he replied, "there's a big mess out there." As he drove away in the Jeep in the direction of Ettelbrück, I realized that it had been stupid of me to give him such a silly answer; I hoped he had not taken my words seriously and had evacuated the hospital. One of the Shermans had meanwhile come back, and the rest of the company under my command was sitting on the two tanks at hand, which were to take us to the edge of Diekirch on the road to Bettendorf and Vianden. Our orders said:

Relief of E Company in Fouhren

Thus the unit which I now commanded consisted of the 2nd (rifle) Platoon and a part of the Weapons Platoon, equipped with heavy machine guns and 60 mm mortars.

So we left Diekirch, passing by the church on a long road lined with big trees, along which the rails of a small railroad line also ran. We were less than two kilometers out of the city when we came under fire shortly before an intersection. In fractions of a second the men jumped off the tanks and looked for cover in roadside ditches, while the Shermans fired on the wooded heights to the right of the intersection with their 75 mm guns. It was obvious that the Germans already occupied the plateau of Longsdorf and thus threatened the road from Tandel to Diekirch. To the left of the roadside, somewhat away from the bend to the left, there was a crossing guard's hut or something similar built of bricks. While the men were still dividing up in the area beyond the Blees bridge, we suddenly came under machine-gun fire from this small building. In the brief exchange of fire, which ended abruptly with a direct hit from a tank shell, two German soldiers were killed.

When we examined the little house more closely, we found a number of Panzerfaust weapons as well as several cases of 8 cm mortar ammunition. The date of manufacture on the inside of the packing cases was November 1944, so the ammunition was brand new. In addition, the two dead men had practically unused equipment and weapons. Yet it was generally known that the German armaments industry was almost ruined and no longer able to rebuild again after being area-bombed. This, though, seemed rather to indicate the opposite; in any case, finding it gave me reason to consider that the situation at the front could be worse that I had thought at first.

After this brief incident, I regrouped my men and we went on in echelon, watching on all sides, in the direction of Tandel. Following the narrow-gauge railway, we reached the edge of town and marched through it without any further incidents. The town appeared to be dead. I took over the leadership of the platoon, followed by the two Sherman tanks. Now and then there were shots on the heights above Tandel. In the distance we also heard the sounds of machine weapons, and again and again the dull blasts of exploding artillery shells.

We were wondering what would happen up on the heights when machine-gun salvos suddenly burst out from the right at the edge of town. One burst of fire tore up the road just in front of me; my men and I instantly took cover in the bushes to the left of the road, and behind the small railroad bed. The ditch that ran parallel to the railroad tracks, into which I had jumped, was half-full of ice-cold water that now penetrated through the collar opening of my jacket and soaked the whole underside of my abdomen. I shivered from the cold and tried to pull myself up somewhat, out of that wretched hole, when the machine gun began to rattle again. The soil sprayed up everywhere in front of me; some shots hit at an angle and ricocheted off the rails with a loud whistling sound. The German machine-gunner, who obviously was located directly opposite me, must have had an excellent field of observation and fire. He really nailed us to the ground and never let us raise our heads out of the ditch or from behind the wall of earth. I called to my men, who were farther behind me and were still near the last houses of Tandel, that they should send the tank forward to wipe out the machine-gun nest. But the tank did not move. I could see that, in its place, a group of "old veterans", including a sergeant with a BAR (Browning Automatic Rifle), were working their way forward. He fired from the flank in the direction from which the machine-gun fire came. He emptied several magazines and obviously was successful, for the machine-gun fire stopped and I liberated myself from my miserable situation. I called to my men to draw back to the foremost tank.

We were fired on again, this time from the rear, and the BAR gunner, to whom I owe my life, was hit and lay there. One of the medics went to him at once and had him brought back. I immediately reported to 1st Lieutenant Witney by radio, and he had the 1st Platoon, under the protection of a tank, attack at once. We ourselves held Tandel until late in the afternoon, when the regimental S-2 officer, who had just arrived, ordered me to break through to Fouhren with my unit at once and relieve the surrounded "Easy" Company. Every minute was precious, he commented.

Some distance outside of Tandel, a field path branched off on the left side of the road. Because of the tree barricades that the Germans had set up without the risk of drawing fire on themselves, this was unusable at the time, so that only the road itself remained.

When I observed it through my binoculars in the twilight, I saw in the faint light of the fading December day that a machine-gun hole on the right side of the road was just being abandoned. As we moved forward, I also saw numerous Germans hurry over the hill. It was almost dark as we moved cautiously forward in the direction of Fouhren. Since the field path, which curved away to the left of the road, was unusable because of the tree barricades, we moved ahead on the right side of the road, which was lined by shrubbery which more or less protected us from being seen. Then the two tanks following us suddenly stopped; their commander refused to accompany us in the dark unless the terrain ahead of us had been scouted in advance to see if the enemy was present. In addition, sufficient infantry protection had to be given to the tanks to protect them from the danger of lone German fighters of a tank-destroying team.

I myself then went at the head of the group, my weapon ready to fire. My pulse was beating loudly. Carefully, avoiding any noise, we very slowly approached the curve to the left ahead of us. From a distance we could already see the flickering fire that illuminated the left side of the valley: Fouhren was burning. The Sherman tanks stayed back. In the faint light of the flickering fire, I suddenly noticed that numerous troops had dug in on the declining slope to the right of the road, and I immediately thought of the E Company, which had obviously taken up a new position here after a hard fight. I called to them: "Easy, here's Baker!" – but I got no answer. The figures kept on digging. Something inside me impelled me to try it in German: "Hände hoch und rauskommen, wir werden nicht schiessen!" The reaction was immediate: machine-gun bullets whistled toward us.

As quickly as we could, we divided up and took the slope under fire. From the rear, one of the Sherman tanks opened fire and hurled numerous shells and .50 machine-gun salvos at the German position, but obviously could not score any noticeable hits because of the darkness. When I thought I had found a target in the sight of my M-1 carbine, weakly illuminated by the glow of the fire, I pulled the trigger. I must actually have fired at a German, for I could just barely see that a dark form threw itself down but got up again shortly thereafter. It held something in its hand, which I could recognize as an MP 44 machine pistol by the characteristic shape of the magazine. I estimated the distance at 60 to 70 meters as I fired again. When the shot hit, there was a metallic ring and sparks flew; obviously my shots had hit his weapon and bounced off. I heard the German cry out and could see that he ran away. My shot had grazed him after all.

A hearty exchange of fire resulted, and shortly after that we were fired on from the left in the flank and the rear. I also noticed that, in the middle of the fight, a group of Germans ran off to the side to attack us in the flank. Sergeant Donahoe, who was at my side, was grazed on the head by a shot as a German bullet bored through the side of his helmet and came out the front. He was really lucky. We could not go any farther here and made our way through trackless country back to Tandel, where we immediately dug in at the edge of town. Here we again met the rest of our troops, who had stayed behind to guard the village. By radio we immediately ordered ammunition, especially hand grenades and machine-gun ammunition, as well as K-rations. A tank coming in from Diekirch was to provide the transport.

About 3:00 AM I heard the sound of a motor and saw that a Sherman was in fact approaching from the direction of Diekirch. I ran out to the road at once to stop it, but it moved toward me so fast that I had to jump hastily to the side to avoid being run over. It hurried past me . . . in the direction of the enemy!

Shortly afterward we heard several explosions as well as machine-gun fire, then the sound of a motor coming toward us. Again the tank hurried past us, ignoring all our signals. We never received the requested ammunition. I heard later that the battalion's S-4 officer was on board himself to find out what the situation was. But because of the extremely poor visibility, he could not see anything. In addition, making contact with the commander of the tank turned out to be impossible. So the tank, as soon as it came under the German fire from which we had miraculously emerged unscathed, immediately turned back, since Tandel was thought to be occupied by the Germans.

The Germans are in the majority

Even before daybreak, a patrol brought the news that the Germans had indeed made their way closer to Tandel during the night. Under the protection of fire from the two tanks as well as the Weapons Platoon with its 60 mm grenade launchers, the 2nd and 3rd Platoons moved along the road again in the direction of Fouhren.

We could not have gone more than fifty meters when we were struck by a murderous fire again. I ordered the men to move to the left side of the road immediately, from where we could attack the German flank better. By walkie-talkie I requested mortar fire, and the first shells flew at once. But they fell too far to the left of the road, and too short. In fact, two shots fell into my own line. Thank God nobody was injured, and I was able to adjust the fire correctly, so that it now fell exactly on the German position.

Yet we received an order from the company commander to return to Tandel, since an attack on the German lines was too risky and would result in too many losses. Shortly afterward the radio set was hit by a shell fragment and radio contact broke off. I noticed several Germans moving toward us and fired two magazines at them from my position, protected by a tree. My men also fired like mad. The Germans suffered numerous losses and went into cover.

Down below along the road, the Sherman opened fire on the Germans. We raced past the tank toward Tandel when another tank with a white star approached. Thank God for the reinforcements!

But the tank suddenly fired its bow machine gun at us, and right after that a shell from its 75 mm tank gun hit the Sherman farther up the road. It all happened so fast that I came to the conclusion that it could be a German tank with a star painted on it. But it actually turned out to be one of our tanks that had fallen into the hands of the Germans.

Horrified, we sprang into the bushes on the left side of the road and threw ourselves into the brook. Here we found two of my men from the other platoon with four German prisoners, seeking cover in the thick underbrush. The men were bewildered. There were crowds of German infantrymen all around. Surely our own troops had left Tandel already. The German prisoners explained the situation and assured us that the best thing to do was to surrender. After I had made clear to them that we would shoot them on the spot if they made the slightest move, we waded through the high water of the brook and reached a bridge, across which the road we had been on ran. At this point the water was almost up to our hips and frightfully cold. So we stood under the arch of the bridge with our prisoners when, shortly afterward, German troops in company strength marched over the bridge in the direction of Diekirch. After things had become somewhat more quiet, I gave the order to march on. We waded through the "Tandel Brook" for a distance of about 300 meters and reached the rest of B Company in the thick underbrush outside of Tandel. We turned our prisoners over to them and, at their instructions, turned off toward Bastendorf. This was all done at high speed, and it is a wonder that the Germans, who had occupied Tandel already, did not follow us farther; in any case there was no further exchange of fire aside from a few single shots.

At the bend in the road were some of the men of the G Company of our 2nd Battalion, who directed us to a steep slope beyond Bastendorf, where we dug in. As night fell, it began to rain and snow. Freezing, shivering and hungry, we spent the night in a hastily excavated dugout, and I tried to dry out my clothing and shoes as best I could.

Orders to Retreat

The night was comparatively quiet. Only now and then did we hear the thunder of artillery and the rumbling of motors in the distance. During the next night of December 19-20 there came an order from the regiment to drop back to Ettelbrück. So we crossed the "Herrenberg," where we again exchanged fire with German advance units, and reached the road to Erpeldange. But the German artillery had found its range superbly by then. Our withdrawal route to Erpeldange and Ettelbrück was constantly under fire as the companies, in the specified order, left their defense lines. Ahead of us went the hard-hit A Company, then we followed, and finally the G Company of the 2nd Battalion, which had suffered numerous losses from the effects of German artillery fire. It was obvious that E Company, which we had been supposed to relieve in Fouhren, had been completely wiped out or defeated. A sad result! South of Ettelbrück we crossed the Alzette and dug in. From our position we kept the road to Feulen under surveillance. Early in the morning of December 21 we saw a German infantry company moving along this road in loose marching formation. One of our tanks fired two explosive shells into their ranks. Thereupon our machine guns and mortars all fired on them. I cannot say for sure how many German soldiers fell in this surprise attack, but the result was great panic, and the greater part of the enemy company was left lying on the road.

But the regiment ordered us to drop back farther. We were told that the 80th U.S. Infantry Division was advancing to take over the sector. During our change of position I saw through my glasses that there was a German up on the hill. Obviously he had not yet seen us, and I waved to one of our sharpshooters; the German fell head over heels down the slope. He cried out horribly and crept around on all fours. His face was a bloody mass; we had hit him in the head.

One of our medics crept forward and pulled him to our trench. He looked bad. The bullet had entered his cheek and come out the back of his head. Obviously the man could no longer see. It turned out that he was an officer of an artillery unit who had been supposed to measure our position as an observer.

The man would scarcely have a chance of surviving, I thought as he was taken away. When I asked our medic why he had spontaneously gone into enemy fire to rescue a badly wounded enemy, he replied that it was his duty to helped a wounded man, but in this case it had been the German's huge binoculars that had caught his eye.

From our cover we observed individual German soldiers climbing the hill. We did not fire, so as not to betray our position needlessly. About an hour later, after we had worked our way back somewhat, we were stopped by two soldiers with fixed bayonets. Americans! Their insignia was the "Blue Ridge" patch of the 80th Infantry Division. They identified themselves as scouts of the 319th Regiment and inquired about the enemy's position. The advance guard of their company arrived very soon. At the same time we were withdrawn, and I believe I remember that the 319th Regiment marched out in the direction of Ettelbrück toward evening of the same day.

Surprise Attack in Gilsdorf

We spent the night in the castle of Colmar-Berg, where we could finally recover somewhat from the strains of the past days. Numerous troop units were present, and there was finally hot food to be had again. Although the front was dangerously near, we spent several days in the castle, until early in the morning of December 24, when my B Company received orders to take part in a combined action, a local counterthrust on the Sauer river, in which the village of Gilsdorf, which according to intelligence reports was in German hands, was to be liberated. About 9:30 AM trucks drove up and took us through Cruchten and Schrondweiler to a wooded hill. We had to search the nearby woods for Germans immediately. Meanwhile several tanks of the 10th U.S. Armored Division had moved up to support us in the attack.

We cautiously approached, reaching a specified assembly point near Folkendange, about three kilometers away from Gilsdorf.

Shortly before the order to attack in the late afternoon, several young Luxembourgers turned up and identified themselves as resistance fighters. Some of them wore U.S. Army jackets, were armed with German carbines, and insisted on taking part in the attack on Gilsdorf, their home town. After checking out their identities, the commanding officer of the task force agreed, and the young Luxembourgers offered to lead the attack on account of their knowledge of the area, and climbed onto the tanks.

Although it seemed too foolhardy to me to let my own men, who were supposed to provide protection for the tanks, ride on the Shermans, the Luxembourgers would not let themselves be talked out of it, but were very eager to be active at last. From Folkendange we now set out in the direction of Gilsdorf along a snow-covered road, for a lot of snow had fallen meanwhile. At the head of the battle group were the two Shermans on which the Luxembourgeois (Ben Bauler, Charles Breyer, Emile Pesch, Jean Haendel and Louis Dupont; author's note) had taken their places.

By a narrow lane which led steeply downhill into the village we reached the edge of town, and the first tank immediately opened fire on a corner house at the bend in the main street. After additional houses had been fired on with explosive and phosphorus shells, our infantry attacked, along with the brave Luxembourg boys. In the ensuing combat among the houses, in which I must stress the extraordinary courage of the "Maquis", we were able to drive the Germans out. Several of them were so surprised when we disturbed the Christmas celebration that they had begun that they let themselves be taken prisoner without resistance.

Our Luxembourgers "scouts" also proudly brought in prisoners after they had "hauled out" a crew from a cellar with a hand grenade. All in all, this operation, which was later named "Task Force Rudder", was a great success, since we had scarcely any losses to report. A similar operation was said to have been carried out farther to the east, near Moestroff, by the same command. As we searched through the houses, a shepherd dog suddenly came at us, placing himself in our way and growling menacingly. To the horror of the inhabitants of the house, one of my men took aim at the dog and shot it. I regretted this incident very much, but war is war, after all.

Later in our search of the houses we heard sounds from a cellar. After calling out twice in German, we received no reply. A hand grenade was activated and thrown down the stone steps to the cellar. We were extremely shocked when, after the ear-splitting explosion, we stormed the room and discovered a stunned old woman behind a bin of potatoes, holding her ears. Thank God the grenade had exploded in an anteroom, and miraculously, none of the fragments had penetrated. This incident encouraged us to proceed more carefully in our further searching.

We spent that day, along with the tanks, in readiness at Gilsdorf, from which we could look toward Diekirch. Unfortunately, Gilsdorf had been seriously damaged during our attack; several houses were badly damaged or were burning. We received no order to push forward toward Diekirch, since the city was obviously more heavily occupied.

Toward evening of the same day we received a hot meal as a Christmas greeting, consisting of the traditional turkey and baked potatoes, which had been brought up in a thermos container from a nearby field kitchen.

On December 25 every house was searched again before we left Gilsdorf. Then we arrived again at our point of departure, the castle of Colmar-Berg, where we were allowed to rest for two more days.

Finally several trucks came and took us to St. Hubert. Here I was personally given instructions to make contact, as communications officer, with the nearby British units. Thank God the worst was now over for us. The fighting in the Hürtgenwald, Tandel and Ettelbrück will always remain in my memory.

Albert Dogan, "C" Company

It was quite by chance that, among a group of U.S. veterans of the 109th Infantry Regiment during their stay in Diekirch in September of 1984, a former rifleman of C Company (109th Infantry Regiment) recognized himself in a well-known photograph that was taken by an American army photojournalist in December of 1944.

The account of Private Albert Dogan is no less interesting and thus deserved to be spotlighted:

After going through hell in the Hürtgenwald, where I just barely survived, we were loaded into army trucks and taken directly to Diekirch, Luxembourg. It was said that the city was in the "quiet sector", and we were directed to several modern apartment houses that were to serve as our quarters. The houses were located directly on a main street, and from their back yards one came directly to the bank of the Sauer River.

I still remember that each of these houses consisted of four apartments as well as a big ground floor on the same level as the rear entrance. There was hardly any furniture inside, but this scarcely bothered us, for we regarded these houses as a luxury in comparison to the snow and mud that we had just left.

Small stoves were quickly set up in almost every room, and briquettes provided a warmth that did us good. We received three hot meals every day from the field kitchen that was located right next door.

But I was miserable!

My stomach could no longer stand any real food, since we had lived almost exclusively on K rations for almost two weeks; I had to throw up often. In addition, I had a bad case of diarrhea, the result of having frequently drunk melted snow or water from any available mudhole.

Along with all these troubles, my feet were so swollen that I could not possibly wear my shoes any more. Since the same problem had befallen many of the men, we were issued galoshes (rubber overshoes) that we wore without shoes. It helped, and the swelling soon decreased.

From November 8 on, until our arrival in Diekirch, we were constantly outside in the snow, dirt and mud, so that we were constantly wearing the same pieces of uniform clothing. The constant fire did not even allow us to loosen the laces of our shoes. Until then I had never heard of the term "trenchfoot", much less known the consequences of it.

After a few days we were on our feet again. We spent most of our time resting and were allowed to go out in the evening. Although this was the quiet sector, we were made aware of the fact that the front was just a few miles away. Now and then we saw German soldiers for a moment on the banks of the Our, and it seemed as if a sort of "gentlemen's agreement" at the time stopped both sides from shooting at each other, although there were often opportunities. I remember that one evening, in a tavern with several GI friends, I met an older man, who turned out to be a wine and liquor dealer and came from Clervaux. He was very friendly, very devoted to us, and did not charge us. He also gave us many postcards with pictures of Clervaux, which we were to keep as souvenirs.

At that time the situation was actually so quiet that we were allowed to tell our families in our letters that we were in Luxembourg. So I immediately sent one of those postcards to my parents.

After several days of rest, we were reminded of our duties again, and drills were held. The training program included, among other things, training with the "bazooka", with which every man was supposed to become familiar. We were immediately divided into two-man teams, one man as the gunner, the other as loader and ammunition carrier.

The responsible instructor chose as our target a big tree that stood about 50 meters away from us. According to instructions, the fired rocket projectile was supposed to hit the trunk three feet above the ground. Six or eight such teams fired one shot each without even grazing the tree. When it was my turn, I took my time, aimed very calmly and fired. The shot hit the tree right in the middle, a little higher than four feet up. Thus I became a bazooka-man.

That meant that had to carry around not only the bazooka, which could be broken down into two pieces and carried over the shoulder, but also an M1 carbine. Unfortunately, my loader was a 37-year-old draftee from Missouri, who constantly complained that he was over 35 years old and was not supposed to be drafted into the army.

On Wednesday evening, December 13, we discovered a barbershop in Diekirch, and many of us got our hair cut.

The Rush of Events

The radio in the shop was turned on, and a program in the Luxembourg language was in progress. The barber was very excited and stammered in strongly accented school English that something terrible was about to happen, and we asked him what was troubling him so much. He told us that it was said in the newscast of that 13th of December that great concentrations of troops had been observed by several people on the German side of the Our (see Vol. I: The Germans). This absolutely did not perturb us, since we had become accustomed to the calm situation for some days, and we adhered to the apparently prevailing agreement that "if you don't shoot, I won't shoot either." But the barber became more and more nervous, though we just laughed about it and did not trouble ourselves.

On December 16 we were jolted out of our sleep spontaneously in our quarters around 5:30 AM, as artillery shells exploded everywhere at very short distances, and powerful spotlights lit up the cloudy night sky.

We immediately received orders to leave the upper floor and go to the cellar. After about an hour everything was quiet again. Almost all the glass in the greenhouse near our quarters was shattered. To the best of my knowledge, nobody in our unit was injured. So we went back into the house and waited. As we did every morning, we went to the nearby field kitchen to get our breakfast, and while we were still eating, we received the order to go back to our quarters at once, polish our shoes, take the camouflage nets off our helmets and stick a "Red Keystone", the emblem of the 28th Infantry Division, on the front. We were to make our uniforms look as neat as possible, since a parade had been scheduled for 10:00 at the market place in Diekirch.

No sooner said than done. Cursing, we walked out of our quarters and marched in rows of three up the street to the market place by the church. Several other units of the 1st Battalion had already arrived and were waiting.

We had not yet taken up our assigned position when suddenly a Jeep, followed by a cloud of dust, came racing up at top speed and stopped on the "parade ground." In no time flat we received orders to go back to our quarters in double time and be ready at once in full battle dress, with camouflage nets on our helmets.

When we were transported out of Diekirch in trucks shortly after that, we saw the damage that had been caused by the German shelling. In the railroad-station area there were fires in numerous places.

Since my unit, the C Company, belonged to the reserve battalion in Diekirch, we were driven hastily to Brandenbourg, where we took up positions around the castle ruin. Finally we received definite information about the situation and learned that the Germans had broken through and were advancing, and that we were to fight against units of the 5th Paratroop Division, which threatened the positions of the neighboring 110th Infantry Regiment on our left flank. I had my carbine and a brand new bazooka with me. My loader with the ammunition pouches had obviously gotten on another truck, and I never saw him again.

When we were to make our way to the castle ruin, it was already dark, and the lock that held the two parts of the bazooka barrel together rattled with every step, so that my nervous comrades growled at me that I should get rid of this "cowbell." That was the end of my bazooka . . . no great loss, for I did not have the ammunition with me anyway.

After a night in the castle ruin, which was obviously a thousand years old, we were directed early the next morning to positions on the highlands that overlooked the only approach road to Brandenburg. We could clearly hear the noise of battle coming toward us from around the bend in the road, and rumors went around that heavy street fighting was going on in the nearby village (Bastendorf). We quickly dug foxholes halfway up the slope from the road, but nothing moved here.

We changed positions and gathered in a clearing near a path through the fields. It was cold, foggily gloomy and extremely damp; the ground was very soft and all the field paths were muddy. The situation was very confused; nobody was responsible! Two small U.S. tanks clattered up, and some of us were given orders to get on them at once . . . I never learned why. Except for gathering here, we had not yet done anything, and now we were already being ordered to withdraw, as we were told suddenly that the road on which the two tanks drove away from us was blocked by numerous German assault guns. It was not long before shots were exploding all over the place. Tracer bullets whistled over our heads. We were completely bewildered and looked for an officer who would lead us. There were about a dozen of us left there, and someone among us noticed, somewhat off to the side with a smaller group, a soldier with a carbine, a pistol holster and a jacket that an officer rather than an enlisted man would wear. In this group there was also a U.S. Army photographer, who immediately took a picture as we met to discuss the situation.

(25 years later I recognized myself in this picture, and it appears to have been published several times in books about the offensive as well as about the 28th U.S. Infantry Division.)

Was the person in question an officer or not? In any case, he took on the leadership of this assembled lot of men and marched at the head of us. For hours we wandered around through the thick woods, and it seemed as if we were going in circles. Finally, in a similar clearing, we came upon several GMC trucks close to a bumpy field path. Other soldiers had already boarded them, and we were ordered to get aboard as fast as possible. We drove only a few minutes; the trucks stopped at a road, and we had to get off and wait, since food would be brought to us at once.

We were given orders to move about fifty meters into the woods and fire three clips of eight rounds each at a wooded slope opposite us. Then we had to get back onto the trucks as fast as we could . . . without food. What was all this about? Only later did I learn that this shooting had the purpose of drawing enemy fire at us so as to learn where the enemy's position might be.

From here on, as I recall, we were driven to an orchard on a hill beyond Ettelbrück and unloaded there. Around midnight I was chosen, along with three other men, to work our way forward to the center of town and find out whether the enemy had already moved in. Almost every minute, or at almost regular short intervals, a medium-caliber shell exploded on the blown-up bridge on the road into town. Thank God our four-man patrol encountered no signs of the enemy, and so we went back to the assembling place more quickly.

I picked up a frozen apple and ate the side that was not rotten in three bites . . . it was the best delicacy I'd had in weeks! On the next day we were loaded onto the trucks again and drove along a straight road past a steel mill and directly into the forecourt of a castle-like villa, as we thought. Later we heard that it was the palace of the Grand Duke of Luxembourg, the capital of the country of the same name, and that this residence had served the officer corps as a gymnasium during the four years of the German occupation. That was probably also the reason for the almost complete lack of furniture.

Still shaken by everything that had happened to us, we decided to spend the first night in a kitchen in the cellar, but the next day we moved up to the first floor after we had been assured that no combat was going on in the immediate vicinity of Luxembourg City. I remember several large oil paintings, probably portraits of ancestors of the grand ducal ruling family, leaning against the wall in a huge hall. I assumed that the pictures had been brought here after Luxembourg was liberated, in expectation of the return of the ruling family. We also learned that the head of the Luxembourgeois dynasty was named Grand Duchess Charlotte.

We spent some days in the capital, and the only reason for it was probably the protection of General Bradley's headquarters, which were also located here, in case of a German attack. But our good luck lasted all too short a time. Very soon after that we were transferred to the bitterly cold vicinity of Sibret (on the Bastogne-Neufchâteau road). Here I suffered frostbite on both feet, and on New Year's Day, after receiving medical treatment, I was sent to a hospital, an evacuation hospital in Sedan.

Since my condition did not improve markedly, I was transferred to a gigantic military hospital in Bristol, England. By mid-February the war in Europe was over for me, as I crossed the North Atlantic by liberty ship for further treatment in New York.

A Nineteen-year-old Machine Gunner's Story
Report on the Action of D Company
Like so many soldiers of the 109th Infantry Regiment, David Skelly will never forget the retreat combat in the vicinity of Diekirch in December of 1944. He was the gunner of a heavy, water-cooled Browning machine gun M 1917 A1 in the D Company of the 1st Battalion. He tells his story:

"Our first arrival in Diekirch was greeted most heartily by the inhabitants, and in addition, a Red Cross canteen pampered us for the first time since we had left the USA; we worn-out soldiers were given hot coffee and freshly baked doughnuts by friendly Red Cross nurses. We were sent to take quarters in a hotel, where I immediately made friends with several civilians.

We were constantly surrounded by children who always asked us for chewing gum and chocolate. To my astonishment, there was among them a ten-year-old girl who understood a little English and even spoke it. I became especially fond of her and often brought her something to eat.

When I ran out of chocolate, I often bought some baked goods in a bakery in Diekirch. I did not enjoy them myself; the pastry looked better than it tasted. Sugar was obviously in short supply. Something similar happened to me when, during a patrol, a friendly farm woman offered us coffee that did not taste at all good to us. It turned out that this coffee was a kind of surrogate, consisting of malt, chicory and toasted acorns.

Fortunately we had our field kitchen, which always pleased us with a varied and nourishing menu. Very often there was roast meat, vegetables, soup, pancakes, etc. Even the K-rations that we had previously lived on for a long time gradually became strange to us. After several days of rest in Diekirch, we were transferred to the front line, which was formed in our sector by the course of the Our. At first we had to expand the existing gun positions and observation bunkers, some of them built by previous U.S. units, and reinforce them with wood. As a "heavy infantry company", my unit was spread out through the entire sector and was supposed to provide the necessary fire to protect the units that were equipped only with light weapons, in case of an enemy attack. My loader and I had dug out a T-shaped hole for our heavy water-cooled machine gun, which was mounted on a massive tripod. We placed the weapon itself on the raised T, surrounded by a trench about four feet wide. Around this position we placed numerous wooden poles about a meter high.

Only the front side of this fortification remained open, giving us a 90-degree field of fire.

The whole thing was covered with two rows of fir-tree trunks, which were camouflaged with earth, branches and straw. The rear entrance was widened so that a quick change of position was possible at any time.

According to regulations, we also had to dig out a second position somewhat off to the side, which could be occupied at once in the case of enemy sighting of our main position. Somewhat farther down the slope there was an extended row of the gun positions of A, B and C Companies.

Many times I had to fire the gun on orders from the regiment and shoot off a specified quantity of ammunition within a very short time, to unnerve the Germans, as it was said. Then our whole defensive line suddenly became very active. Otherwise, especially at night, a spooky quiet prevailed. During one such firing by us, my machine gun sustained damage to its barrel, so that it jammed from then on, which resulted in loading difficulties. I reported the event and received a barrel from the supply company at once. Although according to regulations the cooling hose and the water container had to be on the machine gun, I removed both, since they constantly caused trouble, and besides, the machine gun was heavy enough anyway. The ammunition was divided up so that I could be supplied immediately from nearby gun positions in the event that I used up my six cases of 250 rounds each. In addition, we were directed to a position behind our lines where an ammunition depot had been set up, and where ammunition had to be available at any time. Somewhat farther to the rear, the 81 mm mortar teams, who likewise belonged to our "heavy" company, had also gone into position. They too were supposed to cover the valley with defensive fire in the event of an enemy attack, so as to support the infantry companies.

At this point in time, almost all the officers no longer wore insignia of rank, neither on their helmets nor on the shoulder patches of their jackets. Obviously there had been several casualties among them caused by German sharpshooters. Many lower-level officers had now followed their example and likewise removed their chevrons. Only a dull white stripe, painted horizontally or vertically on the back rim of the helmet, let us know whether the man was an officer or NCO (officers had vertical stripes, NCOs horizontal).

The nights became increasingly colder, the morning fog often lasted until midday, accompanied by drizzling rain. Thus we spent the nights huddled together and wrapped in additional blankets in our gun holes, which were padded with soft branches, and waited impatiently for the 3rd Battalion to replace us.

Days went by without anything happening. In my hole I also had a radio set and was in communication with an observation post of a rifle platoon somewhat farther down toward the valley. From here too there always came only the same reports: "Everything quiet, nothing new." Shortly before December 10, though, it became generally noticeable that when night fell, dogs ran through our lines more and more often and disappeared into the darkness. It turned out later, after the German attack had already begun, that the dogs had been sent out from Diekirch. After a dog had been shot shortly before December 16, a small cardboard container with sketches and information about the position of the 109th Regiment, and especially about the garrison in Diekirch, was found attached to his collar. The "spy" was also said to have been found, as we learned later. It was supposed to have been a shoemaker who lived in Diekirch who worked for the Germans as a communications man and sent information to them via trained dogs. According to rumors, he was said to have been arrested by Luxembourgeois militiamen. (see Vol.I: The Germans)

When the offensive began on the morning of December 16, my company, which was then back in Diekirch, was just about to come forward for awarding of decorations. Because of the sudden beginning of artillery fire, this ceremony, scheduled for noon, was canceled. After the terrible news had arrived that the enemy was crossing the river and had already begun to attack our defensive line and barricades, our company was transferred to defend militarily important points in and around Diekirch. I myself occupied a hastily prepared gun position near the railroad bridge in Diekirch.

From here we could hear very clearly the sounds of battle that came to us from a distance of four to five kilometers. Heavy traffic prevailed in Diekirch. Off-road vehicles constantly brought wounded men back from the front lines, as well as German prisoners.

On the afternoon of December 19 we were informed that the front could no longer be held and our troops were to be pulled back. We ourselves were loaded onto Jeeps and GMC trucks before nightfall and taken to Ettelbrück to set up a defensive line there to cover the withdrawal of the companies of the other two battalions, which were drawing back. When we had left Diekirch, the convoy came under German artillery fire on the main road. As we came into Ettelbrück, a truck behind us that was loaded with ammunition was hit and blew up. More German shells flew our way and struck the first houses. We jumped out of the Jeep and ran into a house on the left side of the road to seek shelter from the shell fragments.

In the living room on the ground floor we found a frightened young woman with eight-month-old twins. The woman did not want to move. We tried to explain to her that she should go to the cellar at once. Finally there was nothing else for us to do but take the children away from her and move her to the cellar. A short time later the house was hit in the gable and the roof began to burn.

We hurriedly evacuated the woman and the crying babies to the center of town, where a medic took care of them. I only hope that this poor woman could be brought to a safe place in time. At the edge of Ettelbrück there were fires in several places. White phosphorus sprayed around from the exploding 81 mm shells that were in a burning U.S. truck and now went off by themselves and spread their deadly contents at irregular intervals.

During the night our troops moved soundlessly out of Diekirch and, like us, reached Ettelbrück, where we were immediately directed farther by guides. Two days later a cohesive unit had been formed again beyond Ettelbrück, and now it was applied to fight off the German advance toward Ettelbrück. In fact, the German troop soon turned off and pushed forward in a westerly direction.

I myself no longer took part in this defensive fighting, for on December 22 I was subordinated to a task force at Berg. This task force was to push forward again over footbridges to the Sauer in connection with a tank battalion and tear a part of the south bank of the Sauer away from the enemy.

It was our company's task to support the B Company, chosen to attack, with our heavy weapons. In this respect the 81 mm mortars stood out particularly, and during the attack on Gilsdorf they had fired a deadly hail on the edge of the town. When we ourselves returned, Gilsdorf was already partially cleaned out of enemies. So there was at least an "earned Christmas vacation", since after this successful move, which had been arranged by Lt.Col. Rudder, we stayed in Gilsdorf one more day.

Finally, on an ice-cold December 27, we were taken out of the southern sector and transferred to Belgium to defend a threatened area around Petit Voir and Recogne.

Allow me to make one more personal observation here: It may be said that I am not proud of all that I did during the war, but as a soldier of the United States I am certain that I did my duty and thus contributed a small part to the victory over Nazi Germany. Among our countless prisoners there were many with whom I was able to make friends for a short time. Thus I would like to keep permanently in mind only the "human" and the "good" that was still to be found here and there in this war.

An Unusual War Diary

Written on empty cigarette packs in the first days of his imprisonment, is the diary, consisting only of phrases, of Martin Slota.

The former sergeant served at the headquarters of the 2nd Battalion, in the S-2 (intelligence) unit, and led a team of five men. It was his job to obtain and evaluate militarily important information, concerning the enemy's position on the line held by the 2nd Battalion (thus approximately in the Vianden-Longsdorf sector), for his staff. On December 16, 1944 he himself was at the headquarters of the 2nd Battalion on a large farm in Bastendorf. To this day he maintains that the first wave of German attackers at Fouhren consisted partly of soldiers in civilian clothing, but also in part of German soldiers in American uniforms. He also maintains that he saw a German truck, with infantrymen in U.S. uniforms sitting on it, drive through Fouhren. To date Martin Slota is one of the very few credible witnesses who confirms the rumor that units of Volksgrenadiers within the 7th Army fought while not wearing regular uniforms.

Author's note: As for the soldiers in civilian clothing, it is most probable that they were ditch diggers who had to help build bridges in Gentingen and Ammeldingen, but who could also have taken part in the attack on Fouhren (because they might possibly be needed for mine-removal work). But there have been numerous reports of German soldiers in American uniforms. In this case they do not necessarily have to be troops who were intended to cause confusion (such as Panzer Brigade 150, commanded by Obersturmbannführer Otto Skorzeny, within the framework of the 6th SS Panzer Army). It is probably a case of soldiers who, because of a shortage of clothing and equipment in winter conditions, put on coats, jackets, footwear and the like from captured American supplies and thus were often misidentified. Often such misidentifications turned out to be fatal (as with GR 916 and GR 915 in Bettendorf; see Vol.I: The Germans).

But back to the diary of Martin Slota, which he wrote later in Bitburg shortly after being taken prisoner. Although it unfortunately exists only as a fragment, the brief phrases provide sufficient information about the fate of the E Company, which was put fully out of action near Fouhren. In its unabridged original form (phrases), the diary confirms, on many points, the statements of other soldiers on both sides. Here are the contents:

Diary of a Prisoner of War
Bastendorf, Saturday, December 16, 1944:

Brother Henry's birthday. 0530-0615 hours. Enemy artillery fire awakens us abruptly in the houses that served as our quarters.

0630 hours. My buddy Alexander and I go to the command post of the E Company in Fouhren. Jeep driver Bellawa returns to the headquarters. Alex and I examine reports concerning the crossing of the Our by the "Jerries" near Bettel (the military boundary between Luxembourg and Germany).

0700 hours. On the way to Bettel – the other observation posts report "Jerries" on our side of the river, plus one death among our men.

1000 hours. The "Jerries" encircle Fouhren, cut off our supply route and fight against our troops at the western edge of town. I myself take part in the fighting and fire my first round since landing in France, shooting a German.

1200 hours. The "Jerries" withdraw somewhat out of the fight – the supply route remains cut off – no food. Andy Pallo is with E Company. Permanent alarm level all through the night.

Sunday, December 17, 1944

Fouhren, Luxembourg. All quiet in the morning – still no food.

1400 hours. The "Jerries" close the circle – take the village, part by part. Our own artillery fire is very badly directed.

1500 hours: The "Jerries" capture the company command post (the artillery). The building is in flames. Four German tanks on the opposite hillside fire on us and approach. The cook and I fire on the "Jerries" from the third floor of a house. The enemy comes in greater numbers by the light of the houses that are in flames. As darkness breaks (Saturday-Sunday), there is lasting and heavy German artillery fire.

1800 hours. Discussion of "surrendering." Decision to surrender. Leave the burning house without weapons. I worry about how Mother will take the news if I were to be missing in action. The enemy searches us for weapons and marches away with us. Andy Pallo surrendered with us and the E Company.

1900 hours. The "Jerries" lead us through Bettel. We pull a wagon with wounded U.S. soldiers and "Jerries." Cross the river on a wooden bridge built by the "Jerries" and leave the wounded back at a German medical station.

2100 hours. Still marching.

2300 hours. Stop and spend the night in a barn – still nothing to eat.

Monday, December 18, 1944:

0900 hours. The march continues. Are questioned (during the day) –and march on. Still nothing to eat – only a few apples that I picked up off the ground.

Tuesday, December 19, 1944:

0300 hours. Reach a small camp near a hospital in Bitburg. Russian and Polish prisoners of war work in the hospital. 0900 hours. Meet three of my men: Brendal, Van Vorst and Schmidt, who were likewise taken prisoner. Alexander (Alex) is with me.

1400 hours. U.S. planes bombard Bitburg. Direct hit on the Polish camp and German building. Air pressure blew up the housing of the Americans. Numerous U.S. soldiers wounded.

1500 hours. Must bury the dead . . .

Mousetrap Fouhren

The small village of Fouhren located on the high ground northeast of Our valley with a direct view on the German border area lay right in the line of attack of the 5th German paratroop division. It was vital for the Germans to secure the village and its crossroad leading in the direction of Diekirch. For the unfortunate men of E company, 2nd Bn, 109th Rgt, Fouhren became a nightmare during the first couple of days of the "bulge."

Bill Alexander was a member of the intelligence section, 2nd battalion, 109th Inf. Rgt. at the time of the battle of the bulge. Along with his outfit, he arrived in the Diekirch-Fouhren area around Thanksgiving time after the battle at Huertgen forest in late November 1944.

"We were certainly well received by the Luxembourg people at that time," Bill recalls. "My Thanksgiving dinner consisted of – not turkey, which most of the American troops got at that time – but of a roast goose, prepared by one of the Luxembourg families for myself and the members of our unit. I believe at first we were stationed at Bettendorf; later on our unit was moved to Bastendorf – that's where our battalion headquarters also were. Prior to the battle of the bulge, our particular mission was to maintain an observation post in the castle of Vianden. We were on the post on alternating shifts, 24 hours by 24 hours. Usually there were two men in the castle for 24 hours and then they were relieved the following day. There was also down in Vianden at that time a squad of men from the third platoon of E company billeted in the Heintz hotel, as well as members of the "Miliz" (local resistence/partisan group) who were in Vianden. It was only a few years ago that I learned of one of the members of the "Milz," Leo Hansen – the only member of the group who spoke English – and I had contact with him during that time. We must have been at that castle probably for about two weeks, continuing this observation of the Germans. From the castle, we could look across the Our river on the other side of the hill where there is a sanatorium, which turned out to be the Germans' observation post. They were watching us and we were watching them watching us. There was little really that we could see going on around us. We had no phone line on the castle; any message that we wanted to get through back through the battalion would have to go through E company (in Fouhren) through the men at the Heintz hotel. They did have a line that ran down there. There was also a line that ran down to the "Miliz" wherever they were in Vianden.

The intelligence section was headed by Sgt. Martin Slota; the other members, 6 PFCs in total, were J. Byrne, J. Smith, P. Gollobor, F. Van Vorst, and Hans Breandl, who was a German alien – he had been in Germany and he acted as our interpreter for the time being – plus two others and myself. Probably around December 6, on several nights, we could hear movement of some kind across the river. We didn't see anything of course. On one or two occasions there was a light snow on the ground and in the morning you could see that there had been something moving up and down across the Our river on the other side of Vianden.

Fatal decision

On the morning of December 16, (I was billeted in a house in Bastendorf near the battalion headquarters), probably around 5:30 or 6 a.m. in the morning, a dozen or so shells fell into the small village and woke up the entire community. During the shelling, along with the occupance of the house, I went down into the basement, and when the shelling stopped, I came up and moved to the square in front of the church close by the headquarters of the 2nd Bn. There I met Martin Slota, and he had received orders from our section leader, Lt. Barry Gotski, I believe was his name. I had been wounded just before joining the unit, I did not know him too well.

The lieutenant and Martin had received an order to proceed with another member of the unit up to Fouhren to confirm a report the Germans had built a bridge across the Our river at the town of Roodt. We operated our unit on a rotating basis so that each man picked up his turn and sequence on any mission that was assigned to us.

It was not my turn to go, but I had known Martin for a long time, so I decided I'm going to go with him. I didn't want one of the younger members who had just joined the intelligence section to go with Martin on what would be his first patrol. He and I and a corporal Roode, who was our driver, proceeded from Bastendorf down the road and up through Tandel to Fouhren at the intersection of "Tomm" road and the street leading down to the church, where we contacted the sergeant who had led the patrol down the road the night before and had reported the Germans' coming across the river early that morning.

I happened to know the sergeant, because I had been a member of E company before I joined the intelligence section. His name was Maynard Midthun; he was a divinity student, and everybody called him "deacon." We located "deacon" and told him that we had been sent out to confirm his report that the Germans had come across the river, and asked him to lead us down there. "Deacon" for the first time in his life used profanity in saying he would certainly do nothing of the kind because he had just got out there with the skin. So Martin and I started off together in the direction of Roodt off the two-track, and we had maybe gone 800-1000 yards, when Martin motioned up, and . . . coming over the hill was a column of German troops. They didn't look wet, and we decided whether they had a bridge or not it was obvious that they were moving around Fouhren, where E company's CP was located somewhere north.

We then decided we would go back and report to the E company commander what was going on and what we had seen. So we negotiated our way back to Fouhren up to the Vianden road up to a large house there on the corner of the road, which was owned by the Betzen family. We reported to captain Brown what we had seen and this really should have concluded the mission that was assigned to us. However it became apparent to us that there was going to be a firefight there sooner or later; maybe E company could use a couple more rifles. So Martin and I decided we would stay with E company and we sent our driver, CPL Roode back to Bastendorf. I learned somewhat later that CPL Roode had been ambushed near a viaduct and had been killed. Martin and I stayed in the Betzen house then. We made ourselves available to CPT Brown and the squad leaders of E company to prepare for the defense of the area. During the day, probably around 10 or 11 a.m. in the morning, we became aware of German troops moving across the Vianden road to the west of the Betzen house. E company called down for artillery fire on that particular building. At that time there were also some mortar units of the weapons' company in the area, and they had mortar fire directed on the German troops crossing the roads.

One of the means the Germans were using to move troops across the open area across the road was by means of stretcher bearers wearing red cross armbands. They would move across the road further to the south with four men carrying the stretcher, and they came back with only two. They were doing this for some time until we brought fire down on the red cross bearers or . . . looking like red cross bearers at least. Later that afternoon we thought we heard some tanks approaching and we thought the Americans are coming to help us here. But nothing developed; we heard nothing more beyond that and I don't know whether any tanks ever got near Fouhren or not. There had also been a column of Germans across the ridgeline east of the house. They had driven back in the company CP in the Betzen house two or three squads that were out there with machine guns.

Also, some civilians and some members of the "Miliz" had come up from Vianden to some of the houses west of us. Later, they all wound up in the Betzen house as the pressure was increased by the Germans closing in around us. But that night, everything remained fairly calm. We just sat there hoping that there would be some relief coming. That night, I was posted as a guard on one of the wings of the Betzen house. I suddenly heard a noise, and I thought it was a cow coming down the road . . . clip, clap . . . and then stop, and then it continued for some time until I could see against the skyline the outline of a German soldier, a German helmet and equipment. We halted him and called him in towards the house towards the center of the house. I asked the other fellow that was with me to cover me and I stood up, partially at least, and came out to bring him in. He had his hands up, but as soon as he got up within ten feet of me, he slipped the assault rifle off his shoulder; he was very anxious to get rid of all the weapons he had. He also pulled up a couple of grenades, which he handed to me, too. I kept him with his hands up; we brought him in and got him inside the light where we could see him. It developed that he was an Austrian who had been drafted into the German army and the last thing he wanted to do was to fight. He was trying to surrender. We brought him in and introduced him to CPT. Brown, who had no use for him at the time. We had no interpreter who could talk to him. All we got was an Austrian . . . and he was finished. So I said, "What do we do with him?" The captain said to take him down to the basement and hold him down there.

Earlier the next morning (December 17), the Germans began to push further on behind us and circle the entire town, which they hadn't done before. They eventually pushed far enough ahead to cause our artillery support to withdraw, and we soon lost any capability of directing artillery fire on units coming in close – which they did, gradually pressing closer throughout the afternoon. It was getting dark – it must have been around 5:30 p.m. – when they came down by a line of trees, almost directly from the south. It was apparent that one of the members of that enemy column was carrying on his back a flamethrower, which was kind of disturbing to us, because there was no way for us to get out of there at all. We directed rifle fire on him and he was stopped and knocked down.

A little later, someone managed to get closer by the end of the road to throw a concussion grenade at the corner of the house where I was, but as he rose to throw it, we fired upon him and he went down. His grenade did explode and I got a little piece of tin in my leg. Sometime after that – maybe half an hour or so – the Germans managed to set fire to the upper story of the house by firing tracer bullets into the hayloft. The fire spread rather quickly beneath the net portion of the house which would be the western wing. There were several horses and some cattle in there. The fire panicked them, and it panicked us, too. It spread rapidly, and we now could no longer expose ourselves in position, because we would be silhouetted against the flames. One of the other E company members, I believe his name was Kahn, and apparently the only Jewish member inside the company, stood up against the backside of the flames; he was cut down and killed. I am sure he was the only man in the house that was killed that night.

The fire continued to spread, and we knew that we couldn't get out of there unless we did surrender. Captain McBride, the 2nd Bn executive officer, who had also been in the house from the beginning of the day of the 16th December, urged us to keep resisting. We did try to keep calm and wondered what would happen when they really assaulted us. However, the Germans held back – it must have been some time around close to midnight – the house was pretty well in flames in the western and southwestern corner. The word came through – I don't know how it was given or directed to every member of the unit – that the Germans have said "you have five minutes to come out or stay there and cook." At that time there were probably 70 or 80 men of E company that were in the large U-shaped house in addition to several members of the Betzen family and people from Vianden and inhabitants from neighboring homes. While the flames were building up, a German soldier ran in through the open door of the courtyard, got into a jeep that was parked there and took off. Very shortly after that the order came down to come out and surrender.

Martin and I, who were down in the root cellar, threw our rifles out into the fire and came upstairs. I think we were the last of E company or of the 2nd Bn to come out of that house. The men were crying or cursing as they came out. We were taken shortly after that across the Our river – there was a bridge at Roodt – and were eventually moved to Bitburg. The German soldiers who captured us, were of a paratroop unit. They treated us well. I remember one of them searching me, put his hand in my pocket and I said, "Cigarettes." "Ah, Zigaretten," he said and made a motion for me to take them out and I thought that this was my last draw. I handed them to him and he said, "Ja, Zigaretten," and put them back. That was probably the nicest thing that happened to me that night! Most of the Germans were very young, they may have been seventeen or eighteen. We were kept that night in a barn or shed in the little town of Obersgegen, and the next day they marched us off to Bitburg. But they let us go to an orchard on the hill to pick up some fallen apples. That was it. I was liberated in May 1945 and returned to allied control on May 17.

CHAPTER *VIII*

COMBAT IN THE
3RD BATTALION'S SECTOR

The 109th Regiment, with its commander, Lt.Col. James Rudder, originally had its headquarters in Diekirch, and then, after the regimental boundary had been determined by the division, moved to Ettelbrück on December 12. Two of its battalions had permanent sentry duty on the already mentioned defensive line, while the third remained in Diekirch in mobile readiness as an operational reserve.

Battalion Situation

Each battalion was supposed to have two weeks of front service and then one week of rest. On December 16, 1944 the 1st Battalion formed the reserve in Diekirch, while the 2nd and 3rd Battalions were in defensive positions along the Our. According to reports from reconnaissance troops as well as intelligence reports from the division, the opposite sector was occupied only sparsely by the 915th Regiment of the 352nd VGD. Only now and then did medium-caliber German artillery shoot harassing fire for short periods (probably to prove their presence) into the American positions. According to observations, even the gloomy bunker life of the Germans seemed to have its favorable aspects, since feminine forms ventured into the German lines often as night fell, seeking their way back to the neighboring Eifel villages behind the lines in the first light of morning.

The weather became increasingly colder from December 1 to 16. Powdery snow often fell, turning to a damp fog or a cold rain after a few hours. The nights became bitter cold, and every GI probably dreamed of warm quarters, the traditional turkey dinner and the promised end of the war for the coming Christmas of 1944.

When the 3rd Battalion of the 109th Regiment settled down to rest on the front line late in the evening of December 15, 1944, it was located at the right (south) end of the division's defensive line. To the right of it, the 60th Armored Infantry Battalion of the 9th U.S. Armored Division had taken up positions. For its neighbor on the left it had the E Company of the 2nd Battalion, likewise in a defensive position along the Our. Its own sector accordingly stretched from Reisdorf (roughly to the confluence of the Our and the Sauer shortly before Wallendorf) approximately to Longsdorf. This position had been occupied shortly before by the 1st Battalion, which was now resting from its guard duty in Diekirch since December 11.

The defensive sector of the 3rd Battalion was organized and occupied by the I and L Companies. The K Company remained back in Moestroff to serve as so-called "firemen" (mobile reserve). In addition, every front-line company had a platoon armed with heavy machine guns of .30 and .50 caliber, as well as a "team" of 81 mm mortars, supplied by Heavy Infantry Weapons Company M, the main part of which remained back in Bettendorf along with the battalion headquarters.

The 57 mm antitank unit was likewise held in reserve at Bettendorf. Its commander, Captain Paul Gaynor, had set up its command post at Gilsdorf.

The actual front line ran some 250 to 600 meters away from the right bank of the Our on the heights that were regarded as a major obstacle if the enemy should attempt to achieve a mass crossing.

Only in two places south of Longsdorf did open country prove to constitute a gaping hole in the front, an ideal spot for defense. In order to provide sufficient protection no matter what, the surveillance of this gap was turned over to a .50 machine-gun unit in Longsdorf, supported by a "rifle squad" of the I Company. At other spots which could not be kept under surveillance, numerous parachute flare mines and anti-personnel mines were laid, as well as charges of TNT in trees and hand grenades equipped with trigger and trip wires, so-called "booby-traps."

These traps turned reconnaissance trips, especially at night, into a dangerous risk, for there were only two known safe paths indicated on the map of the area, and these were always used by the battalion's reconnaissance patrols.

The actual strength of the 3rd Battalion as of December 15 amounted to about 80% of its specified strength.

In general, it was a rather relaxed unit that turned in for the night on December 15, 1944, not dissatisfied with this "quiet" sector, and certainly dreaming of the coming Christmas celebration, with letters and parcels of presents from family members in America.

Surprise Attack

About 5:30 AM on December 16, 1944 the battalion was awakened abruptly by the thunder of massive artillery fire and the whistling of shells and Nebelwerfer rockets at very close range. At first it seemed as if the fire would concentrate on the command posts, supply depots and information transmission system, but then it fell on the flanks and rear of the battalion in its sector.

The battalion staff's building in Bettendorf (the Schauls farm?) was now somewhat damaged, and the command post of Company L, a farm on the Bettendorf "Niederbierg", went up in flames.

Telephone connections that linked the battalion with the regiment in Ettelbrück as well as with its own companies were badly damaged or completely broken; despite the immediate use of signalmen, the connections were extremely bad. Fortunately radio transmission, generally carried on by a few SCR-300 radio sets, was functioning.

The battalion commander, Major Jim McCoy, immediately directed all the units into their combat positions, but it turned out that surprising, concentrated enemy fire had already implemented his orders. A parade planned for 10:00 AM at the "Kluster" in Diekirch, in which several soldiers of the 3rd Battalion were supposed to be decorated for bravery during the fighting at Hürtgen and Vossenack, was immediately called off.

About 6:30 AM the greatest part of the indirect enemy fire was directed at the defensive line itself, the strongest of it at the right side, which was held by Company L, as well as at the center of the battalion's line.

Only around 9:00 AM did the situation gradually become known, when Company L reported by radio that they had made contact with the enemy at double company strength. I Company likewise reported an attack by numerous enemy infantry platoons. Probably the enemy, under cover of darkness and the spooky morning fog, had already crossed the Our even before the fire began. Many of the attacking Germans screamed and shot blindly around themselves until machine-gun fire and exploding mines suddenly brought the first wave of attackers to a stop on the high plateau near Reisdorf and Hoesdorf.

Most of the German soldiers who were captured or wounded on this first day were still very young, half children, and some of them carried a small bottle of whisky or brandy. Some of them asserted fanatically that the Wehrmacht would celebrate a great victory festival in Paris at Christmas! The two front companies, I and L, commanded by 1st Lieutenant Bruce Paul and Captain Embert Fossum, reacted vigorously to the attack and laid a heavy fire upon the enemy by the .50 machine-gun teams detailed to them, also receiving invaluable help from the 81 mm mortars of the M Company, plus the regiment's cannon company (105 mm howitzers) and the 107th and 108th Field Artillery Battalions of the division's artillery.

The order to ration ammunition was immediately countermanded by the division staff for all the artillery and mortar units. About 9:30 AM, two units of the heavy .30 machine-gun platoon of M Company had come from Bettendorf and reached the sector of I Company, where they were of great help in repelling an attack that had just begun. The same small unit immediately undertook a position change in order to regroup. At the same time, the "mess sergeant" of M Company left Bettendorf with two men in a Jeep in order to supply the small crew on the left flank with food and maintain contact with Company E of the 2nd Battalion. He never came back, and since neither phone nor radio contact from Longsdorf existed any longer, everything suggested that the situation here was extremely bad.

Applying their full infantry firepower, Companies I and L were able to beat back the second enemy attack without losing ground. Although under pressure, the Germans did not draw back, but gathered on the west bank of the Our, protected by thick shrubbery, underbrush and steep slopes.

When a third attack again failed, the enemy did not at first undertake another attempt, but rather seemed to wait for reinforcements. Late in the afternoon of December 16, Company L called for mortar fire when a German patrol tried to break into the company's right flank. This defensive fire ended further German attacks in that sector for the day.

About 2:25 PM Company F of the 2nd Battalion made contact for the last time and reported a strong German attack by three assault guns (probably from Assault Gun Brigade XI of the 5th FJD. Author's note), supported by infantry at Walsdorf, as well as from Fouhren in the direction of Tandel, the sector of E Company (2nd Battalion), from which there was no longer any contact with the 3rd Battalion.

The 1st Battalion, which had remained in Diekirch at the highest level of readiness, was already mobilized in the morning, and its A Company, supported by a platoon of Sherman tanks from the 707th Tank Battalion, hurried in the direction of "Seltz" but was stopped shortly before Longsdorf in the country near Fouhren by the three assault guns. In the fight that followed in the twilight, a Panzerfaust shot hit the leading U.S. tank, and although the shot glanced off, the tank had to be abandoned on account of motor damage. As night fell, the other two Shermans drew back somewhat; it seemed as if the German assault guns would not move farther forward because of the danger in the dark.

Now and then one could hear the dry bursts of machine-gun fire and the whistling of tracer bullets that lit up the scene. Early in the night of December 16-17, German artillery, "Nebelwerfer" and heavy mortar fire began again, aimed at the sector of the 3rd Battalion. Observation and listening posts of Companies I and L reported enemy movements, the sounds of motors, and the crunch of tracked vehicles on the German shore of the Our. Company K in Moestroff was ordered to take action immediately at any dangerous point on the regiment's defensive line. During the night the front units were supplied with food and ammunition wherever it was possible, wounded and dead were picked up, and damage to communication lines was repaired. All through the night the sounds of heavy harassing fire were heard, alternating with U.S. fire on the German crossing points, until early in the morning of December 17, when fire from fog launchers shook the entire front line. This heavy fire lasted barely an hour and then fell silent altogether. At about 7:30 AM the first light of morning allowed a view of several hundred meters in open country, and one could, even though unclearly, catch sight of enemy artillery that was moving toward the positions of I and L Companies. For two hours, machine guns and light mortars dueled; Company L maintained its position, as its own mortar fire and requested artillery support fell on the Germans, who were advancing extremely slowly and constantly regrouping. Company I, though, soon reported that it had lost contact with its right platoon in the thick woods, and it was feared the platoon was in danger of being rolled over. Little by little, though, the platoon's defensive fire was heard, but as no machine weapons were at hand other than a few BARs (Browning automatic rifles), it became weaker and weaker and finally fell silent.

At about the same time the news came from the regiment that Company A, which had hurried to help the unfortunate platoon of E Company in its hopeless defensive combat near Longsdorf, was holding its positions only with difficulty on account of the arrival of German tanks, supported by paratroopers and infantry as far as "Seltz" and Bleesbrücke.

Major McCoy, Commander of the 3rd Battalion, immediately transferred a platoon from Company K across the Bettendorf road to relieve A Company of the 1st Battalion. Company I was still holding its position. The main part of Company K, held in readiness in Moestroff, reported no direct contact with the enemy, so that an additional small patrol was ordered to go to A Company at Bleesbrücke and "Seltz." The regiment also made known that the antitank company had taken positions on the hills overlooking the Diekirch-Bettendorf-Vianden intersection, and around 10:00 AM it had driven back an attack of German assault guns with returning infantry, which already had broken into a position of A Company. Two 40 mm Bofors anti-aircraft guns of the 447th Anti-Aircraft Artillery Battalion, in ground combat at the foot of the "Herrenberg", also provided great assistance to separate the tanks from their accompanying infantry.

Although the loss of two 57 mm antitank guns to direct hits, and the loss of their crews, had to be taken in the bargain, the other gun crews scored numerous hits on the assault guns, but because of their small caliber, no vital damage was caused. In spite of that, the attackers drew back again, and the assault guns turned away (Author's note: these were probably the three "Hetzer" Jagdpanzer, which are hard to tell from an assault gun by an untrained eye or at a distance because of their lack of a turning turret.) The fourth German attack began about 2:00 PM in the sector of I Company, which still consisted only of three incomplete platoons. It was again fought off thanks to the excellently directed fire of the two artillery battalions (107th and 108th) from their positions around the Herrenberg near Diekirch. After this further costly defeat, the German infantry made no more attempts, but only directed poorly aimed medium- and small-caliber artillery fire at the heights. A larger German unit was successful, though, in breaking through the main battle line of the 2nd Battalion, surrounding Fouhren and attacking U.S. artillery units on the Herrenberg by taking roundabout routes through the forest. Lt.Col. "Jungle Jim" Rosborough, Commander of the 107th Field Artillery Battalion, was able to save his threatened guns (105 mm howitzers) and the field kitchen situated farther back, despite serious losses. As a result, the regiment ordered all the field kitchens of the 3rd Battalion were ordered back to Ettelbrück that afternoon. Two halftracks of the 899th AAA Battalion, with quadruple .50 caliber anti-aircraft guns, took up defensive positions in the upper "Bamertal" near "Drei Braaken", so as to use their deadly fire to drive back any possible breakthrough from the northeast slope of the Herrenberg toward the rear of Diekirch.

Alarm

All personnel remaining in Diekirch: battalion secretaries, assistant cooks, mechanics, musicians and transport NCOs, were quickly assembled into an improvised combat unit and immediately sent to the front lines, to strengthen the positions in any case and help to delay the German advance.

The day's results for December 17 were not very encouraging. Company E in Fouhren was completely encircled and cut off. Company C of the reserve battalion in Diekirch had been ordered to join the 2nd Battalion in the Bastendorf-Brandenburg area late that afternoon, which considerably weakened the reserve.

Companies A and B of the 1st Battalion lay motionless in defensive positions around the "Seltz" and near Tandel, in the direction of Bastendorf. During the night before December 18, the usual harassing fire began again, and again the sound of heavy vehicles and motors could be heard from the German side of the Our. Apparently, armored units were moving in.

About noon on December 18, the enemy broke through at one point on the range of hills near Moestroff and defeated one platoon of K Company. Companies I and L were likewise under strong pressure, and their ammunition was gradually running low.

Shortly after 1:00 PM it became known that one German Panzer VI tank and two Jagdpanzer had broken through from Longsdorf and, from a dead angle unreachable by U.S. antitank weapons, had fired on and taken control of the Diekirch-Bettendorf intersection, making it unusable. Enemy infantry had followed immediately, supported by its own 8 cm mortar unit, and was fighting bitterly against what remained of Companies A and B.

In Diekirch, a still available battalion reserve, consisting of 3/4 platoon strength (about twenty men) of the battalion's headquarters company, was pulled together and sent, avoiding the roads, to a hill west of Bettendorf. From here it could, if only "symbolically", protect the rear of the 3rd Battalion and send important data, necessary for the battalion's withdrawal plans, to the regimental commander, Lt.Col. Rudder, in Ettelbrück. These data were evaluated as quickly as possible by the regimental staff and immediately passed on to the commander of the 3rd Battalion, Major McCoy.

Withdrawal to Diekirch
As already mentioned, the presence of the German tanks plus the constantly following infantry made it impossible for the hard-hit and exhausted companies of the 3rd Battalion to withdraw along the Bleesbrücke-Bettendorf road. When the order to withdraw was given to all units at 2:45 PM on December 18, 1944, the situation was as follows: Company L was still in Reisdorf, Company I was fighting hopelessly in the midst of German infantry that was cutting through the defensive line, and was suffering severely from the loss of a rifle platoon. One platoon of Company K had also been completely lost and wiped out. The rest of the company was under German mortar fire, without fire protection, and could not hold out much longer.

Major McCoy had quickly decided to pull back the nearest and most endangered units (I and K Companies) to Bettendorf in a first phase. After that, Company L would cross the Sauer bridge at Reisdorf and move back along the banks of the Sauer via Moestroff. The whole battalion would then cross the river on the still-intact bridge at Bettendorf and reach Gilsdorf along the right bank of the Sauer (the present-day cycle path), then quickly cross the Gilsdorf bridge and finally build up a new defensive line on the heights around Diekirch. The battalion's S-4 officer (responsible officer for material and equipment) and the transport officer were called back from the regimental discussion in Ettelbrück to lead the withdrawal and check out the condition of the route to Bettendorf. This route was already familiar to many officers, since it had been used by the 3rd Battalion as a training zone before December 10, which would simplify their task considerably in the darkness. Meanwhile, the already withdrawn units that remained of the 1st Battalion had taken up defensive positions on the slopes of the "Kleck" (Rue Clairefontaine) and thus could prevent the enemy from advancing directly by way of the Bleesbrücke. Company L, located about five kilometers from Bettendorf, was nevertheless the first to be ordered to withdraw from Bettendorf. In the process, the rest of Company M, the 81 mm mortar unit and the requested artillery support of the 3rd Field Artillery Battalion of the 9th U.S. Armored Division were to provide the needed support at the rear.

Under a smoke screen, the exhausted Company L hastily vacated Reisdorf; many individual pieces of equipment of the individual soldiers, extra rations and

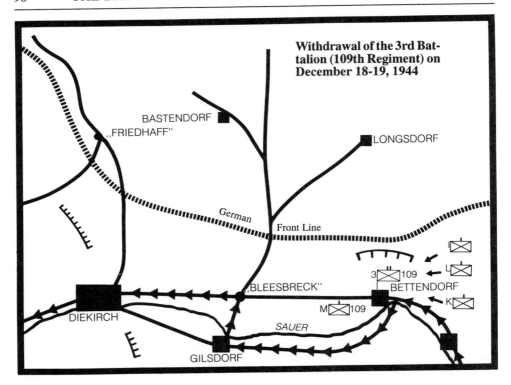

Withdrawal of the 3rd Battalion (109th Regiment) on December 18-19, 1944

ammunition, were left behind undestroyed because there was no more time left. In the panic of this withdrawal a 60 mm mortar was also lost, as German infantry-weapons fire pursued the fleeing company. At Moestroff they were stopped by machine-gun fire from the opposite heights, since the enemy had already broken through I Company's lines at various points. Much valuable time was lost here; finally Company L, badly beaten and scarcely to be described as a combat unit any more, reached Bettendorf and, with its last strength, occupied the slopes assigned to it at the northeast edge of the village.

Thereupon Companies I and K were ordered back and reached their gathering position in the twilight, under considerably less pressure from the enemy. German artillery fire was now directed against main roads and intersections in Bettendorf. Shortly after nightfall, the S-4 officer withdrew all still available vehicles except weapons carriers and command cars, loaded with wounded men, to Ettelbrück via the prescribed withdrawal route.

The staff company of the 3rd Battalion quickly set up a command post in the basement of the Hotel des Ardennes in Diekirch. About 8:00 PM, I and K Companies, followed by what remained of M Company, left Bettendorf, and for a short time L Company protected the rear of their comrades with sparse infantry-weapon fire, until they had crossed the Sauer bridge. Suddenly heavy German Nebelwerfer launcher fire began, bombarding the railroad-station area in Bettendorf with explosive shells. A direct hit fell in the line of the withdrawing L Company and killed ten men. None of the survivors will ever forget the terrible whine of the approaching "screaming Mimies", as the 15 cm Nebelwerfer shells were called in American slang. Meanwhile the regiment had hastily sent a platoon of the A Company of the

The Eternal GI, Ardennes, 1944-45. Photo: US Army

Above: Lt. Col. James Rudder took over the leadership of the 109th Infantry Regiment early in December 1944. Here Lt. Col. Rudder marches at the head of his troops through Colmar, France, liberated in February of 1945. Photo: US Army

A typical scene from those unforgettable days in September 1944. Little Jean Barbel of Ulflingen (Troisvierges) welcomes a lieutenant of the 28th US Infantry Division with a flower on the Rue d'Asselborn on September 12. Photo: US Army

Right: "Luxembourg is free": US soldiers of the 5th US Armored Division in the capital in mid-September. Photo: US Army

Painter Willy Dillenbourg, wrapped in the American flag he made by hand, greeting the American liberators of the 5th armored division on the "Fielser Stroos" in Diekirch. The flag was partly hand-painted by him and the stars were stenciled on. The red stripes were cut out of a swastika flag by Diekirch ladies and sewn on. This flag, recently rediscovered, is to be seen at the entrance of the Diekirch Museum. Photo: Marc Rosch archives

First contact with the soldiers of the 5th Armored Division on the street near the "Pärdsrennen". The Jeep belongs to A Company, 47th Armored Infantry Battalion, 5th Armored Division. From left to right, Pierre Job, Julie Thirifay and daughter, Willy Dillenbourg, Pier Faber, M. Krebs, Pierre Weis, Augustine Weis. Photo: Marc Rosch archives

Painter Willy Dillenbourg proudly poses for the photographer with his handmade "Star Spangled Banner". Recognizable in the picture are Theis Pierchen, Mme. Lily Thilges, Camille Thilges, Franc,ois Bastendorf, Pier Faber and Harry Suttor. Photo: Marc Rosch archives

The first American infantrymen come to the "Kippenhof" from Brandenbourg

Right and below: The Kippenhof-Brandenbourg crossed. The farmer and refractories rejoice as the halftracks drive by. Photos: Mme. Suz. Oesch

*An M-8 "Greyhound" scout car reaches
the "Kippenhof", followed by a Jeep of
the 85th Cavalry Reconnaissance
Battalion of the 5th US Armored Division.
Photos: MMe. Suz. Oesch*

A reconnaissance Jeep of the 85th Cavalry Reconnaissance Battalion of the 5th US Armored Division is greeted by Diekirchers on September 11, 1944. Photo: Jos Ferry

Shortly afterward, the first US tank rolls across the railroad bridge, followed by several personnel carriers and a jubilant throng. Photo: Roland Gaul archives

The liberators: Officers and men of the 5th US Armored Division at the "Sauerwiss" in Diekirch. Photo: Roland Gaul archives

Diekirch, September 1944: Lt. Aloyse Schiltz and the American 1st Lt. Clayton d'Avy (HQ-G2 section, 5th Armored Division) before the house of Prof. Mathias Wagner. Prof. Wagner had secretly built a small radio receiver with special listening devices, which provided invaluable service to the refractories in the church at Pfaffenthal, including René Schiltz.
Photo: René Schiltz collection

General Omar Bradley)right) decorates Maj. Gen. Norman D. "Dutch" Cota, Commander of the 28th US Infantry Division.
Photo: US Army

Group picture of Civil Affairs Detachment B1F1, taken in the Diekirch city park at the end of September 1944, opposite the headquarters at the "Maison Rouge". Front row, left to right: Captain English, Captain Kappanadze, unknown British officer, Major Matthews, unknown British officer, Major Lewis, unknown British officer, Captain Brulle. Photo: Roland Gaul archives

From left to right: Sgt. Charles Frawley, A Company, 1st Battalion, Private Harry Dahm (drowned while crossing the Our), Private Paul Andrus, missing near Diekirch, December 18, 1944 (he was captured). The picture was taken in Diekirch early in December 1944, probably by Jos Ferry, and paid for with cigarettes, coffee and chocolate. Photo: Charles Frawley archives

Private Bob Meyer, machine gunner of A Company, 109th Infantry Regiment, was captured by the Germans after attempting with his unit to rescue a surrounded US unit near Longsdorf. Photo: Roland Gaul archives

1st Lieutenant Jim Christy, Executive Officer of B Company, led the attempt to relieve the surrounded E Company of the 2nd Battalion near Fouhren. In the picture he has a German 08 pistol in a holster made by a Diekirch shoemaker. Photo: Roland Gaul archives

"For this purpose, a parade was held on a square near the church, with a musical group from the division band." These two pictures were taken at the "Kluster" (Place Guillaume) on December 15 by a private photographer, while the Germans were making their final preparations for the attack. Photos: Roland Gaul archives

One of the best-known photos of the 28th US Infantry Division, December 1944. Center, with woolen knit cap: Private Albert Dogan of C Company, 109th Infantry Regiment. Photo: US Army

Private Albert Dogan in dress uniform. Photo: Albert Dogan archives

Pfc. David Skelly, machine gunner of D Company, 1st Battalion, 109th Infantry Regiment. Photo: Roland Gaul archives

Martin Slota, Intelligence Unit, 2nd Battalion, 109th Infantry Regiment, was captured by the Germans at Fouhren on December 17, 1944. This picture shows him during training at Camp Livingston, Louisiana. Photo: Roland Gaul archives

Lt. Col. James Rudder, Commander of the 109th Infantry Regiment, photographed at Pointe du Hoc, Normandy, June 6, 1944. Lt. Col. Rudder was formerly Commander of the 2nd Ranger Battalion. Photo: Col. Harry M. Kemp archives

From right to left: Major Jim McCoy, Commander, 3rd Battalion, 109th Infantry Regiment; Major Harold S. Martin, Executive Officer, 2nd Battalion, 109th Infantry Regiment; 1st Lieutenant Norman Stiles, Motor Officer, 3rd Battalion. Photo taken April 1945. Photo: Col. Harry M. Kemp archives

Captain Harry M. Kemp, Executive Officer, 3rd Battalion, 109th Infantry Regiment, shown as a major in Germany, April 1945. Photo: Col. Harry M. Kemp archives

An 81 mm mortar ready to fire, with a stack of explosive shells propelling charges fixed to their tail fins. The gunner is receiving data for indirect fire on the field phone. Photo: US Army

The railroad bridge and the Sauer bridge at the edge of Diekirch, blown up during the withdrawal of the 109th Infantry Regiment on December 20, 1944. This photo was taken late in January 1945, after US engineers had spanned the Sauer with a Bailey bridge. Photo: US Army

Photographed in Diekirch, early December 1944: Left: Captain Fred Winterbottom, Battalion Adjutant; center: 1st Lieutenant Norman D. Stiles, Transport Officer, 3rd Battalion; right: Major Harold Martin, Executive Officer, 2nd Battalion. Photo: Roland Gaul archives

Sgt. Ralph Boettcher, Marlene Dietrich's chauffeur in Diekirch and Ettelbrück on December 10-11, 1944. The M.G. on the armband means "Military Government". Photo: Roland Gaul archives

Clowning to pass the time at a gun position, Diekirch, November 1944. Photo: Roland Gaul archives

Cannoneer Bob Davies at his battery's firing position on the "Herrenberg" near Diekirch, November 1944. Photo: Bob Davies

A gun position of the 107th FA Battalion on the Herrenberg near Diekirch (late November 1944). Photo: Roland Gaul archives

A 105 mm howitzer ready to fire, with is crew of B Battery, 107th FA Battalion, later in the offensive (December 1944). Photo: Roland Gaul archives

A 155 mm howitzer of the 108th FA Battalion later in the offensive (probably in Belgium, January 1945). Photo: Roland Gaul archives

Lt. Col. James Rosborough, Commander of the 107th FA Battalion, called "Jungle Jim" by his men, received the Distinguished Service Cross for outstanding leadership of his unit in the face of the enemy. Photo: Mrs. J. Rosborough

Left: Captain Paul F. Gaynor, Commander of the AT Company, 109th Infantry Regiment; right: his brother, Captain Robert M. Gaynor, Company Commander in the 110th Infantry Regiment. The picture shows them meeting (as majors) in Germany, April 1945. Photo: Robert M. Gaynor archives

155 mm explosive shells (as used by the 108th FA Battalion) are brought to a gun by two ammunition carriers. There the fuzes are attached. Photo: US Army

This Sherman tank was knocked on its side by the explosion of a heavy Nebelwerfer projectile near the brewery in Diekirch, as described in the eyewitness report of Sgt. Robert Martens. Photo: Roland Gaul archives

1st Sergeant Robert Martens, Commander of a Sherman tank in C Company, 707th Tank Battalion. Photo: Bob Martens archives

103rd Engineer Battalion there, and while the withdrawal of the 3rd Battalion was still in progress, this unit made the last preparations for blowing up the bridges in Gilsdorf and Bettendorf.

When the last platoon of L Company had crossed the Gilsdorf bridge in the direction of "Rue Clairefontaine" (Diekirch), two explosions in quick succession rang out. The last bridge was nevertheless not fully destroyed because of a "hangfire" (detonation defect); a gaping hole in the middle of the bridge was later to be hastily repaired by the advancing Germans and made passable for small vehicles.

In addition, in the confusion of the withdrawal it was forgotten to blow up the row of plane trees that ran along the small railroad line in the direction of Bleesbrücke, although they had already been prepared by the engineers on the previous day.

Every unit, including the last platoon of Company L with Captain Embert Fossum, at whose command the bridges had been blown up at the right time, was now received by officers of the regiment's headquarters company and directed to a gathering place for a new defensive line around Diekirch.

During this maneuver, which was time-consuming and completely confusing on account of the darkness, the commander of K Company, Captain Simpson, and his executive officer, 1st Lieutenant Sheehen, were wounded by shell fragments. The two could not be evacuated until December 19; a platoon leader, Lieutenant Tropp, took command of the company. The men spent the rest of the night looking for better means of taking cover, and dug improvised foxholes in the hard-frozen ground to the extent that it was possible. Only a few men were able to get any sleep before the 19th of December dawned. The morning found the situation as follows:

The 3rd Battalion lay in defensive positions on the northwest heights around Diekirch, with Company I on its right wing, L on the left and K as a reserve back in Diekirch. The hastily constructed positions of K Company extended about to the middle of the "Kleck."

Every company, as far as possible, was assigned one or two groups of 81 mm mortars from Company M. The battalion's antitank platoon secured the "Kleck" (Rue Clairefontaine) with its remaining 57 mm guns, since the German advance on Diekirch was expected in that direction.

All the troop units were fully exhausted from their superhuman exertions. Above all, they lacked warm winter clothing, overshoes, woolen blankets and rations of food, in addition to sleep. During the last three days the companies had been able to get a hot meal only twice, and K and C rations were also running low gradually.

About 10:00 AM the first enemy patrols were sighted at the "Kleck." From far up in the "Seitert" and the "Friedbesch", artillery and machine-gun fire could be heard. Thanks to the favorable observation posts, the 81 mm mortars could lay precise fire on the advancing Volksgrenadier troops. The first attack on Diekirch was beaten back, and the Germans occupied the houses at the end of the "Kleck" as far as the "Bleesbreck." Numerous German prisoners, who were brought out of a house by gendarmes, auxiliary police and militiamen (resistance fighters), supported by a tank of the 707th Tank Battalion, were quickly taken to Diekirch and turned over to the regiment in Ettelbrück for questioning.

About 2:00 PM Company L and the 2nd Battalion to their left reported that the enemy was now in complete possession of Bastendorf and was approaching the

Herrenberg with armored personnel carriers. On the Diekirch-Hosingen highway, nicknamed "Skyline Drive" by the Americans, there again occurred bitter fighting and close combat near "Friedhaff"; in the end the Americans, who had to endure heavy losses, had to give in to German pressure. Despite opposition, the Germans continued to gain ground in the Bamer Valley and "Kalebesch."

On the afternoon of December 19, German artillery fire caused great destruction in the railroad-station area of Diekirch, where German shells had already set the Hotel du Midi afire when the offensive began on December 16. At the same time, the regiment in Ettelbrück was informed by the G-2 officer of the 28th Infantry Division (Intelligence Section) that German tank attacks could be expected during the same night, or in the early morning of December 20 at the latest. (Only on December 19, 1944 were German engineers able to move heavy material, particularly artillery guns and Jagdpanzer of the 352nd VGD, across the Our.)

The regiment was finally ordered to give up Diekirch and move farther back to the south, beyond Ettelbrück. In the process, they were to make absolutely sure that all approaches to Ettelbrück were to be either mined or blown up!

But what would now become of the civilian population?

Until then, they had always been assured that there was no reason to be nervous; but now it was clear to the American leadership that Diekirch could no longer be held under these conditions.

Diekirch is Evacuated

On the morning of December 19, the Battalion Commander, Major McCoy, was hastily given the task of exploring the situation all along the defensive line that had been set up quickly the previous night, and empowered his executive officer, Captain Harry M. Kemp, to set up a command post for the 3rd Battalion in a suitable and more or less safe building in Diekirch. He was to make absolutely sure that several telephone lines to the regiment in Ettelbrück as well as to the front-line companies were set up simultaneously. In addition, Captain Kemp was empowered to supervise all transportation personally, so as to guarantee the supplying of the combat units with ammunition and the evacuation of the wounded. On the evening before December 19, the Battalion Adjutant, Captain Fred Winterbottom, and two non-commissioned officers of the Staff Company had quickly been ordered from Bettendorf to Diekirch in order to locate and set up a suitable building to serve as a command post.

Shortly after midnight, Captain Kemp, along with other officers of the battalion's headquarters company (staff company), reached Diekirch in a Jeep on having received the aforementioned instructions. The headquarters of the 3rd battalion were thereupon set up in the cellar of the Hotel des Ardennes (today a parking lot opposite the Chateau Wirtgen). The main command room measured approximately five by eight meters and was located seven to nine steps below street level. Three tables offered space for maps of the area, and the battalion's radio as well as two field telephones were also located there, one of the latter being a direct link with the regiment in Ettelbrück, the other leading via a switchboard to the front companies and the other battalions. Three chairs and meager oil lamps and candles were the room's only comforts. The other cellar rooms served the personnel of the staff company. Early in the afternoon of December 19, as German machine-gun salvoes could be heard, recognizably different from the American because of their characteristic sound, Captain Winterbottom was speaking to Captain Kemp and had brought along the Luxembourg Gendarmerie Lieutenant Melchers as well as two other gendarmes, since they wished to speak to the American commander. As already mentioned, Captain Harty M. Kemp was at that time the highest-ranked officer in the battalion in Diekirch, representing Major McCoy, the battalion commander.

Lieutenant Melchers immediately made Captain Kemp aware of the threatened situation of the civilians remaining in Diekirch . . .

Just two days before, rumors had spread like wildfire and caused fear and terror among the population on account of the uncertainty of the situation.

Again and again they were assured by the Americans that there was no danger and therefore no reason for panic. In spite of that, inhabitants attempted more and more often to leave Diekirch in small groups, setting off in a southerly direction with their necessities of life packed onto handcarts or bicycles in order to find safety; every time, though, the worried people were mercilessly turned back by the military police or the militia and informed that they would put themselves in danger unnecessarily, and that the Americans had the situation in hand.

Lieutenant Melchers insisted that the population should be evacuated that same night under cover of darkness, since such a threatening situation to the welfare of the inhabitants of Diekirch could no longer be justified. He requested a written order from the U.S. commander, directed to all posts and making the evacuation possible. While the solution was still under discussion, Captain Kemp received an order by telephone to prepare, without delay, the withdrawal plan for all the units of the 3rd Battalion that were still present. New positions on a defensive line determined by the regiment on the heights around Ettelbrück should be occupied within the next few hours. For this purpose, though, several important pieces of information about the general situation in Diekirch were lacking, as well as those on the use of the approach roads and paths to Ettelbrück, so that Captain Kemp could not give an immediate answer to Lieutenant Melchers' request, but had to disregard the question of the civilians for the time being and ask Lt. Melchers to return at 5:00 PM, as he believed that he would have found a solution by then. In any case, according the regimental command, the withdrawal of his own troops took priority over the evacuation of the civilians in terms of military importance.

During the two hours that now remained, Captain Kemp gathered information and details about the situation of the individual companies, withdrawal possibilities, etc., and passed these on to the regiment, which came to a decision shortly thereafter. The units involved in the defense were to leave their positions in groups, be funneled through Diekirch and reach Ettelbrück via the main road along the Sauer. Since this military operation absolutely had priority, the Diekirch-Ettelbrück road could not be used by fleeing civilians.

Captain Kemp spoke by direct line with the S-5 officer, the regiment's officer responsible for "Civil Affairs" in Ettelbrück, who left it up to Captain Kemp to approve the evacuation of the population, provided they would not in any way interfere with the withdrawal of the troops. Captain Kemp, who found himself under great pressure of time in such a difficult situation, made a decision soon and thereupon gave Lt. Melchers the following handwritten order in the cellar of the Hotel des Ardennes:

"This date it has become necessary in the best interests of the population of Diekirch/Lux. to order the town to be evacuated at 24:00," addressed "to whom it may concern", signed Harry M. Kemp, Ex.-O. 3rd Bn US Army.

Thereupon Lt. Melchers immediately left the U.S. command post, where preparations for the withdrawal of all still-present U.S. military forces from Diekirch were already being made in great haste, and met with Gendarmerie officials, militia and firefighters to plan evacuation measures.

Messengers were quickly sent to the houses to let the inhabitants, most of whom were living in the cellars, know that they should immediately pack their most necessary possessions and report to the railroad bridge at midnight. (The Sauer bridge had been blown up since September, the Diekirch-Ettelbrück road was reserved for the U.S. troops, the northern road from Diekirch to Erpeldange was already in German hands; thus only the railroad bridge remained open for the exodus of the population in the direction of Stegen. Author's note.)

Since individual German patrols had already pushed forward to "Bamertal" by the appointed time and engaged in firefights with the Americans who were still present, the majority of the inhabitants of this part of Diekirch remained in their safe cellars and passed up the assembly, while several messengers had "released"

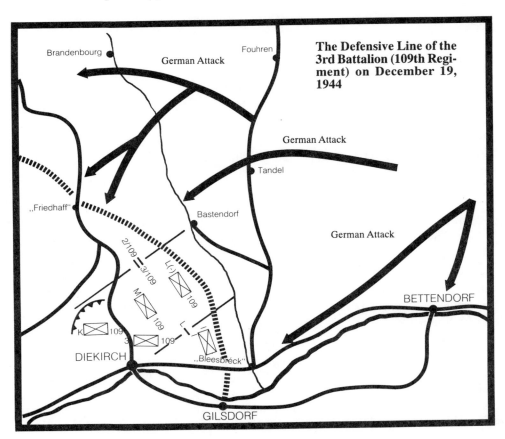

The Defensive Line of the 3rd Battalion (109th Regiment) on December 19, 1944

themselves and reached safety. In all there were 300 to 400 persons who remained in Diekirch until the final liberation on January 19, 1945. Captain Kemp himself was no longer able to supervise the evacuation that he had begun, but left the responsibility for it to the Luxembourg authorities and auxiliary police on the scene, under the command of Lt. Melchers. Captain Kemp personally led the withdrawal of his battalion to Ettelbrück and had the bridge at the edge of the city blown up under German artillery fire. The battalion moved back according to plan and occupied the heights around Ettelbrück on a new defensive line planned by the regiment. Only here did the fully exhausted soldiers finally get a hot meal, rations and, above all, warm clothing that a field hospital unit had left behind.

At the moment when a mighty explosion (the blowing up of the bridge) had resounded through Ettelbrück, the railroad bridge in Diekirch (today the Red Bridge in the city park) was the scene of an indescribable confusion and incredible panic, accompanied by the impacts of German artillery shells in the upper city as well as on the roads to Ettelbrück. Everybody wanted to be the first to cross the bridge; the few Gendarmes and auxiliaries who were still on hand were not able to master the situation.

Gendarm Huss was only able to prevent any use of flashlights or oil lamps. A seemingly endless column of fully packed handcarts, wagons, bicycles, baby carriages and even horse-drawn wagons moved across the railroad bridge through the blackness of night with unsteady steps, accompanied by the cries of the fearful children and the whinnying of the frightened horses.

Suddenly a mine attached to the bridge, which the Americans had forgotten to remove, exploded, killed a horse, injured several people and tore a hole in the iron plates of the bridge roadway. The militiamen on hand immediately examined the bridge and removed additional mines and explosive charges that had been placed there by U.S. forces fir the purpose of blowing up the railroad bridge and either could not be removed during the rushed withdrawal or had been forgotten. The mines were thrown into the Sauer at once.

Several inhabitants, who were trying to reach Ettelbrück after midnight in their own or a "liberated" motor vehicle were stopped by the constant fire on the road to Ettelbrück or were turned back by the auxiliary police still on the scene.

Because of the damage caused by the explosion, some of the horses had to be left behind, which meant that larger wagons also had to be given up.

Strewn all over the place were baskets, bedclothes, covers, food, even whole sides of bacon and hams. Many older people suffered leg injuries in the exodus of the population of Diekirch that night and had to be carried. Meanwhile the ghastly whistling of the German artillery shells and the flashing of the impacts farther ahead continued. All through the frightening night the inhabitants streamed to the footbridges at the "Haardt" forest and "Fielser Stroos" (road to Larochette). Only on the next day did the stream of refugees reached Schieren and Cruchten, where most of them were treated by the Red Cross unit of the 10th U.S. Armored Division. Only in Mersch, Moesdorf and Lintgen, where the majority of the people from Diekirch reassembled, did they finally feel that they had reached safety with their belongings and could recuperate from their exhaustion. In the part "Through Civilian Eyes" we shall have a closer look at those dark days for the population.

Source: The account of the military operations within the framework of the 3rd Battalion (109th Infantry Regiment) described here was based on an unpublished manuscript written in the early fifties by then Lt.Col. Harry M. Kemp as a scientific treatise for an "advanced infantry officer's course." This manuscript was amplified by numerous specific details supplied by Colonel Kemp.

The "Bronze Star" Medal for 1st Lt/ Norman D. Stiles, responsible transport officer, HQ Company, 3rd Battalion, 109th Infantry Regiment

First Lieutenant Norman Stiles served with the Headquarters (Staff) Company of the 3rd Battalion of the 109th Infantry Regiment and was responsible for all the transport traffic within the battalion. Through his personal activity during the withdrawal of the U.S. troops from Diekirch as well as the evacuation of materials, he earned the "Bronze Star" for a heroic deed, as can be seen in the following newspaper article:

"1st Lt. Norman D. Stiles recently was awarded the Bronze Star medal for "heroic action against the enemy" during the time that the division (28th Infantry Division), lying in the path of the Germans' all-out drive into Belgium (and Luxembourg) last winter, resisted the attackers with such tenacity that the Nazi timetable was completely disrupted.

Lieutenant Stiles, who is executive officer of the third Battalion, 109th Infantry, distinguished himself on Dec. 18 as a transportation officer when he was faced with the task of withdrawing all vehicles in the face of constant enemy pressure. The Germans had cut the supply routes on both flanks and the battalion was backed against the Sauer river with the enemy also known to be nearing our positions on the opposite side of the stream.

Lieutenant Stiles, acting on his own initiative, collected all battalion transportation and personally led all vehicles through heavy artillery, mortar and machine gun fire to safety in the vicinity of Ettelbrück. He then went forward again through the same fire without regard for personal safety and led foot troops over the only possible route of exit.

Entering the army in September, 1942, he went overseas in October, 1943. He was with the 28th Infantry during its drive through Normandy, Belgium, Luxembourg and finally into Germany."

Norman Stiles, who presently lives in the state of Pennsylvania, offers the following account:

"I served regularly as a detached transport officer with the 3rd Battalion of the 109th Infantry Regiment from the landing of the 28th Infantry Division in Normandy in July of 1944 to the end of the war in Europe. We actually entered Luxembourg twice. The first time was in mid-September 1944, when we hurried through Wiltz after the retreating Germans and pushed them back to the border. We came into Luxembourg a second time when our exhausted division was transferred here after the very brutal fighting in the Hürtgenwald to be refreshed and regrouped here.

Early in the morning of December 16 I was rudely awakened and experienced the heaviest German artillery fire during the whole war. I myself was quartered in Diekirch, while two of our battalions were located eastward of the city in a defensive line set up along the river that forms the natural boundary here. Later I saw a greater percentage of German troops and tanks here than ever before.

Shortly before noon on the first day of the German offensive I climbed onto the roof of the Hotel des Ardennes, in which the staff company and writing room of the 3rd Battalion were located, and could already see German units on the heights beyond the Diekirch-Bettendorf road intersection clearly at this point in time. On December 18 tanks, which I recognized as assault guns Mark IV, were also sighted. On the roof of the hotel, I waved to an approaching airplane, as I believed it was one of our P-47 Thunderbolt fighters. But it turned out to be a Focke-Wulf 190 machine with German markings, coming from the northwest and flying toward Germany. It flew very low, and the pilot could obviously see the general confusion that already prevailed among our troops in Diekirch.

The first columns of our attackers, which approached threateningly, came, I believe, from an easterly or northeasterly direction.

Our battalion commander, Major Jim McCoy, ordered me to go to the headquarters of the 109th Regiment in Ettelbrück at once to obtain clear information as to the regiment's situation at last, since all radio traffic was badly disrupted at the time.

I reached Ettelbrück by Jeep via the bridge from Ingeldorf (roundabout route) and reported to the regimental headquarters. Everybody was surprised at my visit, since the staff had obviously believed the 3rd Battalion had been wiped out. They asked me if it were possible, or if I myself were in condition, to lead the battalion, whose order to withdraw without delay came through now, back to Ettelbrück and a new defensive line.

Since I knew the situation around Diekirch, I offered my services, and thus Diekirch was evacuated by our troops during the same night of December 19-20.

As far as was possible, all available materials and pieces of equipment were loaded up and taken along. Several slightly damaged vehicles which could no longer be repaired, and several supply depots had to be destroyed. In addition, in the overly rushed atmosphere it was no longer possible to have various intersections and approach routes mined by the engineer platoon detailed to us.

We may have been halfway between Diekirch and Ettelbrück when news from the rest of the regiment, also in withdrawal, reported the presence of a German advance unit at the eastern entrance to Diekirch.

The withdrawal proceeded noiselessly; now and then German artillery shells landed at the entrance to Ettelbrück.

The last of our worn-out units had just crossed the bridge at the entrance to Ettelbrück when it was blown up by men of the engineer platoon under the command of Lieutenant Head. I myself directed a large part of the withdrawal maneuver and stood at the bridge in Ettelbrück before it was blown up, in order to give instructions to arriving units.

East of Ettelbrück we formed a new line, which could be held, and was held, for only a short time. After a brief exchange of fire with German advance units, we drew back farther to the southeast. On the next morning, our observation posts reported that German troops had marched into Ettelbrück.

When Patton's Third Army finally arrived, the shockingly high number of losses first became known to us; various companies that had consisted of 210 men since their regrouping in Diekirch now numbered only from 37 to 45 men. I can only hope that their sacrifice was not in vain.

A Portrait Artist as a Spy

Thomas Hickman served as a "scout" in the HQ Company (Staff Company) of the First Battalion in Diekirch, which had set up its headquarters in the Hotel du Midi opposite the railroad station since being relieved by the 3rd Battalion. Although his unit was itself at rest, he was sometimes at observation posts along the front lines. He reports:

"When we were finally transferred to Diekirch after sustaining heavy losses in combat in November, it seemed that the war was over for us, for we had been told that we would be coming into a so-called "rest area" here. For the first time in months, we finally received fresh underwear and some new clothing, could take a hot bath and enjoyed movie shows and similar entertainment almost every day. In addition, parties were held regularly in a dance hall at Diekirch, so that within a short time, each of us had almost completely forgotten the war. In mid-December Marlene Dietrich even came to Ettelbrück to put on a show in the USO program for the jubilant GIs.

But the war was not over, for each of us knew that the front was only a few kilometers from this paradise. During my activity as a scout, I often noticed troop movements on a small scale, about at company strength, on the part of the Germans. In addition, I thought I heard the sound of motors and tracked vehicles now and then at night, which could be heard by us when the wind conditions were favorable. Similar observations, though infrequently, were reported from other observation posts as well. In any case, we immediately passed them on to the battalion, which was responsible for passing the information on to the regiment and the division. We were assured that it was nothing out of the ordinary, since Germany was so weakened militarily that a great expenditure of power and an advance were impossible. Although our observations were considered to be correct, they still drew no attention from our leadership. A fatal error, for early in the morning of December 16 the first German shells fell!

At the time of the German artillery attack, I was in the Hotel du Midi (in the railroad-station area of Diekirch), on the first floor, where I was sleeping along with numerous comrades. After the first explosion had awakened me immediately, I climbed onto the roof and saw the pale yellow detonation flashes of the exploding shells coming closer and closer. Within a short time, most of the men had fled into the cellar. Just twenty minutes later (just before 6:00 AM) the roof and the upper floor of the hotel were shaken by several shell impacts. The ceilings caved in, plaster crumbled, dust penetrated into the cellar rooms, and something inside me moved me to leave the cellar at once and seek shelter outside. Numerous men had already rushed down to the Sauer, leaving their equipment behind. When I had run several hundred meters along the river, I looked back and saw the hotel being hit again. Shortly after that, the ground floor was on fire. As I heard later, several soldiers, including my friend William Manley, were battered by falling sections of the walls, or even choked by the dust. All over the station area, some of the houses, as well as the hotel, were completely burned out. As I heard later, several other company command posts, as well as the battalion's motor pool, were hit precisely by German artillery and mortar fire and burned down. How and why was their targeting so accurate?

Only now do I recall that, several days before, a portrait painter had been among us, attracting attention by his curiosity, and I myself had been surprised that he had known the names of so many officers.

This man, who possessed an extraordinary talent for drawing, was very much in demand. Almost everybody wanted to send a portrait home to his family members in the USA for Christmas. For cigarettes, chocolate and similar goods, which we were now given plenty of, most of the GIs had their portraits drawn by him.

He was an imposing figure, probably over 1.80 meters tall, had a moustache and always wore a Basque beret. He came to us often, as his artistic talent had been talked about by then. Since he spoke fairly fluent English and was trusted by everybody as "the painter", he went in and out of the Hotel du Midi freely.

Since he also knew how to entertain us, it certainly happened that, in talking with many an unsuspecting GI, without creating any suspicion, a great deal of information about our garrison strength, tanks, command posts, etc. was obtained.

Since every one of us believed he was in a safe, quiet region and was looking head only to the coming Christmas holiday, even during our security service there was probably no doubt as to the reliability of this artist, of whom I now believe that he was very probably a German spy and therefore responsible for the very precise direction of the artillery fire that knocked out command posts.

Thus carelessness from the commanders down to the common soldiers cost us a high price." (see also the report of B Company by Lt. J. Christy, and the report of D Company, David Skelly.)

Adored by All GIs: Marlene Dietrich

It would be incorrect to tell only of combat activities and individual experiences without reporting on an event that was downright sensational for Diekirch and Ettelbrück at that time, although scarcely any inhabitants of the two cities got to share in it. This event was planned and carried out exclusively to invigorate the exhausted soldiers in their condition of recovery. It was the appearance of the legendary Marlene Dietrich, idolized by all the U.S. soldiers regardless of rank.

An extraordinarily lucky man to have been chosen to serve the singer as her chauffeur for two days, as he describes himself to this day, was Ralph Boettcher, then a 23-year-old staff sergeant, and also of direct German ancestry. The author interviewed him at a veterans' gathering in Fort Wayne, Indiana in October of 1983:

"After our division had advanced to the German border in September of 1944, I was subordinated by my unit (Regimental Cannon Company) to the "Military Government Unit." The commander of this unit was Major Stanton.

I myself, as a staff sergeant, had five men under me; our main task was to pass on certain regulations made by the division staff for the civilian population to the representatives of the provisional city government and supervise their implementation.

At the end of November 1944, our unit was transferred to Ettelbrück, and we were assigned a certain territory in cooperation with the mayor of the town. Supported by the local auxiliary police, our activity consisted for the most part of supervising the maintenance of the evening curfew time, after which no inhabitant was allowed to be on the street without specific permission, as well as the supervision of travel permits and other special permits.

Although the Germans had been driven out, the exceptional conditions under which the U.S. Army represented the executive powers were still in effect, though somewhat relaxed.

As for vehicles, we had at our disposal not only a Jeep made available by the staff, but usually also several captured German cars of the former Nazi civilian administration.

The headquarters of the 109th Regiment were likewise located in Ettelbrück at this time, and its personnel were active in filling the ranks of the hard-hit troops again. Every one of us was looking forward to the coming Christmas celebration. It appeared that we would receive special supplies of food and drink rations; at least we ourselves had gotten a look into a storehouse set up for that purpose, the goods in which were supposed to be given out to the troops at Christmas.

But a further surprise was to make the soldiers' hearts beat faster. On December 10, 1944 the rumor was finally confirmed: Marlene Dietrich was coming to Ettelbrück and Diekirch.

Marlene's show was part of the USO program that was planned and carried out for the entertainment of the soldiers in places of recovery.

For her brief appearances in the two cities, I was chosen to be her chauffeur and drove a deluxe 1939 model Packard.

The fact that I was chosen for this may have been pure chance, but it aroused the envy of all my comrades.

I myself wrote to my sister in Kewaskum, Illinois, USA about this event. Shortly afterward, my sister allowed part of the letter to be printed in a daily newspaper. I still have it to this day, and it always reminds me of a day that I will never forget. It said: "Dearest Sis: A few lines to tell you of my latest experience and to thank you for the parcel containing the two cans of juice, peaches and candy. Now for the good part.

Last night I gave up my bed and slept in a cold building just so Marlene Dietrich and her mate could sleep in my bed. (Her mate slept in my bed), and we in fact gave her our whole home. But the greatest privilege which was mine, was the honor to be her chauffeur for the night, driving her to and from her performance in a 1939 deluxe model Packard, and to see her early in the morning just as she climbed out of her bed. Now, who can beat that? She also had dinner at our penthouse this noon. The show was very good.

Well, I guess that's about all there is except that I wish I had my camera here, because there's so many pictures that I'd like to get and can't, although I did get a picture of Marlene Dietrich. Not bad!"

(The article above appeared in the "West Bend News" on January 4, 1945.

Germans in U.S. Uniforms?

There are many accounts, from American soldiers as well as civilians, of German soldiers in American uniforms during the first days of the attack in December 1944.

Although they apply exclusively to an "organized" German command in American uniforms, specially chosen and trained by SS Obersturmbannführer Otto Skorzeny in order to create confusion behind the American lines in the northern sector of the offensive, it is said, though scarcely believable, that similar organized undertakings were carried out by Brandenberger's 7th Army.

Without having found any evidence on this point (special German units in U.S. uniforms) in any official U.S. unit's reports from the southern combat sector, the author nevertheless considers it highly probable that individual soldiers of German units gathered and wore U.S. uniform and equipment items to protect themselves from the cold, for lack of winter clothing. But since numerous informants insist that in the first days of the offensive they personally saw Germans in U.S. uniforms, who attracted their attention because of their remarkable behavior, the following report, for the historical truth of which the author cannot vouch, shall be representative of numerous similar accounts. Cannoneer Bob Davis experienced the withdrawal of the 107th FA Battalion, commanded by Lt.Col. "Jungle Jim" Rosborough, on December 18. The unit had supported the hard-pressed 109th Infantry Regiment on the two preceding days. On orders from the division, the guns were taken out of their firing positions on the Herrenberg near Diekirch, after they had been seriously threatened on December 17 and attacked by a strong German patrol on the morning of December 18, so as to be moved to Schieren and Colmar-Berg.

Bob Davis was the gunner for C Battery and remembers the numerous requests for artillery fire that was directed constantly on focal points of the front line held by the 109th Infantry Regiment since December 16, 1944. There is one incident that he cannot forget to this day, namely the encounter with the military police at the crossroads.

"When we hastily left our position at the isolated farm," he tells, "we found ourselves on an unpaved path north of Diekirch. (The position was not far from the Reuter farm on the Herrenberg, today the Diekirch Army Barracks.) We came to a side road on the left side of the path, where there was a guidepost with a sign pointing to Diekirch. Since I had used the same route many times before to report to the headquarters of the 107th FA Battalion in Diekirch, I noticed at once that the sign was not pointing in the right direction. But without giving much thought to the matter, we went on, followed by two other trucks which were towing the guns. Somewhat later we met 12 to 15 military policemen in new-looking uniforms and armbands. They looked like soldiers ready for a parade, since their uniform trousers all were neatly pressed. The MPs all carried Thompson submachine guns and were all remarkably clean-shaven. They stopped the convoy and a lieutenant stepped up to us. From inside the truck I heard how, in perfect English, he persuaded the driver to take a different route, so as to reach Diekirch via the "Little Bridge." The other MPs did not say a word during this conversation. Only now did I remember the road sign pointing the wrong way, and I whispered to Staff Sergeant Phil Marino, who sat next to me, 'I think these MPs are Krauts'.

Since the driver hesitated, the MP lieutenant drew his pistol and three of his men cocked their weapons and pointed them at me as I tried to load my M1 carbine. Sergeant Marino growled at me: "Do you know what you're saying?' and ordered the driver, Ed Kowak, to take the prescribed route.

Somewhat later we heard machine-gun fire.

We never reached Diekirch, but later I took the liberty of mentioning my observation to Lt.Col. Rosborough, whereupon he answered me only with 'Shut up'."

As Members of the Division's Artillery, the two Field Artillery Battalions 107 and 108 distinguished themselves particularly in the defensive fighting of December 16-19, 1944 in the defensive sector of the 109th Infantry Regiment, both units having been intended to provide fire support since the division's arrival in Luxembourg in November.

The division owes it to the two artillery battalions that despite strong pressure from the enemy, most of the endangered U.S. units could be withdrawn at the right time.

The commander of the 108th Field Artillery Battalion was Lt.Col. Bernard Major; his executive officer at that time was Major Frank Towned, who visited the former combat area in the spring of 1982 and provided information about his unit:

"Our battalion, the so-called medium battalion of the division's artillery, included three batteries of four 155 mm caliber howitzers each. I myself served as S-3 (Operations Officer), but at the beginning of December I was replaced in this function by Major Houser and named Executive Officer. In the southernmost sector of the division's line was the 109th Infantry Regiment, to whose direct support the 107th Field Artillery Battalion under Lt.Col. Rosborough had been assigned.

At the specified time, our unit was likewise in the same sector, but without having been intended to support a specific unit. Our command post at that time, as well as the fire direction center for the batteries, were in a large room on the ground floor of a modern apartment house in Diekirch (today the Junker-Schwinninger House on the Rue de la Brasserie). Strict blackout measures as well as sandbags reminded us that despite the unbroken quiet, there was still a war on.

At the beginning of December this command post was given up and vacated. The staff moved into the cellar of the present-day Gendarmerie (barracks) and set up an extensive telephone network from there to all the observation posts of the "firing batteries" as well as to the 109th Infantry Regiment in Ettelbrück.

Several observation teams, consisting for the most part of a lieutenant and three men, were alternately in action on the front line along the Our and made technical firing entries on the maps, so that the division staff could aim harassing fire precisely at the German West Wall bunkers, especially at night. The distance from the observation post to a gun position was very variable, but on the average (at Diekirch) it was between four and six kilometers.

In addition, one or two men had been detailed to every infantry company on the front line whose task it was to send the battery the technical firing data in the respective map quadrant immediately in the event of an attack in the company's area, as well as passing direction corrections on to the calculating unit. Here too, radios were in use.

Early in the morning of December 16 I was in the cellar at our command post when the first German shells took us by surprise, landing in the railroad-station area around 5:30 AM. Minutes later, a shell exploded in the garden near the cellar window and wounded two men. Additional shells exploded close to the building and broke numerous telephone cables, so that for a time there were no telephone connections to the batteries or the observation posts.

Shortly after that, shell fragments also hit the cable to the generator that supplied the inside rooms with electricity for lighting, so that the staff was compelled to work by makeshift lighting. Another shell hit the gable of the house, also near the cellar window. Nobody was injured, but the air pressure flung several sandbags and the blackout tarpaulin onto one NCO.

When the dust had cleared, the man lay on the ground, very pale, with half the tarpaulin wrapped around him.

Only at noon, when connections had been set up again, did we finally learn what the situation was.

Feverishly, the batteries were now in contact with our fire direction center, which received the targeting data from the observation posts. It was our task to convert area targets that had become known into technical firing data and then pass these numbers on to the number two gun of a battery. The 155 mm gun, previously aimed in a basic direction according to terrain map and artillery compass, was now 'corrected' on the basis of these data. The other three howitzers then received the aiming data directly from the battery commander and deviated somewhat from the aim of the original gun so that as extensive area fire as possible could be achieved.

We generally made the mathematical horizontal and vertical deflection corrections on the basis of special calculating devices and passed them on at once. Observation posts then reported to us by radio as to the accuracy and effect of a salvo.

We remained at this command post until Monday, December 18, when the order came to move the batteries back.

One of our shooting batteries, I believe it was B Battery, had its firing position along the small brook below the "Friedhaff" northwest of Diekirch. The guns were about 150 meters apart in a meadow that could be reached from the road by a field path. Several poplars stood along the lower edge of the meadow. The distance of 150 meters was chosen so that in case of enemy fire, an exploding shell could disturb only one gun, the fragmentation radius of the German shells then in use being what it was.

Still farther back was the ammunition supply, normally six tons per battery, which was brought up by the service battery.

From a specified point, carrier trucks supplied the guns with explosive or white phosphorus ammunition. Approximately one ton of 155 caliber ammunition was normally supplied to each gun, and had to be on hand immediately.

To guarantee sufficient safety from shell fragments, ammunition holes were also dug along the guns, depending on the nature of the soil, and surrounded by sandbags. In a second hole was the steel container for the ignition charges.

Two types of charges were used: the 'green bag' and the 'white bag' charges. Since the 155 howitzer fired a caseless shell, the charge determined by instructions (firing data) from the fire direction center for the range of fire had to be pushed in behind the shell. The 'green bag' had a measured charge consisting of four partial cartridges of propelling powder, which were sewn into small bags. The 'white bag' consisted of seven increment charges and was intended for a greater distance.

As the enemy came closer, the charges became smaller and smaller. I remember that the gun crews were frightened when, hours before the evacuation of the guns, the order came: Charge 1, the smallest charge, enough for a maximum of 1200 meters.

I myself was with this battery at the time and kept an eye on the situation, but then I had to return to the command post.

In the afternoon of December 18, the news reached us that German tanks, coming from an easterly direction, were advancing on Diekirch. I myself drove a Jeep with four man armed with bazookas to the Diekirch-Bettendorf-Vianden intersection (Bleesbrück), where heavy fighting was going on, in order to examine the situation. At that time the tanks could not yet be seen; besides, it was impossible to order area fire when they appeared without seriously endangering our own men.

I drove back to the command post, where similar information had been received. Our fire was now (in the afternoon) aimed principally at the woods around Longsdorf and Tandel, which were full of German infantry. For this area fire, only explosive shells with very sensitive impact fuzes were used.

Shells were aimed so as to explode in the trees, in order to achieve as great a fragment field as possible from above.

Although the artillery had been partially equipped with brand new proximity fuzes for testing purposes, to my knowledge these were not used, since the troops were not yet familiar enough with their handling. They were an invention in which an electronic transmitter built into the head of the fuze sent out a signal, which was reflected by the target. The distance between the shell and the target was 'preprogrammed', and after covering the predetermined trajectory, an impulse ignited the shell. The igniter was called a 'proximity fuze', 'pozit fuze', or 'Bonzo' fuze, and was used principally to ignite the shell just above the ground, since with a normal impact fuze a large part of the explosive power is lost in the ground.

Late in the afternoon of December 18 the order came from the division to give up the gun position, since there was danger of being overrun by the enemy. One battery of the 107th FA Battalion, which was farther to the northwest of us, had apparently been attacked, and Lt. Col. Rosborough had only been able with difficulty to fight their way out again. In the process, the gun crews had fought bravely as infantrymen. When night fell, the trucks towed the guns out of the meadow and drove quickly in the direction of Ettelbrück. Leaving behind numerous rounds of ammunition and fuzes which there was no time to destroy, but without losing a gun, the battery took up a new position near Berg, from which it fought against the approaching Germans in the ensuing days."

Epilogue: Two Great Soldiers

Two former unit commanders, whose names and actions are directly related to the events of the war around Diekirch at that time, have not been forgotten. Both of them have died some years after long illnesses. Universally admired by their troops as officers and "shining examples" of selflessness and bravery, no matter how serious the situation, were Lt. Col. James Rosborough (107th FA Battalion) and Captain Paul Gaynor (Antitank Company, 109th Infantry Regiment), still fondly remembered to this day by many veterans of the 28th U.S. Infantry Division. Through their exemplary actions in the leadership of their units, as well as through outstanding bravery in the face of the enemy in an almost hopeless situation, both officers gained one of the highest American decorations, the "Distinguished Service Cross" or DSC.

Lt. Col. James Rosborough came from Pennsylvania, the home state of the 28th U.S. Infantry Division. After serving in many capacities as an artillery officer, he was given command of the 107th Field Artillery Battalion, which he commanded in an exemplary manner until the war ended.

This unit, consisting of three batteries of 105 mm howitzers, was attached to the 109th Infantry Regiment since the combat in the Hürtgenwald to provide its artillery support.

Lt. Col. Rosborough had his batteries take up positions at the foot of the Herrenberg between Diekirch and Bastendorf. This superb situation on the upper heights of the high ground overlooking the Sauer valley made possible an excellent defense against the attacking enemy.

An additional position was located on the high plateau of the Herrenberg (today a military training ground).

When a German patrol succeeded on December 18, after several unsuccessful attempts on the previous day, in breaking through the American lines near Bastendorf and attacking the artillery positions, Lt. Col. Rosborough reacted lightning-fast. With a hastily assembled task force of all available forces, he was able to free and evacuate the surrounded battery after a hard firefight.

The 107th FA Battalion then provided valuable support in covering the withdrawal of the 2nd Battalion (109th Infantry Regiment) along the road to Erpeldange and Ettelbrück.

His popularity was based on the fact that Lt. Col. Rosborough was always with the fighting troops, and with his men in the foremost line, which won him the nickname of "Jungle Jim."

For his heroic deed he was decorated with the DSC, and he left the army at the beginning of the sixties as a brigadier general.

His 1944 uniform and the DSC, given by Mrs. Rosborough, are in the National Museum of Military History in Diekirch today.

Captain Paul Gaynor was the commander of the Anti-Tank Company of the 109th Infantry Regiment since the 28th U.S. Infantry Division entered Luxembourg. His command post, originally set up in Medernach, was moved to Gilsdorf at the end of November. Although Captain Gaynor constantly had to undertake scouting missions along his regiment's entire line, he still made numerous contacts with the civilian population of Gilsdorf. To this day, people in public life at that time still remember him fondly.

When the Germans attacked, Captain Gaynor's 57 mm antitank guns were hastily placed in positions around Bleesbrück, a militarily important intersection, but on account of the meager penetrating power of their caliber, they could accomplish little against the three German tanks that came on the scene.

In spite of that, Captain Gaynor's guns proved themselves in fighting off numerous infantry attacks in the "Seltz." Through his outstanding bravery, he won the DSC here. The certificate of award cited the following basis for the decoration:

"When the AT company saw itself compelled to give up its positions, Captain Gaynor stayed behind alone to cover their withdrawal.

With his carbine he put eight Germans out of action and wounded several others. Under heavy enemy fire, he then plunged across an open field to rejoin his company again."

Paul Gaynor's brother, Brigadier General Robert Gaynor, now deceased, fought in the same division as his brother but had already been badly wounded in September of 1944. He also received the DSC for his extraordinary service.

The Gaynor brothers, incidentally, are the only brothers who, fighting in the same unit (28th U.S. Infantry Division), both received this high American decoration. Captain Paul Gaynor, who visited his friends in Gilsdorf as a colonel in 1958, died of lung cancer in 1978. He was buried with military honors at Arlington National Cemetery, Virginia."

The 707th Tank Battalion

Another support unit for the infantry battalions of the 28th Infantry Division, the 707th Tank Battalion, was kept in the division's reserve from December 1 to 15, 1944.

The units of the battalion, equipped with Sherman tanks, were quartered in the following towns:

The Headquarters Company was in Merkholz, A Company in Drauffelt, B Company in Pintsch, C Company in Heiderscheid and D Company in Brachtenbach.

The tank crews, consisting in part of recruits, spent their time preparing materials for use, taking courses in the technical area, tactical training in the field and target-shooting practice. Numerous officers of the battalion were trained as advanced observers, so that if need be, the Shermans could also be used for artillery support and indirect fire.

The bow machine gunners of the tank crews were likewise trained in the use of the flamethrower, which could be installed in the tank in place of the machine gun. Since this was planned for the foreseeable future, numerous demonstrations of the use of this weapon at distances under 100 meters took place in the country.

On December 16, 1944 the battalion was already called to alarm readiness by the G-3 (operations) officer of the division before 7:00 AM. On orders from the division, Companies A and B were immediately assigned to the 110th Infantry Regiment, C Company came under the command of the 109th Infantry Regiment and D Company went to the 112th Infantry Regiment. The tank crews were immediately placed under the direct command of the individual regimental commanders and were to operate according to their instructions.

In this brief overview of the 707th Tank Battalion we shall look exclusively at C Company, since only this unit saw service in the area of the 109th Regiment treated in this book.

Around 11:30 AM the commander of C Company went to the command post of the 109th Infantry Regiment in Ettelbrück and was given the order to assign one platoon of his company to the 1st Battalion of the 109th Infantry Regiment, then in reserve at Diekirch. The 1st Platoon, consisting of four Sherman tanks, reached Diekirch about 1:15 PM and was immediately ordered to support units of the 1st

Battalion (probably Companies A and B; see reports of Lt. Christy and Pfc. Meyer: author's note) in their counterattack in the direction of Longsdorf, where it appeared that some eighty Germans had been sighted. About 3:30 PM tao tanks, followed by infantrymen, attacked at the bend in the road to Longsdorf. The houses along the road were already occupied by German troops. About 5:30 PM the German defensive fire in the trackless country, supported by antitank weapons, became too strong, so that the 1st Platoon's Sherman tanks received an order not to venture any farther forward in the darkness (because of the danger of German troops armed with Panzerfausts), but rather to remain with the infantry units that had dug in for the night and be ready to protect them. About 7:30 PM the commander of C Company (707th Tank Battalion) ordered the 2nd and 3rd Platoons to go to Diekirch and build a defensive barrier on the threatened approach roads in the direction of the German border. By 8:30 PM the 2nd Platoon received instructions from the commander of the 2nd Battalion (109th Infantry Regiment) in Bastendorf to move toward Brandenburg at once, in order to prepare to defend the town along with units of G Company (109th Infantry Regiment).

At 7:45 AM on December 17, 1944, the attack in the direction of Longsdorf was resumed along with A Company (109th Infantry Regiment). The commander of C Company of the 707th Tank Battalion returned to Diekirch in his tank to make a report about the efforts to relieve E Company in Fouhren, which were to be carried out by B Company with tank support. He left Diekirch again about 2:00 PM and, on the road south of Tandel, encountered a trap. A long fight took place. About 5:00 PM radio contact with the commander of C Company (707th Tank Battalion) was lost. (See the report of Lt. Christy, B Company. Lt. Christy states different times for the same events, but it is definite that this tank fell into the Germans' hands intact: author's note.)

The 2nd Platoon of C Company (707th TB) was now instructed to undertake a counterattack east of Brandenburg along with G Company (109th Infantry Regiment) around 8:30 AM on December 17, in order to relieve the threatened F Company (109th Infantry Regiment). This was successful, and the commander reported around 10:30 AM: mission carried out successfully." In the afternoon, though, around 4:00 PM, the Shermans encountered a column of German assault guns in the country. In the ensuing tank battle not far from Kippenhof, four German assault guns or self-propelled mounts were knocked out.

The 3rd Platoon of C Company (707th TB) received instructions to move in the direction of Hoscheid along with parts of B Company, to the extent that this was possible, in order to relieve the hard-pressed units of the 110th Infantry Regiment there. But this was not successful; the German resistance was too tough, and without sufficient infantry support it was impossible to advance. The commander of that task force thereupon received orders to set up a defensive barrier, which had previously been formed by engineers, at "Flebour, on the road to Hoscheid." But around 2:00 PM there already came a new order to withdraw immediately to establish contact with a battery of Lt. Col. Rosborough's 107th Field Artillery Battalion.

Around 3:30 PM a vigorous firefight took place against German units which had already worked their way up to the gun positions by 3:00 PM. The Germans were defeated and the Shermans stayed to protect the guns, which were firing constantly.

The 2nd Platoon of C Company had been supplied with fuel and ammunition during the night. Then the other two platoons (1st and 3rd) were to be supplied, but on account of too-strong German patrol activity, this was no longer possible. On December 18 the 1st Platoon, after having lost one Sherman tank, was located in defensive positions very near the intersection at the "Bleesbréck." The platoon leader immediately requested supplies of ammunition and fuel.

Around noon, two half-tracks carried out this mission successfully. But it was only possible to refuel one tank completely; the others, farther forward in the field, could not be supplied because of too-heavy German artillery fire. Around 1:00 PM an attack was made by two or three German Jagdpanzer from the direction of Longsdorf. During a brief exchange of fire, one Sherman tank was hit by a shell from the 75 mm gun of the "Hetzer" and began to burn; the crew was able to get out in time.

The German pressure gradually became too strong, so that the intersection on the Bleesbréck could no longer be held for long. During the afternoon, two tanks of the 1st Platoon hurried to take up positions in the "Kleck" not far from the bridge to Gilsdorf, and the retreating infantry units of the 3rd Battalion (109th Infantry Regiment) dug in on the northern and eastern heights around Diekirch.

During this time the 2nd Platoon of Sherman tanks formed a roadblock near Bastendorf and stayed back to cover the withdrawal of the infantry units from the town. During the firefights that flared up continually around Bastendorf, a German heavy machine gun, a mortar and a fully loaded ammunition truck were destroyed by a Sherman tank. The 3rd Platoon of C Company was still in a defensive position at the Herrenberg near the gun batteries of the 107th FA Battalion. About 1:00 PM the order to withdraw to Diekirch came from the command post of the 109th Infantry Regiment in Ettelbrück. Some of the 105 mm guns were thereupon hooked onto the Sherman tanks. While this maneuver was underway, the column was attacked by enemy infantry. The Germans, who stormed the column in open country without any cover, suffered heavy losses above the 'Bamertal'. Around 6:00 PM, additional Sherman tanks were sent out to strengthen the roadblock formed by only two tanks at the Gilsdorf bridge. All through the night of December 18-19, the Bleesbréck and the road to Diekirch were under irregular German artillery fire. Since there was still no information as to the whereabouts of the commander of C Company, who had last been seen in Tandel the previous day, 1st Lieutenant Ryan took over the leadership of the company.

On December 19 the remaining tanks of the 3rd Platoon remained in the roadblock at the entrance to Diekirch. Around 9:00 AM, auxiliary policemen reported to the platoon leader that there were numerous German soldiers in the houses around the Bleesbréck, about 500 yards ahead of the roadblock. In a firefight that was supported by a tank, the Americans and the Luxembourg auxiliary police and resistance fighters were able to take numerous German prisoners. During the same night, the remaining tanks of C Company secured the withdrawal of the 109th Infantry Regiment to Ettelbrück.

Only on December 24 were the other ten tanks of C Company transferred from Schrondweiler to Stegen. About 1:00 PM, two tanks took part in the preparations of the "Task Force Rudder", consisting of elements of the 1st Battalion (109th Infantry Regiment) as well as units of the 90th Reconnaissance Cavalry Squadron of the 10th Armored Division, to recapture Gilsdorf.

After Gilsdorf was taken, all the Shermans of the 707th Tank Battalion that were capable of action were first ordered to Sedan, France, for maintenance, and then saw action in the defense of Neufchâteau with the 28th Infantry Division.

CHAPTER IX

THE 9TH U.S. ARMORED DIVISION IN ACTION

As already mentioned (preceding chronological overview, 109th Infantry Regiment), the 2nd Battalion of the 109th Infantry Regiment was relieved by the 60th AIB of the 9th U.S. Armored Division on December 10, 1944, so that the regiment's boundary was now near Wallendorf. Thus the specified defensive sector that had been assigned to the 60th AIB for surveillance stretched from the confluence of the Our and Sauer about to Grundhof. The 60th AIB was a young unit, still without battle experience, with a specified strength of 800 men. Fully motorized by half-tracks, the battalion was divided into four rifle companies, one headquarter and one service company. The half-tracks of the rifle companies were equipped with .30 and .50 machine guns, the vehicles of the heavy companies also with 81 mm mortars. The commander of this well-tested unit was Lt.Col. Kenneth Collins.

As a report of its action we have the memoirs of the former commander of C Company, Captain Roger Shinn, who was captured by the Germans in the Beaufort-Emsdorf region during defensive combat with the 276th Volksgrenadier Division (see Vol.I: The Germans, GR 986, P. Engelhard). Captain Shinn's report will provide a representative overview of this hotly contested sector, even though it is somewhat outside our area of study. Captain Shinn writes in his monograph "Wars and Rumors of Wars":

"The 15th of December was a day like any other for us. From our positions we had an extensive view across the Sauer and Our to the Siegfried Line, and now and then we saw individual "Jerries" moving around; really nothing extraordinary. Normally they were out of the range of our rifle and machine-gun fire, but as soon as several of them showed themselves incautiously, the artillery observer normally sent several shells their way.

The region around our positions along the Sauer was relatively familiar to us. C Company had occupied this area now for five days, the same area where it had occupied positions in November. In spite of that, we were spread out too much; I was certain of that. As company leader, I had to watch, or to hold, a strip of land that normally would have to be defended by a battalion, or if necessary by a regiment. Thus there were gaping holes in the defensive line that were guarded by nobody. To have a sufficient overview all the same, the platoons, and even the individual squads, were in communication with each other by telephone lines.

Our left flank was formed by the anti-tank platoon, which regularly undertook patrols as far as our neighbor to the left, the 109th Infantry Regiment, so as to establish necessary communication regularly in a northwesterly direction. Vigorous patrol activity also prevailed among the "Jerries." Now and then a few German shells fell on our line, which were returned tenfold by our side. Ammunition had been rationed by both sides, but our supplies were far greater. Just two nights before, I myself had led a patrol and a reconnaissance party to a projecting hill from which an excellent field of vision toward Wallendorf unfolded. Our mortars fired illuminating ammunition across the Sauer. We stared into the eerie-looking and destroyed village but could see no presence of enemy activities. Everything was uncannily quiet.

In the afternoon, after the cold, damp fog had dispersed, I made a checkup trip to all the positions of my company by Jeep, and then, when that was finished, drove to the battalion's command post. This was located in a hotel in Beaufort. Then, with the information I had just received, I returned to my own company's command post in an isolated house on the road that led steeply downhill to Beaufort. I had chosen this house as our headquarters just three days ago because it offered far more comfort than a thoroughly soaked dugout on the front line in the woods.

At nightfall three German shells fell in the company's sector, the only three on that day. Nothing out of the ordinary! The mess sergeant was just driving the prepared food to the positions. I myself gave the individual platoons routine instructions for their actions and surveillance activities during the night. This Friday also ended like any other day.

A Thunderclap awakened me abruptly early in the morning of December 16, and chunks of plaster and dust rained down from the ceiling of the company's command post. The building trembled, the ground shook. Shells exploded everywhere, such as we had never experienced before. Our senses were no longer capable of reacting reliably for a moment, for we were all so shocked and confused. The entire crew was awake at once. I called to the sentries outside the door to find out what was going on, and sent messengers out immediately to bring in information about this heavy fire; the vigorous fire kept up, and the shells exploded with glaring flashes. Soon one group returned and brought along a huge iron fragment that they had found in a shell crater several hundred meters from the house. Undoubtedly a thick chunk! One NCO from the front line rushed in excitedly and reported having heard suspicious sounds on the other side of the river just before the firing began.

I made a note of his comment and sent him back to his platoon. Dozens of calls reached me now from my company's positions. Every caller reported the same thing: flashes along the entire front from the muzzle flash of the German artillery.

I immediately got on the main line and had myself connected with "Comfort 6", the battalion commander, Lt. Col. Collins. He reported that his command post (Hôtel Belvedère) had been hit several times and he had therefore moved his command post as well as the telephone switchboard to the cellar without delay. The quarters of the reserve company (B Company) nearby had taken several direct hits, resulting in dead and wounded. I was reporting our own situation to him when the connection was broken. Numerous telephone lines had been so damaged by shell fragments that at first we had telephone contact only with our own platoons. The troubleshooters set out at top speed and repaired the broken lines despite the shells that fell. Since we were so isolated from each other, good vocal contact was of great importance. The firing continued until the morning broke and then continued only at irregular intervals, so that we could make good use of the individual pauses for further examination of the situation.

There was still no report of enemy movements! But A Company, our neighbor to the right, was already involved in a firefight, for one could hear the noise of machine guns clearly.

I immediately telephoned to Lieutenant McCarthy, the officer leading the right platoon, that he should order particular watchfulness on our right flank. The gap between him and the A Company was very large, so that a large unit of "Jerries" could slip through before one of the two companies noticed it.

During the morning the Germans attacked McCarthy's platoon. Suddenly they swung out of the sector of "Able" (A Company) at our right-flank positions.

McCarthy's men, most of whom had taken up excellent firing positions on projecting rock formations in the thick woods, drove off the first German attack in a hail of bullets. Many Germans had already fallen in these first morning hours.

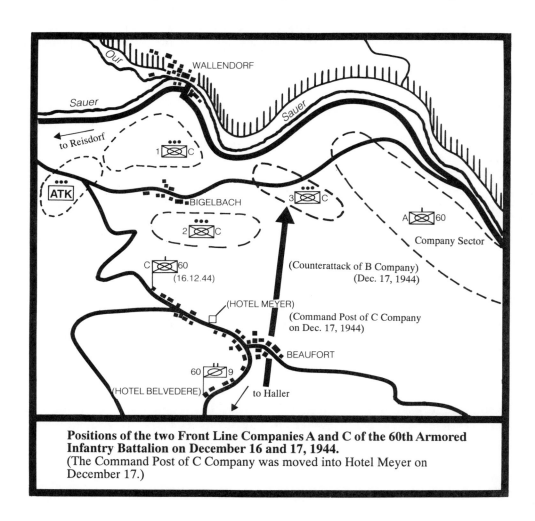

Positions of the two Front Line Companies A and C of the 60th Armored Infantry Battalion on December 16 and 17, 1944.
(The Command Post of C Company was moved into Hotel Meyer on December 17.)

But it became serious when the Germans suddenly emerged from the under-brush to our right.

"Able" was in the greatest danger of being surrounded, as the enemy was push-ing forward through the gap. I immediately ordered the small company reserve (about twelve men strong) to strengthen McCarthy's right flank. The young officer was even able to move his men forward somewhat, so as to gain a more effective field of fire, thanks to which he was doubtlessly able to decrease the pressure on "Able" somewhat. But more and more Germans broke through . . . and it looked bad!

Again I called "Comfort 6" . . . "Hello, Ken, this is Moe." (For reasons of security, all military courtesy was done without, and calling and recognition names were given only in the form of nicknames.) "The Germans are in the majority, Mac can't possible deal with them." For Lt. Col. Collins this was the first major combat, as it was for us, too. He tried to stay calm and answered me: "Can you direct mortar fire onto them?" – "The woods are too thick to achieve sufficient success; besides, we would endanger 'Able' with stray shots. Has 'Baker' (B Company, the reserve company) been transferred already?" I asked. "Baker is undertaking a relief thrust between 'Charlie' (C Company) and 'Able'; pass this news on at once to avoid confusion," was his answer.

I reassured myself that other than the right platoon, nobody in my company had had contact with the enemy up till now, and I hurried away in the Jeep. Shortly before the sector of the 3rd Platoon I left the Jeep and hurried through the woods to McCarthy. He took me to an artillery observation post, from which I could see far to the right. We saw numerous "Jerries" on the bank of the river there but could not spot a crossing point. Our artillery (3rd FA Battalion) was doing outstanding work, using their steady fire to prevent the enemy from gathering again. Then we hurried to the right, where the underbrush through which the enemy was moving began. Many dead men lay along the edge. McCarthy himself had suffered numerous dead and wounded, whom the medics were taking care of.

On the right flank, Americans and Germans were fighting it out at the closest range. As long as the soldiers used the tall trees or rock outcrops as cover or stayed in a gully in the woods, they were hard to hit. Now suddenly both sides fired just a few shots. Nobody could advance without letting himself be slaughtered.

My men did an excellent job in their "first real battle." They were all very well known to me, since I had commanded and trained the same unit in the USA. I myself was encouraged by their positive attitude. Even the NCO in charge of the mail brought up ammunition. I simply could not grasp the fact that an older but conscientious official who always had a good sense of humor had become a "fight-ing soldier" in this situation. How he suddenly got here from the staff company I did not know. In any case, his unaccustomed activity brought him into great danger. Suddenly a messenger called to me and brought me the alarming news that our blockhouse had been taken. Bad news! The blockhouse, occupied by a unit in sec-tion strength, was an observation post in the woods on the extreme left flank of my company. In the morning we had already heard nothing from them, since the tele-phone lines there could not be repaired.

I raced back in the Jeep to the command post, from which I had better telephone contact with the individual platoons. There I finally learned the truth about the blockhouse. The left platoon reported that a number of Germans had suddenly come at it from the rear and attacked the men. Apparently there were no survivors.

I was still waiting impatiently for a report from McCarthy, who was to provide the confirmation. "Baker" had begun a counterattack, but no call came. Instead of that, I received the shocking news that the enemy was now in the area of the 2nd Platoon too, thus in the center of the company's line. The platoon chief had not been reachable since the early morning hours. I ordered his deputy to hang on, so as to set up contact with the right platoon in case of a German breakthrough, so that it could not be cut off and isolated. The 1st (left) Platoon reported that the enemy was attacking from the right and trying to surround the unit.

Meanwhile a German artillery shell struck the building of my command post and the roof caved in. I quickly decided to get out of this building and set up a new command post not far from this place. While the men were in the process of loading the telephone switchboard, as well as the field phones and other materials, hurriedly into the Jeep, a terrible howling was heard suddenly. I threw myself into the ditch and there was an ear-splitting blast; clumps of earth rained down on me. We got up immediately and hurried in the direction of Beaufort, where we hurried into a house on the edge of town so as to be better protected from shell fragments. Again we heard this dreadful howling in the air! More explosions followed, one after another.

These were the so-called "Screaming Mimies" or "Nebelwerfer" shells, whose nerve-numbing screech as they arrived had an even more paralyzing effect that the explosion of the shell. The bombardment went on. It was area fire that struck the entire edge of the town. We were completely helpless in the face of the situation. Nobody would have bet a nickel on his chances to survive.

Then it was still. I got up to see what damage had been done, when a hysterically screaming woman ran across the street, her face bleeding. A medic ran after her and brought her, along with three wounded company clerks, to a bandaging station in Beaufort. I could not believe that we only had two wounded men as a result of this terrible fire. Later I heard that the German "Nebelwerfer" shell, which our troops had nothing to equal, was used only for the destruction of blocks of buildings. Although the terrible howling noise frightened all the soldiers, its shrapnel effect was quite meager, since the explosive charge was screwed on in back of the rocket propulsion motor unit. The air pressure was all the greater and caused extraordinary damage in surface fire. We set up the command post some 500 meters farther, in a house on the right side of the road, and quickly reestablished telephone connections to the platoons. The house was very solidly built and the cellar would surely offer sufficient protection.

While the cable-layers were still working feverishly, I hurried to the battalion headquarters to learn some details of the general situation. It appeared as follows: "Able" was under heavy fire; for two hours now nothing had been heard from "Baker", which was supposed to carry out the actual relief thrust, and "Charlie", my company, had sent a message from the left platoon via a mortar unit, since the direct line had been broken, that they were almost completely surrounded and urgently needed ammunition as well as medical supplies. Lt. Col. Collins told me there was some hope for reinforcements . . . but this was not certain.

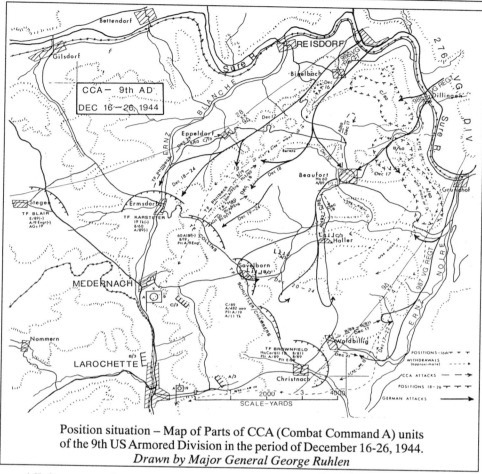

Position situation – Map of Parts of CCA (Combat Command A) units
of the 9th US Armored Division in the period of December 16-26, 1944.
Drawn by Major General George Ruhlen

All the reports from neighboring units were unclear. It seemed, though, as if the enemy's main pressure was being applied farther to the left and in a northerly direction. But we ourselves believed that we were located at a focal point and did not understand why the corps did nothing and threw all available units into the battle.

I hurried back to my command post. A frightened family and the village policeman sought shelter in the cellar. We spent a sleepless night; most of the phone connections were broken again. The German fire began again.

I decided to look for the left platoon in the darkness, along with my company sergeant. We approached cautiously, as we were inclined to believe the last news of a possible encirclement. But this was apparently not yet the case, and we got through without difficulty. The small village of Bigelbach at the foot of the hill occupied by the left platoon was in flames. Besides, as it turned out, the enemy was occupying it.

Great gatherings of searchlight beams groped toward us from the opposite shore. Obviously the Germans were very confident, since they operated by artificial light without any means of shielding it.

Crouched down in a ditch, I then learned the true circumstances. The platoon had come under a hail of shells, but few of the dug-in men had been killed or wounded. The Germans had not made any further attack after that, but had turned away.

Thus the platoon's readiness to provide defense, in connection with the anti-tank platoon, had been proved despite the shortage of ammunition.

Just a few hours remained until the dawn of December 17. A sentry reported illuminating rockets in the sky. A quick look brought the certainty that the tracer ammunition was German. A German patrol approximately 800 meters to the left of my command post was firing flares as if they were fireworks. A 60 mm mortar undoubtedly could have wiped them out, but we had no mortar at our headquarters, and there were too few of us to fight them from our hiding place. Obviously the enemy patrol did not know exactly where they were at a given time, but in daylight they could be dangerous to us. In spite of that, we did not want to let ourselves in for a firefight.

So we left this building soundlessly and set up a new command post for the third time, this time in the center of Beaufort. The Hotel Meyer was just the right place. Although German shells had wrought desolation all around, the main building was still in good condition. In my ensuing first talk with the headquarters of the 60th AIB, I received an order from Lt. Col. Collins to undertake a counterattack at nightfall. A reconnaissance company in a light armored scout car was supposed to push forward along the same lane where "Baker" had attacked yesterday in order to reestablish connections with the companies. In addition, he had meanwhile assembled a battalion reserve, a minor miracle of organization, consisting of one remaining platoon of "Baker 3", light tanks of the 3rd FA Battalion, and men of the 89th Reconnaissance Squadron. The commander of this assembled unit would be Captain John Hall of the staff company.

He was to apply his thus-constituted unit anywhere where it was needed as "firemen."

The undertaking began at 7:30 AM in the vicinity of my command post (Hotel Meyer). It caused some difficulties to push forward through the uneven woodlands under German artillery fire. Parallel to this, my men made an attempt to reestablish telephone connections to the first platoon. The houses at the edge of Beaufort were already occupied at this time by the Germans, who now began to have sharpshooters fire at us. I myself thereupon posted several snipers in the houses around the hotel to protect my command post. As soon as a German steel helmet showed itself at a roof window or gable, my men opened fire. Obviously they were successful, for after two hours the German rifle fire stopped. Later in the day, though, individual groups of "Jerries" sneaked around. The German artillery likewise became active again. But Hotel Meyer was a very solid building. So we stayed there.

As our Jeep with a reel of telephone cable set out, it came under fire. The sergeant was wounded and the Jeep went into a ditch. The German sniper was spotted at once. But there was no point to attacking him openly without accepting the loss of several men in the bargain. So Captain Hall's tanks stormed the house and took it under fire. Part of the house collapsed under the hail of shells. Late in the afternoon, a reconnaissance party was able to reestablish contact with McCarthy. A medical Jeep hurried after them and evacuated the wounded men of the 3rd Platoon. On the way back they drove into a trap but were able to escape.

But McCarthy urgently needed ammunition.

A half-track was quickly loaded with ammunition and food rations. The halftrack vehicle, equipped with a .50 machine gun and several riflemen, set out and came back some time later, after carrying out its mission successfully. On the return trip it too was fired on.

The half-track set out on a second trip.

Most of the men finished this second day since the German surprise attack with several bars of strengthening chocolate (D-rations), which had just been delivered.

Shortly thereafter, the scouting party returned. In the thick woods they had to give up several vehicles on account of Panzerfaust damage. In the darkness Captain Harder, commander of B Company, tried to push forward to Beaufort with a half-track in order to fetch hot food from a field kitchen for his exhausted men. But the very heavy German fire forced him to turn back. I ordered several machine guns set up on the first floor of the hotel. Everyone was informed that he had to draw back into Hotel Meyer without delay if the danger became too great. The hotel was a kind of fortress!

State of Siege

Shortly after I had returned to the hotel from an inspection tour, "Nebelwerfer" and artillery fire began anew. The building trembled but held out, although it had taken several hits on its gable. Through a splintered window, I could now see the fiery glow of the burning houses, with numerous "Jerries" very close around them. In a matter of minutes we were surrounded. A firefight commenced. We were in a kind of fortress; its forces were several cooks, mechanics and scattered soldiers from other units . . . but we had enough ammunition! No telephone lines were working any more; we were cut off! The Germans had quickly spotted our weakness and fired on us from all sides. I hurried to the second floor, from which I could see the Germans better. Most of their bursts of fire struck the stonework and did not damage. But soon several of them had worked their way up under cover of fire and threw hand grenades through the windows. The men near the windows stayed under cover behind stacked-up pieces of furniture, in order to fire on any intruding enemy after the hand grenades exploded.

Before the entrance to the hotel stood one of our Jeeps in flames. In the flickering light I spotted the outlines of several German soldiers, stuck the barrel of my M1 carbine through a broken window and fired. One fell to the ground immediately. Obviously I had hit him; he was the first human being I had directly and visibly killed.

While I was still looking out, a burst of machine-gun fire splintered the bricks of the window frame. I threw myself to the floor at once.

Our defensive fire from the windows was now quite impossible, since the muzzle flash of our weapons immediately drew the attention of the alert German machine gunners. So we resorted to our hand grenades instead, pulled the pins and threw them out the windows.

Meanwhile the Germans had blown up the main door and pushed into the lobby. Things were getting hot!

A German machine gun rattled in the long main corridor of the ground floor. After two or three bursts of fire, two Germans stormed ahead. One of my men, firing from a dead angle of the stairway, quickly put them out of action. Another of our hand grenades, that exploded at the entrance to the building, killed another German. But how were we to hold out here? Surely it would not take very long until a whole German company would storm our hotel. And fire constituted an even greater danger. The Germans had meanwhile begun to fire incendiary shells which, thank God, exploded before they reached the windows, on account of the long distance from the mortars, and so scattered the greater part of their burning contents short of the gables. Close to the hotel was a barn stuffed full of straw. To this day it is not clear to me why the Germans did not set fire to it; the fire would have spread directly to the hotel. There was still bitter fighting, and chocking smoke filled the ground floor.

Our half-track parked near the gable was in flames, a great danger for us all! There were still some sixty gallons of gasoline in its tank, that would cause a tremendous explosion.

Several minutes later the German infantry-weapon fire stopped. Instead of it, I heard throaty sounds and then crunching steps in the midst of the crackling fire: the handful of surviving Germans drew back. Quickly it ran through my head: they have certainly called for artillery fire, and I called to my men: "We have to get out of here!" – "We'll fight our way out in groups of three" –"Look out for snipers or a trap!" I ordered. – "We'll meet at the castle ruin near the battalion's command post."

We used the rear entrance and were thus out of the light of the burning half-track; I was the first to go out, glided soundlessly across the ground and went onward, followed by two others. But soon I noticed that there were seven of us who were following me, in spite of my instructions to make our way out in small groups. Although the danger of being spotted by the enemy was now greater, I let them stay with me and crawled onward.

Then we heard Germans very close to us. They were directly between us and our path to the castle ruin, our meeting place. So we had to take a long roundabout route, crawling on our bellies most of the time. We always oriented ourselves according to the hotel, which had gone up in flames half an hour after we broke out and thus provided a frightfully beautiful orientation and reference point.

Ammunition that we had left behind exploded at irregular intervals. We slipped by close to a German unit's location. The German soldiers were just in the process of eating beside a house by the light of flashlights. How easily we could have wiped out the few incautious Germans, but we did not do it because we would have lost our lives as a result. We crept on through Beaufort's numerous gardens and livestock pens in a wide curve that brought us to the main road in about the center of town. Obviously, the upper part of Beaufort had not yet been occupied by the enemy, or only slightly. As if the town would hear us, we crept silently to the street, stood up and went onward without hurrying, so as not to draw any attention to ourselves.

We arrived at the castle ruin but found no more of our men there. Obviously the others had gone astray, fallen into the hands of the Germans or had somehow reached our lines by another route.

Very cautiously we approached the battalion's command post (Hotel Belvedere). It was empty. Since only one road was available for withdrawal leading out of Beaufort, exactly in the opposite direction to the enemy, the personnel of the battalion's command post had presumably utilized this route. Without losing time, we likewise marched along the same road in a spread-out column until, after about a mile and a half, we came upon units of our own division's artillery (3rd Field Artillery Battalion), which was likewise withdrawing. The commander of the artillery battalion (LTC Ruhlen) took me in his Jeep to his command post, which was located at a farm. I asked him to make immediate radio contact with our battalion commander, Lt. Col. Collins. While the radioman was trying all the channels, I quickly ate a C ration and then I must have fallen asleep, for half an hour later someone shook me awake and reported:

"Sir, it's the battalion headquarters on the phone for you."

Counterattack

"Come to the command post at once," Lt. Col. Collins ordered. A truck picked me up and took me there. The truck stopped by a downhill road at the edge of the woods, and a sentry picked me up. We set out. It was so dark that I could scarcely see the man who marched through the underbrush ahead of me.

I almost hit my head on the battalion chief's command tent. Inside I found Lt. Col. Collins, several of his staff officers, plus a table of maps.

The colonel was very happy to see me again; they had thought we were already lost. He explained to me that, at the division's command, Combat Command A (of the 9th Armored Division) would now take over the entire sector. Some reserves would make their way to us already tonight, and a counterattack had been ordered for daybreak tomorrow. For it a task force had been assembled, which would be supported by a company of Sherman tanks, a platoon of light tanks (M5 and M24) and two platoons of engineers, applied as infantrymen.

The mission consisted of breaking through the German lines to Beaufort, getting our surrounded units out, and returning.

The colonel asked me for my opinion. "Beaufort is crawling with Germans, but they are not cohesive," I told him. A major of the tank company commanded the task force. Only with difficulty could my tired eyes study the map, for the sector of terrain that we were to use was unknown to me.

I also heard that the present command post occupied the same site as our "motor pool." Several half-tracks in well-camouflaged positions took care of its protection. I lay down and fell asleep at once. The day dawned, but we waited one more hour. Then we set out. The tanks pushed forward on a broad line, followed by our half-tracks. Numerous dead German soldiers lay on the ground. Suddenly German rifle fire began – sharpshooters. One of the tanks took a hit from a Panzerfaust shot. Two of its crew members sustained life-threatening injuries and were evacuated immediately. The tank's radio set no longer functioned. I got into the tank and took over its command. Then we heard that farther off on our flank, two light tanks had been hit and gone up in flames. Three Panzerfaust hits, even before the attack had begun: a bad omen. The engineers were now ordered to protect the tanks as an advance unit and were to comb through the woods. Suddenly German artillery fire began as we left the forest and open country stretched ahead of us. The unprotected engineers suffered losses from the German artillery fire. The 76 mm guns of the Sherman tanks smashed the thick underbrush and set fire to a house near the woods.

Then a shell tore a cow wandering around ahead of my tank to pieces, two other tanks were damaged and unable to maneuver. Medics ran around and rescued wounded men, among them Captain Hall, who had sustained a shrapnel wound on his leg. Thus our headquarters company no longer had any direct leadership, as Lieutenant Ruder, the adjutant, had been killed the previous night. We came to a stop and quickly called for artillery support. Moments later, the 105 mm shells from our 3rd FA Battalion were whistling over our heads and smashing into the woods this side of Beaufort. It was an uncanny scene. One could no longer make out the individual explosions of our artillery fire, since the fire was so heavy. During the fire, German infantrymen stormed out of the woods, their hands over their heads, and ran toward us. They surrendered by the group, even by the platoon. More than a hundred of them were taken prisoner and guarded by some of our slightly injured soldiers.

Most of the Germans were very young, dirty and hungry. The German return fire continued.

The engineers, the group ahead of us who had suffered the most losses, climbed onto the half-tracks as fast as they could and we set out to attack. The Sherman tanks took the lead. I could not inquire about the situation in my tank, because of the defective radio set, as the tank platoon, to which I too now belonged, got underway. Now we drove through a wide clearing. Suddenly I saw a single German soldier jump onto the path, raise a Panzerfaust and aim at the leading tank. Although the lieutenant in the tank had seen him in time to throw a hand grenade at him, the hollow charge of the Panzerfaust exploded on the side of the tank. The German was, to be sure, wounded by shrapnel, but the tank was in flames.

The panic-stricken crew got out of the burning tank. A machine-gun burst mowed them down from the turret. Only one survived, but he was badly burned from the explosion.

For unknown reasons the track of the tank I was in broke; thus the tank was unable to move but fired its turret machine gun at the underbrush from which the German fire had come. The other tanks also fired into the woods now; again numerous Germans surrendered.

Now I got into a half-track. We drove quickly through the clearing and approached the edge of the woods again. A few Germans who wanted to detain us here were mowed down. But the path ended here. I myself had no map and therefore did not know our position. Still in all, we had to be close to the front and thus near my surrounded platoons. The major who commanded the task force studied his maps but was not sure where our front lines were. Did they, in fact, still exist? We noticed numerous German telephone cables that ran through the underbrush. A bad sign! It meant that the enemy had built up a communications network behind the surrounded men! I myself cut several cables and ordered the men to do the same, in hopes that we could cause the Germans just as many difficulties with broken telephone lines as they had caused us. Gradually it got dark.

The major had lost almost half of his tanks and did not want to put the rest of them in danger needlessly in the dark. He ordered us to draw back somewhat.

So we drove back and passed the Sherman, which was still burning; ammunition was still exploding noisily.

After we had crossed another clearing on our way back, German mortar fire suddenly fell on our column. In no time all the men had left the vehicles and disappeared into the forest. The iron fragments of the exploding shells hissed menacingly. Two men were wounded. No medics were available, so I stayed with the wounded men, who were squirming with pain, until the fire let up somewhat. The first half-track that had followed the column of tanks was at the edge of the clearing behind us. I hurried to it and ordered the driver to move ahead and pick up the two wounded men. The empty vehicle drove up and immediately evacuated the two men. Along the edge of the road in a ditch there were two German 8 cm mortars with ammunition and propelling charges. Our own mortar unit had lost their weapons in an ambush the previous day and now used the German mortars to fire in the direction from which the fire on our column came. In addition, we were able to fire our own remaining mortar ammunition effectively, since it was basically the same caliber.

I reported our misfortunes to Lt. Col. Collins, After some time the S-3 officer received permission to bring back the surrounded men by a night exfiltration. He himself tried to reach the command of McCarthy's 3rd FA Battalion to pass the order to break out on to him.

What is the situation of the rest of your company?" the battalion commander asked me. "They are obviously still standing fast," was my answer, "but for how long?" – "What are the chances of a small patrol pushing through to you if no connections can be established?"

"About 50-50," I replied; "the German lines before Beaufort are heavily manned, to be sure, but there are numerous gaps."

"Select some men immediately," I thought it over for several minutes. The handful of cooks, mechanics, and the rest of the soldiers who had come through since the combat at Hotel Meyer formed only a hopelessly small group. I myself wanted to lead the undertaking and chose one more NCO; the rest of the men would only weaken the undertaking rather than being of any great help to us. Captain Harder had meanwhile chosen men too, to go in search of his own cut-off B Company. We agreed that the first of us who would reach the lines was to inform the rest of the units of the order to break out without delay.

Taken Prisoner

In the little daylight that remained, we assembled and studied the map to decide on a route. Each of us ate a K ration. I was fairly weak and worn out from exhaustion, but the excitement and my will power ameliorated those feelings. We swallowed a few benzedrine pills and put two packages of strengthening chocolate in our pockets.

I took off my heavy underclothing and removed everything that could make a sound from my pockets. I handed my personal effects as well as my binoculars over to a sergeant to keep for me. Then Sergeant Ziringer and I set out.

"If one of us should be killed or wounded," I ordered him, "the other must work his way onward no matter what. If we are called to, I'll try to answer in German, and you fight your way through. If we are discovered and surrounded, let's try to break out at any cost."

On our way we passed several of our own sentries from tank destroyer and reconnaissance units of the 89th Recon. Cavalry Squadron. Once we were fired on by our own men and had a hard time making ourselves known and getting the fire stopped. In Haller we learned that a battle group of the 89th Recon. Cavalry Squadron had no success in trying to recapture Beaufort. The enemy controlled the edge of town, it was said. To my surprise, though, I found two of my lost men from the first platoon here; they had fought their way through and were now at the command post of the unit in Haller. They had been given the task of establishing contact with the 3rd Field Artillery Battalion. Both of them were wounded but had carried out their task. "The platoon is still holding its position," they confirmed.

On account of the enemy's present position, we saw ourselves compelled to take a new line of march. Advance posts showed us where German positions were located several hundred meters from the edge of Beaufort.

Relying only on the map and the compass, we circled around Beaufort and reached the end of a rocky ridge in the woods. It was too risky to go around it, since we could fall off it easily in the darkness.

The tip of a fir tree rose close beside the rocky cliff. We climbed down the trunk of the tree and reached the bottom several meters below. According to the map, we had now covered the greater part of the route, but we were totally exhausted. Our eyes flickered, and everything around us was blurred. The sky above us was cloudy; the pale moonlight just barely came through. I myself thought I saw the landscape move; that shows how tired I was.

It was already midnight. We had to hurry. I avoided cautious movements now. Hoping for good luck, we now walked on quickly, standing straight up.

We walked faster and faster.

I hope that this kind of walking would make our movements less suspicious in enemy territory. We had apparently walked on for several minutes now. Nothing had happened!

This confirmed our opinion, and we walked even faster. Suddenly we heard from one side: "Halt!"

I came to a sudden stop. In a fraction of a second I had to make a decision. As weakened as my senses were by exhaustion, I was unable to recognize whether the voice was that of an American or a German. I stood still. My eyes struggled to see something.

Sergeant Ziringer and I recognized the barrel of a weapon that was pointed at us from a foxhole. We heard a whistle. Several men hurried toward us. They took our weapons from us, searched us and led us away. We were in German captivity!"

The 3rd Armored Field Artillery Battalion

The 3rd Armored Field Artillery Battalion, under its commander, Lt. Col. George Ruhlen (now Major General, retired), had already entered Luxembourg within the 9th U.S. Armored Division on October 18 and 19, 1944. At this time the same division was assigned to serve as the corps reserve and support the infantry units present in the corps' sector.

It is interesting to note that the following order was given to the 1st, 3rd, and 9th U.S. Armies in Luxembourg from Eisenhower's headquarters as early as September 21, 1944. This order was secret and was not allowed to be received in writing. It was to be passed on only by general officers. It said, among other things: ". . . as long as sufficient supplies and stocks have not been brought in to fill the supply gaps resulting from the too-quick advance through France and toward Germany, the 1st, 3rd, and 9th U.S. Armies will remain on the defensive for the time being. So that the enemy learns nothing of this, in no case are clearly defensive-appearing maneuvers to be carried out. These include, among others: the construction of defensive positions, fortifications, the laying of anti-personnel and antitank mines, barbed-wire barriers, road blockades, mine traps, etc. The only exception will be contact mines." This order remained in force until the German breakthrough on December 16 put an end to it. "This order was also one of the reasons," as General Ruhlen reports today, "why the Germans advanced so quickly on the first days of the offensive, a point that is all too often neglected by most historians."

The Combat Command B of the 9th U.S. Army was originally located around Ettelbrück, but was then transferred to Ulflingen (Troisvierges); the division's own reconnaissance unit, the 89th Recon, Squadron, went to Clervaux, from which vigorous patrol activity was carried on. Other unit positions of the 9th Armored Division were: the 52nd Armored Infantry Battalion in Bettendorf, the 73rd Armored Field Artillery Battalion in Christnach, and the 3rd Armored FA Battalion around Consdorf.

Only on December 10, 1944 was the whole division assigned its own front sector, which had been occupied previously by units of the 8th U.S. Infantry Division on the "defensive line." This sector stretched from Wallendorf approximately to Medernach-Reuland, an area that appeared to have an almost natural boundary, formed by the courses of the Black and White Ernz Rivers. Somewhat later, the sector beyond Wallendorf was moved farther to the right, roughly to Grundhof. The division's reserve, formed by CCR, was transferred to Allerborn and Longvilly, thus to the Belgian border. Combat Command A (CCA) to which the 60th Armored Infantry Battalion, 19th Tank Battalion, 3rd Armored FA Battalion, the A Company of the 9th Armored Engineer Battalion and the A Company of the 131st Ordnance Maintenance Battalion belonged, under the complete command of Colonel Thomas Harold, thus entered the area around Beaufort. Later CCA was strengthened by two units of the 89th Reconnaissance Squadron, the A Battery of the 482nd Armored Anti-Aircraft Battalion, and two companies of the 811th Tank Destroyer Battalion.

Lt. Col. Ruhlen's 3rd Armored FA Battalion took up positions somewhat west of Haller on December 14. His unit consisted of three "firing" batteries, each with six M7 105 mm howitzers, mounted on Sherman tank chassis (called "Priest" because of the pulpitlike machine-gun casemate) of 105 mm self-propelled howitzers, a HQ (headquarter) Battery, a "Service Battery" and three tanks of the Sherman or M-24 "Chaffee" type for reconnaissance. The unit was fully mobile, with half-tracks for the crews. In all, the 3rd FA Battalion included approximately 480 men, with an effective combat strength of 350.

"On December 15, 1944," General Ruhlen reports, "we were busily at work laying telephone cables to our advanced artillery observation posts, which were located on the Reisdorf-Wallendorf-Bollendorf line. The gun batteries around Haller dug themselves in on uncovered country at my command. Somehow I personally had the feeling that something was "brewing" on the German side. Numerous observations confirmed my suspicion again and again. Since October 24, when my guns had taken up positions around Consdorf, our side had fired day after day on German transport columns in the Siegfried Line, as well as on troop concentrations around Echternach.

At this time, only half of Echternach belonged to the Americans. Several times my observers reported the visits of German officers in black leather coats to the bunkers of the Western Wall. We ourselves had picked up three Polish forced laborers and several German runaways who had swum the Sauer to surrender to us. They all reported that a gun or tank was hidden under almost every large haystack or barn in the Rhineland, and that fresh German divisions crossed the Rhine almost every night. That was taking place around December 12.

In addition, we had often been under German artillery fire from various directions from which we had never been fired on before. Somewhere in my subconscious mind I remembered the history course at West Point, the chapter on World War I, when the Germans began their last major offensive just at the moment when everybody firmly believed that the Imperial Army was completely beaten.

"A dull rumble" was heard in the early morning hours of December 16, but the first shells, which I could identify from shell fragments as being 105, 150 and 170 calibers, came howling toward Haller only after 6:15 AM. The intensity of the fire increased, the echoes of the shots resounded down in the Sauer valley. Every one of us ran for cover. It became known very soon that this time it was not a local firefall, nor was it return fire in answer to our fire the previous night. In Haller and the surrounding villages, church bells rang to sound the alarm. German shells and Nebelwerfer projectiles rained down ceaselessly, and I estimated that in the time from 6:15 to 7:15 approximately 800 shells exploded in and around Haller. Clouds of smoke and dust from tremendous explosions could be seen clearly from the direction of Beaufort. Nebelwerfer rockets, recognizable by their howl that penetrated to the bone, exploded not far from my dug-out gun positions. These were located on both sides of the road that ran downhill from Haller to Beaufort (the low-lying meadow behind the Hotel Alff). An advanced observer reported that some sixty Germans were in the process of crossing the Sauer near Dillingen on a narrow footbridge.

All the phone lines were broken, only the phone connection with the command post of the 60th Armored Infantry Battalion was still operating.

By radio (we had radios with fifty modulated frequencies on five channels, as well as twelve radio-amplifiers with a range of twenty miles) there came imprecise reports of the surrounding of the companies of the 60th Armored Infantry Battalion. The attacking German units, which turned out to be troops of the 276th Volksgrenadier Division, were immediately taken under fire by my guns. While this fire from our side continued, the observation post of my B Battery was hit and the entire crew wounded. Although one of them was lost, the crew held out and directed fire onto the crossing point by radio.

Around 4:00 PM news reached us from the headquarters of the division's artillery; among other things, the attacked sector was to be defended only by CCA, and my 3rd Field Artillery Battalion, as well as one platoon of the 19th Tank Battalion, had to supply the necessary artillery support. Further reports told us that the positions previously occupied by the 73rd Field Artillery Battalion had taken about 150 accurately aimed direct hits. So the Germans apparently knew the exact location of our positions along the Sauer. Fortunately, I myself had never occupied these positions, as I had been advised to by the division's artillery.

Although Haller was still under fire, our positions here apparently had not yet been discovered. Captain Golladay spoke up and reported that the Germans had obviously occupied Berdorf already, and that our previous gun positions had all taken direct hits. He had immediately transferred the staff battery to a farm (the Pletschette Farm). Late in the afternoon, B Battery just barely missed a direct hit from a salvo.

In spite of that, we kept on firing; even routine tasks were still carried out despite the German fire. Sergeant Westenfelt, C Battery's Mess Sergeant, spent the whole time taking hot food to his battery in Haller, and Corporal Dean continued to deliver the mail.

The German fire continued during the night and was aimed principally at the main street of the town, as well as exactly in front of the battalion's headquarters and the Fire Direction Center in Haller. Early in the morning, alarming news reached us. The reserve unit of the 60th Armored Infantry Battalion had just been mobilized. One company of the battalion apparently had been surrounded, another was in danger of being cut off. Lt. Col. Collins, Commander of the 60th Armored Infantry Battalion, had immediately requested tank support from the division's headquarters, but this had been refused him, since it became known later that only a single company of Sherman tanks form the division's reserve for the Luxembourg area, and it was already subordinated to the 4th Infantry Division. In order to help Lt. Col. Collins all the same, I ordered Lt. George Potter to take our three observation tanks to Beaufort to get the infantrymen who were enclosed and cut off in the houses there out. This was partially successful. Our tanks destroyed several German machine-gun nests and quickly evacuated the wounded from the village, which was under strong pressure.

About 3:00 PM we heard that all the infantry companies along the Sauer were cut off without contact to each other and surrounded by the enemy, and that heavy street fighting was going on in Beaufort.

Lieutenant Smith telephoned and reported that his communications half-track and a part of his men, with additional infantrymen of the 60th Armored Infantry Battalion, were surrounded in Hotel Meyer at the edge of Beaufort. Sergeant Rudi was able to storm through the corridor of the hotel, which was under machine-gun fire, and break out with five men. Two of my men, Sattler and Farrel, were no longer able to leave the hotel and fought on with hand grenades and a bazooka until the building was stormed and began to burn. Haller was still under fire, and soon B Battery was hit by countless shells. From Berdorf the enemy had an extensive view of Haller, so that the smallest position change of B Battery immediately brought on several artillery salvos.

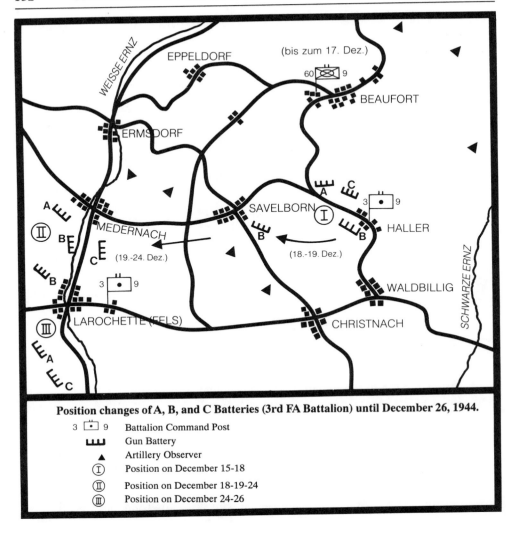

Position changes of A, B, and C Batteries (3rd FA Battalion) until December 26, 1944.

3 ⊡ 9	Battalion Command Post
⊔⊔⊔	Gun Battery
▲	Artillery Observer
Ⓘ	Position on December 15-18
Ⓘ	Position on December 18-19-24
Ⓘ	Position on December 24-26

Thank God that many of these shells were duds!

Our position in Haller could not be held any longer. Despite our answering fire, I could no longer justify this position. At my request to the headquarters of CCA, I was given permission late in the afternoon to move the guns to Savelborn. Approximately a quarter of the crew of my B Battery was dead or wounded!

During the position change, the pilot of the artillery observation plane, while flying over the eastern Sauer valley, spotted five German artillery batteries that were shooting. Now he directed the fire of my other two batteries (A and C) on them, and within a short time three German guns were put out of action by direct hits.

About 8:00 PM, numerous half-tracks and trucks drove through Haller. They belonged to the Staff Company of the 60th Armored Infantry Battalion, which was also withdrawing to Savelborn. Beaufort was already in German hands, it was reported. This meant that there were no longer any American troops of my C Battery there. About 9:00 PM, while C Battery was firing defensive fire, a German shell hit two ammunition locations farther to the rear, which caught fire. In no time three soldiers extinguished the fire with earth, so that an explosion could be prevented. Our muzzle flashes were obviously betraying our position, for shortly after we fired, we were fired on. The German artillery observers must therefore be very near us. So I ordered C Battery to take up new positions on the heights east of Medernach.

At the same time there came an order from CCA, saying that on the next day a task force would push through Haller, and that we had to make sure that no German patrols could sneak into the village during the night. I ordered forty of my men, plus part of the medical unit with four half-tracks, to remain in Haller. During the night they, along with the A Battery of the 482nd Armored Anti-Aircraft Battalion, were to protect the village from German attacks.

The withdrawal from Haller to Savelborn and Medernach was a risky situation, since the exit route was constantly under harassing fire. On our way we came upon numerous men of the 60th Armored Infantry Battalion and the 89th Reconnaissance Squadron, who had broken through the German barrage and were fighting their way back. We picked them up and drove them back to their unit later. Many of them wore blankets and German helmets, and in their flight they had passed through Beaufort, which was apparently full of drunken German soldiers.

"When they were called to from afar and ordered to halt, they simply shouted 'Heil Hitler!' and kept on marching." Obviously the trick had worked; the Germans had let themselves be bluffed.

The Headquarter battery took up quarters in Medernach, I set up my command post between Savelborn and Medernach, the Service Battery in a villa near Medernach (now the Fondation Arend-Fixmer), but was transferred to Larochette later, since the staff of CCA took possession of the building.

On December 17, a company of the 19th Tank Battalion had already been ordered to Ermsdorf in order to protect the northern flank of the sector; in addition, the A Troop of the 89th Reconnaissance Squadron had been sent into the vicinity of Waldbillig.

The strength of the enemy was estimated at about one battalion in Beaufort plus two others in Mullerthal. The counterattack planned by the staff of CCA was to be carried out as follows:

Task Force Hall, composed of the remaining parts of the 60th Armored Infantry Battalion and some engineers, was to push forward through the woods to the strip known as "Berens" in the Beaufort Heath, and thus advance to the edge of the village. Task Force Philbeck, consisting of Sherman and M-24 tanks of the 19th Tank Battalion as well as an engineer unit, was to attack Beaufort on the north side to the left of Task Force Hall and then swing to the south. Finally, Task Force Chamberlain was to attack Beaufort via the direct route from Haller with the rest of the 89th Reconnaissance Squadron as well as the quadruple .50 machine guns, mounted on M-16 half-tracks, of the A Battery of the 482nd AAA Battalion.

To make our job easier, two companies of the 811th Tank Destroyer Battalion (from Waldbillig) were detailed to us.

My battalion was to provide the necessary artillery-fire support for the three attacking units. The counterattack, which would begin about 8:00 AM on December 18, had an assembly point near the positions of my B Battery. My A Battery was located some 400 yards ahead of the line of attack.

Task Force Hall ran into a trap and lost several vehicles. Lieutenant Perry, one of my communications officers who was with the remaining unit of the 60th Armored Infantry Battalion, directed my defensive fire precisely at the flank of the German line. On account of my battalion's extremely heavy artillery fire, connections between the units on the German line were broken. This resulted in some of them surrendering at once, while the rest of the enemy troops, in small groups, became involved individually in forest combat. Meanwhile Lieutenant Brown in the observation plane had spotted an enemy artillery position near Beaufort that was firing on Waldbillig. By fire excellently directed from the plane, I was able to knock out this battery within a short time.

Task Force Hall got no farther, while Philbeck's battle group was still moving forward on the "Beauforter Heed" in the direction of "Berens." At the same time, a local attack of German infantry on Ermsdorf, supported by mortar fire, took place. But the village was held!

Shortly after 12:00 noon, A and B Batteries came under mortar and machine-gun fire. The direction from which the fire came was to the right of B Battery, in a wooded area. Through the use of explosive shells with "Superquick-Fuze" ignition, which exploded in the trees, the German fire was brought under control.

In addition, my cannoneers often had to reach for their rifles and machine guns as German infantry threatened to storm the guns. Still the Germans were able to make a strong attack on the northern column near Haller. A breakthrough resulted in a split of Combat Command A and thus a turn to the Larochette-Mersch road. To our misfortune, Task Force Chamberlain had also been pushed back to Haller, having lost several tanks. They themselves had been able to advance no more than 1.5 kilometers.

The woods around A and B Batteries filled with German troops. Our defensive fire, part of which was carried out using our .50 caliber bow machine guns, was successful. Direct attacks on our guns came to an end. Suddenly the German artillery fire fell silent too. Later we found out that the German artillery observer, a lieutenant, had been hit by fragments of a shell from B Battery. Shortly after that, my two batteries put a Nebelwerfer battery out of commission after it had been spotted from the reconnaissance plane.

About 4:00 PM the communications officer of the hard-hit 60th Armored Infantry Battalion reached me and reported that the men would dig in for the night. This was the first report of the general situation that I had received since the beginning of the German attack. Thereupon I moved my A Battery, which was somewhat more than two kilometers away from them, as far as Medernach.

Under the fire support of C Battery, the M7 "Priest" vehicles of the two batteries drove to high ground west of the Larochette railroad station. Along the way, A Battery was fired on from a patch of woods. B Battery, which was driving behind A Battery, covered the woods with a deadly hail of shells. At that some 120 Germans, all members of the 986th Volksgrenadier Regiment, surrendered. I set up my command post in the same building as the CCA headquarters in Medernach. We called it the "Japanese House", as there were numerous Japanese woodcuts and drawings in the interior of the building (Fondation Arend-Fixmer). As quickly as possible, a communications network to all available units was set up, so that it was possible at last to get some clear information about the situation on our very incomplete front line. I ordered eleven observers to go to the front line at once; from then on, they steadily communicated firing missions. From then on our defensive fire was so effective that every German attack that began was shattered in its initial stages. The Commander of CCA, Colonel Harold, called this tactic "defensive with fire." On the basis of precise maps, it was now easy to lay coordinated artillery fire on an area of land with precision.

About 2:45 PM on December 19, an attack on Waldbillig, carried out by two German infantry companies supported by three assault guns, was recognized and reported. Again I drove this attack back. Shortly after that, German infantry units attacked Savelborn. While I fired shells at Savelborn, several half-tracks of the 482nd AAA Battalion with quadruple .50 machine guns pursued the fleeing Germans and almost completely wiped out the enemy units. The survivors, who surrendered, spoke in terror of an American secret weapon. That is how murderous the "Quad Fifty", known in soldier slang as the "meat chopper", was. A further attack on Waldbillig was also fought off; the German units lost two assault guns in the process.

Late in the afternoon my observation plane spotted another target area. Two enemy infantry and vehicle columns were jamming the approach road and the small bridge near the point where the headquarters of the 60th Armored Infantry Battalion had been located previously. Several salvos of high explosive and incendiary ammunition, equipped with time fuses, caused the enemy considerable losses and, on account of the towering outcrops of rock, they could retreat in only one direction.

During all of this combat activity since December 16, one of my forward observers and fire direction officers, Lieutenant Cravens, and his observation unit (belonging to C Battery), had been completely cut off from our unit. In spite of that, they continued to fulfill their mission to the rear of the enemy. Their reports by radio were of great value to us. Lieutenant Dale "Ira" Cravens had spotted targets and made sure that our fire did not fall on the lines of the enclosed troops of the 60th Armored Infantry Battalion.

Via the same radio, Lt. Col. Collins gave the order to break out to his three cut-off companies. During that night the 320 brave soldiers, who had already held off every enemy attack, fought their way through to our lines under the leadership of Lieutenants McCarthy and Cravens. Before the night breakthrough, they had buried all their equipment in the woods and mined their half-tracks.

It was learned from a captured German messenger that CCA was in the attack area of the 276th VGD. When this division attacked with two shock-troop regiments, Waldbillig, Ermsdorf and Medernach were to be captured on December 19, and Reuland, Fels and Mersch on December 20. The division was composed chiefly of replacement personnel from the navy and Luftwaffe.

On December 21, 1944 the 423rd Field Artillery Battalion of the 10th U.S.

Armored Division reached us to strengthen us more. Meanwhile I had my C Battery take up positions south of Larochette, south of Ernzen.

About 3:30 PM an observer from the 423rd FA Battalion reached us by radio and reported that the enemy was about to undertake an attack, supported by five armored scout cars and assault guns. After brief artillery fire, which was also supported by Nebelwerfer rockets and heavy launchers, a massive attack indeed developed from the direction of Waldbillig. Our two artillery units fired like mad, and after thirty minutes the attack came to a standstill.

At this time Troop C of the 89th Reconnaissance Squadron was located at Savelborn. Freskeisen was defended by the A Battery of the 482nd AAA Battalion.

While the German infantry units were scattered, three assault guns had succeeded in working their way up to the edge of Savelborn and seriously threatening the anti-aircraft batteries of the 482nd AAA Battalion.

Sergeant Forke of C Troop (89th Reconnaissance Squadron) was able to set fire to the motor of the first assault gun with five rounds from the 37 mm gun of an M-8 armored car. The disembarking crew came under rifle fire. Under the fire protection of the armored car, Lieutenant Lawson and Sergeant Chartin then worked their way with bazookas to the second assault gun at the Savelborn-Haller-Freckeisen intersection and put it out of action with two shots from short range. The track was blown off the assault gun, which slid off the road and came to a stop against a stone wall. The third assault gun, which wanted to withdraw along the road to Haller, was hit by our artillery fire and went up in flames.

Then a German battalion tried to advance from Waldbillig to Christnach. Here too, the attack had to be called off on account of many losses. To our surprise, one of the three shot-down assault guns bore SS markings. Until then it had not been known that SS units were present in the southern sector! (Author's note: There is no precise explanation for this.)

Numerous Germans who surrendered after this combat had American jackets and equipment, Many of them even wore the emblem of our division on their coats and jackets. Those who were found with pieces of American uniforms had to remove them; this also applied to shoes. Thus they marched shivering toward the prison camp near Fels.

A certain ruthlessness came over us after we had found numerous dead American soldiers with head wounds or ripped-open bodies, with pieces of German equipment that had been stuck into them. In this area the Germans were making short work of American prisoners who were caught with German materials.

While our defensive fighting continued, General Patton visited CCA on December 20 and ordered that the line be held at any cost. He had likewise given the VIIIth Corps at Bastogne the order to hold on, and instructed the IIIrd Corps to attack as soon as possible.

On December 22 the CCA was combined with the newly arrived 10th U.S. Armored Division. The Third Army feared a German attack on Mersch and then into the flank of the units pushing forward from Luxembourg to Bastogne. This would cause serious difficulties for the American supply columns and communications network.

Separated from units of the 10th Armored Division, my 3rd FA Battalion drew back to Meysembourg, and I moved my command post into the castle there. From now on our task was to guarantee CCA of the 10th Armored Division general support, as well as to strengthen the firepower of the 423rd FA Battalion. Nothing was said about supporting CCA itself. An attack on the part of CCA of the 10th Armored Division, supported by units of our division's own 19th Tank Battalion, proceeded only slowly. In the vicinity of Beaufort this task force suffered numerous losses of tanks and infantry from the Nebelwerfer and anti-aircraft fire in ground combat of a German 8.8 cm battery. Only a battle group of the 19th Tank Battalion succeeded in recapturing and holding Eppeldorf. Thus the danger in the northern part of the perimeter was avoided.

Christmas brought new rumors of relief for our worn-out units, but probably not for the artillery, on which the army leadership had to depend permanently. Waldbillig and Haller had meanwhile been liberated by units of the 5th U.S. Infantry Division. Positions that had been given up near Medernach were recaptured despite Nebelwerfer fire. At noon on December 25 it became known that the enemy was in retreat and was hurrying toward the Sauer. On the following day, the 19th Tank Battalion was relieved around Eppeldorf by units of the CCA of the 6th U.S. Armored Division; in addition, the 5th Infantry Division then took over the sector. In the west, the 80th Infantry Division pushed forward from Mersch. During the past ten days, my artillery battalion had fired over 26,000 rounds. From December 16 to 23, we had theoretically fired an average of one round every forty seconds. The highest shot cadence was achieved on December 21 and 22. On each of these days we fired approximately 7100 rounds.

Day and night, the ammunition vehicles of our Service Battery rolled out of Larochette and Altlinster in order to supply the guns with urgently needed ammunition. The loaders and truck drivers ate while they drove; we ourselves, according to army orders, had absolute priority for being supplied with ammunition from one depot, since we were known to be the only artillery unit in this threatened sector for days.

Although we had suffered numerous reverses, the CCA of the 9th U.S. Armored Division had nevertheless succeeded in halting and scattering the advances of the 276th VGD, carried out with massive artillery support. This division itself was one of the hardest-hit units in the whole German Army. After its withdrawal to German territory, it was still supposed to be used in the northern part of Luxembourg." – Here the memoirs of General Ruhlen end. Countless tactical details and other items concerning his unit are still available, but their scope would vastly exceed the limits of this book.

Combat Command A of the 9th Armored Division was detailed to the 4th Armored Division, and the 3rd Field Artillery Battalion was transferred from Meysembourg via Angelsberg, Mersch and Arlon to Neufchâteau. From here a successful attack was made on the main approach road to Bastogne, in order to free it for the breakthrough. The 3rd FA Battalion fought off German attacks on Sibret, Villeroux and Senonchamps until January 4, 1945.

After the 9th Armored Division had been reconstituted in France, Aachen was taken at the end of February. But its chief claim to fame in the history of World War II was that the 9th Armored Division took the Ludendorff Bridge in Remagen intact on March 7, 1945 and thus became the first U.S. unit to cross the Rhine; in fact, it was the first successful battle group to cross the Rhine since the Romans. (Note: In the daily report of Company L of the 109th Infantry Regiment, Captain Embert Fossum mentions, among other things: ". . . and received valuable help from an artillery battalion that is unknown to me. The code name for the telephone communication was 'Cobblestone'." Major General Ruhlen offers the following explanation: "'Cobblestone' was the code name for the command post of the division's artillery. My own was 'Commerce'. Since we were known to be the only artillery battalion in the sector in question, I certainly supplied the support fire for the threatened L Company on the Our front. All the code names of the units of the 9th Armored Division began with the letter C.")

The 19th Tank Battalion in Ermsdorf
The last unit to be treated in this report on the 9th U.S. Army will be the 19th Tank Battalion, which was transferred to the left flank of CCA and thus to Ermsdorf, in order to bar a suspected enemy breakthrough of the thinly occupied sector. The following notes come from a published war diary written by Captain Edgar Terrell, then Company Leader of D Company of the 19th Tank Battalion.

About 3:00 PM on December 16, after the staff had gained clear knowledge of the seriousness and the extent of the German attack, the Commander of D Company, as well as the Commanding Officer of the 19th Tank Battalion, were ordered to the command post of CCA (Combat Command A of the 9th Armored Division). After a brief discussion of the situation, the orders were given: D Company was to go to Ermsdorf immediately, secure the village and protect the left flank of CCA, which had taken over the section of country south of Ermsdorf in order to oppose the attack of the German units which had crossed the Sauer near Grundhof.

From their position, which was located approximately 20 kilometers from Ermsdorf, the company reached the village about 8:30 PM. The weather was cloudy, damp and cold. Immediately the Sherman and M-24 "Chaffee" tanks of the company left the "Service Company" of the 60th Artillery Battalion, which departed on the following morning.

The Commander led the First Platoon of Shermans along the uphill road toward Folkendingen and to the edge of town. The 2nd Platoon was ordered to take a position at the northern road out of town (in the direction of Eppeldorf), and the 3rd Platoon established connections to the 60th Armored Infantry Battalion in an easterly direction.

On December 17 the 1st Platoon was separated from the company and had to move to Haller at nightfall. On the way to Beaufort, where the headquarters of the 60th AI Battalion were located (in the Hotel Belvedere), Lieutenant Krumm, who commanded the 1st Platoon, learned that the upper part of town was already surrounded by German troops, and that the troops still on hand would fight their way back to Savelborn. Without making any contact with the enemy, the tanks then went to Savelborn, where they remained overnight. On the morning of December 18 the 1st Platoon led the attack of Task Force Philbeck (named after the Executive Officer of the 19th Tank Battalion, Major Tom Philbeck) in the vicinity north of Savelborn and attacked the enemy even before the first light of morning. It turned

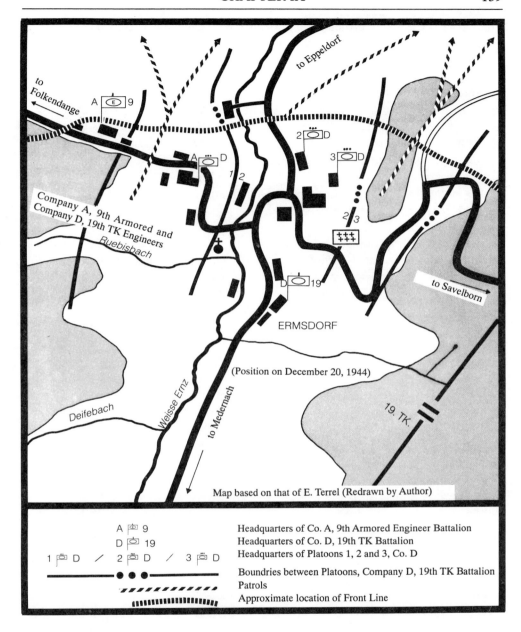

to Eppeldorf

to Folkendange

A ⬭ E ⬭ 9

2 ⬭ D

3 ⬭ D

A ⬭ D

1   2

2 / 3

Company A, 9th Armored and
Company D, 19th TK Engineers

Ruebisbach

to Savelborn

D ⬭ 19

ERMSDORF

(Position on December 20, 1944)

Weisse Ernz

Deifebach

to Medernach

19. TK.

Map based on that of E. Terrel (Redrawn by Author)

A ⬭ 9	Headquarters of Co. A, 9th Armored Engineer Battalion
D ⬭ 19	Headquarters of Co. D, 19th TK Battalion
1 ⬭ D / 2 ⬭ D / 3 ⬭ D	Headquarters of Platoons 1, 2 and 3, Co. D
━━━ ●●● ━━━	Boundries between Platoons, Company D, 19th TK Battalion
⁄⁄⁄⁄⁄⁄⁄⁄	Patrols
ⅢⅢⅢⅢⅢ	Approximate location of Front Line

out that the enemy had already pushed forward to the assembly place the previous night. The advance had taken place so quickly that it had not been noticed that the Germans had already dug in just a few hundred meters from the American lines.

As was learned later from captured German documents, the attack began minutes before a planned attack by the enemy. B Company, which formed the main component of the task force, was able to scatter the enemy, so that the German attack could not be carried out. But this bold maneuver had its price. Several tanks had been damaged and shot down by Panzerfaust hits. Late in the afternoon, the 1st

Platoon of D Company turned back to Ermsdorf, having suffered losses, and occupied its original position at the northwest edge of town. From then on, until about December 26, the company held Ermsdorf. Position changes of the individual platoons were carried out very rarely. Yet it was of major importance to weld the advance posts together into a solid line. For this reason, one platoon of the A Troop of the 89th Reconnaissance Squadron was detailed so as to establish a firm connection to the 60th AI Battalion.

Numerous patrols from Ermsdorf to Eppeldorf were undertaken, with or without tank support, on orders from CCA, in order to keep track of the enemy's situation regularly.

Lieutenant Casey's and Lieutenant Dahn's armored reconnaissance troops often had contact with enemy patrols north of Eppeldorf. One of these patrols is mentioned here:

"In the evening twilight of December 21, Sergeant Willaert's tank had just reached Eppeldorf. The driver, Tec 5 Krainz, left the road and took up a position alongside a house, in order to have a better view of the scouting troop whose protection he was to provide. Suddenly several Germans, coming from various directions, stormed the street and fired on the tank, bringing it to a stop. The driver's hatch door was still closed, but the prismatic periscope had been hit by a shot, so that the driver could see nothing. In his eagerness to turn the tank in another direction via the speaker system, Sergeant Willaert unknowingly ripped out the microphone cable, so that Driver Krainz could not receive any instructions. But he himself, though without being able to see, had taken the initiative and turned the tank around out of fear of Panzerfaust attack as the battle around the houses intensified. He turned around very sharply, rattled along a downward-sloping side road and drove blindly into the house out of which most of the infantry fire was coming. The crew of the tank, who already thought their situation was hopeless, found to their great surprise that some of the Germans surrendered."

On December 19, engineers of A Company of the 9th Armored Engineer Battalion, which was now located to the left of D Company (19th Tank Battalion), were on hand to prepare the bridge over the White Ernz in Ermsdorf for demolition, so that in the event of a withdrawal, the enemy's advance could be delayed. For a time, Ermsdorf was pinpointed by German artillery fire, though without any success in locating the artillery observer. Two tanks were damaged and had to be sent to the field repair shop. On their way there (one of them had to be towed), they were fired on by 8.8 cm shells, but were not hit. On the day when the 10th U.S. Armored Division relieved CCA, Major Philbeck was given command of a newly assembled task force, whose task it was to protect, from Medernach through Ermsdorf to the enemy lines behind Eppeldorf, the right flank of the task force of the 10th Armored Division, which was attacking from the west out of Eppeldorf on the same day. As night fell, this task force, consisting chiefly of the C Company of the 19th Tank Battalion, moved back to Ermsdorf. Major Philbeck's tank rode at their head. On account of the unevenness of the road, caused by the previous German fire, and with extremely poor visibility limitations, the tank drove too near the edge of the road, slid off and turned over before it came to rest in the high waters of the White Ernz. Most of the crew members were thrown headfirst against the armor plate and trapped inside, unconscious. Major Philbeck himself, who was sitting in the turret of the tank, was drowned by the inrushing water before a recovery tank could pull the tank out and rescue the rest of the crew. Captain Crayton took the place of the unfortunate officer.

Aside from the tragedy of the combat, several other incidents deserve to be cited which kept the troops' morale high. The auxiliary cooks did their best to deliver hot meals regularly.

Supply NCO McPeck, who was regarded by the company as an excellent "morale-booster" because of his sense of humor and his good nature, unintentionally put on a "show" that made everybody burst out laughing in spite of the tense situation. One day later, when D Company had taken up its position near Ermsdorf, he was towing the company's armored scout car (M-8 Greyhound), which also served as a supply vehicle. He himself drove ahead in a Jeep. In the twilight his eyes sought the company's command post. But instead, he stopped in front of the cafe in the village (Cafe Weyrich) and inspected the barroom, where there was still beer on tap. While he was happily enjoying a beer and being happy to be sitting in an upholstered chair at long last, there was a burst of German fire. None of the men had yet told him that the front was so close by. The men were laughing so hard that they almost forgot to take cover when the burly sergeant took one jump and hid behind the door of the toilet, which he mistook for the entrance to the cellar.

Another unforgettable event for the men of D Company was the traditional turkey dinner on Christmas Day in Ermsdorf. Shortly after that there was once again nothing but C and K rations for everybody. On December 26 the order to be replaced finally arrived, and D Company rejoined the battalion they belonged to at Angelsberg and continued from there to Arlon.

CHAPTER X

FROM THE JOURNAL OF THE U.S. 10TH ARMORED DIVISION "TIGER DIVISION"

Historical Background

In general, the division's journal concerns only the military operations on a higher unit level and thus includes exclusively the main movements and actions of the entire division. This journal is a concise summary of the "daily unit reports" of all the units subordinated to the division. These reports, which are presently stored in the division's archives, served to keep the Adjutant General in Washington, D.C. informed of the completed combat actions.

In order to afford the reader a clear overview of the actions of the "Tiger Division", the journal was condensed as much as possible; important events that took place in our region were separated and treated at length.

On December 16, 1944, thus at the beginning of the offensive, the 10th Armored Division was taking part in a training program in the vicinity of Apach, Germany, Waldweistroff and Königsmacher. The division's artillery also supported the 3rd Cavalry Group in the Saar area. The division's headquarters plus all the unit commanders of the 10th Armored Division were working feverishly on a plan for the further extension of the bridgeheads at Dillingen and Saarlautern, which had been gained by the 90th and 95th Infantry Divisions. For that reason, preparations, terrain studies and maneuver plans were being made for an advance undertaking into the Rhine valley.

At 5:50 PM on December 16, the XXth Corps alarmed the division's headquarters and gave the order for a breakthrough at daybreak on December 17. The division commander, Major General Morris, was to report without delay to the headquarters of the VIIIth Corps (General Troy Middleton) in Bastogne. After a discussion of the situation and the extent of the commenced German attack on a front more than 100 kilometers long, the 10th Armored Division was released from being subordinate to the XXth Corps and, effective at 6:00 PM, was assigned to the VIIIth Corps. The situation in General Middleton's corps was extremely alarming; an enemy focal point was located on the Our front, the main sector of which was defended by a thin line of the 109th Regiment of the 28th Infantry Division. On the night of December 16-17, a message from the division's headquarters was received at 3:30 AM. The order from General Middleton appeared as follows: The division was to move to Luxembourg immediately, and in the process, a combat command was to advance to the northeastern outskirts of the capital city, while the other units moved in a southwesterly direction.

Luxembourg City had to be circumvented in any case. With Combat Command A (CCA) as its advance guard, the division crossed the Moselle near Thionville and Cattenom at a speed march. Since the capital city was closed as a transit route, CCA had to advance over various detours to the specified gathering place.

Around 3:00 AM on December 18 the change of position was completed; the division itself had covered the distance of some 12 kilometers in approximately 18 hours.

When the command was given at the headquarters of the VIIIth Corps in Bastogne on December 17, the division had received instructions to destroy enemy focal points in cooperation with the 4th Infantry Division, and to relieve threatened American units in Consdorf, Berdorf, Echternach and Osweiler. General Morris thereupon immediately made contact with General Barton (Commander of the 4th Infantry Division) at his headquarters in Luxembourg. Here, among other things, it was decided that CCA would take over the Echternach-Waldbillig sector. Early in the afternoon of December 17, the division commander ordered the commander of CCA in Lintgen to establish contact with the 4th Infantry Division immediately and attack enemy units that were cutting through the Muller Valley, if the fading daylight still allowed. Task Forces Chamberlain and Standish (both of CCA) were to establish contact with Task Force Luckett (12th Regiment, 4th Infantry Division) but to delay their planned attack until the following morning so that a coordinated counterattack could be achieved.

CCB reached its prescribed position west of Luxembourg at 10:00 PM on December 17, 1944. At this time it became known that the headquarters of the 28th Infantry Division were under great danger and the enemy advance on Bastogne was to be taken very seriously. As a result, Colonel Roberts, Commander of Combat Command B (CCB), received the order to defend Bastogne, which constituted an important communication point. Thus CCB advanced to Arlon, where the D Troop of 90th Cavalry Reconnaissance Squadron was subordinated to it. Only around 2:00 PM was the marching destination of Bastogne taken up. General Middleton gave Colonel Roberts the order to hold Bastogne and to defend the endangered communication points. These localities were Noville, Longvilly and Bras, which were occupied immediately between twilight and 10:00 PM by the battle groups (teams) of Desobry, Cherry and O'Hara, so named after their commanders. Immediately after arriving in bastogne, CCB was put under the command of the commander of the VIIIth Corps.

In the night of December 18-19, the G-2 Section (Intelligence Section) of the 9th Armored Division, as well as of the 12th Army Group, informed the division headquarters that an attack by two German divisions had taken place in the gap between CCA of the 9th Armored Division and the 109th Infantry Regiment of the 28th Infantry Division. General Morris met with Lieutenant General Patton at the headquarters of the XXth Corps on December 19 and was named commander of the corps and thus of the subordinated 4th Infantry Division for the time being.

On the morning of December 19 it was reported to the division headquarters that the enemy had reached the Bastogne-Arlon-Luxembourg road. A platoon of light tanks and a platoon of Troop B of the 90th Cavalry Reconnaissance Squadron were immediately assigned to check out the situation. This unit made contact with the enemy near Bastogne, but the road in question was still open. An additional patrol was sent to the Arlon-Luxembourg road as well. At approximately the same time, the remaining 90th Cavalry Reconnaissance Squadron was sent quickly to Stegen, in order to fill the gap in the front line, in a line to Schieren, between CCA of the 9th Armored Division and the already withdrawing 109th Regiment. This maneuver was completed about 3:00 AM in the early morning of December 20. On the same day, General Patton subordinated the 5th Infantry Division, then withdrawing from the Saar, the CCA of the 9th Armored Division and the 109th Infantry Regiment to the command of General Morris' temporary corps, which was then given two tasks: 1. Hold up the enemy on the south flank (Mertzig-Ettelbrück) until a purposeful attack could take place, and 2. Attack St. Vith around 4:00 AM on December 22.

The 5th Infantry Division (Red Diamond), although now subordinated to the temporary corps of General Morris, was still located in Thionville at that time, and arrived in Luxembourg only around noon on December 22. In a discussion with the division commanders at the headquarters of the 3rd Army in Luxembourg on December 21, General Patton planned to attack with the IIIrd and XIIth Corps. The Commander of the XIIth Corps, Major General Eddy, was present at this meeting and was given the command of General Morris' provisional corps. On December 22, General Morris informed the newly appointed commander of the situation. The date of the attack planned by General Patton, though, was postponed.

Thus as of 10:00 AM on December 22, the Commander of the 10th Armored Division assumed the responsibility for the sector of CCA of the 9th Armored Division as far as the border and between the IIIrd and XIIth Corps.

On the morning of December 23, CCA of the 10th Armored Division moved into Larochette and made preparations for an attack on enemy positions along the Sauer, in order to get the river crossings back into American hands. This succeeded, and units of CCA remained at critical points along the Sauer, ready to intervene at any time.

Even before this attack, the 90th Cavalry Reconnaissance Squadron, which had filled the actual gap in the front line, had succeeded in freeing the area between Ermsdorf and Gilsdorf from enemy forces. Thus the approach to the Sauer was already open two days before the planned attack by the Corps. In addition, this action made it possible to occupy numerous chosen observation posts. On Christmas Eve, CCA and the Standish and Rudder Task Forces attacked in a northwesterly direction and pushed forward to the Sauer, where it built up a defensive line on December 25 which was later taken over by the 5th Infantry Division. Relieved briefly by Task Force Rudder, consisting of units of the 109th Infantry Regiment, parts of the 707th Tank Battalion, a part of the 90th Cavalry Reconnaissance Squadron and the A Company of the 609th Tank Destroyer Battalion plus several artillery units, the 10th Armored Division was called back to a gathering place around Metz as of December 26.

Liberation of Gilsdorf and Moestroff on December 24, 1944 by the 90th Cavalry Reconnaissance Squadron

Although this fully motorized and armored reconnaissance unit was not at full strength during its attack on the Gilsdorf-Moestroff area, in which five Luxembourg citizens also took part, it was able, with infantry support from B Company of the 109th Infantry Regiment and the other already mentioned units, to take both villages in surprise attacks and hold them until it was relieved. For this reason, the 90th Cavalry Reconnaissance Squadron deserves closer attention. The unit was composed of seven so-called troops. Troops A through D were the actual reconnaissance units. One troop was itself divided into a staff unit plus three platoons of three sections each. All the units were designated "mechanized", meaning motorized. For example, every section had two Jeeps, which were not called "Jeeps" but rather "Peeps" in the jargon of the American armored troops. One "Peep" was equipped with a .30 or .50 caliber machine gun on a mount, the other with a 60 mm mortar. Every section possessed, among other things, one M8 "Greyhound" armored scout car equipped with a 37 mm gun. Every vehicle was also equipped with heavy radio equipment for its main task was locating enemy positions and reporting them to higher staffs. In most cases, the 60 mm mortar, worthless to a fast-moving reconnaissance unit, was replaced by a large-caliber .50 Browning machine gun, a weapon that was very popular among the troops. On account of its great range, it was often used to inspire the enemy troops in a suspected position to return fire, whereby they then betrayed their position. In addition, the .50 machine gun was very useful in providing anti-aircraft protection.

For direct artillery support of the four aforementioned troops, the E Troop formed a mobile artillery unit, consisting of eight 75 mm howitzers on self-propelled mounts of the "Carriage, Motor 75 mm How M8" type. F Troop, or F Company, consisted of light tanks of the M 5 (Stuart) type, which were replaced, on account of their small caliber (37 mm), which was completely useless against German tanks, by M 24 "Chaffee" tanks with 75 mm guns as of the end of December. One staff and repair troop and the squadron headquarters completed the 90th Cavalry Reconnaissance Squadron, making it a fully combat-capable and self-sufficient unit, although its tasks were limited exclusively to acquiring knowledge of enemy positions and targets. Like every unit of an armored division, the 90th Cavalry Reconnaissance Squadron also possessed half-tracks to transport its men.

Supported by the B Company of the 609th Tank Destroyer Battalion, equipped with M-10 tanks (caliber 76 high velocity), the B Company of the 109th Infantry Regiment (see Lt. Christy's report), and the other units already mentioned, parts of the B Troop and F Company of the 90th Cavalry Reconnaissance Squadron were able to capture and secure Gilsdorf. In a similar action, Moestroff was liberated. It is interesting to learn from the preparatory maneuvers of the "daily S-2 and S-3 reports" (Intelligence, Operations) which units carried out these actions. In the original text we read:

Troop Locations: Squadron Headquarters: Cruchten
     Troop A: Stegen
     Troop B: Cruchten
     Troop C: subordinated to CCA
     Troop D: subordinated to CCB
     Troop E: Essingen
     Company F: Cruchten
     Staff and Repair Company: north of Kehlen

Weather report: Snow during the day, poor visibility. Night clear. Barometer pressure 751 mm (read in Cruchten at 11:00 PM on December 22).

Operations

Troop A held its line from Stegen to Schieren for the time being. German patrols were driven out of Stegen around 5:30 AM. No enemy contact in the Diekirch-Ettelbrück zone. Two patrols carried out. Observation posts occupied on the range of hills south of the Sauer. Enemy movements sighted north of the Sauer. Troop B occupied positions along the Schieren-Schrondweiler road. The remaining part took over the guard of all explosive traps prepared in the sector of the 9th Armored Division.

December 24
Weather Report:

Cold and clear. Barometer pressure 751 mm (at midnight in Cruchten). Operations: A maintains the prescribed line, B Troop left in the direction of Diekirch. C Troop divided from Ermsdorf in the direction of Diekirch. In the process, it captured two German scouts on bicycles. (Both scouts were members of the 276th VGD). C Troop: Passed observation posts of friendly units of the 109th Infantry Regiment. Occupied line along the Sauer as far as the heights beyond Moestroff. D Troop remains subordinated to the CCB. E Troop: continuing artillery support from Stegen. F Company (minus two platoons) remains in reserve at headquarters in Cruchten. One platoon detailed to C Troop, the rest of the platoon supports the attack on Gilsdorf.

B Company of the 609th Tank Destroyer Battalion takes up firing positions along the Sauer.

Result of operations: Team Layton captures Gilsdorf, supported by units of the 109th Infantry Regiment. Continuing direct fire on the north bank of the Sauer. Positions set up as far as Moestroff. On the left flank, contact with the arrived 80th Infantry Division.

Enemy Units:

A captured German made known that he belonged to the 1st Company, 914th GR, 352nd VGD.

Enemy movements: Limited to patrol activities. Busy vehicle traffic north of the Sauer confirmed by observation posts. Artillery and Nebelwerfer fire on our positions directly south of the Sauer. Unknown number of tanks heard. Three of them spotted and destroyed. Artillery and antitank positions sighted and fired on: 4 guns destroyed.

Sector was fired on by German Jäger around 6:10 AM. German engineers blew up the half-destroyed bridge at Gilsdorf. Numerous German troops on bicycles spotted and wiped out on the Gilsdorf-Diekirch road.

This authentic report in concise form also includes countless details of the combat activities of the entire unit, though its size is too great to include here. Now let us hear the words of the officer in charge of the operation, Major Gilbert Layton, Executive Officer of the 90th Cavalry Reconnaissance Squadron:

"On December 19 we arrived at our headquarters in Cruchten, which we reached via Mersch and Schieren. Our commander, Lt. Col. Licherie, was immediately occupied with a problem that was hitherto unknown to us. I remember that in the same night a stream of refugees coming from Stegen had blocked the streets in Cruchten and influenced our movements greatly. It was bitter cold. Women with crying infants, children with fully loaded baby carriages and handcarts, adults and countless old people streamed toward Cruchten all through the night. Since we ourselves did not know the situation and nobody knew just where the enemy actually was, we remained in Cruchten. On the morning of December 20, we took part in helping to evacuate the refugees to Lintgen. But more and more kept coming, pursued by panic fear, so that we were faced with an insoluble problem. In addition, dozens of mentally ill patients who had come from the Ettelbrück hospital had arrived. It was no longer possible for us to take all of these people to safety. Thus the medical service of our unit took over this task in collaboration with the service company, which took the people out of the danger zone on trucks. Among the countless refugees there was a Catholic nun who spoke excellent and unaccented school English. She unselfishly delayed her own evacuation as long as there were still refugees in Cruchten, for it was her duty to stay with the people wherever they were.

Meanwhile the B Troop had undertaken a reconnaissance trip to Ettelbrück and reported that very few, if any, Germans had advanced as far as Ettelbrück. Only A Troop reported a meeting with an enemy patrol in Stegen. After a brief exchange of fire, the Germans had been driven off. These incidents confirmed our suspicion that the combat was taking place north of Cruchten. Thus we again had some time to take care of the homeless refugees.

On the following day, several farmers reported and insisted on looking after the cattle in their abandoned farms. They asked for U.S. patrols to accompany them for their protection.

After a discussion, Lt. Col. Licherie agreed, since these local farmers could be of use to us, as they knew every bit of this region. So every day we made numerous trips, which we jokingly referred to as "milk patrols", to the farms in and around Stegen. The representative of the farmers' group also spoke English, though with a thick accent. To my question of where he had learned the language, he told me that for seventeen years he had been a farmer in the American state of Iowa. This fascinated me, since I come from Iowa.

He also told me that he had saved money in America in order to come back to Luxembourg, marry his school sweetheart and take her to Iowa. When he had enough money and returned to Luxembourg, the war broke out. Fate . . . !

At the same time, I found out that several young Luxembourgers actively supported the A Troop. They were very familiar with the region, and them themselves led patrols under the leadership of Lieutenant Meisner. In the process they proved to be excellent artillery observers. Some of them wore red scarves sewn-on initials along with their uniforms, which were provided by the U.S. Army (Vianden Militia).

Much later, when the 10th Armored Division had been withdrawn to Metz and I was carrying out an inspection of the troops, these young Luexmbourgers were still in our ranks. They had decided to stay and move with us. This was against all the regulations, and several commanders were criticized most severely by the staff. The commanders of Troops A and B, in which the Luxembourgers were, had simply supplied them with complete uniforms bearing the insignia of the 10th Armored Division and forbidden them to go on wearing the scarves, which attracted too much attention. After a long discussion, Lt. Col. Licherie recalled their services to our troops and allowed them to come along. They fought like real soldiers until the end of the war. So as not to cause any trouble because of their illegal status, the Luxembourgers were not mentioned in the unit's reports, although some of our success was attributable to them.

When we had moved almost all the civilians out of Cruchten, a young woman in a shocking emotional state was found in one house. We learned through a soldier who could speak French that her elderly father had fallen into the water from a bridge in Ettelbrück during the chaos of the evacuation and had been swept away. Unfortunately, we could do nothing for the woman.

As I searched the other houses for remaining civilians, I found two elderly women and one old man sitting in a dark room around a glowing stove. The man was wrapped in blankets and was obviously in shock. One of the soldiers told me that they had fished the man out of the water the previous night. Then I realized who he was. So there was at least one happy note amid all the misery of the refugees. The man was immediately given medical care and, along with his daughter, evacuated to Luxembourg.

Meanwhile the order had come from headquarters to send a scouting party to the Sauer. A strong patrol, consisting of parts of B Troop, a platoon of tanks (Chaffees and Shermans) of F Company, also supported by an additional platoon of M-10 tank destroyers of the 609th Tank Destroyer Battalion, as well as an infantry company of the 109th Regiment, were to attack Gilsdorf, ascertain the enemy's strength and, if possible, drive him out of the area. Before the order to set out arrived, the tank destroyers took up a position on the heights, from which they could take Diekirch as well as the Diekirch-Gilsdorf road under direct fire. We ourselves moved to an assembly point in Stegen. From here we had already reached an isolated farm in Folkendange around 9:00 AM. The headquarters of the attacking unit were immediately set up at the farm. From the edge of the woods, just to the right of the farmyard, a V-shaped notch in the ground afforded a view into Diekirch. Several tank destroyers thereupon took up this position. Later it turned out that this position could also be seen by the Germans on the hills northwest of Diekirch (the Herrenberg).

The first attack took place at 9:30 AM according to the prescribed schedule. The leading attack column had just reached open country along the road when the German artillery suddenly went into action. Numerous shells fell on the road, in the fields and the forest short of the farmyard. They tore ugly black holes in the snow-covered landscape. Within minutes we drew back again and looked for cover as best we could. The land right around the farmyard was hit especially hard, so that the farm could no longer be used as a command post, since the enemy now knew our position.

Along with all this misfortune, the tank destroyer platoon had suffered some losses from shells that exploded in the trees. Among others, a German direct hit had

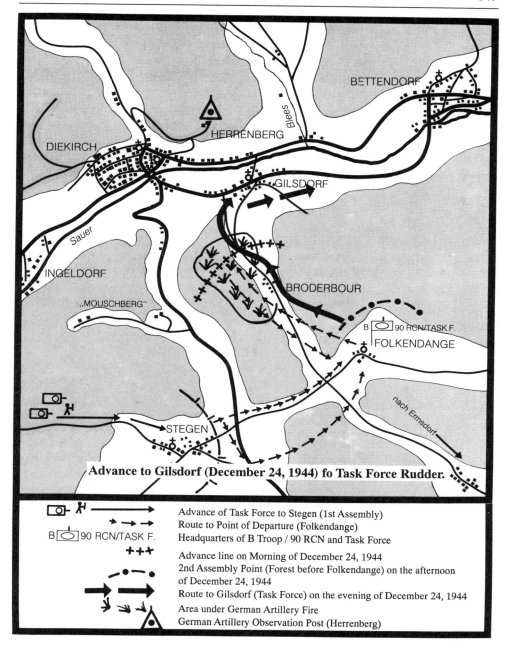

Advance to Gilsdorf (December 24, 1944) fo Task Force Rudder.

	Advance of Task Force to Stegen (1st Assembly)
	Route to Point of Departure (Folkendange)
B ⬭ 90 RCN/TASK F.	Headquarters of B Troop / 90 RCN and Task Force
+++	Advance line on Morning of December 24, 1944
	2nd Assembly Point (Forest before Folkendange) on the afternoon of December 24, 1944
	Route to Gilsdorf (Task Force) on the evening of December 24, 1944
	Area under German Artillery Fire
▲	German Artillery Observation Post (Herrenberg)

wiped out a tank destroyer on the road and killed the crew. (Tank destroyers have an open turret!) The unit commanders immediately gathered, and we decided that there was no point to continuing the attack in this manner. A push through to Gilsdorf in daylight would have resulted in the heaviest losses, especially as the German artillery positions could not be spotted, so we waited for darkness and remained under cover. Meanwhile sentries who had been posted along the road had encountered four young Luxembourgers who wanted to go to Folkendange. Since they wanted, as they said, to fight against the Germans themselves, they offered to guide us along a good road to their home village of Gilsdorf. To our surprise, they also gave us considerable information about where the Germans were quartered in the village. They were given back their weapons, mostly German carbines, and I sent them to the infantry (B Company, 109th Infantry Regiment; see Lt. Christy's report).

We waited until the light was just sufficient for us to just see our direction of march, but dark enough to prevent the German artillery observers from seeing across the Sauer. Thin wisps of fog that appeared late in the afternoon favored the developing undertaking. The men of B Troop, along with the Luxembourgers, then got aboard their tanks, which had gathered several hundred meters farther back along the edge of the woods. The infantry company followed.

At top speed the tanks left the forest, drove along the road and hastened along a steep road toward Gilsdorf. Firing from all their guns, the tanks reached the edge of town and fired into the first rows of houses, where there were presumably Germans. The surprised enemies, who stormed out onto the street, were mowed down by the rattling machine guns of the tanks. Within minutes some fifty Germans lay dead amid the total chaos on the pavement of the village street. The infantry then cleaned out the houses of Gilsdorf under the protection of the tanks. Numerous Germans, who had been taken completely by surprise during their Christmas celebration, surrendered without offering any resistance. Shortly after midnight we had all of Gilsdorf under control. We remained in the village on December 25.

In the first light of morning the tank destroyers, still camouflaged on the heights, fired from under cover on a German vehicle column on the Bettendorf-Bleesbrück-Diekirch. Numerous trucks and several tracked vehicles were destroyed or damaged. They also caused serious losses to a cycle company that had been the advance guard. One gunner even claimed to have scored a direct hit on an individual rider. In the afternoon of the same day a similar undertaking against Moestroff was to have begun from Folkendange. As retribution for our "raid", German artillery and Nebelwerfer shells suddenly rained down on the unsuspecting infantry unit on the high plateau around Folkendange. The infantrymen, who were to lead this attack with tank support, suffered numerous losses. Although they had been warned by us that their position was in the enemy's direct view, the incautious and overly zealous commander had probably told them to march on.

In spite of that, we were able to drive some of the Germans out of Moestroff in the evening hours. We ourselves spent Christmas Day evacuating our own wounded. As far as I know, there were no casualties in our unit the night of the surprise attack on Gilsdorf. Thus the southern shore of the Sauer remained under American control. The enemy withdrew to the highlands on the other shore, and had surprisingly blown up the partially damaged bridges (blown up during the withdrawal of the 109th Regiment, 3rd Battalion; see Col. H.M. Kemp's report), so that we could not use them for an attack across the river.

In the night of December 25-26 the "Task Force Rudder", as the undertaking was later named, was withdrawn and the 90th Cavalry Reconnaissance Squadron was once again subordinated to the division's headquarters. On December 26 we were moved, along with the entire division, to Metz."

A Luxembourg "GI" in the Ranks of the 10th U.S. Armored Division

The number of Luxembourgeois who volunteered to join the American troops and fight against the Germans since the liberation of their country in September of 1944, after deserting from the RAD or the Wehrmacht, and often after months of concealment, is very small.

Although these "non-regular soldiers" were strictly banned by the American leadership on account of their non-military status and their nationality, there still remained a few of them in various units, usually unknown to the higher officers, who provided valuable assistance to the Americans, as happened all too often, because of their knowledge of the locality and the language.

One of these Luxembourgeois "GIs" was André Flesch, likewise a forced recruit of the Reich's Labor Service (RAD), who deserted during a front furlough.

After deserting, André Flesch made his way to the "Maquis Belge" and even to the "Chef de Camp" of a large group of members of the "Mouvement National Belge." Returning to his homeland immediately after the liberation of Luxembourg, André Flesch was contacted by the mayor of Pétange with the request to support the "Veiner Miliz", which had suffered one fatality and several wounded during a fight with a strong German patrol on November 19, 1944.

"Although many contacts between the 'Armée Blanche' and Luxembourgeois resistance groups existed," André Flesch tells, "I had never before had connections to the militia (partisan group) from Vianden.

I agreed and thus went to Vianden. One part of our group was quartered in the Hotel Heintz, the other was divided among the houses. Our uniforms looked very colorful, consisting for the most part of pieces of U.S. Army uniforms, Wehrmacht jackets, sometimes with spots of paint as camouflage, German "Knobelbecher" jack-boots, Boy Scout hats and such. Our armaments were just as varied, ranging from captured German machine guns to U.S. carbines and Italian or British submachine guns.

From Vianden we mainly undertook patrols to the Our, for German scouting parties went there almost regularly at night. Vianden had become no-man's-land in the late fall of 1944; very rarely, if at all, did one still see individual civilians on the streets. In the cellar of the Hotel Heintz there was an American telephone switchboard with a three-man crew. From here they were in direct communication with their regimental headquarters in Ettelbrück by radio and phone. At the end of November we came upon a German patrol, and in the ensuing firefight, in which the Germans tried to smoke us out with hand grenades, only one man of us was slightly injured. The Germans lost several men and withdrew. From then on, the castle, on which a machine-gun sentry of ours was posted, was regularly fired on from the bunkers behind the sanatorium. There had already been several such encounters with German soldiers, but we were always able to drive these patrols away. At the beginning of December a group of us brought in three Luxembourgers, who had been surprised by a German patrol and dragged off to Germany a short time before, near the Bivels mill.

They told excitedly of troop concentrations along the border, of concentrations of tanks and artillery guns (see report of Mme. Linden, Bivels, Vol.I: The Germans) Since we considered these observations to be correct, we took these people to the Americans, who had them tell their stories in greater detail.

During the night of December 15-16 I was not able to get any sleep. The sound of motors could be heard constantly, and then all was quiet. After a short time, similar noises could be heard. Something did not make sense here; all of us sensed it. Around 5:30 AM we knew for sure when the first shells howled over and struck beyond Vianden with ear-splitting explosions.

I had never yet experienced such a heavy fire; it was indescribable. After about an hour the heavy fire let up, but in its place we received alarming news. About 8:00 Germans were seen in the upper city by a double sentry of ours. Shots were also being fired by the Our already; obviously a fight with Americans was already in progress there. As quickly as we could, we left the Hotel Heintz and hurried to the farmhouse somewhat farther up. The owner, who returned to Vianden from time to time to look after his house, had offered us his farm as a hiding place. From the straw-covered floor, a ladder led to the roof, right at the slope to the road running from Vianden to Fouhren. The roof was almost at the same level as the road, so that we could reach it with no trouble.

We had received instructions to fight our way through in small groups, and to meet again at a previously selected gathering place in Ettelbrück. We were able to get past local firefights between the Americans and Germans, crawling on our bellies almost all the way and taking numerous detours, and reach Diekirch late in the afternoon of December 18. From Fouhren we had crawled across the fields to Bastendorf; from there we chose a path through thick underbrush across the Herrenberg to the upper city. Shells often exploded very close to us. As if through a miracle, we remained undetected and unharmed. In Diekirch itself an indescribable confusion prevailed. Many people hastened to pack up their most necessary possessions and tried to get to Ettelbrück. The area around the railroad station was on fire, and the road from Diekirch to Ettelbrück was still under sporadic German artillery fire. Other groups of ours had already arrived here, as the auxiliary policemen and militiamen posted on the roads out of town reported to us. As they told us, they had the job of preventing civil chaos and sending the people home again. This had been ordered by the Americans, as the approach route from Ettelbrück absolutely had to remain open.

The sentries, who recognized us by our "VEIANEN" insignia, let us through at once. Under steady German fire, we reached Ettelbrück toward evening; unlike Diekirch, it showed relatively little shell damage. Shortly after our arrival a column of American vehicles coming out of Diekirch drove past us. Several trucks were filled with wounded men, including Germans.

During the course of the night, all of us arrived at the agreed-on gathering place, the hospital, and we decided to make our way onward to the capital.

From Militiaman to GI

So we set out on our way. Flickering light behind us showed that several villages on the heights, including Bürden, were on fire. In addition, the water of the Alzette was high at this time of year. It had overflowed its banks and flooded everything around the bridge to Schieren. In a nearby store, the water reached the door. Numerous packages of food and tobacco were floating in the water, indicating that the flood water had already been inside the store. Three days later, German soldiers, hit by shell fragments, lay dead in the same location. Most of the people were already in flight, so that indescribable confusion also prevailed in Ettelbrück. Along with the stream of refugees, we passed by the 'Maison de Santé' (hospital for the mentally handicapped).

But then we waited for the morning light and moved on; the road was now almost empty. Schieren looked to be practically dead. The only person we met was a poor, mentally ill man. He was completely naked, and all his hair was cut off. He had wrapped a blanket around himself, and he said he wanted to go home to his mother. What could we do with this unfortunate man? He had surely fled from the asylum and had gotten lost during the hail of shells. We had to help him, or he would surely freeze to death.

While we were standing there talking it over, an American Jeep suddenly rushed up to us and stopped. With their weapon ready to fire, the soldiers forced us to throw our rifles and submachine guns away and put up our hands. After they had searched us and found no proper identification, they made us and the mentally ill man get into the Jeep and drove away with us. Our clothing, part of which came from American stocks, had surely angered them. And not one of us could communicate with them.

It was fortunate for us that the officer, a Lieutenant Colonel to whom they took us, spoke German, so that we could explain to him that we were active resistance fighters and were fleeing from the Germans to Luxembourg. After many questions, the colonel let us go and explained to us that he commanded a scouting unit of the 10th U.S. Armored Division. He also asked if we were willing to serve as scouts in his unit, but only for a limited time. I volunteered.

We were given back our weapons and got into the Jeep. Two of my comrades stayed in Schieren at the headquarters of the 90th Cavalry Reconnaissance Squadron, as the unit was called, while Pit "Pete" Hansen and I were driven to Stegen. Here we were quartered for the night in the last house in the village. Numerous U.S. soldiers were already in the same room and looked at us questioningly when we came in. There were about forty soldiers there, who constituted the military occupation of Stegen at that time. Several armored cars and Jeeps with machine guns on them were also standing ready.

On the next day we were finally given a hot meal by the Americans and got some rest. Around noon the commander of the occupying troops in Stegen appeared with a French-speaking interpreter. First Lieutenant Meisner briefly explained to us the planned operation, which was to be carried out the next morning. I spent the rest of the day with 'Frenchie', as I later nicknamed the interpreter, and asked for information about the unit. Aurel Lachance, as he was named, was of French ancestry and remained my best friend in the unit until the war ended. Our mission was to scout the area along the Sauer between Diekirch and Ingeldorf and report anything that happened.

Striking a German Convoy

Early in the morning of December 21 we set out. During the night it had snowed, and we stomped through deep new snow. Besides Lt. Meisner the group included another artillery liaison officer, two radiomen, 'Frenchie", Pit Hansen and I. After

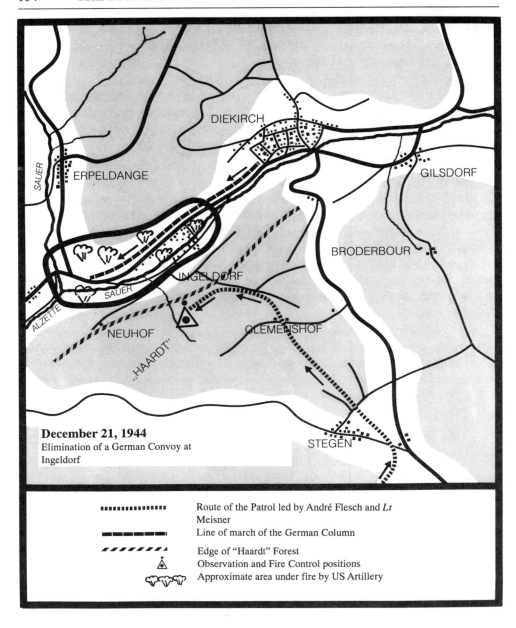

December 21, 1944
Elimination of a German Convoy at
Ingeldorf

▪▪▪▪▪▪▪▪▪▪▪▪▪▪	Route of the Patrol led by André Flesch and *Lt* Meisner
━━━━━━━	Line of march of the German Column
⁄⁄⁄⁄⁄⁄⁄▲	Edge of "Haardt" Forest
⚠	Observation and Fire Control positions
🌩🌩🌩	Approximate area under fire by US Artillery

about ninety minutes on difficult paths through rough country and underbrush, we reached the edge of the woods. So as not to leave any unnecessary tracks in the snow, we all marched in a row, one after the other. The first light of morning appeared. It was uncannily quiet. From our position, concealed by thick brush at the edge of the 'Haardt' woods, a narrow field path led down to the bridge to Ingeldorf. An extensive field of vision lay before us, reaching from the railroad station in Diekirch to the curve at the entrance to Ettelbrück. Only a small, gurgling brook off to the side broke the ghostly silence.

To our amazement, a swastika flag flew on the gable of the first house in Ettelbrück. So the Germans had already advanced that far. Probably it was only an advance group that was supposed to mark the foremost line for fighter planes that might come later. With our field glasses we examined the area part by part; from the road to the hilly terrain across from it, then from the highlands back to the road. It must have been around 10:00 when Lt. Meisner suddenly saw a number of cyclists coming from the direction of Diekirch. I too could now see that they were German soldiers. Somewhat later another group of cyclists followed them, along with horse-drawn wagons and fully loaded infantry carts, accompanied by motorcyclists.

At further intervals there followed infantrymen, trucks, guns that, along with their ammunition limbers, were pulled by horses, several prime movers and three or four turretless tanks. Additional infantrymen marched at the end of the column.

Spread out over some distance, this convoy approached the first houses in Ingeldorf. The advance unit immediately spread out in the village. Then everything happened lightning-fast. The officer accompanying us radioed some firing data to an artillery battery (near Grentzingen, Walsdorf and Colmar-Berg), and moments later we heard the soft whistling of the first shells over us, followed by the dull rumbling of the explosions. The first salvo went too far, and the shells exploded over the railroad tracks.

In no time the Germans had scattered in all directions. After two more salvos had fallen short, the fourth salvo was right on target. The shells caused frightful destruction in the column, which was not able to leave the road in time to seek cover. Horses reared up and were hit by shell fragments, cries were heard, men's bodies were flung around by the air pressure and shock wave of the exploding shells. Numerous vehicles caught fire. The Germans had quickly left the road and tried to save themselves in the houses of Ingeldorf. The guns and tanks disappeared from our field of vision. The Germans blindly returned fire in what they suspected was the right direction. Our fire continued about two hours; the artillery officer continued to give firing adjustments, until anti-aircraft shells suddenly began to explode in the treetops above us. So the Germans had spotted us and fired 2 cm shells at the edge of the woods. We drew back and returned to Stegen around 2:00 PM. From there we went right on to Schieren by Jeep to report to Lt. Col. Licherie. While I waited in front of the command post, an excited young man came up to me and inquired about Ingeldorf. He told me that his sick, elderly father had stayed at home there, and insisted on evacuating the man from the danger zone.

Although the place was still full of Germans, I agreed and volunteered. During the same night we again reached the edge of the woods via Stegen. I had left my Beretta submachine gun behind and carried only a German pistol. The village itself was full of Germans. But they were still frightened by our effective firefall; they kept quiet and treated their wounded.

We were able to get the old man out of the house and persuade him to come with us. We waded through a shallow place (the water still came up to our chests) in the icy Sauer and reached the other shore unseen.

On the next day (December 22) I took part in a reconnaissance mission in an armored car that first took us to the 'Maison de Santé'. Several mentally ill patients were still there. Since the waterpipes had been damaged by gunfire, the poor people tried to quench their thirst with pieces of ice and snow. Before we went on, we made some hot coffee for them on our burner. Down by the blown-up bridge there were several dead Germans in the water. Some of them no longer had shoes on their feet. They had probably tried to get new shoes out of the shoe store and had been scared away and shot down by sudden American artillery fire. (See Vol.I: The Germans).

Then we drove through the cemetery to just behind the railroad station in Ettelbrück. There were a lot of Germans there. An officer thought they were scouts who had been assigned to check the condition of the railroad station, which might be of use to them. Then we drove back and tried to go in a northwesterly direction. Very close to the burning agricultural high school building we took two prisoners who, as it turned out, belonged to an advance unit.

When we had returned to Schieren, the U.S. artillery again fired on the entry to Ettelbrück, so as to delay the advancing units.

In Cruchten I received not only my first turkey dinner but also a new uniform with the 10th Armored Division's insignia sewed on. During the same night we packed up hastily, for our unit was to be transferred. I was ordered to the colonel, who informed me that I could still stay for a short time, but then we Luxembourgers would have to leave the unit, since we were not regular soldiers.

The division was moved back to Metz. Side by side with 'Frenchie', I continued to fight in the ranks of the 90th Cavalry Reconnaissance Squadron and remained in the unit until the war ended."

CHAPTER XI

THE GERMAN FRONT ON THE SAUER COLLAPSES

While the 5th U.S. Infantry Division with two of its regiments (2nd and 11th) on the attack, was still able to achieve military success on the Siegfried Line around Saarlautern, the situation in the Ardennes was gradually becoming more and more threatening for the surprised Allied fighting forces.

Intervention of the 5th Infantry Division "Red Diamond": Historical Outline
As quickly as possible, General Omar Bradley, Commander of the 12th Army Group, ordered the 3rd Army of Patton, which was subordinate to him, to attack from the south in order to relieve the threatened units. Patton immediately pulled the 4th Armored Division out of the Saargemünd sector, as well as the 26th Infantry Division that was recuperating in Metz, and attacked in a joint maneuver with parts of the 80th Infantry Division. The main purpose of this movement was to hurry at once to relieve the enclosed 101st Airborne Division in Bastogne.

In order to relieve the hard-pressed and hard-hit 4th Infantry Division on the lower Sauer, and to protect Luxembourg City, the vital site of numerous Allied headquarters, General Patton called on Major General Stafford Leroy Irwin's "Red Diamond" Division (5th Infantry Division).

Thanks to unbelievable speed in their own internal troop movements, outstanding leadership and, above all, the courage, tenacity and bravery of the soldiers, the 5th Infantry Division found masterful ways to fulfill the tasks it was given.

The first unit that hurried to help the 4th Infantry Division, was the 10th Regimental Combat Team, consisting of infantry (of its own 10th Infantry Regiment) and artillery units of the division transferred from the region west of the Saar. All of the infantry troop units were fully motorized and therefore capable of moving quickly. Around 5:00 PM on December 20, 1944 the first troop transports arrived in Luxembourg, and they reached their assigned positions even before midnight.

Even before the last units had been withdrawn from the Saar district, the head of the column was already on the road out of Metzervisse, which was softened by rain and snow. Their visibility was so limited by the driving snow that the transport column had to drive with all lights on despite orders to the contrary.

The 2nd Regiment had just reached Metzervisse when an order insisted that they push on farther at once and stop only in Niederanven. In fewer than 22 hours, under constant artillery fire near Saarlautern and Ittersdorf, the Regiment reached the new assembly point around 4:00 PM on December 22 and awaited further orders.

Just 48 hours after their departure, the 10th Regimental Combat Team, which was subordinated to the 4th Infantry Division, attacked.

Originally, the 10th Infantry Regiment (5th Infantry Division) was supposed to relieve units of the 80th Infantry Division, but this plan was given up. Two battalions of tank destroyers were added, and this unit was then supposed to go on the offensive immediately on December 22.

On the night of December 21-22, Colonel Robert Bell (Commander of the 10th Infantry Regiment) took part in a staff discussion at the command post of the 4th Infantry Division, in which the attack plan was changed. According to the new orders, the 10th Infantry Regiment was to attack objectives south of Echternach, pass the "critical" defense line of the hard-pressed units of the 4th Infantry Division, and push forward in an easterly direction from Scheidgen.The planned time of the attack was set at 12:00 noon (December 22). Among other things, a company of the 4th Infantry Division, which had been cut off completely from their regiment by the enemy, was supposed to be liberated near Michelshof.

Counterattacks by the enemy were thrown back by precise artillery fire. In the process, the Germans suffered remarkably heavy losses. On December 23, the 11th Regiment, which had arrived at Imbringen-Eisenborn-Bourglinster on December 21, received the order to drive out the enemy north and east of the Sauer and shatter the established enemy bridgeheads. During the same night, the German Luftwaffe flew a mission over the Sauer front in which bombs were dropped. An alarming report that later turned out to be false urged the units on the Sauer front to be must watchful. It was said that German paratroops had landed there.

Observation posts of the 11th Regiment only encountered a five-men enemy patrol, which was driven away by infantry-weapon fire, near Schoos.

Around 11:00 AM on December 24, the 11th Regiment, accompanied by tank units detailed to it, left the "jump off" line that ran south of Freckeisen to Christnach. On its right flank was the 2nd Infantry Regiment, while the Savelborn-Eppeldorf line was still held by units of the already mentioned 9th Armored Division.

After heavy artillery preparation, the 3rd Battalion (of the 11th Infantry Regiment) attacked with Companies K, L and I and occupied the region around Haller. The Germans who had lost their lives to the artillery fire there belonged for the most part to the 988th Regiment of the 276th VGD. The attack was continued on Christmas Day and began with a TOT (Time on Target: every available gun in the division fired at the same area target at the same time) of the division's artillery and shattered a beginning German counterattack around 6:30 AM. Thereupon the artillery fire turned to the German troops in the villages of Waldbillig and Haller, with a withering effect.

As far as it was possible, the companies received their rations of turkey dinner. But the war went on ceaselessly.

On Christmas night the battalions of the division's artillery, for the first time, fired shells with the new proximity- or pozit-fuze, At the beginning of January the first and third battalions of the 11th Regiment were in defensive positions along the south shore of the Sauer. Reisdorf had been designated as the regimental boundary, but the village itself was in the territory of the 10th Infantry Regiment.

Now and then German artillery and Nebelwerfer fire strayed into the Bigelbach-

Beaufort-Haller triangle. Searches of the houses in this sector often turned up numbers of German soldiers who had hidden there to surrender.

All along the division's line, barricades and minefields were set up at strategically important intersections and approach routes. The unit staffs worked feverishly on planes to carry out a broad spectrum of patrol activity on the north shore of the Sauer. The purpose of this mission was the determine the strength of enemy troop assemblages, but even more so to bring in prisoners for questioning about the situation.

Almost every night, German reconnaissance aircraft flew over the positions of the 11th Regiment. Haller and Christnach were fired on several times a day in a surprise attack by numerous aircraft.

The first patrol, consisting of seven men from I Company, crossed the Sauer in a rubber boat around 10:30 PM on January 5. The country was covered with deep snow, and the men wore homemade camouflage outfits made of civilian bedsheets. At that time the Sauer was approximately fifty meters wide and slightly frozen in places. The patrol reached the north shore without being seen and searched the terrain in a northeasterly direction. No contact with German troops resulted, but it was learned that the shore was heavily mined in numerous places.

A similar undertaking, which was to be carried out on the following night, was postponed because of too-bright moonlight. During this period the 10th Infantry Regiment of Colonel Robert Bell was taken over the responsibility for the Reisdorf-Gilsdorf area. Through regular replacement and exchange of troop units, two battalions remained permanently on the Sauer front, while a third was quartered in Medernach in a mobile reserve position. Numerous observation posts were established, and defensive positions whose task it was to watch the three bridges (at Gilsdorf, Bettendorf and Moestroff, all blown up) were strengthened. The headquarters of the 10th Infantry Regiment were located at that time in the present-day "Fondation Arend-Fixmer" in Medernach. On account of the excellent visibility from the highlands, busy enemy activity could be observed in Fouhren, Walsdorf, on the Tandel-Bastendorf road as well as in the upper part of Bettendorf. Numerous small reconnaissance parties from the individual companies crossed the Sauer every night, but the information they brought in was unsatisfactory.

Hussar Tactics in Bettendorf

The Allied strategy had planned on keeping constant pressure on the south flank of the attacking German divisions and therefore required prompt, precise and detailed information on the enemy's position and strength even at this point in time for the defensive action on the Sauer front.

On January 9 the commander of L Company of the 10th Infantry Regiment received an order to assemble a battle group consisting of a reinforced "rifle platoon" to destroy known enemy positions in Bettendorf and bring in prisoners. This undertaking, which was to be carried out for the most part by soldiers of the 1st Platoon of L Company, was put under the command of Lieutenant William Longpre. For this dangerous mission, the 67th Photo-Interpretation Team of the division made up a map of the village. Indications of enemy positions and quarters were entered on the basis of aerial photographs as well as numerous observations that had been evaluated by the S-2 (Intelligence) section of the regiment. Using this map, the battle group in their white camouflage suits silently reached the bank of the Sauer around 2:00 AM on January 10. The men carried six rubber boats camouflaged with bedsheets but used only one of them to cross the river.

The shore was quite frozen, and this caused some difficulties to ferry six men across each time, including Sergeant Rogers, who carried the heavy radio set. After the group had assembled on the "German shore" without attracting any attention, the men silently reached the upper part of town from a westerly direction. Sergeant Stegmann cut numerous telephone cables that ran along the village street. Then the platoon divided up among the blocks of houses.

A German sentry noticed the patrol as it slipped past and opened fire. A submachine gun burst knocked the German out of the fight, and several hand grenades were thrown into the inside of the house. Numerous Germans came rushing outside and surrendered. A machine gun rattled from the second floor but was silenced by a rifle grenade.

After the patrol had quickly made sure that there was no one left alive in the house, the group advanced to the main street and cleaned out another quarter. Here too, prisoners were taken. One other prisoner was taken by Sergeant Testino after a short exchange of fire from a position at the edge of town. Then the patrol disappeared quickly across the blown-up bridge, along with the prisoners. The group had been in Bettendorf approximately 90 minutes. At a signal, the division's artillery fired a TOT (Time on Target) hail of shells at the surprised troops occupying Bettendorf. One of the German prisoners, a non-commissioned officer, carried a messenger's pouch with several important documents, including a complaint from the regimental commander of GR 915 (Major Hoffmeister) about the insufficient security measures of the forces occupying Bettendorf. There was also an order from the regimental commander to mine the shore of the Sauer without delay. Obviously he had suspected something, but too late (See Vol.I: The Germans).

Further information about the fortified positions around Bettendorf was gained from questioning other prisoners taken on this "raid." The focal points of the German defense, as it turned out, were in fact Bettendorf and the "Rue Clairefontaine", the approach road from Bleesbrück to Diekirch. With the exception of the sporadic, meager German artillery fire, no enemy operations were to be expected in the immediate future.

This spectacular undertaking was followed by further night patrols, and on the night of January 15, 1945 the 2nd Battalion of the 10th Infantry Regiment extended its defensive line to the left, in order to take over the range of hills behind Gilsdorf along with units of the neighboring regiment (the 2nd Infantry Regiment). Thus the fortification of the two regiments on the Sauer front was guaranteed. At the same time, a part of the 8th Regiment of the 4th Infantry Division took over the Bettendorf-Moestroff sector of land on the south bank of the Sauer, in place of the 3rd Battalion of the 10th Regiment.

The 46th Field Artillery Battalion maintained its gun positions in the vicinity of Ermsdorf until January 16, when a new position near Folkendange was taken up, in order to support the infantry units of the "Red Diamond" in an attack across the Sauer between Bettendorf and Ingeldorf. Until the division attacked, the front re-

Lt. Col. Kenneth W. Collins, Commander of the 60th Armored Infantry Battalion, 9th US Armored Division. The photo shows him as a major general shortly before his retirement. Photo: Roland Gaul archives

Center: Lt. Col. George Ruhlen, Commander, 3rd Field Artillery Battalion, 9th Armored Division. Photo: Frank Rockenbrod collection

M7 "Self Propelled 105 mm" (Priest) armored howitzer of the 3rd FA Battalion, 9th US Armored Division, armed with one 105 mm howitzer and one .50 caliber machine gun on ring mount. Photo: Roland Gaul archives

M7 in camouflaged position near Kalkesbach (Berdorf). Photo: Fred Karen archives

Three pictures of a gun position of the 3rd FA Battalion at the Osterholz farm (Consdorf), late October 1944. Photo: Fred Karen archives

The handy M-24 "Chaffee" tank, armed with a 75 mm tank gun, a .50 machine gun, and two .30 machine guns. Crew: four men. Photo: US Army

Halftrack command car of the CCA, 10th Armored Division, at Berg (Colmar-Berg), December 1944. From left to right: Brigadier General Althouse, Commander, CCA, Lt. Col. J. R. Righley, Commander, 21st Tank Battalion, Lt. Col. James O'Hara, 54th Armored Infantry Battalion/Team O'Hara. Photo: General George Ruhlen archives

André Flesch, Luxembourg GI in the uniform of the 10th Armored Division. Photo: André Flesch collection

Left: 1st Lt. George T. Meisner, Troop A, 90th Cavalry Reconnaissance Squadron, André Flesch's chief; right: André Flesch, who remained with the 10th Armored Division until the war ended. Photo: André Flesch

A Jeep of Troop A, 90th Cavalry Reconnaissance Squadron, with a .30 Browning machine gun. Driver: Aurel Lachance, known as "Frenchie". Passenger: André Flesch. Photo: André Flesch

Through heavy snow in the night, units of the 3rd Army, including the 5th US Infantry Division, reached Luxembourg from the Saar in the afternoon of December 20, 1944. Photo: IWM, London

Units of the 2nd Infantry Regiment reach their readiness area on the Sauer. The vehicles belong to the 3rd Battalion, as can be seen from the bumper lettering of the second Jeep.

Men of the 1st Battalion (probably C Company), 11th US Infantry Regiment, take up positions near Gralingen on January 22, 1945.

105 mm gun of the 50th Field Artillery Battalion, 5th US Infantry Division. The battalion supported the attack of the 2nd Infantry Regiment after the Sauer was crossed. The soldiers had explosive ammunition ready: cases with appropriate propelling charges and explosive shells with screwed-on fuzes were assembled only immediately before firing. Photo: US Army

Empty steel cases for the much feared, very effective German 8.8 cm PAK 43 gun near "Friedhaff", Diekirch. All photos by Jean Crombach, spring 1945.

An abandoned American bazooka, found in the "Seitert", Diekirch.

Hundreds of 105 mm brass cases in the "Haardt", probably fired by the 50th Field Artillery Battalion, which supported the attack of the 2nd Infantry Regiment when it crossed the Sauer on January 18, 1945.

A German soldier's grave, inscribed: "Fallen Jan. 3, 1945." Thus the soldier probably died in a US artillery attack in the first days of 1945.

A well-camouflaged and covered observation post for a German advanced observer at the edge of the "Seitert."

A German machine-gun bunker, covered with several layers of logs, in the "Seitert." Left of it is a "Deiwelchen" stove, taken from Diekirch.

Colonel Worrell A. Roffe, Commander, 2nd US Infantry Regiment, 5th US Infantry Division.

Lt. Col. William Blakefield, Comnander, 1st Battalion, 2nd Infantry Regiment. His unit crossed the Sauer at Ingeldorf, took the village and liberated Erpeldange before advancing farther to the north toward "Friedhaff" and "Koeppenhaff".

Lt. Col. William Blakefield, Commander, 1st Battalion, 2nd Infantry Regiment (1944 photo). Photo: Roland Gaul archives.

After Diekirch is recaptured, four men of the 2nd US Infantry Regiment are trying on civilian nightshirt as snow camouflage. The photo was taken in front of the 'Suttor' house on 'Alexis Heck' Street. Photo: US Army

Lt. Col. Robert Connor, Commander, 3rd Battalion, 2nd Infantry Regiment, which finally liberated Diekirch on January 19, 1945. Photo: Roland Gaul archives

Diekirch, January 19, 1945. Two men of the 3rd Battalion search an abandoned German vehicle. The former Hôtel de l'Europe can barely be seen in the background. Photo: US Army

Captain Harry J. Gray of B Battery, 50th FA Battalion, forward artillery observer and artillery liaison officer to the 2nd Infantry Regiment. Thanks to his observations, most of the German positions in Diekirch were successfully destroyed before January 18, 1945. Harry Gray, who has had a prominent career in the technology industry since the war, is now the greatest patron of the Diekirch National Military History Museum. Photo (taken July 1944): Roland Gaul archives.

January 19, 1945: A unit of the 2nd Infantry Regiment moving along the slope of the "Haardt" on its way to the Sauer.
Photo: US Army

A U.S. observer in a snow suit provided by the British Army. Photo: IWM, London

A unit of weary GIs of the 2nd Infantry Regiment are relieved at the "Friedhaff" on January 21 and return to rest at Diekirch. Photo taken in the "Bamerdall" not far from "Drei Braken." Photo: US Army

North of Diekirch, men of the 5th US Infantry Division have chosen a forest hut as their place of residence. The man on the left carries a captured German P-38 pistol in a "remodeled" Wehrmacht holster as his personal side weapon. Photo: US Army

During a front-line inspection at the end of January, the Commander of the XIIth Corps, General Manton Eddy, gives some K-rations to an elderly lady (Catherine Back) in Ingeldorf. Photo: US Army

Every US soldier's dream: These visibly satisfied GIs of the 2nd Infantry Regiment, awaiting transport at the end of January, wave their newly issued furlough forms. Photo: US Army

Pvt. Bowell with non-uniform headgear and two "Luxembourg girls" from Bourglinster. A village boy sits beside them, obviously bored. Photo: Fred Groh archives

After the liberation of Diekirch, a member of the 2nd Infantry Regiment burns maps of the Metz-St. Avold area, where the division had fought in October and November of 1944, in the yard of a farm (Diekirch, probably "Kreuzstrasse"). Photo: US Army

From left to right: Lt. Col. William Breckinridge, Regimental Executive Officer, Colonel Robert Bell, Commander, 10th US Infantry Regiment, Major Marsch, Regimental S-2 (Intelligence) Officer. Photo: Roland Gaul archives

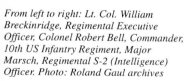

Private Charles Preston of the 5th US Infantry Division removes the snow from his water-cooled Browning 1917 A1 machine gun. Its cooling mantle was filled with anti-freeze liquid. Photo: US Army

mained fairly quiet, and with the exception of the "raid on Bettendorf", no infantry combat took place. On January 13, U.S. heavy bomber units flew over the lines of the 5th Infantry Division on their way back from Germany.

Attacking and Crossing the Sauer

According to the order from the corps, the 5th Infantry Division was supposed to cross the Sauer between Ettelbrück und Bettendorf as a surprise move, without artillery support at first, and push forward to Hoscheid-Dickt. This movement was supposed to drive a wedge 15 kilometers deep into the German front for the purpose of breaking the enemy's southern defensive line. The division planned to carry out this attack with two regiments, these being the 2nd Infantry Regiment on the left and the 10th Infantry Regiment on the right wing of the division's line. The division's 11th Regiment was to be available as a mobile reserve, able to be sent to help units under pressure at any time. After the shore of the Sauer had been scouted carefully for crossing points, the hour of the attack was set for 3:00 AM on January 18.

A close look at the regimental journal in its compiled form provides specific details of the course of the attack. The combat actions of each regiment are presented separately in chronological order, so as to provide a better overview.

The 2nd Infantry Regiment

On January 16, 1945 the headquarters of the 2nd Infantry Regiment were located at a farm near Schrondweiler, and the C Company of the 91st Chemical Mortar Battalion (an independent unit of Patton's 3rd Army, with 4.2 inch mortars) was assigned to the regiment for support. The division's 3rd Battalion replaced the 2nd battalion on the front line; the latter was pulled back to Stegen in the evening. Several patrols, which had the task of drawing German fire along the Sauer to themselves so as to betray enemy positions, were undertaken. The scouting troops who were sent out encountered considerable difficulties in this undertaking; the Sauer had meanwhile frozen over, but they were able to reach the north shore. Heavy machine-gun fire struck them in the Diekirch-Ingeldorf area, and although no German prisoners were brought back, they were successful nevertheless in providing some vital information for the planned river crossing. For example, it became known that in numerous places the bushes along the Sauer shore had trip flares in them. During the same night, the staff's preparations for the attack moved toward their conclusion.

January 17, 1945

In the morning, the 1st and 2nd Battalions (of the 2nd Infantry Regiment) took up their "jump-off" positions before Diekirch and Ingeldorf. The 3rd Battalion remained in an intermediate position, ready to provide fire cover for the first wave of the attack if necessary. After that it was to follow without delay. Silently the first companies reached the Sauer shore via the slopes of the "Hardt" (on the night of January 17-18).

In the area of the 1st Battalion, engineers of the division's own 7th Engineer Battalion were supposed to erect footbridges, when heavy German defensive fire suddenly broke the silence of the night. Company K (3rd Battalion), which immediately advanced to provide support, was not able to reach the planned crossing point. But soon the German machine-gun positions had been overrun by engineer units which had crossed the river in boats, and the 1st Battalion crossed over. Company C (1st Battalion) was thereupon ordered to push forward to Erpeldingen. Precise German artillery fire began too late. Artificial fog screens obscured visibility, and the snow suits, some of them homemade, proved to be excellent.

January 18, 1945

Under German artillery fire, the 2nd Battalion crossed the Sauer early in the morning of January 18 and immediately marched toward Objective 2 (Diekirch). The 1st Battalion had meanwhile reached Ingeldorf when its C Company reported heavy German artillery fire shortly before Erpeldange. Numerous bunker positions on the Sauer near Ingeldorf were destroyed. The following 3rd Battalion had likewise finished crossing the river by now and set out to take Diekirch in a pincer attack (from "Floss" and "Goldknapp"). By early afternoon, 158 prisoners had already been brought back. Heavy Nebelwerfer fire landed on what the Germans suspected were the crossing points. The approach routes to Diekirch from the Sauer were partially impassable because of numerous mines and had to be circumvented. In Ingeldorf several houses had to be blown up by engineers with heavy charges of TNT before the Germans surrendered. All the prisoners in this sector were members of the 914th Regiment (352nd VGD). The crossing had been achieved, but at a price. One officer and 16 men were dead, six officers and 81 men wounded, 30 men missing.

January 19, 1945

The regiment's headquarters had meanwhile been moved to Schieren. Company A was in a vigorous exchange of fire in the "Friedbesch" on the "Erpeldinger Koeppchen." Company C tried to take the road to Diekirch (Goldknapp) from Erpeldange.

In the lower town and railroad station district of Diekirch, street fighting was going on, and numerous fortified enemy machine-gun positions in the houses were being smoked out by the Americans. (See Vol.I: The Germans) Around noon the 3rd Battalion had cleaned out the greater part of Diekirch and reported that the city was heavily mined. An advance guard of the 2nd Battalion reported very strong resistance at "Friedhaff." After the 3rd Battalion had cleaned out Diekirch, it was immediately ordered back to Ingeldorf as a reserve unit, but was also partially detailed to the 1st Battalion.

Around 3:00 PM the 1st and 2nd Battalions directed a combined attack on Objective 12 (Kippenhof). Several prisoners from this sector were members of the 79th VGD, which had been partially transferred into the Brandenbourg sector. The commander of one battalion of the same VGD was likewise taken prisoner. Heavy artillery shells and Nebelwerfer rockets fell singly at the spearhead of the attack.

January 20, 1945

The 1st Battalion was the first to push forward in the direction of Kippenhof and immediately encountered a locally limited counterattack. In addition, there were numerous fortified positions in the forest here, which made any advance impossible. Large-caliber German artillery fire caused the battalion heavy losses. The 2nd Battalion was still trying to make connections. After hard fighting and numerous troop movements, it was still able to fight its way out of the belt around Kippenhof. The 3rd Battalion immediately relieved various hard-hit units and was given the task of cleaning nests of resistance, which had been circumvented, out of the forest.

The 2nd Battalion was called back to Diekirch again and formed the regiment's reserve from then on. After the hard fighting in the forest, the enemy left a remarkable quantity of materials behind, including captured American weapons and equipment. The German prisoners and wounded were members of the 352nd and 79th VGD. They said that ammunition and fuel could not be delivered to them.

January 21, 1945

The 1st Battalion immediately pushed forward in the direction of Objective 16 (Fléibour). Only around 1:00 PM, after costly forest combat, was the battalion able to overcome the German nests of opposition. In the course of the afternoon, Lipperscheid was liberated. From then on, units of the 11th Regiment took over the further attack on Lipperscheid-Delt and Hoscheid, and the exhausted 1st Battalion was brought back to Ettelbrück. The 3rd Battalion solidified their own lines during the night and was replaced on the right wing of the regiment's boundary by other units of the 11th Regiment. Then it too was brought back to Ettelbrück to regroup. The 2nd Battalion, located in Diekirch, was detailed to the 4th Infantry Division for the time being and given the task of fortifying and guarding all the Sauer crossings that had been gained. Later in the month of January, the 1st and 2nd Battalions alternatively were subordinated to the 10th Regiment and took part in its battles. At the end of January, the regimental headquarters were located in Brandenbourg. There follow several memos from the S-4 Section (material and suppy units), taken from the regiment's daybook between January 1 and 30, 1945, which refer to the consumption of foods and pieces of equipment used in winter combat.

Rations of food were taken from the division's stock on a daily basis. The cold rations distributed were mainly of types C and K. Only 1/3 of D rations (chocolate) could be distributed. Additional rations included instant coffee, powdered milk and sugar.

New pieces of equipment and clothing were ordered on a weekly basis. There was a heavy demand for winter clothing, overshoes, gloves, sleeping bags and sweaters. Woolen blankets and rubber boots could be delivered as alternatives.

Ammunition was distributed every day, since enough was on hand. There was, though, a shortage of spare parts for defective weapons.

515 U.S. rifles, six grenade launchers, eight machine guns, and numerous pieces of American equipment and radio sets were recaptured. (Note: Source: Divisional and regimental journals).

The 2nd US Infantry Regiment
(Brief Report based on notes by the late Major General William Blakefield, former Commander of the 1st Battalion, 2nd U.S. Infantry Regiment (as Lieutenant Colonel)

On December 28, 1944 the units of the 2nd U.S. Infantry Regiment, after bitter fighting against the attacking 276th VGD in the "Müllertal", were relieved by the 1st and 3rd Battalions of the 12th Regiment of the 4th U.S. Infantry Division "Ivy Leaves." After the planned position change was completed the 2nd Infantry Regiment fortified its positions in the vicinity of Stegen and south of Diekirch along the Sauer, where it in turn relieved the 44th AI Battalion of the 6th U.S. Armored Division. All troop movements were already completed by 2:00 AM on the night of December 29. According to orders from Colonel Worrell A. Roffe (the regimental commander). the 2nd Battalion was responsible for guarding the MLR (Main Line of Resistance), while the two remaining battalions (1st and 3rd) remained in alarm readiness in Schoos and Stegen respectively. Observation posts of the 2nd Battal-

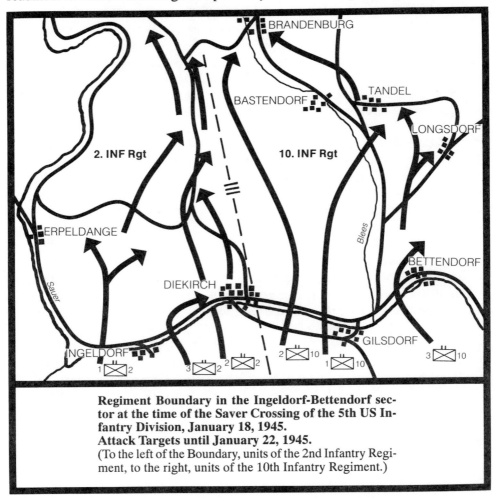

Regiment Boundary in the Ingeldorf-Bettendorf sector at the time of the Saver Crossing of the 5th US Infantry Division, January 18, 1945.
Attack Targets until January 22, 1945.
(To the left of the Boundary, units of the 2nd Infantry Regiment, to the right, units of the 10th Infantry Regiment.)

ion, commanded by Lt. Col. Ball, on the Sauer line reported brisk enemy activity in Diekirch and on the road to Vianden. The German Luftwaffe often appeared in the sky with individual fighter planes, but without attacking the U.S. lines.

On New Year's Day the 2nd Battalion was relieved on the Sauer line by the 1st Battalion (Lt. Col. Blakefield); the former was designated the corps' reserve. During the first days of the new year, the enemy activities did not increase; the German artillery fire continued to be sporadic. Thus two very cold weeks passed on the frozen front line along the Sauer. Patrols and anti-patrol fighting on a small scale, as well as insignificant, locally limited artillery duels, were conducted by both sides, while the staff of the 2nd Infantry Regiment, on orders from the division, worked feverishly on a plan of attack in the prescribed sector (Diekirch-Ingeldorf). The date of attack ("D-Day") was set by the corps as January 18; the time ("H-Hour") was set at 3:00 AM.

"Sauer River Crossing"

The winter of 1944-45 was particularly rough. Thirty centimeters of frozen snow covered the sector in which the regiment was supposed to attack. A temperature of about 18 degrees below zero was recorded when the attacking units were directed into their readiness areas on the night of January 17-18. The main crossing point on the Sauer for Colonel Roffe's regiment was located southeast of Ingeldorf. As opposed to many assertions that the attack in the Sauer Valley was a successful surprise maneuver (which is right up to a point), General Blakefield noted that every man of the 2nd Infantry Regiment who survived the combat to the end of January asserts the opposite.

On January 16, 1945 the headquarters of that battle-tested regiment had already been moved to a farm in Schrondweiler. On instructions from the division, the regiment was reinforced by a higher authority (XIIth Corps) by the C Company of the 91st chemical Mortar Battalion, which was directly subordinated to Patton's 3rd Army. Shortly before the attack began, Lt. Col. Connor's 3rd Battalion had replaced the 2nd Battalion on the front line in the highlands to the south of the Sauer. Lt. Col. Ball's 2nd Battalion, which had taken over the sector in the last few days before the beginning of the attack, came back to Stegen as the corps' reserve. Numerous patrols, which had the specific mission of drawing fire from infantry weapons on the enemy's side of the Sauer, were sent out by the 3rd Battalion.

These reconnaissance parties, consisting for the most part of only three to five men, had some serious difficulties in crossing the icy Sauer in a rubber boat, but along with small groups of engineers they were able to reach the north shore. Many times, despite excellent camouflage and poor visibility because of heavy fog, fire from automatic weapons came at them, and although they were not able to bring in any German prisoners, the patrols acquired important information about the condition of the enemy's shore of the river (water depth, current, ice cover, minefields, etc.).

In addition, it became known that in numerous places the brush on their own side of the river was loaded with flare and anti-personnel mines, which had probably been placed there by the Germans by the end of December. After two engineers had lost their lives on the slopes of the "Haardt" between Diekirch and the

Sauer when a mine had exploded a few days before, special search troops of the engineers worked night after night under cover of darkness to locate explosives hidden under the frozen snow. In this way, numerous "booby traps" in the orchards on the slope down to the Sauer, which had been camouflaged with fallen fruit by German engineers, could be rendered harmless. In the early morning hours of January 17, 1945 the regimental staff's preparations, being made at Colonel Roffe's headquarters in Schrondweiler, were being finalized.

Late in the afternoon of the same day, as night began to fall, the 1st Battalion (Lt. Col. William Blakefield) and the 2nd Battalion (Lt. Col. Ball), brought up from Stegen to take part in the attack, took up their positions of departure before Ingeldorf and Diekirch respectively.

Lt. Col. Connor's 3rd Battalion itself was waiting in an intermediate position, ready to provide infantry fire support if it was needed. All the men had made their own white camouflage shirts out of civilian bedsheets, since not enough snow suits could be distributed; even the wooden assault boats and the individual weapons were covered with white cloths.

To provide artillery support in this sector, not only the already mentioned 91st Chemical Mortar Battalion but also the 50th Field Artillery Battalion (with 105 mm howitzers) was on hand. One of the latter's communications and forward observer officers, Captain Harry Gray, had already successfully directed fire several times on German positions in the inner city of Diekirch, discovered thanks to the smoke of an incautiously lit fire.

Silently, the first companies left the protection of the "Haardt" at 3:00 AM on January 18 and, via the snow-covered slopes, reached the icy shore of the Sauer, where several engineer platoons waited with assault boats for the first wave of the attack.

In the area of Lt. Col. Blakefield's 1st Battalion, the advanced engineer unit was supposed to set up a bridgehead west of Ingeldorf, but suddenly it received heavy machine-gun fire from the enemy side of the river. Company K of the 3rd Battalion immediately was given the order to fire on the German shore while engineers and infantrymen feverishly worked to launch the first assault boats into the water at the predetermined sites. Here the first losses were suffered! Several boats took direct hits from well-aimed German mortar fire and sank at once; the crews, insofar as they were not killed instantly by shrapnel, drowned in the icy waters and were carried downstream.

Wounded men were quickly rescued by medics under unimaginable difficulties while the battle went on, and evacuated on improvised sleds up the steep slope to the "Haardt" and on to Stegen. Soon the German machine-gun positions along the Sauer were pinned down by the heavy fire of the platoons which had crossed the river and were now attacking, and the other men of the 1st Platoon crossed the Sauer in the early morning hours. Lt. Col. Blakefield ordered his C Company to push forward to Erpeldingen without delay, while the 7th Engineer Battalion began to build a pontoon bridge in the same sector. German Nebelwerfer and artillery fire began too late to shatter the American attack, which was now proceeding smoothly. Additionally aided by the smoke screen laid by the 91st Chemical Mortar Battalion, the further course of the operations proceeded, while the 105 mm guns of the

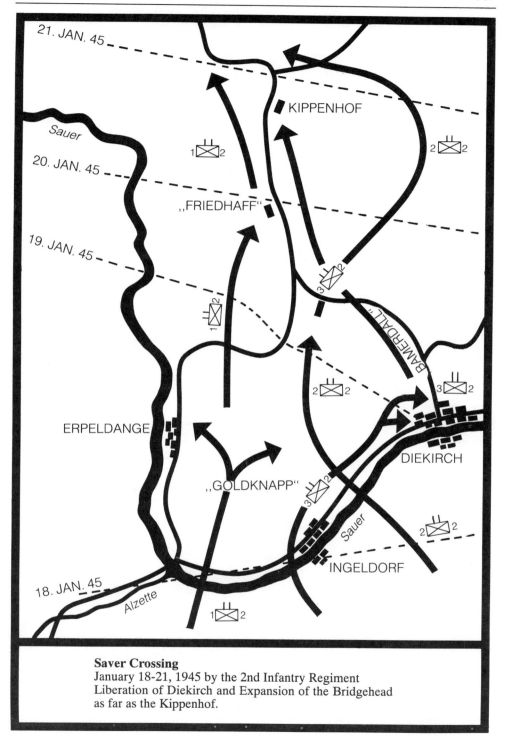

Saver Crossing
January 18-21, 1945 by the 2nd Infantry Regiment
Liberation of Diekirch and Expansion of the Bridgehead
as far as the Kippenhof.

50th Field Artillery Battalion covered the enemy's high ground with explosive-shell fire.

On the morning of January 18, the situation was as follows: Under sporadic German artillery and mortar fire, which fell on the Sauer Valley from the Herrenberg and Kippenhof, Lt. Col. Ball's 2nd Battalion crossed the river after two attempts to erect and assault bridge had been unsuccessful. Finally a third attempt, in collaboration with the engineers, was successful; the 2nd Battalion crossed over and immediately marched on the northwestern heights beyond Diekirch.

Although the enemy shore was now held by American troops, the enemy fought bitterly and tenaciously from well-camouflaged positions that were located farther back in the gently sloping terrain. It took some time before a correct report of the targets could result in successful attacks.

During the river crossing, Private Charles H. Schroder, a BAR gunner, was wounded but declined to be evacuated to the rear. Instead he remained with his company, lying with his weapon in open country between the Sauer and the "Goldknapp" hill and fired constantly at enemy machine-gun positions on the heights, so that his own platoon was able to drop back before the German defensive fire. Permanently without cover, he drew the enemy fire on himself until he fell to a direct hit from a mortar.

During the same attack, Technical NCO 5th Class Calvin Randolph, a company medic of the H Company, learned that three wounded men were lying on the slope of the "Goldknapp" without cover. Although heavy German mortar fire was falling in the sector, Randolph ran out without hesitation, and although a splinter shredded his clothing and slightly wounded him, he was able to rescue the two wounded men. When he tried to evacuate the third wounded man, the brave medic lost his life.

At this time the 1st Battalion was able to push forward in a northerly direction, capture Erpeldange and surround parts of the "Goldknapp" before it moved forward with one company toward the "Friedhaff" on the next day, despite inhuman combat and knee-deep snow.

Meanwhile the 2nd Battalion, after cleaning out the highground from Ingeldorf to the plateau, swung around to the back of Diekirch and left the capture and liberation of the city to units of the 3rd Battalion. Through the movements of the 1st and 2nd Battalions, the presumed German artillery observers on the "Goldknapp" (Erpeldange) and "Heimricht" (Diekirch) were supposed to be put out of action, in order to allow the 3rd Battalion to work its way along the Sauer to the edge of Diekirch. On this subject, the former battalion commander, Lt. Col. Robert Connor, reports: "Since I myself did not know the exact strength of the enemy in Diekirch, I decided to attack the city from the rear (thus from the west end) in a two-part attack wave. One spearhead was therefore to work its way forward to the cemetery in Diekirch, while the other was to advance in the direction of the railroad station. About 3:45 AM on January 18, my I Company crossed the river, being the first unit of the 3rd Battalion that had been ordered to provide direct infantry fire support on the Sauer; it was led by a platoon of the 7th Engineer Battalion and followed later by Companies K and L. Company I succeeded in overrunning two German bunker positions and capturing the crews, members of GR 914.

After the 2nd Regiment had the Diekirch-Ingeldorf bridgehead securely in hand, I gave the order to capture the spooky-looking town. Meanwhile German artillery shells began to fall on the Sauer Valley. I Company came under heavy machine-gun fire at the edge of town and in the station area and was at first detained there.

After the first dead and wounded had been rescued, I myself, along with Captain Gray, the artillery officer detailed to me, evaluated what the situation was, and attempted, at first by means of the artillery fire of the 50th Field Artillery Battalion, to knock out the presumed enemy batteries.

According to our plan, I then ordered K Company to push in to the left of I Company and attack Diekirch from the northwest. K Company quickly came forward and reached the first houses and orchards behind the snow-covered cemetery, crossing open farmland (the present-day industrial zone of Diekirch). Meanwhile the German artillery fire had abated somewhat, but our tanks were not yet across the Sauer.

Working its way farther forward, K Company came upon resistance from automatic weapons not far from the cemetery. Only in the afternoon did I bring up L Company, which was still guarding my battalion's crossing point, and thus set up contact between I and K. As night fell, we reached the edge of the downtown area without any great difficulties and pushed into the area near the Hotel de l'Europe.

A large number of American pieces of equipment showed that the hotel had served as quarters for a unit of the 28th Infantry Division (in December), recognizable by the division's emblem on numerous objects!

On the next morning, after we had received three Sherman tanks of the 737th Tank Battalion as reinforcements, we systematically searched the ghostly-looking rows of houses, some of which were burned out and badly shot up; only seldom did we come upon individual nests of resistance, which were eliminated with tank support or hand grenades. It seemed as if the Germans had retreated leaving a few points of resistance at various intersections in that part of town. Nevertheless we took 158 prisoners, some of them very young, exhausted, frozen and half-starved German soldiers. Among them there were also numerous wounded and sick men who had been left behind by their unit when the remainder of Diekirch was given up by the Germans almost without a fight. Almost all the German soldiers were members of the 914th GR or engineers of the 352nd VGD."

Silas G. Cole, then a 21-year-old soldier and member of the I Company, remembers January 19, 1945:

"After our company had suffered numerous losses at the northwestern edge of Diekirch on January 18, 1945, we were able to push forward to the center of town by nightfall and secure it against possible enemy attacks.

On the next morning, every platoon of the company made several men available for the thankless task of going inside the shot-up houses to search them for German stragglers. It happened that on several occasions booby traps were found inside the houses, so that the greatest caution was urged. I was afraid!

I wore a white snow suit that was already rather dirty from a lot of movement in the country, as well as a white-painted steel helmet. My weapon was a Thompson submachine gun, along with several magazines of .45 ammunition and hand grenades. A submachine gun is better suited to house combat at short ranges.

We moved forward as far as the church without trouble. Several times the third group, to which I belonged, had hauled stunned Germans, who offered no resistance, out of the damp cellars of houses; they looked miserable and yet relieved . . . for them the war was over. In one jump we crossed an intersection where there was also a small railroad line which showed signs of damage.

Everything was uncannily quiet as I walked into the forecourt of a large complex of buildings. To my right were silos that were badly damaged by shell fragments. Many footprints could be seen here in the frozen snow, leading to a small flight of stairs by a ramp. Great caution was urged, for we were the first American soldiers here. With our weapons loaded and ready to fire, the fear of a sudden surprise making me shiver, and my finger on the trigger, I walked along an arched passage some ten meters long (today the entrance of the 'Historical Museum' of Bamertal-Diekirch). A small room to the left was completely empty. I moved along slowly and came to a black hole that opened before me like an abyss, and where a flight of stairs went down. Nothing happened!

Since I had no flashlight with me, I searched the next room . . . and was scared almost to death when I saw an old man sitting silently against a white tiled wall. He looked very sad and said not a word. Next to him an old woman lay lifeless on the concrete floor . . . stiff. She was dead. Several dead civilians were found in open coffins in the building across the street. The people here had probably died of neglect and hardship. We found no Germans, and I left the ghostly, uncanny place and made a report. I learned only later that it had been a brewery. Somewhat farther up from the brewery, a few shots were heard. As evening came, all was quiet and Diekirch was in our hands!"

The Last Phase
On January 19 the regiment's headquarters were moved from Schrondweiler to Schieren. Company A of the 1st Battalion got into a vigorous exchange of fire at the "Friedbesch" on the "Ierpeldinger Keppchen." An advance guard of the 2nd Battalion reported bitter enemy resistance at the "Friedhaff." After the 3rd Battalion had cleaned out Diekirch, it was at first called back to Ingeldorf as a reserve unit, but some of its units had to be detailed to Lt. Col. Blakefield's 1st Battalion.

Around 3:00 PM the 1st and 2nd Battalions set out toward "Objective 12" in a coordinated attack. This objective was the "Kippenhof." But the resistance became tougher, so that no contact between the two units was possible. A few German prisoners, who came out of earthen bunkers half frozen, belonged to the 79th VGD, part of which had been transferred to this sector from Brandenbourg. The commander of the 208th Grenadier Regiment (Major Schiffer) of this division was taken prisoner at the "Friedhaff" on the evening of the same day. Occasional Nebelwerfer rockets were fired toward the spearhead of the attack. (see Vol.I: The Germans)

January 20
The 1st Battalion was the first to move in the direction of "Kippenhof", where it ran into a local counterattack. In addition, there were numerous forest positions here, which at first made progress without tank support impossible. German artillery fire caused Lt. Col. Blakefield's battalion several losses. The 2nd Battalion still had not

been able to make contact. After hard individual close combat fighting in the bitter cold, as well as numerous troop movements, it was finally possible in the evening to break the defensive belt around "Kippenhof."

The 3rd Battalion immediately relieved several hard-hit units and was given the task of clearing circumvented enemy positions out of the woods in the vicinity, with tank support from the 737th Tank Battalion. The exhausted 2nd Battalion was then ordered back to Diekirch to form the regiment's reserve. After two days of forest combat and without any relief, the enemy left a great quantity of materials behind, including captured American weapons and equipment, practically undamaged. The half-starved and freezing German prisoners told us that they had been on their own without any supplies.

Later on January 21 the 1st Battalion was able to surround Lipperscheid and destroy the bunker positions around it. On the same evening, a unit of the 11th Regiment of the "Red Diamonds" took up the continuing attack on Lipperscheid-Delt, and Lt. Col. Blakefield drew his exhausted battalion back to Ettelbrück. The 3rd Battalion consolidated its own lines during the night and was likewise replaced by the 11th Regiment on the right wing of the regiment's boundary. In further operations undertaken by the 5th U.S. Infantry Division until the end of January, the 1st and 2nd Battalions in turn were temporarily attached to the 10th Regiment (Colonel Robert Bell) and took an active part in the fighting. On January 30, 1945 the regiment's headquarters of Colonel Roffe were located in Brandenbourg. The "Red Diamonds" had achieved the desired success. No soldier who took part in the murderous combat around "Friedhaff" and "Kippenhof" will ever forget his worst enemy: the extreme coldness of that winter of 1944-45 in Luxembourg. "How human beings could endure this continuous fighting in sub-zero temperatures is still beyond my comprehension!" – a quotation from General George Smith Patton, Jr.

Fred Groh

Supply Sergeant Fred Groh of the I Company (3rd Battalion) of the 2nd Infantry Regiment had asked me to include some of the pictures "shot" by him during the Ardennes offensive in this book. Some of his experiences are thus captured in the following lines:

"After a troop transfer out of the Echternach sector, where our regiment had rushed to assist the hard-hit 4th Infantry Division, my I Company moved to Stegen on December 29, 1944 to become part of the regiment's reserve. That winter in Luxembourg was really hard, and the life of the troops in the rifle pits on the defensive line was a question of survival in that barbaric weather, especially at night. We considered ourselves lucky to form the reserve, since we were quartered in houses that way. My quarters in Stegen were in the blacksmith's house, opposite which I set up our supply depot as well as the company's kitchen in a farm with a large yard. One night four of us sat around a small stove in the smithy and warmed up. The walls of the workshop were filled with horseshoes, pliers and other equipment; the rust everywhere indicated years of hard work.

We were in the midst of a conversation when the whistling sound of an approaching shell was heard suddenly, followed a fraction of a second later by an earsplitting explosion that ruined our 'idyll.' Thank God the shell had exploded on the gable of the house next door, where it had torn a big hole.

The wave of air pressure from the explosion knocked all the equipment from the walls. Horseshoes (which normally bring luck), rust, coal and other stuff flew around. The room was filled with a black cloud of dust that was so thick that one of us could scarcely see the others. We stumbled out of the smithy into the open and burst out in loud laughter that quickly helped us overcome the shock; every one of us looked just like a chimney-sweep.

Since we were involved in combat during the Christmas holidays, we had our promised 'Christmas turkey' only two weeks after Christmas. Our field kitchen prepared the traditional dinner at Stegen, and the platoons came into the yard at certain times to pick up the long-awaited dinner. For example, the 2nd Platoon, which was quartered in a communal building at the eastern edge of town, came in to get their food and got a fright. Just as the soldiers were happily eating their turkey in the yard by the field kitchen, a German shell came whistling along, shattered the window on the front wall of their quarters, and exploded in the second floor. Sleeping bags, blankets and individual equipment were shredded. If the platoon had been there, not one of them would have escaped with his life.

One night my driver and I were supposed to take hot coffee to the advance guards on the front line by Jeep when we suddenly saw white figures appear just ahead of us on a bumpy and snow-covered field path. In no time we had our weapons ready to fire, and we called to them.

It was Sergeant Jeffries with a six-man patrol. He told us that their mission to bring in a German prisoner from the far shore of the Sauer had unfortunately failed. To be sure, they had been able to overpower a German, but he had put up such a fight that they had had to kill him with a combat knife. Still it seemed a senseless death to me.

After the liberation of Diekirch and the advance to Hoscheid, we were finally relieved and, after long movements back and forth, finally reached Bourglinster on the night of February 4-5. This was a very welcome way station; we lived in a nice little house where it was particularly warm, with very friendly local people. Finally there were movies for us again; I still remember seeing the film 'Going My Way' with Bing Crosby and Barry Fitzgerald.

When we left the movie theater, which had been set up in the city hall, it was a pitch-dark night. Nobody spoke a word or made a sound other than those made by our boots. I think everybody, in his thoughts, was at home . . . far away from everything here.

On February 15 we relieved the 10th Infantry Regiment near Bollendorf, Germany and on the 16th we attacked, with Schankweiler as our objective. Thus we set foot on German soil for the second time."

The 10th Infantry Regiment

In the period from January 1 to 18, 1945, the 10th Infantry Regiment held the Sauer sector of Gilsdorf-Bettendorf until shortly before Reisdorf, with two battalions on the highlands south of the river valley, while a third remained in Medernach as a mobile reserve. In all, the smaller front units were changed 45 times before the time came for the division to attack. This made it possible, among other things, for the individual companies to gain a thorough familiarity with the terrain. The main observation posts were on the wooded hills overlooking Moestroff and Bettendorf.

These observation posts were maintained and extended until January 15. Front units regularly carried out reconnaissance missions to the Sauer, and sometimes ventured behind the German lines. As already mentioned, Bettendorf itself was the site of a spectacular raid, when on the night of January 9-10 a strong battle group pushed into the village and took numerous prisoners after destroying several German quarters and positions.

On the night of January 15, the 2nd Battalion, on the left wing of the regimental sector, took over a part of the right wing of the neighboring 2nd Infantry Regiment and thus extended its own defensive sector about as far as the "Haardt", situated between Gilsdorf and Diekirch, often referred to in the division's reports as the "Clairefontaine Sector" (because of the Rue Clairefontaine or "Kleck"), on the road from Diekirch to the Gilsdorf Bridge. At the same time, the 3rd Battalion of the 8th Infantry Regiment of the 4th Infantry Division took over a part of the right wing, which had previously been occupied by its own 3rd Battalion. The 3rd Battalion of the 8th Infantry Regiment thus at first came under the command of Colonel Robert Bell's 10th Infantry Regiment. Despite this takeover of the sector by parts of the 4th Infantry Division, the observation posts continued to be manned by the regiment's own men, who were relieved only later.

Until the beginning of the attack, every battalion, on orders from the division, carried out scouting trips to locate shallow crossing points on the Sauer in its respective sector. The planned objectives of the attack were principally in the highlands north of the Sauer, directly opposite the regiment's line, as well as the hills to the northwest of Bettendorf.

About 3:00 AM on January 18, the 2nd and 3rd Battalions of the 10th Infantry Regiment began to cross the river, while their own 1st Battalion remained in a reserve position in the quarries at "Broderbour" near Gilsdorf. During the course of the day, the 3rd Battalion reached the "Niederberg" near Bettendorf, where it faced strong opposition from the enemy at company strength. The attack was beaten back and one company of the 3rd Battalion occupied the road coming into Bettendorf. The 2nd Battalion cleaned out Gilsdorf and occupied the strip of land called the "Muergeflesschen" on the road to Bettendorf. At the same time, Company B, along with one platoon of Company C (of the 1st Battalion), followed the units of the 2nd Battalion to prevent a possible enemy attack on the regiment's flank from the direction of Diekirch.

On January 19, the 2nd Battalion captured Bastendorf and left one company behind to guard the village. Around 6:30 PM a German counterattack on Bastendorf took place. About fifty infantrymen, with three tanks (Hetzer) and weak artillery fire (see Vol.I: The Germans) to support them, attacked from the northwest, but were pushed back by strong American artillery fire after a half-hour firefight.

The 3rd Battalion then pushed farther forward to the north and captured the highlands east of Tandel. Even before night fell, the newly captured areas were reinforced and observers were sent farther to the north.

The 1st Battalion remained north of Diekirch and displaced Company C as far as the isolated farm on the Herrenberg, which overlooked the Sauer. On January 20 the 1st Battalion again took up its attack route, pushed forward to Brandenbourg, took the village after a short fight and then extended its sector as far as "Frengerhaff."

The 2nd Battalion reached the edge of Walsdorf on that day and occupied the surrounding woods, while the 3rd Battalion was relieved by units of the 12th Infantry Regiment (of the 4th Infantry Division) near Tandel. Then it was moved off to the west, in order to reinforce the left wing of the 1st Battalion until its attack.

On January 21 the 1st Battalion cleaned enemy pockets of resistance out of the high plateau to the north and west of Brandenbourg. Meanwhile the 2nd Battalion pushed somewhat farther forward, took Walsdorf and occupied the village. The following day, 3rd Battalion occupied Landscheid and sent out one company to cut off Landscheid from the north. On January 22 the 2nd Battalion was involved in forest combat, but it later able to defeat the enemies, who were in retreat. Thereupon the 2nd Battalion turned off to the left in order to replace units of the 1st Battalion on January 23. The 3rd Battalion cleaned out the woods around Landscheid during the course of the day and extended its line as far as the "Hiermesbaach."

On January 23 the 1st Battalion had fought down all nests of opposition and was now at "Groesteen" and "Puhl", as well as "Mont St-Nicolas." In the early morning hours of January 25 it began its attack on Pütscheid with Companies A and B. The 2nd Battalion thereupon took over the securing of the road to Vianden and the area around "Puhl", "Ronnebesch" and "Groesteen." Company C captured and secured Nachtmanderscheid, while the Anti-Tank Company of the 1st Battalion went into position on the plateau to the right of Graligen.

On the afternoon of January 24, an advance unit of the 1st Battalion advanced as far as Pütscheid, where the unit encountered bitter resistance from the enemy, supported by numerous tanks and assault guns retreating to the Our. The unit was drawn back at once, and the division's artillery covered the village with a hail of shells.

During this period, the 3rd Battalion reinforced the positions near "Mont St-Nicolas" and thus established contact with the division's other units. The rest of the 3rd Battalion maintained its positions east of Walsdorf and on the plateau to the north (presently Oberbecken "upper reservoir"/SEO). All the units of the 10th Infantry Regiment held their positions on January 25 and 26, 1945.

Around 10:00 AM on January 26, the 1st Battalion of the 2nd Infantry Regiment was placed under the command of the 10th Infantry Regiment and relieved units of the 4th U.S. Infantry Division. Thus the regiment's right wing was extended considerably and now reached the Fouhren-Bettel line.

On January 27 preparations to capture Pütscheid were made, and part of the 2nd Battalion was immediately transferred to the east of Pütscheid to block off the approach road to Stolzembourg. The 1st Battalion's attack began at 6:00 AM on January 28. Company A captured the heavily defended hill on the village street, while Company C pushed ahead toward Pütscheid.

Again the bitterly fighting German defenders were able to push the Americans back. After suffering serious losses, Company C finally had to withdraw. Then Company A attacked the village from the west and Company B from the south in a pincer movement and liberated Pütscheid about 2:00 PM.

The 1st Battalion was then reinforced by elements of G Company of the 2nd Battalion and drawn back to Nachtmanderscheid. During the same night, the 1st

Battalion was relieved by units of the 11th Infantry Regiment, and the 2nd and 3rd Battalions were relieved by the respective battalions of the 2nd Regiment. About 10:00 PM the maneuver was completed and the entire sector was taken over, for the time being, by the 2nd Regiment.

At the end of January the 1st and 2nd Battalions were quartered in Ettelbrück as reserve units, and the 3rd Battalion in Diekirch.

Colonel Robert Bell's 10th Infantry Regiment had thus succeeded in capturing the highlands west of Pütscheid and northwest of Vianden according to plan, and thus to throw the enemy back to the boundary of the Reich. The exhausted German units were never to recover from the attack on the Sauer front by the regiments of the 5th U.S. Infantry Division. The "Red Diamond" Division, though, suffered its heaviest losses, relatively speaking, in the latter half of January 1945.

The officers of the 10th U.S. Infantry Regiment were as follows:
Regimental Commander: Colonel Robert Bell
Regimental Executive Officer: Lt. Col. William Brekinridge
Commander, 1st Battalion: Lt. Col. Frank Langfitt, later Major Stanley Hays
Commander, 2nd Battalion: Lt. Col. Harris C. Walker
Commander, 3rd Battalion: Lt. Col. Alden P. Shipley, later Major Wilfrid Haughey

The combat events were strongly influenced by the bitter cold, and it turned out that the supply of normal B rations was not at all sufficient. The 10th Infantry Regiment tried its best to supply its soldiers satisfactorily with C and K rations. Like the other units in the division, it lacked spare parts and cleaning materials for weapons as well as solutions to prevent the buildup of ice in the mechanisms. Special lubricating oils had to be used.

Medicines for diseases that were not caused by the effect of combat ran short. Almost all the men at the front suffered from coughing, which proved to be dangerous, especially during night patrols. As far as possible, sufficient supplies of fever and cough medicines were distributed to every company.

The number of medics in the division's own 5th Medical Battalion had for a long time been insufficient to rescue the wounded men under the oppressive weather conditions. The division filled in with medics from the corps. Where other motor vehicles could no longer go to bring out wounded men because of the deep snow, the M 29 "Weasel", a small fully tracked vehicle made by Studebaker, proved its worth superbly. Since not enough of these were available, improvised sleds were made. They consisted of a board structure mounted on two skis and were often the only means usable in pathless, show-covered country.

The newly arrived "shoe-packs", nicknamed "Mickey Mouse boots" proved to be far superior to overshoes or galoshes. Through their use as winter footwear, a threatening spread of "trench foot" could be avoided, since these shoes, made half of vulcanized rubber and half of leather, absorbed no moisture even after days of constant use. It was moisture that, sooner or later, caused this feared disease among infantrymen.

The "Interrogation Team" of the S-2 Section of the 10th Infantry Regiment determined, by questioning the numerous German prisoners, that the following units were present during the January combat (January 17-30, 1945):

GR 914, 915, 916, FEB 352, AR 1352 of the 352nd VGD
GR 36, 57, 116 of the 9th VGD
901st, 902nd Panzer Grenadier Regiments, 130th Panzer Lehr.Div.
Heavy Launcher Regiment 22
5th AR of the 5th FJD
226th GR of the 79th VGD
Units of the 406th Volksartilleriekorps (VAK)

Source: S-3 Regimental Journal, 10th Infantry Regiment

Reports from Soldiers of various units of
the 5th U.S. Infantry Division "Red Diamond"
Southern Heights of Diekirch

Even today, the hiker at the edge of "Haardt" who finds himself on the heights south of the Sauer that run parallel to the river from Ingeldorf to Diekirch will find numerous trenches and foxholes, silent witnesses to the presence of the "Red Diamond" Division in the 1944-45 era. At a closer look, one notices that some of these "rifle pits" are considerably deeper and are located only a few meters from the edge of the woods, or halfway up, close to the forest path, with a view of the "Felser Strasse." These holes, some of which were covered with tree trunks years ago, afford a better-than-average view of Ingeldorf and Diekirch, the Sauer Valley and the heights of the "Seitert" that extend to the northern horizon. These pits are so-called observation or listening posts; their purpose was to keep the stretch of country under surveillance day and night, so as to recognize every move of the enemy and report it to the command posts to the rear.

Since the occupants of such positions had strict instructions not to leave their posts unless ordered to, except to obtain a hot meal, which was distributed on a rotationary basis farther back only once a day, the soldiers who took their turns here were precisely those who suffered the most from the bitterly cold and bone-chilling damp weather. The residents of the nearby villages to the south will surely forgive the soldiers for making use of some of their bed linens, blankets and mattresses in these positions, for these were their only means of protecting themselves to some extent from the chilling frost.

One of the occupants of such an observation post, Virgil Gordon of Ohio, located his one time position at the edge of the "Haardt" again in 1981. He recalls:

"I was a member of an I + R (Intelligence and Reconnaissance) Platoon of the 2nd Infantry Regiment. When the news reached us that the Germans had broken through on December 16, my regiment was fighting at Saarlautern. On December 22 we were replaced in the Saar region and, after an unbroken drive through thick, driving snow, reached Luxembourg near Niederanven. Without delay, the 'rifle companies', to which our I + R platoon also belonged as a reconnaissance unit, were transported farther ahead in order to relieve hard-hit units of the 4th U.S. Infantry Division along the Sauer front.

It was our specific task to scan the country with telescopes from a certain position day and night, enter recognized traces or hints of the enemy's presence on a map or sketch-map of the country and pass it on. A second task was sending out four- or five-man reconnaissance patrols in order to gain more detailed knowledge of the situation in the territory occupied by the enemy.

So it happened that we were on the foremost line, several hundred meters ahead of the infantry units to our rear.

For our own protection, though, a gun pit for a large-caliber machine gun was usually occupied between two observation posts.

In such cold weather as we had never before encountered, a comrade and I dug a chest-deep hole in the hard-frozen forest soil of the wooded hills south of Diekirch the night after our arrival – and it was mighty hard work. A plate of sheet metal from some barn or other covered the two-man hole, so that only a lookout slit, 30 centimeters high, was left open. The hole was open to the rear. So as not to betray ourselves by the dug-out soil around us in the snow-covered woods, it was covered with fir twigs and thin branches, which were then covered with snow. Although we had several woolen blankets with which to upholster the hole, I still froze miserably. The damp cold, which occurred especially in the early morning, also gave us trouble. In our position we had a field telephone which provided a connection to the regiment via the 'Cannon Company.' If this should fail, we had a multi-channel radio set on hand. As our weapons we had M-1 carbines with us. In addition, I had acquired an M-3 submachine gun, known as a 'grease gun' to us, from a knocked-out American tank, and I usually took it with me on night patrols. Because of its handiness and great firepower, the 'grease gun' was especially popular among reconnaissance units, where it was important to be quickly mobile and not to carry any awkward pieces of equipment. I myself took part in only two night patrols from there, and they turned out to accomplish nothing. Our nightly equipment consisted only of the standard winter uniform without a steel helmet, the submachine gun with several magazines of ammunition, and several hand grenades. As headgear I wore an additional cloth cap over my woolen hat to protect me from the biting cold. During January we were also issued white camouflage suits that, it was said, had been made by the civilian population of Luxembourg.

About 200 meters behind our observation post there was our tent, also camouflaged in white, where we could take turns sleeping lying down. Since it was almost impossible to anchor the wooden tent pegs firmly in the frozen ground, every eyelet of the tent canvas was also tied tightly to the leafless trees. Still farther back was our Jeep, which we could share with another crew.

After we had excavated our hole, we spent the frosty night in a two-man tent. It was uncannily quiet; nothing moved. When we went to our hole at daybreak the next morning, we saw that we could see almost the entire valley through the trees. To the right of us, off to one side somewhat, was an abandoned cafe (Cafe Greisen) on a road. This served as the quarters of the companies on the front line as long as the men did not have 'foxhole duty.' How we envied our comrades from the infantry! At least they had a genuine roof over their heads and could make things cozy in the cellar.

Before we began our observation activity, the previously known enemy situation was explained to us: it was said that the Germans occupied Diekirch on the northern side of the Sauer. During the very same night I heard that the something moved now and then in the 'ghost town' ahead of me. My comrades on the 'listening team' also picked up the sounds and could indicate the direction and distance on the basis of the measured sound waves. On the next day, with the aid of a powerful telescope, I actually saw footprints in the snow in front of a house near the bridge. It was very probable that this house was occupied, and some of the footprints were surely made by a sentry who, shivering from the cold just as we were, jumped up and down several times or walked up and down to keep his circulatory system working. The Germans, though, were very cautious and avoided making fires to heat the rooms in which they stayed; at least I hardly ever saw any smoke. Only once at night did a light shine for a few seconds in Diekirch, and then it was dark again. Certainly a careless person had not thought about keeping the area dark when he went outside.

Naturally these reports (and there were numerous similar ones) were carefully noted and passed on by telephone. Thus in the course of time the Regiment was gradually able to form a picture of what part of the city the enemy occupied most heavily.

Scouting trips that we made to the Sauer completed our surveillance of German sentry posts on the north shore.

During the night before January 1, 1945 General Patton had "new year's greetings" fired on Diekirch. At least, so it was said. Every available artillery gun, mortar, tank and tank destroyer shot a deadly fire at the enemy positions all along the Sauer front. In particular, the companies of the 91st Chemical Mortar Battalion subordinated to the 5th U.S. Infantry Division took part, firing some well-aimed incendiary shells into Diekirch.

As a result, several blocks of houses where we had spotted enemy movements went up in flames. The 4.2 inch mortars were frightful weapons. Their great range and the explosive power of their shells had a murderous effect.

Panic broke out among the Germans in Diekirch and Ingeldorf. Obviously they feared that an infantry attack would follow the shelling, and they fired blindly across the Sauer. They covered the slopes in front of us with heavy machine-gun and mortar fire. Several shots struck close behind us in the woods. Nobody was wounded! Purely a waste of ammunition . . . just to calm themselves down!

When the "Red Diamond" Division went on the offensive with the 2nd and 10th Infantry Regiments in the Ingeldorf-Bettendorf sector on the night of January 17-18, we received the order to remain at our observation posts in order to continuously report enemy movements.

When day broke and infantry combat raged down in the valley, we suddenly received a report that General Patton was on his way to our observation posts in order to have a look at the situation personally. We were all excited about the news of a visit from "Old Blood and Guts." I myself was worried, for German shells constantly fell in the woods behind us. The appearance of several vehicles would surely draw the German defensive fire in our direction. The regimental headquarters inquired about the extent of visibility and the visible situation. I could only answer that the fog in the valley still limited the view considerably and nothing could be seen clearly. Shortly after that the regiment telephoned all the observation posts to call off General Patton's visit. We heaved a sigh of relief!

Instead of him, several reporters and cameramen suddenly approached from the right, coming from the cafe. They had also been informed of General Patton's visit and wanted to meet him.

They moved incautiously straight along the slope to our position. I called to them, saying they should immediately leave the open area ahead of us, since they were directly exposed to the enemy's view. But they did not let themselves be persuaded and stomped on through the snow. Obviously they had not yet heard anything about the cancellation. Suddenly a number of German mortar shells exploding around them taught them a lesson and they quickly disappeared over the hill.

The battle was still raging in the lower part of Diekirch and on the rising terrain along the road to Ettelbrück. Even before the fog filled the valley on the late afternoon of January 18, we could see individual Germans fleeing over the hilly country to the northwest. Shortly after that, shots from the 4.2 inch mortars rang out behind us. The shells whistled over our heads and tore ugly black holes in the snow-covered landscape. All through the night they chased the fleeing Germans, and they probably killed many of them.

Days later, after we had been quartered in Diekirch and were now on duty within the regiment's sector, searching the woods beyond Diekirch for scattered Germans, we saw the destruction that had been caused by our own artillery. But war is simply war. Dozens of dead German riflemen lay on the open highlands, frozen stiff, where they had been hit by shell fragments. When I looked back across the Sauer from there to where we had come from, I could see in the distance the edge of the forest where our position had been. These dead men must surely have been members of the columns that we saw fleeing. In addition to numerous dead men, we found a number of badly wounded or sick German soldiers in the forest along the hill road that ran out of Diekirch in a northerly direction. At the end of January we were taken out of the combat situation for a short time and could finally warm up in heated rooms, for the worst enemy of the soldiers in this terrible battle was the dreadful, unaccustomed cold that I shall never forget!"

Reports on the 10th Infantry Regiment from interviews with
Major General William M. Breckinridge, former executive officer.

Major General (ret.) William Mattingly Breckinridge was, so to speak, born into the 10th Infantry Regiment. His father was already the commander of the B Company of this battle-tested unit in World War I and received numerous high honors for outstanding leadership and bravery.

William Breckinridge served during the Ardennes offensive at the rank of a lieutenant colonel, as Executive Officer of the 10th Infantry Regiment, whose successful breakthroughs during the combat in January were attributable for the most part to his extraordinary abilities in coordination.

After the war he took on the leadership of the 5th U.S. Infantry Division and finally became a staff officer in the Pentagon. Named an honorary citizen of the city of Ettelbrück in 1952, he visited Luxembourg several times (especially Diekirch) since then and always maintained that the inhabitants of the country had his complete respect, since they cooperated 100% with the U.S. armed forces present there, despite danger and deprivation, and contributed their share to the final liberation of the country.

General Breckinridge began his military career in 1924 at the U.S. Military Academy at West Point, where he was graduated with honors four years later. As a green second lieutenant, he was given command of the E Company of the 29th Infantry Regiment and, after training at the Infantry School at Fort Benning, was ordered to Panama, where he commanded several units of the 14th Infantry Regiment stationed there.

His superb knowledge of the French language was remembered, and he was sent back to West Point, where he taught French to the cadets for four years.

When large-scale maneuvers were held in Louisiana and Georgia in 1939 and 1940 within the framework of the newly reorganized U.S. Army, Captain Breckinridge was given command of the G Company of the 10th Infantry Regiment, which he already knew well from his father.

After completing large-scale training, he was given the news by the "company sergeant major" at Fort Thomas, Kentucky one evening – the unwelcome news that he would soon be sent back to Panama, whose climate had an adverse effect on his health. That fact was of no avail!

But Captain Breckinridge did not give up, and after ten months of correspondence with the Army command, he finally returned to the 10th Infantry Regiment at Fort Custer, Michigan, becoming the executive officer of the 2nd Battalion. The regiment itself then belonged to the so-called "Task Force 4", the advance guard of the planned American expedition to Iceland. Task Force 4 was a mobile unit that could be used any time it was needed.

Even before the 10th Regiment was shipped out, a personnel change took place in it, and Captain Breckinridge, newly promoted to Major, was given command of the 1st Battalion, with a strength of 800 men. In Iceland, where Task Force 4 was to spend the next two years (to 1943), Major Breckinridge's unit, which had been strengthened by a British machine-gun company, two Navy Construction Battalions and one Coastal Defense artillery and anti-aircraft unit, was assigned to guard an area of some 800 miles of coast, which extended to shortly before Reykjavik. This was not exactly an easy job with the totally insufficient forces available, in view of the huge, bleak area. Let us let Major Breckinridge tell the story:

"In Keflavik, where I set up my headquarters, there were only ten men to defend it. After some time, Lt. Col. Robert Bell (we two were the 'Iceland Oldtimers') was given the command of the 10th Infantry Regiment, and the 2nd Battalion had just arrived from the USA and joined the regiment. I myself thus became Regimental Executive Officer at the rank of Lieutenant Colonel, a function that I was to retain until the German surrender. Colonel Bell and I got along splendidly; he was an outstanding officer.

Our task in Iceland was to guard the coast, build and equip docks, unload cargo ships and, finally, continue training the troop units in this rough climate, which in the end prepared us very well for what awaited us in Luxembourg. In 1943 Iceland became a gigantic supply base for the expeditionary forces that were soon to be shipped from the USA to Britain in order to concentrate the fighting forces for the planned invasion of Europe. There were very few pleasures for our men during their leisure hours in Iceland, and there was enemy activity as well. The German espionage tried with all its might to build up a "5th Column" through Icelandic stringers and win over U.S. soldiers. Prostitutes and tavern-keepers, and even priests, worked as agents of the German secret service, which meant that increasing strong surveillance and arrests had to be carried out. Captured agents were turned over to the British by us.

I was one of the very first officers to reach Britain with the advance guard. Our 10th Regiment was transported there in stages and issued completely new equipment and uniforms. New arrivals reached us in Northern Ireland, and the regiment finally attained its full fighting strength.

We devoted the next nine months to attack training; the men were thus hardened and steeled, and a corps spirit developed that was to prove itself later under the worst conditions imaginable. Most of the training was done partly with live ammunition, and the 47th FA Battalion (105 mm) was definitively assigned as the artillery support unit, a task which it fulfilled masterfully until the end of the war.

32 days after D Day the 10th Infantry Regiment landed in the Omaha Beach sector of Normandy. We replaced the 1st U.S. Infantry Division and encountered the 2nd German Panzer Division near St. Lo, later also the 15th Paratroop Regiment (which was likewise assigned to the offensive in December 1944).

In the numerous minor conflicts the German losses climbed to some 1600, while we had only 350 dead to report. Within the framework of the 3rd Army, we broke through at Avranches as the foremost unit.

There followed bitter fighting at Montreux, Reims, Epernay and Verdun (Fort Douamont), until we finally reached Metz. For two and a half months, combat went on around the Fortress of Metz and Arnaville. The division's own 11th Regiment suffered high losses! When the final attack on Metz began, which finally brought Metz into the hands of the Allies, our losses were likewise so frightfully high that we had lost almost a battalion's strength.

After brief refreshment and new arrivals, we were taken out of that region and transferred to the Saar district, in the vicinity of Differten, where we protected the flank of the 85th Infantry Division. Our regiment itself carried out countless small-scale attacks on the Siegfried Line and was just about to relieve the 11th Regiment on the main battle line when the news reached us from the VIIIth Corps that the Germans had begun a large-scale attack on the front lines on the morning of December 16.

Events in Luxembourg

About 4:30 AM on December 20, I reached the Luxembourg border in my staff vehicle. It was bitter cold. When we arrived, many things were unclear, for we did not know the corps or the corps commander to which the division was to be subordinated. Our job was to push the Germans, on the southernmost flank of their attack, back across the Sauer as fast as possible. Thus the 10th Infantry Regiment attacked near Altrier and Michelshof in the Echternach region and relieved the hard-hit units of the 4th Infantry Division. Shortly thereafter, our headquarters were transferred from Junglinster to the neighborhood of the division's headquarters in

Larochette (Hotel Tschiderer), where it was only a short time before I set up the regiment's command post in Medernach (now the Fondation Arend-Fixmer). This location was fairly close to the front, and we set up an excellent telephone network. After Christmas, when the enemy had been pushed back to the north bank of the Sauer again, the division ordered a broad spectrum of patrol activity, the purpose of which was to become familiar with the terrain by day and night, as well as to locate and report enemy positions. At regular intervals, our artillery fired on spotted targets and positions. The gun positions were located in snow-covered country near Haller. The men, in their observation posts and gun positions on the heights south of the Sauer, froze miserably. Many of them came down with a bad cough and fever, trenchfoot and frostbite. We made every effort to obtain the necessary additional winter clothing, 'shoe-packs' (a kind of snow shoes, half leather and half rubber), woolen blankets, camouflage clothing, medicines and calorie-rich rations from the G-4 officer (officer for material procurement, at division level) as quickly as possible.

The Intelligence Section (S-2) of our regiment found out that the German defense along the Sauer was concentrated mainly on Bettendorf and Moestroff, but the observations brought in by night patrols were far from sufficient to provide a clear picture of the enemy's situation and forces in these two locations. Therefore I ordered all the front companies to take turns pushing forward on the enemy's shore in order to determine the enemy's strength and bring in prisoners. Numerous sketch maps that had been made by the S-2 Section were available to acquaint the companies with the different parts of the towns. Several rubber boats were delivered and were to be used to cross the Sauer, which was only partly frozen.

The patrols found out that the majority of the Germans stayed in the basements of the houses, and that only a few occupied the positions along the Sauer. But the Germans had laid numerous mines along the shore; most of the minefields were known, so that it was possible to draw a path through them into the site map as a narrow passageway. But several patrols had suffered losses from mines and had to return.

The Germans were well aware of our presence and activity, but refrained from sending out opposing patrols in this sector.

The men of L Company were able to pull off a real 'stunt' when a strong patrol under the command of Lt. Longpré successfully carried out a mission ordered by me to bring in prisoners from Bettendorf. As far as I can recall, this patrol was led by Luxembourg 'scouts' (Albert Feck, Thill) to a place where they could make a good crossing by rubber boat. Lt. Longpré had no losses to report and, after a brief firefight in which several German positions had been set afire by incendiary hand grenades, brought in two German prisoners. One of them was an Unteroffizier (NCO) who had just returned from the command post of Major Hoffmeister, the commander of the 915th Regiment (352nd VGD) in Hoesdorf and was supposed to deliver a report to the local commandant of the German defensive forces in Bettendorf, Oberleutnant Schubert (See Vol.I: The Germans).

This news fell into our hands and revealed the German regimental commander's dissatisfaction about a 'false sense' of security.

This and other information, such as the names of officers, conditions in Bettendorf, etc., allowed me, out of joy about the success of the mission, to write a leaflet in ironic style about the hopeless situation of the German defenders on the Sauer, to our joy but surely much to the anger of the enemy. This leaflet was duplicated and I had it signed simply 'Jones.' The artillery then fired hundreds of these leaflets into the German lines by means of propaganda shells. Ironically, it was noted that this leaflet was not to be read by any enlisted men, but was purely 'a matter for officers.' In this sector the enemy actually had no reserve forces any more, so that we were able to take Bettendorf on January 18 and 19 with meager losses. Numerous civilians were still living in the cellars; for a month they had lived among the German occupying forces on supplies of preserved foods and pickled meat. Many of them were sick and weak, and were cared for by our medical section.

One of my officers, who gave excellent service in the attack on Bettendorf, was Captain Martin Gemoets, Commander of the K Company. He relates:

"The Germans were completely surprised when our actual attack began at 3:00 AM on January 18, without artillery preparation. We circumvented several German positions, which were known to us, under cover of darkness. In white camouflage suits, which had been delivered by the division at the right time, we crossed the Sauer in small boats. The enemy did, of course, fire at the attack wave with tracer bullets, but the defensive fire, mainly from machine guns, was so weak here that it did not prevent us from pushing forward. During our advance, we cut all the German telephone cables. During the fighting in the upper part of Bettendorf we captured several communication line troubleshooters, a sign that the German command was powerless without contact to the individual fortifications. Among the defenders there gradually developed a wild confusion when they received fire from us in their backs. Meanwhile various troop units had already succeeded in reaching the hills beyond Bettendorf and the farms located there. There was only a little resistance in the village, which ended with the arrival of our tanks two days later. After the final liberation of Bettendorf, the 3rd Battalion under Lt. Col. Shipley turned toward Bastendorf and Brandenbourg after the artillery (47th FA Battalion) had been brought in. By the end of January, after bitter fighting in brutally cold weather, we finally got to Diekirch and were given front furlough passes. Although we had the hardest fighting to withstand in Luxembourg, I will always hold a fond memory of that small country."

One last comment from Lt. Col. Breckinridge, who was promoted to Colonel shortly thereafter, refers to a new type of fuze that the 47th FA Battalion used against the German artillery positions (of AR 1352) near Frönerhof and Nachtmanderscheid in the Brandenbourg area.

"At the end of January 1945, the 47th Field Artillery Battalion, which was assigned to the Regiment as direct artillery support to us, fired the new Pozit-Fuze, the "secret weapon", so to speak, of the U.S. Army, for the first time. This was an electronic time fuze known as VT (variable time) which, by igniting in flight, but still in the shell's trajectory, even dug-in targets could be hit by fragments coming from above.

Our artillery fired over our quarters in Brandenbourg after the enemy had been cleaned out of the town. The mass of the medieval castle ruin had a disturbing effect on the sending and receiving electronic impulse of the activated proximity fuze, so that there were numerous premature explosions which resulted in several wounded and a perforated field kitchen. The artillerymen simply had not been given sufficient training to be familiar with the use of the U.S. wonder weapon of World War II, about which it had been said that with its use, the greater part of the German offensive could be smashed."

General Breckinridge, who returns to Luxembourg almost every year, now lives in Florida.

The "Bettendorf Raid"

The "raid" already mentioned several times must be regarded as a real "Hussar stunt" that a heavily armed patrol of L Company of the 10th Infantry Regiment carried out successfully and without losses on the night of January 9-10. By order of the regiment and even the division, it had been arranged to bring in prisoners for questioning, so as to gain a clear understanding of the extent of the German forces on the Sauer front. This task was carried out in masterful fashion by the men of L Company. To this day. the onetime participants are still justifiably proud of this "spectacular trick" that they played on the Germans. Among them was a soldier named George Bryant, whom the author contacted in 1982, and who related:

"Our patrol gathered in the company area in the stone quarry between Gilsdorf and Bettendorf, and we put on the snow suits which had just been issued to us, and which were usually worn only for similar undertakings. Since there was a shortage of regular snow suits at that time, we had to return the suits, as often before, after carrying out our mission.

Meanwhile a Jeep with a fully loaded trailer had driven up and we were given extra ammunition, rifle and hand grenades. Several men also had to carry extra machine-gun belts, since the usual metal canisters could make noise that was clearly audible at a distance during a night patrol. Everyone made sure that he did not overload himself, for we had a fairly long distance to cover through knee-deep snow. Shortly before our departure, we were 'briefed' once again, and every man received his specific instructions.

Then we set out. We got into motion without a sound; everybody kept in mind the spirit of the 'briefing' in which the layout of the blocks of houses and the streets in Bettendorf had been stressed. We carried six small rubber boats, which were covered with bedsheets as camouflage.

Under cover of darkness we finally, after we had left the open country via a field path that led out of the quarry (our gathering place), reached the banks of the Sauer at the west end of Bettendorf. After we had made sure that there were no mines there, and that nobody had seen us, we silently crossed the partly frozen Sauer. Only one boat was used for the crossing; the other five were hidden along the shore and covered with the sheets.

The north shore of the river was somewhat steeper and very slippery, being covered with ice and snow. Only at one point was it somewhat less steep. The boat had to make the trip six or seven times until all the men were on the far shore. After the patrol had cautiously covered about 400 meters at the edge of town, we crossed the main street unnoticed and, going in a northeasterly direction, reached the wooded and rising terrain behind Bettendorf. Thus we were now at the back of the village, which rose up before us.

The quietness that prevailed there was almost unnerving, indeed oppressive! At a field path that we had to cross to attain a better view halfway up the hill, aligned with the church, we noticed several colored telephone cables that ran across the path.

Lt. Longpré ordered that these be cut immediately, so that the Germans could not send out a large-scale alarm in case we were spotted prematurely. Sergeant Testino and I cut all the wires with wire cutters after the patrol had crossed the path. We took several pieces of cable along and threw them away somewhat farther on, so that the Germans would be missing several meters of wire. We reached the first houses from the east and waited several minutes. Lt. Longpré gave instructions to divide up. Each group, always keeping in touch, was to assault and take certain specific houses, known from previous reconnaissance of the S-2 Section, to be used as housing by the enemy. I took over the covering of one group and slipped along the side of the house after them. Out of a window on the second floor there hung numerous telephone cables, and we stopped . . . and waited. Nothing happened!

Cautiously I pulled on one of the wires; I heard the field telephone fall in the house. With my nerves tensed to the breaking point and my finger on the trigger of my submachine gun, I waited. But nothing moved. I pulled on the cable again, and the telephone slid across the floor of the room, – finally the cable pulled out. The telephone must have gotten caught on something. Obviously there were no Germans in that room; they were probably sleeping in the cellar. Shortly after that we received orders to work our way up to the main street. Then suddenly shots were fired.

Sergeant Testino hurried forward to see what had happened. Machine weapons were barking and hand grenades exploding everywhere. A German machine gun that began to fire was silenced by a rifle grenade. Moments later, Lt. Longpré rushed back to us and shouted that we should provide concentrated covering fire. His group had taken three prisoners, and so we ran down the lane to the street. We threw hand- and incendiary grenades into every window that we ran past and fired into them on the run. To our amazement, the Germans scarcely returned any fire at all; in any case, not one of us was injured. At a run, we and the three Germans reached the destroyed bridge of Bettendorf down by the railroad station as our own artillery began to lay a fire of TOT (Time on Target) shells on the village. We crossed the Sauer on the concrete blocks of the destroyed bridge that were lying in the water, and within a short time we reached our lines.

The men congratulated us on this success when they saw the Germans, who were now taken to headquarters.

We were brought a hot breakfast, and Lt. Longpré joined us and passed out bottles of whisky. 'A gift from the regimental commander . . . for you boys – You earned it . . . You deserve it!' he rejoiced as he drank to us. Since I myself did not drink, I went back to my foxhole, that overlooked the Sauer from the edge of the woods, and my 'buddy' got an extra ration of whisky, which he accepted enthusiastically. As we heard later, one of the three prisoners was an Unteroffizier with several important papers in his messenger's pouch. Thus the success that had been hoped for had been achieved.

Out of joy and the feeling of victory, we set up a .50 machine gun and fired bursts of tracer bullets into Bettendorf.

When the 5th Infantry Division went on the attack on January 18, 1945, our company used the same Sauer crossing that had been used on our mission. Only on January 28 were we relieved, and our battalion was sent back to Diekirch to rest.

Our platoon was quartered in a big house with a glassed-in veranda near the Sauer. From the field kitchen, which was located in the back yard of the brewery, we received three hot meals every day. Our frozen spirits were reawakened gradually. But the weather continued to be frightfully cold. Since I came from Florida, I had never before experienced such temperatures. Almost every one of us used a beer mug we had found as a coffee cup. When I poured hot coffee from a thermos jug into the beer glass, the glass broke precisely at the 'full' line. I would gladly have brought this souvenir from Diekirch home to Florida with me as a memento of the terrible weather!"

The Liberation of Hoscheid
(from unpublished manuscript by former Cpt. Richard Durst,
Co "G" Co, 11th Inf. Rgt.

Our division resumed operations during the night of January 17/18 when the Second and Tenth Combat Teams set out to force a crossing of the Sauer River near Diekirch and push north along the Diekirch-Hosceid Road. Its mission: to drive a wedge in the German salient's southern flank and force the enemy back across the Our River in our zone of action.

As usual, the weather was terrible. A foot of snow blanketed the area. The temperature hovered about the freezing mark during the day and plummeted to zero at night. Everyone risked frostbite. The wounded faced almost certain death unless they received prompt attention. The water froze in the jackets of water-cooled machine guns. Mortarmen had to hack away at the frozen earth to emplace their base plates. Tank and TD treads slipped on the icy roads. It was brutal!

Although Bell's combat team managed to force a crossing and capture Bettendorf without too much trouble that day (January 18), Roffe's combat team was less fortunate. Ball's Second Battalion ran into all sorts of trouble at Ingelsdorf.

When their supporting engineers' bridging operation failed, Ball's men marched down to the river and literally blasted the enemy from the opposite bank. Alas, their accomplishment went for naught. The Germans were back in position by the time they got across. And they fought as though they were possessed.

Fortunately, the Germans had no monopoly on determination. Many young Second Infantrymen lay down their lives for their country that day. The story of Private Charles H. Schroder, an automatic rifleman in "F" Company, was especially poignant. According to eyewitness reports, Schroder refused to be evacuated even though wounded during the crossing. He continued on across the river, occupied a position out on the snow-covered flatland, and continued supporting the remainder of his platoon until killed.

Schroder's heroism, and the heroism of countless other young men, enabled the two combat teams to carve out a bridgehead one mile deep and five miles wide that day. Quite an accomplishment!

Colonel Roffe's combat team warded off a company-sized counterattack, cleared Diekirch, and captured Friedhof Farm, on January 19, despite a dense fog which shrouded the area until almost noon. In fact, it even managed to overrun several enemy units and capture the entire staff on the 208th Volks Grenadier Regiment during the hours of poor visibility.

Bell's combat team warded off a battalion-sized counterattack launched by the German 226th Regiment, captured Bastendorf, and occupied the high ground from Tandel to Longsdorf that day.

As elsewhere, Bell's men encountered unmistakable signs of American defeat in Bastendorf: bullet riddled clothing and equipment which bore the markings of the ill-fated 28th Infantry Division, directional signs, and piles of American dead . . . many stripped of their clothing and/or shoes.

To practically everyone's surprise, both the Second and Tenth Combat Teams were able to continue their advance northward on the twenty-first despite terrible weather conditions and what often approached fanatic enemy resistance. In fact, Roffe's combat team was able to occupy Lipperscheid, and Bell's combat team was able to occupy the high ground southwest of Walsdorf, prior to dusk that evening. Regrettably, they suffered many casualties in doing so.

Concerned by the great number of casualties within the Second CT, General Irwin directed our Eleventh CT to pass through it that night and continue the attack northward in conjunction with Colonel Bell's outfit the following morning (January 22). We complied. Our Second Battalion was on the combat team's left (west) and had the mission of capturing Hoscheid. Schell's First Battalion was on its right (east) and had the mission of capturing Gralingen. Birdsong's Third Battalion was in regimental reserve at Ettelbruck.

Alas, "E" and "F" Companies, our battalion's leading elements, came under heavy artillery, mortar, rocket, and tank fire from the vicinity of both Hoscheid and Gralingen the moment they commenced advancing across the broad, open plateau just north of Lipperscheid. The men were caught out in the open, snow-covered fields without cover and/or concealment. They were unable to advance or withdraw. All they could do was dig in and take it.

When Major Acuff recognized the plight of his attack units he ordered me to swing my company westward through Lipperscheid, to advance northward along the wooded Sûre River valley, and to seize the high ground south of Schlindermanderscheid so that we might attack Hoscheid from that direction.

I complied with my instructions. I led "G" Company westward through Lipperscheid and commenced advancing northward along a narrow trail midway up the valley's steep wooded eastern slope. Far below us, at the base of the narrow valley, lay the winding Sûre River (our division's boundary with the 80th Infantry Division) and a fine secondary road (Route 27). An equal distance above us, extending for a considerable distance to the east, lay a broad open plateau where members of "E" and "F" Companies were encountering so much trouble. Ahead of us, dug in along the narrow icy trail, was what proved to be the major portion of an enemy infantry rifle company.

During our frightening advance, because the fire of one well-placed enemy machine gun could have eliminated every last one of us with the greatest of ease, PFC Sergeant, my lead scout, observed an enemy machine gun dug in alongside the trail a short distance to his front. He signaled for his fellow soldiers to halt, climbed up to a nearby overhang, pulled up his automatic rifle with a rope, and commenced firing at the enemy machine gunner. The result was absolutely amazing. When the firing ceased, one German soldier lay dead, three others stood alongside the trail with their hands above their heads, and a fifth could be seen racing northward along the trail.

Sergeant sprayed the trail in front of the rapidly disappearing soldier with fire. The enemy soldier stopped, wheeled about, raised his hands above his head, and began shouting "Kamerad" at the top of his lungs. To Sergeant's and his fellow soldiers' surprise, this response precipitated a similar response on the part of 20 other enemy soldiers there on the trail. Regrettably, Sergeant's joy was short lived. He was killed a bit later while attempting to roust another group of enemy soldiers from their position just north of Fischeid.

Unbeknown to me at this time, we captured 42 prisoners during our advance.

Major Acuff directed "E" and "F" Companies to withdraw to the wooded area just north of Lipperscheid when my company and a detachment from our division's 5th Cavalry Reconnaissance Troop got into position about mid-afternoon. They had been out there in that open field for almost nine hours. They had suffered more than 60 casualties, more than one-third of their combatants. They needed to reorganize, to resupply themselves, to evacuate their dead and wounded, and to revive their flagging spirits after the terrible mauling they had just received.

"E" and "F" Companies resumed their attack on Hoscheid early the following morning as Birdsong's Third Battalion passed through Schell's First Battalion in Gralingen and pressed the attack northward.

I assembled my platoon leaders late that morning – some time after "E" and "F" Companies resumed their attack – and led them to the peak of a nearby hill to observe the terrain over which I believed we would be directed to attack Hoscheid.

Unlike the other hills in that area, this particular one was covered with underbrush and deciduous trees whose leafless branches stood out in stark contrast with their snow-covered surroundings.

Minutes later, midway to our destination, we encountered a small clearing in the woods. Recalling previous training, I stopped, signaled the other members of my tiny party to halt, and commenced scanning the edges of the clearing for signs of the enemy. And I was delighted that I did. I soon observed two white-clad figures silhouetted against the trees at the opposite end of the clearing. Being obvious that they weren't Americans, I commenced firing my carbine into the ground near their feet, and directed that they come forward and surrender. Contrary to my instructions, the two men dropped down into their foxholes and continued standing there with their hands atop their heads.

I directed Tech Sergeant Jones, one of my rifle platoon leaders, and Pfc Uram, my radio operator, to converge on them from the two flanks while I kept them pinned down with my fire.

Everything went well for some time; then all hell broke loose. A third German, one who had hitherto remained in hiding, attempted to kill all three of us with one burst from his automatic pistol when Jones, Uram, and I came into alignment. Off to my left, Jones slumped to the ground, his body virtually riddled with bullets. Off to my right, Uram lay sprawled on the ground with bullet holes in his helmet, his radio, and the stock of his carbine. I, on the other hand, remained standing there, unscathed, firing my weapon. Miraculous? No. Jones' body had shielded me from harm.

Our reaction to the ambush was spontaneous and violent. All of us rushed forward, spraying the area with rifle fire, cursing our would-be killers, and casting sidelong glances at our fallen comrade.

Alas, my reaction to the situation was a bit too slow. I permitted my men to take the three Germans prisoner rather than killing them on the spot. Consequently, I had the onerous task of deciding what to do with them. On the one hand, I wanted desperately to avenge the death of the young former college student who had just saved my life. On the other hand, I realized that I'd be committing murder – just like the Germans at Malmedy and scores of other places there in the Ardennes – if I had them shot after taking them prisoner.

Contrary to my every inclination, I couldn't bring myself to order them shot. I did, however, direct that the man who did the actual shooting carry Jones' bloody body all the way back to the battalion aid station in Lipperscheid. Carrying Jones' body all that distance – over a mile – along that icy trail would make him wish he had never seen an automatic pistol. At least, I hoped so! I desperately hoped so!

Ironically, all of our efforts – and the sergeant's tragic death – went for naught. You see, Major Acuff soon directed that I turn my position over to Company "K", 2nd Infantry early that evening and join "E" and "F" Companies on the battalion's opposite flank. I complied.

Once in my new assembly area near Markenbach, I learned that our battalion was to resume the attack, in a column of companies, at 0530 hours the following day (January 24). Company "E" was to lead off followed by Company "F." My "G" Company was to remain in reserve initially, prepared to exploit the success of whichever company succeeded in establishing a foothold in the town. There was to be no artillery preparation prior to the attack. We had no supporting tanks. We were to push northward astride Route 7, seize the town, outpost it, and be prepared to continue the attack northward on order.

Our battalion reconnaissance platoon (Sergeant Horvitz's) probed Hoscheid's southernmost limits and members of the Third Battalion's "L" Company probed the wooded area between our two battalions later that night while most of the men caught a few minutes of well-deserved rest. As expected, Sergeant Horvitz's personnel determined that the Germans still occupied Hoscheid's southernmost houses, and Company "L's" personnel determined that they still occupied the wooded draw between our two battalions.

I left my company assembly area about 0500 hours, January 24 and walked up to a large farmhouse just south of Hoscheid which I believed would be serving as our battalion's Forward CP. I wanted to be immediately available to Major Acuff when the attack commenced. As usual, PFC Uram, my radio operator, accompanied me. The night was quite dark. It was extremely cold. The deep snow crunched beneath our feet. An occasional artillery round whistled overhead.

To my surprise, I encountered no one there from battalion headquarters. To my even greater surprise, I discovered that Captain Dodson, "E" Company's commander who was using the building as his CP, still hadn't issued instructions for the forthcoming attack. Since Dodson had previously served as my Assistant Company Commander, since there was no one there from battalion headquarters, and since the attack was supposed to commence within 30 minutes, I directed that he "get off his duff" and get moving. For similar reasons, apparently, Tom chose to comply.

Needless to say, our attack didn't commence at 0530 hours. In fact, it didn't commence until 0700 hours. Dodson, Captain Jack Brown, the commander of "F" Company who had just returned from three days leave in Paris, and I spent the interim coordinating our plans and issuing instructions to our personnel.

As expected, "E" Company's leading echelon came under heavy small arms fire the moment they moved out. To make matters worse, Dodson permitted these men to remain in the snow-filled ditches where they took cover rather than insisting that they take advantage of the darkness by rushing forward.

Dodson contacted me by radio a few minutes after the commencement of his ill-fated attack, informed me that his company was unable to advance, and stated that he personally was unable to continue. Although I was situated in a position to know that only his leading elements had been pinned down, I felt sorry for both him and his men. They had been through hell those last 48 hours. They had suffered grievously. So, without pausing to consider the propriety of my action, I told him to stay where he was and that I'd take over.

"Now listen, Tom," I stated near the end of our conversation, "you bring your men on into town and occupy the houses east of the road when I've taken five or six of them. As we agreed, Brown and his men will occupy the houses west of the road and swing west when we reach the main crossroad." He agreed.

Satisfied that the matter had been resolved, I returned to my company assembly area, informed my platoon leaders of the situation, and directed Lieutenant Anderson, my Executive Officer, to take two rifle platoons into the wooded draw off to our right – the one "L" Company's personnel had found to be occupied by the enemy – to attack Hoscheid from the east, and "to get a couple of houses before daylight." This accomplished, I returned to the farmhouse which Dodson had been using as a CP, notified him, Brown, and battalion headquarters of my action, and located a suitable location to observe Anderson's progress. Somewhere en route, I've forgotten just where, I learned that matters weren't proceeding according to plan. I discovered that my Weapons Platoon had accompanied my two rifle platoons when they departed. That left me only one under-strength rifle platoon as the battalion reserve. God help me if things went wrong!

Fortunately I had little time to fret. I soon observed Anderson's force making its way across the snow-covered slope off to my right. Unlike me, the Germans in that particular section of the town weren't observant. They permitted Anderson's men to approach within a few yards of the buildings before firing on them. That was far too late. Anderson and his men simply dashed on into the town and took them prisoner.

As hoped, the Germans vacated Hoscheid's southernmost houses once Anderson established a foothold inside the town. Brown's and Dodson's men reacted accordingly. They pushed on into the southern portion of the town and occupied the houses which had been vacated.

The enemy's resistance increased dramatically with daylight. The town's defenders, members of Germany's elite 212th Volks Grenadier Regiment, commenced pounding the buildings we occupied with everything at their disposal. Their possession of the local church steeple enabled them to adjust the fire of their support weapons with deadly accuracy. Their possession of excellent firing positions for their armored vehicles enabled them to virtually preclude Anderson's forward progress. All that he and his personnel could do was seek shelter in the basements of the buildings they occupied and strike back with artillery and mortar fire. Unfortunately, even the latter presented a problem. You see, they had no maps of the area, and no one inside the town was able to adjust our supporting fire. I had to submit all of our requests with the aid of but one small aerial photograph, and adjust all of the fire from my location in the farmhouse.

Due, at least in part, to the preceding, Anderson and his men were unable to make much headway until 1100 hours when a platoon of tanks from the 737th Tank Battalion's Company "A" arrived to support us. They knocked out two of the enemy tanks which had been giving us so much trouble, reducing the pressure on Anderson and his men and allowing me to take the remainder of my men into town and assume personal control of the operation.

My personnel and the newly-arrived tankers spent the next several hours supporting one another as we pushed northward. First, one of the tanks would fire its 76mm Cannon at a particular house. Then, on signal from the tank commander, one of my rifle squads would rush forward and occupy that building before its occupants had an opportunity to recover from their shock. One it cleared the building, its leader would signal the tank commander, and the process would commence all over again with another set of participants.

Although efficient, this procedure was extremely time consuming. Consequently, we were unable to reach the center of town until approximately 1400 hours.

"F" Company – which had been held pretty well in check by several enemy armored vehicles located near the center of town – swung westward along Hoscheid's principal east-west road at this juncture and "G" Company continued northward along Route 7. To our surprise and relief, we found the going much easier from this point onward. The enemy's occupying force either fled northward or surrendered. Consequently, our battalion was soon in possession of a good-sized town – one of considerable importance to the Germans – 50-some prisoners, and a large cache of enemy material. Due to the methods employed during our advance, we suffered relatively few casualties that day. I never learned how "E" and "F" Companies made out, but "G" Company suffered only 2 killed and 8 wounded. Quite a difference from the two preceding days!

Battalion headquarters assumed control of the operation at this point and we rifle companies spent the remainder of the day consolidating our positions, establishing our outposts, evacuating our casualties, and resupplying ourselves.

Unfortunately, our ordeal had not come to an end. The enemy's artillery, mortar, and rocket fire continued pummeling us all that afternoon and far into the night. Apparently, our enemy wanted to inflict as much damage on us as humanly possible for seizing one of the key points in their scheme of defense. On the other hand, a far more pleasant one, several enemy appeared in "F" Company's area that night and asked to be taken prisoner. Needless to say, Lieutenant Farmer and Sergeant Hayes, the individuals to whom they made their appeal, were only too happy to oblige.

Major Schell's First Battalion passed through our position early the following morning (January 25) and continued northward along Route 7 to the high ground approximately 2,000 meters north of Hoscheid. To practically everyone's surprise, the battalion's advance precipitated little reaction; a fact which permitted "A" and "C" Companies to occupy the battalion's objective with relative ease. Alas, the situation changed dramatically when the battalion's supporting armored vehicles commenced moving into position. The enemy commenced pummeling Schell's position with everything at their disposal at this juncture: artillery, mortars, rockets, and even tank fire.

Although Schell's battalion continued on to Hoscheiderdickt that afternoon, it was unable to capture the town prior to nightfall.

Unlike the three preceding days, life within our Second Battalion area was relatively serene that day (January 25). We personnel rested, enjoyed some hot food, shaved, and remained indoors to avoid the cold temperature and incoming artillery fire. The only items of any great significance were that "F" Company sent patrols out to occupy Knapp Hill (to the southwest) and make contact with elements of the Second CT north of Schlindermanderscheid (to the west), Company "H's" mortars engaged targets in and around Consthum, and we personnel received a shipment of shoepacks. Needless to say, the latter certainly raised our morale. They would go a long way to alleviate our problems with trench foot and frost bitten feet. What a shame we couldn't have received them earlier!

Schell's First Battalion overcame the enemy resistance in and around Hoscheiderdickt, Birdsong's Third Battalion completed clearing Merscheid, and our Second Battalion occupied the high ground west of Walhausen on January 26. The German forces which had smashed their way into Luxembourg on December 17 were withdrawing to their homeland under pressure.

Although our Second Battalion wasn't in direct contact with the enemy that day, I shall never forget it. And for the strangest of reasons. First, because it was the first time we had an opportunity to wear our newly-issued shoepacks. And secondly, because our advance took us along one of the roads on which our supporting artillery and the XIX Tactical Air Command had decimated an enemy column some four days earlier.

The scene of the latter sickened even the most hard hearted of our number. It was terrible! The battered remnants of enemy motor vehicles, horse-drawn conveyances, artillery pieces, and miscellaneous other equipment along with the mutilated bodies of scores of enemy personnel and horses virtually filled the road along which we were marching, the roadside ditches, and the adjacent snow-covered fields. I cringed at the sight. I hadn't observed such destruction since back at St. Lô during

August. Fortunately, the temperature had remained well below the freezing mark since their massacre. Consequently, their bodies hadn't commenced to decompose. Still, the sight of those mutilated bodies, many frozen into grotesque positions, was dreadful to behold. It made a person question the very concept of war.

Acuff and Birdsong commenced formulating plans for attacking Walhausen and Weiler early the following day (January 27) when reconnaissance patrols from our two battalions succeeded in entering the two towns without too much difficulty on the preceding night. As might be expected, we company commanders commenced inching our way forward to have a look at our new objectives a short time later, when we learned of our upcoming assignments. Alas, our eagerness proved to be ill advised. At least it did in my case.

My misadventure commenced shortly after noon when I walked over to a house located on the Holzthum-Weiler Road just west of Walhausen with a small party to have a look at the town. A short distance behind us, sprawled in the snow alongside the road, lay six American GIs with bullet holes in the back of their heads. Although uncertain, I assumed that they were members of the ill-fated 28th Infantry Division which had been overrun by the German juggernaut some nine days earlier. Ahead of us, in an apple orchard just west of the town, sat several enemy machine gunners raking us with long range machine gun fire.

Angered by the apparent German atrocity, I directed a couple of my companions to take up positions in front of the house, and "give the bastards something to think about."

When a handsome young Corporal – one of the NCOs who had joined the company back in Haller – looked at me with an askant expression, I exclaimed: "Don't be afraid, son. You'll be all right! They won't be able to harm you if you keep firing at them!"

What rubbish! The rosy-cheeked young teenager lay dead within a matter of minutes – the victim of one of the enemy machine gunners. I felt terrible. Seventeen days earlier, he had joined me back in Haller with approximately 60 other NCOs. When I requested that all of them be reduced to the grade of private without prejudice, I was instructed to delay my decision until I had observed them under fire. With the corporal's death, the matter was purely academic. I had none to consider! I had lost all of them, every last one of them! I would remember that young man's death until my dying day!

Birdsong's Recon Platoon and Company "I" captured Weiler shortly after dark that evening, as Dodson and I prepared to attack Walhausen.

Our attack commenced at 2115 hours with a 15-minute artillery preparation. Once the preparatory fires had lifted, all of us climbed out of our shallow snow-filled foxholes – which we had blasted out of the frozen earth with quarter-pound blocks of TNT – formed into skirmish lines, and moved out. It was cold and pitch black. We could see virtually nothing. We had to rely on our compasses for direction.

Our companies' situation improved somewhat when we cleared the rise above Walhausen. We could detect the outline of the town's buildings and guide on them.

Contrary to our expectations, we were soon observed and fired upon. Enemy artillery commenced raining down on us and enemy machine gunners in the orchard northwest of town commenced raking us with fire. We pressed on, crossing the snow-covered slope east of the Holzthum-Walhausen Road and dashing inside the darkened houses. Alas, they were of little value. Most of them had been booby-trapped.

As might be expected, the preceding slowed our progress dramatically. It took us until well past midnight to clear and outpost the town. It took our battalion A.&P. Platoon until approximately 0400 hours to locate and neutralize all of the booby traps.

Sergeant Wright brought me a prisoner who stated that his platoon was located in a nearby woods and wished to surrender during the latter stages of our operation. He was willing, he stated, to lead someone back to where they were located and arrange for their surrender.

"To hell with them!" I blurted heatedly as I recalled the fate of the Ranger NCO at Fort Plappeville and Sergeant Jones near Fischeid. "If they want to surrender, let them come in and surrender! I'll be damned if I send anyone out after them!"

Having expressed my views on the matter, I had Wright return the man to where the other prisoners were located and get them started back to battalion. I continued standing there in the dark after he left wondering whether I had made the proper decision. My intuition told me that I had.

Our Eleventh and Colonel Bell's Tenth Combat Teams pushed eastward and captured the high ground overlooking the Our River in our zone on January 28. Our task of driving a wedge into the German salient's southern flank and pushing the enemy back across the Our River in our zone was complete. Regrettably, as is often the case in generalizations, that statement fails to indicate the Churchillian "blood, sweat, and tears" involved. I could still recall some of that blood, sweat, and tears; and it pained me deeply.

I spent much of January 28 in my company OP directing the fire of my mortars on an enemy strongpoint located midway between us and the town of Unter Eisenbach. Unfortunately, I was unable to inflict much damage on its occupants until late that afternoon because they had burrowed into the walls of a quarry-like depression. I dispatched one of my rifle platoons and my attached tank platoon out to occupy their position immediately thereafter. Alas, as in the case of several other recent decisions, this one proved to be a poor one. You see, my personnel were subjected to intense long range machine gun and artillery fire the moment they commenced crossing the large open area east of Walhausen.

Although the tanks had little difficulty silencing the enemy machine guns, neither they nor I could do anything about the artillery fire. Six of my men lay dead and several others wounded when it lifted.

Undaunted by their misfortune, the remainder of the platoon struggled to their feet, brushed the snow from their clothes, and continued plodding eastward through the ankle-deep snow. Seeing those dark blobs in the snow – some shell craters; other, the bodies of my men – virtually overwhelmed me. Why in God's name had I insisted on dispatching them prior to darkness? I kept asking myself. It could have waited! There was no great rush to take that damned location!

Feeling as I did, I decided against visiting their location until the following morning. I needed time to regain my composure. I needed time to work up enough courage to look them in the eye without breaking into tears.

Contrary to my expectations, no one mentioned their deadly ordeal when I visited them the following morning. Nor did anyone ask why I insisted on sending them out during daylight. They appeared to be taking the incident in stride . . . like the many other hardships which they had been called upon to suffer recently. It made me feel downright awful. Stupid. Uncaring.

Needless to say, I didn't tarry any longer than absolutely necessary. I summoned my radio operator and headed back toward Walhausen the moment I finished inspecting their position and making a list of their needs.

PFC Uram and I stopped minutes later – midway across the large open field – and loaded the bodies of the platoon's six dead on the ski litters we had used to carry supplies to the outpost.

The remainder of the trip proved to be a veritable nightmare. There, on the litter behind me, lay the frozen bodies of three of my men; one with his eyes dilated and his mouth agape, one with the lower portion of his face shot away, and one with his frozen arm dragging along through the untrampled snow. Although certainly no stranger to violent death, I was completely unnerved by the sight of that boy's arm ploughing along through the snow. My eyes brimmed with tears. A lump formed in my throat. Why, I kept asking myself, had I been in such a hurry to take that position. Unfortunately, I had no answer. I just had, and it had cost me dearly.

I continued onward laden with guilt, trying desperately to avoid looking back at the body-laden litter and the ghastly trail it was leaving in the pristine snow. Ultimately, I failed. The recollection of that sight will haunt me until my dying day.

Acuff summoned all of us company commanders to his CP to confer with Colonel Black, our regimental commander, shortly after I returned from my outpost. As expected, much of what the colonel had to say was complimentary, and thus immediately forgotten. One of his comments did, however, perplex and intrigue me. After his comments to the entire group, Black walked over to where I was sitting, smiled benignly, and exclaimed: "I understand that you think you have quite an outfit, Durst!"

"Yes, sir, I do," I replied. "It's a great outfit!"

"Well let me tell you something, Dick," he continued in a fatherly manner. "When things go right in your unit, it's your NCOs who are responsible. On the other hand, when they go wrong, it's you, the commander, who is at fault. Remember that!"

I nodded, although I hadn't the slightest notion of what he was talking about. Moments later, seemingly as an afterthought, the colonel looked over at me and added: "That certainly was some morning report you submitted the other day! I understand that it went all the way back to Army . . . through command channels."

I was, unfortunately, unable to pursue the matter. Acuff chose that moment to approach. Even more unfortunately, Sergeant Wright disclaimed any knowledge of a "special" morning report when I questioned him about it. Consequently, I had no idea of what the colonel meant until much later when I received a copy of the division's history. Yes, indeed, it was some report.

All of Field Marshal Model's forces had been pushed back behind the line they occupied prior to their offensive, General Hodges' First Army had returned to

Bradley's 12th Army Group, General Devers' 6th Army Group had contained the German thrust toward Strasbourg, and the Russians had commenced smashing into eastern Germany by the end of January.

Although encouraging, these events did not, in and of themselves, assure our success. It was imperative that we continued our drive eastward while the enemy was still disorganized. So, our battle-weary GIs reached down within themselves for the courage to continue as our senior commanders put the finishing touches on plans for continuing the attack. In the north, Montgomery was preparing to send his 21st Army Group southeastward to encircle the Germans in the triangle formed by the Maas and Rhine Rivers. Farther south, Bradley was preparing to send Hodges' First and Patton's Third Armies driving eastward toward Cologne and the Rhine. Still farther south, General Devers was preparing to send Patch's U.S. Seventh and Lattre de Tassigny's French First Armies driving eastward just south of Mainz.

Several rungs down the command ladder, General Irwin was preparing plans to force a crossing of the Sauer River just north of Echternach, Luxembourg. (Note on the Author: Richard H. ("Dick") Durst was born and raised in Akron, Ohio; graduating from its university during June of 1940. He joined the 11th Infantry Regiment at Fort Harrison, Indiana, immediately after graduating and spent the next four years training personnel in the U.S., Iceland, England, and Northern Ireland. A young captain when his regiment was deployed to France shortly after D-Day, he spent most of World War II as a member of the 5th Infantry Division, part of General Patton's famous Third Army. His combat service was terminated during early February of 1945 when he was seriously wounded while leading Company G, 11th Infantry across the Sauer River near Weilerbach, Germany. Dick returned to his regiment during mid-1946 and spent the next 20 years serving in various capacities in the U.S., Europe, Vietnam, and South America. Colonel Durst returned to Purdue University during late 1965 where he earned a Ph.D. in Educational Administration. He then served as a dean at Salem College, in West Virginia, and St. John's Military Academy in Wisconsin, before retiring a second time. Mr. Durst currently resides in Akron, Ohio, with his wife, Helen.

"Deepfelt respect for that Luxembourg mother"
(Report of a soldier of the 11th Regiment, 5th U.S. Inf. Div.)
Among the numerous memories that James W. Carroll will keep forever his meeting with a Luxembourg family during the hard fighting around Hoscheid-Dickt. "Luxembourg can be proud of that mother and her family, of the behavior of that woman under conditions that I can only hope never occur again; her helpfulness and selfless sacrifice for foreign people who pushed into her house and thus endangered her is practically heroic," reports James Carroll, who tried, through the use of a sketch, to remember the events at the end of January 1945.

His story is limited to the impressions that the young soldier acquired during the advance on Hoscheid-Dickt.

James Carroll was a rifleman in the 1st Group of the 1st Platoon of C Company of the 11th Regiment. The mission of the 11th Regiment, which had previously formed the reserve of the 5th Infantry Division since the Sauer had been crossed, consisted of passing through the lines of the 2nd Infantry Regiment shortly before

Hoscheid and fighting to free the road to Hosingen, liberate Hoscheid-Dickt and hold Objective 32 (the "Schinker" crossroads) until relieved.

"When we left Hoscheid, still in total darkness, our 1st Platoon was at the head of the advancing C Company, followed by the 2nd and 3rd Platoons. Then there came the 'Weapons Platoon', which was to supply the necessary fire support at close range with their heavy machine guns and 60 mm mortars. The pale moon was reflected from the frozen, snow-covered landscape, and it was bitter cold; an icy wind, that really cut into our bodies, blew over the hilly terrain. We left the edge of town and plodded off through the country to the right of the village street, where drifts of snow, often hip-deep, slowed our advance considerably. Several times we had to cut through wire barriers and fences.

We plodded along and always kept an eye on the road to the left of us; thus we apparently did not notice that there were numerous German machine-gun positions located along a long hedgerow in the deep snow. Either the Germans were asleep or they wanted to wait until the 1st Platoon was close enough to the edge of Hoscheid-Dickt, where, as it later turned out, another enemy machine-gun nest was located, so as to fire on us from two sides. When we had come to about 300 meters of the first house, one of the Germans jumped out of a gun hole and ran into the house. We shot at him immediately, but he disappeared lightning-fast into the house. At the same time, the machine guns started to fire on our right flank, where the 2nd Platoon was just behind us.

In no time every man threw himself down on the hard-frozen, snow-covered ground, tried to find cover and returned the fire. Someone up ahead shouted, horrified, that we were in a minefield. One group then tried, crawling on their bellies, to examine the blanket of snow, and actually found numerous hastily laid anti-personnel mines as well as tellermines.

Meanwhile the German who had just run into the house tried to get back to his machine-gun hole several meters away, but our shots drove him back into the building again. At this moment our lieutenant jumped up and called 'Let's go!', and we ran through the minefield in the direction of the house, shooting from the hip. The platoon sergeant fired several shots from his submachine gun through the door of the house and commanded in German: "'Rauskommen und Hände hoch!' (Come out with your hands up.) The door of the house led directly to the cellar via a narrow hallway. To our surprise, sixteen frightened young German soldiers, most of them in their underwear, appeared, followed by a young mother with her two small sons and an older man, probably the grandfather of the two children.

Our lieutenant recognized that these were Luxembourg citizens and allowed the small family to seek shelter in the cellar again immediately, for seconds later, mortar, artillery and antitank shells exploded around the house, quite apart from the many mines that, unconcealed, surrounded the house. After the spontaneous fire had abated, the Germans were allowed to put on their clothes and shoes quickly, and we decided to take them to Hoscheid as fast as possible, in order to turn them over to the 2nd Regiment there.

As we learned from the Germans, who surrendered without resistance, the other houses were likewise occupied by the enemy.

The lieutenant chose me and one other young GI to take the prisoners back. We could not possibly take the same route on which we had come, on account of the minefields and the still-threatening machine-gun positions along the hedgerow. But what could we do?

So we had the Germans march ahead of us; after all, it was they who had laid the mines! We had scarcely passed the badly laid and amateurish-looking minefield when the German machine guns took us under fire. Didn't the Germans know that they were firing at their own men, among others, for there were only two of us to guard sixteen prisoners.

How often we threw ourselves down and then quickly sprang up again to run a few short meters until the machine-gun fire began to mark again! We ran right across the field and reached the edge of the road, to which the 2nd Platoon had withdrawn to take the German position under fire from there.

Three or four American soldiers lay dead in the roadside ditch, shot in the head. Obviously they had been hit by a burst of machine-gun fire or by a sharpshooter. The men of the 2nd Platoon, who returned the fire, trembled wit rage as we came running up with the prisoners; some of them threatened, out of blind desire for revenge, to shoot the Germans down.

Although the salvoes were still flying over our heads, we jumped up and raced down the road to Hoscheid.

After we had taken the prisoners to a house beside which an abandoned German anti-aircraft tank stood, it took almost forever before we got back along the snow-covered road to our platoon in Hoscheid-Dickt.

Loving Sacrifice

We were horrified to learn that half of the platoon had meanwhile been killed or wounded, in some cases badly. The lieutenant himself had lost an arm to a hand-grenade fragment, the platoon sergeant had several shots through his leg. In the afternoon they had attacked several houses along the road to Hosingen and captured them, but had to draw back to the first house at nightfall for lack of ammunition and bandages.

Since there was no medic on hand, the young woman and the older man willingly took on this task. She had indescribable sympathy and treated our wounded comrades, groaning from pain, like a mother. She really did everything that was in her power, spoke words of courage and comfort to the wounded men in her native language, and tried as well as she could to protect them with blankets and bedsheets from the damp coldness that prevailed in the cellar.

I helped her and the old man, and it became clear to me that this must be a terrible burden for the woman, especially as the two small children had to see and hear everything. In addition, the woman was surely aware that wild shooting was still raging around her house. I do not understand to this day how that young woman could stand those terrible conditions.

It seemed to me to be too dangerous to evacuate the little family out of the house to Hoscheid, for German mortar projectiles were constantly exploding very nearby, aside from the machine-gun fire and artillery shells.

Although I had volunteered to bring the woman, her children and the man to safety, we agreed that it would be better to stay in the cellar.

In any case, the hard-pressed woman probably would not have wanted to leave her house anyway. At any moment a German counterattack could take place, and there were only a handful of us men who could undertake the defense.

The worst feature at Hoscheid-Dickt was that the houses were several tens of meters apart, so that every crossing could result in sure death.

Almost Fatal Zeal

But the situation remained unchanged until January 26, when engineers of the division's own 7th Engineer Battalion cleared out the minefield so that our tanks could drive through the area around the houses safely.

I had to leave the family and the wounded man behind, in hopes that help would soon come from the following units, to take part in the further course of the battle.

The attack took place under cover of darkness, and with the tanks leading the way, every house was cleaned out. After the 'tank destroyers' had fired heavily on the houses, we attacked. Shortly after that, about 120 German soldiers, many of them no older than eighteen, surrendered.

But our attack rolled onward.

When we reached the last house before the intersection (Objective 32: 'Schinker'), we saw that this building was in a dead angle in relation to the other houses. Until now, we had encountered no civilians in Hoscheid-Dickt other than the inhabitants of the first house, and we prepared to assault this house.

As the barrel of the M-10 Tank Destroyer turned its muzzle toward the house, threatening to fire the first 76 mm explosive shell into it, an unidentifiable voice called out from inside the front room.

The officer who led the attack ordered a search, and to the horror of us all, the house and the attached barn and stable were full of civilians, mostly mothers with their children. Thank God the tank had not fired! How easily we could have taken innocent lives with one shot. When a number of us had seen the freezing families, we pushed farther forward and reached the appointed crossroads without any enemy resistance.

How gladly I would have exchanged a few words with these hard-pressed people, but I had to go on. That is the fate of the infantryman! As soon as one point is reached or passed, you rarely return.

Days later, when we were relieved and transported by truck to our lines at Weilerbach and Echternach, from where we were to cross the Sauer and attack the Siegfried Line at the beginning of February 1945, we passed through Hoscheid-Dickt again on our way back.

We drove fairly fast, so that I could only get a brief look at the house where the young woman had done so much for us, and so I went my way with thoughts of her and her family. It warmed my heart when I thought of them; I wonder what became of her and the children!

The house appeared to be deserted, and only the ugly black holes in the torn-up mantle of snow that had been caused by shell explosions, and the German mines dug up by the engineers and stacked up in the front yard, still bore witness to the fighting that had raged around the little country house just a few days before.

The small country of Luxembourg can really be proud of this person, whose name I never knew; her conduct was, in my eyes, more heroic than all the military virtues!"

Memoirs of an Artillery Observer

Just as the 2nd Infantry Regiment, like the 10th Infantry Regiment, had their own support, the 50th Field Artillery and 47th Field Artillery Battalions, so was the 19th FA Battalion, likewise equipped with 105 mm guns, and detailed to the 11th Infantry Regiment for its direct artillery support.

Lieutenant Frank Breitbarth served in January of 1945 as a "forward observer" in the A Battery of the 19th FA Battalion.

Using a city map of Diekirch, he was able on his visit in the spring of 1983 to identify precise locations in the city on the Sauer.

"After Beaufort had been cleaned out of the enemy late in December, the 19th FA Battalion was located in a well-camouflaged position in the vicinity of Haller to provide support for the 11th Infantry Regiment. Right after the formation of the bridgehead on the Sauer by the 4th and 5th Infantry Divisions, the artillery battalion was brought in with all its guns, and we reached Diekirch around 11:00 AM on January 19. My group consisted of a Jeep driver, a radioman, a non-commissioned officer and me. We immediately took up quarters in the cellar of a house on what today is 'Rue Neuve.'

The 2nd Battalion of the 11th Infantry Regiment had its headquarters in the basement of the school, and in fact in a room that afforded a good view of the 'Rue des Ecoles' and 'Rue de l'Hôpital' from its narrow cellar windows.

Since an attack in the direction of Hoscheid was in preparation at that time, I spent the greatest part of January 20 in the warm cellar, which was faintly lit only by army petroleum lamps. Three or four infantry officers and several battalion clerks sat at the table with me, and we were talking about everything imaginable when someone called "Attention!" Right after that someone walked into the room.

Since I believed it was a trick played by a sentry, I did not get up until I saw, in the faint light, two stars on the shoulder flaps of the man who had come in.

General Irwin (Division Commander of the 5th Infantry Division) immediately commanded "at ease.' The Division Commander shook hands with everyone present and offered each of us a cigarette. Then he held a discussion with the officers and inquired about the division's situation in general. Among other things, he told us that the 11th Infantry Regiment would leave Diekirch that same night to lead the attack on Hoscheid.

Even before midnight we left the center of town, and the artillery observers gathered at the last house on the 'Huelewee.' Exactly at 12:00 midnight the order to set out came and we went on our way.

On a snowy, steep and bumpy field path that divided the woods on the heights (the present-day Fitness trail) we reached the high ground road that ran from Erpeldange to Hoscheid. Almost exactly at the fork in the road we ran into German mortar fire.

I was standing in front of Private Null beside the Jeep in order to orient myself through the use of the map when we both heard the first shell whistling toward us.

I grabbed him by the arm and we threw ourselves to the ground at once. The shot exploded to the side, near Null, and he received several fragments in his back. Medics from the following column were on the scene at once and they came to him, put him on a stretcher and took him away.

I heard later that the fire was falling so close to the path that the medics had to drop the stretcher several times. For Private Null, who was, thank God, not badly wounded, this was surely a very painful way back.

After the launcher fire had let up somewhat, we moved along the street and spent the rest of the night here in the barbaric cold. On the next morning we followed the road and went past a small farmhouse with a stable attached (probably 'Friedhaff'). Three or four emaciated cows, all skin and bone, were still chained up in the stable. The farm had been abandoned by the farmers and the beasts had been without fodder for days already; they mooed miserably. Since I could not find any more straw in the barn, I released them from their near-fatal situation and drove them out to where they could at least find something green under the blanket of snow at the edge of the woods. There was nothing more that I could do for the animals.

Then we went on along the road in the northern direction.

On January 22 we encountered bitter German opposition in the country, and the commander of the cannon company immediately sent for me to help him direct the 105 mm guns into the right position. As quickly as possible, four light howitzers were put into firing positions along a curve, from which they had a large part of the road under control. On January 23 the advance guard of the 19th FA Battalion reached Kippenhof and went into position there. An accident almost took place there. The infantry had meanwhile worked its way forward to just short of the edge of Hoscheid, and the E Company of the 11th Infantry Regiment took up a position in the first houses, setting up their command post on the right side of the road in a woodshed. It was located not far from a fork in the road but was some 400 meters away from the nearest houses and protected from direct view by an area of high ground. Lieutenant Jakes took four men on a patrol in the twilight in order to determine the enemy's situation in Hoscheid. They started from the street and went around Hoscheid close to the edge of town, through deep snowdrifts. They came back several hours later and reported that part of the village was still heavily occupied. On the next morning the artillery was to lay barrage fire on Hoscheid, to enable the following infantry to approach. I myself was chosen to direct the fire, and in fact so that the infantry could attack behind the slowly advancing barrage fire.

While the companies were already marching toward Hoscheid, I had one gun fire; the shell exploded in the center of town. I had the gun set back 400 mills and, to my horror, the shell exploded right next to the site of the advanced command post of E Company. I immediately had the fire halted and urgently requested checking of the technical firing data. It turned out that the gun in question had already fired more than 10,000 rounds, thus far more than the prescribed life span of a gun barrel.

For the safety of our own troops, a combined attack on Hoscheid took place without artillery support, and bitter house and street fighting took place.

After the village was taken and the troops moved on to the north, the artillery set up its command post and fire-control center in a tavern with a bowling alley.

On January 31, I received a front furlough and spent one more night in Diekirch before I was allowed to go to Paris for three days. A very pleasant change!"

The 7th Engineer Battalion

Like every American division, the "Red Diamond" also had its own engineer battalion. In this case the 7th Engineer Battalion was divided up so that each of the three infantry regiments was given one company of "combat engineers" for its direct support. During the establishment and training of this outstanding unit at Fort Custer, Michigan, men were particularly sought after who had been locksmiths, mechanics, carpenters or builders. The officers were generally engineers, architects or qualified technicians. Thus during the course of its training period in the USA and in Iceland or Ireland, a unit that was to prove itself often was formed, living up to the motto of the U.S. Engineers: "They build till they have to fight, and then they fight like tigers." Even General Patton preferred the "Red Diamonds" on account of their engineers when river crossings had to be forced and bridgeheads built, saying: "Leave it to Irwin's division; they'll do it!"

The Commander of the 7th Engineer Battalion was Lieutenant Colonel Hugo Stark. The Chief of the A Company 2, Captain Charles Marks, reports: "it was our task to get the actual fighting troops (infantry) across a river, so as to establish a bridgehead. As a mobile troop, we had light 12-man boats that, coupled together and covered with planking, formed a footbridge that could also carry the weight of light vehicles such as "Jeeps." We had nothing to do with the construction of "Bailey bridges" of steel sections; that was done by corps and army engineers.

The planning for setting up a bridge over a river, such as at Diekirch, Ingeldorf and Bettendorf, took place as follows:

The division assigns to every regiment a precisely delineated sector of land which normally affords a wide view over the river valley, and organizes reconnaissance missions and patrols so as to gain a picture of the nature of the land, but particularly of the two banks of the river. This is a specific job for us engineers, who, in collaboration with the regiment's S-3 (operations) Officer, seek out favorable sites in terms of approach routes, attack possibilities, cover, artillery support, supply routes, etc. After the crossing point has been determined precisely, It is solely the responsibility of the engineer commander to see that the infantry reaches the opposite shore by the fastest possible means. The first attack wave was usually formed from several engineer platoons, since they knew the terrain on the other shore.

In addition to that, it was also our task to search the opposite shore, often under heavy enemy defensive fire, for mines, dispose of barbed-wire obstacles and remove road barricades.

My company, along with the 50th FA Battalion, had been detailed to the 2nd Infantry Regiment. As I recall, the A Company, which I commanded, crossed the Sauer just this side of Diekirch, followed by parts of the 2nd Infantry Regiment. We erected three footbridges that were made of assembled readymade components, and somewhat later we put up a pontoon bridge made of twelve-man boats. My company's command post was set up the following day in a three-story house in Diekirch, from which we had a free field of vision to the Sauer.

Further river crossings that were built by the A Company were south of Bourscheid, near the railroad tunnel, where the Germans had left behind a heavy gun on a railroad car, and then in February of 1945 over the Our near Vianden."

Staff sergeant Russell J. Hunt served in the B Company in the 2nd platoon (of the 7th Engineer Battalion) and was an explosives expert as well as a specialist in disarming German mine traps, the so-called "booby traps." He himself was seriously wounded by shell fragments on the night of January 17-18, 1945, during the first attack wave from the "Haardt" between Diekirch and Ingeldorf toward the shore of the Sauer, which resulted in a long hospitalization. Russell Hunt, who returned to Diekirch in 1980, still remembered the events of that time very clearly:

"On December 20, 1944 the B Company was serving as a support unit near Saarlautern, when we were taken out of that combat area late in the afternoon and immediately transferred to Luxembourg because, as it was said, the 'Krauts' had surprisingly made a breakthrough.

It snowed endlessly! During that same night we drove more than seventy miles; I myself drove with Lieutenant Miller, our platoon leader, in an open Jeep in a column behind a Sherman tank – it was a very long night with bitter, driving snow and biting cold!

When we arrived in the sector occupied by the 4th U.S. Infantry Division (in the Echternach area), where we were to attack, we simply lay down in the snow on our woolen blankets and fell asleep from exhaustion. On the second day after that we were given our first mission, since during the previous night an infantry patrol of ours had run into a German minefield near Consdorf and there had been several casualties.

Since the infantry still wanted to reconnoiter this area further, the engineers had to do the job.

Thus Lieutenant Miller, my men and I set out. The snow on the roads was several centimeters deep, and we finally reached a snow-covered field path that led us to the site. From far away in the snowy landscape, we could already see the place where several mines had exploded, the helmets lying around, the dirt thrown up and the smears of blood still bore witness to the explosion.

I knelt down cautiously on the snow-covered ground and began to search through the blanket of snow one centimeter at a time. Carefully I felt and probed around with a steel rod until I came upon a tripwire two fingers deep in the blanket of white. The wire itself was relatively loose, so that I could cut it. It led diagonally across the field path, and at the end of it was a prepared explosive charge with a pull fuze screwed onto the side of it.

The men found three similar mine traps as well as two tellermines (heavy German anti-tank mines), which likewise were fitted with several tripwires and pull and release fuzes for use against troops on foot. After we had neutralized the fuzes, we removed the mines and marked them, so that they could be exploded later. We now had to carry out similar jobs every day.

At the end of December there was an accident when, despite all precautions, one of the men presumably overlooked a tripwire and caused an explosion in which Lieutenant Miller and two men were wounded. Thus I at first took over the command of the platoon where we were transferred to Heffingen to prepare for the attack on the Sauer valley along with the infantry.

Here we were finally quartered in a house again, where some of us could sleep in beds and some in sleeping bags on the floor or in the kitchen.

Two of our trucks regularly stood in the cobblestoned forecourt, which also served as an engineer equipment depot. Among other things, the trucks regularly carried specialized equipment and hand tools which were issued immediately on request. In addition to numerous explosives such as TNT, Tetrytol, Comp 2, Nitrostarch, Pentolite hollow charges, Bangalore torpedoes (explosives in tubular form to remove barbed-wire entanglements), detonating (prima) cord, mines and fuzes, blasting caps and blasting generators, every truck was equipped with power saws, axes, splitting hammers, picks, borers, winches, steel wire, cable and a great many small tools. Light bridging equipment, assault boats and rubber boats were transported separately. Every truck had a .50 machine gun on a circular mount for its protection.

Preparing to Cross the Sauer

Captain Manos, our company leader, now received instructions to send out patrols from Heffingen to the Sauer in the Diekirch-Ingeldorf sector, their mission being to search the shore for minefields and locate favorable crossing points.

Since snow suits which would have camouflaged us from the enemy's reconnaissance in the snow-covered terrain at night were lacking, we had to improvise, and thus we made snow jackets out of the white inner linings of our sleeping bags by slitting them along the sides and cutting three holes in them. The sewn-on hood was also separated and served as a helmet cover. Along with our mine-seeking gear, we normally carried wire cutters and were armed with a submachine gun, the M 1 carbine, and hand grenades. I myself took part in numerous reconnaissance missions as far as Diekirch and Ingeldorf.

We normally drove by Jeep from Heffingen to Stegen to reach the rim of the 'Haardt' on foot via field and forest paths. From there we had an excellent view over the Sauer Valley and to the highlands that stretched out to the north and northeast.

We began to search the edge of the woods and the slope systematically and found a number of badly camouflaged mines and charges, most of which the Germans had covered with fallen fruit (there were numerous apple trees on the slopes near the Sauer) on account of the hard-frozen ground. The slope was particularly loaded with wooden anti-personnel mines, a 250-gram explosive charge that was activated by a shear board in a wooden box by means of a pressure fuze, the latter made of bakelite, which made the mine very hard to locate with a mine detecting device.

On the riverbank itself there were numerous concrete mines called "stock" mines. They consisted of a hollow body made of cast concrete into which iron and glass splinters had been molded, and which contained a blasting cartridge of 'engineers' explosive. The cylinder-shaped mine, slightly pointed on top, was normally stuck on a piece of wood 30 centimeters long and was activated by a pull fuze. We also found several S mines, called "bouncing Betty" in our jargon, that were particularly feared, since after the three-prong fuze had been activated they were ejected at a man's height and, in the resulting explosion, scattered hundreds of small steel balls or metal scrap in all directions at very high speed. Often these mines were also linked to other mines by two tripwires, which normally resulted in the explosion of the whole field.

This type of mine was usually hard to locate without detecting equipment, since the fuzes looked like dead blades of grass and often projected only a few millimeters out of the ground. Thank God the Germans had not dug these infernal machines in very deeply because of the frozen ground, so that we were often able to recognize them by a slightly raised area and disarm the fuzes.

Since all these deactivations could only be carried out at night, and we had, other than the moon, no source of light, which would have betrayed us at once, what with the enemy's presence, many people now understand why we had been trained in defusing drills with blindfolded eyes. The training we had undergone in the last four years proved itself here, where it really mattered; the men worked primarily on the basis of their sense of touch. During a further reconnaissance mission along the Sauer we suddenly noticed a German sentry on the other shore. Silently we lowered ourselves to the ground and melted into the darkness with the snow. Yet something must have startled him, for we clearly heard him release his rifle's safety and take a few steps. He picked up an object and threw it into the frozen reeds along the shore. Relieved, we breathed more easily and relaxed our nerves as two frightened ducks or waterfowl flew away. We waited a while longer, lying on the ground, then we cautiously set out on our return trip over the steeply rising hill.

Several times we noticed tracks in the snow that had not been made by our men, since we and our infantry always used the same paths. Obviously, therefore, they were made by German scouts who were operating in our lines. In fact, it is said that there were several firefights between patrols near Stegen and Schrondweiler. In mid-January, I was given the task of pushing forward as far as the railroad bridge in Diekirch to check its condition and carrying ability. In a night of intense cold and frost, our new platoon leader, with two men and me, reached the bridge, which had been prepared to be blown up by the Germans. Avoiding any sound, we followed the railroad line and found out that several steel plates were loose. In addition, there were numerous tellermines with electric fuzes on the supports of the steel structure. The bridge itself was fitted with S mines in several places. During the night we severed the wires, again trusting in our sense of touch and our sixth sense, and observed the shore a little longer. Again Germans were in the vicinity, for with the favorable wind we could hear their voices clearly. I am still surprised to this day by their lack of caution!

Wounded During the Attack

On the night of January 17, Captain Manos, our company commander, the platoon leaders and platoon sergeants went to the banks of the Sauer again to find an ice-free place for the attack, which was scheduled for 3:00 AM on January 18. We spent the rest of the night transporting the assault boats, which had been brought as close as possible by truck, to the edge of the woods at the 'Haardt' and placing them in readiness, camouflaged with white sheets. Then we cut the barbed wire that separated the woods from the pastures and the orchard. At exactly 3:00, as planned by the division, twelve men with a boat, followed by numerous infantrymen with machine guns, climbed down the snow-covered slope and began to cross the river. My platoon remained on the near shore until a specified time and helped bring the white-camouflaged boats to the shore. I myself was about halfway up the slope (approximately at the Diekirch-Ingeldorf turnoff) with a team of infantry that we were to bring down the hill, when infantry-weapon fire suddenly rang out and the Germans began to cover the slope and the edge of the woods with mortar fire.

Taking our boats, we charged toward the Sauer as fast as we could. Suddenly a shell exploded by a fruit tree directly ahead of my group. The air pressure threw us to the ground, and I felt a raging pain in my legs. Two of my comrades were killed instantly. I myself had taken a fragment which had torn through my upper calf and penetrated my other leg above the kneecap.

Half unconscious from the pain, I tried to stand up as our attack proceeded amid the German defensive fire, but I was unable to. I raised my arm and called for help. One of the medics who were hurrying after us came to me and immediately gave me a morphine injection before he called two stretcher bearers.

The two had to make a tremendous effort to reach the edge of the woods in the midst of the fire – and in deep snow!

Here other medics carried me along a forest path to a collecting point for wounded, where a vehicle waited. From the moment when I was loaded onto it, I can remember nothing more until I woke up in the living room of a house that, as I learned later, was located on the other edge of the woods before Stegen (Mouschberg, Clemens Farm). Here the 5th Medical Battalion of the division had set up an emergency hospital.

I was operated on, the fragment removed and the wound treated. Then I was put into a heated room and slept for several hours. When I woke up again, someone called out, to my surprise: 'Hello, Russell, did they get you bad?' To my joy, in spite of my condition, I recognized a medic who had been in the same barracks with me in 1940 during our basic training at Fort Knox.

It did not take long before we were taken by 'ambulance Jeep' to an evacuation hospital in Luxembourg. From there, my path led to recovery in U.S. military hospitals in Paris, London, and then to the USA in April of 1945. In September of the same year I was discharged."

The First Attack Succeeded

While Staff Sergeant Russell Hunt was receiving first aid on the hillside and waiting to be evacuated out of the combat zone, the first twelve-man boats with the engineers of the B Company were crossing the partly frozen Sauer.

Staff Sergeant Martin Stoekl, was one of the first soldiers to cross the river.

"The first three boats were already in the water when the German machine-gun fire swung over to the riverbank. The first two boats took direct hits from mortar shells. In the same moment, additional boats with heavily armed infantrymen entered the water somewhat off to the right. My group and I were almost to the other shore when our own artillery and heavy mortars took the German gun positions on the highlands opposite us (Seitert) under fire. In the midst of the lashing machine-gun salvoes, we reached the enemy shore unharmed and immediately threw ourselves to the ground to return the fire. My machine-gun group fired blindly in the suspected direction until, just seconds later, a target had been spotted.

Under the fire protection of a following infantry platoon with a light 60mm mortar, my group, followed by numerous infantrymen, stormed ahead. Our fire was so heavy that it really nailed the German machine-gun crews to the ground. Finally we rolled over the excellently camouflaged position, an earthen bunker behind a chestnut tree close to the Sauer shore, and took the four occupants prisoner. While storming the machine-gun nest, my best buddy, Donald Ickes, fell, shot through the head. Fighting continued on the shore of the Sauer until the early morning hours; then the infantry crossed the road that led from Ettelbrück to Diekirch and tried to take Diekirch from the rear over the highlands that lay before us.

Street fighting at the edge of town and near the railroad bridge, in which we engineers did not take part, took place later. On the evening of January 18, 1945 part of Diekirch had already been combed through, so that we were pulled back for guarding and stayed in a house with two elderly ladies to await the coming day.

Diekirch was really a ghost town. The station area and some of the houses around the little church were badly damaged and burned out. Drinking water was melted from snow and ice, and I remember how our captain was always annoyed when we answered nature's call in front of the house where we were staying, since one of the two old ladies was always fetching snow to melt from outside the front door in a pot.

I myself learned here that the 'Preisen' (Prussians [the "Krauts"]), a word I had never heard before, had locked numerous inhabitants in the church as hostages in December, and had constantly searched the empty houses for something to eat.

In spite of that, the Germans had not succeeded in seizing all the food supplies in Diekirch, for in a cellar we found several bottles of brandy that was happily shared by the company as 'war booty.' After we had been quartered in Diekirch four or five days, we followed the advancing infantry of our division. Somewhere north of Diekirch my Jeep drove over a mine near a small village on January 29, 1945. My driver was killed instantly, and I myself took several fragments in my leg; with that the war was, thank God, over for me."

"The many wounded men, who came back from the front line every day, were a great problem, for often the front hospitals were so overfilled," tells Dr. Harvey Tousignant, surgeon of the 7th Engineer Battalion, "that room had to be made in the quickest way for the wounded men brought in later. The U.S. Medical Corps was organized as follows:

Soldiers wounded at the front were immediately (insofar as the combat situation allowed) evacuated out of the combat zone as quickly as possible by medics and stretcher bearers and brought to the battalion aid station. These first medical first aid depots were normally manned by two or three surgeons, along with personnel consisting predominantly of students who had not yet finished their medical studies, as well as officers who had served for years with a Red Cross unit.

In addition, we had trained medics and helpers whose job it was to give the most necessary treatment to wounded men in the combat zone, give them morphine injections and provide transportation to the aid station. Several heated ambulances and Jeeps specially equipped to carry stretchers were available.

At the battalion aid station, after the wounded were examined and given first aid, a selection was made. I myself was allowed to handle only cases where surgical intervention proved to be necessary for survival. Wounded men who did not have to be treated surgically immediately and whose condition allowed it, were immediately sent, after the clerks at the aid station had filled out the reports on the basis of the doctor's examination, to a clearing station subordinated to the division. Before the wounded men were sent there, each one received a sheet of paper and a tag with his medical history and medical instructions.

The remaining slightly wounded men were given medical treatment and, if possible, returned to the front after a short time, or depending on the nature of their wounds, were transferred to serve with the non-combat troops, such as transport units.

The actual surgery, which was performed with the most modern medical equipment, took place at the medical clearing station. Here cases were treated whose condition allowed transportation or whose condition did not make immediate surgery a matter of life and death.

Here too a sorting took place. Long-term patients normally were sent to an evacuation hospital that was located farther back in the hinterlands. Here the chief surgeon decided whether to send them back to their unit after several months of treatment or to transfer them to a general hospital in France, Britain or even in the USA, with the progress of the patient's recovery again making the difference. The supplying of medicines and medical equipment was done by two means. Routine articles such as bandaging material, disinfectants, burn salve, ointments, etc. were supplied by the quartermaster service, which also supplied the combat troops with equipment. For medicines, blood plasma or specific articles there was a medical quartermaster corps that was involved exclusively with the supplying of material to the units of the Medical Corps.

Among the countless wounded men who were brought in there were also many German soldiers. Here it should be noted that, except for minor wounds that did not demand immediate treatment, neither of the two warring nations was given priority. Whether American or German, wounded men are human beings who need to be helped at once.

At the beginning of January, after the danger of an enemy attack on Echternach had been averted, our battalion aid station was transferred there without delay. My medics had chosen a building for it that, as we learned later, had been the residence of a clergyman.

The men set up the operating room and the writing room in the previous resident's study and thoughtlessly cleared the room by taking all the objects in it, including a library that was obviously very valuable, and throwing the books and volumes out the window into the snow. War is war and shows no respect for private property.

It grieved me to see such old leather-bound volumes, real treasures, being ruined, and I ordered my men to pack all the books in cases, which we later turned over to the pastor in Consdorf, whose acquaintance I had made previously, for safekeeping. The pastor was extremely happy about that and told me that the library belonged to a priest in Echternach who had been arrested and deported by the Nazis. We did not stay long in Echternach, but as I recall, we were moved to a vacant farm not far from Stegen. Here I had my hands full until January 20, 1945, operating on the men of the 5th Infantry Division who had forced the crossing of the Sauer; some of them had been badly wounded by shell fragments or machine-gun bullets. After the attack, most of them were immediately sent to the 34th Evacuation Hospital, which had been transferred to Luxembourg from Nancy.

From there we made our way to Diekirch, where my staff was quartered for a short time in the Hotel Beau Site (now the Hotel de Ville, Diekirch). But we constantly followed the combat troops. In the process I had my first meeting with wounded civilians. After the infantry had captured a villa somewhere north of Diekirch that had been occupied by the Germans, my men, while searching the house and making space in the barn, which stood off to one side, found two terrified women. Both of them had numerous small phosphorus burns all over their bodies and required treatment quickly.

After I had treated their wounds with special ointment, the women were given warm outer clothing and woolen blankets, for it was still bitter cold outdoors. A hot meal reawakened their will to live, and the older one told me that her husband, since deceased, had been a judge before the war. The other woman was their housemaid. I had both of them evacuated to Luxembourg without delay.

Throughout the war, and especially toward the end of 1944, two diseases occurred more and more often and caused many more absences from our division than war wounds.

During the final phase of the battle around Metz, and especially in the Saar region, diarrhea afflicted numerous soldiers very suddenly and at an advanced state. Although it was not dangerous, this disease made many of the combat troops incapable of fighting and thus seriously weakened the combat forces. After these cases had occurred more and more frequently, Washington even sent out a special commission to investigate the causes. After this committee, consisting of military doctors, had almost been captured by the Germans, the investigation was called off. Much more serious was the so-called 'trench foot' that could often result, in an overly advanced state, in the amputation of both feet. Thousands of soldiers showed the first signs of this disease, which was already feared in World War I, as a result of wearing poor-quality footgear with insufficiently thick soles, which they often could not change or take off for days in the combat zone, and had to be treated quickly. Even later in Britain I treated double amputees who had lost their feet to trench foot.

I myself came through the war without a wound, but I will never be able to forget all the misery that I saw."

1st Lieutenant Florence Webster, a trained nurse from New Windsor, reported on the conditions in a military hospital in Luxembourg: "Since doctors and qualified nurses had completed their training, they were given the rank of officers. Most of the nurses thus held commissioned ranks and served in military hospitals and medical clearing stations.

At the beginning of January, my unit reached the capital of Luxembourg with an ambulance convoy and additional sections of the 240th General hospital from Nancy.

The landscape resembled that of my home area with one difference: that a war was raging here. Shortly before nightfall we reached the city, of which we could see practically nothing on account of the blackout regulations, and were transferred to the hospital area without delay. It consisted of a gigantic two-story building that was subordinated to the 34th Evacuation Hospital. The ground floor served as dining rooms for the slightly wounded as well as quarters for the medical personnel.

During the same night, numerous wounded men arrived in a heavy snowfall and were immediately taken up narrow stairways to the upper floor. The roof was partly damaged and the cracks in the roof had to be plugged several times to keep out the penetrating wind and snow, so that the patients gathered here and waiting for treatment would not catch cold too. They all lay on field beds and stretchers and were covered with several woolen blankets; the spaces were filled to the last man and the corridors loaded with wounded men. The hospital became hopelessly packed by the end of January.

Yet the morale of the wounded men was relatively high, for they knew that they were now in a safe place and getting treatment. In order to provide enough shelter for the wounded, the medics and almost all the other hospital personnel were finally quartered in tents in the front yard. Although double tent canvases were used, the icy wind still penetrated. There were seldom enough stoves on hand to heat the tents of the personnel, since they were used to prevent the wounded men from becoming too cold. I myself worked in the reception room. The wounded soldiers, brought here from the front on stretchers, immediately had their uniforms removed and were quickly provided with fresh bedclothes after they had been washed and shaved.

If the wound allowed, they were immediately given a hot meal and hot tea, and were given the necessary medication either orally or intravenously. This was the job of the nurses, on instructions from the doctors. Patients who had to be operated on were housed in a hall where they were treated by nurses.

Many of them needed help in writing to their families in the U.S., for many of the wounded had amputations or suffered severe burns. At times movies were shown in the waiting rooms to keep up the wounded men's morale.

When patients died, which unfortunately happened often, the body was taken over by the Graves Registration Service and the time of death, cause and further data were noted on the 'emergency medical tag', a kind of patient record, before the body was prepared for burial. The number of people working in a military hospital varied greatly with the combat events, but it was always expected of the organization of an evacuation hospital that if need be, it could still perform its service satisfactorily with half of its personnel."

Memoirs of an Army Chaplain

Military clergymen of all faiths had been declared "non-combatant" soldiers by the Geneva Convention and therefore carried no weapons. The clergymen likewise held the rank of officers and had a white cross painted on the front of their steel helmets, or a Star of David and the tablets of the Ten Commandments if they were Jewish clergymen, for recognition as a "Chaplain" or "Padre", as they were called by the troops.

In addition, since they were subordinated to the Medical Corps, they wore a Red Cross armband, which was also meant to identify them as non-combatant soldiers.

Colonel (Ret.) Chaplain Harold O. Prudell, Former Chairman of the present 5th Infantry Division Association, experienced the Ardennes offensive with the 5th Infantry Division, which he had already served as "assistant division chaplain" in Iceland. He gave the author the following account:

"I myself was permanently attached to the 5th Division Medical Clearing Company, to which all badly wounded soldiers, including wounded prisoners of war and civilians were sent for the purpose of being sent on to military hospitals by this unit.

This unit was normally found very close to the combat troops, so that we were often near the front. It was my job to stay with the wounded, give them courage and hope through faith, hear confessions, give the holy communion on request or, in extreme cases, give the death sacrament of extreme unction if a doctor informed me that a patient was near death. Since such cases could take place 24 hours a day around the clock, I slept in my sleeping bag in the 'medical clearing' tent.

The chaplains normally had, in addition to their bible and stola, a prayer book with them during field service. These were distributed to all Catholic military clergymen in the Army, Air Force and Navy, and allowed the clergy to hear the confession of a wounded man who was unable to speak.

Not all chaplains spoke German or French, so that the book was printed in several languages, even in Japanese. A translation into Latin enabled the clergyman to understand the points to which a wounded man or prisoner pointed with his finger to the respective place in his own native language. I often had the opportunity to hear confessions of wounded Germans in this way, before I met a German military chaplain in a prisoner-of-war camp late in the war, and he did that from then on.

Since the 5th U.S. Infantry Division consisted of numerous subsidiary units, I often made visits to the combat troops when I was allowed to in order to hold a field service or field confession when the opportunity allowed. I remember clearly that the bad weather and the endless icy rain and snowstorms made things difficult for the 3rd U.S. Army since its march into Luxembourg. On account of the weather and the constantly overcast sky, the Luftwaffe was powerless, and numerous tank attacks could not be carried out effectively.

On December 22 and 23, 1944 every single soldier of the 3rd Army received a card from the army headquarters in Luxembourg. The front contained a prayer to God, written by Reverend O'Neill, for good weather, so as to end this war as soon as possible; on the back a Christmas message from General Patton was printed. I believe that the greater part of the troops were clear as to the seriousness of the situation, since the U.S. Army Air Force could not be used to protect them, and our tanks sometimes presented 'targets' on the roads, as they threatened to sink into the soft ground.

As if by a miracle resulting from this prayer card, the weather cleared up and the temperature sank more and more after Christmas, so that within a short time the soil in the country froze rock-hard, so that the tanks could be used effectively and in groups.

But with the clearing of the skies, German fighter planes also appeared again, even though in very small numbers. Among them there were even said to have been some captured American fighter planes, which fired suddenly on unsuspecting troops. One of these incidents occurred not far from Larochette, as an ambulance on its way to Luxembourg was attacked by a German pilot in a P-47 plane, in contravention of the Geneva Convention. The driver and several badly wounded men burned to death in the vehicle! (Author's note: This incident, which is backed up by photos, is still purely hypothetical. It is more likely that the ambulance was destroyed by an American fighter by mistake. Friendly fire unfortunately takes its toll in every armed conflict.)

This reinforced the rumor that Germans in American uniforms were amid our troops and were supposed to carry out acts of sabotage behind our lines.

In spite of that, our continuing march was unbroken, and the halting of the German offensive was inevitable.

After Ettelbrück and Diekirch had been recaptured, I looked after the civilians who had been left behind. The cellar rooms of the hospital in Ettelbrück were overfilled with homeless and sick people, who had been cared for lovingly and unselfishly by Catholic nuns during the whole offensive, despite all deprivation. The sisters asked me to say a mass in a room on the lower floor. All the people attended, and one could really see the relief in their faces now that they were finally liberated. As it turned out, many of them had found their way back to God in their time of need.

Since I myself spoke no German, or only a very few words, the nuns asked me to hold the mass in Latin, since this was apparently the custom in Luxembourg.

I offered the holy communion, and at the end of the mass I distributed rations of soap, a rarity, a little treasure that the people accepted thankfully.

Similar conditions prevailed in the hospital in Diekirch, were several old people had meanwhile succumbed to the results of deprivation and could not be buried because of the steady fire on the city by our artillery, but had to be laid out in the icy upper floors of the building or hastily buried in the garden of the hospital. Numerous people also clung to life in the vaulted cellar of the brewery until Diekirch was finally liberated in mid-January.

All of this misery was only to end in May of 1945."

Chaplain Prudell, who holds the rank of Colonel in the U.S. Army, lives in retirement today as the seminary director of the Sacred Heart School in Wisconsin, after having served as a military chaplain for 15 months in Korea and in Vietnam until 1972.

CHAPTER XII

"IVY LEAVES" - THE U.S. 4TH INFANTRY DIVISION

Another unit that fought side by side with the 5th U.S. Infantry Division (Red Diamond) within the framework of the XIIth Corps General Manton Eddy) and made significant contributions to driving the enemy out of the Sauer front and throwing them back to their starting points in the West Wall, is General Raymond Barton's 4th Infantry Division (Ivy Leaves), which deserves to be featured here, since it also saw action in the geographical sector covered in this book.

The following report is intended to offer a thorough account of the military operations within the division's own 8th Infantry Regiment, which, in cooperation with the already mentioned 10th Infantry Regiment, the "Red Diamond", liberated the Bettendorf-Reisdorf sector from the remaining units of the 915th GR of the 352nd VGD and the 79th VGD to just short of Wallendorf in the period of time from January 18 to 24, 1945.

The Commander of the 8th Infantry Regiment was Colonel R.G. McKee; the respective battalion leaders were:

1st Battalion: Lt.Col. Cyril J. Letzeler (as of 1/15/45 Major L.W. Leeney)
2nd Battalion: Major George L. Mabry
3rd Battalion: Lt.Col. Fred Collins.

The following historical account of the regiment, a very condensed compilation from the 'unit reports' of the 8th Infantry Regiment, can be divided into two distinct phases, of which only the latter will be handled.

In the first half of January (1/1-1/15/45), the 8th Infantry Regiment saw service mainly on the defensive along the Moselle and Sauer in order to prevent an extension of the German attack on the southern flank of the offensive. In the period of time from 1/15 to 1/26/45, the regiment was transferred to the Sauer front near Bettendorf, it attacked on January 18, crossed the Sauer, which formed the front line, and on the following days, which were characterized by inhuman weather conditions, finally worked its way to the west bank of the Our, the base from which in February of 1945 the breakthrough of the West Wall was achieved by the 319th Infantry Regiment of the 80th Infantry Division, the "Blue Ridge Division."

After the division's own 8th Infantry Regiment had thus prepared the way for an attack onto German soil, it was taken out of this sector on January 26, 1945 and, after regrouping, transferred to Lommersweiler, Belgium, in almost the same region that it had reached after a hasty advance through France and Belgium in September of 1944.

The mission in the Sauer sector consisted in taking over the defensive line along the Sauer, held by the companies of the 10th Infantry Regiment, by withdrawing from the Grevenmacher area. Through this replacement maneuver it was intended that the 5th U.S. Infantry Division could occupy their defensive sector as far as Ingeldorf, following the course of the Sauer upstream. According to an order from the corps, the 8th Infantry Regiment, in cooperation with units of the 10th Infantry Regiment, was supposed to cross the Sauer in a northerly direction, take possession of the line on the western shore of the Our, and create and consolidate a new defensive line or front line there.

Historical Chronology

On the morning of January 15, 1945 a discussion was held by staff officers of the two divisions, in order to work out the final details of the takeover of the 10th Infantry Regiment's sector of the front by units of the 8th Infantry Regiment.

After the 1st and 2nd Battalions of the 8th Infantry Regiment had determined a strong enemy presence in the Hinkel-Rosport sector, as spotted by several patrols, the preparations for the withdrawal of the regiment and its respective support units (Company A, 4th Medical Battalion; Company A, 91st Chemical Mortar Battalion; Company A, 70th Tank Battalion; 29th Field Artillery Battalion; and Company A, 802nd Tank Destroyer Battalion) were already in progress. About 4:25 PM the 3rd Battalion, which had been held in reserve, became the first unit to be taken out of the sector, and around 9:10 PM it reached the specified positions, which it took over from the front companies of the 10th Infantry Regiment in the Moestroff-Bettendorf sector.

After the 3rd Battalion, as a sort of advance guard of the 8th Infantry Regiment, had moved into its position, the 1st and 2nd Battalions were withdrawn from the Rosport-Echternach area (which was now defended by the 346th Regiment of the 87th Infantry Division) the next day, and reached their specified position about 5:10 PM.

The 17th of January was used by the regiment to set up communications between the newly arrived units and to extend the defensive line farther. Meanwhile the last discussions for the XIIth Corps' attack were held by the staff. The enemy activity on that day was limited to the usual harassing fire and a four-man patrol, which was discovered near Moestroff and driven off.

At 3:00 AM on January 18, 1945 the 8th Infantry Regiment attacked. Together with the 10th Infantry Regiment of the neighbor division, and supported by its own regimental units, an objective was to be attained that was represented on the map by a line of hills, the Gentingen-Ammeldingen-Hoesdorf heights, extending to shortly before the confluence of the Our in the Sauer near Wallendorf. The attack wave took place with the 3rd Battalion on the right wing of the regiment and the 1st Battalion on the left flank. The 2nd Battalion formed the regiment's reserve.

While the attack was in progress, the division's own 22nd Infantry Regiment simulated a "Sauer crossing" farther south (at Wallendorf) to draw the enemy's artillery fire onto that sector.

The attack of the 8th Infantry Regiment moved ahead smoothly at first, since the German opposition seemed to be only weak and disorganized. But the German defenders had quickly overcome the element of surprise, and their own artillery and rocket launcher fire increased when, between 5:50 and 6:30 AM, Companies A (1st Battalion) and L (3rd Battalion), as the advance guard of the attack wave, crossed the Sauer in rubber boats and each stormed an objective on the enemy shore, which were taken only about 8:50 and 10:20 AM.

The construction of a first infantry bridge, which was commenced by the division's engineers at the place called "An der Grô" near Moestroff, was finished about 8:30 AM. During the course of the afternoon, a second bridge was erected under heavy German fire 200 meters upstream and finished at 7:25 PM.

Over these makeshift bridges the remaining companies of the attacking battalions now stormed, following the spearhead after the latter had achieved a bridgehead on the enemy shore, but fought on only with difficulty, for the German defensive fire had grown considerably heavier in the meantime. Along with all this, small fights flared up again and again, especially in the rising country; at this time they were all still dominated by the Germans, giving them an excellent field of vision and fire.

Progress was also made more difficult by the rushing river (Sauer), the current of which carried the boats away again and again, as well as by the relatively poor view and the terrain covered with deep snow.

Around 8:25 AM, two platoons of the B Company, after having crossed the Sauer under considerable difficulties, had pushed forward to the edge of Bettendorf and fought off a counterattack that had just begun there. About 4:30 PM the company leader reported that all the units in the attack wave had reached the enemy shore, so that now the reserve unit (2nd Battalion) could be sent after them.

This unit had already begun to cross the river along with Company F about 1:00 PM at a point some 400 meters away from the edge of Reisdorf. Here unexpected heavy machine-gun and mortar fire struck them, so that several boats took direct hits and capsized in the rushing waters. Even so, it was like a miracle that on that day, except for two men who were drowned, the rest of the men swam to shore. At 2:30 PM Company F reported that the unit, remaining effective, had reached the enemy shore, but could not work its way forward because of too-strong defensive fire.

Company E and the remaining part of F were immediately ordered to cross over the relieve the advance units of Company F, which were under great pressure.

The 2nd Battalion now had the task of capturing Kleinreisdorf (that part of Reisdorf in which the present-day Sauer bridge is located). After the two companies had reached the shore held by Company F late in the afternoon, under cover of the gathering darkness, the objective of Kleinreisdorf was immediately attacked in a combined action. It turned out, though, that the small locality was too heavily occupied by the enemy, so that several attacks were driven back and the companies had to withdraw with numerous losses. Meanwhile, in order to close the gap in the reserve, the 2nd Battalion of the 12th Regiment was placed under the command of the 8th Infantry Regiment as its reserve unit and moved to Medernach.

On the same day, the 8th Infantry Regiment contributed actively to the capturing of parts of Bettendorf. Companies B and C of the 1st Battalion secured the various Sauer crossings, so that the supply units could move in, and the engineers began to build several pontoon bridges that could support the weight of tanks.

On January 19 the enemy's pressure increased considerably and there were isolated counterthrusts in the area of the 1st Battalion on the Niederberg beyond Bettendorf. Kleinreisdorf had not been captured yet, on account of the vigorous opposition.

The villages of Reisdorf and Bettendorf were now under extensive heavy Nebelwerfer and artillery fire. The pontoon bridge not far from the railroad station in Bettendorf, as well as both shores of the Sauer in this area, were hit about 100 times on that day, which made the transportation of heavy materials considerably more difficult.

Company B was immediately withdrawn from the shore of the Sauer in order to make contact with the hard-hit A Company, which formed the spearhead of the attack on that day. In the upper part of Bettendorf there was bitter house combat again and again, for the village was not yet completely cleaned out of enemies, and isolated resistance flared up again and again.

Late in the afternoon the 1st Battalion was given the task of taking the "Bilgeshof-Kranzenhof" line. Thus the companies, supported by four Sherman tanks, turned in this direction, but immediately after they had left the edge of Bettendorf, they came under heavy mortar and machine-gun fire, which could be opposed successfully only when the tanks were brought in.

While parts of the 2nd Battalion had reached the old lime pit, their new "Objective 1", before Kleinreisdorf, Companies E and F still had not succeeded in taking the "little village." Only after a platoon of the anti-tank company had been thrown into the battle with a number of guns was it finally possible to surround the village. But resistance did not seem to diminish even then!

Company K of the 3rd Battalion had been ordered to clean out Moestroff. To their amazement, the men found scarcely any opposition there, for most of the Germans had already left the town the night of the attack. Only a few well-camouflaged machine-gun nests were located on the shore of the Sauer, meant to delay the American advance. Moestroff was taken almost without a fight, and numerous Germans surrendered without opposition, so that the village was reported as free of enemies after about forty minutes.

Around 2:45 AM on the night of January 20, the 2nd Battalion of the 12th Infantry Regiment, which formed the reserve unit of the 8th Infantry Regiment, was ordered to the road out of Eppeldorf, and from there it crossed the Sauer about 7:00 AM on a footbridge at the bend between Moestroff and Reisdorf, then moved along the Sauer as far as Bettendorf and took over the occupation of the town and the hilly area known as "Am Gruef" around 1:00 PM to relieve the 1st Battalion. Additional tanks and guns had just arrived across a "Treadway bridge." During the same night, the enemy had surprisingly withdrawn from Kleinreisdorf, so that around 7:45 AM the 2nd Battalion, supported by the B Company of the 70th Tank Battalion, found the houses empty after the infantry had moved forward with tank support.

On January 21, the 8th Infantry Regiment, despite the absence of the tanks, which could not be used actively in the rough, snow-covered country, nevertheless reached the area of land opposite Gentingen. Here, though, the German resistance appeared again in all its vigor. A planned attack on the fortified bunkers in the forest by tanks had to be called off because of the icy approach roads.

On January 22 a large enemy vehicle and troop movement near Marxberg in the direction of Bettel and Gentingen was reported. After the A Company of the 802nd Tank Destroyer Battalion had been able to maneuver into a favorable firing position around 10:00 AM, the M-10 tanks took the forest bunkers under fire. The German positions, made ready to be assaulted by some 160 rounds of explosive and armor-piercing ammunition, were finally taken by the infantry, which thus captured the "Kranzenhaff" region. From the West Wall, though, there again came heavy defensive fire from heavy mortars, aimed at this strip of land.

The 8th Infantry Regiment, though, received remarkably valuable artillery support from its own 29th FA Battalion, as well as from the A Company of the 91st Chemical Mortar Battalion, so that the enemy no longer ventured a counterattack. Enemy activity was limited only to returning fire at a distance, using 12 cm mortars and Do-launchers (heavy Nebelwerfer).

All the objectives were attained in the following days, and the German bunkers on the slopes above the Our on the Luxembourg side were taken after units of the 8th Infantry Regiment had been transferred several times. On January 25 the regiment thus controlled the west bank of the Our from Gentingen approximately to the confluence near Wallendorf. After the newly established front line had been strengthened, the engineers of the 4th Engineer Battalion mined the entire shore on the Luxembourg side, so as to prevent a possible enemy attack, especially on Hoesdorf. The sector was taken over on January 26 by units of the 319th Infantry Regiment of the 80th U.S. Infantry Division, and around 10:00 PM the three exhausted battalions of the 8th Infantry Regiment moved out to Bettendorf, Medernach and Hoesdorf, in order to be transferred to Ulflingen the next day.

Addendum: The 12th Infantry Regiment

As already described, the 2nd Battalion of the 12th Infantry Regiment was assigned to the 8th Regiment on January 19, 1945 as a reserve and support unit. The 1st Battalion of the 12th Regiment likewise crossed the Sauer in the early morning hours of January 19, under heavy artillery fire, and in the next few days, in cooperation with its own 2nd Battalion, which had been returned to the regiment again, liberated the "Seltz", Longsdorf and Marxberg.

The 3rd Battalion, brought in from Eppeldorf and previously forming the corps reserve (XIIth Corps, General Manton Eddy), liberated Tandel, Walsdorf and Fouhren on January 21 and 22, and then pushed forward to the highlands just short of Vianden. On January 24 the villages liberated by the 3rd Battalion of the 10th Infantry Regiment were taken over.

Walter Berry took part, as a 19-year-old rifleman of the G Company of the 8th U.S. Infantry Regiment, in the crossing of the Sauer at Moestroff. The former Private First Class, who died not long ago, had grown very fond of Luxembourg and, during a trip through the country, related his recollections to the author:

"Late in the afternoon of January 17, as darkness fell, we reached Eppeldorf. It was known to us that we were to cross the Sauer shortly; we just did not know whether it was to take place tonight or on the next morning. It was dreadfully cold.

We settled down in an abandoned house – the inhabitants of the village all appeared to have fled – and spent the night there. The room in which I tried to sleep on the floor was a bedroom under the roof, without a single piece of furniture. Only a wall clock still hung on the wall of the bare, damp room. The thought of the river crossing that awaited us made me nervous, and I could nod off for only a few minutes at a time. In the extremely quiet night I heard only the ticking of the clock and its monotonous striking of every half hour. Subconsciously this reminded me of the church bell in my home town.

Although it was frightfully cold, and we were not directly on the front line, we had been forbidden to make a fire, and we spent the night in full battle dress, rifle at hand, on the bare wooden floor, expecting at any moment to hear the order to move out. It was a sleepless night!

Finally the early morning broke, they woke us and we left the house. We went across the fields through open country to a wooden range of hills that overlooked the river. Our planned crossing point over the Sauer was located at a bend in the river between Moestroff and Reisdorf, but somewhat nearer to Reisdorf. The river did not seem to be very wide, but its current was all the stronger.

Our engineers made every effort to try to push the available assault boats through various clumps of trees and down the snow-covered slope to the riverbank. Several boats slipped out of their hands on the ice-covered ground and slid several meters downhill before they came to rest against a tree trunk farther down the slope, naturally not without a cracking noise. The Germans were not inactive. We were not yet down to the river when Nebelwerfer rockets, the so-called "screaming mimies", and mortar shells fell on us. So we remained in cover on the range of hills almost the whole day and waited. Since the terrain formed a single white landscape, I wore, like almost every one of us, a snow camouflage suit with a hood that was worn over the steel helmet. Since our company had intended to cross the Sauer immediately, and we had not expected such heavy defensive fire from the Germans, nobody had dug a fox hole on the line of departure.

When the first salvoes of Nebelwerfer rockets howled toward us with their horrible whistling sound, I instinctively threw myself to the ground at once and dug my fingers into the snow. The earth literally shook from the pressure wave caused by the exploding grenades.

Suddenly I felt something hit me in the back, near my spinal column. I was sure I had been hit and somehow felt that I was bleeding. Seconds later, when the German artillery fire landed farther back, I crawled to an officer and reported to him that I had probably been hit in the back by a fragment. He examined me and told me that a fragment had entered my gas-mask pouch, pierced it and been caught somewhat deeper in my fatigues. Thank God the hissing piece of metal had hit with its flat side, so that I had fortunately received only a bruise.

When the engineers were finally able to bring some boats to the Sauer late in the afternoon, it was still very difficult to cross the icy river, on account of heavy machine-gun fire from the other side. Only as darkness came on were we able to cross the Sauer along a rope stretched by the engineers.

Scarcely had we reached the enemy shore after great physical exertion than the Germans began to fire flares and white phosphorus shells. With every exploding flare cartridge, which bathed the whole terrain in a blinding light for a few seconds, we froze in a standing position, so as not to betray ourselves prematurely by thoughtless movements.

In spite of that, they must have seen us somehow, for when we finally moved on after a few minutes, the first artillery shells fell, in thick clumps! In a fraction of a second we split up and every man tried to take cover.

I fell into a hole, probably a bomb crater, that had been more or less covered by new-fallen snow, and had a hard time getting out again. Finally I ran to a nearby patch of underbrush that was full of mine traps. Among us there were soldiers who twisted through and tried to get themselves out of the combat through self-inflicted wounds. Some of them simply ran away.

Most of us had landed on D-Day and had not had any furloughs since then!

Yet our company succeeded in taking the prescribed objective, and we immediately tried to dig ourselves into the hard-frozen forest floor. We were just in the process of putting our equipment down and had just begun to dig the first few shovelfuls when a murderous German machine-gun fire rained down on us. The Germans fired tracer bullets at us this time too, and several men of my company were hit before they had even comprehended what was going on. All through the night we could not move, so heavy was the artillery fire that followed the machine-gun fire.

On the next morning I was so frozen through that I could hardly move. It took some time before my joints became more or less supple and I began to feel life in my finger joints again. I still remember how I broke a piece of ice out of a puddle in order to make myself a cup of hot coffee. The coffee helped me get back on my feet again, and gradually I felt warmer.

When we had drawn back somewhat, I stopped in front of a German earth bunker where our company commander, Captain Devine, had spent the night. The bunker was made of tree trunks that had been rammed deep into the ground, the roof had two layers of fir wood and was also covered with a thick layer of forest soil. In the inside it smelled unpleasantly of rancid scraps of food and damp canvas. All the blankets we found inside the bunker were mildewed.

During our withdrawal we were suddenly flown over by a U.S. artillery observation plane. The plane probably belonged to our artillery battalion. All at once there was a loud crash; all that we saw after the explosion was parts of the airplane that sailed through the air and came crashing to the ground!

We had obviously moved forward too fast and had partially circumvented German positions on the slopes north of the Sauer, from which we were now attacked from the rear.

We finally withdrew back to Moestroff. Here we were taken care of, but the officers received extra rations that we simple GIs did not get. Captain Devine, who knew of my frozen limbs, called me into his hastily erected command post in the cellar of a massive house. He gave me a cup of 'Johnnie Walker' Scotch whisky and told me I should drink it instead of using it to massage my frozen hands and feet.

During our stay in Moestroff, Sergeant Joe Columbus found a black horse that was running around somewhere in the village. He caught it and tried to ride it.

On the same afternoon, several war correspondents and photographers came to Moestroff and wanted to take some 'action photos' for several newspapers that were reporting on the action of Patton's 3rd Army. Since everything was quiet at the moment, a 'realistic-looking scene' was to be staged. We were supposed to cross the bridge at Moestroff at a run under artillery fire. No sooner said than done! The engineers attached a charge of TNT to the chimney of our command post near the bridge. The photographers took their positions, and the company crossed the bridge. When the chimney exploded, unfortunately too early, the cloud of black soot was followed by . . . a swarm of bees or hornets that had been rudely awakened. As far as I know, nothing became of the planned photo.

A piano was also found in Moestroff by Sergeant Humphrey; some GI had dragged it out into the street and offered to give us a concert. It turned out that he could play only religious music, which was certainly appropriate to the situation that we were in. In spite of that, we had expected happier music.

Somewhat later the photographers were able to take some pictures that managed to look realistic. We took up our positions again and raced across the engineer bridge to 'liberate' the village of Moestroff again. In one of these pictures, which the author of this book showed me in 1984, I actually recognized several of my comrades of those days again!

Only around January 25 did the units of the 8th U.S. Infantry Regiment succeed in capturing and holding the heights of the German West Wall until the 319th Infantry Regiment of the newly arrived 80th Infantry Division relieved us there."

The 91st Chemical Mortar Battalion

This unit, consisting of four "firing batteries", was first called to life on February 15, 1944, after numerous preceding tests had proved the effectiveness of this heavy high-angle weapon.

The 4.2 inch chemical mortar (counterpart to the German 12 cm mortar) was originally intended to fire gas shells or projectiles with similar chemical materials; in actual use, though, only explosive and white (smoke) phosphorus ammunition was used. This battalion was placed directly under the command of the 3rd Army and could be detailed to a division at any time. In January of 1945 the unit was subordinate to the 4th and 5th U.S. Infantry Divisions on the Sauer front.

"The 4.2 inch mortar was extremely effective," writes Corporal Russell Hall, former gunner of the D Company, "not only because of its great range, but also because of the frightening effect of the white phosphorus ammunition.

The mortar itself had a rifled barrel and broke down into three loads, which could be carried on a special trailer. Except in extreme cases, the firing position had to be prepared in advance, meaning that the mortar had to be dug in, so that only the muzzle of the barrel projected out of the position; this was a safety measure in case of an explosion in the barrel, which happened at times on account of manufacturing faults in the ammunition. The bottom plate, weighing approximately 150 kilograms, was also weighted down in its position with sandbags to avoid sliding after the recoil. It was aimed according to its elevation scale and with aiming stakes which were set up as a zero line, and according to which the barrel was aimed.

The technical firing data such as the elevation of the barrel, were provided by the Fire Direction Center, which also passed the aiming adjustments that had been received from an observer on to the gun crew and determined the prescribed charge for the appropriate range. The charge consisted of plates of propellant with a central hole, which were slid over the hollow tail of the shell, which was fitted with a primer cartridge. With the maximum charge, a range of almost five kilometers could be attained for high-angle fire. Only after the propellant cartridge had been ignited in the barrel did the driving band of the cartridge move out and press into the riflings, which afforded the cartridge a stabilizing trajectory.

After numerous premature explosions had occurred on account of faulty ammunition, we received instructions to fire the launcher only by using the trigger line from some distance away.

Only on December 22 was the entire 91st Chemical Mortar Battalion withdrawn from Lorraine and placed under the command of the XIIth Corps for its support, as well as being divided between two divisions (the 4th and 5th Infantry Divisions). On December 23 the unit arrived in Luxembourg fully effective: A and B Companies were assigned to the 4th Infantry Division, C and D Companies to the 'Red Diamond'. On December 25, Company A was detailed to the 8th Infantry Regiment of the 4th Infantry Division and was to be transferred from Gonderange, where it was quartered, to Lellig. On the way there, the column was attacked by a P-47 fighter with American markings. It apparently turned out later that this was a captured American plane with a German pilot. (See Chaplain Prudell's report and author's note.)

In this attack, two trucks were badly damaged, one ammunition carrier exploded, three men were killed and four badly wounded. Only toward the end of 1944 did the four companies of the 91st Chemical Mortar Battalion, after several changes of position, receive their first firing missions.

On December 31, Lieutenant Parker was killed during an observation mission at the edge of Reisdorf, which was still in German hands at that time. He had been the observation officer of the D Company.

On January 5, 1945 came the order for the whole battalion to be transferred into the respective sectors of the 4th and 5th Infantry Divisions on the Sauer front. But even before this date, the C Company had taken positions near Eppeldorf and Folkendange. Every day all the mortars fired harassing fire at the request of the reconnaissance patrols that crossed the Sauer. On January 13 the 2nd Platoon was firing on Erpeldange with four mortars when the order came from the fire direction center to swing the barrel 500 mills to the right and continue firing without delay. One day later it became known that this firing mission was aimed at a factory in Diekirch that had become known to the 2nd Infantry Regiment of the 5th Infantry Division to be occupied by the enemy. For three days this factory (the Richard Candy Factory in Diekirch) was fired on, partially with white phosphorus and partially with explosive shells, and burned down completely.

Similar targets were identified and fired on during the month of January, so that by January 17, 1945 there were four different locations in Diekirch that were burning."

The following diary contains records in concise form, from the viewpoint of a member of the D Company:

"From Consdorf to Medernach; fired on for the first time here / Pop Larkins finds four hams, otherwise just K and C rations with bad coffee; FDC (Fire Direction Center) is located in a modern building with a cellar made of concrete / Crossley milks cows next door / 3 German 8.8 shells interrupt our Christmas dinner, coming damned close / return fire with phosphorus at a recognized enemy troop concentration / numerous German casualties / New Year's dinner / fire on Diekirch and Gilsdorf from Eppeldorf; comfortable position: straw, candles, stove, breaks in the telephone lines and connections / almost everybody suffers from diarrhea: rumors of polluted water, act of sabotage? Lt. Smith brings along reinforcements from Luxembourg / fishing in the brook with hand grenades / excellent trout / hot showers in Larochette / clean ammunition / on January 1 orders to fire at 11:45 PM; then champagne again (after the liberation of Diekirch), quarters in Diekirch ... 'Heinies' fire on Gilsdorf; destroy German mortar position in Bastendorf / castle of Brandenbourg; movies shown in Diekirch brewery and barrels of wine / Pop Larkins' cabaret in Diekirch / phonograph found plus record: Merci mon ami / ... numerous dead cattle ... transferred to Echternach."

On January 19 the attack of the 4th and 5th Infantry Divisions could no longer be stopped, and the 91st chemical mortar battalion was brought in immediately. Company A followed to Bettendorf, Company B took a position in Warken and C Company came to Erpeldange during the day. The positions were only occupied during the night, though, since the enemy still had a partial view into this sector.

On January 20 the D Company set up its command post at the east end of Diekirch and its firing position near Bastendorf.

During this part of January, the 81st Chemical Company was also detailed to the battalion; in cooperation with its smoke generators, it produced artificial fog in order to conceal bridgebuilding work at Diekirch, Ingeldorf and Bettendorf. This action was likewise supported by the C Company of the 7th Engineer Battalion, which produced artificial fog directly on the Sauer through the use of HC smoke buckets and smoke bombs, in order to protect the bridgebuilding from being seen by the enemy.

On the same day, the A Company fired on Longsdorf, the attack target of the 4th Infantry Division, and put three 8.8 antitank guns out of action there.

Following the 5th Infantry Division on their further attack, the C and D Companies finally reached Hoscheid before they were withdrawn from the northern sector and transferred to the Echternach area.

It was learned later that in the liberation of the Sauer Valley, the 4.2 inch mortars of the 91st Chemical Mortar Battalion were of greater use to the infantry than the artillery in supporting their attack, because of their precise targeting and the effect of their white phosphorus shells. Although numerous houses in Diekirch fell victim to the shells of the C and D Companies and went up in flames, this fire ultimately helped to hasten the liberation of the Sauer Valley and prevent much loss of life among the American liberators.

CHAPTER *XIII*

THE FINAL PHASE

After the Sauer Valley had been liberated by the 4th and 5th Infantry Divisions, the American units hurried ceaselessly after the hard-hit enemy, who was in total retreat, so as to push him back across the German border. But this maneuver resulted in a huge expenditure of supplies.

Blown-up bridges, snow-covered roads, minefields, road barricades, shot-up villages and icy roads delayed, sometimes considerably, the advance of fast-moving units of General Manton Eddy's XIIth Corps, to which both of the divisions named belonged.

Therefore supply lines had to be established in the fastest way, so that the attack would not lose momentum and the enemy could not gather himself for a counterattack. But this was the work of specialists of the corps units, who carried it out in masterful fashion. The battalion chronicles of the following three units give information about the construction work that was carried out in record time. As opposed to the divisions' own engineer units, whose tasks consisted for the most part of removing mines and road barricades and, in cooperation with infantry shock troops, capturing the riverbanks occupied by the enemy, so as to establish an initial bridgehead, the corps or army engineers had very specific jobs and tasks – the moving of heavy equipment and the building of steel bridges out of prefabricated components.

These bridges differed in terms of carrying capability, length and design and generally bore names such as "Bailey", "Treadway" or "Heavy Pontoon Bridge." The 133rd Engineer Combat/Construction Battalion, the 150th Engineer Battalion and the 166th Engineer Battalion all belonged to the 1135th Combat Group, a large unit of assault and bridgebuilding engineer battalions subordinate to an army group. All three were active on the Sauer and Our, and the bridges built by them served as makeshift bridges long after the war. One of the countless "Bailey Bridges" is still in use today at the Luxembourg "Ponts et Chaussées" (bridge and road administration) as, so to speak, a preserved relic of 1945.

The 133rd Engineer Combat/Construction Battalion
The following operations report comes from an interview of the "historical section" of the XIIth Corps with Pfc. Frank Albertson, who took part in the 10th U.S. Infantry Regiment's crossing of the Sauer and participated in the building of a bridge in Gilsdorf by his engineer unit.

"We left our assembly point around 6:00 in the afternoon and reached a position some three kilometers south of Gilsdorf where the bridging equipment and the rubber boats were ready. The night was pitch black and it was snowing lightly. An advance group followed the infantry to Gilsdorf; the village was under artillery fire. Several heavy German shells exploded in the center of town and caused some serious damage. We divided into groups and set out for different points at the edge of Gilsdorf.

At that time a few houses were still occupied by Germans, so that there were small battles. While the infantry cleaned out the blocks of houses, we pushed forward to the south end of town and kept ourselves ready, for the companies could arrive with the rubber boats and bridging equipment at any time.

In the early morning hours of January 18 the materials were at hand, and we began to pump up the rubber boats with hand pumps. Unfortunately, the expected compressor had not been delivered.

Two men required about fifteen minutes to pump up a boat. The inflated boats were stored in the front yard of a farmhouse.

Finally the time had come: Company F was to cross the Sauer. The infantrymen, almost without exception, wore snow camouflage suits. Since we ourselves had none, bed linens and nightclothes found in the village were quickly pulled over us. One of our platoons was to be the first unit to cross. Our orders said, among other things, that later in the course of the night one platoon was responsible for the crossing of an infantry company. So we carried the first eight boats out of the farmyard and along the railroad tracks, reaching the meadows on the shore of the Sauer, where the barbed wire had to be removed first.

Not a single shot was fired, so that we believed everything was all right. The Sauer was swollen and the current, which sometimes carried blocks of ice along with it, forced us to put up a line onto which the boats that followed could hang so as not to be carried away. The boats were numbered and were additionally marked with luminous white tape. The shore was also marked with luminous tape, so that the infantry could immediately find the place at which the boats were waiting.

Without making a sound, we let the first boats glide into the water, occupied only by engineers with light weapons and coils of rope. I myself was in boat number three when we were pushed away by the current. When all the boats were in the water, several shots fell, and then the German machine-gun salvoes hammered at us. Mortar fire immediately began to fall on the middle of the river. Only the first two boats reached the shore, although boat number two was hit by shell fragments and five men were killed. Another boat capsized five meters from the shore and the men fell into the water. Boats five and seven lost several men to machine-gun fire and were swept away.

Under heavy fire, we ran back to the railroad line, where we thought we were safe. But here too we came under fire, so that the survivors drew back to the house nearby. At daybreak several quadruple .50 machine guns that had been brought up behind us opened fire on the shore occupied by the enemy. This fire also put the German observer in the church steeple, who, as it turned out, had been sending information on our mortar positions by light signals, out of action.

A young GI of the 10th Infantry Regiment. For lack of camouflage clothing, he had added white paint to his battle dress. His weapon is the .30 caliber M-1 "Garand" rifle. Photo: US Army

Soldiers of the 1st Battalion, 10th Infantry Regiment (Lt. Col. Frank Langfitt), in the vicinity of Nachtmanderscheid. They were men of the D (heavy) Company. Note the second man with the base plate, the fourth with the barrel of an 81 mm mortar. Photo taken on January 24, 1945. Photo: US Army

Intelligence and reconnaissance patrol by H Company, 10th Infantry Regiment, on a snowy slope near Landscheid. Photo taken around January 23, 1945. Photo: US Army

Two men of the 10th Infantry Regiment ready a Browning .30 M 1917 machine gun in the Brandenbourg area.

The three battalion commanders of the 10th US Infantry Regiment, from left to right: Lt. Col. Frank Langfitt (1st Battalion) Lt. Col. Harris C. Walker (2nd Battalion) Lt. Col. Wilfrid H. Haughey, then a major, who took command of the 3rd Battalion from Lt. Col. Alden Shipley on February 9, 1945. Photos: General Breckinridge archives

Sgt. Lawrence Thorn and Pfc. Preston Erwin load their Browning 1917 A1 machine gun in a position not far from Brandenbourg. Photo: US Army

A hastily erected US field hospital of the 5th Medical Battalion of the 5th Infantry Division in Diekirch. Photo taken January 22, 1945. A wounded man of the 2nd Infantry Regiment is just being brought in. Photo: US Army.

January 20, 1945: Units of the 11th Infantry Regiment walk the "Felser Strasse" toward Diekirch to relieve the exhausted companies of the 2nd and 10th Infantry Regiment north of "Kippenhof." Photo: US Army

On January 22, 1945 a patrol of the 5th US Infantry Division, supported by an M-8 "Greyhound" armored car, advances to Michelau to search the village for strayed Germans. At left is a shot-up RSO (full-tracked prime mover). The soldier in front carries an M-1 rifle with M9 A1 rifle grenade, the man at right an M-3 "grease gun" submachine gun. Photo: US Army

An abandoned Sherman tank near Brandenbourg. The tank, from the 737th Tank Battalion, slid off the icy road and down the slope until it came to a stop. The 737th Tank Battalion was assigned to the 5th US Infantry Division. Photo: US Army

A patrol of the 10th Infantry Regiment in white camouflage suits, being briefed before a reconnaissance mission. The man on the left carries an M-3 "grease gun" submachine gun, a favorite weapon of the reconnaissance teams. Photo: US Army

Right: Pvt. George Bryant took part in the Bettendorf Raid on January 10, 1945. The picture was taken in Germany, March 1945. Photo: Roland Gaul archives.

Group picture of a platoon of L Company, taken in March of 1945. Photo: Roland Gaul archives

Private James Carroll (second from right), rifleman of C Company, 11th Infantry Regiment, took part in the combat around Hoscheid and Hoscheid-Dickt. Photo: Roland Gaul archives

Soldiers of C Company in March 1945. Three of them carry German handguns in Wehrmacht holsters, a common GI practice. Photo: Roland Gaul archives

Two photos, taken in Wahlhausen, northeast of Hoscheid-Dickt at the end of January 1945, after the 11th Infantry Regiment had reached "Objective 32", the "Schinker" intersection. They show men of the 110th Infantry Regiment of 1st platoon, I Company, who appear to have been killed by the Germans after being captured, since the bodies all (?) show head wounds. Note that none of the dead men is still wearing shoes.

An abandoned German Flakpanzer (3.7 cm AA gun on Panzer IV chassis) at the Hoscheid-Merscheid intersection. This very rare version of a Flakpanzer probably belonged to a unit of the 79th VGD or Panzer Lehr Division. According to witnesses (US soldiers), the tank was burned out, and the driver's charred body was still inside. Photo: Roland Gaul archives

After the liberation of Hoscheid, an abandoned Panther tank sits in front of the Welbes-Marnach farm. The tank probably belonged to the "Panzer Lehr" Division and was left behind for lack of fuel and because of a defective track. The lowered barrel of the 75 mm Tank Gun 42 suggests that the gun was damaged internally by an explosive charge. The nickname of the Panther was "hell-hound." Photo: François Schroeder

A group of US soldiers of an infantry platoon, in makeshift camouflage clothing, moves forward along a snow-covered road in the cover of a hedge. The picture shows conditions similar to those at Hoscheid-Dickt. Photo: IWM, London

A US Army engineer with a mine detector, checking a roadside ditch in the Ardennes of Luxembourg. Photo: US Army

An explosives expert of an engineer unit ignites a fuze that, via detonating cord, explodes the charge of German mines, Panzerfausts or hand grenades to destroy them. The longish objects in the foreground are German Riegel mines that, equipped with several detonations, were extremely dangerous. Photo: US Army

Staff Sergeant Russell J. Hunt, then temporarily platoon chief of B Company, 7th Engineer Battalion; beside him Private Harry Spaulding. The photo was taken early in January 1945 in Heffingen, in front of the house where they were quartered. Photo: Roland Gaul archives.

A GMC truck of the 4th US Infantry Division coming from Eppeldorf is stopped at the edge of Bettendorf by a flat tire on January 19. At that time, part of Bettendorf was still under German artillery fire. Photo: US Army

A "floating bridge" is crossed by two Jeeps of the 5th Infantry Division on January 21, 1945. The photo was taken upstream of the railway station in Bettendorf. Photo: US Army

Men of the 1st Platoon of G Company, 2nd Battalion, 8th Infantry Regiment, cross the Sauer on a Bailey bridge in Moestroff on January 21, 1945. Some can be identified: 1. Pfc. Howard M. Hubbard (at left, with two rifles), 2. Sgt. Gaetano Fiorino, 3. Pfc. Raymond G. Bowker (rifle grenade), killed 1/30/45, 4. S/Sgt William R. Humphrey (left, behind first three), leader, 3rd Squad, 1st Platoon, 5. S/Sgt Edward Ference (bedroll under arm) Photo: US Army. Identification: William Humphrey, Jean Nesser

The same soldiers as in the photo opposite below, advancing through Moestroff. The man in the middle is the interpreter of G Company, Sgt. Arnold Erbstoesser. Photo: US Army. Identification: Walter Berry

Photo sequence from a US Signal Corps film, taken in Bettendorf on January 21, 1945, on the way from . . .

. . . the station to the Sauer in the area of the present-day Sassel-Schmitz farm . . .

. . . The soldiers belonged to the 4th Medical Battalion, which . . .

. . . carried urgently needed medicines and bandages from Eppeldorf across the Sauer by boat. US Signal Corps; Roland Gaul archives

We had received orders to try to cross the river again in one hour when we heard that our D Company up the river had received no enemy fire and had succeeded in erecting a footbridge on a row of rubber boats, on which the infantry had already advanced to the road that ran parallel to the Sauer. At the first light of day the Germans fired on Gilsdorf with a Nebelwerfer battery. These shells made a horrifying howling sound as they approached and caused tremendous air pressure when they exploded. Thank God, only a few salvoes were fired, but they caused great damage to the row of houses. The infantry company that we had been supposed to ferry across (Company F, 10th U.S. Infantry Regiment) now used the completed footbridge and crossed the river as early as 7:30 AM. We ourselves now brought up our necessary equipment and began to build a support bridge. Again we came under machine-gun and artillery fire, and numerous men were killed. We could have built the bridge in one or two hours, but under the sporadic harassing fire the construction went on until 2:00 PM. But at this time the infantry had already stormed the hill ahead of us and cleaned out the houses along the Sauer (Rue Clairefontaine, Gilsdorf). When the bridge was finally finished so that the Jeeps could cross it, we drew back until about 6:00 PM, when we were withdrawn, along with the equipment that had arrived, to Diekirch, which was still partially in German hands. Here we took up quarters in a house near the Sauer, and about 10:00 PM we began to build another footbridge. This, too was still under German artillery fire, but units of the 5th Infantry Division pushed across the bridge and reached the upper part of town around 3:00 AM on January 19. Our company itself had lost sixteen men dead and 53 wounded...a high price. All the medics, with just one exception, had been wounded in Gilsdorf."

The 150th Engineer Battalion
(Ettelbrück-Diekirch-Lipperscheid-Schlindermanderscheid)

The commander of the engineer battalion was Lt.Col. Bruce Reagan, who had been a bridge engineer by profession in civilian life. His knowledge was a big help to his unit and surely contributed to its success. He had already been decorated with the "Distinguished Service Cross" in December for successful and vital jobs carried out, and he often returned to Luxembourg after the war. He himself wrote the text of the activity report for his unit.

"On December 22 we were alarmed and left the Saar district around 6:00 AM, reaching Luxembourg via Metz. We received orders to stop in Bertrange, regroup and make the necessary equipment ready immediately.

On December 24 we were moved to Mersch and, despite all the confusion, received a Christmas dinner with the traditional turkey.

It was the task of General Eddy's XIIth Corps to stop the south flank of the German attack front in the Ardennes and close off all the approach roads to Luxembourg City before the Germans could recover and start a counterattack. Thus our first mission in Luxembourg consisted of a series of defensive measures. Reconnaissance troops from all the present engineer units noted defensive sectors, on orders from the corps, and passed information on focal points on to the staffs of the engineer battalions. Bridges were prepared for demolition if necessary, minefields were laid, trees notched and fitted with explosive charges along important roads.

On December 29 this work was finished according to plan, and we received orders to take over the guarding of these points ourselves. In addition, we had to make sure that the MSRs (main supply roads) remained open, for heavy snowfall limited traffic. Thus the greater part of the battalion was busy spreading sand, which was obtained from a pit, on the roads regularly. For this we received two bulldozers. Experiments showed that a mixture of sand and salt worked best. The ice on the roads melted and the sand provided good traction for the trucks. To open snowed-in country roads we were also supplied with a Sherman tank equipped with a hydraulic shovel. While this work went on day and night, the first preparations for the coming operations in the Sauer Valley were already being carried on by the corps. The battalion was charged with carrying out experiments in the preparation of pontoon bridges, that is, every rubber boat was already to be inflated and directly loaded with an attached section of deck made of boards, so as to shorten the actual time needed to erect the pontoon bridge.

During the night of January 17-18, 1945 the Battalion , with Company C alone, set up an eighty-foot bridge in Ettelbrück, and later on the 18th a second Bailey bridge north of the city, despite heavy enemy artillery fire. While the engineers of the 133rd Engineer Combat Battalion built footbridges near Gilsdorf, the A Company of our battalion built a Treadway bridge, 144 feet long, over the actual Sauer bridge blown up by the Germans in Gilsdorf. The work had to be interrupted several times on account of heavy German mortar fire. B Company was to begin the work of building a heavy pontoon bridge in Diekirch on January 19, but the presence of numerous minefields and mine traps on both sides of the Sauer delayed the work at first. After the minefields had been removed, the work was begun quickly; the job was finished at 10:30 AM on January 20.

While the engineers were still searching the Diekirch-Ingeldorf road for mines, C Company was already erecting a D-D bridge (Double-Double: a doubly reinforced prefabricated steel element bridge) over the damaged railroad bridge, which was linked to a Bailey bridge farther to the east, built by the newly arrived A Company, by an approach ramp. This bridge now linked the road to Luxembourg via Larochette with Diekirch. Thus there were now three bridges in Diekirch over which supplies and arriving units rolled northward. The last bridge had to be reinforced again to be able to carry the weight of the tanks. After the work was finished, 642 additional German wooden mines, called "Schu"-Mines", 18 tellermines and nine American tank mines were destroyed in place by Company A.

Individual platoons meanwhile carried out routine work on the supply routes; shell craters were filled, ditches opened, melt-water drains laid, etc.

During the course of the advance farther to the north, the XIIth Corps urgently needed new bridges. On January 23, bridges were built in Lipperscheid, a T/S bridge over the railroad line a mile north of Bourscheid, and another bridge, 110 feet long, in Schlindermanderscheid.

In addition, the bridge erected in Gilsdorf the night of the attack was rebuilt and reinforced again after a gridwork structure had been built on the pillars of the old Sauer bridge, which served as a solid supporting foundation.

At the end of January the battalion was drawn back to Colmar-Berg and replaced by the 133rd Engineer Combat Battalion. In February the 150th Engineer

Battalion provided invaluable assistance in helping the 319th Infantry Brigade of the 80th U.S. Infantry Division cross the Our near Moestroff."

The 166th Engineer Battalion

Lt.Col. Olen B. Curtis' 166th Engineer Battalion was transferred from Merl to Altlinster on December 24, and at first took over the protection of the headquarters of the 1135th Engineer Combat Group. On December 27, after the battalion had been attacked several times by German fighter planes, it was detailed to the 80th Infantry Division and began without delay to take defensive measures in the region around Ettelbrück, Schieren and Colmar-Berg.

Every preparation was made so as to be able to act at once in an emergency; explosive charges were brought up and roads were mined.

In addition, the battalion's snow plows kept the roads open while 24-hour readiness groups spread sand and salt on the icy roads. On January 5, 1945, Company A was given the task of building a Bailey bridge across the upper Sauer river at the Heiderscheider Grund. Intensive German artillery fire disturbed the work; in spite of that, the work of constructing a 96-foot Treadway bridge over the pillars of the blown-up Sauer bridge was completed, at a cost of 16 wounded engineers, some of them seriously wounded. In connection with that, Company B began without delay, as soon as the components were at hand, to build a double Bailey bridge in Esch on the Sauer. The work had to be interrupted numerous times on account of a German firefall, but late in the afternoon of January 7 the bridge was usable. Later in the month the battalion had the task of guarding the approaches to the bridge and continue to keep the approach roads open with snow plows and sand. Only on January 18 did Company B set up a 48-foot Treadway bridge near Tadler under intensive fire, without suffering any losses itself. Smaller Treadway bridges were built by Company B in Merkholz and Wilwerwiltz on January 24 and 25 respectively. In cooperation with the 80th Infantry Division, with the staff of its 318th Infantry Regiment, Lt.Col. Curtis began preparations to cross the Sauer. Dillingen was chosen as the crossing place.

While the companies gathered the bridging equipment and rubber boats, a scouting patrol left Mersch on February 6 and reached the highlands south of Dillingen. During the same night, the American artillery fired on the enemy shore while the first attack wave, consisting of two platoons of Company F (of the 18th Infantry Regiment) crossed the river in the boats. The men had just reached the shore when a murderous fire brought the undertaking to a standstill. Under cover of darkness on the following night, after the artillery had kept the enemy-occupied highlands under fire, additional parts of the regiment were able to cross. The bridgebuilding itself took six days, since it was interrupted again and again by heavy Nebelwerfer fire. The losses were frightfully high in Dillingen alone. From February 9 to 16, 72 men had lost their lives or were badly wounded. Numerous engineers drowned in the waters of the Sauer after a raft ferry capsized as a result of being hit.

But the American advance was unstoppable; numerous troops streamed over the bridge in Dillingen toward the enemy, while the rest of the battalion blew up circumvented bunkers and eliminated minefields. After successfully crossing the Sauer, the 166th Engineer Battalion was subordinated to the 4th U.S. Armored Division.

CHAPTER XIV

THE 8TH U.S. ARMY AIR FORCE OVER LUXEMBOURG

"Klette's Wild Hares" was the Air Force jargon nickname of the 324th Bomb Squadron, detailed and directly subordinated to the 91st Bombardment Group, which participated within the framework of the extensive military operations of the 1st Air Division as well as the entire 8th U.S. Army Air Force.

The nickname of this unit refers directly to that of the echelon commander, Major Immanuel Klette, one of the most decorated U.S. pilots of World War II.

Both the 8th and 9th U.S. Army Air Forces deserve much credit for the successful nature of the Allied advance after the extraordinarily bad weather, that at first made any possible military attack on enemy units in the Ardennes from the air impossible, gradually dissipated after Christmas 1944 and the skies cleared.

While preparations by the OKW for the German offensive were already underway in the late autumn of 1944, and the military units, plus supplies of materials, ammunition and equipment were slowly brought to the respective sectors of origin on the West Wall, the 8th U.S. Army Air Force, with the 324th Bomb Squadron under Major Klette as its "leading force." and with a total of 1291 bombers of the B-17 and B-24 types, escorted by 954 fighter planes, set out on November 21, 1944 to deliver a crushing blow to the Wehrmacht command, which surely contributed to the postponement of the day of the attack, originally scheduled somewhat earlier, to December 16. On that day, and again four days later, the attack was made chiefly on the Leuna fuel refinery near Merseburg, one of the main facilities for German production of fuel, which was needed more urgently than ever by the Wehrmacht.

Although the weather on that November 21, according to reports, was the worst ever recorded in all the action of the 8th U.S. Army Air Force, the success was nevertheless noteworthy despite numerous planes being shot down.

In that dangerous mission, Major Klette stood out particularly, and shortly thereafter, despite his 27 years, he was promoted to Lieutenant Colonel for his extraordinary abilities as a pilot and leader. Major "Manny" Klette is also the pilot who scored the highest number of missions and enemy encounters in the European Theater of War, as well as the greatest number of flight hours during combat missions (total: 689 hours, 25 minutes). Included is a mission that was carried out by twelve B-17 "Flying Fortress" bombers of the 324th Bomber Squadron on December 18, 1944. This mission of a very special nature, which required five and a half hours of time, applied to Luxembourg. Its name was recorded in the logbook of the echelon commander as, "Screening Force Mission."

"Screening Force Mission"

Despite complete surprise at the beginning, the Allied command very soon attained a clear awareness of the extent of the German attack. Since the thin American units all had to drop back according to plan at first until new forces could intervene, it was necessary to use all means to prevent the unification and coordination of the German combat units, including those that were first to cross the boundary at the West Wall.

It was necessary above all, since the U.S. Air Force could not intervene directly because of the bad-weathjer zone, to concentrate on massive disturbance of enemy air traffic and crippling of information centers. At higher command from the 8th U.S. Air Force, Major Klette was ordered to lead one of these operations just two days after the beginning of the German offensive.

His task was to disturb any radio traffic within a limited air space (ground to ground, ground to air and air to ground). This was to be accomplished by the massive dropping of aluminum paper strips and scraps.

Thus on the morning of December 18 the echelon of "Klette's Wild Hares" took off from the 8th Air Force field at Bassingbourne (near Cambridge, England) on that mission, flew over the English Channel, then set a course over The Netherlands and approached Luxembourg, where from an average altitude of 31,500 feet aluminum strips were dropped from air space position 5035 N-0603 E to 4935 N-0625 E (approximately Monschau-Remich).

Tons of these shreds, called "chaff", bundled and equipped with small explosive charges which caused their dispersal, were hung in the bomb shafts of the B-17 aircraft in place of the usual bomb loads. In addition, several men in every aircraft, especially the machine gunners, were to push out parachutes filled with the same material.

The entire drop took place in formation flight, in which Major Klette's B-17 flew at the head of the left wing. This formation, consisting of twelve aircraft and escorted by several high-flying fighter planes, returned to England unharmed and without making any contact with German fighters, after successfully carrying out its mission. Within the framework of a larger offensive action of the 8th U.S. Army Air Force, the 91st Bombardment Group, including "Klette's Wild Hares", took part in numerous subsequent large-scale air attacks. After no flights could be made for about five days on account of very bad weather, as of December 24, 1944 circa 2000 bombers were applied against various targets in Germany, particularly Luftwaffe support points, railroad junctions and cities occupied by the military forces.

The 91st Bombardment Group established packs of bombers for an A Force to bomb the airfield at Merzhausen, as well as a B Force to destroy the Luftwaffe support point and airfield at Kirch-Gons. The latter unit was composed, among others, of a high-flying echelon (381st Bomb Squadron), a low-flying echelon (389th Bomb Squadron), and "Klett's Wild Hares (324th Bomb Squadron), which undertook the leadership of the attack on Kirch-Gons under the command of Major Klette.

The weather was relatively clear, so that the bombing could be done by sight. Kirch-Gons was totally destroyed in this attack; the airfield with its runways showed numerous bomb craters, so that this support point became unusable. When the units returned from their successful mission, they came into a bad-weather zone with zero visibility over the Channel.

Because of these extraordinarily difficult weather conditions, which lasted into England, the base at Bassingbourne, where the 324th B.S. was stationed, could not be reached, and the squadrons had to land at the totally overfilled air base in Bury St. Edmunds.

The further missions of the 8th U.S. Army Air Force in which the 91st Bombbardment Group participated were directed primarily against the German supply network. Thus Bitburg, Prüm, Wittlich, Koblenz-Lützel, Remagen, Cologne, Bonn, Mainz, Ludwigshafen and Kaiserslautern were bombed regularly until mid-January 1945. So "Klette's Wild Hares" helped to destroy the German supply network, a hard blow that finally brought the offensive to a standstill.

Major Klette's squadron was identified by a letter A in a red triangle on the tails of its B-17 planes. The A indicated that they were members of the 91st Bombardment Group. The letters DF painted along the fuselage were the identifying mark of the 342nd Bomb Squadron whose radio identification sign was the word "dimple." Major Manny Klette's plane bore the registration number 224, as well as the nickname "Oklahoma Yankee."

The squadron that dropped aluminum strips over Luxembourg on December 18, 1944 was constituted as follows:

B-17 number 224: Major Klette, Commander
"   "   174: Lt. Maplesden
"   "   889: Lt. Raisin
"   "   205: Lt. Bowlan
"   "   772: Lt. Boies
"   "   946: Lt. Emerson
"   "   568: Lt. Gaines
"   "   944: Lt. Kimmel
"   "   988: Lt. Adams
"   "   880: Lt. McDovel
"   "   993: Lt. Laws
"   "   151: Lt. Balaban

Total: 12 aircraft
Mission time: 5.5 hours
Mission location: Line approximately Monschau-Remich

Surely many Luxembourgers still remember the rain of aluminum strips that fell from the sky on December 18, 1944, scattered in all directions by the wind, and probably used as makeshift tinsel to decorate many a Christmas tree, which no GI, no German soldier or villager wanted to go without despite those hard times.

Christmas 1944: An Airplane Tragedy near Diekirch

As already related, as of December 24 massive air raids against German supply routes and freight yards, on which all the supplies of the already bogged-down German offensive moved, were flown by the 8th U.S. Army Air Force for strategical bombing, and by the 9th U.S. Army Air Force for tactical air strikes.

The comments of several inhabitants of Diekirch about a four-engined American airplane that crashed on the "Goldknapp" (between Diekirch and Erpeldange) awakened the author's interest. On the basis of a "missing aircrew report", and finally thanks to the interviews of two survivors of this crash, the fate and the fateful mission of this bomber crew could thus be reconstructed.

This is what the surviving co-pilot of the airplane, Lt. Alfred J. Walterscheid, now living in New Mexico, wrote to the author:

"Our machine, a four-engined B-17G, belonged to the 570th Bomb Squadron of the 390th Bombardment Group. This unit itself was part of the 13th Combat Wing of the 3rd Air Division of the 8th U.S. Army Air Force and was stationed in southern England from 1942 to 1945. Our Bomb Squadron itself came directly from Geiger Airfield, Washington, USA, and had been stationed at Parham Airfield near Framlingham in Suffolk since July 4, 1943. The unit was commanded by Flight Captain Richard "Dick" Perry, a still young but extremely capable officer. The plane whose co-pilot I was bore the number 44-8323, as well as the nickname 'Blonde Bombshell'. A bright yellow letter J was painted on the rudder as an identifying mark. Normally we flew missions in a formation of 18 to 21 planes. My crew was composed as follows:

Pilot: 1st Lt. Elwood Lee
Co-Pilot: 1st Lt. Alfred J. Walterscheid
Navigator: 1st Lt. Loran A. Steen
Bombardier: 1st Lt. Roland E. Weber
Upper Machine Gunner: Tec. Sgt. Robert de Orsay
Radioman: Tec. Sgt. Coy D. Pledger
Bow Machine Gunner: S/Sgt. Paul C. Roberts
Fuselage Machine Gunner: S/Sgt. Stanley V. Wrubleski
Tail Machine Gunner: Junior Sgt. Eddie C. Skindingsrude.

Early in the morning of December 25, 1944 I did not yet know what was waiting for us on that day. Our whole unit went to Christmas mass at midnight, and Chaplain Daniel Lanahan gave us the holy communion. Around 5:00 AM we were awakened. After a brief but ample Christmas breakfast we were then briefed by Captain Perry. Our mission on that fateful day, on which six crewmen in our plane were to meet death, was supposed to be a routine flight. The bridge near Morscheid (Trier area) was to be bombed and destroyed because, according to information from headquarters, an important railroad line that transported ammunition for the German attacking units, which had already come to a stop in the Ardennes, ran across it. That flight was our 28th mission.

According to our briefing, our plane was to take position number 4 in the formation, thus directly behind the squadron leader, the plane of Captain Perry. Every plane carried a normal load of explosive and incendiary bombs. Our flight went off without problems at an altitude of 19,000 feet, but the target was to be overflown at an altitude of 25,000 feet, from which height the bombs were to be dropped."

Co-pilot Walterscheid was flying the "Blonde Bombshell" himself when heavy anti-aircraft fire began unexpectedly in the Eifel, short of Bitburg. His report continues: "I saw an explosion on the right side of the cockpit; the next one was a direct hit on engine number 4, which immediately caught fire and exploded. The plane slowly began to dive. I tried to control it ... without success. The pilot, Lt. Lee, was also helpless. He gave me the thumbs-down sign; not a good sign. To be ready for anything, I instinctively reached for my parachute behind my seat, but at the same moment the airplane turned to the side, made a tight circle, so that I was not able to lift my arm right away. Then everything happened so fast that I have a very hard time remembering the order of events.

A second explosion, caused by another direct hit, probably tore the cockpit away. An ice-cold gust hit me in the face; when I regained consciousness, feeling numbed, I saw nothing but blue sky behind me, plus an empty pilot's seat. At my side was my chest parachute. I reacted lightning-fast, pulled it to me and hooked the D ring of my harness into the carbine hook of the parachute. I released my safety belt, was immediately pulled away by the airstream and thrown out of the cockpit, which was falling to earth. I pulled on the rip cord, and as the parachute opened with a jerk, a carbine hook that had not been secured hit me above my right eye. The ice-cold wind blew me over a small village before I landed in a snow-covered open area.

I had also lost one of my fleece-lined left aviation boot. I looked up to the sky and, a relatively long distance away from me, two parachutes floating to earth. A dull thud behind me, then at a distance to the southwest a black cloud of smoke ... It was not long after that when three German soldiers took me prisoner and led me away.

I spent that night in a cow barn, under guard. The cows that were still there warmed us, and I joined in, in English, when the German soldiers sang 'Silent Night'. On the next morning, after being questioned by a young officer, I was allowed to make an improvised foot covering out of old sacks. Then we went off on foot, until after an exhausting march, we arrived that afternoon at a German prisoner-of-war camp, where I could count some 200 interned American soldiers. To my great amazement, I met two members of my crew.

Roland Weber and Coy Pledger, the bombardier and the radioman.

First Lieutenant Weber told me that he could remember only a noise; then he was thrown out of the airplane and hit by a scrap of plexiglas. His parachute opened normally. Tech Sergeant Pledger remembered only a rough landing after he had jumped out.

Days later we arrived in Wittlich; the city showed much damage. In Koblenz we were subjected to stringent questioning, and all our personal belongings were also taken away from us.

Five months later, after a lot of misery, we were finally liberated by the russians from Stalag III on the Baltic Sea. Only now could I communicate with my family. I am sure that during my 28 flights I caused a lot of destruction and human misery. Therefore I cannot be proud, but rather feel that I made a small contribution to the fight against Nazi Germany." Thus ends Lieutenant Walterscheid's report.

The bridge at Morscheid took four direct hits from 1000-pound bombs on that day, and several hits on the south end. The railroad tracks were completely destroyed.

Lieutenant Lee's "Blonde Bombshell" was the only loss in this mission on Christmas Day 1944. No one knows exactly what happened to the plane, but from the missing aircrew report no. 11115 of March 1, 1945, the following can be learned:

An additional witness (a civilian from Diekirch), who was on the "Mouschbierg" between Diekirch and Stegen shortly after 12:00 noon on that 25th day of December, reports: "A large burning airplane, with a national emblem that I could not recognize at once, came from the direction of Gilsdorf toward Diekirch at a low altitude, badly hit. Several explosions on the ground followed, probably from bombs that were thrown or fell out. The burning plane then 'flew' in the direction of Ettelbrück and I lost sight of it but still heard the dull thud. It must have exploded in the air!" The MAC (missing aircrew report) report confirms this. After the offensive, the plane was found in several pieces strewn on the plateau on the southern slope of the Goldknapp called "op Héimricht." Among the ruins were the battered bodies of five crewmen. The same eyewitness (Michel Hamen of Diekirch), who had already returned to Diekirch at the end of January, was present when the bodies were taken away by the American authorities. He also had to bring two horses to take away several bombs that lay on the slope to the "Waalebrouch" and had not exploded.

For Wrubleski, Skindingsrude, Roberts, Steen and de Orsay, the "Héimricht" became their fate. Pilot Elwood Lee had met death shortly before the fatal explosion, presumably still on German soil, when the cockpit tore off and he was flung out. The six unfortunate crewmen were buried at the U.S. military cemetary in Hamm, Luxembourg; the mortal remains of Paul Roberts, Loran Steen and Eddie Skindingsrude were reinterred in the USA in 1951 at the request of their families.

Lieutenant Walterscheid lives in retirement in New Mexico today; Lieutenant Roland Weber runs an insurance agency in Fort Wayne, Indiana; Sergeant Coy Pledger lived in Oklahoma after the war and died a few years ago after a long illness.

Psychological Warfare
Enemy Propaganda Operations (December 1944-February 1945)

Psychological warfare is not a modern-day invention. Psychological warfare used as a weapon is as old as mankind itself, and was already used successfully by parties that waged war in ancient days. Fully based on the degree of effectiveness, especially in critical and clearly hopeless situations, psychological warfare and the propaganda operations that were related to it were used with great effectiveness in World War I. As an important component of the higher staffs (army corps, army, army group), there were many special "Psyops units" (on the American side) or propaganda units (in the Wehrmacht) in World War II, whose task it was to weaken the enemy psychologically in the hope of encouraging him to give up. It was the purpose of this type of warfare to deliver purposeful information to the enemy deliberately to encourage him to think about his situation. Psychological warfare is partially based on the inmost human feelings, in the hope that they, through utilization of an existing unpromising situation in which he is at at a given point in time, can inspire the enemy to change sides. In this process, psychological warfare makes use of various types of "propaganda", which can be designated either "white", "black" or combined "gray" propaganda. By white propaganda is meant the revelation of truths that have heretofore been deliberately concealed from the enemy by his own side, for whatever reasons, since they could lead, with some certainty, to unwanted actions (for example, the political, economic or social situation in his homeland, far away from the front). Black propaganda is based chiefly on plausible-sounding lies and untruths or fictionalized ideal concepts that will be regarded as plausible by the enemy and inspire him to change his combat morale. Gray propaganda is a mixture of accurate information and rumors.

The propaganda units existing at the higher service levels work closely with the G-2 or S-2 "intelligence" units (news services, in the Wehrmacht, called Ic or "Abwehr"), which evaluated and disseminated details of the enemy's situation that could be used for psychological warfare or deliberate propaganda action. Such information generally was gained through interrogating deserters and prisoners, came from information provided by the civilian population, or was gained through aerial reconnaissance.

The information that was usable for psychological warfare was, after being prepared, usually written up in the form of "propaganda" leaflets or broadcast on known enemy frequencies or enemy radio waves. Radio Luxembourg, under the code name "Radio Annie", was used particularly during the Ardennes offensive when numerous Americans of German descent in the Psyops section of the XIIth Army Group, including the subsequent ex-GDR author Stefan Heym, sent anti-German or demoralizing messages into the air from the Villa Louvigny in Luxembourg. Heym described his experiences as a psychological warfare agent or "sky warrior" for Radio "Annie" Luxembourg in the book "Reden an den Feind" (Addresses to the Enemy), written by him in 1986. On the other hand, the leaflets, printed by the thousands (by both of the opposing sides), were either scattered over the front area by low-flying aircraft or fired by the artillery in so-called "propaganda shells." In the Wehrmacht in particular, there were already propaganda troops at the beginning of the war whose task it was to "cover" the enemy liberally with leaflets through the use of either artillery or gas balloons.

For this purpose there was even a special kind of ammunition produced, the propaganda rocket missile 41. A normal artillery propaganda shell, generally of 10.5 cm caliber with a maximum range of 10 kilometers, consisted of a hollow steel body equipped with a time fuze and containing 250 to 300 leaflets. A small ejection charge of black powder was mounted behind the leaflets to scatter them, either on impact of the shell or during its trajectory, so as to achieve a better dispersal. The wind then took care of distribution. How much value the Wehrmacht placed on this type of warfare is shown by the example of "propaganda rifle grenades" which could be fired directly at the enemy by the infantry at the shortest ranges (circa 150 meters) by using a cup-launcher. The Americans generally preferred the distribution of leaflets by their artillery. So there were "propaganda rounds" of 105 mm, 155 mm and, in rare cases, even eight-inch (203 mm) calibers. The propaganda rounds were not standard ammunition, but merely "smoke" or colored-smoke marker shells from which the smoke containers had been removed and replaced by leaflets.

Unfortunately, supplies and statistics as to the effect of the psychological warfare during the late 1944-early 1945 period were very sparse or not available at all at the time of this book's publication.

Yet it can be noted in conclusion that the possession of enemy propaganda by men of the Wehrmacht was punishable by draconian measures – especially in the case of soldiers who carried enemy leaflets on their persons and were regarded as possible deserters and saboteurs – and the military courts often sentenced them to death.

The following is a small assortment of propaganda leaflet text found in the Luxembourg front area:

Security First, a German leaflet that was very probably fired into the sector of the 3rd Battalion of the 109th Infantry Regiment of the 28th U.S. Infantry Division on December 16 or 17, 1944, thus right at the beginning of the offensive. The original, which can be seen in the Musée National d'Histoire Militaire in Diekirch, was kept as a memento of the war by a GI of the 28th Infantry Division. It is astonishing how well informed the German defenses were about the opposing U.S. troop units or knew the unit's previous history.

Safe Conduct – one of the most widespread U.S. leaflets used on the western front, signed by the Commander of the Allied Expeditionary Forces, General Dwight D. Eisenhower. It was probably printed by the millions. On the back of the leaflet, which exists in both red and green, the rules for treating prisoners, based on the principles of the Geneva Convention, are printed. As a soldier of the 109th Regiment recalls, a German soldier surrendered at Bleesbrück on December 18, 1944 with the copy shown here. The "safe conduct", which had thus fulfilled its purpose, was then sent to America as a souvenir.

Job on Two Fronts – German propaganda leaflet from mid-December 1944. "He earns fifteen dollars a week and risks his life – he earns 45 dollars a week and is safe at home."

Merry Christmas: Hark . . . the Herald Angels Sing! With these leaflets the Wehrmacht tried to persuade the Americans to desert shortly before Christmas of 1944 by appealing to his inmost desire for a Christmas celebration with his loved ones in the U.S.A. The second leaflet did not even rule out the possibility of spending Christmas 1944 at home – the way to do it was through illness and recovery leave in the U.S.A. at Christmas.

That was a dream, 5 minutes after 12, and We ask for information! Three U.S. Psyops propaganda leaflets that were meant to make the German soldiers see the undeniable reality. Probably distributed at the beginning of 1945.

U.S. instructions for lifesaving – German soldiers who could not understand English were taught the life-saving words "Ei ssörrender – I surrender" phonetically. January 1945.

3x Field Post, January 1, 1945 issue (front and rear). White propaganda representing the reality of the situation as a penetrating antidote to the Wehrmacht reports that whitewashed the situation. The U.S. gains of territory in the Wiltz, Diekirch and Echternach areas indicate the middle of January 1945. "One month of war history" – U.S. reference to the failed offensive and parallels from the eastern front. Mid-January 1945. This leaflet, with about 200 other copies, was found only in 1989 in an unexploded 105 mm U.S. shell.

Field Post, February 7, 1945 issue. In the Prüm-Echternach sector, West Wall fortifications are threatened with being surrounded. It was probably fired by the 5th U.S. Infantry Division shortly after the Sauer crossing on February 7, 1945.

Without a doubt, the frightening specter of "Germans in U.S. uniforms" behind the American lines can be regarded as a successful factor in German psychological warfare during the entire course of the offensive. Several "Skorzeny" men of Panzer Brigade 150 crossed over with the mission of appearing in U.S. uniforms and creating confusion and sabotage on the U.S. front in the northern region of the German attack. They caused rumors of the massive use of similar commands to spread like wildfire all over the front area. The result of this "psychosis" led to genuine Americans often being questioned for hours because they did not know the correct password at checkpoints. A similar incident, in which Prince Felix of Luxembourg was examined stringently when in the uniform of a British brigadier general, can also be seen as a result of this. The newspaper article on the subject appeared in the February 1, 1945 issue of "Stars and Stripes."

Radio Luxembourg During the Ardennes Offensive

As already mentioned, the transmitters at the Villa Louvigny and Junglinster were used by "Radio Annie", run by the OSS (Office of Strategic Services) for psychological warfare. Under orders from Lieutenant Colonel William Harlan Hale, "Radio Annie" broadcast demoralizing "greetings" and messages to the German front every night (with a short interruption during the first days of the offensive) from the end of November 1944 on. The transmitting facilities, which had already been taken over by the Americans in mid-September 1944, remained under the control of the OSS until the beginning of April 1945. The code name "Annie", incidentally, came from the first name of Miss Anni Esch, who worked in the record archives of Radio Luxembourg, and who was courted by several members of the psyops warfare section.

It was quite by chance that in 1985 the author met the chief engineer of Radio Luxembourg at the time after the transmitter had fallen intact into American hands in 1944.

Without going into excessive details, the following report, based on an interview with Donald V.R. Drenner, will offer a brief overview of the effective use of this station, which is world-famous today, with its present headquarters and main transmitters still in Luxembourg.

On September 10, 1944 Donald Drenner, a civilian radio expert with special military status, arrived in Luxembourg with the units of the 5th U.S. Armored Division, after having worked for the BBC for months. The transmitter with the 147-

kilowatt equipment had remained intact, although it had been prepared for demolition by the Germans. The German radio engineers had simply removed several parts and taken them with them.

But the two Luxembourgeois engineers also showed initiative that paid off. Shortly before the Germans returned, Metty Felten and Nicolas Schmitt had been able to convince the German personnel at the station that the best way to make the transmitter unusable to the Americans consisted of destroying switches and removing the big tubes. The German technical personnel, not very gifted technologically, followed these directions. Meanwhile, though, the two Luxembourgers had secretly removed certain important components and hidden them. For example, one tube was hidden for a time under a huge pile of straw in a barn near Diekirch.

"For this reason it was a minor matter to make the transmitter functional again within a few days," Donald Drenner reports, "after we had taken it over. There was just no more contact between the radio station in the Villa Louvigny and the transmitter in Junglinster. Since this break was caused by a damaged connection that was mounted in the bridge near Eich and blown up by the Germans, this damage was also repaired quickly. Within days we were 'on the air' again. The necessary energy of 20,000 volts was supplied by a heavy Diesel generator, for which I immediately ordered . . . and received . . . a thousand gallons of fuel.

At the Villa Louvigny a party was held after the transmitter was functioning again. There I made the acquaintance of a girl employed by Radio Luxembourg, Annie Esch, whose first name was probably used as the code name for Radio Annie when the OSS got interested in Radio Luxembourg in mid-November 1944 and the transmiter was thus placed under the control of the secret service.

Within the parameters of psychological warfare, several German prisoners of war from the fighting around Aachen who had volunteered were used to read demoralizing letters from German soldiers. Radio Annie became active at night; then it was switched to the frequency of Radio Berlin, which we knew, and our broadcasts could thus be heard by the entire German population. To protect the transmitter in Junglinster, where work went on day and night, a few tanks and several soldiers stood by. During all this time I was assisted by the Luxembourgers Ferd Scholtes.

The headquarters of the OSS, whose communications officer, Lieutenant Sam Rotterman, took control over all activities, were located in a command car by the Villa Louvigny. To this car, which was guarded stringently, I myself had no access, nor did the personnel subordinate to me.

When the German offensive began on December 16, 1944 and it became known that a possible German attack from Echternach on Junglinster could not be ruled out, it was decided to shut down the transmitter. As quickly as possible, we took the tubes out of the amplifiers, loaded them onto a 6x6 Dodge and drove to Luxembourg. Only on December 23, after the German advance had finally come to a standstill in the endangered area, did we again get a green light from the Army Group Command. During the very same night, about 11:30 PM, Radio Annie became operational again. On the following day the Luxembourg Military Band gave a concert at the Villa Louvigny, which was broadcast. During the nightly broadcasts of 'Annie', a propaganda program was always introduced by 'Yankee Doodle',

'Lili Marleen' or selections from operas by Schubert or Strauss. Numerous OSS personnel, including several American agents of German origin, regularly gave information, the purpose of which was to use the radio to damage the morale of the German troops, who were already on the defensive. After the offensive ended, Radio Luxembourg remained under the direction of Colonel Rosenbaum, Lieutenant Colonel William Harlan Hale as station chief, and me as Chief Engineer, and under Allied control until the beginning of April 1945."

Here are some excerpts from broadcasts by Radio Annie, consisting for the most part of interviews with prisoners from the 5th Paratroop Division in an American prisoner-of-war camp.

"Our radio truck is now in an American prisoner-of-war camp, a transit camp behind the front in the Ardennes. We have called a German Unteroffizier (NCO) in a blue uniform to the microphone. "Herr Unteroffizier, was is the significance of your blue uniform? Are you in the Luftwaffe? What is the meaning of the emblem on your left side?"

"The emblem on the left side of my uniform means that I am a pilot. It is a symbol of activity, and . . ."

"Were you in action as a pilot?"

"No, I never had the good luck to go into action as a pilot; I was sent into action as an infantryman, as a paratrooper."

"When were you active as a pilot?"

"I was a flight instructor and trained trainees for the front."

"Why were you not used as a pilot?"

"That is the way it was with us; we not only had a shortage of gasoline, but also of aircraft, for the American Air Force was so superior to our planes that we could no longer venture on missions against England." – "So, and why were you then transferred to the paratroops?" – "Along with me there were other comrades, some of them with high honors, who came from the front, who were transferred to the paratroops. We came to Gardelage, a transit camp. Here Wehrmacht members of all kinds were gathered. From there we were divided among the close-combat schools; these schools were where we were supposed to be trained for the infantry." – "And so you were retrained to be a paratrooper?" – "Yes, we are paratroops, but we never jumped out of an airplane, that is, when one was a pilot and he had bad luck, naturally he jumped out, but the specific paratroop training, that we never had. We were taught only the necessary basic concepts, but very poorly, there was no real weapons teacher to instruct us."

"Didn't you ever have genuine infantry training?"

"No, the infantry training was very faulty."

"And what happened to you in action?"

"Well, in action it happened that it was very difficult for us, only for the men who came from the combat squadrons or the flight units." – "Were other former pilots in service there?" – "Yes, we had a captain, he was the company chief, he was . . . as a human being he was fabulous, he got along fine with the men, the men liked him. One day, though, he and his company had moved quite far ahead and enemy tanks came along. The superior power was clear to see. He ordered his men to drop back somewhat and gather together." – "Yes, and then?" – "The men moved back, and the regimental commander of the 15th Regiment held this captain responsible, he was court-martialed and sentenced to a year's imprisonment and the loss of his rank. It was too bad for the man, for he only wanted the best for his men." – "That was in the 5th Paratroop Division?" – "Yes, that was in the 5th Paratroop Division in this regiment." – "And what happened to you as a former pilot; how did you like it?" – "Well, waging war is simply a matter for men; it is pleasant when the march goes forward, when you have weapons; but it is hopeless, sad, when you sit in a hole in the ground, facing a force, facing soldiers who have fully automatic weapons, who have artillery support, who are well-fed. We certainly had brave hearts, but the heart alone is not decisive in war, we lacked the weapons." – "What was lacking?" – "Well, we had only the carbine, for example, and with our carbine you had to load every round; on the other hand, the American soldier had a self-loading rifle that had eight or nine rounds in it, and he can fire it like a pistol." –"What was it like in this good weather in the last days? Did you see a lot of airplanes?" – "Yes, we saw a great many airplanes, but unfortunately only American airplanes; if we had seen one of our airplanes, we would have been happy, but . . . we slowly began to feel hopeless and didn't understand why we airplane pilots were sent off into the ground – ah – ground combat, where an air force is necessary. If we . . . the American air force with its fighter-bombers gave us a lot of trouble." – "Well, thank you, Herr Unteroffizier." – "You're welcome."

Often the psychological warfare put on programs on Radio Annie about the extremely miserable food supplies of the Wehrmacht in action in the Ardennes, so as to lower the German morale.

Here is an excerpt from a similar interview of a captured member of an artillery regiment of a Volksgrenadier division:

"How was your food?" – "Well, with the food it was like this: it was always brought in at night, and everything was cold; sometimes . . . we got no potatoes, just a casserole, always a one-dish meal, and later meat and potatoes were requisitioned from the civilians because none was available as supplies."

"How was that done, the requisitioning, what did they do?"

"Well, a requisition order was shoved into their hands, and then pigs, cows and so on, and potatoes were simply taken away." – "Why was the food always cold, as you said?" – "Food containers were brought forward, and on the way they always got cold." – "Was the kitchen so far away?" – "Yes, it was far away." – "How far was it, how many kilometers away was it?" – "Ten kilometers, at least, and all under artillery fire." – "Oh, and what was the situation with equipment and clothing?"

"I personally had good equipment, but other comrades were not sufficiently equipped; they had no head protectors, they had only a pair of thin gloves and socks, thin ones, and so they always had wet feet, the whole time. An awful lot of comrades had their feet frozen off." – "Couldn't you warm yourself up? Wasn't there a stove or any such thing there?" – "We had no chance."

The prisoners were regularly asked about the morale of the troops, probably the most important factor in psychological warfare:

"What was actually the mood, the opinion of the soldiers about the offensive that was begun on December 16, and what do they think about it now?"

"In December it all seemed as if it was still going well, as if we still had enough forces there, but when the offensive came to a stop and we kept trying to push the wedge farther and that didn't succeed, then we realized that a bad mistake had been made by the leadership in having started the offensive in the first place, for it cost a terrible lot of human lives." – "In your unit too?" –"Yes, there were very many dead and wounded." – "You were in Luxembourg at the end, weren't you? And did you talk to the civilians there?"

Yes, we were quartered in Luxembourg several times, and it happened that the civilians always showed us the difference between German and American soldiers." – "What did the civilians say about the Americans?" – "They always said they had behaved perfectly . . . the people, well, they always gave them something willingly, but the Germans came in and took all the hay and fodder out of the barns, took private quarters and never asked if they were wanted there at all. The mood among the Germans was very bad."

Another example of a broadcast was the following:

Willi von Manstein: "I am an American prisoner. I am all right. I ask that my family be notified. My address is Berlin N 65, Bankstrasse 78. Willi von Manstein."

"Comrades, I speak to you from imprisonment. I can only tell you it is better to be imprisoned by the Americans than to be in our Wehrmacht. Not just the food, no, one is treated like a human being here. Full of trust in the strength of the American army, I see the end of the war ahead and the awareness that there are still sensible people, there are leaders with character and humanity." (a member of the 5th Paratroop Division)

It is noteworthy than Radio Annie also broadcast to Germany the report of a Luxembourgers who fled from Germany. He told the OSS agents the following:

"I fled from Germany a few days ago, and I was lucky to reach Luxembourg safely. If I just make a comparison between here and in Germany, then I ask myself how it is possible that the Nazi criminals could still pull off their last disgraceful act. What I am talking about is the Volkssturm, in which older fathers, grandfathers, lame and asthmatic man are forced in without differentiation. This is the worst crime of all time. But I also know the attitude of these, Germany's truly last battalions. I saw twice how they assembled in a village in the vicinity of Mayen. There was no trace of courage or confidence in victory to be seen. Some of them wished often and loudly: 'If only the Americans were here, then at least we would have peace and quiet.' Others said: 'We're not coming here any more; there is no reason to hang around here; I would rather stay home and muck out the cowbarn.' There was no trace of weapons to be seen. I asked one man about fifty years old, who walked with a slight limp: 'What would you do if you were lying behind a bush with a weapon and the Americans came by close to you?'

He answered: 'First I would let out a yell of joy, throw my weapon away and greet the liberators.'" (Source: tape recordings of Radio Luxembourg, in: Deutsches Rundfunkarchiv, Frankfurt am Main.)

CHAPTER XV

THE CIVILIANS

The last part of this book is dedicated to the very compassionate and hard-pressed civilian population between the Sauer and the Our. Of the numerous inhabitants of the villages around Diekirch, there were many who could not reach safety in the hinterlands at the right time or be evacuated from the combat area later by the Americans or the Germans during the course of the offensive, so that they had to endure sufferings and fears that are almost unimaginable to us today amid the barbaric weather conditions, in the dim candlelight of a cellar room that offered them some measure of safety.

At this point I would like to mention the excellent work of Abbé Fritz Rasqué, who worked hard to gather the firsthand experiences of the inhabitants of all the villages in the Ösling and Echternach areas as early as 1945 and publish them in his book "Ösling im Krieg."

Unfortunately, this book is out of print today, and I consider myself lucky to possess a copy. Throughout the years it has provided me with a basic knowledge of the events that took place in the area (from the civilian standpoint), and has helped me in my research and interviews with eyewitnesses from the various villages around Diekirch. The works of Josef Maertz and E.T. Melchers have also contributed to this chapter and provide an extensive overview of the life of the civilian population during the offensive.

For practical reasons, I have limited myself only to villages and farms that are in close proximity to my home town of Diekirch. In addition, the accounts and comments of the civilians enhance the chapters in the German and American sections, so that the reader receives a well-rounded picture of the events. Often it was possible to locate individual experiences precisely in this way, and the historically factual and objective portrayal resulted from the comparison of the three different viewpoints. In this way the attentive reader may note names, dates, incidents, etc. that, presented in different ways, attest to the veracity of a historical event.

In addition, the following accounts shall be representative of the entire population of the Ösling (Luxembourg name for the Ardennes) area, whose courage and endurance are remembered to this day by so many soldiers, whether Americans or Germans. In conclusion, I would like to express my heartfelt thanks to all those people, including those who wished to remain anonymous or who provided only a few comments.

Tandel (Interview with Felix Leonardy)

This quiet and charming village on the road to Vianden was liberated on September 12, 1944 by the units of the 85th Reconnaissance Cavalry Squadron of the 5th U.S. Armored Division, which immediately established an advanced command post in the Leonardy house on the main street. For its protection, a platoon with three newly arrived Sherman tanks was quartered in the village.

In the days that followed, many scouting trips were made by Jeep along the Our in a northerly direction, and some of them resulted in conflict with German patrols. In one such mission, unfortunately, a small troop, including a captain of an American unit stationed in Tandel, was captured by the Germans.

The replacement of the troops by units of the 8th Infantry Division was carried out along with a field service, which was conducted by an American military chaplain in the overfilled village church in Tandel. The new commander, Captain Inge, was very happy that Frank Hansen of Ettelbrück, who had meanwhile taken on a special status in the U.S. Army as a "Luxembourg" GI, was in Tandel at that time to assist the Americans on numerous patrols as an interpreter with knowledge of the locality.

The forest lanes and trails that led from Tandel to the German lines were mined and equipped with trip-flare by the American engineers on account of nightly infiltrations by German scouts. The "U.S. Command Post", which was still situated in the Leonhardy house, was likewise protected by a belt of mines and numerous tripwires for the same reason.

Almost every day in October and November the militia (resistance fighters) made its way from Vianden to Tandel in order to obtain information, equipment or necessary rations from the Americans. Because of their closeness to the front line, the village on the Our were evacuated, as was the village of Vianden, and the local militia had partially taken over the task of guarding them. Captain Inge was very happy to take part in the local fair as an honored guest of the population of Tandel and dine at the fair table in dress uniform with the Leonhardy family. Without exception, the inhabitants received special permission to go shopping in Diekirch. In addition, several inhabitants preferred having their hair cut by a chosen American soldier to making their way into Diekirch to go to the barbershop!

At the end of November this unit in turn was relieved, and to the amazement of astonishment of the inhabitants of Tandel, there appeared the smoke-blackened, unshaven, exhausted, ragged and totally worn-out soldiers of the 28th Infantry Division, which had been brought there by truck directly from the Hürtgenwald to recover from the strains of the bloody battles there. On their helmets and the sleeves of their jackets there was a red spade-shaped emblem. The captain of the unit that was quartered in Tandel from then on bore the name of Lewentis, which indicated his Greek ancestry, and had been given the task of keeping an eye on the population in the Tandel area that was friendly to the Germans, since it appeared that numerous German night patrols were making their way to the Valerius farm on the road to Diekirch, as the tenant farmer there at that time was a German.

Captain Lewentis also questioned numerous people from Bivels at his command post, as they could cross the German border unnoticed at the beginning of

December after they had been evacuated to Germany and had observed large troop concentrations in the Eifel Mountains. After an initial report, Captain Lewentis had these people, who had been brought to Tandel by the militiamen from Vianden, sent immediately by Jeep to the regimental headquarters in Ettelbrück, where they could be questioned more thoroughly.

Shortly before the start of the offensive, Tandel was only lightly occupied by troops of the 109th Infantry Regiment. In the meadows around the village, three light howitzers had taken positions, and a field kitchen provided for the physical well-being of the always-hungry soldiers. The activities of the troops consisted almost exclusively of standing guard on the range of wooded hills toward the Our and making reconnaissance trips.

The peaceful life that had returned to the quiet village since its liberation in September came to an abrupt end in the early morning hours of December 16 when a tremendous burst of fire suddenly made the air tremble and the first enemy shells exploded in the village. Almost exactly at 8:00 the German fire ceased as the first advance guard of a German unit pushed through Bastendorf and Seltz to the intersection in the vicinity of Tandel shortly thereafter. In the woods across from there, individual firefights were already flaring up between German patrols and Americans posted there, and the population of Tandel was already making attempts to flee to Diekirch in haste that day. Many of them, though, hastily decided to turn back to their houses, since the intersection to Bastendorf was under German mortar fire. When numerous inhabitants had been injured by shell fragments there and a few had even been killed, the people quickly sought shelter in their cellars. Aside from limited local combat, the situation was quiet in Tandel all that Saturday. But around 5:00 PM the first individual houses were already occupied by the Germans. Under cover of darkness, about forty Americans moved in and occupied every window and doorway of the Leonardy farm with one or more riflemen.

In the morning hours of December 17, commands rang out from a German lieutenant who was supposed to capture the farm held by the Americans. Shortly after that the lieutenant fell from a fatal shot in the storming of the farm. The rest of the young German soldiers were obviously embittered about the fact that there had been three fatalities among the civilians in the cellar when the Sinner house was stormed, including the Polish maid Marie Dusynska as well as Pierre Winter and Pierre Ney of Fouhren; thus they hesitated at first to attack the Leonardy house after their leader had been killed by an American sharpshooter.

All through the day the Americans defended themselves superbly and held the house. They were given food by the inhabitants. Eight soldiers at a time were given roast venison and baked potatoes from the Leonardy family's kitchen. The bullets were flying everywhere in Tandel, so that it was impossible to localize the individual exchanges of fire. Toward evening, three American tanks and nearly a hundred infantrymen approached from the direction of Diekirch and cleaned the Germans who had advanced out of the village. The inhabitants and evacuated persons from the lower houses in Tandel, as well as the American cook with his field kitchen, quickly used this opportunity to escape to Diekirch during the short time that the road was still open.

All Hell breaks loose!

The three Sherman tanks now took up positions in the yard of the farm and thus blocked any and all traffic to Diekirch. Meanwhile the Germans tried to set fire to the barn, which stood next to the house, by firing incendiary bullets from the underbrush across the road, but every time a few brave American soldiers were able to extinguish the fire.

All through December 18 the German artillery fired shells on the village, while the infantry was able to lure the three tanks out of their positions by localized combat during the brief pauses in the artillery fire, and destroy all three of them by direct Panzerfaust hits. The commander of the leading tank, who fired his machine gun at the German positions from the open turret of the tank, was thrown out of the turret by the force of the explosion and was able to escape, while the rest of the crew inside died in the flames. (He himself, who wrote to various people in Tandel after the war to inquire about the fate of his men, wrote that hell had really broken loose on that day; shells of every caliber had struck and caused a great deal of damage.) Of the approximately 100 soldiers who had hurried up to defend Tandel, most of them, all but about thirty, were able to escape. Now the road was open for the German advance, and German assault guns appeared immediately and surrounded the village. The Germans captured the remaining Americans and numerous inhabitants and took them away. One officer climbed out of an assault gun and looked at the prisoners. When he pointed to three young inhabitants, he claimed that they were partisans who were to be shot at once.

But immediately a young German soldier, who had been captured by the Americans the previous day and had spent the night at the Leonhardy farm, stepped up and informed the lieutenant that he had been treated well and properly, that there were no partisans involved, and that the lieutenant should bear that in mind. But the grim officer would not let himself be persuaded and intended to hang the three young men. The Americans were then relieved of their equipment and their gloves, and their chocolate and cigarettes were taken from them. The hungry Volksgrenadiers, assembled from all branches of the service, had orders to requisition food and now began a systematic search of the houses and farms. Now the Americans and the Leonardy brothers were placed before one of the assault guns and were to be taken away over the hill to Bastendorf in the midst of an assault. But the American artillery observer had a sharp eye, and very soon the first shells came whistling from the Herrenberg and exploded in the ranks of the Germans. Obviously the U.S. artillerymen did not realize that they were thus firing at their own countrymen. When the front wheel of the leading assault gun was damaged by a shell fragment and the order came to draw back again to Tandel, the civilians used this moment of confusion to flee into the woods and cover themselves with leaves in the underbrush.

Meanwhile the soldiers in the village had fled into the vaulted cellars from the American artillery fire, and the remaining civilians, fearing for their lives, had to seek cover in less safe cellars, stables and sheds. The icy cold bothered them particularly. Several days later, to the horror of the remaining inhabitants, not to mention many a young German soldier, the Gestapo appeared; among the many SS and SD men was SS Sturmbannführer Hans Klöckner, who had formerly spread fear and terror in the occupied Diekirch district as security officer, who now threatened executions. As it turned out later, there were also several Luxembourg collaborators who knew the area with him; before the liberation in September they had been able to get to Germany, and now they set out to plunder the houses in Diekirch.

The male civilians of Tandel were now compelled, on pain of death for disobedience, to bury the dead people and animals under U.S. artillery fire. Many of the Germans who had been killed came from the Navy, as their uniforms showed.

Finally the field police arrived, to the fright of the young Volksgrenadiers. These "chained dogs", as they were called, were looking mainly for deserters, and militia personnel in the area. While searching the inhabitants, the brutes found a pair of pliers in one jacket pocket and a jar of honey in the other pocket of an inhabitant of Fouhren. When one of the tough guys asked why he carried the pliers with him, since they could be used to cut telephone lines, the good-natured man replied that no good drayman would go without pliers. "I have never yet seen a drayman with pliers," roared the monster at him. When the brave man asked if he had ever seen a drayman with a jar of honey, the brutal field policeman poured out his anger at the local man, punching and kicking him to the ground.

A young refractory, who was also among the civilians, saw his last hour coming and used the opportunity, during the fuss about the jar of honey and the pliers, to step out of line unnoticed, slip back and act as if he was going to take a milk can and bring water from the nearby brook. The sentry standing guard in front of the farm, who was also afraid of the "chained dogs", let the young fellow from Tandel go past unstopped.

Thus he went with his milk can through the German lines and across the meadows without attracting attention, until he came to the hills on the other side. There he was fired at several times when he did not stop when a sentry called to him but fled immediately. It took him two days to make his way to a farm near Walsdorf seven kilometers away, where he had previously hidden from the Germans for ten months. The whole house was full of German soldiers, who behaved without exception like normal, well-meaning people. Felix Leonardy even received treatment from a medic, as he has suffered severe frostbite on his hands and feet, and he was able to await the return of the Americans there.

At the end of 1944, Tandel was fired on almost daily from the U.S. artillery positions at Stegen and Folkendange. Whoever wanted to come out of the moldy cellars in Tandel and breathe some fresh air had to do so between 8:00 and 8:30, since the Americans obviously took a coffee break in that short period. Fortunately, most of the family members and inhabitants of Tandel, since they were farmers, had sufficient supplies of wood for heating, as well as potatoes, by eating which they could cling to life. Most of the cattle had been slaughtered by the Germans; only a few cows were allowed to live, so that the children of the inhabitants could at least have milk. Numerous cows had also been driven across the border, where they supplied the German field kitchens with fresh meat. Now and then the inhabitants received meat to add to their meager food supplies, and sometimes also moldy Kommissbrot. The Russian "Hiwis" and Turkestanis who had deserted to the Wehrmacht and now served with an engineer unit in Tandel were experts at slaughtering pigs. They were actually more interested in pork than in the Wehrmacht.

The first German troops were already withdrawn from Tandel shortly before Christmas. But there was still plenty of excitement: One day an SS officer from the Sudetenland appeared and, during a house search, wondered why American carbines and hand grenades were still lying around everywhere. Under threat of the most severe punishment, he ordered that all civilians had to turn over all weapons and ammunition, to the last cartridge case, by twelve o'clock.

The inhabitants of the Leonardy house now searched through every corner of the house. On the ground level, the floor was covered with ten centimeters of straw, and manure was piled up in the hall. Numerous rifles that were found in living rooms were thrown onto a pile in the yard. While searching the attic, the inhabitants found a "corpse" wrapped in several blankets; it turned out to be a half-starved and almost frozen but still living American soldier who had hidden there to await the return of his comrades.

He could no longer stand up, and could scarcely speak.

The Germans wanted to force him to say that he had been hidden and fed by civilians, or at least given water, but thank God, he always answered "no", though semiconscious.

What would have happened if the poor fellow had said "yes"? Everywhere in the village there were signs with regulations, threatening death for disobeying them. On New Year's Day, American white phosphorus shells set fire to several barns, which burned to the ground.

Almost all the inhabitants suffered from digestive ailments and intestinal infections, but they were happy to have at least part of a heated cellar. A week after the Germans had evacuated the village, all the inhabitants were driven into an unsafe horse barn to make room for wounded men in the cellars.

After hours of heavy fire, Tandel was liberated on January 22, 1945.

A Frightful Day in Tandel
(December 17, 1944)

It has already been mentioned several times that, at the Sinner house in Tandel, three civilians were shot by German troops who had captured the village on December 17. In several publications that appeared right after the war, it has often been stated [erroneously; the author] that it was troops of the SS, Gestapo or Grossdeutschland Division who were alleged to have committed this crime.

Although the shooting of three innocent persons cannot be denied, the author has attempted, on the basis of several bits of information as well as the following eyewitness report of a person who was directly involved, to reconstruct the actual course of events. The conclusion drawn by the author at the end of the report could be a possible explanation of why and how the shooting took place.

But let us listen to the then twenty-year-old Marianne Sinner:

"About 9:00 AM on December 16 there were still a few shells falling on Tandel, so that we remained in the cellar longer, to which we had fled in panic when the terrible thunder of the German artillery had awakened us in the early morning hours. My uncle, who had just come to us a few days ago, and my father insisted that as long as there was time, we should leave Tandel and go to a safe place. But they soon gave up this plan when they heard, while still packing some things onto the horse-drawn wagon, that there was a dead man among the fleeing civilians down at the intersection of the road to Bastendorf, a man who had tried to flee by motorcycle. It was so dangerous that most of the people who were already in flight had gone back to their cellars in Tandel as quickly as possible. Outside it was extremely dangerous, for the Germans were now firing steadily on the village with mortars.

This fire only let up during the afternoon. Shortly thereafter, our farmyard filled with refugees from Fouhren who knew our house. They asked for shelter, since our farmhouse, centuries old, offered safe protection from shell fragments with its thick stone walls and solidly built cellars. They also told us that the Germans had already reached the edge of Tandel, for a short time ago a militiaman (resistance fighter) in flight had shot a German scout, apparently a lieutenant, whose body lay out on the road.

The people from Fouhren had all fled in panic and had scarcely anything with them, except Mr. Pierre Winter, who carried a leather briefcase with important papers and did not let it out of his sight. We immediately took the poor people to the cellar, which actually consisted of two vaulted rooms connected by a hall.

Most of them, especially the children, immediately lay down on the straw that we had hastily fetched from the barn, and went right to sleep. I did not want to do without my bed, and I went upstairs to my bedroom for a few hours. But when the shooting started up again in the early morning hours, I became nervous and soon sought the shelter of the cellar again. About 6:00 AM on December 17 we heard machine-gun and rifle fire down by the Tandel brook. From the nearest (Theis) house we also heard shots. The Americans who had been quartered here several days ago must therefore be shooting back. It was not long until we heard knocking at the front door. At first nobody wanted to open the door, but when the knocking continued, my father opened the door. A lone German soldier stepped into the house and asked whether there were any Americans in the house. Pierre Winter came up and said there were none. He assured the German that there were only civilians, including small children, in the house. My father confirmed this. How surprised we all were when the soldier, without searching the house, appeared to believe our words; in any case, he behaved very correctly and left the house again.

So Sylvie Winter and I, who had ventured out of the cellar, returned to its protection again and found Marie, our Polish servant, in the cellar in tears. Since the girl spoke and understood only Polish, as she had been in our house only a few months, I was not able to understand what was bothering her. She has been assigned to us as an agricultural helper by the county authorities in Diekirch in the summer of 1944. Apparently, as we had learned from Mr. Wovkiev in Diekirch, she had been abducted by the Germans and had spent some time in Germany. Her name was Marie Duszynska.

Now as Sylvie and I tried to console her somehow, we realized that her clothing was thoroughly soaked. Shortly before that, Marie had taken her clothes from the washline and put them on, although they were not yet dry. 'You'll catch your death of cold,' I had tried to tell her and went upstairs with her to have her put on dry clothes. I gave her some of my mother's clothing to put on. Then Marie tried to explain to me that she preferred to be alone, and she lay on her bed with the clothes. She continued to cry . . . as if she foresaw her death.

So I went back to the cellar. After some time wild shooting began around the house; shells exploded as well, and we could not distinguish individual explosions. Suddenly I noticed that my father was no longer in the cellar. Mr. Winter was also gone. I was struck with fear. So I was no longer thinking about our Marie when I looked for the two of them in the other cellar.

I ran up the steep cellar stairs and shouted: 'Are you crazy? Come back down to the cellar . . . at once!' when I saw the two of them standing in the hall. Finally they moved and came with me. I followed them and had scarcely been in the vaulted cellar room, which was poorly lit by two candles, for two seconds when a machine gun began to hammer in the garden and a burst of bullets tore up the wooden cellar door that led out to the garden. Some of the bullets marred the crude whitewash in the room where we were. I can still hear Pierre Ney today saying: 'Man, was I lucky today!', for a bullet had just missed his head by a few millimeters and gone into the cellar wall. He was to die a few minutes later.

Although the cellar walls were very thick, we heard two dull thuds upstairs in the house, followed by several short bursts of fire. An instant later we heard outside: 'There where the wires go in, that's where they must be!' These words petrified us with fear. We hoped the Germans would not throw any hand grenades through the cellar window.

We all shouted as loudly as we could: 'Stop, there are only civilians here, we have small children with us . . . stop!'

The cellar door that opened into the house was smashed in brutally and several heavily armed German soldiers rushed into the cellar: 'Pigs, swine, get out! Hands up, out! One after the other!' Suddenly the house was full of German soldiers.

I could scarcely see anything. It was dark and a noticeable, acrid blue smoke filled the hall. Suddenly my foot hit something soft. Then I saw that it was Marie who lay on the floor in a huge pool of blood, with her face to the floor. I was just about to bend down when the German pushed the barrel of his rifle into my back and brutally ordered me to go on. Suddenly the thought struck me: My God, Marie . . . we had forgotten her!

The Germans drove us out to the paved courtyard, which was bathed in blindingly bright light. The whole length of the roof of the cow barn was on fire. The cattle roared pitifully.

One after another, we had to place ourselves along the stone bench against the wall of the house, with our faces to the yard. 'Hands up!' one of them shouted, 'Whoever puts his hands down is dead!' Then there were shots, Pierre Ney, quite close to me, fell, mortally wounded. Another man, an inhabitant of Vianden, was shot in the shoulder. Then panic broke out. Sylvie Winter, her brother Camille, her sister Alice and her mother, who stood at the edge of the road, used this moment when everyone was looking at the dead men to flee. Then I myself made an attempt to flee but could not go farther when I thought of my father. Although I probably could have made it, I stayed out of concern for my father and uncle. 'One more step and you are dead!' one of them screamed at me. I went back and raised my hands. – 'Where is the swine with the leather jacket?' – 'He just ran away with the women,' another soldier replied. Then I suddenly saw that Mr. Winter was also lying dead on the ground, down near the 'Baakes' (bakery house). His briefcase lay beside him.

Obviously he had tried to flee in the direction of the brook and had been shot immediately. 'Come on, down to the meadow,' a gruff voice shouted, 'and take the dead along'. Several men carried the two dead men and put them down in the 'Paesch' (orchard). Then we were lined up. 'Men to the right, women to the left, all of you take your hats off. Hands up, whoever moves will be shot.'

We were searched brutally for weapons. The Germans found nothing, other than American chocolate, and a few brandy bottles on the men, which they scornfully threw into the field. As if by a miracle, the small bag of Mrs. Scheidweiler was not searched. Otherwise we all wound have been shot. Much later Mrs. Scheidweiler almost dropped dead of fright when she found an American army pistol, which her son, a refractory who had saved himself by immediate flight on December 16, had left in her bag without her knowledge.

So we stood there and shivered. Then I saw three men step up and put loaded magazines into their machine pistols. There were loading!

I closed my eyes and thought, 'it is over, I hope they start here so that you don't have to see your father die!' Seconds seemed like hours – but nothing happened. When I opened my eyes again for a second, the soldiers were still standing there, their weapons ready to fire.

The cattle were lowing frightfully. Then one of the Germans ordered me: 'Hey, you there, go on, let the cattle out!' In no time a soldier was behind me, chasing me to the stables. When I saw the bodies of the two men as I passed by, I could not go any farther. 'Then don't,' the German shouted, 'get back!' Suddenly I fell down on the soft ground of the meadow, and the German behind me fell, too. When I tried to get up, I noticed that he was gasping and bleeding from the neck. A shot had hit him. (Only much later did I learn from neighbor Theis, who had been with the Americans in the house near our farm, that an American sniper in the cellar of our house had observed us and, since he knew me, had shot the German on the way back. But since I had also fallen down, he had blamed himself, thinking his shot had also hit me. But Mr. Theis saw me running onward and told him so.) I fell down a second time when I stumbled on account of my wooden shoes. Back with the other people, I was screamed at: 'So that's the way you do it, you take a German soldier along and lure him within range of the American rifles so he can be shot like a rabbit.' None of the people who were still standing there with their hands up would have bet a penny on my survival at that moment. But the Germans didn't shoot me.

The Americans, though, had hidden in the Theis house. There were about ten men, the same ones who had moved in with us several days ago and had stayed in our office, where the wires still hung out the window. 'That damned yellow house has to be set on fire," commands rang out again as some of the Germans drove us down to the Tandel brook below the meadow, where we had to stand with raised hands for more than two hours. Here there were dozens of Germans standing ready, having sought shelter in the bed of the brook from the well-aimed American shots. Only we remained standing and looked into the barrels of the guns aimed at us. Several incautious German soldiers, who raised their heads too far, fell before our eyes with a bullet through the head. Meanwhile the shots and the cries continued. Several times an assault on the theis house was undertaken, but every time men fell dead, shot in the head. The Americans fired very precisely! 'You stay here until the yellow house is in flames,' an Unteroffizier shouted to us.

Finally the German artillery began to fire shells at Tandel. Our guards and the rest of the Germans made use of this moment to run toward the house, driving us ahead of them as a 'protective shield'. They locked us in the workshop-garage. Just beside it, in the coach house, were many of their wounded, crying miserably. The shells fell to the left and right. The fragments cut noisily into the wood of the garage and whistled over our heads. We lay on the ground, one on top of another, crying and praying. When things became a little more quiet, we noticed that, as if by a miracle, none of us was wounded. Nor had any of the Americans fired when the Germans drove us here; that became clear to us only now.

Somebody broke the door down; there were no more Germans there. 'They are in the cellar,' several people from Vianden called to us. Only now did we notice them in the unburned wing of the cow barn; while we were standing by the brook, they had sought shelter there after they had reached Tandel. After the gunfire had stopped completely, my father went into the house to get some bread. He had to pass by Marie's body, which was still lying in the hall in a pool of blood. A German who had seen him called to him: "It's no use, you are going to a place where you need no food and no clothing.' My father gave me a coat, which I quickly put on, for I was terribly cold. But we were not taken away. Suddenly two or three tanks rumbled up and took the meadow between the Theis house and our farm, in which the Germans were, under fire.

The Americans in the Theis house, who had run out of ammunition (this was confirmed later by Mr. Theis; they were already making a white flag in the cellar and intended to surrender) were thus saved as if by God's mercy. The Theis family was also taken out of the danger zone quickly by them.

In no time the Germans, who had been in the farmyard with us, were in the cellar again. German artillery fire began again. We ran and, for a few minutes, sought shelter in the Theis house, which was completely abandoned and on fire. 'My God, where are Mr. Theis and his family?' I wondered as we ran farther amid the whistling shell fragments. After throwing ourselves down, getting up again and running farther about a hundred times, we finally reached Bastendorf during the night, where, in panic fear, we knocked on the door of the first farmhouse and called: 'Let us in! Open up!' An American soldier opened the door, shook his head and said only, "I think these people are crazy.' Here we were given a cup of coffee. Only now did I notice that my coat and my stockings were torn to pieces.

Our flight continued through the fields in the direction of the 'Friedhaff', where we were stopped by a U.S. patrol close to the road. Here too there was already fighting and shooting in the surrounding woods.

Early in the morning the Americans took us along to Diekirch, where we rested until evening.

When we wanted to go on to Ingeldorf early in the morning of December 19, the militia stopped us from going farther. 'Nobody can stop us any more,' was our explanation, 'after all we have been through . . . we'll never again fall into the hands of the Germans! – If you won't let us through, you'll have to shoot us,' was our answer.

From Ingeldorf we went to Warken, from Warken to Feulen. When the Germans were just outside Ettelbrück, we went farther, some on foot, some in a horse-drawn wagon from Feulen, until our flight finally ended in Eash on the Alzette. I will never forget this terrible 17th of December."

Why Were the Three Civilians Shot?
Possible Conditions, and Author's Comments
(see also Vol.I: The Germans)

1. Marie Duszynska

The German shock troops, which had worked their way up to the Sinner house from behind, surely noticed the telephone wires left behind by the Americans and leading to the office window. Just to the left of them was the side door of the house. The Germans obviously assumed that the Americans were still in the house. Now the house was stormed by them. A hand grenade was thrown in the window, a second in the doorway, after the door had been broken open (these two explosions were heard by the people in the cellar, directly under the office). (The author personally verified the traces of the two exploding hand grenades in the house.) Probably several German soldiers immediately rushed into the house and, while in motion, fired a few bursts from their submachine guns. Marie Duszynska, who had hurried down the stairs in terror, was surely hit by the second burst of fire from the submachine gun of a German, who fired instinctively. A second possibility is that the girl, on account of poor sight and the smoke of the two explosions, was mistaken by a soldier for a fleeing American and shot. In any case, Marie Duszynska was hit by numerous bullets, as confirmed by the men who took her body to the cemetery in Tandel later.

2. Pierre Ney (35 years old)

Pierre Ney left the house with the other people from the cellar and had to line up with his hands raised. He certainly wanted to try to escape in the direction of the road, and was shot instantly when he put his hands down. Probably he had not seen the German rifleman because he was blinded by the fire blazing in the stables ahead of him. (The prisoners were standing with their faces toward the farmyard – thus looking into the fire.) The second shot, which hit the other man in the shoulder, suggests that Pierre Ney was likewise shot by an automatic weapon from which two shots were fired, since the second shot hit and wounded the man standing right next to him.

3. Pierre Winter (59 years old)

probably also attempted to escape downhill. Since he was shot in the 'Baakes' (bakery shed), it can be assumed that he was trying to run through it to the meadows in the direction of the Tandel brook.

On December 20 the three dead were buried in the churchyard beside the village church by boys from Longsdorf, whom the Germans had forced to bring them to Tandel (see report on Longsdorf, J. Sinner).

Longsdorf

Longsdorf, that peaceful little village that lies beyond the Diekirch-Vianden road, retains to this day a connotation of costly combat for numerous veterans of both warring nations who experienced the first days of the offensive. Since Longsdorf and Marxberg, the latter situated on higher ground, are located only two kilometers from the German border, the territory around it had been, since the liberation of the sector in September by the 5th U.S. Armored Division, the site of numerous patrols, but also of counter-patrol activities. Correspondingly, the local population was often not sure whether they had to deal with Americans or with Germans in U.S. uniforms, who appear to have slipped into the village at twilight on numerous occasions. Joesph Sinner, then fourteen years old, remembers that time of privation.

"The first Americans whom we saw at all were a motorized scouting party that pushed forward from Gilsdorf to the Seltz on September 12. While the Gilsdorf Bridge was guarded by U.S. soldiers and several militiamen, several lightly armed infantrymen advanced to the Seltz-Bastendorf intersection, followed by several tanks, and took up positions there to secure the roads to Tandel and Vianden. Only two days later, after almost all the inhabitants of Longsdorf had already greeted the American liberators jubilantly at the Seltz, several Jeeps drove into the town, and their crews took up quarters in the farms. Now an interesting period began!

During the following days the Americans made regular reconnaissance trips to the Our, behind which the bunkers of the West Wall stood threateningly. One day, while gathering wood on the Marxberg in company with an older comrade who, as a student, was compelled to serve with a German anti-aircraft unit in Esch on the Alzette, I was spoken to by an American patrol. I understood no English, so my comrade talked with them. It turned out that the sergeant wanted to persuade us to drive our horse and wagon down to the bank of the Our and find out whether the bunkers off to the right, just this side of Gentingen, were occupied by German troops. Thank God my comrade prevented me from agreeing, enthusiastic as I was at first. But when, on September 16, a small column of Sherman tanks, all of which bore an orange-red identifying mark, advanced in the direction of Niedersgegen while several Lightnings flew over, we gradually lost our shyness and felt confident in moving farther and farther out, even to the German border, to gather wood.

An American reconnaissance unit was quartered at our house, but we seldom got to see them. The handful of soldiers disappeared remarkably early in the morning and only returned to the barn that served as their quarters as night was falling.

Somewhat later, observation posts, which were occupied day and night, were set up in the church and in a house on the Marxberg. So the days passed in routine field work, which we carried out without any noteworthy events happening. In short, the everyday life had taken over again.

In mid-October there was suddenly a German attack on the Marxberg, which was occupied by the Americans. Obviously the German artillery observer had spotted the quarters, perhaps on account of silly, overly confident, and incautious behavior by its U.S. occupiers, and now wanted to give the 'Amis' some trouble. Several shells strayed into the brush behind my family's house, but without doing any damage worth mentioning. The barn on the Marxberg, though, where the little

U.S. occupying force had put up placards for the election of the U.S. president, burned to the ground as a result of a direct hit. For reasons of safety, the farmers now drove their cattle into the barn every night, since there had likewise been numerous cows wounded by nightly harassing fire, and they had to be slaughtered. Late one afternoon, while I was helping with work in the fields and had gone some distance out, several Germans sprang out of a hedge and forced me at gunpoint to keep calm and answer their questions. Among other things, they wanted to now what the noise in the village meant, and whether there were U.S. tanks there. I explained to them that it had nothing to do with tanks, but was almost always made by the farmers who were running their harvest, gathered late in the year, through the threshing machine, and the motors would keep running until nighttime. After they had questioned me further about the Americans and I had given only evasive answers, and after they had decided that I was alone on their area, they disappeared just as quickly, threatening to shoot me if I told on them.

Naturally I reported the incident at once, which resulted in the Americans arriving shortly thereafter in an armored scout car, which made daily scouting trips through the region from then on. A similar incident took place after the troops in Longsdorf had been relieved by units of the 8th U.S. Infantry Division. As I was driving the cows from the pasture on the Marxberg down to the stables, I noticed several American soldiers down by the spring in the twilight, filling their canteens. Though the others did not say a word, one of them walked up to me and asked in German about the quarters of the unit. I could tell immediately by his accent that he could not possibly be an American . . . so they were "Germans in U.S. uniforms."

Thereupon the soldiers of the 8th Infantry Division undertook several house searches, since they suspected there was an enemy radio transmitter somewhere in Longsdorf because of the regular harassing fire of the German artillery. In addition, they mined places they could not keep under observation, and in the evening they attached hand grenades with tripwires along the field path. One day there was an accident there when a farmer who was looking for his cows was badly injured by an exploding tree charge. From then on, no inhabitant of the village dared to go into the forest on the border any more, since this too appeared to have been heavily mined by the Americans, in order to fight against enemy night patrols that might come through. American patrols also came in with German prisoners who had fallen into their hands along the Our. Although life was back to normal again, the inhabitants of Longsdorf were still well aware the actual front, even though it was quite peaceful except for German harassing fire, was nevertheless just outside their doors.

From the Front in the Hürtgenwald near Aachen, the filthy, exhausted soldiers of the 'Bloody-bucket' or 'Spade Division' (28th Infantry Division) finally came to relieve the unit in Longsdorf at the end of November 1944 and fully occupy two houses on the Marxberg. With them came five tanks, which took positions at the edge of the village and fired at regular intervals on the bunkers of the West Wall. As soon as the shots rang out and the windowpanes rattled, we village boys could no longer be held back. Every one of us took dozens of empty 75 mm shell casings home as 'spoils of war'! Twice a day a Jeep drove up and brought the men hot food and coffee. Although the Americans frequently traded their rations for civilian food and brandy, they did not talk much and preferred to avoid us. Only one of them, who was a farmer in civilian life, was very interested in our agricultural equipment. He was very friendly, visited us often and was always a welcome guest at our table, despite the language problems.

Early in the morning of December 16 there was again a firefall from the German side, but its intensity was indescribable, being not at all inferior to the earlier ones. This time the Nebelwerfer rockets, which approached with a horrible howl, were particularly thick. Although the farmers were already accustomed to regular fire, this time they hurried into the cellars of their houses. Our house itself was hit three times in the upper stories, and the roof was badly damaged. When it finally became somewhat quieter around 8:00 a.m. and we came upstairs to get a better look at the damage, we suddenly heard outside in the road: "Upstairs, second entrance to the right," and in no time there were Germans all over the house and yard. Two shots rang out as the fully unsuspecting U.S. Jeep with the usual morning food approached the bend in the road. One shot smashed through our front door and bounced off the wall tiles. After the Germans had captured the shocked driver, we had to come out to the paved yard with hands up, and the house was searched.

The Faust family next door was already out on the road under guard. We looked at each other in despair. Nobody dared to say a word. Shortly after that the Germans came out of our back yard with two American soldiers who had hidden in the barn (see Vol.I: The Germans).

Meanwhile a young German soldier drove the captured U.S. Jeep into the yard, and the other soldiers eagerly rushed toward the thermos container filled with coffee and the doughnuts, a kind of American circle-shaped bakery goods known to us for only a short time. All day there was shooting on the Marxberg, until the infantry weapons suddenly fell silent late in the afternoon. Shortly after that the Germans took the entire U.S. force, which had gone into the church and defended themselves, and of which a number had been wounded, away through Longsdorf in the direction of Tandel. Thus the village was already in the hands of the Wehrmacht on the first day of the German surprise attack. The Americans, numbering about sixty, were all taken prisoner, except for the few dead. On Sunday all the inhabitants had to leave their houses and go, on orders from the Germans, to the cellar of the neighboring Theis farmhouse, since the other vaulted cellars had been turned into command posts by the Germans. But they let us look after the cattle and bring the most necessary things that we needed for survival from the houses. On the afternoon of December 17, Longsdorf was full of Germans. There must have been several hundred of them!

Toward evening there came two horse-drawn wagons from the Seltz, carrying wounded Germans who were treated at the bandaging station set up at the Theis farm. This was located in a side room of the cellar of the farmhouse, so that we had the opportunity to talk with several wounded men. Some of them told us they were from the Hamburg area and came from the Navy. Down on the road to Tandel there had been a fight with tanks and infantry, in which the Americans had killed numerous Germans. There was shooting all over the place now, and the mood on the cellar became gloomier from minute to minute (see Vol.I: The Germans).

All through the night, the automatic weapons fired from the fields in the direction of Tandel, and not one of us dared to leave the cellar. Several wounded German paratroopers were brought in. The Germans really seemed to have thrown every branch of the service into the battle. Then, early in the morning of December 18, a messenger rushed into the bandaging station and reported excitedly that 'our' tanks had finally arrived. Moments later, the cellar walls actually shook, and through the small window I saw several assault guns, tanks and heavy, half-tracked prime movers with infantrymen riding on them, armed to the teeth.

One unmodified civilian vehicle and several Kübelwagen drove past the Cafe Faust. Several officers got out and made their way to the lower part of town, despite the steady U.S. artillery fire. Shortly after that I heard that the regimental command post was supposed to be set up in the cellar of the restaurant. That afternoon, when I was allowed to look after the cows, which were bellowing from hunger, I saw that our house was also full of Germans, who had also set up a command post and intelligence headquarters down in the cellar.

Two days later, all the male civilians were called out of the cellar and taken to Longsdorf, and we had to go to Tandel under guard. Many grim Gestapo officers, among them SD Sturmbannführer Hans Klöcker, whose name was know to us from the Diekirch district government as a symbol of terror and power, had arrived in a black limousine.

Klöcker himself questioned us about our experiences with the Americans. Several inhabitants of Tandel and Fouhren, who had been in flight despite the ban and had been rounded up by the German troops, were now sent off to Germany. Now, on orders from Klöcker, we had to bury the two men from Fouhren who had been shot disgracefully, and the Polish girl, at the edge of the woods. We still could not understand this horrible deed. And they had all been dead for several days!

When evening came, we sought out the safe cellar of the Leonardy farmhouse to spend the night there. The kitchen was filled with countless soldiers who were having a meager meal there. A young soldier, or Volksgrenadier, as the soldiers were called, joined us, and we talked about various things. One of them even explained to us the functioning mechanism of a stick hand grenade.

On the following day, during a further search of the houses, the Germans found an American soldier, paralyzed with fright, in the attic of the Leonardy house. Thereupon a thoroughgoing search of the village for further hidden Americans was made, and we ourselves, under a heavy guard, had to gather up and deliver the U.S. hand grenades, rifle ammunition, weapons and pieces of equipment that had been left behind. They allowed us to keep only the chocolate and soap that numerous dead Americans who still lay there had in their coat pockets. In addition, we also had to gather mines after a German explosives specialist from an engineer group had inspected and disarmed them.

On the next day, Klöcker and his assistants got into his limousine; it was said he wanted to go to Diekirch! At our insistence, he issued us a pass allowing us to pass the sentries and go back to Longsdorf, for I had heard no news from my parents since then. Surely they had not been able to get any sleep for worry about me. On the roads out of Tandel there were suddenly lots of military police, who were extremely annoyed at the presence of civilians on the roads. One of them even shouted cynically that all these Luxembourg civilians ought to be done away with. But they did not dare to cancel Klöcker's orders and let us go. The road was a sea of mud. With roaring engines, a column of heavy Wehrmacht half-tracked vehicles towing guns approached the Seltz. One heavy antitank gun or howitzer took a position above the Seltz and threateningly pointed its barrel in the direction of the Sauer.

When we were almost to our village we could see twelve guns being put into position in the fields beyond Longsdorf. On the following morning, after we had spent the night with the other inhabitants in the cellar of the Theis farmhouse, nothing more could be seen of the guns. Instead the open field had been covered with bushes in several places, so the Germans had worked through the night to camouflage their guns. At irregular intervals all through the day they fired across the Sauer. The Germans were very thrifty with their ammunition. But the U.S. artillery was all the more active!

It got colder and snowed steadily. The icy wind howled horribly through the shot-up roofs of the houses and tore at the loose sheet-metal panels of the barns. On Christmas Eve, young soldiers came to us and asked us if they could invite us to a little Christmas dinner in my parents' house. I agreed nervously, for I too wanted to return to our house.

In our dining room there was a slightly decorated Christmas tree, around which several candles were burning. The smell of pine needles and burning candles, very familiar to us, filled the gloomy room. A Feldwebel played 'Silent Night, Holy Night' on his harmonica, and we all sang. A grenadier who came from Oldenburg told of the heavy fighting beyond Ettelbrück, with heavy losses for the Germans. But most of the young soldiers were very curious and eager to learn more about the Americans. This was probably the reason why they had invited us in the first place. They were all rather surprised at the way we described the U.S. soldiers! On Christmas itself, a military chaplain was supposed to hold a mass for the soldiers and for us, but an unexpectedly heavy U.S. artillery firefall prevented this.

Two days later an explosion down in the meadows awakened our curiosity, and we looked out through a window. The Germans had blown up a tank, which obviously could no longer be repaired and had been sitting motionless for several days already, with a Panzerfaust. Close to ninety men must have been quartered in Longsdorf by the end of the year; at least the cook who had set up his field kitchen in the stable behind the Cafe Faust said he had to cook for ninety men. The cuisine was very limited. There were potatoes and turnips of all kinds, but rarely a piece of meat or broth. But in our need and privation, even Kommissbrot (hard, black bread) tasted good to us! Just before the year ended, the soldiers suddenly came to life when it was said that 'the General' was in the village. (Author's note: presumably Oberst E.O. Schmidt, Commander of the 352nd VGD, probably promoted to Major General at that time.) We actually saw an older officer get out of a staff car that drove up and go into the cellar of the Cafe Faust, where the command post was set up. After a while he also looked in on us and asked how many civilians were still in the village, if we had enough to eat and if nobody was injured.

At the beginning of the year an Oberleutnant Vogt was quartered in our house. He was obviously not very popular among his men. Right after his unit had been pushed back from Ettelbrück, he seized our house. Until the German retreat from Longsdorf he remained the 'local commandant'. On the day after he had moved into our house, I saw to my horror, as I returned to the neighbors' cellar after taking care of the cattle, that the valuable old oak furniture that had been in the family for generations had all been thrown out the window of the upstairs bedroom. What could I do? My mother was very attached to this furniture. There it lay now in the snow and dirt, some of it damaged!

I never learned the reason for this; perhaps the room was too small for the new master of the house!

An old Unteroffizier who had noticed me excused himself, saying that he had not been able to prevent it and regretted very much that such valuable things had simply been thrown in the dirt ruthlessly. To do something for his probably genuine guilt feelings, he visited me later in the cellar and gave me a new U.S. overcoat.

On January 3, 1945 several soldiers from Diekirch drove into our yard in a private car taken from a dealer. The car needed repairs, and they told us young fellows to have a look at the motor.

In order to tow an infantry gun, another group of soldiers, at the command of Oberleutnant Vogt, tried to get our old tractor to run; but on the first day of the German advance into Longsdorf I had already anticipated the situation and removed several ignition cables and spark plugs.

The soldiers from Diekirch had brought along piles of white cloth, bedsheets as well as tablecloths, and the women in the cellar had to help make camouflage suits of them.

All the men who were able to work now had to help a small group of soldiers, under the command of a staff sergeant, to gather up and bury the dead men, who were still lying on the ground, frozen stiff. The ground was frozen so hard that we could scarcely put the dead men under the ground. The frequent snowfall made the blanket of white thicker, and the fog also impeded the view.

Finally we received white snow jackets, picks and shovels, and had to report for work every day. Mainly we had to keep the approach roads from Tandel and Fouhren open, remove snowdrifts and build corduroy roads, while under guard.

In addition, numerous tree-trunk barricades were built. Several times, when the wisps of fog had cleared somewhat, we were spotted by a low-flying 'Piper' which directed a hail of shells at us in seconds. Only one of us was wounded.

At the beginning of January the U.S. artillery sent their terrible greetings to Longsdorf more and more frequently. While we trembled in the cellar, our house took several hits; the stables took direct hits and many cows died instantly of their wounds or had to be slaughtered by the Germans shortly thereafter. I myself had to help several times to butcher the cows after the shooting.

The greatest part of the meat was sent back over the border to the field kitchens on the German side, which had been moved back there for safety's sake. The remaining pieces, mostly scraps of meat that looked rather meager, were prepared by the troops in the kitchen of the Café Faust. So despite the situation, we were happy to get at least a little meat as a change from the daily potatoes and the thin barley soup.

The German troop doctor came by every day to take care of the wounded and sick civilians; two medics often changed their bandages. One man had gotten an infection as a result of a shrapnel wound, but could not be treated on the scene because the necessary medications were not available.

They gave him a white camouflage jacket and sent him to the chief bandaging station in Vianden. After several days he came back to us on foot and told us that his wound had been treated properly there. In mid-January an Unteroffizier insisted on taking me to Fouhren in a Kübelwagen on account of my knowledge of the area. But my mother energetically held me back, although I myself would have gone along gladly just to get out of the stuffy cellar for a few hours.

So the days passed by; individual artillery duels broke up the monotony until suddenly, in the latter half of January 1945, wild shooting broke out in the woods before Longsdorf and on the 'Bettenduerfer Bierg.' When we woke up on the morning of January 23, the Germans had disappeared from the rooms upstairs. But there was constant shooting. From our cellar window I saw a German column creeping up the ascending road to the Marxberg, while one of their machine guns covered their retreat with ceaseless bursts of fire. Around 11:00 AM we looked through the back windows and saw the first Americans who, likewise in white camouflage suits, were taking positions down in the meadows at the edge of the woods. We waved to them through the narrow cellar windows. But the shooting continued. Only late in the afternoon did the Americans, accompanied by eleven tanks, come along the village street. One of the Shermans immediately took up a position in our yard while the infantry searched the houses and barns. Suddenly there was a firefall of German artillery, in which our barn was hit more than once. My friend was wounded in the leg by a shell fragment and evacuated immediately.

On January 24, U.S. trucks drove up, and the rest of the civilian population, which had held out for more than a month under unimaginable privation and fear, quite aside from the hygienic conditions, was liberated from the gloomy cellar and evacuated out of the war zone to Heffingen."

Unwelcome Guests at Café Faust, Longsdorf

Situated directly on the main street of Longsdorf, a country inn has been run for about a hundred years by the Faust family in their farmhouse, more than 300 years old, next to their farm.

Before the German offensive, seventeen American soldiers of the 28th Infantry Division were quartered there, to the pleasure of the family. There were as good as no language problems during the social evenings, for the Polish maid Julie Pzil, who had lived with the family since 1937, was able to converse in her mother tongue with several American soldiers of Polish ancestry.

Raymond Faust, then sixteen years old, still remembers to this day how the Americans gave their extra food to the family again and again, or were always happy to trade their rations, so desired by the civilians, for Luxembourg brandy. The activity of the Americans in December was limited mainly to patrols as far as the German border, carried out partly on foot, partly in a scout car which was stationed at the restaurant.

"A few days before the German surprise attack," says Raymond Faust, "the Americans left us and took up quarters in a house on the higher ground of the Marxberg, since they had a better view of the West Wall from there. Since German scouting troops had apparently advanced as far as Longsdorf a few days before, the Americans advised us urgently to stay in the cellar from then on. For after all,

Longsdorf was just a short distance away from the front, and now and then there was a German firefall.

Thus since about December 10 we spent the nights in the cellar of the house on beds that consisted only of mattresses with straw under them, and a few blankets. A stove provided pleasant warmth in the room, for the weather had meanwhile become considerably colder.

A terrible burst of thunder early in the morning of December 16 awakened us abruptly. The shots fell very close to us. The ground around the farmyard actually trembled. We heard a shell fall on the neighbors' house, and some of the shell fragments tore holes in our roof.

About 7:00 it suddenly became quiet again. It was still dark when shouts, footsteps and knocking on the big gate of the farmyard were heard. 'Open up!' was screamed outside. It took our breath away; the Germans were there again. At first none of us dared do go through the low cellar door into the front yard to open the heavy wooden gate. When even our hired man did not want to, my sister finally went into the yard with the Polish girl and pushed the bolt aside. 'Hands up! Everybody come out!' In no time there were two dozen German soldiers and several officers in the yard, and they searched the cellar, barns, stables and house. After the officer had been convinced that there were no longer any Americans in the house, we were allowed to go back into the cellar, where we could sit down on the potatoes, straw sacks, mattresses and blankets . . . for the room in which we had previously stayed was immediately seized for the Wehrmacht. Through the cellar window we could see the village street, where shortly afterward, along with the seventeen Americans from the Marxberg, we were led away in the direction of Tandel. It was not long before countless Germans came along with their fully packed infantry carts and stopped at the Sinner, Kaellen (Theis) and our house. Radio sets, telephone switchboards, antennas, telephone cables and a lot of equipment were unloaded and carried into our cellar as quickly as possible. More than a dozen soldiers were busy cleaning out the root cellar. All the turnips (about thirty horse loads) were thrown into the farmyard, where they rotted in the course of the coming days. In this cellar, which formed the largest room, the Germans set up a communication post. A thick bundle of cables that ran out of the cellar very close to the entrance to the dining room indicated that an important command post was located in the house (see Vol.I: The Germans).

That same afternoon our hired man was forced to drive our farm wagon, pulled by three horses, to the Seltz under guard in order to pick up wounded soldiers there. After about two hours he came back; a shell had ruined the wagon, but thank God, nothing had happened to him or the three horses. The two other wagons, which were driven by German soldiers, were fully loaded with gasping soldiers who had terrible wounds. The wounded men, most of whom died in our cellar during the next few hours, were quickly brought inside. I had never seen anything so horrible. Abdominal injuries with half their intestines hanging out, head wounds, limbs torn off, bodies torn to pieces, faces burned or smashed until they were unrecognizable. An awful smell spread through the cellar, a smell of burned human flesh, manure, pungent-smelling medicines and vomit. The doctors and medics worked feverishly.

But as evening came, we had to leave the cellar. They advised us to stay in the cellar of the Kaellen (Theis) farm across the street, where our neighbor and his family were already staying. While we packed up the most urgently needed things, we saw that the U.S. prisoners, several of whom were wounded, were being brought back to Longsdorf under guard. Obviously the Germans had used them as shields on their advance to Tandel and were now taking them away in the direction of the Our. In silence we took leave of the poor fellows with whom we had spent pleasant hours in December; we could not help them. A German field kitchen drove up and set up shop in the barn to the rear.

Finally, when it got dark, we were settled with the neighbors. In the same room where the people of Longsdorf found shelter there were also two young German radiomen with their transmitters.

At night, gunfire from the German side in the direction of Tandel and Bastendorf began again. On the morning of December 18, two shells fell in our farmyard not long apart. One shot, that fell too short, came over the roof of the Sinner house and struck the angle of the farmyard wall, right near the main gate, where it tore a big hole. Apparently a German officer, who was standing right under the arch of the gate at the moment the shell exploded, having just left the cellar by the side exit, was wounded there.

All through the day, hundreds, if not thousands, of German soldiers, all fully camouflaged, flowed down the road with packed wagons and infantry carts in the direction of Seltz, Tandel and Fouhren.

On December 18, Longsdorf was likewise the scene of indescribable confusion. In the early morning hours one could already hear from afar the lowing of cattle. Shortly thereafter, whole herds of cows and beef cattle arrived from various directions, probably coming from Tandel, Bastendorf, Brandenbourg and Fouhren, and now being driven away in the direction of the German border. We had to watch powerlessly while the greater part of our livestock and our neighbors' was driven out of the stalls and into the German Reich.

In the afternoon there came the first German vehicles: off-road vehicles, tracked vehicles, armored troop carriers, heavy towing tractors with guns in tow, turretless assault guns and tanks, and to our surprise, numerous luxury cars from Luxembourg . . . The Wehrmacht's supply lines ran through Longsdorf.

Squeaking sounds from our farmyard led us to believe that the Germans were in the process of slaughtering our nine pigs; the usual squawking of the chickens also fell silent soon. Finally, out of the chimney in the rear shed came clouds of smoke that smelled sweet, and we knew that the German occupying troops were also processing the mashed pears and distilling them to brandy in our workshop. It was said afterward that one of the soldiers, from the area around Trier, knew the handiwork involved and turned out some 700 liters of 'Birendrepp' (pear brandy) by the time the Germans withdrew from Longsdorf.

We had practically nothing to eat but mush, which my mother cooked from wheat flour and sugar.

One day it was even said . . . the general had been here and had been angry because there were still numerous dead men who had not been buried. So the troop veterinarian was given the job of having the dead, who had been stacked back in the shed, buried quickly. Thus a small cemetery of German soldiers' graves came into being in the meadow behind the farmyard and near the crossroads.

But there was also a pleasant event. The wife of the Kaellen family's hired man gave birth to a baby in the shed, delivered by a German army doctor. The father was so happy that he got drunk and, in his intoxication, did something stupid that, if it had been discovered by the Germans, would surely have cost him his head and perhaps cost us ours, too.

The two radiomen who were in the same cellar with us at the Kaellen farm had a chicken cooking in a pot on a small stove. When the drunken hired man believed he was unobserved, he opened the lid of the pot and . . . urinated into the broth. We were horrified at it and scolded him, but none of us dared to tell the German radiomen, who ate the chicken and the soup with a hearty appetite some time later . . . !!

So the days went by, until the American artillery became very active at the beginning of January, and one of the cellar dwellers was wounded in the head by a shell fragment during a firefall. Thank God the wound was not life-threatening, and after a German medic had provided first aid, the man was sent to the hospital in Vianden on foot, where a doctor treated the wound.

It could be noticed gradually that the Wehrmacht was in retreat. Almost every day, motorized units rolled through Longsdorf in the direction of the border. A tank that was probably no longer usable because of motor damage was blown up in the meadow by the Germans. At night we heard shooting along the Sauer. Then one morning we noticed white-clad figures at the edge of the woods, about 400 meters away from the Kaellen farm – Americans. There was hardly any shooting. Several hours later our liberators arrived; the Germans had given up Longsdorf almost without a fight. There were firefights only on the Marxberg and in the last houses in the direction of the 'Kranzenhaff'; unfortunately, several houses caught fire. When we were evacuated to Heffingen on U.S. army trucks, U.S. tanks were rolling toward Longsdorf. One of these tanks must have been hit from the edge of the woods by a German soldier with a 'Panzerfaust' as it advanced toward Hoesdorf, for there was still the burned-out wreck of a tank there in March. For a long time, a heavy German antitank gun in a field in the direction of Fouhren bore witness to the intensity of the combat during the German withdrawal. The towing tractor for it stood off to the side, burned out, with its ammunition strewn over the field from the explosion caused by the fire. Countless bunkers and big roofed-over command posts were found in the woods around Longsdorf. A gigantic piece of work . . . but useless. A terrible smell soon emanated from the hedges and the fields, from the rotting corpses that still lay all over, and that I had to pass every time with the plow. In addition, we all suffered for a long time from diarrhea, which we all had caught in those unforgettable days in the damp cellar with a limited diet and without any medical treatment.

In the Midst of the Battle!: The Villages of Bettel and Fouhren
(From the recollections of a farmer from Bettel)

"As early as September 11, the first U.S. units broke through the Siegfried Line beyond Bettel with numerous tanks as the advance guard of their division, and met scarcely any German opposition. In the ensuing days, the U.S. armed forces advanced to Sinspelt and Shankweiler, Germany. Between Sinspelt and Mettendorf, though, the German units, with tank support, undertook several counterattacks, in which the Americans had to suffer numerous losses.

Day after day the American aerial surveillance flew over Bettel in the direction of the West Wall, in order to direct the U.S. artillery fire accurately at the German bunkers and the tank units that were farther back. The remaining U.S. attack units, though, were withdrawn after just a few days, without having advanced farther toward Germany. Since Fouhren offered an extensive field of vision and its location was better suited than Bettel to afford a view into Germany, numerous observation posts were set up there by the American reconnaissance units. These observation units remained in Fouhren until the beginning of the German offensive.

At almost regular intervals, though, U.S. patrols, often followed by several tanks and scout cars, passed through Bettel and made sure again and again of the situation in the German bunkers, close to the German side of the Our. From now on (early October), the U.S. artillery batteries placed in positions around Bettel fired every night at the Siegfried Line near Neuerburg; several times the Germans returned the fire with large-caliber guns, resulting in many dwelling houses and barns in Bettel being hit. Otherwise the Americans were inclined to be mistrustful and avoided making contact with the inhabitants. At certain times of the day Bettel was unoccupied by the Americans, so it was not surprising that the Germans used those times for their own reconnaissance and pushed forward to Bettel with small scouting parties. Often there were also SD or SS men among them, who tried with threats of deportation or shooting to force the inhabitants of Bettel to give information about the nearby U.S. positions. In a similar action, Jean Scholz was shot when he tried to escape from the Germans; another person was injured at the time. On October 10 a German night patrol tried to persuade us to leave Bettel without delay and gave us until midnight. But since we knew that the Germans just wanted the farmers' food supplies, we stayed.

There were often encounters between patrols along the Our. Then the automatic weapons clattered, one heard cries as well as the explosions of hand grenades. A short time later, the dominant U.S. artillery again aimed at the enemy shore. But the Germans were able again and again to get to Bettel with small groups and get away unseen. I myself noticed that in a similar patrol, which had slipped into our house, there were also civilians, mainly Luxembourg collaborators who had fled since September and were looking for our food supplies. Cows were also said to have been stolen from several farmers in the lower part of town, a sign that the food supplies for the men in the West Wall were running very short. A mighty clap of thunder that was heard early in the morning of December 16 drove us to the safety of the cellar as the shells exploded all around and our house took several hits. When it became light, the Germans were already in the village. It was crowded with soldiers, naval men who had been sent to the infantry, paratroopers, anti-aircraft men, etc., all of whom tried to advance to Fouhren. The U.S. soldiers stationed here defended themselves bravely and held the Germans up for several hours by well-aimed mortar fire. Then the resistance fell silent and countless small German bands followed, for several bridges and footbridges had meanwhile been erected over the Our in the Bettel-Hoesdorf sector, and the attackers were now coming across them with their war materials.

At the beginning of January, numerous Germans returned with inhabitants from Bettendorf, for things had become rather quiet in Bettel since the German troops had passed through. But one heard artillery duels down along the Sauer now and then. In our cellar, which we had managed to insulate against the ever-worsening cold, damp weather, we continued to share our fate with two families from Bettendorf. Now and then we were visited by German soldiers who guarded the bridge by Roth and were constantly in search of something to eat. Most of them were very young and behaved properly, in fact they even felt sorry for us to the extent that they often gave us some of their meager rations of bread. But how senseless it all was . . . children at the front! (see Vol.I: The Germans.)

In mid-January there were usually only five soldiers of an observation unit left in the rooms of the upper story. Two of them were Austrian, one was Polish, and their chief was a fanatical Nazi party official who had been drafted into the army. Again and again the other four tried to convince him that the war was long since lost for Germany, and that it would be better to surrender. In one of his outbursts of rage about that, there must have been a fight, in which one shot was fired. We did not dare to come out of the cellar.

Later, when they surrendered to the Americans, who attacked from the direction of Longsdorf on January 25, 1945, the Nazi lay dead in the barn with a combat knife in his heart . . . stabbed by his own men. With raised hands, the four Germans ran toward the Americans, and we followed with the children. We were quickly evacuated by an arriving U.S. unit.

Only on March 2 did we return to shot-up Bettel, which made a sorry scene. An indescribable mess of destroyed German vehicles, including several tanks, lined the Our. They had tried in vain to cross over to Germany. Two assault guns and several anti-aircraft guns remained back in Bettel and were towed away by the Americans not long afterward. In Bettel itself, 128 dead German soldiers were found, who were buried together in the woods near Poscheid. Apparently the Germans had partially booby-trapped the houses during their retreat.

Several Americans are said to have been killed when the charges exploded. Among the victims was also Félix Petry, who was killed when a mine trap exploded as he opened the door of his house. Only in mid-March were all the families who had fled since October back home again." (Source: Petry Family, Bettel.)

Fouhren

"On December 15," the Goebel family recalls, "the Americans were still celebrating in Fouhren, which they had occupied since September, and from which they undertook numerous reconnaissance expeditions to the Our. In the village itself there were several observation posts, which were occupied day and night. One of these observation posts was connected by field telephone with a handful of Americans, as well as with the militia partisans in Vianden.

We ourselves had no American soldiers quartered in our house, and for that reason it seemed very remarkable to us that about 10:00 PM there was suddenly a knock on the door, several Americans in very new-looking uniforms walked in and inquired about the local command post. We ourselves knew that it was on the

'Tomm', since Captain Blum, the company chief of the unit quartered in Fouhren, who was often in town, was located there.

By the broken English that they spoke, and finally the German that they tried to disguise with a fake English accent, it very soon became clear to us that they were Germans in American uniforms. Therefore we gave no answer and avoided their further questions. As surprisingly as they had come, they disappeared again. Later in the night, sounds of a power saw in Walsdorf reached us again and again; probably the Americans were building roadblocks out of fallen trees. Since there was often talk of German patrols, we decided to look for Captain Blum the next day and report this unusual occurrence to him.

But Fouhren received heavy artillery fire even before dawn. The inhabitants immediately disappeared into their cellars. The whole morning of December 16 there was wild shooting outside the house. The Germans reached Fouhren that afternoon; paratroops, it was said, were moving in the direction of Poscheid, a small village, consisting of only three houses, in the woods this side of Walsdorf. Fighting was going on all over. The few remaining Americans forced the people who tried to flee to stay in the cellars. The artillery fire continued into the evening. According to stories told by the advancing German soldiers during the night, there had been numerous deaths and wounds caused by their own artillery fire during the evening. When we fed the cattle in the barns around midnight, the infantry combat in Fouhren had quieted down. A column of U.S. prisoners, under guard, went along to road to Bettel, scarcely recognizable from the narrow cellar window. A German captain in our yard shot off several flares, in order, as it was said, to signal 'our location'. Shortly after that, in the early morning hours of December 17, 1944, numerous German paratroops came up from Bettel and began at once to search the houses, sheds, barns and stables for hidden Americans. But since they found no more American soldiers, they fell, half-starved, upon the potatoes, apples, bacon, ham and other food (see Vol.I: The Germans).

Only up at the crossroads on the way to Fouhren, in the direction of Longsdorf, was there still shooting now and then. For a short time, Hauptmann Metzler (Commander, 2nd Battalion, FJR 13) had his command post in the cellar of our house.

Cattle killed by shell fragments were gathered up and taken to the field kitchen. On December 18 the house shook when a German assault gun, its motor thundering, took up a position behind the wing of the house. Shortly after that the tank drove ahead a little way on the road to Diekirch. But since it was fired on, it came back behind the wing of our house. A clap of thunder rang out. An American tank shot at the German assault gun right through our house from down at the bend of the road to Diekirch, though the gun was not visible from that position.

When the gun drove out again and returned fire, almost all the windows in the first two stories shattered from the air pressure of the shot. The U.S. infantry in the woods beyond Fouhren was still able to hold off the German assault. Then more assault guns were deployed against them. The assault gun behind the wing of our house changed its position immediately after the arrival of the other armored vehicles and drove off along with another assault gun, firing into the woods now and then while in motion, in the direction of Tandel, where the Americans were still holding out bitterly.

On the same afternoon, a number of German soldiers with radio sets occupied our house. Among them was an officer wearing the Knight's Cross; he advised us to remain in the cellar.

Later in the course of the German offensive, an American airplane was hit by the German anti-aircraft guns posted near Roth and Bettel, and crashed (see Vol.I: The Germans). The pilot was able to parachute out and save himself, but in a short time he was captured by the Germans and taken away. This was reported to us by young soldiers who remained on guard in our house at that time. Now the Germans began to remove U.S. mines from the tunnel of the 'Benny' (narrow track train line). Fouhren was constantly occupied by the Germans until late January of 1945. Ragged and hungry soldiers often came from Diekirch and Longsdorf and searched the houses for something to eat, which they took away in baby carriages and infantry carts. Stoves and blankets were also requisitioned and taken away. Once there was a fight when a group of soldiers coming from Diekirch were chased back mercilessly by an officer with the excuse that they did not belong to this unit.

In the first few days, though, a number of people had been able to flee and find shelter with acquaintances in Tandel. The families of Betz, Winter and Goebel, who stayed behind, spent the entire offensive in the cellars of their farmhouses under great privation. A person by the name of Haentges, who had been taken away by the Germans, returned at the beginning of January and was housed with us as instructed by the occupiers. Only on January 24, after the Americans has won part of Fouhren, were the unfortunate families evacuated at once by truck to Reuland."

Events in Bettendorf

The "Niederberg" that stretched as far as the Our behind Bettendorf was the site of hard fighting in the first days of the offensive, when German units, chiefly of the 916th GR, which had not succeeded in taking the high plateau of Hoesdorf, now tried to fall upon Longsdorf by crossing the Niederberg. Several separate and isolated farms were and are still located on the Niederberg. The residents of the "Webeschaft" told their story: "On December 15 several German propaganda shells exploded in our neighborhood and covered the meadows with leaflets. These leaflets, which were meant for the Americans who were in the rifle pits on the hilltops of Bettendorf, were printed in English on both sides and showed a picture of a pondering U.S. soldier, which was supposed to encourage the GIs to surrender. Other leaflets were supposed to remind the Americans of their relatives and the coming Christmas holiday.

But very early on December 16, shells of all calibers fell, first down by the Sauer, but soon they made their way up to the Niederberg. Rockets were also fired, rushing toward the valley with a terrible whistling and whining sound and a long fiery tail. Numerous shells, though, landed squarely on the U.S. defensive line in the forest, and thus close to the farm. We sought the shelter of the cellar as fast as we could after the roof of the house had been hit several times by big shell fragments.

In the afternoon, our father could no longer stand the uncertain situation and climbed from the cellar to the storeroom after the artillery fired had died down, in order to get a view of the country from the rear window of the storeroom. To his horror, he found that there was already a crowd of Germans behind the farmyard. One of them must have spotted our father and fired a rifle grenade from his carbine in the direction of the window, but fortunately it missed its target and exploded below the window.

Shortly after that there was banging on the front door. 'Get up and come out!' Numerous soldiers in new-type quilted camouflage suits filled the yard and searched the barn and sheds with their weapons ready to fire. They even looked for hidden American soldiers in the storeroom. After the Germans had convinced themselves that there was not a human soul in the whole house other than our family, some of them left at once in the direction of the valley, and thus toward Bettendorf. There was wild shooting shortly after that, as a number of Americans from the 'Moetschenhaff' about two kilometers away raced by in a Jeep in an attempt to reach the lower village on the Sauer. (see Vol.I: The Germans.)

In the evening the German artillery became active again, with a firefall on Bettendorf. Numerous houses, especially in the 'Fraeschegaass', took direct hits and began to burn. During the same night a German patrol came back with four captured American soldiers whom they had overwhelmed on the upper Niederberg. They came into our kitchen and demanded water for themselves and the prisoners.

On Sunday, while the German rocket launchers fired in the direction of Beaufort with their awful howling sound, a strong German patrol again searched the underbrush behind our farm; now and then the soldiers, including some who were wearing U.S. overcoats, fired blindly into the brush.

We had come to the decision to flee to Diekirch and had already stowed some food and blankets in a cart and wanted to set out at nightfall, when a German sentry spotted us and sent us back.

One evening seven trucks came past the farm and drove along a rocky field path in the direction of the German border. On the next morning they came back loaded, in part with fresh meat and other provisions. Numerous wounded men were treated in our dining room at Christmas. Later, though, the bandaging station was moved to Reinigshof, where an ammunition depot had apparently been set up as well.

American fighter planes often flew over Bettendorf in order to fire their deadly machine-gun salvos at anything that moved. At night it could be seen by the flickering flames that the Hamen farm by the Blees bridge was burning.

The Germans were celebrating Christmas in Bettendorf when American launcher fire suddenly fell on the lower part of the village and the exploding phosphorus shells caused great damage.

As several young soldiers reported, the Wehrmacht had been pushed back and now occupied the north bank of the Sauer. At the beginning of January new troops arrived, having been withdrawn from the Wiltz area. Many soldiers in fact wore pieces of clothing, which came from a clothing store in Wiltz, under their uniforms on account of the icy weather. Many of them asked for paper with which to insulate themselves further, for paper and old newspapers kept out the strongest wind. The food supplies of the field kitchen gradually ran out. On numerous occasions cattle were requisitioned from us and slaughtered, and seventeen-year-old Hitler Youths stilled their hunger with potatoes. In addition they tried to get our ox to move a heavy infantry cart. The beast, though, was so stubborn that the soldiers finally gave up after several attempts.

Numerous officers, including a major (Author's note: Probably Major Hoffmeister, Commander, GR 915), were quartered in our dining room, since it, as they said, was safer up here than down in the village. The sentries around the farm-yard were increased, and additional pits and fox-holes, equipped with machine guns, were dug around the house and the observation posts. Some of them were covered and camouflaged from enemy view with white bedsheets from our house. Two days after the officers had moved in with us, the family, except for the mother and a sickly child, were taken away by the military police to be housed with the Petry family in Bettel.

Before that, though, it had come to our attention that, during a previous night, American patrols had slipped silently into Bettendorf, where several Germans, including a courier, had fallen into their hands, to the fury of the major.

So we were moved under guard past the Reiningshof, which likewise looked like a fortified bulwark. The sentries called to us to cross the mountain at once and not to continue along the ridge to Hoesdorf in order to make our way to Bettel on the road along the Our. When we reached Bettel, there was a German field kitchen not far from the Petry premises. In the house itself there were numerous soldiers, among them a Pole whose teeth an officer had knocked out with his fist when he learned to his anger that the Pole had wanted to surrender. The officer was later stabbed by his own men.

When the Americans came nearer, the Germans in the house decided to surrender and made a white flag out of bedsheets. We accompanied them under American guard to Longsdorf, which was already in American hands. We were immediately given a hot meal by the Americans, who had set up their command post in the Faust Cafe, and then were taken by Jeep to Gilsdorf, which was partly on fire. After brief questioning, we finally reached Larochette, where we were in a safe place at last.

Our farm buildings themselves had taken four direct hits, and the livestock was reduced by shrapnel to a few half-starved cows that had not been taken away or slaughtered by the Germans. After our return we found the seventeen-year-old German soldier who had stilled his hunger on potatoes so often, lying dead with a bullet in his head in a rifle pit not far from the barn . . ."

The Other Side of the Valley
Schroederhof and Keiwelbach

After the terrible artillery attack, an American patrol appeared in Schroederhof in the early morning hours of the following day (December 17) and asked the worried inhabitants if any Germans had been seen there yet. One of the American soldiers spoke perfect German and told them he came from a unit that was stationed in Folkerdange at that time. Late in the afternoon the patrol returned from Moestroff and brought three prisoners along. Some of these were from a German advance unit which had already advanced to the Sauer on December 16 and overwhelmed an American position in close combat. On that day the Germans themselves had taken two U.S. prisoners, whom they brought with them. One of them had lost an ear to a bayonet attack in hand-to-hand combat. The wounded man, as well as the German prisoners, were sent to Ermsdorf by Jeep at once. The ensuing days passed fairly quietly, until numerous U.S tanks came from Folkendange and Ermsdorf on Christmas Day 1944 to take up positions at Schroederhof and cover the territory in the direction of Moestroff and the Sauer with shells. After a cannonade lasting for several hours, they turned back to Keiwelbach.

Here the Americans had set up their headquarters at the Schuhmacher farmhouse, as well as a bandaging station, which was located in the living room. The Americans ruthlessly moved out the pieces of furniture and even used some of them as firewood.

The remaining inhabitants received one hot meal a day from the Americans, who had set up a field kitchen at Schroederhof in January. But after the Americans had ascertained that a woman who lived in Keiwelbach who spoke English had listened in on their conversations and discussions around the card table, they became mistrustful, and the civilians were taken away to Larochette, where they remained through the rest of the offensive, until the danger was over. Although Keiwelbach was not particularly damaged by artillery shells, the houses nevertheless showed considerable interior damage from the ruthless Americans, as well as damage around that had been caused by their armored vehicles.

The Mill in Bettendorf served as housing, and a fairly safe haven, for most of the remaining inhabitants of the village on the Sauer during the German offensive. The former employee of the Zettinger-Hoffmann mill, Jean-Pierre Graf of Bettendorf, recalls:

"I was the 'maid of all work' in the mill since 1941, from truck driver to caretaker of the machines and drive train. So it was not surprising that my boss, Mr. Hoffmann, sent for me at once on the morning of December 16, 1944, after the unexpected and extremely heavy German artillery fire on Bettendorf, for I had not shown up for work on account of the danger.

Mr. Hoffmann was full of anxiety that the Germans would come back, for this firefall suggested that they would, and told me to drive to Esch with his family. I ran to the mill at once. The lower village and the railroad station of Bettendorf had taken several direct hits, and scarcely a single house had escaped without shrapnel damage.

Mr. Hoffmann also ordered me to bake several loaves of bread quickly in the oven of the mill and, while they baked, to load the truck with clothing, bedding, household goods, etc. We also loaded a big barrel with preserved meat, several cases of wine and brandy, and foodstuffs onto the truck and carefully stowed everything between the hastily packed suitcases.

Since I wanted to stay behind, Dr. Joris, a friend of the Hoffmann family, offered to drive the truck. We said good-bye hastily; then the family drove away. Instead of turning left in the direction of Eppeldorf, Dr. Joris chose the route to the right across the plateau, where the truck finally skidded into a ditch. Suddenly German mortar fire began again; the people in the truck abandoned everything and came running back.

Mr. Hoffmann's son Georges had rushed ahead and asked me how we could get the truck going again. I had an idea and ran with him to see Farmer Weyland, who had four horses that could surely do the job. Scarcely had the farmer led the first horse out of the stable into the farmyard when another salvo of shells struck. The horse shied and ran away. We rushed into the shed and took cover under the machines. The fire continued for almost half an hour. Americans were running all over the place nervously, also seeking cover from the German shells. Suddenly there was a pungent smell . . . fire; the house and stables were burning. It was impossible to extinguish the fire, as it was too dangerous to stay outside. So we ran quickly back to the mill. On the way we found the runaway horse dead on the road; a shell fragment had killed it.

In the mill we felt fairly safe. The ceilings of the cellar rooms were, in fact, made of reinforced concrete. Mr. Hoffmann was bewildered and completely demoralized. He gave me the keys to the wine cellar and I hid them in the root cellar behind the garden door, in a corner with old sacks that were stacked up there. There were some 300 to 400 of them, and I took several to make myself a soft bed, for I intended to stay in the mill, since it was my place of work. So I lay down that evening and tried to sleep, but I did not succeed. Explosions and weapon noises that I could hear from the Niederberg disturbed me constantly. The German artillery had meanwhile stopped firing on Bettendorf at irregular intervals; not a good sign.

When I made coffee at the first light of dawn, I looked through the window and saw German soldiers who made their way along a hedgerow on the slope and into the upper village. I almost stopped breathing. Mr. Hoffmann had been right!

But we only came face to face with the first of them on the following day. Our hearts were pounding. The door was bashed in and a lieutenant and three soldiers with pistols ready to fire pushed into the room. 'Who are you?' the officer yelled at me. I answered that I had stayed behind to look after the cattle and guard against fire.

He took a list out of his jacket pocket and asked for my passport. After a brief check of my name, he gave me the passport back again without saying a word. What was this all about? Were the Germans looking for somebody? I did not dare to ask. Then the Germans began to search the upper stories of the mill and plundered all the food that was still there. On the afternoon of December 19, Mr. Zettinger and his wife, who ran the mill in Moestroff, came with some eighty people from the village. He told us very sadly that the Germans intended to evacuate them to Germany that night, since this was the front area, and civilians had no business being here. But the lieutenant let himself be persuaded, and so the people were allowed to stay and sought shelter in the silo of the mill. But in the cellar below the miller's house there were already more than twenty people from Hoesdorf, plus several neighbors of mine from Bettendorf. Fortunately I had quickly hidden two rolls (about 200 kilograms) of cornmeal. Otherwise this too surely would have been taken away in the direction of the Reich border. Our food offered little variety. Everything in the way of canned goods that the people had brought with them was shared. Generally we had 'Sterzelen' (grey millet flour dumplings), which were easy to prepare. And every other day we had some bread that we baked ourselves. As of January, when the U.S. artillery began to fire on Bettendorf regularly, there was sometimes a piece of meat from a cow that had been killed. Most of the livestock, though, cattle, pigs, geese and chickens, had already been slaughtered or taken away by the Germans previously. For almost four weeks we were hermetically sealed off from the outside world. The Germans allowed us to get a little fresh air at night, but only for a short time, since U.S. artillery shells were constantly exploding in the area.

Now and then we heard machine-gun fire from the south. They did not let us go into the village itself. Thus we held out until mid-January 1945.

Liberation

When the U.S. fire unexpectedly fell heavily on Bettendorf on January 18 and 19, 1945, we all knew it. The Americans were attacking. On the morning of January 18, infantry-weapon fire began to be heard around the mill. A German machine gun that had taken a position in the yard of the mill fired now and then in the direction of the Sauer. I heard from the Germans that the Americans had crossed the river and surrounded Bettendorf. There were frequent exchanges of fire (see Vol.I: The Germans).

All at once two men wounded by shots were carried in. One of the Germans had been shot in the head and groaned loudly as they carried him into the cellar. The American fire grew heavier and heavier. None of us in the cellar dared to move, out of fear. Many of the men prayed.

Toward morning a few German soldiers came running to the mill from the village. They counted their remaining bullets. When they found that they altogether had exactly sixty bullets left, they gave up.

I assured them they had nothing to fear from the Americans and should wait for them here. Surely it would not be much longer. They threw their rifles in a heap and we went into the front room. Suddenly the mill was shaken by a clap of thunder. We heard cries. An American tank had fired two shots at the silo tower . . . in which close to a hundred civilians had been staying, and which they were now leaving in panic fear. Several of them had been wounded from shell fragments.

After about two hours the time had come. Through the window I saw several Americans advancing on the mill. Carefully I pushed the door open and stepped to the doorstep with my hands raised. Not a shot was fired. I let the white-clad, heavily armed U.S. soldiers in, and they immediately captured the Germans and led them away. When I finally stepped out into the open again, I saw that the Americans were already searching many prisoners at the castle garden before they took them away. The Germans had to get onto a truck and were driven away. Only now did I see the pontoon bridge that the Americans had erected behind the mill, and over which troop carriers with reinforcements were rolling.

The people were crying for joy. Finally the danger, the privation and the thousand fears were gone. I went into the cellar with our liberators and got out several hidden bottles of wine and whisky. We celebrated and drank for several hours, until the Americans had me summoned in the evening and said that there must be more German soldiers on the third floor of the silo, for they had seen a light there.

Although I denied it, I had to go to the silo with five soldiers and one NCO and search it. With drawn pistol, the NCO pushed the door open and jumped into the room. Thank God we got there at that time. The light was not made by German soldiers, but by a white phosphorus shell that had exploded; its deadly contents were now burning on a machine. The flickering fire was extinguished quickly and we went back to the cellar. An indescribable joy prevailed among the people; the feeling that they had come through all the misery inspired real floods of joyful tears. But the thunder of cannons continued to rumble outside.

The Americans brought small stoves into the mill, so that the people could finally get warm, for it was a very cold winter. Finally we had light in the mill again, after I had gotten the generators in the cellar to work again.

Several people told me that they had been treated respectably by the German soldiers, but not by the German military police, who had threatened, on pain of death, to evacuate several people from the upper village to Germany. They had in fact arranged for ten people to set out in the direction of the border under guard. The two guards, though, two young Wehrmacht soldiers, had a heart for the people. Up on the ridge of the Niederberg they let the people go free, and they happily returned to the cellar.

On January 21, 1945 most of the people were evacuated to Junglinster by the Americans, leaving only a few who stayed behind to feed the remaining cattle and clean up the place.

I stayed there willingly, for there was a lot of work to be done. I kept the generators working; thus at least a few houses had light again. About a hundred balls of wheat had fallen out through the holes in the silo, and they spoiled in the cold, damp winter. The roof of the mill alone had been shot through fifteen times. It would still take weeks until the damage in the mill could be repaired and grinding could begin again."

The Gilsdorf Militia (Resistence)

The preceding reports of the B Company of the 109th U.S. Infantry Regiment, as well as the 90th Reconnaissance Cavalry Squadron of the 10th U.S. Armored Division, have already portrayed the surprise attack on Gilsdorf on December 24, 1944, which resulted in a German company being cleaned out of the village. Although often mentioned by the Americans themselves, it is much less well known that several young men from Gilsdorf participated in this operation. The Gilsdorf chronicler Jean Haan has already written several articles in the early fifties about the Gilsdorf Militia boys. One of them is Charles Breyer, who was interviewed by the author concerning the events of that time.

Charles Breyer (a former by force conscripted of the Wehrmacht) of Gilsdorf-Broderbour went into the service of the American liberators as early as mid-September 1944, after he had succeeded in escaping from the Germans again. Although he had lived for months in the woods of Broderbour in privation, hunger and constant fear of being captured, he was eager to be active again at last and "pay back" the Germans when, on September 11, 1944, the first Americans appeared in Folkendange with their tanks. His reminiscences provide an extensive picture of the events in that quiet village on the Sauer.

"After Emile Pesch and I myself," Charley Breyer reports, "had hidden from the Germans, partly in a burrow in the Broderbour Forest and partly at Goberhof near Reisdorf, and I myself had just managed to escape the grasp of the Gestapo at my parents' house several times, we immediately offered our services to the Americans as they advanced from Folkendange in the direction of Wallendorf.

On September 11, several Sherman tanks hastily took up positions at Broderbour and fired over the Herrenberg at the fleeing Germans. In the ensuing days the Americans set up several big tents and a field kitchen at Broderbour; heavy artillery guns took up well-camouflaged positions, invisible to the enemy, in the Walch Quarry, just a few hundred meters away from my parents' house.

Several tanks were also kept there and waited under camouflage nets to be utilized soon. The kitchen was moved to the Geisen quarry somewhat later, so that its smoke would be less likely to be seen by the enemy. Unfortunately, though, J. P. Lorentz of Gilsdorf was shot mistakenly by a U.S. patrol in the field.

Although the Americans were mistrustful of us at the beginning, we nevertheless were given pieces of clothing and captured German weapons by them at the end of September. From now on we were given orders to guard the bridge in Gilsdorf and the uphill road to Bettendorf alongside the cemetery. Double sentries were also posted for this purpose, while another group of militiamen (Bernard Bauler and Jean Haendel) patrolled the field paths along with the Americans.

When the 5th U.S. Armored Division was relieved by units of the 8th U.S. Infantry Division, we kept our 'job', although nothing worth mentioning had happened in all that time.

Late in November 1944 an anti-tank unit of the 28th U.S. Infantry Division was quartered in Broderbour, and some of their light anti-tank guns were located in the quarry. Two trailers with heavy quadruple machine guns served to protect them against any enemy planes that might attack, and were towed into a favorable firing position close to the edge of the woods above the quarry. While dugouts were being excavated and reinforced with tree trunks, the population of Broderbour became annoyed with the Americans for staying in that hill town isolated from Gilsdorf, and blamed them for the mysterious disappearances of hams and other pieces of smoked meat. Then, to our complete surprise, on December 16 the first German shells fell precisely on Broderbour. A rocket launcher, known as a Nebelwerfer, scored a direct hit on a 105 mm gun of the U.S. 'Cannon Company' and killed the entire crew which was standing ready. The Americans replied to this fire by firing shells at the Seltz, the Herrenberg and 'Fouerbierg'. On December 18 the Americans led numerous ragged and wounded German soldiers through Broderbour to Ermsdorf.

The Americans gradually made it clear to us that we, not being regular soldiers, wound undoubtedly be shot as partisans if we happened to be taken prisoner, and they insisted that we should 'suppress' ourselves. The remaining occupying forces in Gilsdorf withdrew silently the night before December 20. A gun still standing near the water house in Broderbour was quickly taken away to Stegen by an American unit on December 21, after the lower village was already in the hands of the Germans. On December 22, 1944 the first Germans appeared in Broderbour. A scout or motorcycle rifleman on a DKW 500 cycle was shot by an American sharpshooter while riding at top speed along the road just outside Folkendange. Thereupon I decided to join the people of Broderbour and Folkendange and flee to Stegen. Meanwhile heavy snow had fallen and the Americans tried to camouflage the trucks and tanks in Stegen from enemy sight with bedsheets. Many tanks bore a red spot of color on the white sheets as an identifying mark. I was arrested and taken into custody by an American patrol immediately on my arrival in Stegen because I was wearing an American jacket and trousers. They took me to the school, where a U.S. command post was set up in a classroom. Here I was questioned and, on account of my papers, released again after a short interrogation. Since I still had my 'laissez-passer', I was allowed go move around Stegen freely. On the road to Medernach was a column of camouflaged American trucks and tanks in readiness, and on account of the heavy snowfall and their white camouflage, they were extremely hard to spot at a distance.

On December 23, we as 'militiamen' were not only allowed but instructed to work our way forward to Broderbour and scout the area.

We were given back our weapons and went to Folkendange in the afternoon. Shortly before that, two men from Diekirch had arrived in Stegen in an American Jeep. They were Louis Dupont, who came from Cruchten, and Mich Hamen, who had shown the Americans field paths unknown to them leading from Schieren to Schrondweiler and the "Tschiddeschmillen'. Louis Dupont joined us, while Mich Hamen stayed with the Americans in Stegen to show them other field paths off the beaten track, which he knew like the back of his hand.

At the edge of Folkendange we immediately noticed several light tanks forming a barricade to prevent any possible attack on Stegen by the Germans. We found Broderbour unoccupied, but for our safety in the darkness we attached an American hand grenade equipped with a tripwire to a fir tree along the road that goes past the dump of the quarry. On the next morning we found the shattered body of a German scout beside the road!

During the same morning, the Americans began to attack Gilsdorf from Folkendange. But scarcely had the tanks, followed by an infantry company, left Folkendange when artillery fire began to fall. The Americans suffered several losses and drew back. At our urging, they then allowed us to take part in the undertaking to clean the enemy out of Gilsdorf, which was postponed until darkness fell.

December 24, 1944

So Ben Bauler, Emile Pesch, Jäng Haendel, Louis Dupont and I climbed aboard the tanks and led the battle group through the 'Aal', a narrow lane, toward Gilsdorf to its intersection with the village street. The first tank immediately fired at the shortest range, without warning, one shell followed by another . . . to the despair of Emile Pesch, at his parents' house, which appeared to be occupied by Germans. Further shells exploded in the Schaack distillery, which was immediately stormed by the advancing U.S. infantrymen. I myself followed the Americans into the house, and we captured a group of German soldiers, all of whom were drunk and offered no resistance. When we searched the uninvited 'occupiers of the house', whom we had disturbed during their Christmas celebration, outside, the battle group with the tank had already pushed forward to the main street of Gilsdorf. I quickly took a pair of binoculars from a German and ran after the others, after several Americans had taken the Germans away. Several houses unfortunately went up in flames or were destroyed, for the Americans ruthlessly, blindly fired tracer and incendiary bullets into the rows of houses. With the help of hand grenades, Ben Bauler smoked out several cellar rooms. The Germans offered scarcely any opposition. In all, we

Gilsdorf men were able to haul twelve men out of a cellar ourselves without any of us being wounded in the shooting. Most of the Germans carried machine pistols and assault rifles, which we immediately took possession of and kept for the duration.

Near the cemetery on the 'Huurkels', the Americans had spotted a machine-gun nest that offered bitter resistance. Under the cover of fire from a tank, four U.S. soldiers, Ben Bauler and I worked our way forward over the railroad tracks to get in back of them. When the gun pit was stormed after the tank had fired a shell into it, it was empty. The Germans had fled at the right time.

After Gilsdorf had been completely cleared of the enemy early in the morning of December 25, the Americans began to mine the bridge approaches and the Sauer shore in Gilsdorf. The mines themselves were laid according to plan, so that they, as it was stated, could be removed later with no danger. Only on the evening of December 25, after we had celebrated our surprise attack and drunk to it sufficiently, did the Americans go back to the quarries in Broderbour. We ourselves went with a patrol to Mersch, where we were to find further activity.

On December 27, 1944 we took the oath as auxiliaries of the U.S. Army in shot-up Ettelbrück, and received blue armbands with the letters CIC as identifying marks. We also received a complete set of American equipment and battle dress without insignia. We were allowed to keep our German weapons. From now on we regarded ourselves as 'soldiers', and took part in many patrol missions and stood guard at the blown-up bridge in Ettelbrück and in Warken, until the U.S. attack on Ingeldorf and Diekirch in mid-January 1945."

Diekirch

The following reports are based on the stories of numerous elderly inhabitants of Diekirch, whom I listened to intently on long winter evenings, beginning in my boyhood, and who knew how to describe the events just as they saw them. The subject of the Ardennes offensive was a favorite topic of conversation during the long evenings in the 'Uucht' for folks gathered around the stoves in many farmhouses, and I still remember them with happiness and sadness today. Unfortunately, this hardly ever happens any more; this good old Luxembourg tradition has been lost. For that reason I have not added anything to these narratives except a few additional notes and anecdotes that go with these stories of history. My thanks go out particularly to the inhabitants of my beloved home town who have shown great interest in and understanding of my work. From a plentitude of information from people of various age groups, I have chosen only the following, since all the other reports that I have collected in the course of eight years are similar to them, and a complete presentation would far exceed the bounds of this book. In addition, it should be mentioned that the last two reports came from the writings of Michel Preisen and J. Zeyen, from their respective diaries written in December 1944 and January 1945 in the 'Bamerdall', and have already appeared in 1945 and 1946 in the 'Landwirt' and "Nord' (two bygone local newspapers) respectively.

Michel Hamen is probably one of Diekirch's best-known personalities. Thus it is not surprising that I, as a native 'Bamerdaller', having spent my youth running around with a bunch of boys that often hung around Hamen's Mich, turned to 'Mich', among others, at the beginning stage of my publication, for he knew how to tell exciting stories out of the history that he himself experienced. My interview with 'Hamen's Mich', in very abridged form, provided the following scenario:

"As I recall," tells Michel Hamen, "the first shells in the early morning of that fateful Saturday in December fell on the upper city, not far from the bend to the 'Rue Jean l'Aveugle', but without directly causing great danger. Gradually, though, the explosions of the shell salvoes, which hissed over from the direction of Longsdorf, came closer to the Bamertal, where they exploded regularly at intervals of one to two minutes with a dreadful noise. Somewhat later we noticed the harsh detonation flashes of the heavy-caliber shells on the slope of the Herrenberg facing the Bamerdall, until finally the Bastendorf House was hit. In no time, all the inhabitants of the Bamer Valley had disappeared into their cellars without wasting a second. It got serious, in dead earnest.

When the ear-splitting fire swept on over us, to end finally around 8:30 AM, Jemp Gaul came coughing into our cellar, all stirred up, and reported breathlessly that 'd'Preisen' ("the Krauts") had been seen down in the Kleck (Rue Clairefontaine), and that a German shell had wiped out three American soldiers in front of the Olinger house, near the city hall (today the city music school).

This alarming news, which spread like wildfire, inspired most of the "Bamerdall" farm families to pack their horse-drawn wagons and carts as quickly as possible with whatever they needed most to survive, in order to hurry off in the direction of Ettelbrück and safety. Other preferred to take their belongings and head for the partly vaulted cellar of the private brewery, built in the previous century, that stood below the 'Kalebe"sch', in order to seek shelter there, since they simply did not believe that the Germans were coming back, being of the opinion that the Americans would soon put an end to these 'spooks', but had been filled with panic fear by the unbelievably heavy fire.

But the fleeing "Bamerdall" folks were turned back mercilessly by the U.S. military policemen and militiamen posted at the edge of Diekirch, with the simple explanation that there was absolutely no danger of an enemy attack on Diekirch, and that the situation was already under control. The confusion on the roads would now result in needless panic among the people. On the evening of December 19, though, several firefighters hurried from house to house throughout the "Bamerdall" and excitedly reported that Diekirch would be evacuated that same night. But in view of the preceding sleepless nights, many "Bamerdall" folk scarcely paid attention to this warning, and so they missed the information, having already dozed off in their cellars during the afternoon after the noise of exploding shells had let up.

Around midnight the railroad bridge on the 'Rue de la Gare' became the scene of a mess of confusion. Inhabitants from all parts of the city, with handcarts, horse-drawn wagons, coaches, fully packed bicycles and such, tried to seek shelter for themselves and their families in the direction of Stegen, since the road to Ettelbrück was under German fire and was in any case closed to civilians because of the withdrawing Americans. Witlessly we stared at the American infantrymen who passed silently before us and moved past the shell-damaged houses in the station area in the direction of Ettelbrück. Gendarm Reiles strictly forbade the use of flashlights and stable lanterns, since these could well result in a firefall.

The noise of clattering machine guns could be heard from the 'Kleck', where there was obviously heavy fighting already. One inhabitant even tried to cross the bridge in a delivery van, but got stuck between the rails and was forced to turn his vehicle around. But he got to Ettelbrück later on foot, along with many individual stragglers, after he had been able to circumvent the sentries just at the right time, before the bridge at the entrance to Ettelbrück had been blown up by the U.S. engineers.

In despair, the people of Diekirch, seized by fear and panic, pushed across the railroad bridge to reach the other shore of the Sauer and thus the road to Fels. When I myself, with the horse-drawn wagon on which my family had found space to squeeze in with our most necessary belongings, tried to cross the bridge in the midst of the refugees, we were turned back by the militia, who gave the reason that the horses could shy on the bridge and injure refugees who were crossing the bridge bunched together. The same thing happened to other farmers. Then I decided to go back to the "Bamerdall" and wait a bit, until the stream of refugees had let up somewhat. Napping in our stable, we were frightened out of our sleep when, around 4:00 AM on December 20, a new firefall on Diekirch broke the nightly stillness. About 4;15 AM we were on the bridge again, where the exodus had already ended. Clothing, bedclothes, shoes and food lay strewn all over the street and the approach to the railroad bridge; it had been left behind by the inhabitants as unnecessary ballast. A dead horse with its abdomen ripped open lay on the shore of the Sauer below the bridge, in which it had been killed by an American mine that was still there. Another one still lay on the bridge and had been shot on account of its injuries.

The hole in the roadbed of the bridge, which had been made by the exploding mine, had been covered hastily with planks from the Schou firm's storehouse, so that the wagon could get across the bridge. As I found out later, several old people suffered leg injuries on the rails and had to be carried. People hurrying out of the "Bamerdall" who joined us, reported that numerous houses here had been hit and, among others, the church steeple had taken two shells. Through the ironwork of the steel bridge I saw parts of Gilsdorf in flames as we reached the other bank of the Sauer. We were probably the last big family that could still leave Diekirch. Behind us there was another flash as the 'Maison Rouge' (today the Hôtel du Parc) took a direct hit from a shell that had happened to come this way. Early in the morning of December 20, dead tired and freezing, we and our exhausted horse finally reached the edge of Stegen, where an American patrol in a Jeep caught up with us and told us not to take the road to Schieren. Instead they detoured us through Schrondweiler, where we could continue on our course to Mersch and Lintgen. On the next day we arrived in Lintgen exhausted but happy to find the Dudzinski family, which had left Diekirch before us, there. They told me that the great majority of the fleeing Diekirchers had found shelter in sheds or with various families in Mersch until the Americans were able to evacuate them to Luxembourg. They had even been given a stack of old railroad ties to burn for heat, for the weather was terribly cold and damp. After I had made sure my own family was safely settled, curiosity got the better of me. With several other men from Diekirch, we wanted at least to inquire about the situation, so we drove back to Cruchten with an American patrol that was driving there. We pleaded with them until they finally took us along.

The farmers from Cruchten told us that from Colmar-Berg on the road to Schieren was closed to all civilians. There were many U.S. troops, tanks and scout cars everywhere. After I had gotten some rest at the home of a friend there, I went to Stegen to get more exact information. On my way there, heavy snow began to fall again. Just this side of Stegen, seven or eight U.S. tanks had taken up positions at the edge of the woods. I had not yet reached the edge of town when I was stopped again by an American patrol and taken into a house where there were already numerous civilians from Cruchten and Stegen. But since most of the inhabitants had fled from Stegen, a captain allowed us to stay in the village, at least to help the remaining people feed the livestock. At the Matthey farm there were lots of U.S. vehicles of all kinds, and many soldiers. Exhausted soldiers in full battle dress were resting on the floors of the rooms in the Lentz farmhouse. So I spent the day with the soldiers and offered them Quetsch (plum brandy), which a farmer had brought to safety earlier, and which we now traded for coffee and the tasty, desirable U.S. rations.

The captain, who forbade the trade as soon as he found out about it, later gave his permission, after he had noticed that his soldiers were wild about the Luxembourg 'firewater' and he could not stop them. Finally he himself asked for a bottle of booze. During the night we were awakened by footsteps, then calls to halt. Germans? No! It was people from Bastendorf who had reached Stegen by roundabout routes and reported that the Gestapo was in Bettendorf. On the morning of December 24, some 300 soldiers assembled in the church in Stegen, though there was not enough room for them, to celebrate a holy mass with a chaplain. Five soldiers and I helped the chaplain prepare this early midnight mass, at the end of which the chaplain heard confessions and gave absolution. Obviously, this troop was going into action soon. Every sign pointed to it.

Early in the afternoon I was called to the captain, who asked me if I was familiar with the area around Folkendange, Gilsdorf and the vicinity. I said I was, whereupon he asked me if I was ready to show a reconnaissance unit various field paths on the way there, and perhaps to lead a tank unit there with a group of soldiers. Naturally I agreed, and at my request I was given a U.S. overcoat, a helmet and two hand grenades, which I stuck into my coat pockets. So we drove through several snowy country lanes in a Jeep to 'Tschiddeschmühle' and Folkendange. Here there were already numerous soldiers and tanks under cover at the edge of the woods. Some of them had been wounded by a previous German artillery attack and were being treated by medics in a house.

Here I also met several boys from Gilsdorf who belonged to the militia and had volunteered to lead the U.S. attack on Gilsdorf, which had been planned for midnight, as far as the center of the village. I myself got onto a tank at the end of the column and rode along to Broderbour, where the shattered body of a German motorcyclist still lay in the dirt. I thought about my family and changed my mind, for there would be fighting in Gilsdorf in a short time, so I jumped off the Sherman and headed back to Stegen, which I reached early in the evening, for the attack had been rescheduled. On the way to Colmar-Berg I suddenly heard the booming of the tank guns. When I reached Cruchten, the guns of the U.S. artillery were thundering, probably firing on Ettelbrück and Diekirch.

It did not take long before I began to look suspicious to the Americans on account of my half-military, half-civilian clothing, so that I was searched again by a security patrol and taken to a U.S. command post in Schieren.

The colonel by whom I was questioned was a tall man who spoke excellent German. After checking a few details, he asked me if I was ready to accompany a motorized patrol to Ettelbrück, in order to get into various parts of town more quickly thanks to my knowledge of the place. The purpose was to find out had already withdrawn from the town completely or were still occupying the station district.

I accompanied the patrol, as a passenger in a Jeep equipped with a machine gun, as far as the edge of town, not far from the 'Maison de Santé', and showed them the way to the railroad station via 'Stackels' before I returned to Schieren and Stegen. Shortly before noon on December 25, a squadron of twenty to thirty U.S. Flying Fortresses flew over the Mouschbierg in the direction of the German border. Minutes later, a burning plane without a recognizable national symbol, wreathed in smoke, came back from that direction, turned off over Bettendorf, rapidly lost altitude and flew over the Sauer Valley. I could see that only one engine on one wing was still working. Finally I lost sight of the plane because of the terrain; only a thick plume of black smoke remained visible for a long time. Seconds later a deafening crash from the direction of Diekirch broke the silence!

On December 26, my desire for adventure having meanwhile been satiated, I turned back to Lintgen and my family, who had worried greatly about me.

Only weeks later, after Diekirch had been liberated in mid-January, did we become one of the first families to return to our village. We found a grim scene of destruction in the Bamer Valley. Dozens of inflated and rotting animal carcasses lay along the edge of the roads amid the dirt and the charred remains of the roofs that had caved in. An awful smell permeated the air. The bodies of several soldiers, unrecognizable as Germans or Americans on account of the dirt, were also lying around unburied. According to what people who had stayed behind told us, approximately sixty Germans who had hidden in the brewery cellars along with the freezing civilians surrendered without a fight when the Americans arrived in the Bamer Valley. My house had been hit several times; in the back barn there was still a heavy German Tatra half-tracked prime mover with a load of Panzerfaust weapons and crates of mines."

The Farm on the Herrenberg

Up there where the Diekirch barracks of the Luxembourg Army stand today, there was a farm overlooking the Sauer Valley until the end of the forties. Because of the splendid view, it was once a popular place for excursions, and not just for the populace of Diekirch, as postcards of earlier times indicate.

The Reuter family, which occupied the farm at that time, was one of the few families from Diekirch that could not be informed of the evacuation of the population on December 19, 1944 at the right time, and thus spent fearful weeks amid privation and cold in the cellar of the stately farmhouse, the upper floors of which were occupied by the Germans, and which served them as an advantageous observation point above the Sauer Valley, until the final liberation of the city.

Before the offensive, numerous captured Luxembourg 'collaborators' were assigned to the farm for forced labor in the fields under guard, and housed in the barn at night. In mid-December 1944, just before the German attack began, there were also some fifty American soldiers quartered on the Herrenberg. They were the crews of a battery of guns, and lived in part in tents, in part also in the warm stables of the farm. Their guns, which now and then fired shells in the direction of the West Wall, stood for the most part on the northwest slope of the Herrenberg in the places known as "Schwéngsgronn" and "Märtesdelt" (107th and 108th FA Battalions). On the plateau of the Herrenberg, two armored personnel carriers with quadruple machine guns had taken positions near the farmyard to protect the Sauer Valley against possible enemy air raids.

The first German shells that exploded near the farmyard in the morning of December 16 caused great confusion among the American artillerymen, who saw their guns sacrificed to the German firefall. When explosions were heard in Diekirch itself, the Reuter family was urged by an American officer to seek shelter at once in the safe cellar of the house. On the same evening, a young French-speaking officer and two soldiers drove up to the battery position in a Jeep and reported of infantry combat in the "Seltz." Shortly after that, the American guns were heard again, after they had spent the whole afternoon firing their shells at the attacking enemy at irregular intervals. On the morning of December 17 the quadruple anti-aircraft guns were towed away and placed in positions on the "Schetzebierg", probably to attain better control over the road running down from the Herrenberg to Diekirch. The noise of infantry weapons could be heard all day from the Seltz and from Bastendorf. There was also combat on the slopes toward the Blees bridge. Toward evening, all remaining U.S. soldiers left the farmyard with their weapons and equipment, after the officers had once again urged the inhabitants to continue to seek shelter in the cellar. Then they went away, and all through December 18 the thunder of U.S. cannons was mixed with the threatening sounds of infantry weapons that came nearer and nearer.

"In the night before December 19, a three-man German reconnaissance party surprisingly appeared and asked us about the location of the U.S. soldiers. There were two young fellows and an Unteroffizier in camouflage suits and carrying rapid-fire rifles. After they had searched the house and every corner of the farmyard and the barn and made sure that there were no longer any Americans in the immediate vicinity, although combat was going on in the area, they came back to us in the cellar, asked for some apples and a ball of straw so they could get some rest, for they said they had not gotten any sleep since December 16. At the first light of day on December 19 they disappeared again. Only late in the afternoon, after things had become fairly quiet on the Herrenberg, did a platoon of communication men arrive with telephones, radio sets and cable drums, which they had packed on infantry carts and laboriously pulled up here from Bastendorf.

Among them were several soldiers with unusual helmets without the noticeable rim; paratroopers, as they explained, but as soon as they had laid telephone wires across the farmyard they marched on into the valley. (see Vol.I: The Germans).

Communication and Observation Post

During the course of the evening, several soldiers with various equipment joined them, and the front rooms with a good view of the Sauer Valley were set up as observation posts, while the intelligence switchboard with all its wires and radio sets was located in a small cellar room. In our cellar there were, in addition to my family, also two former Luxembourg collaborators assigned here, who now, along with me, had to dig out several rifle pits around the yard. Later we also had to shovel out trenches in the snow along the road; even my wife was not spared this work. From Stegen we heard artillery shots again and again, followed by the explosions at the foot of the Herrenberg.

Early in the morning of December 20, while it was still dark, an infantry company took up quarters at the farm and replaced part of the communications unit, which climbed into a truck that drove up and rode away to Diekirch. From the company leader, a lieutenant, I heard that the civilian population had fled from Diekirch the previous night along with the Americans, and that the city was in German hands. He allowed us to stay at our farm and even had me drive a horse and wagon to the "Bamerdall" to get some food there. The great majority of the houses in the "Bamerdall" had already been searched for anything edible by the extremely hungry German soldiers; even the brandy bottles and cider barrels at the Hamen farm and the Reding mill had already been found by them. So I drove on to the center of Diekirch and found a group of inhabitants who were staying in the vaulted cellar of Dr. Sinner's house. Otherwise Diekirch had become a ghost town. I talked to the people in the cellar and decided to bring my wife and the children there, as it was probably safer there. I myself intended to stay at the farm in order to take care of the livestock but to go to Diekirch once a day. It turned out, though, that this was extremely dangerous, for the Americans were firing from the 'Haardt' at everything that moved. For this reason, no German soldier ever showed himself on the street in daylight. Only now and then did one see a figure sneaking around, usually civilians going to collect drinking water or looking for food in the destroyed grocery stores in the city.

On December 22 the lieutenant forbade me to go to Diekirch, for the artillery fire was falling on the hill road to 'Friedhaff' and on the "Bamerdall. So nothing came of my plan to house my family in Dr. Sinner's cellar in Diekirch. So I returned to the cellar, where about twenty soldiers were resting while the communications men were at their phones making connections amid the gunfire.

Upstairs in the dining room there sat several Unteroffiziere at their observation posts and maintained contact by field phone with an artillery position at the Kippenhof. Unaimed American harassing fire fell around our farm all day. Obviously the Americans had not yet noticed any sign of the German presence.

Two days later I observed through a shear telescope, which a bragging officer allowed me to use, that German artillery shells were falling on 'Mouschbierg' and the village opposite us, called 'Bloen Eck', near Stegen. A few minutes later he gave the Unteroffizier who was there, and who attentively observed the effect of the shots, an American tank as a new target. Through the shear telescope I could actually see in the white landscape, after the ensuing shell had torn a black hole in the blanket of snow, how a white-camouflaged tank was moving backward behind a clump of fir trees. As quickly as possible, the Unteroffizier calculated the firing adjustments and gave them to the battery by telephone. The fourth shot hit the target. Although I could not see the hit clearly, a cloud of black smoke rose up from behind the clump of trees after the explosion.

On the following day, the U.S. artillery became active again. On Christmas Day, white phosphorus poured down on Diekirch. Whole groups of houses were burning in several places down in the valley. Several shells, which were probably guided toward us by the Piper airplane, also hit the farmyard, but without directly causing any great damage. As the fire became heavier and heavier and the cellar walls actually shook with every explosion, the collaborators, who came from Hosingen, Fouhren and Stegen, went out. Only one of them came back after several hours . . . for Stegen was in American hands. The U.S. gunfire had resulted in the telephone lines being broken several times, and a crew had to get underway at once to repair the damage.

Now and then the German observer's command to fire could be heard from his vantage point in the dining room. At one time there was a loud exchange of words between the battery and the fire-control position: "Bad business . . . waste of ammunition,' and so forth.

So we stayed in the cellar permanently for several days, for it was too dangerous outside. We ate mainly potatoes, bacon, apples and Kommissbrot, which we obtained from the soldiers. An American shell exploded in the stable and tore up four cows, whose remains quickly were added to the meager meat rations of the Germans. I myself ate nothing but meat for the next few days, although that was not my habit. But when all the other provisions ran out, several patrols with small boatlike sleds were sent to Diekirch every day on orders from the commander in order to scrounge up food. We still had flour left, and some yeast; so my wife baked several cakes, although baking could be very dangerous, for the smoke that came out of the chimney betrayed the source of the fire and showed that the farm was occupied, and in similar cases the Americans had not differentiated between German soldiers and civilians. Everything that moved was shot at by the U.S. artillery.

From then on there was a hot, watery vegetable soup for the soldiers once a day, located, according to the food carriers, at the Fromes Mill in Bastendorf and brought up to our farm in a thermos container. As the snow got deeper and deeper, the German occupiers finally requisitioned my three horses for various transportation; my chickens and ducks had been slaughtered some time ago and had disappeared into the hungry stomachs of the Volksgrenadiers.

On January 8, 1945, there was a fire on Brabanterstrasse in Diekirch after a rain of white phosphorus shells from the 'Haardt' had fallen on that part of town. On the following day, a German officer came up from Bastendorf and was very annoyed to find that there were still civilians at the farm. The collaborator who had meanwhile returned from Stegen, though, was very devoted to us and made sure that my family and I could stay in the cellar.

But I also heard that some of the civilian population remaining in Diekirch had been forced to move out to Brandenbourg the previous night. The U.S. incendiary fire was given as the reason for it.

Surprisingly, on the morning of January 18, after it had grown quiet in the meantime except for the usual U.S. artillery fire, machine-gun fire was heard down in the valley along the Sauer. A short time later, German shells flew over the roof from the direction of Kippenhof and struck down in the valley. There followed several salvos from a German Nebelwerfer battery also posted there; the rockets, with their characteristic howling sound, flew their courses over the farmyard. It was not long before dozens of U.S. shells were exploding around the house. The house was damaged by them, as were the stables. Toward midday an Unteroffizier reported over the radio: 'It seems to be serious.' On the night before January 20, shouts were suddenly heard from in front of the farm. Numerous U.S. soldiers charged into the house with their weapons ready to fire and took the few remaining Germans prisoner; they surrendered without resisting. Some of them were still in their underwear and socks. The Americans pushed into the cellar, and my wife tried in vain to make our little daughter cry, in order to make it clear to the Americans that the cellar was occupied by civilians. But it did not help. So we all shouted together. In no time two white-clad U.S. soldiers rushed into the dark room . . . and we heaved a sigh of relief; the Americans were here again.

While the Germans, who had been allowed to get their clothes on quickly, were lined up outside the house and searched, one of them was able to escape. A submachine gun was fired but did not hit him. On the following day, some two hundred exhausted, white-clad U.S. soldiers arrived. They were so frozen and soaked they thoughtlessly set a fire that evening that was noticed by the German reconnaissance shortly afterward. Several German shells hit and set the barn and stables afire. Ammunition that the Americans had hauled up and stored in the stable exploded all over the place. Six cows and two horses could be rescued, but the rest died miserably in a roaring sea of flames. A parked Jeep with an ammunition trailer caught fire, exploded and burned out. We watched helplessly as the hungry flames also reached out for the house, part of which also burned down. The greater part of our property thus fell victim to the flames on account of the carelessness of the U.S. liberators. When daylight came, we saw several dead German soldiers in the fields, plus numerous dead and already frozen cattle that had been killed by shell fragments. An abandoned U.S. truck stood in the field, riddled with bullets.

Finally a Jeep drove up and took us to Diekirch in the afternoon, where we were not allowed to stay on account of approaching U.S. units and tank columns. In the 'Kleck' we were loaded onto a GMC truck along with several other people and taken to Medernach, after Diekirch had come under German fire again a short time before. In Medernach my last two horses, which I had taken there, died; later we buried them beside the road.

Here we finally found a place to stay with a family. While a U.S. engineer squad searched the approach roads for mines, the collaborator H., who had come along willingly, was arrested by the militia. On January 23 I rode as a passenger in a U.S. truck to Luxembourg to get a 'Laissez-passer' at the office of the Civil Affairs unit. Here there were already several people from Diekirch who were waiting for the same document.

When I returned to my native village as one of the first inhabitants of Diekirch since the final liberation, I saw a hopeless scene of destruction and desolation that the last German offensive had caused.

When I wanted to look at my farm on the Herrenberg, I was stopped by a U.S. patrol, but they let me proceed after I showed them my 'Laissez-passer'. With heavy heart I had to accept the fact that outside of our lives themselves, practically nothing else remained for my family and me." (Source: Etienne Reuter, Diekirch.)

A Craftsman of German Ancestry

A craftsman of German ancestry and his family were likewise among those inhabitants who could not leave Diekirch at the right time and thus spent their perilous lives in the cold, damp cellars of their dwelling houses until their final liberation by the 5th U.S. Infantry Division in January 1945.

Long before the war, Pierre Carl, who came from the Eifel area, had settled in Diekirch, where he operated a blacksmith shop. Despite his German ancestry, "Schmatt Karel" soon became a fully integrated and respected citizen, who felt more and more united with Diekirch and its inhabitants. He felt this all the more so during the difficult times during the German occupation. But unfortunately, especially since the liberation in September of 1944, there were provocations and insults by hotheaded 'patriots', who suddenly felt justified, having a gun in their hand, in being as zealous as they pleased.

Although Pierre Carl and his family had to put up with all of that, they bore this injustice passively, for they regarded themselves as citizens of Diekirch.

It is not the author's intentions to tear open long-healed wounds and bring up again sad episodes, but rather to portray the situation objectively; in this sense, let us let "Schmatt Karel" tell his story:

"Since the arrival of the Americans after the battles around Aachen in late 1944, we had several soldiers quartered in the house and also in the storeroom of the workshop, and we also fed them numerous times. Among them were two who spoke and understood some German, which contributed considerably to understanding and, despite the friendly welcome of the people in Diekirch, helped to dissipate the remaining slight mistrust of the civilians by the GIs. Louis Schmitz also had several soldiers of a resting company in his house. The U.S. garrison set up a field hospital on the present-day football field, and since the arrival of the unit, it was visited regularly, for numerous U.S. soldiers were suffering from digestive disorders and diarrhea. Not far from the railroad station there were an American motor pool and gasoline station behind the Haentges Hotel, which went up in flames at once in the early hours of December 16, 1944, when the first German shells exploded in the station district. It was not long before people were talking of acts of espionage in Diekirch, as well as informants among the population who must have directed the fire precisely at U.S. troop quarters and material concentrations. After the German fire had finally stopped in the afternoon and the soldiers quartered at my house had quickly departed, the alarming news was heard that the Germans were already just short of Diekirch, for down in the 'Kleck' (Rue Clairefontaine), militiamen had shot a German scout. Bit by bit, this rumor was confirmed as, on the next two days, the Germans attempted to push their way through the 'Kleck' and from the Herrenberg into Diekirch.

U.S. Jeeps and trucks coming from the front filled with groaning wounded men and captured Germans gave evidence of the threatening situation. When the inhabitants noticed that the Americans were slowly moving back, there was panic in Diekirch, and people tried to leave the city with hastily packed carts as quickly as possible, despite the firefalls that kept falling. But the militia and the military police would not let the people out of the city and sent them back into the cellars, explaining that there was no danger.

In the yard of the old brewery in the "Bamerdall" several U.S. mortar teams had taken up positions and were firing their mortar ceaselessly over the south slope of the Herrenberg in the direction of the Blees bridge. Several U.S. half-tracks with anti-aircraft machine guns mounted on them, occupied the exits from Diekirch in the 'Kleck' and at the Hotel des Ardennes. A few hastily prepared dugouts along the street on the 'Esplanade' were equipped with light machine guns, for they apparently expected the main thrust of the German advance there. Toward evening, numerous American foot soldiers passed by the street barricades, all in retreat, when suddenly German artillery fire began to fall again, this time on the center of the city. Only later did we hear that the inhabitants of Diekirch had left town during the same night . . .

The morning of December 20 was uncannily quiet. Only around noon was the sound of engines heard from the 'Kleck', and two German assault guns rattled over the paved street and stopped at the corner of the Rue de Brabant, while German infantry searched the rows of houses. Through the cellar window, through which I had watched the German approach, I called to them that there were only civilians here, whereupon several soldiers with submachine guns ready to fire came into our cellar and searched everything thoroughly. They went away again silently, and I ventured out of the house to get a look at the situation. This advance guard was followed by countless other soldiers, ragged, dirty, exhausted and starving. Some of them came past with fully packed baby carriages and milk carts, onto which their weapons and equipment were tied, in the direction of the church. A real parade of beggars! (see Vol.I: The Germans).

I felt sorry for these obviously exhausted soldiers, who looked scarcely older than seventeen; but what could I do? When an American shell suddenly hit the gable of the Felten house, the tanks drew back into the Rue de Moulin, where they were out of sight of the enemy behind the high walls of the old brewery. The tank commander, who had just surveyed the area with his field glasses from the cupola, said with a defiant air: 'That will stop at once. Nothing can stop us now; we have just "killed" two Shermans near Tandel.'

Somewhat later, several fully camouflaged tracked vehicles and armored personnel carriers with infantry riding on them drove along the Esplanade and turned off in the direction of the railroad station. One heavy prime mover pulling a Nebelwerfer recognizable by its characteristic bundle of barrels drove up into "Bamerdall" and took up a position in front of the Villa Lola (this was told to me later by several "Bamerdall" folks), from where it fired several salvoes of rockets in the direction of the 'Haardt.' Then the gun crew made a position change and drove in the direction of Kippenhof.

The German field police, which had arrived by then, began to barricade the empty houses and post regulations, though after most of the Volksgrenadiers had already made off with everything edible. A German tracked vehicle drove up, and a young officer, who got out of an off-road vehicle that followed it, asked me to show him the way to the Villa Faber and the hospital. I recognized Miss Holweck inside the car; she had been badly wounded by a shell fragment and urgently needed medical care. So I got into the vehicle and rode along to the hospital, where two German medics immediately took care of the badly injured woman. Then we drove on, for the young lieutenant was in a hurry to reach the Villa Faber, where there was apparently a larger command post.

We had not yet passed the Girls' School when suddenly a low-flying fighter-bomber passed by and fired its machine guns at the street. Thank God the bullets hit some distance away, and in the next moment the vehicle disappeared behind the villa in question. The lieutenant took me along and led me into the cellar room, where several communication men were working at their telephones. Somewhat later, several messengers also arrived. The mood of the soldiers was obviously troubled . . . the morale of the troops did not seem to be the best.

As we drove back, the young officer told me that he himself was a student and would like to desert, since it was impossible for the Germans to win the war under these conditions, and his troops had already suffered considerable losses. Besides, everything was lacking: food, warm clothing, weapons, ammunition, fuel. All of this was already strictly rationed and had become rarities.

He even tried to win me over as a middleman and look for the Americans in the 'Haardt' forest on the south heights overlooking the 'Sauer' river. When I made it clear to him that even the slightest mention of desertion could cost him his head, he quickly put those ideas aside . . . for the much-feared military police were still in Diekirch. Meanwhile, several "Bamerdall" inhabitants had been locked in the church as hostages, since, as an Unteroffizier claimed, they apparently had cut telephone cables. When the young lieutenant had left, I was taken away too. At the last moment, though, one of the tank drivers, with whom I had talked a bit previously, prevented my being locked in the church too.

As I later found out, the terrified men were set free again after Diekirch had been searched thoroughly.

Late in the afternoon, an officer and three soldiers came into my cellar, in which we had already settled as best we could, and insisted that I go with him to the Café Back (now Café Radar), since it appeared that numerous armed civilians would hold out there. One of the sentries apparently had seen a young fellow with a rifle running into the building. The officer had the three soldiers load their weapons, placed himself in front of a window and shouted harshly: 'Hands up and come out. If you fire one single shot, you'll all be shot!'

Thereupon he ordered me to call to the young men and insist that they lay down their weapons at once and come out without delay. I talked to them and they recognized the seriousness of the situation; shortly after that they came out with hands raised, were roughly lined up against the wall and searched. A hand grenade was found on one of them. When one of the soldiers brought several weapons out of the café, the officer became furious and wanted to have the young fellow shot. I begged and pleaded with him, saying that they were just adventurous fellows, and thank God, he gave up his plan, and the three disappeared at once with several girls who had also been in the café.

The local savings bank in Diekirch had been hit several times. At the side of the street lay a heavy money safe that had been opened by force. For several days, paper money that had come back into circulation since the liberation in September turned up, but the robbers, who turned out to be former Luxembourg collaborators who had followed the combat troops to resume their activities in the Nazi party leadership, soon learned that the money was valueless.

More and more often, U.S. artillery spotter planes now flew over the city, which was also being fired on just as regularly by the U.S. artillery. A sign at the entry to the "Bamerdall" reading "Attention: Enemy View" warned against thoughtless movement during the day. From now on we no longer left the cellar. Only now and then did I venture outside in order to get water and a hot meal, which the Germans had promised us, from the German field kitchen that was set up in the alley behind the Felten house. Thank God we had enough provisions in the house, for the soldiers' meager casseroles were not very nutritious.

When the Americans began, as of New Year's Eve 1944, to set whole rows of houses afire with incendiary shells, most of the inhabitants fled into the vaulted cellar of the old brewery (now the National Museum of Military History), which was well below ground level, and whose meter-thick outer walls offered protection against any kind of weapons. The few Germans, who sought shelter during the U.S. artillery firefalls that grew more and more frequent early in January, all wore white bedsheets and cloths as snow camouflage. They told of an anti-aircraft battery up in the "Bamerdall", as well as a heavy mortar unit in the courtyard of the 'Butzeschull' (boys' school), that now and then fired back at the 'Haardt'.

When the conditions had become worse in mid-January, we were evacuated at night by the military police."

Interrupted Studies

It is known that Diekirch developed more and more into an educational center since the turn of the century, especially on account of the boys' junior college, the 'Dikricher Kolléisch', where increasing numbers of the sons of Ösling farm families continued their studies with the thought of one day becoming teachers in their home towns or making careers as public officials.

One of these students was Emile Post of Drinklingen, near Ulflingen, who began his studies in 1942 as a thirteen-year-old scholar and boarder at the so-called "Bullett", the boarding school of the academy. Mr. Post is now a reverend in Luxembourg.

As a sixteen-year-old student, he likewise missed the news that the population of Diekirch was leaving the city in the night of December 19-20, and thus remained there, without his parents having received the slightest news from him. The following has remained in his memory since those perilous days:

"As of 1943 we had classes at the 'Kolléisch' only in the morning, since the afternoons were usually filled with 'mandatory duty activities' organized by the Nazi Party and the Hitler Youth. Although we had numerous school subjects to learn, which the professors, Schlim, Lacaf, Thibeau, Zahnen, Kremer, Goergen, Weis . . . drilled into us, the studies in those uneasy times were not approached very seriously, and the school's directors, Dr. Buerner and Dr. Würz (two German secondary-school teachers), preferred that we took an active part in the Hitler Youth, which we could not avoid despite the objections of our parents. At night, especially during January of 1944, there were often air-raid alarms, in which, according to the prevailing school regulations, the bedrooms had to be evacuated in the shortest time possible and everybody had to get to the air-raid shelter. We were also given training in firefighting and first aid. In the spring of 1944 we also had to take part in a military training program, which was conducted by soldiers with front experience, and under the supervision of the police, in an empty wing of the academy. It consisted mostly of stringent physical exercise, military drill and small-arms shooting. Naturally, the shooting was a lot of fun for us; so it was not surprising that we ran around our bedrooms in the evening with a few old hunting rifles that we had found in the theater wardrobe of the boarding school. Early the next morning, the German police were already at the school searching for the weapons, which we had already hidden hastily in a clothes closet. Somebody had squealed on us? The weapons were found, there was a gigantic fuss, and a lot of disciplinary actions followed. But this did not bother us much, especially as everybody knew that the Americans had landed and the downfall of the Third Reich was now just a matter of time. One of us, a clever hobbyist who wanted to become an engineer, had built a primitive-looking radio receiver out of many separate components, and it actually worked. In our eyes, that was a minor sensation. So small groups of us often listened to the Allied broadcasts at night and thus were constantly kept up to date on events at the front.

Somehow it was found out. Our poor 'genius' had to answer to Dr. Buerner, who became furious, confiscated and destroyed the radio.

Weeks later, we were suddenly told one afternoon that the Americans were at Verdun and were advancing on Luxembourg. During that very same night, Wehrmacht trucks drove into the schoolyard, and the German students who were in one class with us had to pack their things hastily and assemble in the schoolyard. Then they got into the trucks with their luggage and drove away . . . to their homeland.

On the following day (about September 3, 1944) we gave free rein to our joy and held a demonstration, destroying a portrait of Hitler outside the window of Dr. Buerner's study and riding over it with our bicycles. The director and the other German professors hit the road that same afternoon.

On the next morning there were no more classes; I packed my belongings neatly onto the luggage rack of my bicycle and rode past the Germans, who were fleeing to the German border, to my family in Drinklingen, where I got to see the first Americans on September 12.

In mid-November 1944 we were informed that classes at the 'Kolléisch' would begin again and we should return to Diekirch. Since the boarding school was closed, I shared a room with two younger students, Robert Kails and Jean-Pierre Spaus, at Mrs. Nosbusch's house on Palace Street. Our landlady, Mrs. Nosbusch, who came from Vianden and was acquainted with my family, welcomed us and took good care of us. The school studies were continued and life slowly returned to its usual pace. Diekirch had meanwhile been occupied by numerous U.S. troop units, and between the soldiers and us boys there developed true friendships, not just on account of chocolate and chewing gum, but also because of the English language, which each of us proudly tried to master.

Not far from our housing, by the house of Professor Lacaf and Attorney Reuter, there was an American field kitchen . . . a real attraction on Palace Street. We slowly assimilated a completely new vocabulary from the 'boys from overseas', the land many a Luxembourgeois dreamed of, and of which there was so much talk in the villages of the 'Ösling' (the Luxembourg Ardennes), for almost every family somehow had relatives or friends who had emigrated to the USA in the previous century. There were words in the U.S. jargon that could not be found in any "Oxford" English dictionary, but that quickly became part of our vocabulary.

In Diekirch it had become so quiet that the war had almost been forgotten, although the U.S. Civil Affairs office still enforced emergency measures.

Completely by surprise, the first German shells exploded in Palace Street on the cold morning of December 16, 1944. In no time we were all out of bed and, along with Mrs. Nosbusch, sought shelter in the cellar. We were completely baffled. Nobody had expected any such thing at all. We stayed in the safety of the cellar all day – our school classes did not meet.

Militiamen, from whom we heard that the Germans had very probably launched a large-scale surprise attack, advised us to stay in the cellar, for fire was resumed that same evening. On December 18 I saw a column of German prisoners being led to our high school by Diekirch militiamen. It dawned on us slowly . . . the situation was more serious than we had assumed.

Mrs. Nosbusch was obviously aware of the danger, and after we had packed our most necessary clothing, bedding and food supplies, we moved to the 'Megonsvilla'. There we settled in the cellar of the house, which belonged to friends of Mrs. Nosbusch. Besides us, there were a girl from Vianden and the hostess of an inn in Diekirch, named 'Lizzi', there. During the same night, German anti-aircraft and tracer shells came from the direction of the Herrenberg and exploded in Palais Street. So as not to let any light be seen, we hung several potato sacks over the big cellar windows and spent an uneasy night there by the faint light of lanterns and candles.

Early in the morning of December 19, shells fell on Diekirch again, and we decided to spend the whole day in the cellar.

At the first light of day on December 20, it had become uncannily quiet. After two hours of uncertain waiting, I could not stand it in the cellar any more and I decided to find out what the situation was. So I went down from the 'Megonsbierg' to the post office, where I met two people who told me that the militia had evacuated Diekirch during the night. Hadn't anyone informed us of it? I said no and decided to pack up my things at once and ride home to Drinklingen and my parents on my bicycle as fast as I could. I got the house key from Mrs. Nosbusch and packed my suitcase. As I was about to go back across the 'Kluuster' (main town square) to the 'Megonsbierg', I saw a German assault gun rattling down the 'Bamerdall' with infantrymen sitting on it. Behind it marched the 'Bamerdall' people, followed by armed soldiers. To the left and right, German scouts with submachine guns walked along the road. I was just about to hurry away when one of them shouted 'Halt!'

Hostages?

Paralyzed by fright, I stopped, turned around slowly and saw that two Germans were coming toward me. I was hastily searched and questioned; then I had to join the people who had been brought out of their cellars. Several German sentries with loaded guns encircled the church, and we had to line up in front of the door. Other civilians were brought here from different parts of the city. Among them there was a young militiaman (partisan), scarcely older than I, about whom one of the Germans said he had been caught with a rifle. When the assault gun turned away, many of the people, especially the women, believed they were going to be shot.

As one of the sentries made a show of loading and cocking his assault rifle, we believed our last hour had struck. But suddenly there was an American firefall from the 'Haardt'. With ear-splitting crashes, the shells exploded on the 'Kluster' and spread their fragments in the direction of the church and the post office. The young militiaman must have used this moment of confusion to disappear, for he was no longer there when the Germans drove us into the church for protection from the shell fragments. So now we sat in the church and froze. The German guards did not say a word. Only one of them kept grinning at us as he fumbled with his assault rifle and its curved magazine. Toward evening there was a second firefall, and when the first shot broke through the roof of the church and caused a lot of damage in the main choir, we all crouched down behind the heavy stone pillars and waited nervously until the shooting ended.

Finally the Germans pushed us outside . . . and let the women go. All the men, of whom I was the youngest, to the best of my knowledge, now had to move along the deanery to the cellar of the sacristy, where the Germans locked us in with several guards. What was the purpose of all this? Were we just hostages, or were we going to be shot? Only now did one of the guards say a few words. 'Well, you probably didn't believe we would come back so soon, did you?' He received no answer. Someone had discovered several crates of apples, and we went at them eagerly, for we had nothing to eat for a whole day. I was rather tired from the previous sleepless nights and made myself a 'bed' out of a few coke bags. Surprisingly, the Germans let us go the next morning, without a word of explanation. They had probably held us here until they had searched Diekirch thoroughly for so-called 'partisans' or Americans.

Survival

As fast as I could, I went back to the 'Megonsvilla', where Mrs. Nosbusch had been very worried about me. Meanwhile the Germans had also been there and had checked the identities of the cellar dwellers, but without giving them any trouble.

So we set out to survive here. We had several rabbits, chickens, even a piglet that must have known we were in need, and I had to slaughter it with a kitchen knife. We heard that a man from Vianden was baking bread at the 'Fischer' bakery and gave it out to the remaining people every other day. Every morning before it was light, we three comrades took buckets, milk cans and pots and went up to the well in the upper brewery to get fresh water from a cistern. Very seldom did we get to see a German. Everything was deathly still. We could move around only in the dark, for there were wooden signs on the 'Kluster' and the 'Bamerdall' road with a skull and big lettering warning against movement during the day, for the Americans in the 'Haardt' fired at any careless movement. Numerous dead cattle lay in the 'Bamerdall'. The sidewalk was littered with empty and broken bottles.

Constantly searching for food, though we ourselves had enough to eat, we reached the Masseler butcher shop on the 'Esplanade'. The meat we found here, though it was already turning greenish, was taken along all the same and eaten after being thoroughly cooked.

At the end of December, Diekirch suddenly became livelier, as German troops, who had been hit hard beyond Ettelbrück and had to leave a large portion of their war materials behind, took up quarters there. The Germans gradually settled into a purely defensive type of warfare in Diekirch. Even we boys had to take part. Although we were not under pressure, we had to help break down the wall of a farmyard on Hospital Street with picks and heavy hammers, so a heavy machine-gun position could be set up. A similar machine-gun bunker position was established in the firehouse.

On the following day we had to dig trenches, as well as firing positions for heavy grenade launchers, in the yard of the 'Butzeschull' behind the church. It took some time and cost us a lot of energy and effort before the dugouts and the ditches were deep enough for the heavy circular base plates of the mortar barrels to be lowered into them. From the cellar windows of the 'Megonsvilla' we could observe the mortar batteries firing steeply over the damaged roof of the church in the direction of the 'Haardt'. We could even clearly hear the explosions of the shells at the edge of the woods, which were occupied by the Americans.

But the Germans had to ration their ammunition, and almost every mortar was answered by many shots from the American artillery. It did not take very long before the Americans had presumably figured out that the position was near the church.

During the same night there was a terrible firefall, in which the upper story of the 'Megonsvilla' took several direct hits. Almost the entire facade collapsed. Chunks of plaster, dirt and sand fell from the ceilings down the cellar stairs and into the room where we were. The sacks were torn from the windows by the air pressure, our carbide lanterns were extinguished; none of us could see each other any more because of the dust; our teeth grated on the sand in the air. Then we decided not to stay there any longer, and we went to the 'Old Brewery' in the 'Bamerdall', since we had already heard that numerous people were staying there. On a winding stone stairway, we carried our food and some blankets into the deep, vaulted cellar, the floor of which had been covered with straw. We found many old people here, who had been brought here from the overcrowded hospital, because the thick walls of the old brewery offered sure protection. The Germans, who also stayed here at times, had broken a hole through the outside wall from which they had immediate access to the Esplanade.

Through this hole we could also slip out in the twilight, and with a few jumps, protected from the view of the enemy, we came quickly to the center of Diekirch whenever we went in to get bread.

In another cellar room with rounded arches there stood a stove where a woman cooked for the people in the cellar. Several German soldiers were also fed here. One day a shot was fired in the front part of the brewery, and the noise reached us through a long underground passageway that connected the two cellars. It turned out that a sentry had shot a cow that had fallen down the cellar stairs in the other building and broken a leg. The emaciated animal thus provided us with meat for a while.

At the beginning of January the Americans began to fire incendiary shells. The whole Esplanade went up in flames. Burning white phosphorus cascaded down the fronts of the houses like oatmeal! Suddenly there was a dull thud, and a white phosphorus fragment fell onto the stove through the hole in the cellar window through which the stovepipe went outside. The stove was immediately in flames. Cries were heard, but the fire was quickly extinguished with sand, which was then thrown outside, where the fire flared up again. It took some time before the acrid smell of white phosphorus was gone from the room. Unfortunately, several old people died here in the cellar, and their bodies were placed in simple coffins without lids in the next room. The sight of the dead people did not affect me at all, for each of us was just concentrating on keeping himself alive. We also had no more sense of time. Our thoughts were so dulled that we had even forgotten that two days ago it had been New Year's Eve, the night when the Americans had fired so heavily on Diekirch.

When our food supplies ran out, we decided to look for the local German commander of the garrison billeted in and defending Diekirch, and ask him for permission to go to the refrigerator building in the station area and search for meat.

When we forgot to give the Hitler salute, we received a good chewing out. In spite of that, he gave us permission, and so we set out with a sled and brought back several thick chunks of meat, which the soldiers posted there gave us.

The homemade brandy from the wine and whisky bottles that we brought from the Müller liquor shop across from the brewery helped to improve the atmosphere in the cellar somewhat. I caught a fever and became so weak that I could hardly stand up.

In spite of everything, the German military police came on January 15, 1945 to drive us to Brandenbourg, since it was considered safer there. I stumbled after the sled, which was pulled by comrades, and on which we had packed what remained of our possessions. My head threatened to burst at every step. Up in the 'Bamerdall' was a German anti-aircraft gun, with its crew standing ready. Via the Kippenhof we reached Brandenbourg, where I immediately lay down in a stable and covered myself with straw, because I felt so wretched.

After two days, though, my fever was gone, but hunger made me miserable. A young soldier gave me a chuck of Kommissbrot and some rancid butter to make a 'war sandwich'.

On the following day, at our insistence, the local commander in Brandenbourg gave us a permit that allowed us to cross the area occupied by the Wehrmacht on our way home. We reached Hoscheid on foot. Here we begged until an older German soldier gave us a ride on a horse-drawn wagon. Shortly before the 'Schinker' crossroads he called to us, 'Hang on tight, you're going to experience something now.' – But his colleague replied, 'Man, don't scare the boys.' At the next moment he swung his whip with both hands, and the horses almost jumped and crossed the intersection at a fast gallop. Black holes to the right and left showed that the crossroads was often under fire, and the ammunition drivers had to look out for U.S.

artillery fire. Through the ruins of Hosingen we reached Fischbach, where the local commander only allowed us to proceed on the next day, after we had gotten some food from the field kitchen there. On our way to Binsfeld we passed a column of German vehicles near Rossmühle. They sat there motionless, without a drop of gasoline. On January 23 my home town was liberated."

The Diekirch Hospital During the Offensive
The hospital in Diekirch, built in the previous century and run by the order of the Sisters of St. Elisabeth, developed during the course of the offensive into a unique community of fate and suffering.

The conditions prevailing there, which grew noticeably worse from day to day, cannot be described in words. The following report is based on what was told by Sister Consolata and Mr. Jean Weber, then an orderly in the hospital, as well as a newspaper article written by Ben Molitor, which appeared in the Luxemburger Wort in 1979 as "Diekirch Mosaic: the Diekirch Hospital."

Although the country had been liberated by the Americans in September and the living conditions had improved markedly, the war was by no means over yet. This became all the more obvious to the doctors, Dr. Sinner, Dr. Tandel and Dr. Hetto, and to the personnel of the Diekirch Hospital when, in October, a resident of Bigelbach was delivered, one leg half torn off by an exploding mine and the other badly injured. The one leg was amputated at once, by the medical care had come too late. The man, who had lost too much blood during transport to the hospital, died at 6:00 AM on St. Elisabeth's Day, the day of the patron saint of the order.

On November 19, 1944, three young men of the Vianden Militia (P. Gleis, M. Schneiders and J. Corring) were hastily brought in with bullet wounds, some of them serious, after they had been hit during a fire fight with a German shock troop at the castle in Vianden.

"Their uniforms were full of blood," recounts Jean 'Jängi' Weber, who had to cut off their clothing to expose their wounds before Dr. Tandel could treat them. Since the hospital was already full of old and sick people at that time, they were provisionally placed in the delivery room. Somehow Jean Weber had contracted a serious case of blood poisoning in his arm and hand during the ensuing days. His right hand swelled alarmingly, so that he had to be operated on and could only resume his work as an orderly again in mid-December of 1944. Since there was a shortage of space, he had to share his room, which was right next to the main door, with an old man from Bettel. As on every other day, "Jängi", as he was called by everybody, got up very early on the morning of December 16, 1944 to help the sisters prepare to treat the patients. "Suddenly there was a terrible explosion that rocked the whole building. Before I knew what was happening, there were two more explosions at the front of the building, close to the entrance. When I hurried down the hall to the door to see what was wrong, the old man came toward me, as white as chalk and trembling in his nightshirt. A German shell had hit right in front of the entrance and torn a big hole in the building. A part of the wall that separated my room from the entrance corridor had caved in. The room was full of pieces of stone and dust. The hail of shells lasted for about two hours.

When it had quieted down, Dean Colling came hurrying into the hospital and told us the alarming news that the Germans had very probably launched an offensive, and the first scouts had already been seen in the 'Seltz' that afternoon."

Sister Consolata tells: "Measures were taken at once to move the badly ill patients out of the upper floors of the hospital and transport them to Luxembourg. Sister Yvonne, the Mother Superior, was aware of the danger and gave every sister of the order the choice of leaving while there was still time or staying and doing her duty. It was purely a question of conscience. It was even suggested that every sister who would go along to Luxembourg be given not only a supply of bedclothes and underwear but also a certain sum of money, although this had never been done before. Not one single sister left the hospital. The old Pastor Miller from Berlé and 'Jängi' stayed with us.

As quickly as possible, the other patients, mostly old and infirm people, were moved into the various cellar rooms. Since the elevator no longer worked, this was all done by hand on the stone stairs. Unfortunately, the cellar of the hospital was divided into various small rooms that were connected by a hallway. For this reason it was not possible to give everyone a bed. Many of the people had to sleep on the floor after the sisters had made them a resting place of mattresses and bedclothes. Meanwhile other patients were brought in from the neighboring villages. "Although the cellar rooms were already fully occupied," Sister Consolata recalls, "no one was turned away. Since the roof had been hit several times and the icy December wind howled through the stairwell, nobody could stay in the upper stories any more. An improvised kitchen was hastily set up in the cellar, where several sisters were constantly occupied with preparing at least one hot meal a day and hot tea from the food supplies that were still available. At certain times of the day, shells always exploded in the vicinity of the hospital."

"The hygienic conditions worsened increasingly in the cellar," says Jean Weber; "there was only one toilet bucket, which stood in the middle of the room, for some ten to twelve patients. How often the sisters and I had to help the old men relieve themselves. Along with the bad smell, fever and dysentery were soon added. Later in the course of the offensive it was life-threatening to go outside and empty the toilet bucket in daylight. Thank God we had our own water supply, which was still functioning."

From the approximately 200 people who left the hospital, where they had sought shelter, in the early morning hours of December 20 to find a safe haven in the upper brewery in the "Bamerdall", the staff of the hospital learned that the population of Diekirch had left the previous night, and the Americans had also withdrawn. It did not take long until the first Germans pushed into the hospital later in the day and immediately searched it for Americans. After they had assured themselves that there were only old and sick people in the cellar rooms, they made no further searches, but took possession of the ground floor to set up a 'suitable' bandaging station.

When heavy U.S. artillery fire thundered down on Diekirch on December 24, the last 'tough' patients, who had not wanted to leave their rooms previously, left the rooms on the first floor and sought shelter in the cellar. Thus the number increased to almost 160 people: staff, patients, homeless, wounded.

"Pastor Miller had set up a makeshift altar in the middle of the place," Jean Weber reports, "for the midnight mass. By the light of candles and oil lamps he gave the holy communion while the shells howled outside. He fell down several times as he stumbled over the patients lying on the floor, so that I constantly had to support him as he passed by everyone and distributed the communion. At the end of the mass he gave a general absolution."

During this night, great portions of Diekirch were on fire.

Using the flour that was still available, the sisters had baked eighteen cakes and 26 fruit tarts as a small treat and Christmas gift for the patients. After Christmas the temperature dropped sharply. The icy, damp, cold wind blew through all the cracks into the cellar. The first sick people died . . . among them also the very ill Sister Erasmina. What was to be done with the dead, whose numbers increased every day?

Sister Evarista and Jängi Weber buried two of the dead in the hospital garden, although this was very dangerous. Several times Jängi had to hit the ground as he was fired on by U.S. artillery from the 'Haardt'. It took a long time before the ditch in the rock-hard frozen ground was deep enough to be able to take the body. To make later identification of the bodies easier, an empty medicine bottle with a note bearing information had been tied around each one's neck before they were tied inside a bedsheet. A sister carefully noted the day of death. By mid-January the number of dead had risen to eighteen, who lay in a cellar room. The icy weather prevented decomposition.

"In order to identify the hospital for friend and foe," Sister Consolata reports, "we had fastened a big red cross made of cloth on the snow-covered lawn in front of the entrance. Neither the Americans nor the Germans respected this. The hospital was constantly under U.S. fire, and the Germans, in the 'protection' of the red cross, had parked several trucks loaded with ammunition behind the laundry room, as they thought they were safe there. In addition, there was a German anti-aircraft gun close beside the hospital, but it was removed in mid-January. During all of this time, the Germans left us alone and even allowed us to make trips to Diekirch after our food supplies ran out."

Various chosen sisters, as well as Jängi, marked with a red cross over their clothing, took turns going with a sled to fetch flour and other food from abandoned stores. Everything was carefully noted as to quantity and weight, in order to reimburse the proprietors later for this necessary 'robbery'. Several times the sisters also came under fire as they crossed the 'Kluuster'.

From the Wiltgen Pharmacy, Jängi 'liberated' the remaining medicines. "Diekirch was one big heap of rubble," he tells. "After a firefall I saw that the Germans were busy gathering up their dead in a side street, in the midst of dead cattle, rubble, dirt and charred beams. Diekirch was no longer recognizable. In front of the Reding Shoe Store there lay a gigantic heap of shoes of all kinds, all mixed up, in the dirt of the street."

When the water pipes froze on account of the barbaric temperatures, drinking water had to be acquired by melting snow.

In the cellar, we prayed every day. Even men who had neglected their faith prayed devotedly with their rosaries.

Then, about 9:00 AM on January 19, after shooting had been heard near the hospital early in the morning, the Americans were suddenly there. An indescribable joy broke out among the patients, who had expected to die there after they had rejected the Germans' offer to evacuate the hospital on January 17. Tears of joy, prayers of thanks, words of welcome . . . all were mingled together.

On January 20, 1945, Army ambulances drove up and the Americans began to take the patients, every one of whom suffered from dysentery, away to Luxembourg. The dead were registered and buried in a mass grave in Ettelbrück, from which their families could remove them later. Seven sisters remained at the hospital: Perpetua, Rosa-Maria, Amanda, Evarista, Evalda, Leocadia and Consolata, to begin the unselfish work of cleaning out the place. The work of rebuilding the hospital, though, would take until 1950."

Juvenile Frivolousness

"How easily all this could have backfired, now that we think coolly about it today," recalls Pierre Prim of Diekirch, who then, barely seventeen years old and living in the 'Kléck', hurried along with the retreating U.S. units in the direction of the Blees Bridge with several comrades of the same age, in order, in their youthful enthusiasm, to shoot at the 'Preisen' ("the Krauts") and not miss any of this excitement. – "We were all unashamedly lucky, for several times we could have been killed. From somewhere we had obtained two German carbines, the operation of which I had to learn previously in a mandatory war training camp during the nazi occupation of Luxembourg. So we were eager to become 'active' and imagined that the war was a kind of adventure or sport – having weapons in our hands made us terribly strong in spirit and caused lightheadedness.

So on the afternoon of December 17 we ran down to the Blees Bridge, since the news had come that the first Germans had been seen there early in the morning of the previous day, shortly after the terrible firefall.

At the fork to Gilsdorf there stood militiamen, auxiliary police and some forty U.S. soldiers ready for action. When they immediately turned us around and sent us home, we tried to go over the ridge of the Herrenberg and pushed through the sloping meadowlands as far as a promontory on the heights by the 'Bleesmillen', somewhere below which there was a well-camouflaged U.S. machine-gun nest.

We slipped ahead to the Americans, who noticed us only later and probably could no longer send us away because of that. There was shooting all over on the other side and in the direction of Tandel. We tried to make clear to the machine-gun crew that we wanted to stay and shoot at the Germans. I borrowed a telescope for a moment and could actually observe a German soldier running down the path below the quarry on Bettendorf Hill with two ammunition cases. Now and then he threw himself to the ground, then jumped up lightning-fast and ran farther. But the machine-gun crew had already spotted him, and I was scared when the machine gun right beside us began to rattle. Shortly after that, the German fell in a hail of bullets. Killing at a distance! . . . for I had observed it all through the telescope . . . this made me stop and think for several seconds. But when the machine gun fired on the same area again a short time later, these thoughts disappeared again and we were filled with excitement. Full of fighting spirit, we also fired blindly over at the opposite slope.

Later I could also see, or believed I could see, that the hedges were moving in the fields near Fouhren and Longsdorf. Was it only a figment of my imagination, or was it camouflaged German vehicles. In any case, it did not take long before several shells howled across from the American side and exploded on this strip of land. Shortly after that the 'hedges' had disappeared. When we went home that evening, after German mortars had begun to take the area around the Blees Bridge under fire, a dead American soldier with a radio set smashed by shell fragments lay in the roadside ditch very close to the Welfring house. This was the first dead man I had seen up close; he was badly mangled.

On the next morning, two or three Sherman tanks took up positions at the approach to the Gilsdorf Bridge, in order to form a barrage against any possible German attack in the direction of Diekirch.

When we heard that the Germans had occupied the Cafe Breyer and the houses on the bend this side of the Blees Bridge the next day, auxiliary police and militiamen, followed by the three of us, worked their way up close to the houses in the shelter of the slope to the right of the railroad tracks. There was a lot of shooting.

Shortly after that, I crept on my belly to the edge of the side road and took cover behind one of the massive plane trees that lined the edge of the road. Up at a window of the first house I saw the barrel of a gun . . . I raised my head, lifted my carbine and fired one shot in this direction, a shot that did not hit. I was immediately fired on by a submachine gun and let myself roll back. Since we were in a dead angle from the houses, protected by the slope, the German infantry fire was not able to reach us.

Meanwhile we had gotten behind the tank again, where several auxiliary policemen were already negotiating with the commander to get him to advance and fire on the house so they could storm it. Several Germans had been seen with Panzerfaust weapons; this was obviously the reason for the commander's hesitation. We ourselves also urged the tank officer to do something. Several minutes passed while the shooting between the German occupiers and the auxiliary police and militia continued. Suddenly there was an ear-splitting crash. We who stood somewhat behind the tank saw that its entire body slightly shook from the force of the detonation. We also felt the air pressure of the muzzle flash. When the cloud of dust around the first house had dissipated, we saw that the explosive shell had torn a big hole in the gable, which encouraged us. The shooting went on and the house was stormed. A large number of Germans surrendered at once to the militiamen and police, whom we now joined. Similar actions were to take place twice in the early afternoon. Again Germans were taken prisoner. On 'our' side, only Militiaman Winandy was injured by a shell fragment. Every time, we helped eagerly in searching and disarming the prisoners. In this way I acquired a German assault rifle with a lot of ammunition, which was smaller than the normal carbine bullets. (see Vol.I: The Germans).

We all felt like heroes. Our chests puffed out mightily as we led a group of German prisoners back through the 'Kleck' and several inhabitants of Diekirch who had ventured out onto the street saw us. I myself, who had learned the basic concepts of German barracks-yard drill at the military training camp, commanded several times, with the assault rifle ready to fire: 'In unison, forward march, march!'

or 'A song!' On this day a lot more prisoners were brought in and taken to the Hotel du Midi, part of which was still on fire, where they were turned over to the American CIC. Late that afternoon, when we wanted to go back to the Blees Bridge to appropriate some of the equipment left there by the German prisoners when they were searched, the Hamen farm was blazing brightly. Intense infantry combat was also raging everywhere in the 'Seltz' and on the 'Bettenduerfer Bierg'. The noise of battle came gradually nearer.

So that evening we hid in a house at the 'Neelcheswee'. During the night, though, the inhabitants fled out of Diekirch. Auxiliary Policeman Thull hurried along the 'Kleck' and spread the news that all the inhabitants of this part of town who were still there should go to the Sauer Bridge without delay. We ourselves, though, did not take this warning very seriously, since we were still excited by our dreams of victory and imagined ourselves to be heroes.

On the Morning of December 20 we were awakened by the sounds of motors from far away! I was almost scared to death when I looked down to the 'Kleck' from the front door and saw a German tank rattling up the road. In no time we were all on the move. I sprang out of the house, but had completely forgotten to leave my weapon back in the house as I ran down the Esplanade. There, at the intersection of Brabant Street, the so-called 'Redingsbiergelchen', two German soldiers blocked my way and forced me to surrender and hand over my assault rifle. They tore the assault rifle out of my hands and had me stand up against the wall of the Reding Shoe Store. From the corner of my eye I could see the tank, with a German cross painted on it, rumble by in the direction of the church. What happened then I do not understand to this day. The two soldiers, who were scarcely older than I, and who obviously came from the 'better strata' of society, let me go. I simply could not understand it. After I had overcome my fear, I wanted to get away from there as fast as possible. As if possessed, I ran through the 'Grousgass' down to the Sauer and to the railroad station. Too late; the station district was already occupied by the Germans. They marched silently past the city park, with their weapons, equipment and ammunition on army carts or even on requisitioned baby carriages and carts. Only now did it become clear to me how serious the situation really was. I ran back in the direction of the Esplanade and was stopped here again by an approaching German column.

After I had come to a standstill immediately at the first cry of 'Halt!', I saw a soldier aiming at me. – 'What are you doing here?' – 'I stayed behind to feed our cattle,' was my spontaneous answer, which had occurred to me immediately, thank God.

I was searched on the spot, and thoroughly this time. When the soldiers found an American marching compass on me, they became mistrustful. One of them stuck the barrel of his submachine gun in my back and ordered me to put my hands up.

They marched me in front of the church, where a large number of local men, as well as several women from the 'Bamerdall', were already standing under a heavy guard. What did the Germans have in mind? What fate were we to expect?

Suddenly there was a firefall and several U.S. shells exploded on the 'Kluuster' close to the post office. In no time my guards hit the dirt and, driven by panic fear, I used that moment to flee. Gasping, I reached the Café Back, where we had planned to rendezvous. My two friends had also escaped and were in the attic of the abandoned restaurant.

Things Happen Fast

Late in the afternoon of December 20, we were horrified to see a group of German soldiers with an officer and a civilian come down the street and approach the cafe. In no time the Germans had surrounded the building, and the officer ordered us to throw out our weapons at once and come out. Only now did we realize that the civilian was the blacksmith Carl. He also spoke to us and tried to make it clear that a thoughtless act could cost us our lives.

We did not think it over for long, but raised our hands and went down the stairs. We were taken into custody brutally and placed against the wall with our hands up. The officer ordered three of his men: 'Load your weapons – if one single shot is fired, shoot them at once!' Then he ordered the house searched. We were terrified and in a cold sweat. Seconds and minutes turned to hours. After some time, one of the soldiers returned with two U.S. hand grenades and a carbine. The officer was beside himself, for it was a German carbine, and he swore we must have shot one of his men. Thoughts raced through my mind like lightning.

I was thinking of throwing myself at one of the guards in the next moment when Carl the blacksmith suddenly spoke to the officer and pleaded with him that we were just boys who had taken a weapon, which we had probably found, with them out of a desire for adventure. There followed seconds that were a matter of life and death. The officer was finally persuaded by the smith and gave up his plans. After a thorough search we were allowed to stay in the house.

Two days later, though, we were abruptly awakened when several Germans demanded that we go to the Villa Conter immediately. To our horror, the sinister Gestapo official Klöcker was there; he forced us to carry trunks and load plundered goods into several luxury civilian cars. I noticed that there were several people from Diekirch, who had belonged previously to the Nazi Party and had fled to Germany before September 10, among his helpers. They too were busy looting and handling the stolen goods.

So we spent the whole morning hauling crates and carrying trunks, until suddenly there was another firefall. In the confusion, and amid the exploding shells, we disappeared as fast as possible and hid ourselves in a house on the 'Kleck' not far from the pumping station. Close to the house there was a burned-out German truck, plus numerous Wehrmacht bicycles and dead horses. Several dead soldiers lay along the edge of the road and the avenue of trees near the tracks of the 'Benny'. Two days later, when we had used up the food we found there, consisting of jam and canned goods, hunger drove us back into Diekirch.

On 'Nikolaus' Street a shell had torn a hole in the roof of the Huffler store. Although the Germans had already taken practically everything, we were able to find a quantity of canned goods under the rubble, and we stuffed them into our pockets eagerly.

An appetizing smell came from the 'Groussgaass' and lured us there. Numerous refugees had stayed in the half-destroyed Fischer-Thiry bakery, and one of them, Willy Besseling from Vianden, was just baking bread for the civilians who were still in Diekirch, using the remaining supplies of flour. He also gave us some of it, and so we at least had fresh bread. But when the yeast ran out, the bread got thinner and thinner.

At the entrance to the 'Kleck' there was a German machine-gun position by the Faber house. Despite the snow, we recognized several minefields along the Sauer, all the way to the Gilsdorf Bridge. American shells, usually white phosphorus shells, fell on Diekirch more and more often, starting fires in several parts of town.

Constantly searching for food, I was caught by a German patrol on the Esplanade in January and taken to a gloomy cellar on 'Mill' Street, behind Simon's garage, where a German command post was located. An officer sitting at a card table, dimly lit by several candles and oil lamps, questioned me about the general condition of the civilians in Diekirch. After I had told him of our situation, he let me go again, but after that I had to help other civilians several times to dig rifle pits.

So we went on living, and our thoughts were concentrated only on getting enough food to eat. Remarkably, we were awakened abruptly one morning as shooting was heard along the Sauer. Shortly after that we saw the first Americans along the shore of the Sauer, near the Gilsdorf Bridge, and going in the direction of the main road. We ran to meet them, but were treated rather mistrustfully by them. After we and one other person were searched at the 'Kleck' and our identities were checked, we were taken by them to Gilsdorf on a rubber-boat bridge. Numerous civilians, including several wounded people from Gilsdorf and Diekirch, had gathered in the salon of the Café Walch and were waiting restlessly for their evacuation out of the danger zone by the Americans. When several German shells exploded in Gilsdorf, we all flung ourselves on the floor and did not dare to raise our heads any more. A shell fragment broke through the window, bounced off and grazed my cheek. An American soldier was beside me at once and looked at the wound; fortunately it was just a scratch. Shortly after that we got into ambulances and were taken to Medernach, where we got a hot meal at an American field kitchen. After that we went on to Larochette, where we were questioned by the CIC at the Ginter house about the situation in Diekirch during its occupation by the Wehrmacht.

After a few days, though, we three decided to take off and go back to Diekirch. Although we fell into the hands of the American MP in Medernach, a second attempt, undertaken somewhat later, succeeded. We crossed the Sauer on a bridge built by U.S. engineers. When we reached the other shore in the city park of Diekirch, a Jeep, in which Jules Dominique sat along with two U.S. soldiers, caught up with us.

When the first Diekirchers returned at the end of January, we had already scouted the area and eagerly collected war relics, which we found piles of around an abandoned German prime mover on the Herrenberg. Heaven knows what we would have done with all the weapons and ammunition if the Militia had not caught up with us and taken everything away from us!"

The Diekirch Law Enforcement personnel During the Offensive
After daily life had gradually been normalized since the liberation of Diekirch and the surrounding area, the competent U.S. authorities insisted that the Luxembourg Gendarmerie (state police), which had finally been activated again, should take up

its duties as soon as possible. Above all, they should protect those "political prisoners" who were confined in the Glyco building in Diekirch from the wrath of the inhabitants and prevent their property from being molested. Other tasks consisted of conducting patrols and sentry duty along with the appropriate U.S. authorities, for Diekirch and the neighboring villages were still part of the endangered 'front area' after the withdrawal of the German troops behind the West Wall.

There were far from enough trained gendarmes or officials who had seen service before 1940 available for these missions, so that the district commander at the time, Lieutenant Melchers, constantly had to call on auxiliary personnel, some of whom took an oath for this purpose. These auxiliaries consisted for the most part of auxiliary policemen who had volunteered for service, firefighters, and returned members of the "maquis" or the "Armée Blanche."

At the end of October 1944, the Gendarmerie brigade in Diekirch had regained its old effective strength of professional gendarmes. They were Adjutants Peters and Reiles, Wachtmeister Huss, Glesener, Donven and Bredimus. It was a job for engineers that faced the district commander and his subordinates in restoring order in the area that had faced four years of martial law and privation without overly limiting civil liberties, which were still limited to some extent by the U.S. Civil Affairs authorities.

The former Wachtmeister (Police NCO) Roger Huss, who died just a short time ago, then served not only outside but also in the writing room of the Gendarmerie. Here is his report:

"After sufficient auxiliary gendarmes had been enrolled and placed under the direct command of Adjutant Peters, they were immediately divided into groups of two or three for specific missions. Each of them carried with him a pass, issued by the district commander, which was to identify the man as a recognized order-keeping official. The auxiliary gendarmes normally were issued a German K-98 carbine, of which the Gendarmerie in Luxembourg had obtained a large quantity, as a service weapon. At the beginning of their term of service, they accompanied the regular gendarmes on their beats, or stood guard at the Glyco building where the 'political prisoners' were interned.

In addition, they regularly undertook patrols or stood guard at various roads leaving the city. A white armband with the lettering 'Gendarmerie Auxiliaire' was their own piece of uniform identifying them as auxiliary law enforcement personnel. Among the numerous volunteers who were divided among the various offices in the northern part of the country after they had taken their oath, there were also several Diekirchers who thus did service in their home town.

They had all been promised that later they would be given the opportunity to be accepted into the Gendarmerie corps after passing an examination or to enter other areas of service as public officials and civil servants.

The story of the arrest of numerous German soldiers, who had hidden in two houses at the Blees Bridge on December 19, by auxiliary gendarmes and militiamen after a U.S. tank had taken one of the buildings under fire at very short range, is especially noteworthy. After numerous shells had struck not far from the prison in Diekirch and close to the Glyco building, it was decided that the German prisoners, who were being guarded by militiamen and young men from Diekirch, should be turned over to the Americans at once. In addition, the Glyco building should be cleared immediately and all the 'political' prisoners should be transferred to Luxembourg or farther to the south, since their safety could no longer be guaranteed on account of the threatening situation.

Lieutenant Melchers had meanwhile negotiated with the representative of the American commander in Diekirch and had found a solution to the problem of evacuating the civilian population of Diekirch.

After Lieutenant Melchers had received the evacuation order, according to which the city was to be evacuated starting at midnight and without affecting the ordered withdrawal of the U.S. troops from the sector, he immediately called all of the Gendarmerie officials subordinate to him together. Each of us was given a particular task. Since there was only one way for the civilians to leave Diekirch without using the Americans' withdrawal route (Diekirch-Ettelbrück), which was reserved for military use, the people had to be informed quickly. Sentries, consisting of U.S. military police, auxiliary gendarmes and firefighters, were posted at various routes out of the city, under American command, to prevent the people from leaving by those routes and thus to keep the road open for the withdrawing U.S. military forces.

I myself was given a double mission. With two auxiliary gendarmes, I was to warn the occupants of the Esplanade and the 'Kleck" after dark, and then hurry to Luxembourg on a motorcycle to have several city buses hurry toward the refugees to take them to Luxembourg.

The stream of refugees itself was to pass through Stegen and reach Schieren and Colmar-Berg, and be transported on from there by bus.

After the discussion, Adjutants Peters and Reiles went to Ettelbrück, in order to meet the people later in Schieren.

The auxiliary gendarmes were advised to leave Diekirch as soon as possible themselves, since it was feared that they could be arrested by the Germans and shot as non-uniformed 'partisans'.

Evacuation

As quickly as possible, I was shown how to operate the motorcycle that was assigned to me, for I had never before driven one, before I went with Auxiliary Gendarme Gillen and Fireman Thull to the Esplanade and the 'Kleck'. The ominous noise of battle could be heard from the Blees Bridge, where the German soldiers had been captured by our men shortly before. It was already dark when we saw the Americans withdrawing from the lower 'Kleck'. Shortly before that, Lieutenant Melchers had arranged for the gendarmes' families to be taken to a safe place at once, as long as the road to Ettelbrück was still open. So Gendarme Bredimus drove my wife, who was pregnant, to Mersch in the service vehicle, and later to Luxembourg with Lt. Melchers, in order to arrange what was necessary to take care of the refugees.

The evacuation was to take place step by step. I myself had orders to finish it by remaining at the 'Eisebunsbréck' until all the people had crossed and then to drive to Luxembourg without delay in order to arrange further transportation for the refugees. Around 10:00 PM there were already numerous people with their necessary possessions, which they had packed onto wagons, pushcarts, baby carriages and such, making their way to the bridge. At that time it was uncannily quiet in Diekirch. No light; a real ghost town. Silently the worn-out American soldiers moved along the sidewalks on both sides of Depot Street in the direction of Ettelbrück. Their withdrawal was cast in a ghostly light by the fire that still burned in the Hotel du Midi near the station. Finally there was a jam at the bridge, for I could no longer persuade the people to stay back, although they had been instructed to wait until midnight. So I could only prevent them from making unnecessary noise or showing any light, although it was pitch dark.

In panic fear the people pushed forward to the bridge. Several tried to drive horse-drawn wagons along the rails. I saw an incredibly sad picture, which reminded me of the Middle Ages. Old and sick people were carried over the bridge on wagons or wheelbarrows. Artillery fire was suddenly heard in the distance, and several shells exploded in the upper city. Here and there a flare rocket illuminated the horizon with an eerie light. Suddenly there was a loud bang on the bridge. Cries were heard; horses reared up in fright. A mine forgotten by the Americans had exploded and killed a horse. Panic and traffic jams set in. I reached the other shore with the stream of refugees and advised the people to make for Stegen without delay, and go from there to Cruchten and Schieren. Meanwhile, preparations for their transportation further to the south were being made.

Then I quickly set out on the motorcycle for Luxembourg. In Linten I was stopped and checked by an American patrol. Gendarmerie Captain Stein, to whom I reported on the threatening situation as ordered, finally arranged for buses and trucks to be sent to meet the column of refugees.

For unknown reasons, though, the people from Diekirch were only picked up by the trucks after they had reached Mersch and Lorentzweiler after an exhausting march on foot.

Then I was ordered by Captain Stein to go to Ettelbrück and inform Adjutants Peters and Reiles that they should report to the barracks in Luxembourg immediately. Since the direct route from Luxembourg to Ettelbrück absolutely had to be kept open for military columns, I used side roads to reach Cruchten by motorcycle. Not far from the 'Lommelshaff' an American battery had taken a position and was firing toward Diekirch, as I found out. To my question as to why they were firing on the city, I was told that the Germans were in Diekirch and on the move toward Ettelbrück. U.S. tanks were standing ready everywhere. Numerous army trucks lined the streets in Colmar-Berg.

Schieren too was full of American soldiers. I had to pass several checkpoints before I could reach Ettelbrück by motorcycle. I found the two adjutants and gave them the news. Since we also wanted to inquire about the situation, we decided to go on to the center of town. The bridge this side of the sanitarium had been blown up by the retreating Americans, and so we had a hard time reaching the other shore. In the distance we heard the rumbling of the U.S. artillery.

When we had gotten as far as the main street, there was a firefall. German shells exploded in the blocks of houses to our left and right at irregular intervals, and we drew back as quickly as we could. After we had made our reports in Luxembourg, I was allowed to take my wife to my family in Rumelange.

After that I went back into service in the capital city. Only on January 23, 1945 did we return in a service vehicle to Diekirch, which had been liberated just a short time before. Meanwhile several makeshift bridges had been erected by the U.S. engineers, so that we could get through Ettelbrück without problems. Part of the Gendarmerie building was still burning from incendiary shells, and the city looked hopeless. There were destroyed houses, burned-out neighborhoods, black bare walls, rotting livestock, emaciated, badly burned cattle running around. To get our service underway to some extent, we set up a provisional office on Main Street. Along with the returning auxiliary gendarmes, we lived and ate at the hospital, which was also badly damaged, aside from the unending misery of the sick people who had held out in the cellar there for five weeks. My first task was to work with the American graves service in gathering and taking away the numerous dead bodies in the vicinity of Diekirch. In the process, one American lost his life when he went to get the body of a German soldier that had obviously been booby trapped with an explosive charge, which blew up. This is said to have taken place at the 'Flossbach'. The 'Seitert' in particular was full of soldiers' bodies. One dead German found above the 'Floss' was even, to my amazement, wearing my own shirt, which he must have appropriated from the ruins of my home.

It was undoubtedly my shirt, for I recognized it by the manufacturer's label as a shirt that I had bought in France in 1938. While we registered the dead, a group of auxiliary gendarmes was busy clearing out the numerous dugouts. Foods rations that they found were taken along and distributed to the homeless. Since there were numerous German minefields, especially on the 'Erpeldinger Koeppchen' and around Bastendorf, walking in these areas was extremely dangerous and they were therefore closed off.

To remove the explosives, we had a special group, for we were not allowed to touch any of the explosives that lay around in quantities.

In Diekirch itself we had to carry out patrols constantly in order to prevent objects from being removed from half-destroyed houses whose occupants had not yet returned. Later I was also empowered to carry out an investigation of the shooting of three civilians by the Germans in Tandel."

Auxiliary gendarme "Men" Gillen volunteered for police service at the end of September 1944, after it had become known that the Gendarmerie urgently needed auxiliary personnel to carry out its regular services. "After I had turned in numerous questionnaires and school certificates," 'Gillens Men' relates, "I was sworn in along with several other volunteers, who had also volunteered recently, at the boys' school in Diekirch.

Several members of my group came from the 'Maquis' and thus already had a basis of service with weapons; others, and I was one of them, volunteered because we had been promised a job, either with the Gendarmerie or state, later, after we had taken examinations.

Then the group to which I belonged, consisting of P. Klasen, T. Hutchingson, T. Wagner, G. Mont and N. Scholtes, received an identity card and an armband which was supposed to make us recognizable as auxiliary gendarmes. After we had been taken along on patrols by the regular gendarmes for several days, each of us was issued a carbine and had to report to the Gendarmerie building twice a day to receive orders from Adjutant Peters.

The service, which ended daily at 6:00 PM, normally consisted of checking the identity of travelers who were encountered outside the city, insofar as they were not known to us, as well as sentry duty at the Blees Bridge, the 'Fielser Stroos' and the 'Friedhaff'. To some extent we also took over, along with the Americans, the guarding of the 'political' prisoners in the Glyco building, to protect them from the anger of the civilian populace. The very variable service without any noteworthy events soon resulted in boredom and a desire to do something interesting, so we began to have shooting drills (while doing sentry duty), and soon there were only a few isolators left on the high-tension poles. But this was soon to change!

Completely by surprise, the first shells struck in the 'Kleck', where I lived, early in the morning of December 16. The fire was so heavy that at first I did not try to leave the house to report to the office at 8:00 as usual. Only in the afternoon, when the situation had calmed down somewhat, did I go there. Several U.S. vehicles with soldiers sitting on them drove by hastily. Close to the Nitrolux Shoe Cream factory I saw several badly injured civilians, among them a man whose lower arm had been almost completely severed by a shell fragment. I immediately brought help and called an American medic, who took care of the injured people without delay. As I went on, artillery fire began again, but this time at the Herrenberg. The Americans in Diekirch seemed very tense and nervous; everything was in a state of excitement. Hardly any civilians were seen on the street. Adjutant Peters had meanwhile received the command from his superiors to provide a description of the situation immediately. Thus a group of us, reinforced by several militiamen, who also carried weapons, received orders to go to the Gilsdorf Bridge and Blees Bridge in order to find out what was going on. Later three Diekirch boys, whom I knew from my neighborhood, joined us. They also had a rifle and were eager to become 'active'. Although we had advised them to disappear, they did not let us get rid of them and stuck to the Americans. Since we were concentrating fully on our task, we did not worry about them any more. All around the Blees Bridge and on the slopes beyond it, the Americans had dug themselves in. Several antitank guns went into positions here. We learned that the Germans had crossed the Our in the early morning hours. But there was no direct danger, since they had already been stopped, and the U.S. forces who were present had the situation in hand. This was only a precautionary measure, probably just a local attack.

But on Sunday we could already hear the noise of battle from the direction of Longsdorf and from the slopes beyond Bettendorf.

We had orders not to leave our positions by the bridges unless to make a report on the situation.

On December 18, individual American machine guns were firing in the direction of Longsdorf, and several tanks on the Seltz fired on the slopes in the direction of the Our. To provide ourselves with a better picture of the situation, we took the field path that led up from the left side of the road to the Herrenberg to reach the U.S. positions, and the three boys followed us. Above the rifle pits, an anti-aircraft gun stood ready. We joined a soldier but could not communicate with him. He was very excited, pointing with his index finger in the direction of the Seltz and shouting 'Germans, Germans!' So it was serious.

In the afternoon we noticed that something was moving on the horizon. I concentrated my eyes on a hedge that did not look genuine to me. I noted the distance between it and a telephone pole. After some time it seemed to me that the distance had grown shorter, as if the hedge had moved. Moments later, this time moving considerably faster, the hedge was standing in front of the pole! Although I did not have a telescope, it was clear to me that there were camouflaged German vehicles there.

It did not take long, for the Americans had not failed to notice this either, and a 40 mm anti-aircraft gun opened fire. I saw the explosions of the shells on the horizon. Moments later the 'hedges' had disappeared. But now one shot after another was fired by a U.S. artillery unit on the Herrenberg. The shells whistled over our heads and landed with a pale yellow tongue of flame, followed by a black cloud of smoke, on the horizon. The tanks down on the road at the 'Seltz' also opened fire in this direction.

We hurried to Diekirch, where the news was already spreading like wildfire and panic was setting in. Numerous inhabitants were already about to leave Diekirch, but were turned back and sent home by the U.S. military police and militiamen posted on the roads out of town, with the explanation that the Americans were masters of the situation."

The Fight at the Blees Bridge (crossroad)

The extraordinary deed by which the auxiliary gendarmes succeeded in bringing numerous German prisoners out of the houses near the 'Bleesbréck' has already been described in the book "Les Deux Libérations du Luxembourg" by Lt. Col. Melchers. The author thus does not wish to presume upon the author of that book. "Men" Gillen, who was also involved in this battle, tells of it from his viewpoint:

"On December 19 we went back to the Blees Bridge very early in the morning. The noise of infantry weapons thundered everywhere. During the previous night, the German artillery had fired on Diekirch and Gilsdorf again, for fresh impact marks could be seen everywhere. Close to the turnoff to Longsdorf lay a German vehicle and the charred body of its driver. So the Germans had succeeded in pushing forward this far! But the Americans were still holding their position above the road to the Blees Bridge. Several Sherman tanks were standing near the Gilsdorf Bridge. The three boys were also by the tanks near the bridge. We made sure that the Americans were still holding the rifle pits behind the Cafe Breyer, and then made our way down a narrow path that descended steeply to the road. Where we came out on the road there stood a small house that we passed in order to reach the Blees Bridge.

Georges Mont saw a German bayonet lying close to the front door and wanted to pick it up. First he said to me that I should stand off to the side a bit, so I could give him fire protection if necessary. Suddenly something moved in the house, and the first shots were fired. Georges ran back, and we took up a position in the roadside ditch, where we took cover behind several thick plane trees to the right of the rails of the 'Benny'. We immediately returned fire from there. The three boys were suddenly there and firing, too. Meanwhile one tank had driven somewhat farther up the road in the direction of the Blees Bridge. The approach of the tank must have robbed the Germans of their will to fight; in any case, they came out, one after another, with their hands up and surrendered to Georges Mont, who had jumped up at once and, pointing his rifle at them, ordered them to line up along the wall of the house immediately. We searched the prisoners quickly and escorted them to the astounded Americans. First, though, I had assured myself that there were no forced recruits from Luxembourg among them. As I found out, some of the captured soldiers came from northern Germany, while some of them were Silesians. Before the astonished faces of the few people who ventured to their windows in the 'Kleck', Georges and I, along with the three boys, marched along with the prisoners and turned them in at the Gendarmerie, where they were immediately taken over by the Americans.

Until then nobody really was clear as to just how far the Germans had already advanced.

Lieutenant Melchers, who was likewise very astonished by this deed, pointed out to us that the weapons of the captured Germans were probably still in the house, and we should go and get them right away. So we went back and got a small wagon from my neighbors' garage, in which we intended to transport the weapons. Meanwhile numerous militiamen had gotten wind of the matter and accompanied us. Numerous firearms were in fact found in the house, including a machine gun, several carbines, Panzerfaust weapons, and several boxes with belts of ammunition. In addition, we found several weapons with a curved magazine, which we had never seen before, the MP44 assault rifle. One of the boys immediately adopted one of these new-type automatic weapons.

Early in the afternoon, after a number of militiamen had removed some of the weapons, we went back to have another look at the threatening situation. The tanks still stood on the road to the Blees Bridge, and the U.S. infantry had set up a machine gun in the Welfring house. The Americans warned us not to go as far as the Blees Bridge, for the Hamen Café was obviously occupied by the Germans. So Georges and I went along the bumpy path to the left again, behind the small house and as far as the U.S. positions. We looked for an advanced sentry who was sitting in a rifle pit, well-camouflaged by a hedge, some thirty meters behind the roof of the house. He tried to explain to us that the whole house was occupied, fixed a rifle grenade onto his M1, and fired it. The shot penetrated the roof and exploded in the inside of the garage. We hurried back and worked our way along the slope beside the road until we were even with the house. Meanwhile the other auxiliary policemen and several militiamen had put the captured machine gun into position and were firing into the house. The Germans fired from all the windows. A vigorous exchange of fire developed, but it died down to some extent when the machine gun ran out of ammunition. Meanwhile one of the tanks, followed by the three Diekirch boys, had moved forward and fired a shell from a dead angle, which tore a big hole in the house under the roof. Then the tank moved back somewhat and fired again. Georges volunteered to get several cases of ammunition for the machine gun and jumped up. Shots flew around and bounced off the rails of the 'Benny'. I ran after him and we ran to the tank. Here we obtained several incendiary grenades and ran back without the ammunition cases. From the cover of the roadside ditch, George hurled the grenades, which landed in front of the house. I recall that he was even able to throw one of them inside the house through a window. The white phosphorus sprayed around, and thick white clouds of smoke rose up and enveloped the house. That was probably the sign for the tank commander. The Sherman advanced to a short distance in front of the house and fired another explosive shell into it. Georges jumped up immediately and raced to the front door. When the dust of the explosion had cleared somewhat, we were pleasantly surprised to see a whole crowd of German soldiers, who were still in shock, leaving the house. Georges Mont stood at the door with his rifle ready to fire and shouted: "Hands up! Come out!"

The Germans were immediately taken into custody by us, stood in a row and searched. Every one had to put down all his equipment, including his helmet and leather gear. One of them was carried out of the house. I myself took the bread bag from an older soldier, as it was stuffed full of canned goods. When he insisted on keeping it, I gave him two cans back with the comment that the men would be treated well as U.S. prisoners of war.

Then we had the prisoners line up in rows of three, to Georges' orders in 'Wehrmacht tone' and 'Garrison drill tone', and marched them away. The boys, who were still following us with their weapons in their hands, were delighted.

At the city hall we turned them over to the American sentries and were told that we had to report to the Gendarmerie building at once. District Commandant Melchers had meanwhile been in touch with the American commander and had arranged for the people of Diekirch to leave the seriously threatened city at once, but only as of 12:00 midnight. Still in all, this needed to be acted on immediately, so that the evacuation would proceed according to plan without interfering with the U.S. withdrawal, preparations for which were already underway. The Americans had also informed us that the city could no longer be held, out of concern for the civilian population, and the troops who were still present would move into a new defensive position.

After that we were given our orders and the situation was explained. While one group of auxiliary policemen went to find Mayor Theis and Dean Colling to bring them to the Gendarmerie, the others were given the job of informing the population as soon as possible and making it clear to them that they were not to leave Diekirch before midnight, for the U.S. withdrawal had absolute priority. Each one of them was to report to the 'Eisebunnsbreck' (railway bridge) over the Sauer, for all other exit routes had to stay open for military use. I myself, along with Gendarme Huss and Fireman Thull, went to the 'Kleck', where my family lived. Since I knew the inhabitants of this part of Diekirch better, I covered the lower part. Hardly anybody answered the door when I knocked and called. But since I had to cover all the houses, I had no more time to spend a longer time at any one house. Much later it turned out, as I learned after the offensive, that the people did not want to open the door when I knocked, since my hobnailed boots reminded them all too much of the sounds made by the Wehrmacht jack boots, which they had come to know only too well during the last few years of occupation.

It was already dark when I reported back to the Gendarmerie, and Adjutant Peters left it up to us auxiliaries as to whether we would stay in Diekirch or leave. But we were urged earnestly to leave the city at once, since because of our extraordinary status as Gendarmes, we would surely be shot if we were arrested by the

Germans. There was one thing that I did not understand: why we auxiliary gendarmes, along with the remaining officials, militia and firefighters, were not supposed to stay at least until the stream of refugees had crossed the bridge, in order to make sure that chaos did not break out. After all, we were paid to uphold order. But most of the auxiliary gendarmes set out as soon as night fell.

The time grew short, and the U.S. withdrawal was already in full swing. I decided to run back home as fast as I could and get a few pieces of clothing; since I had no backpack, I packed them into a pillow cover and threw them over my shoulder. After that I went to the center of town with my family, and we waited until the appointed time. But even hours ahead of time we saw again and again, among the U.S. vehicles that were moving out in the direction of the station, individual people who were trying to leave Diekirch by horse and wagon or even by car.

Finally the time had come, and we moved silently to the bridge. It was pitch black. Everything was uncannily quiet; only later was the stillness broken abruptly by renewed German artillery fire. The 'Eisebunnsbréck' itself was the scene of one big mess of confusion. Everybody was trying to get his family to the other shore as fast as possible. Horse-drawn wagons bounced across the railroad tracks.

Gendarme Huss was still present and forbade the use of flashlights or lanterns. Several auxiliary gendarmes, who were conscious of their duty, helped older people across the bridge. Numerous sick or aged people sat on a wagon feeling hopeless and depressed. Small children cried . . . a scene of despair. I myself went to Stegen and from there to Beringen on foot. After some time, trucks came from Luxembourg to take the refugees to the safety of the capital city. In Dommeldange I reported to the Gendarmerie office, where I learned that several auxiliary gendarmes had already arrived, and that we were to report to the 'Heilig Geist' barracks. Here we were put back into service and continued to guard the 'political' prisoners. Toward the end of January, I went back to Diekirch with the other auxiliary gendarmes. We still did sentry duty on the roads of town until mid-March, in order to check the people who returned. The first people we allowed in were those who were directly involved with the work of cleaning up the city and restoring the water supply. Numerous houses were badly damaged, and the furniture and goods inside that were not burned had to be secured from looters. Although I had taken pleasure in keeping order, I quit several weeks later and went into an occupation for which I had been trained."

CHAPTER XVI
THE MILITIA IN DIEKIRCH

An overview of the forces of law and order in the period from September to December 1944 would be incomplete if it did not mention the Militia. Militiamen were for the most part volunteers who, although they were not directly under the command of the Gendarmerie or the 'Military Government', usually took on the guarding of 'political' prisoners or, on account of their knowledge of the area, very often accompanied American patrols on scouting trips along the border formed by the Sauer and Our. Best known is probably the 'Veiner Miliz', which was a symbol of armed resistance in Luxembourg since November 19, 1944. In every locality there was militia, from which auxiliary policemen were sometimes recruited.

Here, based on a report, in more or less general terms, is the story of the Diekirch Militia.

The headquarters of the 'Dikricher Miliz' was located in the 'Dikricher Kolléisch' (high school) in mid-September 1944. The group was composed of:

Baulesch, Menn	Lentz, Josy
Beck, Jean Pierre	Lorang, Pierre
Bix, Paul	Ludovicy, Rob
Deloos, Mett	Scheer, Jos
Eischen, Jos	Schmartz, Erny
Gerson, Nic	Weber, Jeng
Gerson, Félix	Weber, Theo "Tuttessen Tit"
Dockendorf, Jos	Winandi, Henri
Kips, Vic	Rischard, Jeng
Lanser, Mett	Wampach, René
Lary, Paul	

The two chiefs of the Diekirch Militia were Vic Kips and Jos Eischen, known as the "Roude Joss." Jean Pierre Beck, then 27 years old, volunteered for the Diekirch Militia after Militia instructor Frantzen of Reimberg, his home town, had written a letter of recommendation for him. Jean Pierre Beck was accepted at once at the headquarters in Diekirch, especially as he owned his own revolver and a K-98 carbine, for the armament of the militia in those days was rather deficient. Since one job of the militia in Diekirch, as well as in other towns in the country, was to arrest known collaborators, so-called "Gielemännercher" ('yellow men', because of the Nazi party yellowish/brown uniforms), foreign militiamen who did not know the persons in question were usually preferred for this thankless task.

"At the 'Kolléisch', our headquarters and office," J.P. Beck reports, "it was like a fair. Countless refugees from the border towns, who had to leave them because of the proximity of the front, had taken over the main building and the Kolléisch courtyard. In the yard itself they cooked, slept and . . . complained a lot. At this time (the end of September) Diekirch was overflowing with refugees and American soldiers who were passing through. There were also all the 'Gielemännercher' from the whole region, so that the prison, right behind the Kolléisch, was overfilled very quickly. So then a separate prison camp was set up for the 'politicals' in the Glyco building, the left storeroom of which was hastily set up as a dormitory with two, and later three, bunks made of wood. The food for the prisoners was prepared in the 'Prisongskichen' under the supervision of Mrs. Weiss, the wife of Prison Director Weiss. The 'Gielemännercher' came in groups, for cleaning-up actions were taking place from Ulflingen to Echternach. Everybody who was under suspicion of having sympathized with the Nazis was brought in. There were hard cases, unrepentant ones, among them, but also many harmless ones who simply happened to get mixed in with the others. But hard case or harmless, no differentiation was made, they all went into one 'pot' of 'Gielemännercher.' There were also those who had the misfortune of being found and arrested by the U.S. Military Police (MP) in Diekirch after 10:00 PM, and who were sent to the Glyco for one night, or sometimes for several days, until their identity could be checked. We militiamen had received special passes from the Americans, so that we could go freely in and near Diekirch at any time. These passes also allowed us to carry weapons, generally confiscated German carbines and submachine guns.

We helped out with so-called 'cleaning-up actions' in Diekirch, but for this purpose militiamen from out of town were called in when a known pro-German had to be arrested in Diekirch.

But the Americans also made use of our services. Every time one of them had to go to Wiltz or Clervaux in a Jeep, one or two men of us were taken along, for the Americans still suspected there were Germans in the woods.

Then, on November 19, the grim story of the shooting of Léo Roger in Vianden was heard. It was known that a few Vianden militiamen, on sentry duty at the castle, were surrounded by the SS, and there was a lot of shooting. Two of them were badly wounded when the Germans stormed the castle. Léo Roger himself was mortally wounded in an alley near the old cloister.

They had immediately sent out two men from Vianden and asked for reinforcements from the Diekirch Militia. The 'Roude Joss' had agreed at once, and so Nikela Simon took the majority of our men, whose numbers had increased considerably by then (50 men), to Fouhren by bus, for Nikela did not dare to go farther. Then we went on down to Vianden, almost in Indian file. Scarcely had we reached the headquarters of Vic Abens, the chief of the Veiner Miliz, than the first German shells fell on us and put us all in a grim mood. The noise was two and three times as loud in this 'mousetrap' in Vianden deep in the Our valley. In the faint candlelight, nobody could see anyone else's pale face. Thank God! For we were asking ourselves: 'Who would stay here willingly?' As far as I can recall, there were Paul Bix, Felix Gerson,

Ted Weber, Menn Bauler, Mett Lanser, Henri Winandi and I. Thus I received my first baptism of fire in Vianden, for the Germans fired at us every day. But we returned the fire with automatic weapons from the armory below the castle. At the end of November the situation in Vianden had gotten back to normal, so that we were released.

December 16, 1944

Around 5:30 in the morning, two shells fell on the street right in front of the Glyco building. Three of us were standing guard in front of the main door, and I never ran so fast in my life as when the second shell came whistling along; I threw myself into a ditch that was half full of ice-cold water. I remained lying there motionless for about ten minutes, for meanwhile other shells were exploding; their fragments flew around our ears. Those of us who had experienced Russia had told the rest of us what the whistling sound of the shells meant. If they whistled a high note, then they were going on over our heads, but woe to us if they made a quavering sound; then we must hit the dirt at once and get our noses down as far as possible. Early in the morning of December 16, 1944, almost all the shells 'quavered', and impact after impact followed. In the Glyco building all hell had broken loose. The 'Gielemännercher' felt their deliverance was near. We fired our submachine guns off over their heads a few times to 'depress' their mood, but probably also to let our nervous tension relax. From the Vianden militiamen we knew that a second German attack was likely. Although the Americans had also been informed of that, they did not take it seriously. But around 11:00 AM of the same day, the greater part of the U.S. occupying forces moved out of Diekirch. This made us even more nervous. Several shells had fallen between the sections of the Glyco building and had done some damage. Thank God nobody had been damaged. Without knowing what was really going on, we set up machine guns at the four corners of the Glyco and waited for whatever might come along. When some of our colleagues from Vianden turned up the next day and reported to us that they had just barely escaped from the Germans, we finally knew what our situation was. After that came a steady stream of terrible news, such as: The first Germans had already been seen at the 'Kleck' (Rue Clairefontaine), Longsdorf was in German hands, or the 'Prussians' were on the Herrenberg.

Then on the following day it was said that Diekirch could no longer be held, that the Americans had to give up the city, and the civilian population had to be evacuated. So there we sat, deserted by God and the Americans, with about 300 prisoners in the Glyco building. What should we do, and where should we take the prisoners? Those of us who came from Diekirch immediately went home to help their family members pack. So there were about fifteen guards remaining, including me. On the night before December 19, 1944 we set out to take the prisoners on foot to Mertzig by roundabout routes. We were not allowed to use the main roads for this, for they, it was said, had to remain open for 'Patton's tanks.' So that none of the prisoners got the idea of trying to escape, we fired regularly past the right and left sides of the columns, and so nobody got away from us. In Mertzig they were all quartered in the school. The school benches were pushed aside and straw was strewn in the rooms. That evening everybody, prisoners and guards, had to go without supper. In Mertzig we were anything but welcome, for the people here were busy packing too. 'Shoot them all', we heard from all sides, 'these lousy guys who have betrayed Luxembourg don't deserve anything else.' And why had we come to Mertzig anyway? I think today that Vic Kips got the idea, since he came from Mertzig.

In the morning we found some bread and potatoes in the abandoned houses. So there we sat, amid the thunder of the guns and the exploding shells in Diekirch and Ettelbrück. The sky was lit up as far as the German lines at night, and we heard rumbling and thundering everywhere. Not a trace of the Americans! The people of Ettelbrück were likewise packing and fleeing, and fired burned in several places in the city. We could see the glow of the fire from Mertzig. The feeling that the end had come prevailed among us, and we had almost 300 'Gielemännercher', bad and not so bad, for whom we all felt responsible. But there they were!

The scrounged-up potatoes were cooked in pork pots in the schoolyard. Everybody received three of them and . . . only water with them.

Then we heard that a special train was ready at Useldingen (on December 20). On the morning of that day we walked on to Useldingen. The prisoners were taken on board, and the train went to Esch on the Alzette, where the Russian prison camp at Beles was available (a former camp for captured Russians who had been taken there by the Germans; today Cité Remmerich). Since the prisoners from Russia among us knew somewhat more about the Russian lice, we slept on tables, while the legs of every table were set in buckets of water.

We were quartered there for about a week, then we went on with the prisoners to Ober- and Niedercorn. In Obercorn some of them were put in an empty movie house, while the rest of them were housed in a school in Niedercorn. There the Esch Militia took over the duty of guarding the prisoners. Since the 'Gielemännercher' were treated quite badly here and I did not want to cooperate, I preferred to return to Diekirch, for curiosity would not let me rest any longer. With Léon Weiss of Stegen and a man called 'Mett' from Diekirch, we hitched a ride on American supply trucks to Mersch, then via Angelsberg to Stegen.

We arrived there by Jeep on December 25. Around Stegen there were several large-caliber U.S. long-barreled guns that fired their heavy shells toward the German side at irregular intervals during the day; the Germans replied, though very sparingly, at night. The first night we sat with some American soldiers in a farmhouse whose inhabitants had fled. Shell after shell landed in Stegen; the house shook from the explosions, and we trembled with the Americans when the plaster crumbled down from the ceiling.

'Mett' from Diekirch and I absolutely wanted to get back to Diekirch; he wanted to go home and I wanted to get the clothes I had left behind at my uncle's house. Naturally there was a lot of curiosity involved, for we were eager to know what was actually going on in Diekirch. So we walked some distance along the 'Fieseler Stroos.' On the heights at the edge of the 'Haardt' woods there was a heavy American tank. Just by chance, one of the crew spoke some French, and so we identified ourselves with our 'laissez-passer' and told him what we planned to do. 'OK', he said, and so we walked on in good spirits. At the left bend of the street there was a stone stairway that came out down in Diekirch at the horse-racing grounds. As we stood on the stairs and looked down into Diekirch, several bullets whistled over our heads, and the ground was sprayed up to the left and right where the bullets hit. Mett and I turned around and shouted: 'Ne tirez pas, Laxenburg Police!' There were Americans there too in a grove of fir trees two or three meters high at the edge of the 'Haardt', who had probably taken us for strays from the Volkssturm, for we looked almost like them. From the 'Luxembourg Police' we had only a white armband with a red lion. We could not get to Diekirch, so we went back to Stegen. The night was unusually cold, and German shells were falling again. Several drunken Americans staggered around. The farmer at whose house we spent the night was the other of a brewery and had canned apples, pears and plums on hand, and since the big wooden barrels smelled of brandy, the GIs had shot holes in them and then held their cooking pots by the holes and drunk the juice, which made them very drunk. Alcohol has a particularly strong attraction to soldiers in a war. The drunken Americans were no laughing matter, so we thought, "we don't want to stay here', and so Mett and I went from Stegen to Schieren, and on January 1, 1945 we arrived via roundabout routes in Ettelbrück. In Ettelbrück it really looked like wartime. There must have been bitter fighting there just a short time ago; several houses on the main street were still burning. Dead Americans and Germans were still lying all over. In the place of show-window dummies there stood several Americans in a clothing store, with their rifles ready to fire. They let us pass, but asked us to look in at the villa at the entrance to Ettelbrück on our way to Diekirch, since they suspected that Germans were still there. So we went into the house, first into the upstairs rooms, then the living room, bathroom, kitchen, etc. Everything was uncannily quiet. We threw two hand grenades into the cellar, and went down only after we heard nothing after the explosions. Where we got all this courage from is a riddle to me today. There had presumably been German soldiers in the cellar, for steel helmets and overcoats were lying around everywhere. When we looked more closely into the semidarkness, we found a dead body lying under a table. Outside we reported to the waiting Americans: 'No Germans.' Although we wanted so much to go to Diekirch, we no longer dared to go there. So Mett went on to Stegen and I went home to Reimberg. But at the edge of Schieren a tall black soldier blocked my way and looked me over, his rifle in hand. 'You're a German spy,' he said. My permit no longer meant anything. He took me about 150 meters to a house where the command post was located. Several of the Americans who questioned me spoke such good German that they reminded me somehow of Germans in U.S. uniforms, about whom I had often heard. I had a bad feeling about this. The Americans did not waste much time on me, they shoved me onto the hood of a Jeep and set out a high speed in the direction of Mersch. Here they unloaded me at the Gendarmerie. Unfortunately they had confiscated all my papers, but to my good luck, there were several men who knew me at the Gendarmerie. I said to them: 'Do me a favor and lock me in a cell, so I can finally get some rest', for I had scarcely slept at all in three days. On the next day I went to Dr. Faber, then the veterinarian in Mersch, whom I knew from the Resistance. He got me my papers back, and with them I hitched a ride to Luxembourg, spent the night there with my sister-in-law there, and took the train to Esch the next day. Meanwhile the 'Gielemännercher' had been delivered to a makeshift camp in Belval-Source.

There I stayed until about the beginning of March, when I went back to Diekirch . . . to the Glyco building. The prisoners were then put to work cleaning out and rebuilding. I often went as a guard with various groups to the nearby farms such as Folkendingen, Mouschbierg, the Bech farm, and to Stegen, where they had to help work in the fields. I was also housed for a month with a dozen men at the 'Friedbésch' in Diekirch, where the 'Gielemännercher' cleaned out the badly damaged forest and disposed of tons of war materiel. The prison camp remained in Diekirch until 1948. After it was closed, I served at the prison in Luxembourg until 1950. Here I guarded Kratzenberg (one of the top local Nazi collaborators) in his death-row cell during his last night. He remained loyal to the Führer to the end."

The 'Veiner Miliz' (The Vianden Partisan Group)
A prominent example of Luxembourg armed resistance, the "Veiner Miliz" or Vianden partisan group was composed primarily of Luxembourg deserters of the German Wehrmacht that had been conscripted earlier by force under the Nazi occupation. Some were lucky enough to be on furlough to Luxembourg from the Eastern front, when they learned that the allies had landed in Normandy. Determined to 'pay back' the Nazis and to fight along with the allies, they hid in the dense woods around Vianden, waiting for the Americans to liberate Luxembourg.

The "Miliz" initially consisted of a handful of young men from Vianden, who because of their great familiarity with the terrain, always escaped German search patrols. When it was learned that the Americans were approaching the Luxembourg border in early September 1944, they started to organize their own guerilla war against retreating Germans. At the beginning there were only few weapons available, ranging from hunting rifles and shotguns to Belgian revolvers and World War I carbines.

With the arrival of the 5th U.S. armored division at the German border, the Luxembourg bordering villages were evacuated of their inhabitants and Vianden thus became 'no man's land.' On September 12, Victor Abens, who had escaped from the Lublin concentration camp and former 'Gendarmerie' officer Jos Kieffer founded the "Miliz" and offered their services to the Americans. Gradually the number of the "Miliz"-men increased to 36. There were also three women of Vianden in the group.

The 'Miliz' was of great assistance to the Americans, escorting I&R patrols, collecting vital intelligence, guarding the bridges, staffing observation posts, and denying access to infiltrating German patrols who crossed the Our to probe for weaknesses in the American positions. There were numerous firefights in and around Vianden, which apart from the 'Miliz' was only occupied by a few U.S. artillery observers and members of intelligence teams headquartered at the Hôtel Heintz. Together with the American artillery observers, the 'Miliz' operated a listening and observation post around the clock at the ruins of the Vianden castle, where every movement on the German side of the Our could easily be spotted from.

The 'Miliz' also prevented looting and driving over of cattle by night time German patrols, often escorted by Luxembourg collaborators. By making good use of the terrain and the excellently-chosen dugouts in town, the 'Miliz' always succeeded in defeating the German intruders, who often had to abandon their mission because of too heavy losses. Thus, gradually, the arsenal of the 'Miliz' was supplemented by German automatic weapons and hand grenades taken from killed enemies.

On November 19, 1944, a strong German company tried to infiltrate Vianden in the early morning hours to destroy the U.S./Miliz observation post at the castle. During the heavy firefight all over Vianden which lasted until the afternoon, the Miliz had one member killed and four seriously wounded. Again, the Germans gave up after suffering sizeable losses. It was from that moment on that the news about the 'Vianden Miliz defeating an enemy four times stronger' flashed around the country and that as a result more young Luxembourgers from other parts of the country joined the 'Miliz.'

To distinguish themselves from other Luxembourg partisan groups, the members of the 'Vianden Miliz' wore captured German fatigues with painted-on camouflage patterns and armbands and badges with the inscription "Veianen" (Vianden) and the Luxembourg "red lion." In addition, they wore red scarves with embroidered initials of their names. French style berets and caps completed the 'unconventional' uniform.

It was the members of the Vianden 'Miliz' who collected the first clues and reports from inhabitants from the small border village of Bivels (who had been Linden-Meier) in early December 1944 that 'something' was 'cooking' on the other side. Aware of the German threat of a possible attack (which turned out to become the 'Bulge') the 'Miliz' immediately took those individuals to the U.S. authorities to report what they had seen. Just before the German surprise attack, the 'Miliz' also captured a German NCO, who during his interrogation also yielded the massive presence of German troops, armor and artillery close to the border.

When Vianden was shelled in the early morning hours of December 16, 1944, the 'Miliz' immediately knew what was going to happen and broke up. Aware of the fact that they would be shot as partisans if caught by the Germans, the 'Miliz'-men retreated through the woods in direction of Diekirch and Ettelbruck. In Schieren they were intercepted and arrested by U.S. troops unfamiliar with them. The 'Miliz' looked very suspicious to those Americans in their strange uniforms and German equipment, especially as the word of "Skorzeny's saboteurs behind the U.S. lines" was in everybody's mouth. After their identity had been thoroughly checked, they were released and continued to serve with the U.S. units, primarily the CIC detachments. One member of the 'Miliz,' Frankie Hansen from Ettelbruck continued to fight with the 8th U.S. Inf. Division in Germany and was even awarded the 'Silver Star' after the war after Congress had passed a bill hereto. Hansen's brother Pierre along with André Flesch were the ones who served with the 10th Armored Div., after they had taken a U.S. artillery observer of the 90th Cavalry Recon. Sq. to a favorable position near Ingeldorf enabling the direction of a devastating fire to an advancing enemy column on December 22.

All members received high Luxembourg decorations after the war.

The "Friedhaff" in Diekirch – Graveyard for many Soldiers

The "Friedhaff" north of Diekirch has already been mentioned many times in this book as the main intersection on the hotly contested highland road to Hosingen, called "Skyline Drive" by the Americans, that was of strategic importance to both sides.

Numerous lists of the dead, especially those on the German side, list the "Friedhof northwest of Diekirch" as the place of death where so many youthful German soldiers had to depart this life. For several months after the war, before their removal to Sandweiler, field graves, marked with a steel helmet on a simple wooden cross, surrounded that peaceful-looking farm and bore witness to the intensity of the fighting.

It is therefore interesting to let the former owners of that farmstead, set apart from the noise of the city, tell their story. Here is what Mrs. Oesch recalls of those terrible days:

"When the first German shells landed near the farmyard very early on the morning of December 16, 1944, we went immediately to the cellar, which could also be reached from the outer yard. After the shooting had let up somewhat and the opposite farm had taken numerous hits, the Americans brought in several wounded men, whom they took away again after some time. All through the day, the noise of battle rose up to us from Bastendorf. Now and then, individual shells landed in the vicinity of the Herrenberg.

On December 17 a firefight suddenly flared up in the 'Hueldaer', in which several Americans and Germans were killed. Shortly after that a German reconnaissance party entered the house and searched for hidden Americans. After the Germans had convinced themselves that there were no longer any 'Amis' in the house, they helped themselves to a portion of our food supplies, giving the excuse that they had not eaten anything for two days and had covered a number of kilometers on foot.

On the afternoon of December 18, a whole group of ragged German soldiers appeared, some of whom were almost children, and brought in numerous wounded men, who were bandaged before our eyes in the cellar. Small-scale combat was still going on in the 'Hueldaer' in the direction of Bastendorf and Brandenbourg. The noise of battle could also be heard from the Kippenhof. (See Vol.I: The Germans.)

A command loaded the numerous dead (meanwhile several wounded men had expired in the cellar) onto a cart that the Germans had requisitioned from our barn, and buried them beside the road to Erpeldingen. We spent the end of the year in the cellar along with German artillerymen, until finally, at the beginning of Germany, a German officer ordered us to leave the farm and return to Brandenbourg. The population of Diekirch, we were told, had already been evacuated to there. When we were reluctant to leave, he said: 'Then we'll take you away, for after us come the chained dogs.' He meant the field police (because of their ID chain). So during the night we reached Brandenbourg, where we found a place to stay with the May family. Here there was a hospital (in the school) to which badly wounded men were brought every day for necessary operations. Those soldiers who died (meaning most of the wounded men) were buried in the garden. Many more were to follow before the final liberation!

On January 16, 1945 a German patrol returned to Brandenbourg and bragged of the numbers of U.S. prisoners that they said they had taken along the Sauer. A few days later, though, the Americans were again the masters of Brandenbourg, and we finally got a hot meal again. Somewhat later, people were sent from Diekirch to take care of the sick people. Only at the end of February were we given permission to return to our farm. It was partly destroyed. We found all the furniture, stoves, mattresses and bedclothes in the abandoned bunkers and dugouts at the 'Friedbesch' and the 'Hueldaer.' On account of the dampness, almost everything was ruined. In the cellar there were still several dead German soldiers. The bodies of other soldiers lay in the back yard and the meadows. In the Friedbesch itself there were many bodies, including Americans, who had died here late in January, as we were told.

Around the house of Dr. Schmol, which was across from ours and almost completely destroyed, lay numerous horribly mutilated and rotting bodies of soldiers. Death had reaped a rich harvest at the 'Friedhaff.'" – Even decades after the war, the Oesch family suffered a cruel twist of fate when an unexploded 105 mm U.S. shell blew up while hedges were being burned down about 300 meters from the house, killing the young wife of the family.

Unimaginable Conditions

Unimaginable conditions prevailed then in the damp cellars, where the people who had missed the chance to be evacuated survived in misery and privation, in fear for their lives, through the constantly increasing U.S. gunfire on Diekirch, recalls Félicie Lanners, both of whose parents died as a result of illness and privation in the vaulted cellar of the "Old Brewery" in the 'Bamerdall.' Miss Lanners was active with the Red Cross, which collaborated closely with the American Red Cross, since the liberation in September of 1944. The biggest problem was providing medical care for the population, as well as taking care of the people who came from the border area along the Sauer and Our, and who had to leave their villages on the German border for reasons of safety, what with the events along the front brought on by the American advance into that area.

"We had to find shelter quickly for these poor people who had to be evacuated; so at first we set up a Red Cross service area in the Hotel des Ardennes in Diekirch where the people could report. Many of them stayed with relatives or friends in the nearby area; it is astounding how need brings people back together.

Many times we had troops passing through who came from the front, and we served the grateful U.S. soldiers hot coffee and doughnuts in a sort of canteen.

Mainly, though, there were several U.S. Red Cross nurses on hand, who were responsible, along with two army doctors and trained medics, for the health of the U.S. soldiers quartered in Diekirch. Many of them were suffering from diarrhea, trench foot and digestive disorders as a result of the privations they had endured. On December 6, I was asked by the officers to play Saint Nicholas for the soldiers who were there, and to their joy, I distributed extra rations. Many of the soldiers played guitars and sang. After that there was again plenty of coffee and doughnuts for everybody. It was a truly moving festivity despite all the problems of the time; many of the American boys were so moved that they could not hide a few tears in their eyes.

Day after day I performed my service in the writing room of the Hotel des Ardennes, until the hail of shells in the early morning of December 16 prevented me from leaving the cellar, where we had quickly sought shelter. Other than my parents and my sister, we still had people from Vianden with us. So we remained in the cellar, terrified, and despite the long pauses in the gunfire, we chose to stay there.

When the heavy fire had let up on December 19, I ran quickly to the Red Cross station in the hotel to arrange for at least my weak, elderly parents to be evacuated. 'You are worrying needlessly,' I was told. 'In a short time reinforcements will arrive here; there is no need for them to leave.' But on the way back, I met nurses from the Diekirch hospital who, along with a helper, were transporting several sacks of flour from the Fischer bakery to the hospital on a handcart. A bad sign? I did not let myself be deluded. I also asked for some flour and yeast, and then I went back.

Meanwhile my sister had made the cellar a little more 'homey.' and had built two beds for our parents by placing boards and mattresses over two stone wash-tubs, for up to now we had slept on the cellar floor. We decided to leave Diekirch and started to make preparations the next day. We packed up, baked bread, loaded supplies of canned goods and smoked meat onto a cart, and got everything ready for the next morning.

Late in the evening there was knocking on the door. My father told me that I should go to the door, but out of terror and fear, I did not want to go upstairs. When there was gunfire in Diekirch later and shells landed very close to us, we ducked under the tables in the cellar and were so afraid that we could not sleep.

On the Next Morning
(December 20, 1944)

The people were all gone when we ventured out onto the street. Instead of them, we saw German soldiers with fixed bayonets on their rifles searching the houses on the extension of 'Rue de la Croix' down to Bridge Street. As fast as we could, my sister and I ran back into the cellar and nervously told what we had just seen.

An hour later there was another knock at the door. This time my father got up and walked up the stairs quietly and calmly. He opened the door and asked the German soldiers: 'What do you want from an old man and his family?' – 'You can see for yourselves that there is nobody else here' was his answer after he had been asked about hidden Americans.

The two soldiers did not search the house; obviously they believed my trust-worthy father and went on. We spent the next two days in the cellar, but tried several times to find out how many civilians were still living on our street. We noticed that numerous German soldiers had taken up quarters in Mr. Thillen's house and barn. They were polite and proper, and gave us some of their food. Yet I noticed at once that their mood was depressed.

On December 22 one other person joined us in the cellar and told us that numerous people had found shelter in the deep, vaulted cellars of the Old Brewery in the 'Bamerdall.' The cellars were especially safe from shells, and it would be better if we would also go there, for in the meantime the U.S. artillery had fired on Diekirch several times. I decided to make my way to the "Bamerdall" in the darkness to find out. Since I saw German soldiers in snow camouflage suits all over, I quickly wrapped a bedsheet around me, so as not to attract attention in the white surroundings. I looked for several people I knew in the 'Bamerdall', found some of them in their own cellars, and heard that the farmer Franz Felten had lost his life when a shell exploded, and old Mr. Preisen had recently died in his bed. When I finally tried to go to the brewery, shells flew over from the "Haardt' and exploded in the center of Diekirch.

Seized by panic fear, I raced past the church and had to throw myself down among the dead cattle on the "Wilhelmsplatz" several times as shells exploded close to the post office. I will never forget the mangled body of a horse, with the guts hanging out, beside which I crouched to seek shelter from the shell fragments.

"Rue Neuve"

There were fires in many places, and the pungent smell of white phosphorus filled the air. The corner house of Pastor Hansen had taken a direct hit. The wall was town wide open and many volumes of his valuable library had also been flung by the force of the explosion into the street, where they lay in the wet dirt.

When I returned, exhausted, to the protection of the cellar, I immediately slept for a couple hours, until an explosion shook the house. When my sister and I had worked up the courage to look, we observed to our horror that the house next door had been hit and was beginning to burn. We all feared that the fire could spread to our house, and we decided to leave the house at once. Then I thought of the nuns in the hospital!

My father advised me to hurry there at once and inquire while they packed all our necessary clothing and additional foods and supplies onto a sled. I ran off, but in Hospital Street a German soldier suddenly sprang out from behind a house and demanded the password. In my fear, and frightened by the muzzle of his submachine gun, I could not say anything but 'Our house is on fire, we have to get out,' and I ran onward. I entered the hospital from the back and went into the cellar. Terrible conditions prevailed there. All the patients, old and sick people, had been moved to the cellar along with their beds, one on top of another. In addition, there were a number of homeless people and refugees in the hospital. A side room of the cellar, which was also occupied, was also set up as a makeshift toilet. On account of the gunfire, the buckets had not been emptied. In addition, several old men had been incontinent and could not be changed by the nuns for lack of clean clothes. Awful smells filled the room and sickened the air, and I heard the whimpering and groaning of the seriously ill patients.

The mother superior made it clear to me that it would be quite pointless to try to house my parents here. Sickened by the smells, which were turning my stomach, I left that place of horror, in which the nuns lovingly sacrificed themselves despite the prevailing conditions, and went back. This time too, the German sentry let me through unhindered. My parents and my sister were awaiting me impatiently, for shortly before that a German Unteroffizier had urged them strongly to go to the Old Brewery in the 'Bamerdall.' The remaining inhabitants of the houses on our street had also been forced to leave their houses. Several soldiers accompanied us there. My mother could not stand all the signs of destruction that surrounded us, and sobbed constantly. Shot-up and burning houses, dead cattle with abdomens swelled from rotting, splintered trees, fallen or bent electric poles, a litter of stuff in the dirt and snow of the street.

In the 'Old Brewery'

We finally found a place to stay in a side room of the cellar, lit by faint candlelight, for the big malt cellars, supported by strong cast pillars, were already overfilled with refugees. The Germans had brought in straw, which helped somewhat against the damp coldness of the stone floor. Here we put down our mattresses and blankets, as well as our few supplies of food.

All of this had to be guarded closely, for in the faint light of candles and oil lamps, food often disappeared. The condition of my parents grew increasingly worse; the sleeplessness of the previous nights, as well as the constant fear that is natural to old people, had worn them out. And now came fever and diarrhea.

A woman we knew from "Neie Wé" hurried home again, slaughtered her chickens and brought them back. So at least we had some meat to eat for two days. We brought water from a spring cistern behind the brewery. Often, though, I took a can of water and some flour and, under cover of darkness, ran down to the Fischer Bakery, where Felix Manon and Willy Besseling of Vianden baked bread. In addition, I often hurried to the Thilmany farm in the 'Gruef', where I was always given some milk for my parents. Likewise I often took part in 'hamster trips', on which several of us from the cellar tried to salvage something from the stocks of the 'Konsum', some of which were still in the half-destroyed building . . . Sometimes we also received some 'Kommissbrot' from the Germans, who were staying in part of the cellar. Two women from "Neie Wé" cooked in a side room when there appeared to be no danger, as the smoke could go into an inner courtyard before it dissipated.

When shells exploded in the courtyard of the brewery on January 5, my aged father had a heart attack. His strength decreased more and more. We could do nothing but pray. I put the rosary in his hands and sat beside him, while my sister tried not to let our feverish mother know of his condition.

Father did not recognize me any more and thought I was Mother; subconsciously he seemed to understand that he had only a few hours to live. I heard him say: 'Thank you for everything that you have done in my life,' then his breathing became weaker. He died shortly before midnight on January 7, 1945. Just two days earlier, Mrs. Knepper and a hired man from the Thilmany farm had died in the same cellar. The bodies were placed in the anteroom of the malt works. On January 13 my mother also died from the effects of a lung infection and high fever. Just after my father's death I had hurried to the hospital and asked for fever medicine. Although I had never before given injections and the sister warned me, I insisted. When the sister explained to me how to give the injection, she warned me again that I would have to deal with my conscience. I gave Mother the injection, but it was already too late. On the next day she died.

With the help of several cellar dwellers, we carried the body upstairs and placed it in a cold storeroom there.

Then I gave a boy some money and had him go with me to the Weis carpentry shop to obtain two coffins. Again we had to cross the church square, and again we were fired on by the Americans. In the midst of the ruins, an old man was crouching with his daughter, who was almost about to give birth to a child. She was already having strong pains, but she would not leave her father. As fast as we could, we

Cpl. Russell Hall, gunner of D Company, 91st Chemical Mortar Battalion, in a Jeep of that unit's A Company. Photo: Roland Gaul archives

The crew of a 4.2 inch chemical mortar setting up the weapon: barrel, baseplate and monopod. Photo: US Army

4.2 inch mortars shortly before firing. To help absorb the weapon's strong recoil, the dug-in baseplates have been weighted with several sandbags. At right, a cannoneer is just attaching the propelling charges to the shells. The shells contained white phosphorus, indicated by the gray color coding. This photo was taken in Germany late in March. Photo: US Army

Above: The Sauer bridge of the 5th Infantry Division in the Dillingen-Weilerbach sector was shrouded by smoke generators and WP smoke shells of the 81st Chemical Company and the 91st Chemical Mortar Battalion early in February 1945. Photo: US Army

Right: A German 8.8 cm antitank gun probably destroyed by the direct hit of a shell fired by the 91st Chemical Mortar Battalion in the Fouhren-Longsdorf sector. The photo was taken in the spring of 1945. Photo: Philippe Gleis collection

Infantry support bridge, 144 feet long, erected by the 133rd Engineer Combat/Construction Battalion in Gilsdorf on January 18, 1945. The roadway rests on several pontoon boats. Photo: US Army

A fully loaded GMC truck, followed by a Jeep, crossing a 120-foot Treadway bridge at Gilsdorf. Both vehicles probably belonged to a supply unit of the 10th US Infantry Regiment. The Treadway bridge, also resting on rubber boats, was also built by the 133rd Engineer Combat/Construction Battalion. Photo: US Army

A bridge at Ettelbrück erected by the 150th Engineer Battalion on the night of January 18, 1945, extended and reinforced later that month. Photo: Roland Gaul archives

Engineers of A Company, 150th Engineer Battalion, move bridge components over the blown-up Sauer bridge near Gilsdorf on January 18, 1945. Photo: US Army

Ettelbrück on the afternoon of January 18, 1945. In the foreground is an infantry bridge, probably erected by the 7th Engineer Battalion, 5th Infantry Division. In the middle is the blown-up highway bridge. In the background is the Treadway bridge built by the men of the 150th Engineer Battalion on the night of January 18. Photo: US Army

Men of the medical unit of the 150th Engineer Battalion, who had their hands full during the Sauer crossing in January of 1945. Photo: Roland Gaul archives

". . . an additional 642 German wood mines, 18 tellermines and 9 US antitank mines were blown up." Here men of the 150th Engineer Battalion are removing mines in Ingeldorf below the "Neyhaff" on the Sauer shore. Photo: US Army

A US engineer using HC "Smoke Pots" to generate a smoke screen in a sector along the Sauer. Photo: US Army

A GMC snowplow truck of the 166th Engineer Battalion in action. Photo: Roland Gaul archives

A snowplow of the 166th Engineer Battalion in action near Mersch, January 1945. Photo: Roland Gaul archives

A Treadway bridge erected by the 166th Engineer Battalion over the frozen Sauer at Heiderscheidergrund. Photo: Roland Gaul archives

The partly finished 270 foot Bailey bridge built by the 166th Engineer Battalion near Dillingen, photographed on February 10, 1945. Photo: Roland Gaul archives

Engineers laying fir trees to prevent snowdrifts on the approach roads, photographed near "Hierheck/Eschdorf" in January of 1945. Photo: US Army

*A second bridge built across the Sauer near Dillingen by the
166th Engineer Battalion (February 1945). Photo: US Army*

Colonel Immanuel (Manny) Klette, seen in the 1960s; as a major, he commanded "Klette's Wild Hares" of the 324 Bomber Squadron and led an attack against German radio traffic on December 18, 1944. Photo: Roland Gaul archives

S/Sgt. Stanley Wrubleski (died December 25, 1944). Photo: Mrs. Wrubleski

The original crew of the "Blonde Bombshell". Front row, center: Pilot Lt. Elwood Lee; second row, second from left: bombardier Lt. Roland Weber. Photo: Mr. Roland Weber

Left: Captain Richard "Dick" Perry, Commander, 570th Bomber Squadron, Below: Co-pilot Alfred Walterscheid, one of three crewmen of the "Blonde Bombshell" who survived the explosion. Below left: Junior Sergeant Eddie Skindingsrude (tail gunner), who lost his life on the "Goldknapp" near Diekirch on December 25, 1944. Photos: Roland Gaul archives

The Gilsdorf Militiamen who took an active part in "cleaning out" their home town on December 24, 1944. Photos with kind permission of families

Emile Pesch

Charles Breyer

Jean "Jäng" Haendel

Bernard "Ben" Bauler

Louis Dupont, a Diekircher who joined the US troops and the Gilsdorf boys to help "clean out" the town.

Farmer Michel Hamen with his wife Ketty and children Roby, Paul and Willy. Photo: Michel Hamen

". . . after they had dozed off in the cellars in the afternoon, after the noise of exploding shells had let up." An unhappy family that missed the chance to be evacuated and had to wait for the final liberation as "cavemen" in the damp cellar. This photo, taken in Belgium in January, clearly shows the pitiless conditions that the civilians had to survive. Photo: IWM, London

They tried, using handcarts, horse-drawn wagons, coaches and fully loaded bicycles, to bring themselves, their families and a few possessions to safety in the direction of Stegen. (Photo taken in Belgium.) Photo: IWM

The Germans leave Diekirch, early September 1944.

Two Wehrmacht vehicles: an armored personnel carrier (above) and a staff car (center), hurrying away while collaborators, party hangers-on and "Gielemännercher" set out for the border of the Reich, some of them on foot (below).

These three unique photos were made by Constant Wolff.

Palace Street in Diekirch during the cleaning-up work in the soring of 1945. The shot damage was caused largely by the US artillery beyond the "Haardt."

A look from New Street at the Majerus Bakery on Palace Street.

"Neiewe/", the shot-up Bintener house, where a German machine-gun nest was located. Photos: Jean Schickes archives

Exhibits at the National Museum of Military History in Diekirch, Luxembourg 1944-1945

U.S. M3 Halftrack, built by White (1941), restored to original condition as staff vehicle of the 3rd Field Artillery Battalion, 9th US Armored Division. Beside it: German "Hetzer" Tank of the 352nd VGD.

American and German infantry weapons, from carbines and pistols to machine guns and edged weapons.

The museum's strong point are the striking dioramas reconstructing real scenes and made up according to interviews with eyewitnesses. Here a U.S. field kitchen with traditional turkey dinner on Thanksgiving Day, 1944.

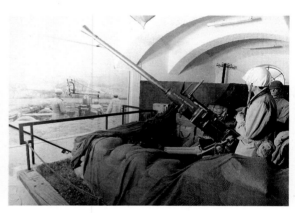

U.S. 40 mm Bofors anti-aircraft gun in position. Foreground: an enlarged photo of the same type of gun, taken in Echternach, February 1945.

Diekirch is evacuated. Civilians in flight with a few of their belongings.

German PAK 40 (75 mm) in a well-camouflaged firing position on December 18, 1944. The antitank gun shown here was left in Diekirch when the Germans retreated in January of 1945. All photos: Rol. Schleich

took the two of them on a wagon to the house of Dr. Sinner, since I knew that a German medic had often treated sick civilians there. As I later heard, the child was brought into the world by a German army doctor in the cellar of the post office. (See Vol.I: The Germans.)

When the boy and I arrived at the carpenter's shop, there was also a man from the Grossgasse there whose wife had been killed by a shell fragment, and who also wanted to obtain a coffin. Since his wife, knowing she would die, had insisted on being buried in her home town of Schifflange, he also scrounged up some sheet metal and some zinc in Petry's hardware store in order to seal the bodies, which could not be buried immediately. When we returned to the brewery and again came under fire, in which phosphorus was sprayed around, we found that a pious German soldier had placed a candle before the bodies in the malt works and was saying a prayer. When he saw us, he hurried away without saying a word. Later my parents were placed in the zinc-sealed coffins, and I took a knife and carved their names in the coffin lids, so that they wound not be mixed up later. We lived on for several days, always afraid and constantly praying, until on January 18, 1945, as we went out for a breath of fresh air around noon, we saw big white wisps of fog slowly spreading through the valley from the 'Goldknapp.' Since the fog smelled strongly of chemicals, we thought at first that it was gas, and we hurried back into the cellar. Toward morning on January 19 we heard shooting down in the Rue de Moulin, and shortly after that the first Americans appeared at the brewery. Without noticing us, a handful of soldiers first searched every corner of the brewery building and found several half-grown German soldiers, who had crawled away and hidden out of fear.

Then medics and a chaplain came and took care of us. We were treated at once, and several hours later we were finally given a hot meal and warm clothing. The chaplain blessed the dead and held a mass, with a generator serving as an altar. He said that the danger was not yet over, and gave general absolution and holy communion. Even the toughest men cried when they realized that they were finally free.

Several days later the dead were gathered and were to be buried in a mass grave in the cemetery, along with others who had died in Diekirch. But I insisted that my parents be buried in our family plot, and dug the graves myself with the help of two men. After the coffins were underground, I became very sick and was hospitalized until the middle of April. Then I again took up my service with the Red Cross.

In spite of everything I experienced, which often comes back to me in nightmares on winter nights to this day, I was fascinated to see that even people who had never practiced Christianity were suddenly impelled by the circumstances to remember their faith and reach for the rosary."

Understanding in Polish

It may seem very surprising that a large number of the U.S. troops who had been quartered in Diekirch since September were of Polish origin, many of them having emigrated to the USA in the early twenties and become American citizens. A particularly large number of 'Polish' U.S. soldiers belonged to the 5th U.S. Armored Division, as well as the 109th Infantry Regiment of the 28th Infantry Division, as the author was told by the Dudzinski brothers.

Czeslaw and Joseph Dudzinski

Dudzinski reached Diekirch on April 20, 1937, following an appeal of the government of Luxembourg for agricultural and service workers. After their arrival in Luxembourg, the Dudzinski family helped to establish a farm in Nachtmanderscheid, which they ran for the next two years.

In 1939 the oldest son, Joseph, was supposed to be drafted into the Polish Army, but he was able, through a request from the government of Luxembourg to the Polish embassy in Paris, to be released from military service. In January of 1940 he moved to Diekirch and found work as a hired man and a home at the Schmitz farm on Stavelot Street. Immediately after the Germans arrived, he had to report at once to the General Staff in Wiltz to get the necessary papers for the employment office of the Diekirch district government. There it was pointed out to him that, since he was born in Stuttgart, he was an ethnic German. His straightforward reply that he was a Pole caused him numerous difficulties and much mistreatment from then on. Shortly after that Joseph Dudzinski and his family, which lived on a farm in Bastendorf, received an order in which it was stated that Jews, Gypsies and Poles were inferior and were not allowed to associate with 'normal' people. The result of this was that Joseph Dudzinski no longer received any food or tobacco rations.

Still in all, he managed to withstand the provocations of the 'master race' during the four years of nazi occupation and survive the war in spite of much degradation and privation.

The 10th of September 1944 gradually came closer. "At the beginning of September," Joesph Dudzinski relates, "I already listened regularly to the broadcasts and reports of the BBC in Polish, in order to gain a picture of the general situation, above and beyond rumors of the approach of the Allied troops. Again and again we Poles were urged to support the Americans as well as possible. When, shortly after that, the German party functionaries absented themselves like cowards and a group of engineers blew up the Sauer Bridge around 7:00 PM, we finally knew for sure: 'The Americans are advancing, the hour of liberation is near!' But on that evening Diekirch looked like a ghost town; there was hardly anybody in the streets, for although the Germans had withdrawn, most of the inhabitants still feared repressive measures if they disobeyed the regulations that had been in force till then. All night long my brother Czeslaw and I stayed awake and watched in the direction of the 'Haardt', where there were still said to be about 180 Germans. Sure enough, in the early morning hours of September 11, fighter-bombers fired on the 'Haardt', the 'Mouschbierg" and the wooded hills beyond Stegen. One wing of the 'Clemenshof' caught fire and burned down. Shortly after that we saw a column of Germans moving along the Sauer from Ingeldorf toward the border. Around 7:00 AM I decided to go and meet the Americans, and took my bicycle out of the garage. Despite many difficulties, I succeeded in crossing the destroyed Sauer Bridge with my bicycle on my back and reaching the other shore. Here I got onto the bicycle and rode to the Cafe Greisen on the 'Fielser-Stroos.' I had not yet reached the restaurant when four Germans rushed out and ran as fast as they could down the slope and through the meadows in the direction of Gilsdorf. I threw myself down at once out of fear, and took cover behind a tree, so as to be safe if there was any shooting. But the four soldiers, who were obviously the last German soldiers in the city of Diekirch, were surely thinking only of flight. I lay on my belly and watched for a while until they finally disappeared in the brush; then I rode cautiously, noticing every sound, on in the direction of Stegen. Meanwhile it was 7:40 AM, and rays of sunlight were breaking through the morning fog of early autumn.

Not far before the turn to the 'Clemenshof' a soldier in an olive green uniform suddenly jumped out onto the road with his submachine gun ready to fire and, waving his hand, forced me to stop. When I heard his 'Stop, where are you going?' I recognized at once, to my relief, that he was an American soldier. Mistrustfully he searched me and looked at my passport. Somewhat surprised, he nodded and said, 'Oh, Polish.' I nodded back in agreement. He called out something, and shortly after that I saw that another soldier, off to the side, got out of a roadside ditch and spoke into a radio set. It did not take very long before, to my astonishment and amazement, about twenty Americans suddenly appeared, all of whom spoke to me in Polish. That was a load off my mind! . . . I couldn't believe it!

A lively discussion developed spontaneously; they asked me where I came from in Poland, how I happened to be here, where my relatives lived, what I was doing, etc. . . . Then a non-commissioned officer inquired about the conditions in Diekirch. I told him that to the best of my knowledge there were no more Germans in the city, but that half an hour ago I had seen four fleeing German soldiers. They offered me cigarettes from the 'New World' and went on talking. I still could not believe it. American soldiers of Polish ancestry, who still mastered their ancestral language perfectly.

Somewhat later, several scouting parties arrived at Clemenshof and reported that the bridges in Ingeldorf and Gilsdorf were intact, but they could not say anything more definite about their exact conditions. Thereupon two more patrols set out.

I myself reported that the 'Eisebunnsbréck' (railroad bridge) across the Sauer had not been blown up by the retreating Germans the previous day, and that there were plenty of beams and planks in the nearby storehouse of the Schou construction firm.

Several tanks approached from Stegen; I put my bicycle on the back and climbed onto the steel giant. Then we set out. Several halftracks full of infantrymen followed us. The tank on which I rode went as far as the Daleiden crossing guard's hut and stopped there. I asked an officer if I could hurry on to Diekirch and inform the people of the long-awaited arrival of the American units. The Captain delayed a while, then he finally gave me permission, plus the order that I should report back to him within an hour.

So I ran off full of joy. I called to all the people I met along the way and gave them the liberating and cheering news. Flags of Luxembourg, which had not been seen for four years, were hastily brought out of their hiding places. My brother Czeslaw and I hoisted a Polish flag to the roof of the Heinz carpentry shop, where he worked. Then I hurried back to the Americans, who were still waiting at the 'Fielser Stroos.'

Meanwhile many people had hurried out to meet the Americans, greeting them with waving flags. Mr. Dillenburg, the painter, had even hastily painted an American flag with the word 'Welcome' or something similar. We even saw a woman who, filled with joy, handed out bottles of wine from a basket to the American soldiers. I reported to the captain, who lost no time in having beams and heavy planks brought to the railroad bridge. Shortly after that the first tank crossed the bridge and was welcomed by a jubilant throng. A real whirl of joy, a flood of feelings of relief, that cannot be described in words, broke out. The crowd of people accompanied the first Sherman tanks, singing and waving flags and flowers, to the market place in Diekirch. The foot soldiers who followed were greeted warmly, given flowers and drinks, kissed by the girls . . . I too allowed myself to rejoice in this moment of true joy at the feeling of being free, and drank more and more of the liquor that I shared with my Polish friends, until I finally began to feel so bad that they had to take me home. Only late in the afternoon did I feel better again, and I looked for the Americans again. I was introduced to a Major Hamberg, whom I invited to dinner.

Only toward evening was the population finally aware that they had finally been freed from Nazi oppression. Swastika flags, Nazi and party effigies were burned publicly, signs with regulations were torn down and smashed.

The people gave free rein to their feelings of hatred toward the Germans; now and then they became so extreme that the Gendarmerie adjutants Peters and Reiles had their hands full keeping order.

On September 12 the first arrests of former Nazi adherents were already taking place. In an attempt to capture the 'Gielemännchen' M.K. at the Blum house, Jempi Preisen was killed by a pistol shot. Finally several U.S. soldiers, who had gotten into the house by going over the roof, succeeded in overpowering and seizing M.K. Blinded by rage at the death of the patriot Jempi Preisen, the stirred-up mob got hold of the captured man and tore him away from his American guards. Several fell upon him like wild animals, hit him and spat on him. As he lay on the ground, scratched and covered with blood, he was dragged through the dirt and over the pavement of the street in the direction of the Sauer Bridge, where he was to be lynched on a tree.

I had previously relieved my brother of two hand grenades that he had obtained; in his overzealous excitement, he wanted to take part in the arrest of the collaborator, and I had tried hard to persuade him not to take part in this mob justice. It horrified me when I saw that even orderly citizens could act like wild animals out of blind rage. I ran quickly to Dean Colling and police Captain Gilson, who had been in charge of the public safety office since September 11, to get them to prevent the lynching.

When we reached the Sauer Bridge, where the furious mob had brought the luckless man who still lay on the ground, we heard that a Diekircher, strong as a bear, had torn down the rope from which M. K. was to hang, and threatened to knock down anyone who would attack the defenseless man. He explained that the man deserved a fair trial, and only for that reason had he rescued him from the whim of the furious mob.

The luckless M. K. looked terrible. Bleeding from many small wounds and scratches, he could scarcely be recognized. He was finally taken away.

In the evening there was celebration everywhere. The beer, wine and strong liquor flowed in rivers. Everybody had his American, whom he invited to dinner and waited on hand and foot. There was dancing, singing . . . drinking! Suddenly the joy of living was brought back to Diekirch at one stroke. But the war was not yet over. This became all the clearer to us when, after several days, the first wounded Americans returned from Wallendorf. Several days later, Chestow Niejawek, a 'Polish' American soldier with whom we were particularly friendly, fell in an attempt to break through a line of bunkers on the Our. At the end of November, new U.S. forces moved into Diekirch.

Again there were numerous soldiers of Polish descent among them. One of them, Bill Lewandowski, was our guest of honor when my brother Czeslaw married Miss Weber shortly after that. Bill, who was often accompanied on his visits by 'Negro-Joe', a black driver, was later killed at Bauschleiden.

On December 16, an explosion directly behind the barn on the Schmitz farm broke the morning stillness. Several explosions very close by followed in fractions of seconds. The Glesener house, located directly behind the garden wall, took a hit; fragments flew around and cut their way noisily into the wood of our barn.

In no time, everybody in the house was on the move and seeking safety in the cellar. After about half an hour the shooting stopped, resuming again with great vigor around 9:00 AM. This time the stable took a direct hit.

For two days we did not dare to leave the house except to care for the livestock under cover of darkness. Several neighbors had already told us that the Germans were probably on the advance again, and that we should leave Diekirch as long as it was still possible. In great haste we packed a horse-drawn wagon and set out around 2:00 AM on the night of December 20 for the 'Eisebunnsbréck' (railway bridge), over which the inhabitants were to leave Diekirch in the direction of Stegen. The horses were frightened by the explosions of shells, which were falling in Gilsdorf and coming closer and closer, and it was not possible for me to get them to cross the bridge. Now and then bright flare rockets exploded and lit up the pitch-black night for a few moments. Since we were overloaded, we drove back in haste.

Farmer Thilmany warned me and urged me to leave Diekirch without losing a minute. He himself would take care of the Schmitz family. After I had said goodbye to my family and my future wife, I hurried to cross the 'Eisebunnsbréck' around 4:30 AM, and reached the orchard on the slope of the 'Haardt.' No German would ever get his hands on me; that was my only thought.

Panting, I reached the edge of the 'Haardt' and hurried from there to Cruchten, where numerous people from Diekirch, who had left the city around midnight, were waiting. I met Val Schmitz, who wanted to go to Lintgen. He was very depressed about his fate, and totally discouraged, so I tried to help him. His morale improved steadily, though, when he found most of the inhabitants of Diekirch there. We found a place to stay in a carpenter's shop, later in the Cafe Wolff, where we also had our meals. To my great joy, I also found my brother Czeslaw and his wife Annie, who had left Diekirch in the stream of refugees hours before me.

Several days later, two CIC officers spoke to us and asked the people to give them statements about various events in the German attack. Since we had also noticed certain things, we reported to them. So they took us along to Mersch, and here we were questioned, mainly about several people who had provided information to the Germans by radio.

At the beginning of the German offensive we could not stand it in Litgen any more on account of impatience and the lack of any news from Diekirch, and so Czeslaw and I decided to slip out secretly, go to Stegen and make our way from there to the Sauer. In Stegen, though, we were stopped by the Americans, who made us round up the cattle that were straying all over the place and supply them with feed.

The Americans often fired toward the Sauer Valley, from where the dull shock waves of the exploding artillery shells could be heard every time. Days later, after we had given up our plans and returned to Lintgen, we insisted on being taken along by a convoy that was to drive to Medernach, in hopes of getting more precise news there.

At the edge of town there we met Victor Abens, Chief of the Vianden Militia, who was helping a U.S. reconnaissance unit with his knowledge of the area. He himself had already taken part in numerous scouting parties, and told us what the situation was. So we got into a Jeep and accompanied the patrol to just short of the Cafe Greisen on the Sauer in Fels. They told us that U.S. units had crossed the Sauer the previous night and occupied parts of Diekirch.

On the following day we advanced as far as the Schou storehouse. This time too, the patrol was led by Vic Abens, as well as Jules Dominique. Only on January 23, 1945 was it made known that Diekirch was fully liberated from the Germans. I immediately requested a 'Laissez-passer', for I insisted on looking for my family, from whom I had not had the slightest news up to then. So Dr. Henri Rosch. Jos Lorang, Jemp Dostert and I reached the edge of Diekirch, where the U.S. military police blocked our way. Once again I had good luck. A captain of Polish ancestry took me to the CIC of the unit and arranged for me to stay in Diekirch. Meanwhile Felix Meyers had been named 'Acting Town Mayor.' To my joy, I found the Schmitz family doing well. They had spent the entire time of the second German occupation in their cellar. The house had taken numerous hits; several head of cattle had succumbed to shell-fragment wounds and malnutrition. Adjutant Peters of the Gendarmerie, who had also returned, asked me to help the Americans and the inhabitants who had remained in Diekirch with the necessary work of cleaning up. But Felix Meyers arranged for me to continue to take care of the cattle that were running loose and supply the remaining livestock of the farmers who had not yet returned with food. On one of my trips I noticed several dead cows that had been killed in a minefield in the meadows near Glaesener Street. Since all the approaches to the Sauer had been loaded with these diabolical German wood mines, I preferred to stay in the city, and did the best I could to take care of the entire complement of cattle until their owners returned."

The Western Part of Diekirch

This area was much more lightly populated forty years ago than it is today. Numerous gardens bordered 'Hospital', 'Flower' and 'Glaesener' Streets along the cemetery. The 'Flossbaach' still flowed, partly uncanalized, through that part of town to which it gave its name. Here too, there were only a few houses. Yet they determined the fate of groups of mostly old people who, since they had missed the evacuation of December 19, had tried to survive in the cellars of the few houses. Scarcely any of them dared to come out of the protection of the houses, since this part of town was in direct view of the American artillery observers in the 'Haardt.' At that time, but especially as of the first week of January 1945, the Americans shot at anything that moved.

Emil Grosbusch

Twenty-two years old at that time, Grosbusch had fled with his parents over the railroad bridge on the night of December 20 and had found shelter with friends in Moesdorf (Mersch), but was too worried about the cattle that had been left behind, and therefore returned to Diekirch on the next day.

"Diekirch looked dead," he related, "after I had reached the railroad bridge over the Sauer by way of Stegen. Although an American sentry on the road out of Stegen had urged me to turn back, I would not be stopped from doing what I intended.

Via the "Lann", I reached my parents' house, went straight to the stable and began to feed that cattle that were tied up there. I had just finished and was about to go out the main door when I heard the sound of motors in Hospital Street. Seconds later, a German tank with infantrymen sitting on it rattled up. Several soldiers with weapons ready to fire and fixed bayonets walked along each side of the street. In no time I had closed and bolted the front door and disappeared into a side room. Then a submachine gun cut loose; the bullets cut through the door and hit the wall of the hall. 'My God, it's all over now,: I thought, for I was eligible for the draft, although I had been postponed. 'Come on out!' one of them yelled. With my hands raised, I came outside and was immediately seized by two soldiers. The tank, which was heavily camouflaged with branches, had meanwhile turned in front of the house, and I had to walk in front of it. Then we went on in the direction of the church. Followed by only two soldiers, I had to go through the yard of the 'Butzeschull' while the tank, accompanied by the infantry, went up the 'Megonsbierg.' There were already dozens of people in front of the church, a mass of men and women who had likewise been driven out of their homes. What was going to happen to us? What did they have in mind?

I quickly took the English-French dictionary, that an American soldier had given me at the time of the liberation, out of my back pocket and hid it behind the big wooden crucifix by the left entrance to the church. Here we had to wait, for people were still coming here under guard. I stood somewhat off to one side and used the moment when they were changing the guard to escape along the church. As fast as my legs could carry me, I ran behind the 'Kluuster' and down 'Palais' Street and finally, out of breath, reached my parents' house, where I immediately hid myself in the barn above the stable. Only when it got dark did I venture back to the house, where I took several U.S. chocolate and candy rations, plus a big loaf of bread that had been left behind, before I crawled back into the straw. I threw some turnips and some more straw to the cows before I lay down to sleep. In the middle of the night I was awakened by voices; my God, the Germans were in the house. Only after they had taken our three pigs away did it become quiet. So I stayed in the barn two days, filled with fear, and did not dare to leave the building. Meanwhile snow had fallen and it was becoming considerably colder.

Through a crack in a bran window I saw several German trucks going up the 'Kockelberg.' Other than that, I saw scarcely any German soldiers.

'Emil, Emil!' a feminine voice suddenly called in front of our house, and I recognized Maria, Farmer Thilmany's Polish servant girl. She explained to me that she needed help milking Mr. Steinlein's cows; would I be willing to come? I agreed, and so we went to his farm. But the cows had not been milked for several days and all had milk fever; it was impossible to milk them. Some of the cows later died.

I learned from the maid that there were still about twenty older people in our street, and I decided to visit them. But when I returned to our house, several young German soldiers had taken up quarters there. What could I do? I explained to them that I did not want to leave on account of the cows, that my brother was with the Wehrmacht in the east, and that I also had to care for the old people who had stayed behind. But all that made very little impression on the Germans. They left me alone. But I let my beard grow, for I was constantly in fear of being taken away and drafted because of my age. During the next few days I supplied the people in the cellars with drinking water from the 'Flossbaach.' For this I had fastened a big cooking pot onto a sled and covered it with a piece of wood. Twice a day I made this trip and bailed out the water with a dipper. But this work was not completely free of danger. Often the American artillery fired from the 'Haardt' across the river, and I had to throw myself down. Since I had to run between the shells, it often happened that more than half the water was spilled. So from then on I only went in the dark. There was a similar firefall when I was on my way back with two sides of beef, which I had taken from the "Kühlhaus" (refrigeration house) near the train station and tied onto the sled. I was just passing the cemetery wall when the first shells from the 'Haardt' exploded. The ground around me was thoroughly plowed up. This firefall lasted more than thirty minutes, and I survived it only by a miracle. Only when it got dark did I venture out onto the street again to deliver the meat to the Biver house. During the same night the meat was cut up, cooked and roasted, since the smoke coming out of the chimney during the day would surely have attracted the attention of the Americans.

From Catherine Rommes we obtained bread, fresh-baked white bread, which she brought from Diekirch, where Willi Besseling of Vianden was baking the remaining flour at the shot-up Fischer Bakery into bread for the people who remained. Nor was there any lack of milk, for our cows were milked every day. One day, though, there was a firefall in the vicinity of my parents' house, and a big shell fragment tore both front legs off our only ox. The animal roared and writhed around in pain. A young soldier finally shot the ox, at my urging. With two other soldiers, we finally moved the carcass outside, and I went to the hospital, since I had heard that there were still a number of people there and their food supplies were running short. I informed the sisters that they could have the meat, so they would at least have meat for all the people for several days. But it was too dangerous for them, as there were constant firefalls around the hospital. There was, in fact, a German anti-aircraft gun there, which fired now and then, but the Americans had not been able to locate it precisely. Only later was a big red cross set up on the roof of the hospital, so as to avoid a worse fate.

I myself no longer dared to go to my parents' house, but stayed in Mrs. Haentges' cellar.

At the end of December

Catherine Rommes asked me if I would accompany her and her brother's wife to see friends at the Froenerhof. The child that had been born in the Diekirch hospital two days before the offensive began had died there, and the woman wanted to go back to her husband. The child, scarcely a week old, was buried in the hospital garden, and the woman insisted on leaving Diekirch after she had recovered from the strain in Mr. Brandt's cellar.

So we set out early in the afternoon, the two women and I. We had taken along Mrs. Rommes' things and some food on the sled. Via the Seitert, where we were out of sight of the Americans, we reached the path to the road to Erpeldingen. Here we met a German sentry, who advised us not to use the road, as the 'Amis' would see us. So we went on across the fields, through the snow-covered country, until we finally arrived at the Kippenhof. We went only as far as Brandenbourg and left Mrs. Rommes with friends there.

My shoes were in such bad condition that I urgently needed a new pair. I had heard that numerous German soldiers had already appropriated 'Tetinger shoes' from Diekirch, so I went to the Reding Shoe Store. I found a hopeless mess in the store. Hundreds of shoes and slippers were all mixed up, some of them in the dirt of the street. Since I could not find a suitable pair, I took a size 43 left and 45 right shoe, and thus again had a pair of useful shoes, as it was extremely cold.

On the way back I ran into the hands of a sentry, who forced me to go with him. 'Whoever plunders will be shot' – this slogan I knew only too well from before – now it is all over, I thought as he shoved me down the cellar stairs of a house in the lane behind the Esplanade.

'What are you doing here in Diekirch?' an officer sitting at a faintly lit table barked at me. 'I cannot go away; I have to take care of thirty old, sick people who cannot take care of themselves', was my answer. After a short exchange of words he let me go, and I ran as fast as possible back to Mrs. Haentges' caller. So the days passed, not one of them without U.S. artillery fire. We had almost gotten used to it.

Hairbreadth Escape

Early in the morning of January 18, as daylight had just dawned, we were awakened by the bursts of fire from a German machine gun very close to us. We got up immediately and crept up to the first floor to see what was going on. Through a crack in the window shutters I could see that there was a German machine-gun crew on the balcony of the Bormann house across the street, firing now and then in the direction of Heimricht. The soldiers were camouflaged in white and could scarcely be seen because of the snow all around. On account of the very sharp angle, I could not see what they were shooting at. Shortly after that, an American machine gun, clearly recognizable by the slower shot cadence, fired back.

Again and again the Germans fired. The exchange of fire continued until afternoon. Then there were suddenly several explosions, one after another. When I looked out again, I noticed that there were numerous black holes in the snow-covered street. – Mortar fire. Shortly after that the Germans were gone. Instead, though, there was shooting right around the house. We no longer had a chance to go down cellar. A submachine gun fired; the women shrieked and prayed. Bullets flew through a window above us. I called to Mrs. Haentges that she should shout something, anything, in English. Then, with one smash, the living-room door was open and I recognized two American soldiers. I jumped right up and wanted to hug them. But one of them poked the barrel of his weapon into the pit of my stomach and pushed me to the wall, where I had to stand with my hands up. Only after Mrs. Haentges had explained to him that I was not a German, they backed off from me, though they remained mistrustful.

Shortly after that, another soldier came into the room. He wore a vertical stripe on the back of his helmet – an officer. He spoke some German. He inquired whether any of us were injured, and then asked if we knew where there were still Germans. I said yes and drew a sketch map of the street on paper. But he insisted that I accompany the U.S. soldiers. Only after the shooting had let up somewhat did I agree to lead them. Most of the Germans surrendered without opposition, including the young soldier in our house who had always begged me to hide him until the Americans arrived. The Americans got as far as the girls' school that day and settled down there for the night.

Dead cattle were lying all over. Two days later I was up in the 'Floss' rounding up straying cattle when I suddenly encountered two ragged Germans. They asked me if I had a piece of bread, and where the route to the German border was. Telling them I would get them some bread and they should wait there, I quickly made tracks along the 'Héimricht.' On the way I found a half-frozen stray piglet that I picked up and took along. A pile of smashed German carbines on the slope down to Diekirch indicated that the Americans had probably taken a number of German prisoners there.

This was also the direction in which the Americans had moved into Diekirch. All of the meadows around the cemetery were heavily mined. I kept the piglet in the stable for several days before I slaughtered it. So at least we had some meat when my parents returned."

The "Bamerdall" During the Offensive

Of all the parts of Diekirch, the 'Bamerdall' was one of the hardest-hit, and it was also the part of town that was liberated last by the Americans. Many people from the 'Bamerdall' missed the news of the evacuation and tried to survive as well as they could, despite the cold, the hunger and the constant danger. Among them was Michael Preisen, who left posterity a manuscript in which he wrote down his observations and feelings every day. This diary, written from the viewpoint of a hard-hit farmer, appeared at the beginning of 1946 in "Nord", a local newspaper from Diekirch, under the title of "The Experiences at a Farm – Dec. 21, 1944." We hereby express our appreciation to the author, who unfortunately died all too early, and who probably could have told a great deal more about his wartime experiences. This report from Michael Preisen shall be representative of the "Bamerdall", where the author of this book also spent the greater part of his youth, and its inhabitants, a large family within Diekirch who are especially dear to him.

A Factual Account (appearing in "Nord" (local newspaper) in 1946)

When the battle was fought not far from Bastendorf and the Americans had to draw back somewhat, the burning question was: Are they coming or not? And they came! The storm broke around 10:00 AM. Accompanied by three tanks, they moved into the city from the north. With the butts of their rifles they smashed the doors in and pointed their rifles at the inhabitants' hearts. Rudely and roughly, they demanded to search all the rooms to see if a hated American or a terrorist was hiding there. At the first shot we would unfailingly be killed! Then they shoved us into the street, dressed in our thin work clothes, without even letting us put on a warm coat. On the street I found – Mr. F, who had already been dragged out, my neighbor F. F., and several others. We had to walk beside the tanks and go along with them until all the houses in the city had been searched. From there to the church square, not one additional man joined us, for all of them had justifiably tried to get away. Here we were then told that we should go into the passageway to the church until the search was finished, naturally in the company of sentries.

Men still arrived gradually, until the search was finished around 2:00. In all, there were between fifty and sixty men. About 11:00 the robberies began. By 1:00 there were already more than a hundred bicycles standing in front of the post office. They appeared to prefer black-painted ones. Stolen motorcycles were passing by, followed by the cars of the Diekirch doctors and businessmen.

Around 2:00 we were standing in a crowd by the entrance to the church when the shells fired from Ettelbrück suddenly fell. We sought cover, but the church doors were locked; only the first door to the choir loft was open, while the other was locked at the top. Some ten to twelve men tried to seek shelter behind the picture of a saint to the left; others occupied the stairs to the second door, and three of us found shelter behind the choir-loft door. The shells fell right and left, and the fragments penetrated the doors and stone walls. Fortunately, nobody was injured, except for one man whose hand was hurt.

It was 4:00 and we still could not leave; we got tired of crouching there; it was cold too, and nobody had eaten. So we stood there until about 6:00 PM. Then we were taken to the cellar of the sacristy, where we were crowded into the narrow space. We were allowed to lie down, but nobody had room to. Fortunately the heating system was more or less working, so that we could stand it. Since the open spaces around the church were filled with a lot of supply trucks, we came under heavy artillery fire again around 11:00 PM. It was fortunate that the schoolhouse was situated somewhat higher and gave us some cover. So we fortunately escaped the shells, but the schoolhouse took several direct hits. It gradually got stuffier in the place, and several old people began to feel faint. Time passed very slowly for us, and nobody knew what they were going to do with us. Some people were even imagining concentration camps, until suddenly, around 10:00, a Nazi woman told us that the seventeen-year-olds could go home; I could not understand the rest of what she said. In fact, though, we all crowded toward the door and all got out without any trouble. On our way home, we came under fire again and had to sneak homeward along the houses.

When I arrived at our farm, I found the whole place full of German soldiers. I went into the house and saw to my horror how much could be torn apart and plundered during one night. The best bedclothes, the best clothing, everything was gone; what remained was strewn in the dirt and stomped on by army boots, the drawers pulled out and thrown away. A mess of devastation, and yet an officer had said as I left that nothing would be touched. It is possible, though, that the soldiers who came later thought the house was empty, for nobody had been at home since I had left, and the houses of the people who were away had been treated even worse. Then I hurried into the horsebarn. Two of the best horses were gone. Since the animals had nothing to eat for thirty hours, I got busy and fed them right away. First I took care of my old father, who was unable to leave his room and had likewise had nothing to eat.

The soldiers had tied all the cattle so close together, so as to have room for their army horses, that it was impossible for me to get through with a basket or bucket. I fed the cattle with some difficulty and then went into the cellar to get some turnips for the next day. When I had been busy doing that for a few minutes, I heard someone call softly to me from a corner of the cellar. I immediately recognized the voice of our hired man, who had now been in the corner of the cellar for almost forty hours. After a year in the east, he had not returned after a short furlough. He should have fled, but he had missed the chance. Suddenly the Nazis were there, and he had to hide in the cellar, dig himself into the turnips somewhat and try to hold out. The two of us were in a perilous situation. If they caught him, it could cost both of us our heads, him as a deserter and me as a harborer. I had to supply him with food every day, which was very difficult, because I had to pass many soldiers every time before I reached him. Although two field kitchens had pulled into the farmyard, I never got to our cookstove, as it was used by the soldiers all day.

I had to supply him with food as well as I could. A little milk, bread and butter, and a few apples, all of which I had to put in my pockets so it would not be too conspicuous.

So we survived the first week, and then things got a little better. When the American tanks pushed their way through above Ettelbrück and stopped the German attack on the third day, all the supply forces from here were given the order to hitch up at once and begin to withdraw to the north, since the 'Esplanade' and the 'Rue Clairefontaine' were under heavy fire from the 'Haardt' batteries. Everything was confused now, nobody could find his horses' harness. People who had never driven a horse were supposed to hitch them up. Meanwhile the fighter-bombers were coming in from the west and shooting off bursts of machine-gun fire. From 4:00 PM to well into the night, the long column was attacked ceaselessly, but the fire must have been imprecise, for when I took the road past the cemetery two days later, I saw only a few dead horses.

Today two dead German soldiers were brought to our farm, left lying there for several days and then buried on the sidewalk above the Villa Lola to the right of the road. Every morning we supplied the people from the bunker opposite us with two buckets of milk. Most of them were poor families with many children, but there were also a few single people, like S.J. and G.; here and there we also see B.B., who also takes care of the Schwinniger house, and who fired two revolver shots through the door at a German soldier because he wanted to get him out of the house.

The fire on the city is becoming heavier all the time, and the soldiers who are still here, most of them being engineers and storm troopers, have to draw back to the upper farms and bunkers, where they are somewhat under cover.

For three weeks I had to bring the fodder for sixty horses, and the Germans took the fodder away only at night, because the hail of shells was too heavy during the day. Because of the darkness they wasted a lot, and then the numerous cows and steers that were running loose came early in the morning and ate up what remained. Most of them had been hit by shell fragments and could only move ahead laboriously, limping. At first I also gave them some turnips, but as time passes, one grows tough; after two weeks, dry-eyed, I chased them away with a stick, because I myself had nothing left for a single cow, since the Germans' horses had eaten up everything.

Then came a rough day for me. I was called to the commander's office. In the drawers of our house someone had found a package of memorial cards for our late son, who had died on the first day of freedom. They claimed that from this memorial they could see that our son had died as a terrorist, and I as his father was to be made responsible for him. I opposed that by saying that only someone who, as a civilian, fired at a soldier, qualified as a terrorist, and I, as the father of a grown-up son, could not be held responsible for him. I was informed that the whole family would be held responsible. On the next day, at 8:00 PM, they would meet again, and if the facts were correct, I would be shot the following morning at 6:00. I went home in despair, lay down in the stable, for there was no room for me in the house, and made plans. I came to the decision to flee. I planned to reach the Friedbusch if possible, spend the night on the upper Sauer, and then to try to reach the American lines between Erpeldingen and Bürden, staying under the cover of the hedges. I followed the bed of the brook through the 'Bamerdall', sneaking past the sentries, and fortunately arrived in the vicinity of the Friedbusch, a hundred meters above the Erpeldingen-Diekirch intersection, where the woods meet the road. I glanced over toward the woods without turning my head, but every fifteen meters there was a soldier in a hole, ready to shoot.

If I took one step into the woods, I would undoubtedly be shot. There was nothing to do; I had to give up. I turned around and made my way back past the other sentries to the house. The next day brought a little relaxation. About 9:00 AM there suddenly came the command for the whole battalion to go back to Bastendorf. We had to help out until we were behind the Herrenberg, but then got back to the house with the horses under heavy fire. The fire became heavier and more precise all the time. Almost every shell took lives, but mostly Wehrmacht lives, those of the men housed in the barns and stables.

The road from below our farm to above the Villa Lola was lined on both sides with dead horses. Here and there among them lay a stray cow that had been hit. A dead German soldier has been lying in our yard for three weeks now; no soldier felt like burying him. They find the occasion to eat and drink, but nobody bothers about their dead comrades. Such is the unity of the people!

Today was a black day for us and our neighbors. Shortly after noon we took three hard hits and our neighbors four. They smashed through the fairly new, strong walls and caused a lot of damage. One Wehrmacht horse fell victim at our place, four at our neighbors.' Afterward we were hit by a phosphorus shell; but we were on guard and had water ready, and were able to extinguish the fire in its initial stage. Then I went with my helpers to look after my father, who had stayed in his room all the time and did not want to come down. We found him in the last stages. Fear and privation had affected the 93-year-old man so much that the end was near. His room, floor, ceiling and walls were perforated in many places by the fragments of the shells that had exploded in the garden. But he had remained unharmed to the end.

After feeding the livestock, I visited the neighbors to tell them of their uncle's death. Afterward Mrs. Lisa asked me to look after her husband, who had been out in the stable for two hours and had not come back into the cellar. I had a bad feeling and went to the place where the shells had fallen that afternoon.

On my way back, my foot struck something soft; it had to be a person. In the first moment I could not determine if it was a civilian or a soldier. Therefore I wiped the dust and dirt off his trousers and saw that it was the landlord. Only now did I see his face. I won't describe it! I ran quickly back to the house to get a blanket and put it over him, so the women in the house would not see him. On the next day, my helpers and I worked hard to dig a grave in the hard-frozen ground, and we buried both of them.

Today the Germans slaughtered my last two pigs. (They slaughtered the first one on the second day, they stole the second one the next night and took it away alive, and now the other two. (One was never asked if one would like a piece too.) At the first notch of the 'Kahlenbesch' lay two big heaps of frozen meat, about 200 quarters, that was captured by the Americans. (This meat was shipped by Luxembourg trucks yesterday, the third and fourth day of the American occupation, and, it was said, shipped to Esch/Alzette.) This meat did not suit the master race. In their own words, they like to eat pork and sauerkraut for life (it makes blood, they say). Then chicken fricassee and rabbit meat. They steal the small animals of the absent people in the light of day, those of the present people in the twilight and at night. Not a day goes by when we don't hear the squealing of pigs and the squawking of the frightened and pursued poultry. But the German soldier understands his work, and he misses nothing. For a week they have been robbing the city. They preferred the morning hours between 8:00 and 10:00, since the fire was lightest then. To conceal themselves better in the snowy landscape, they take bed linens (naturally Diekirch linens), make a cut in the middle, stick their heads through, then come up with a hood and the snowman is finished! Once in a while we also see pieces of clerical clothing. Now the procession begins. With all possible and impossible vehicles, such as handcarts, hand-drawn wagons, baby carriages, pushcarts, doll carriages, even little boys' toy trucks. I saw the little boy's truck, that belonged to Mr. W. the hairdresser, pass by at least forty times; now it lies smashed in a roadside ditch along with the dead horses. They even cut up the people's good fruit-tree ladders and, according to their length, made two or three carriers for plundering. First they took all the canned goods. In the upper city you stepped on broken glass jars every few steps. Their contents lay frozen on the ground. In their hurry, they destroyed at least a third of the stuff. Then the bedclothes were taken; only the best was good enough for the master race to use in their damp bunkers, where most of it is now rotting.

They took everything of lesser value and threw it out the window. They deliberately left all the cellar doors standing open, so the potatoes would freeze! I have never seen a German soldier close a door other than those of their bunkers and cellar holes. Systematic destruction! All the stoves and cookers that they could get their hands on, even those of the poorer and poorest people, were stolen and taken to the bunkers. Then they went into the various stores in the city, naturally to the clothing stores first. The Germans kept two rooms in our house ready to hold the clothing that they brought there. Then for two weeks, every evening between 10:00 and 11:00, a car drove up. A command of five or six men set to work, and in twenty minutes the car raced off toward the Reich.

After that they discovered the M. breweries. Everybody who could walk and was not on guard duty joined the parade, goose-stepping, one after the other, staying close to the houses to stay under cover. In the narrow lanes they crowded more closely together, and in a quarter hour, fully loaded, they began the trip back. They did not build up supplies, but drank all night and began the same game the next day. Mr. M. will probably be amazed to find his tasty Thurgau and Sylvaner gone. His brandy, and that of all the brewers, probably went the same way, so that nothing will be left for the 'Amis.'

After most of the shops had been plundered bit by bit, things became a little more quiet. Finally it was the turn of the stationery shops, since the soldiers lacked writing materials. This evening they brought two of Mr. Reuter's fine horses from the 'Herrenberg' farm into our stable. The soldiers asked me to take good care of the horses, so that no other unit would steal them. A strange system! The Germans steal horses from each other!

Since my neighbors' stable was too much under fire, we took her two surviving horses into our stable. Yesterday along came an officer who said he had to have them, as they would be killed by shells anyway. I told him they belonged to my neighbor who had been killed in the ruins, and asked him at least to have a word with the woman of the house.

The woman defended herself, while we blockaded the heavy doors and climbed out on the roof, and the woman kept her horses.

The last week begins and the gunfire gets heavier and heavier. Shell after shell comes our way; it is almost beyond endurance; the walls are full of holes and no longer strong. One hole is made next to another, and we worry about how it will end. The gardens and orchards behind the houses look disastrous, and there will scarcely be a tree that is able to stay alive. Every two meters there is a shell hole. Today a major fire began in the city. After heavy gunfire, there are fifteen to twenty different places burning simultaneously. We could only see some of the fires, to be sure, but the sky was lit up brightly and we thought the whole city was in flames. The houses of M.H., J.B., H.L., Sch.H. and Widow Z., plus a third of the Esplanade, were burning, and other fires were visible all over.

We limited our rescue work to the B. house nearest to us, that burned down, but we were able to prevent the fire from spreading to the W. house.

These fires were now part of the daily, or rather the nightly, order of things. Every evening at about the same time, several houses fell victim to fire. Today our neighbors' barn burned for the second time. The first time the fire could be limited, but now almost everything burned down. One never sees a German soldier help put out the fires; they all creep off into their holes. The few remaining farmers in the central part of town earn the thanks of those who have left, for they have to feed their own stock under difficult conditions and then, as best they can, the stock of their neighbors, so that thanks to their intervention all will not be lost. Most of the livestock dies, not so much from lack of food as from lack of water, since it is hard to get water in the center of town. The well-known S. deserves special praise. He was the maid of all work. He took several families into his house, fed the livestock, milked the cows, supplied all the people with milk, distributed bread, provided light for many people, in short, he was everywhere, and yet his life hung by a thread. The bunkers and farms in the 'Bamerdall' were cut off from the city for the last two weeks. Whether S. knew of that I don't know. The fact is, though, that he appeared one morning at his parents' house and brought bread to his family. On his way back, though, he was caught and not allowed to go back down. He had to return to his parents' house. After several hours he tried to get through a second time, along with his sister. When the sentry caught sight of him, he aimed at him, but his sister was able to pull him away at the last moment.

In the last few days the bunker across from us got new occupants. Mr. and Mrs. F.I. from Ingeldorf were driven out of their farm and brought here. About 8:00 in the evening they reached the bunker on a sled. Before they could go in, a shell exploded near them. Franz was thrown to the ground, while his wife was seriously injured by shell fragments. Two days before 'the end' we suddenly received the order to go to Brandenbourg at 2:00 AM. None of us felt like obeying, and I had already prepared my hiding place. In the bunker too, they had not yet packed.

After a second demand, they gathered up everything they needed, but it seemed to everybody that it would not last much longer. In fact, about forty people from the brewery were evacuated to Brandenbourg. But the people in the bunker stayed; the day of liberation was near. The attack was initiated at night by heavy artillery fire with air support, which the Germans answered with grenade-launcher fire from the nearby hills. About 6:00 in the morning a furious machine-gun fire set in, and we knew what was going on. The fire continued until late in the afternoon. We were frightened again and again. Would they get through?

Toward evening, the fire suddenly let up; weary and stressed out, some of the Germans returned to their bunkers, but most of them stayed out. About 9:00 in the morning a single 'Ami', followed at a distance of about fifty meters by two others, came cautiously up the road, looking all around, swinging his machine pistol back and forth.

At thirty meters several civilians, including F.I., beckoned to him to come in; the bunker was occupied. He signaled to them with one hand that they should move back. When he reached the bunker, two Wehrmacht men appeared with bowed heads and surrendered.

They had already thrown their weapons away the night before and hidden in the hundred-meter-long bunker with the intention of surrendering. When they iden-tified themselves as two Czechoslovaks, they were treated gently and could set off for the city without 'Hands up!' Now a few more men had arrived, and four or five of them went to the second bunker. There were still some twenty men inside who apparently had no idea that the 'Amis' were in the neighborhood. They were hav-ing an excited conversation when the soldiers appeared at the open door. They looked around, but not one reached for his carbine. A moment of murmuring, and then one after the other set out down the road, goose-stepping, 'Hands up!' In the third bunker the search brought no results. Then the villa across from us was searched, as were our two farms, where nothing was found. In the afternoon a few individuals were hauled out of the forestry building, and then we were rid of those hated faces.

We are all standing before the ruins of our home town. Our farmhouse is still standing, but all the walls are full of holes, almost the whole roof is ruined, no doors or windows are left. The neighbors' farm has been hit even harder. The man of the house is dead, ten to twelve head of cattle gone, the wall caved in, the barn with the machinery burned down. If wet weather sets in now, the whole city will probably be soaked with rain, all the way to the cellars. Almost all of us are faced with the question: Shall we rebuild or give up? It looks hopeless. Somebody told me Prince Félix was here, took a look and said it was worse here than in St. Lô. Build, yes! But it can scarcely be done by our own power, and the state itself is heavily burdened. There would be just one solution: To force the Germans, once the war is over, to rebuild those areas themselves that were destroyed because of them. The whole Luxembourgeois Nazi clique, though, led by the man who had to repeat a year of school here in Diekirch forty years ago and grew a goatee because he had a high opinion of himself, shall and must be turned over to the authorities and punished severely. (Written in a stable during sleepless nights and by faint candlelight during the occupation.)

Original manuscript in the possession of the Wolff-Preisen family, on display at the Diekirch National Museum of Military History

Author's Note
This detailed and precise report written by Michael Preisen reflects very well the feelings of a man who had to suffer much at that time. Some clarification is nevertheless appropriate: In this report there is much talk of plundering and looting by the 'Nazis.' Without seeking any excuse for it, let it be noted that the Wehrmacht soldiers were forbidden on pain of death to seize foreign property. This did, however, not include: food, clothing, footwear and anything that the soldiers could use to survive on frontline duty. Although there were very probably extreme cases, most of the plundering is attributable to the returned Nazi party officials, Luxembourg collaborators who knew their way around well, as well as the helpers' of the Gestapo who were chosen to search for papers at the Villa Conter, which served as Klöcker's headquarters before the liberation in September.

It was exactly this type that Michael Preisen wanted to deliver to the sword of justice, since his son had been shot by a Luxembourg Nazi Party functionary while the latter was being arrested on September 12, 1944.

On orders from higher places in the Wehrmacht, livestock was requisitioned, and sometimes driven back to Germany to be processed at the field kitchens there, for the Wehrmacht was "playing its last card." Food, shoes, clothing, means of transportation: they were short of all these things.

It might also be noted that the bunkers referred to by Michael Preisen, in which numerous families lived as "cavemen", were the cellars of the formerly private breweries carved in the rock in the 'Bamerdall', situated at the edge of the

"Kaalebésch." In these cellars, where a child came into the world under indescribable conditions at the beginning of January, scraps of bedding, furniture and such, that had been brought there, were still found long after the war. After live ammunition had been found by children several times in the early sixties, as well as the mortal remains of a German soldier, the "Bamerdaler Cellars" were finally closed by the local authorities.

CHAPTER XVII

HOW WE SURVIVED THE TERRIBLE DAYS IN DIEKIRCH

The report appearing below this title, of the experiences of Forester J. Zeyen, who then occupied the present-day "Foyer des Jeunes" in the Bamer Valley, likewise appeared in two editions of "Nord" on July 14, 1945.

On December 11, 1944, American batteries, artillery and mortar took up positions in the 'Bamerdall' as far as the "Friedhof" (Friedbusch). Then cannons thundered day and night, and their shells ate and hammered ceaselessly at the West Wall. The food services of the Americans were within our housing, and hundreds of soldiers received their food here; they were really fine young men. They were actually here to rest after the battle of Aachen. The nightly cannon thunder was burdensome to us, for several mortars had their positions close to our house. But we felt very safe and hoped the Americans would soon attack the West Wall in earnest and break the line with their many materials and forces. Then came December 16, 1944, 5:30 AM. I was awakened suddenly by a strange whistling in the air. Farther down in Diekirch there was noise. The American batteries fired their guns regularly. Then there was a hissing again, followed immediately by a detonation in Diekirch. For the third time something hissed past our house, there was a terrible noise nearby, our dining-room window fell into the room with a crash. I jumped out of bed, an American sentry came into the house and advised us to seek shelter in the cellar; he himself took our little Albert out of bed and carried him to the cellar. We followed as fast as we could, shivering from nervousness and cold. It has become certain, the "Prussians" returned the fire of the Americans but were thriftier as to quantity. Soon a neighbor family, laden with clothing and everything possible, entered our cellar. They reported that the "Prussians" would make a counterattack here to take pressure off the combat around Aachen. They would surely not succeed, but could cause a lot of damage. (So they knew more than we did.) When daylight dawned, we left the cellar; shooting continued all day from all sides. The next night we went back into the cellar. The next day was a Sunday (December 17, 1944). There were no church services. Around 3:00 in the afternoon, Mr. Guth came from Wiltz with a wagon to pick up his son, who was living with us as a student. He was very excited and reported that the radio (ours did not work, as the wires were destroyed) said the Germans had attacked from Wasserbillig to Aachen. Diekirch was endangered. Flames rose to the heavens from the neighboring villages. The residents were fleeing with wagons and herds of cattle to the Belgian border. Mr. Guth took little Abby and his mother away, and wants me to come along too. But I don't want to leave my wife and house alone, and did not believe at all that the presumed German offensive would have any success. The American soldiers were very quiet and kept looking toward the Herrenberg. The same things happened on Monday.

Fighting was going on in the vicinity of Longsdorf, Fouhren and Bastendorf. House arrest was announced, and we had no contact with the people from Diekirch, not even with our closest relatives and children, who live in Diekirch. We were completely in the dark as to how close the terrible danger was. Rumors went around that the "Prussians" had crossed the Our and broken into our land in great numbers. The villages on the heights (Weiler and Merscheid) were in flames. The cannon thunder continued without a stop. The German shells landed dangerously close to our house, splintered trees and knocked down the utility poles, but didn't hit the house. On Monday evening the American soldiers packed their things very quietly, the guns left their positions. The soldiers didn't give us any clear information, and about 10:00 the kitchen drove away with its baggage; we didn't even hear a pot rattling. The whole operation seemed very strange. Around 11:00, American infantry took up quarters in the cellar, a nervous captain gave hasty orders. We heard that the "Prussians" are in Bastendorf, and they want to take up a position to oppose them the next morning. On Tuesday bloody battles took place at 'Friedbusch-Hagedörner.' German prisoners were brought in. The American command that is in our house is on the radio constantly. I asked a soldier who spoke some French whether the situation was critical. He answered, "No, the Prussians have been pushed back twelve kilometers." So we are reassured; the Americans gradually left our cellar, and around 11:00 the whole command was gone. We went to bed calmly and fell, after three sleepless nights, into a deep sleep. I can still say we came through it well again.

We heard no more shells explode.

Wednesday, December 20, 1944. After a good sleep, we got up in the morning and everybody went to work. After 9:00 our J. came from Diekirch with his milk wagon and reported: "There is nobody left in the place, even your children from the Esplanade are gone." What did all this mean? I stood at our dining-room window and looked toward the Herrenberg. I couldn't believe my eyes. A soldier with a rifle stepped over a wall. Another looked out from behind a tree in our orchard. There was another one behind another tree. Then I heard the command: "Come on!"

I experienced the most terrifying moment of my life. The "Prussians" were back again. It was incredible, unbelievable. Yesterday there were still the proud American troops here with their strong, fast materials, and now the German soldiers are standing on our property. A German soldier asked my wife: "Where is your husband? – Do you have chocolate?" – My wife called me. I stepped into the yard. Two "Prussians" were already standing there with rifles ready to fire. "You are arrested, come with us", said one of the two. I put on a coat and followed the soldier, limping, still suffering from a bad accident. Along the way they asked me when the Americans had left, where their food depot was, whether they were quartered in the house. Where had their artillery been? And so on. By the next house, German infantrymen were coming down the 'Bastendorferweg', followed by two tanks. "There come our tanks," said one of the "Prussians" proudly.

The soldiers got my attention. I had to observe them more closely. The difference from yesterday was too great; then I still saw American soldiers with creases in their trousers, and these here wore ragged uniforms, had dirty, bearded faces, some were walking with sticks, old men and half-grown boys, all mixed up.

They were wild hordes that approached; they smashed in the locked doors of the houses, screamed at the occupants who came out of the cellars, drove the men who were present into the street. They found many houses empty. A drunken young Unteroffizier screamed: "Where is the civilian population?" Little by little, we built up a troop of men who, accompanied by several soldiers, made their way to the square in front of the church. The few tanks went to the Esplanade and Graben Street to capture the city. More and more men who stayed behind arrived and crowded together, shivering, for it was cold. Suddenly there was an ear-splitting crash; shells hit in and around the church, we moved into the steeple stairway and back to the choir loft. Mortar and windowpanes fell to the ground. As night came on, we were taken to the cellar under the high altar. Crowded closely together, we crouched there. A young Unteroffizier was in charge of our guards and soon began to give orders. "Is anybody armed? If the slightest thing happens in Diekirch or here, you will be shot. It's a good thing for you that the Americans were gone when we arrived; otherwise what happened to the village of Bettendorf would have happened to Diekirch. Did you ever think we would be back so soon? We would rather have gone home and made peace, but there are still so many irrational people in the world who don't want that."

We spent the night worried, thinking of those at home and those who had fled. Shells kept flying over us from the direction of the "Haardt" and Ettelbrück and striking the "Schetzebierg" and Herrenberg. On the next morning, about 9:30, the same Unteroffizier appeared and asked: "Are service-eligible men among you, what age?" We answered: "Seventy, sixty, fifty." "Then everybody out!" We pushed out into the fresh air. The day was gray, gray as the worried faces of the people. Pieces of linen were strewn in front of the deanery. The looting had begun already.

I dragged myself home as fast as possible, along the left row of houses, for shells were falling on the 'Bamerdall' regularly. At home I was greeted as if I had returned from long imprisonment.

My wife told me that yesterday, after I was taken away, a drunken German soldier, his hair hanging in his face, appeared in the house and roared: "Hands up, get out", then he fired his pistol like a madman, at the doors, walls, cabinets, searched some of the cabinets and took valuables, liquor and tobacco away with him.

My wife and her helpers had left the house, gone to the first houses in the 'Bamerdall' and then returned because nobody followed them. They found the house empty. Soon, though, three soldiers of rank came in and demanded a drink; they had bad colds. My wife told the three what had just happened and showed them the damage. They could not imagine a cultivated German soldier doing that. But we were to have further problems with the German culture that we had already 'enjoyed' for four years. – Our house was filled with soldiers, some of them sleeping in the dining room, others cooking in the kitchen.

I withdrew, exhausted by the past night. Soon three young soldiers came to me: "It is really nice here, very comfortable, that's the way we'd like to keep it," and so on. When I did not answer, one of them asked: "Are you sick?" I said yes.

Then they took a different tone, spoke of the behavior of the Luxembourgers during their withdrawal in September, of the plans for the present offensive, about their new weapons. The 'Amis' were running and would not stop any more. Aachen, Antwerp and Liège had fallen. Maybe we'll be in Paris for Christmas, one said with a grin: "We'll surround the Tommies and Amis on the Channel and they won't get home any more. That would be nice for the Amis, if they could go for a walk on the beautiful Rhine."

Then there was a terrible crash. I said: "That one hit us." All the windowpanes on the east side were broken, the cold wind blew through the house. "No, that was from us," said one of the three soldiers, and they stormed out onto the street where a tank was standing. They climbed on and pulled out a dead German soldier. This is what happened:

The man who stayed on guard in the tank had fumbled with the trigger of the gun. It was already in bad condition, and had gone off unintentionally. They buried the dead man in the yard in front of our house; we were not told to keep quiet about this grave. Then I went into another room. Here a soldier (probably a Hitler Youth of seventeen) was giving the same speech I had just heard, about surrounding, new weapons, airplanes without gasoline, but with turbines and water. Nebelwerfers firing rockets from which the 'Amis' ran away, howling and screaming. Shells that fell vertically down on the target and unfailingly hit the target, then the V1, V2 and V3, then a magnet that pulled the enemy aircraft out of the skies and down to the ground. Finally something that would not be mentioned, because of espionage, so that the enemy would not take any countermeasures. So swelled up from bragging but thin and weak from hunger, they went out without food or clothing. For the war lived on itself.

Sickened, I went back to the cellar reserved for us, which we were not supposed to leave from then on. We brought everything we could down to keep with us, for nothing was safe from these robbers. My razor was already gone, combs and hairbrushes, for they needed them, as one could see by their constant scratching. Friday, December 22, 1944: the supply train set out, wagons full of mattresses and bedding headed northward, pulled by stolen farm horses. They used any available vehicles: handcarts, hand-drawn wagons, baby carriages and toy wagons were used. Their army horses were small and skinny. Our barns and stables were full of horses that ate the food, in so short supply this year, that was for our cows. In the evening the soldiers left their quarters and went to Diekirch to go "organizing." At first we didn't understand what they meant, but we soon found out that it was a euphemism for stealing and plundering. Then came the evening of December 24, Christmas Eve. About a hundred men, the 7th Company, moved into our house and cellar with one lieutenant. The soldiers carried stocks of oats from a barn in the field to their camp. I found their mood depressed, the weather was clear and nice; we sat around our stove, which warmed us badly. I heard an old soldier saying: "In the six years that I have been a soldier, this is the first without a Christmas tree."

A terrible night followed: Shell after shell fell over us and around us, even on Christmas Day itself. On December 26 it was said that American tanks were shooting in Diekirch. New hope! The "Prussians" drove their wagons to the north. Infantrymen ran alongside on foot. Several soldiers explained that they wanted to hide and surrender to the Americans, who would soon arrive. But we ourselves were disappointed the next day, for the Americans had withdrawn again.

In the evening the engineers leave their quarters to lay mines along the Sauer. During the day they spread out from Diekirch to the Sauer at Erpeldingen, dig in and set up bunkers in the brush and trees as far as Michelau. Every day groups of soldiers change their positions; "those are candidates for death", one of them explains. These candidates for death go through Hoscheid to Consthum and serve as reserves on the front, to fill the holes. There is talk of a major battle near Bastogne. On Friday, December 29, troops coming from Bitburg march through. They are half-starved and want to sit down here at their comrades' full pots of food. But they are driven away with shouts. Comradeship does not go that far. Every group knows only its own men. The newly arrived soldiers then get their hard 'Kommissbrot' out of their food bags, smear it with some lard (yes, it's supposed to be fat, an old engineer explains) and still their hunger. What a great contrast with the food that we saw in the American army. During this time the firing on Diekirch continues; the Germans explain that the Americans are firing from the "Haardt Heights" and come as close as the houses of Diekirch, on the other side of the Sauer, at night. To the west they have occupied the Feulen Heights. Ettelbrück is no-man's-land. On the night of December 31, 1944-January 1, 1945, the Lieutenant freed them to celebrate New Year's Eve. Supplies of food, wine and brandy were brought up from Diekirch. "They drank and ate until late in the night," as the soldiers expressed it. In the process, they sang their marching songs and drank more and more. Their singing turned into roaring and growling, until finally, about 3:00 AM, even the most stubborn of them shut up and sank into sleep. On the next day, January 1, 1945, the U.S. Air Force took advantage of the clear weather to carry their New Year's greetings to the Fatherland. Soldiers who came to us from the Herrenberg farm told us that the farm is destroyed, horses and many cattle are dead, and seventeen people are sick in the cellar there. Our mother got sick from work and stress, her nerves were shot, she had a lot to take care of. The soldiers caused her a lot of annoyance and stole everything out of her hands. With determination and courage, she grabbed the stolen things out of their arms and set them straight about their disorder and dirtiness, which the men accepted laughingly. The nights were now terrible, there is no chance to sleep, any next shell could bring destruction. During the day too, we are not allowed to leave the house. The "Kalebösch" woods and the trees growing in front of our house were hit by shells that exploded and shattered. At the nearby "Friedhaff", a direct hit killed the cattle and their old caretaker Oesch. The front always stayed the same; it was a positional war that could still go on for months, the soldiers said, and fill the whole area with bunkers and rifle pits. The scrounging soldiers reported that civilians in Diekirch fought with them over the goods and took everything possible out of the houses. This handicraft is quickly learned, and perhaps the people need to do it. On January 7-8 a position change to Consthum took place. Thus a troop movement. Horse-drawn wagons filled with stolen goods headed north. On January 9 there were other units quartered with us; hungry and exhausted, they grabbed for their "Kommissbrot." The SS men from the staff hung around in droves and won; the others suffered in silence. The dirt piled up higher and higher around our house. On January 10, four field policemen took up quarters at our house. The chief ordered four chairs as soon as possible from my wife. The soldiers warned us about the field police (saying they were dirty dogs who had already made trouble for many of them).

Through the little contact that I had with the policemen, I learned that they were absolute loafers; they were also sick of the war and felt that everything could go wrong. From them I heard more about the battle of Bastogne; a whole division of Americans was surrounded, it was hardly to be believed; they even spoke of nine divisions. The outcome would be close.

During the day, 600 liters of gasoline were divided up. The shells whistled over the Herrenberg toward the West Wall. They interfered with supplying. The field kitchen from Walsdorf, from which food was brought here in the evening, was hit. The food was now being brought from a cellar in the "Kalebösch." It was very dangerous to fetch it. The "Bamerdall" was lined with dead horses, cattle and soldiers. Our house was filled again and again with troops. It was not hit, though, despite the heavy fire. "The house in the dead angle," the engineers call it. In the evenings we saw the glow of the burning houses in Diekirch. A group of engineers (scouting party) was supposed to sneak up on and capture the American sentries at the Neuhof the other side of Ingeldorf on the evening of January 13, a young man reported. On the next day I asked him how the patrol had done. He said: "The Americans had posted more sentries than we had men, and we turned back in a hurry." On the night of January 10-11 a wall caved in from a direct hit and crushed Farmer Felten in his cowbarn. At the same hour, the 93-year-old Farmer Preisen died. Such reports made our situation more and more desperate, for there was no end in sight. We had now put a cookstove in our cellar and could cook and warm ourselves whenever we wanted. Our only consolation was the thunder of the American guns; the sound of them being fired not far away confirms that they have not forgotten us, although we sit in a trap and are subjected to a matter of life and death. The decisive battle of Bastogne must have gone badly for the "Prussians"; not one soldier talks about it any more. I asked a soldier about the surrounding of the American troops; "What?" he replied, "We were surrounded" —new hope for us!

Wednesday, January 17. From Tuesday to Wednesday was a rather quiet night; it snowed again. The soldiers who came in from the trenches at night ate their meager meal and talked loudly; I could understand a few words. One of them, who had a very loose tongue, hollered: "Do you know that the Russians are in Kattowitz?" I understood that to mean that the Russians have begun an offensive. That was the first time they mentioned the Russians. A senior paymaster came to our cellar and reported that the civilians from Diekirch were being evacuated to Brandenbourg and had to have left Diekirch by 2:00 AM. We decide not to leave our cellar under any circumstances, and cannot sleep for excitement. On Thursday, January 18, at 3:30 AM, a ferocious American fire began, coming from the directions of the Haardt and Feulen. Hundreds and thousands of shells flew over Diekirch and the vicinity. Nebelwerfers howled, machine guns hammered, rifle shots cracked; all hell has broken loose. Around 5:30 AM the field police brought evacuees who were on the way to Brandenbourg into our cellar; they all had to flee from the hail of shells. They were the Burner family with four people, Mrs. Bauer from Bettel, who had lost her husband, wagon and baggage, Mrs. Ed. Schmitz-Kipgen with four children, Mrs. Thommes-Reger and child, Mrs. Kremer and child. Outside all hell was still raging over the countryside.

The field police came into our cellar with a bottle of liquor and drank to steady their nerves, as they put it. "The Americans have crossed the Sauer at Erpeldingen." While my wife was in the process of cooking a hearty pea soup for the many guests whom we now had to feed (23 people), they asked for a bowl of soup, also to steady their nerves. The soldiers have all left without much noise; they left their gas masks and almost all their equipment behind. One soldier reported to the police that the command had left its position in the "Seiteschgronn." Soon the sentry from the farmyard door came into the cellar and whispered something to the policemen. They hurried away, packed their things, searched for helmets and gloves, and left the cellar without saying a word. Their car is frozen fast. "We'll get through anyway, won't we?" says one of them, and they stride out the gate, following the road to the north. Our house is now rid of the Germans; the shells keep on howling and blasting. Around 4:30 in the afternoon, three soldiers came back into the house, looking around nervously and going from one window to another. They were very unnerving to us, for we suspected they were going to blow up our house. Asked if they were going to take up quarters here, one of them replied nervously: "Oh, the Americans are in the vicinity and have taken prisoners up there." Things are getting better and better, we said to each other hopefully. The three then took the road to the north and were captured. Around 5:00 AM a submachine gun was fired near our house. An American patrol was firing into our barn door and farmyard gate. Our people fled into the cellar and the U.S. soldiers followed their direction. The long-awaited day had become reality: The Americans were here again. We received them with open arms, communicated as well as possible, and they were happy to accept the liquor we offered them. One German soldier crept out of his hiding place and surrendered, smiling and happy to be captured. Then the patrol went away. As I found out later, the American soldiers had crossed the Sauer at Ingeldorf, Diekirch and Gilsdorf. Those from Gilsdorf had reached the Herrenberg farm by 8:00 AM. At 7:30, American soldiers arrived at the bunker of Pierre Witry along the Sauer. At 10:00 American soldiers arrived at the 'Bamerdall' and took prisoners from the cellars of the "Kahlebösch." Our liberators came to us via Ingeldorf, Goldknapp, Friedbösch, Krischend, Herrenberg and Maertesdelt. The civilians who came from Diekirch during the night and settled in our cellar told blood-curdling details of the destruction of Diekirch, the plundering of the stores and the stealing from the private homes. They also mentioned the business houses that had stored incredible lots of goods, even prewar goods, but previously had not had a pair of shoestrings for needy people. The tavern keepers were also mentioned where the Germans had taken hundreds and thousands of bottles of wine but never had a little drink to offer their customers. During the night before Friday, January 19, the heavy fire of the Americans continued. A white phosphorus shell crashed into the right corner of our roof, the first one that hit us. An unusual smell of burning soon assailed us. We looked around the house uneasily without finding anything. A streaming rain had begun at the same time and extinguished the fire. A second shell hit the roof of the barn, a third the kitchen window. So the night of liberation brought the most damage. The hellish noise of the guns continued all morning. The noise came from the direction of Seitert and Friedbösch. Frightened, we asked if the Americans had succeeded in throwing the big-talking "Prussians" out of their positions. In the afternoon the noise of war let up, and soon an American soldier came and asked us whether German soldiers had stayed behind. We turned over one to him, who had climbed in a window of our house to surrender to the Americans. Soon a group of mine seekers came up the road from Diekirch and assured us that the Germans had withdrawn quite far. Now was are completely calm and feel free.

Saturday, January 20. A month has passed since the second German occupation. The surrounding of the U.S. armies has failed. The big-mouthed propaganda of the seventeen-year-old soldiers had no success. They had once again eaten to satiation (one of their expressions), caused incredible damage, murdered, plundered and stolen. Heaps of dirt marked their path. But – They are gone! Forever, we hope. They would not have been allowed to come back. Now U.S. tanks are moving in the direction of Hoscheid and over the Herrenberg. The shells keep flying after the fleeing Germans. The American Red Cross occupies our house; a doctor bandages the wounded. I ask a wounded German soldier where he was in the battle. "Twelve kilometers from here," he said. I found out that he was in Hoscheid. Trucks full of infantrymen drive northward. The front is approaching the border. U.S. quartering is reported. Our cellar evacuees, whom we have now taken care of for four days, must leave us. Some go without a word of thanks!

Now we begin to clean up our house, a gigantic job! Tuesday, January 23: Birthday of the Grand Duchess. The U.S. artillery fires on the West Wall. The heap of frozen meat that was stored beside our house is taken away by the 'Ravitaillement (food office) Luxembourg." Three heavy trucks full. The first to speak for us are Jean-Pierre Dichter, Michael Preisen and Edy Felten. They give us the news that our children have been evacuated to Lintgen. We decide to sleep in our beds again that evening, for in the cellar we are bothered by coughing; the British Lieutenant Félix Meyers, a Diekircher, at that time City Commandant in "Civil Affairs", visits us. My wife had a look at Diekirch today. Diekirch is a burned-out, dead city. A few people still inhabit the cellars and look like death-masks. The house of our children on the Esplanade is completely burned out. At night the noise of gunfire at the West Wall is terrible; German shells from over there come hissing past our house and land in Diekirch. One hits the house of Pastor Boesen in the 'Bamerdall' and kills two American soldiers in bed.

Friday, January 26. The gendarmes make up a list of the present inhabitants and, when possible, the sick. The Dean has returned; he visits the sick and blesses the graves of the dead. We get letters from our children in Lintgen via U.S. soldiers. Every day there are new visits: returning inhabitants and relatives. Many find their first housing with us until they have made their homes habitable again. Life begins, and the people work tirelessly. Fodder must also be brought out of the destroyed barns for the livestock. We gather wood from the bunkers. The roofs are patched as best we can, and all kinds of glass is set into the windows. On February 19 our Ketty and little Albert come back; both have been on a real odyssey for two months: from Diekirch via Wiltz, to Belgium (Lutrebois), then ahead of the returning Germans farther and farther, via Arlon to Garnich and Körich. From Körich to Bonneweg and from there back home. On February 20 the West Wall is finally penetrated, the shots from there toward Diekirch have stopped. They have kept us in tension a long time. The Allied armies now push deep into the heart of Germany from all sides.

The German nightmare was over.

Bastendorf and Brandenbourg

Somehow those two peaceful villages, somewhat off the beaten track, were blessed by being spared the massive destruction caused by intensive artillery fire. To be sure, scarcely any house or barn got away without any shell damage, but in comparison to other villages, most of the houses were habitable after the offensive. But as of January 1945, the two villages had to suffer under sporadic U.S. artillery fire, which constantly sought out suspected German troop assemblages there.

Bastendorf

As if by a thunderclap out of the blue, the inhabitants were rudely awakened here in the early morning of December 16 when the German mortar and rocket launcher salvoes howled over the village and struck on the Herrenberg or in the vicinity of the "Friedhaff." Several salvoes, though, fell too short and landed in Bastendorf, but did not cause any major damage. Thank God there were no civilian victims of the German firefall. At the break of day, most of the people ventured out of their safe cellars to see how much damage there was. Nobody knew as yet what was actually going on. The little U.S. garrison, though, was at the highest level of alarm readiness, and soon the bad news spread that the Germans had crossed the Our in the night and were advancing! By that afternoon, the noise of battle could be heard from the "Seltz" just two kilometers away. "The situation was more serious than we had presumed at first," said

Nic Haentges and Jean Toussaint.

"As fast as possible, everybody packed everything necessary together, in order to leave Bastendorf before nightfall. The Americans, though, assured us there was no more danger; they would soon take care of the Germans. Since shells were exploding now and then on the road to Tandel, most of the people stayed in their cellars. On the two following days, the town was covered with tracer bullets now and then. It seemed as if the Germans were concentrating mainly on the church and the mill at the edge of town in the direction of Brandenbourg. Again and again the Americans succeeded in using well-directed mortar fire to prevent the Germans, who were now in the Seltz, from making an attack on Bastendorf. But this defensive fire was only supposed to cover the delayed withdrawal of the Americans. An American machine-gun nest that had been set up in the attic of the Haentges house so as to have a better field of fire, was withdrawn, after the German mortar fire east of Bastendorf had become too heavy, in the afternoon of December 18. One of the soldiers had been thrown down the wooden stairs and injured shortly before by the blast of an exploding shells at very short range. The midday hours passed very quietly. Again and again, though, new fights flared up not far from the 'Blees' Bridge. Late in the afternoon of December 18, the first German patrols moved hesitantly into Bastendorf. Some of the soldiers fired their submachine guns now and then, wildly sending a few bursts of fire into the front doors and windows. When nothing happened, they immediately pushed their way into the houses and looked for hidden Americans."

"When I heard that the Germans were in the house," Jean Toussaint relates, "I took a white cloth and went to the cellar stairs holding it in my upraised hands. While I was calling to the Germans that there were only civilians in the cellar, I climbed up the stairs. Immediately several soldiers were there, pushed me aside and went down cellar with their guns in hand. After they had satisfied themselves, they left us alone. Some people, though, were driven out into the street by them and had to wait there until the search was ended. Only on the next day did German supply units arrive in Bastendorf. This column was almost completely horse-drawn. Numerous soldiers also brought their weapons and equipment on small carts, even children's wagons.

The unit's field kitchen and supply train were quartered at one end of the village. A command post was also set up in the mill, to protect which several camouflaged earthen bunkers were built in the direction of the Herrenberg. The German soldiers stayed almost exclusively in the woods, so that it was hard to estimate how many might actually be quartered in Bastendorf. All in all, they did not bother very much about the civilians and left them in peace, but were constantly going on patrols to scrounge food in the village.

"Several cows had been badly wounded in the firefall the previous night, so that we had to slaughter them," Jean Haentges reports. "So we had a lot of meat. Along with it, we had flour from the mill to bake bread, milk and canned goods. In the cellar of our house there was a well, which came in very handy. In this way we always had water and did not need to leave the house, for once the weather had cleared up, the village was constantly under surveillance from 'Storks', as the Germans called the American reconnaissance planes. Every incautious movement was immediately replied to from the American side with a few shells from the direction of Stegen. Now and then there was fresh butter. For several inhabitants of the village, though, the American artillery shells were fatal. A ceiling caved in from a direct hit and buried a resident under it. Three others were badly injured by shell fragments and taken to Brandenbourg, where a German dressing station was located. I myself had to help a wounded man, after a German medic had put a bandage on his heavily bleeding head, to get onto a sled and take him to Brandenbourg on the completely snow-covered road. This took almost three hours. But any help came too late! We learned later that the man, whom we turned over to the doctor at the Café Zenner in Brandenbourg, died before he could be treated.

Some people still had electric power in their houses, since the mill was still working. When the Germans found out that radios were being listened to, all the radios had to be delivered to the mill, on order of the local commander.

For Christmas there was brandy that the Germans had brewed. The mood, though, could not be made very happy even by that. Every one of the soldiers seemed to feel it: this was the last Christmas of the war. The U.S. artillery aimed more and more accurately at the village.

Several times at the beginning of January, several men were forced to shovel out the snowed-in approach roads in the direction of the Herrenberg and dig dugouts."

One evening in the middle of January, the sound of motors was heard in the village for a short time," Jean Toussaint tells. "Only on the next day did we find out what this was all about. In the darkness, several German Jagdpanzers had come to Bastendorf, and had taken up positions first by the mill. Somewhat later only two were left there, and the others went on in the direction of Brandenbourg. When it was said that the Americans were on the advance (around January 19, 1945), these tanks were posted at the edge of the village. In our yard a mortar team had already gone into position soundlessly, and we recognized from their equipment that they were Americans. Shortly after that the Jagdpanzer clattered up, passed our yard and drove to the bridge at the edge of town. The Americans had not fired yet, and the Germans probably had not yet noticed that there were already American soldiers in Bastendorf. In a turning maneuver by the bridge, the tank skidded off the icy road and fell into the icy Blees. Two men were drowned. German soldiers hurried to the scene and dragged the two other crewmen out of the tank. One soldier with blond hair still hung out of the turret in the water for days. It did not take long before shots were fired. German artillery fire also fell on Bastendorf later. But the village fell into the Americans' hands almost without a fight. One day later, American tanks followed. On orders from an officer of the oncoming troops, the civilians, most of whom, thank God, had come through the offensive in good shape and gotten off with nothing more than a fright, were then evacuated."

Brandenbourg

On September 11, 1944, things began to happen fast in Brandenbourg. When the first American patrols, coming from Bastendorf, cautiously searched the edge of town for strayed Germans, a single German armored personnel carrier with a squad of men on it charged along the Hohlweg from Kippenhof toward 'Freng' (Froenerhof). Along the way, the Germans used their gun butts to smash at the Luxembourg flags that had already been mounted on the houses. Moments later, the first Americans were in the village. Fortunately for the inhabitants of the village, there was no shooting.

The small American reconnaissance troop, though, was quite mistrustful of the jubilant residents at first. Every movement of the people was followed by a rifle ready to fire. Only when the women picked flowers in their gardens and offered them to their liberators did their tension relax. After they had searched the first houses at the edge of town, the Americans inquired about the Germans. Several orders were given by radio. It did not take long before the first Jeeps, equipped with heavy machine guns, rolled down the main street of Brandenbourg, followed by an armored scout car. In no time everybody was up and about; everybody tried in his own way to thank the American liberators, sometimes with flowers, sometimes with 'Quetsch' liquor. Only after the entire village had been searched for German soldiers and they had made sure that the village was free of enemies, were the Americans more trusting. They gave out chocolate, chewing gum, and soft-drink (lemon juice) powder to the children and accepted invitations.

Hardly an evening went by in those September days without a celebration in the three taverns. Every inhabitant of the village had 'his' American, who usually had supper with the family in the evening. More U.S. troops came to Brandenbourg gradually. A food depot was set up in the dairy. In addition, the American liberators went on daily patrols in the direction of the German border and on the highland road to 'Kippenhof.' Right near the Froener farm and in the fields around the 'Houschterhaff' stood several guns and tanks that fired in the direction of the West Wall at irregular intervals. Several inhabitants, who watched it happen often, often brought empty shell cases back as 'souvenirs.'

Various residents of the village had meanwhile learned a few words of English through regular contact with the Americans, who had meanwhile been replaced, and the GIs were happy about that. Only at the beginning of December did the Americans begin to dig out rifle pits around the castle and along the road to Landscheid and occupy them.

As if out of nowhere, the first German shells whistled over Brandenbourg from the direction of 'Freng' in the early morning hours of December 16, 1944, and landed on the 'Köpp' and near Kippenhof. The inhabitants of the village were greatly amazed. Although no houses were seriously damaged, the people generally remained in the safety of their cellars and only ventured onto the streets in the afternoon. Suddenly it seemed as if the number of Americans now at alarm readiness had become greater. In fact, they had received reinforcements. The greater part of the U.S. soldiers, though, did not stay in the village, but divided up in the country around the Fröner farm.

There were also said to have been fatalities at the "Fischbacher" farm already. When the terrible news that "the Germans are on the advance" flashed through Brandenbourg in the afternoon, most of the inhabitants left the town on foot, with handcarts, over the "Setzdellchen" in the direction of "Fléibour" and Michelau.

On Sunday, though, some people could no longer stand it and returned to Brandenbourg to look after their livestock. To their horror, they found the village occupied by the Germans.

Almost all the houses were filled with men in field grey. It seemed as if the Germans would not be much disturbed by the presence of the returning people; they behaved themselves properly, but by that time a large portion of the food supplies of the farmers of Brandenbourg had been appropriated. Some of the soldiers looked miserable. Among them were some who were only half-grown, as well as numerous older men; nothing was uniform any more. The lower tavern became a food depot. Several rooms were filled with sides of beef and pork from slaughtered cows and pigs. A field kitchen next door was in operation constantly; now and then German troop units, all on foot and pulling their equipment with them on carts, passed through the village heading north.

Somewhat later there came farm wagons drawn by horses, which brought supplies. The upper floors of the houses, as well as the stables and barns, served the Germans as quarters; the residents were allowed to stay in the cellars. Only now and then did American shells stray into the village. But wounded men were brought to Brandenbourg from everywhere, and a dressing station and makeshift hospital had meanwhile been set up in the church, the school and Café Zenners. Those soldiers who died there despite emergency operations were buried in a garden across from the church. One night, though, the people were brought out of the cellars and driven into a barn, the excuse being that a German soldier had been shot in the village.

Nervous hours of uncertainty and waiting went by. They were threatened with shooting if the guilty parties were not found. After some time, though, they were set free again. It turned out that the German soldiers had used the time to search the houses for additional supplies of food. Although they had taken hardly anything, they continued to behave correctly and often gave the people some of their chow and Kommissbrot. When the first snow fell, some of them were busy at a sewing machine in the Weis house making snow camouflage shirts out of white bedding 'organized' in Diekirch.

They did not forget that Christmas was just around the corner. They gathered around a poorly decorated little fir tree that was set up in the living room, drank and sang 'songs of home.' In the middle of the night, female voices were suddenly heard. More than a dozen women in German uniforms took part in the Christmas celebration, and the inhabitants in the cellar gradually heard the sounds of ringing laughter and high spirits. But appearances were deceiving. On Christmas Day the Americans were already firing on Brandenbourg with heavy artillery.

There were dead among the Germans, who behaved somewhat more quietly from then on. Scarcely a day passed on which the Americans did not send a few 'greetings' to Brandenbourg.

In mid-January 1945 the Germans evacuated numerous inhabitants from Bürden, Michelau and Diekirch to Brandenbourg at night, because, as they said, "they were safer there."

On January 20, the first white-clad Americans advanced into Brandenbourg from Bastendorf. The Germans had already departed in the direction of Froenerhof and Nachtmanderscheid hours before, leaving their heavy equipment behind. Only in the hills was there wild shooting.

Weeks after the definitive liberation, the war took a victim in Brandenbourg when Mathias Steffen was killed by an exploding mine near Froenerhof. The peaceful village was ringed by abandoned German war materials. In the meadows by the Blees, a heavy German antitank gun gave the children something to play with for a long time. (Source: Math. Weis family)

She Cooked for General Patton

Although this last story took place in Luxembourg City, it still deserves to be mentioned. It was a particular honor for Mrs. Berthe Simon-Baum, for it was she who, in the kitchen of the "Fondation Pescatore", helped to prepare the Christmas dinner for General Patton and his staff. This very unusual story came about in the following way, Mrs. Simon tells:

"Before the war began I was in service at the "Fondation Pescatore" (a well-known nursing home in Luxembourg) and learned to cook there. When the Fondation became a government building during the Nazi occupation, I got a job as cook for a person nearby who had relatives in America. So it was not at all surprising that this person, simply for reasons of language, since she had already been in the USA herself, regularly had several American soldiers and a few officers as her guests after the initial September liberation. Since two higher officers were quartered in her house in December of 1944, I gained their confidence.

On the day before Christmas, my employer asked me if I would be willing to help prepare the 'Réveillon Menu' at the Fondation Pescatore. Since I was familiar with the kitchen from my earlier service there, I agreed, especially as a Christmas party would be given afterward for the officers, and I was also invited. So my employer and I, wrapped in heavy coats, got into a Jeep that took us directly to the 'Pescatore.' It was snowing lightly.

It was somewhere around 5:30 PM when we entered the dining hall. A gigantic Christmas tree, that had been chopped down in the woods near Strassen a short time ago, had been set up here, and two GIs were busy decorating it with red candles, candy and chocolate. There was nothing else available to use as Christmas tree decoration. The dinner table was also decorated only simply. Only the porcelain, the silverware and napkins of the house adorned the spotless white tablecloth. We entered the kitchen, where five military cooks were already in the process of preparing the holiday meal. I was introduced to them and told what the menu would be. There was chicken soup with rice and wine, turkey with all kinds of vegetables, Christmas cakes with candied fruits as well as a creamy dessert with coffee.

During the work it seemed to me that four cooks were softly humming Christmas carols. Only one of them, a black soldier, had tears in his eyes and regretted that he could not be with his family. We were able, though, to get him into a better mood, and soon enough every one of us was singing along. A wonderful atmosphere of Christmas joy prevailed, so that one could forget that the war was still going on, since it was known now that the enemy had attacked again in the northern part of the country. While one of the cooks stirred the chicken-with-rice soup and now and then added a spoonful of wine to it and tasted it, I cleaned and cut the vegetables to go with the turkey. The turkeys themselves arrived in a frozen condition, already cut into parts, in cartons on the kitchen table.

The turkeys were roasted in the ovens and constantly covered with sauce. Good smells gradually filled the kitchen.

Meanwhile another soldier whipped the dessert cream, which was then put in the icebox until it was served. The red wine was also ready, uncorked and waiting to be served.

Around 8:30 one of the 'boys' in uniform came in and excitedly told us that General Patton would take part in the holiday meal. The name 'Patton' spread through the house like wildfire. And in fact, minutes later the General appeared and got out of a Jeep with his famous dog 'Willie.' One of the soldiers took the dog upstairs, where it had to wait in a room.

Through a food window I saw the General, who was sitting at the middle of the table in a dress uniform. Some twenty officers had likewise taken their places around the table. There was heavy traffic around the food window in the kitchen, for everybody wanted to get a look at the famous general. While several soldiers in ordinary uniforms poured the wine, the soup was brought in. We also noticed that the entire building was surrounded by military policemen outside.

The soup was followed by the traditional turkey, the meat of which was already neatly cut and served on silver platters along with vegetables and gravy. Patton and his staff enjoyed it very much. Meanwhile there was much talk and laughter.

Finally there came the Christmas cake with candied fruits on it. Each of the guests had not yet finished his piece when a messenger came in, and I myself saw that he went to General Patton and handed him a written message. Suddenly everybody was talking at once. One of the cooks explained to me that there was a battle going on near Ettelbrück. Now everybody was on his feet. It was said that Patton himself would go there and set things right.

The cream was not served and the party was not held. The big banquet hall was deserted in seconds. Vehicle motors started up, commands rang out near the kitchen door.

A Jeep took me and my employer home, and I wearily explained to my husband how the Christmas party had to be interrupted. To this day I feel honored that I was allowed to cook for the liberators of our country, and for General Patton.

APPENDIX

THE DIEKIRCH HISTORICAL MUSEUM

Closely linked with the preparation of the two volumes of this book is the origin of the Diekirch Historical Museum. The museum, opened on September 24, 1984 in presence of some 300 U.S. veterans plus several German participants of the Ardennes offensive, offers a thorough portrayal of the battles during the change of the year from 1944 to 1945 in the Diekirch area, with a number of dioramas (life-size scenes), equipment, weapons, uniforms, vehicles and original photos. The purpose of the museum, established by the author in collaboration with F. Karen, J.C. Bachstein, J.P. Sassel, M. Schaaf, H. Makkinga, J. Roulling and F. Rockenbrod, was an unbiased portrayal of both sides. The creation of the dioramas was based on numerous interviews with veterans from both sides, as well as archival material. Great value was placed on displaying exclusively original material and no copies of military equipment.

It was the author's intention to provide those interested in the history of the war in Luxembourg with as true-to-life and objective a portrayal as possible in these two volumes, as well as the museum.

The museum itself, supported by the city government of Diekirch as well as the Luxembourg Army, the Ministries of Justice, Culture and Defense, is located in the rooms of the "Old Brewery", which played an important role during the offensive as a place of refuge for civilians and even for German soldiers. The museum has recently been authorized by the Luxembourg government to convert its name to "National Museum of Military History."

The largest diorama, portraying the crossing of the Sauer by units of the 5th U.S. Infantry Division on January 18, 1945, sponsored by several representatives of this unit, has been made available to the public in 1987.

Fifty Years Later: Clues of GI Presence in Luxembourg
GI Tree Carvings: Their Names Remained
The following pictures are typical of the period from mid-September to mid-December 1944, from after the first liberation to just before the Ardennes offensive. As is known, except for the breakthrough near Wallendorf on September 14 (the bridgehead was abandoned at the end of September), no noteworthy events took place on the front line along the Our and Sauer . . . until December 16. During this period of time, the American troop units in the hills on the south side of the river carried out patrols and cross-country drills and also got a good deal of rest.

To pass the time, or perhaps to leave their mark on the place, many GIs took pleasure in using their bayonets to carve their names and addresses or troop units on the beech trees around their foxholes. Others left behind slogans and what could almost be called works of art. In the postwar years these carvings scarred over so that in some places they are still more or less legible to this day. It is remarkable that most of these extraordinary relics of American presence are found in the area of the Sauer-Our confluence, the Wallendorf-Beaufort region. For this reason it is simple for the interested historian to classify the carvings according to troop units. Inquiries to Belgian historians have shown that similar trees in the Ardennes are almost unknown there – thus this is almost an exclusive historical item for Luxembourg.

The four following pictures were taken on the Hoesdorf plateau in June of 1992 and were certainly made by soldiers of the 5th U.S. Armored Division, as photo 1 confirms.

Photo 1: Paul Zuhlki, 51 11th Avenue, Chicago, plus the triangle characteristic of tank units with the number 5 for the 5th Armored Division. Underneath are two crosses (the meanings of which are not clear), then apparently the number 771 or 17+. The number 771 could refer to the 771st Tank Destroyer Battalion, but that was attached to the division only at the beginning of 1945. The same tree also shows considerable shell-fragment damage, caused by artillery fire from the West Wall – either from mid- or late September 1944 of from December 16-18, three months after Paul Zuhlki had carved his name there.

Photo 2: Elmer Hiott immortalized his love for his country, the U.S.A., on September 24, 1944 (date 9-24-44), on a beech tree about thirty meters from the first one. On September 24 the units of the 5th Armored Division, after costly combat on the German side near Wallendorf, Niedersgegen and Biesdorf, had drawn back to the south bank of the Our near Hoesdorf and Wallendorf. Perhaps Hiott just managed to outrun death there!

Photo 3: September 44: a further indication of the presence of the 5th Armored Division.

Photo 4: A further expression of love of country: the unmistakable heart symbol along with U.S.A. and 44.

It is interesting to note than, in the same area, no similar carvings have been found that indicate the presence of the 8th or 28th U.S. infantry divisions, which later took over the sector.

On the Niederberg near Bettendorf, the legible names of two German soldiers were found carved on a tree a few years ago. Unfortunately, these trees were cut down a short time ago . . .

Other such trees have been found on the heights above the Sauer near Beaufort. The authors of these 'tree graffiti' must certainly have been members of the 60th Armored Infantry Battalion of the 9th U.S. Armored Division, which was there from the beginning –December 17, 1944 – and thus experienced the start of the Ardennes offensive. If one compares the precise positions of the trees with a map used by the 60th Armored Infantry Battalion, it can be seen that the carvings were very probably made by members of the A Company, who passed the time in this manner.

Photo 5: A snake? – or perhaps the course of the Sauer river?? The symbol also bears the term "Devils." Unfortunately, the tree was already cut down some years ago, so that the bark on the underside, that may have contained further graffiti, had rotted away.

Photo 6: "Fuck Hitler" – A GI surely expressed his loathing for the Führer here. The word, not very clean, is nevertheless very common in military jargon.

Photo 7: "Floyd Botts" – without anything else.

Photo 8: This artist came from Detroit, Michigan. He also adorned the Beech tree with a waving flag.

Photo 9: Unmistakable "Baltimore, Maryland, USA, 1944", one of the clearest carvings in this area.

Photo 10: Framed: 1944 OC'T' ABC. OC'T' for October? In that case, the author may have belonged to the 8th U.S. Infantry Division.

Photo 11: "Michigan" and "Texas" along with an unmistakable American star.

Unfortunately, a tree with a stylized head of Hitler carved on it near Grundhof fell victim to a storm in 1990. Surely there must be numerous other mementos, and the author would be grateful for further information.

Photo 1

Photo 2

Photo 3

Photo 4   Photo 5   Photo 6

Photo 7   Photo 8   Photo 9

Photo 10   Photo 11